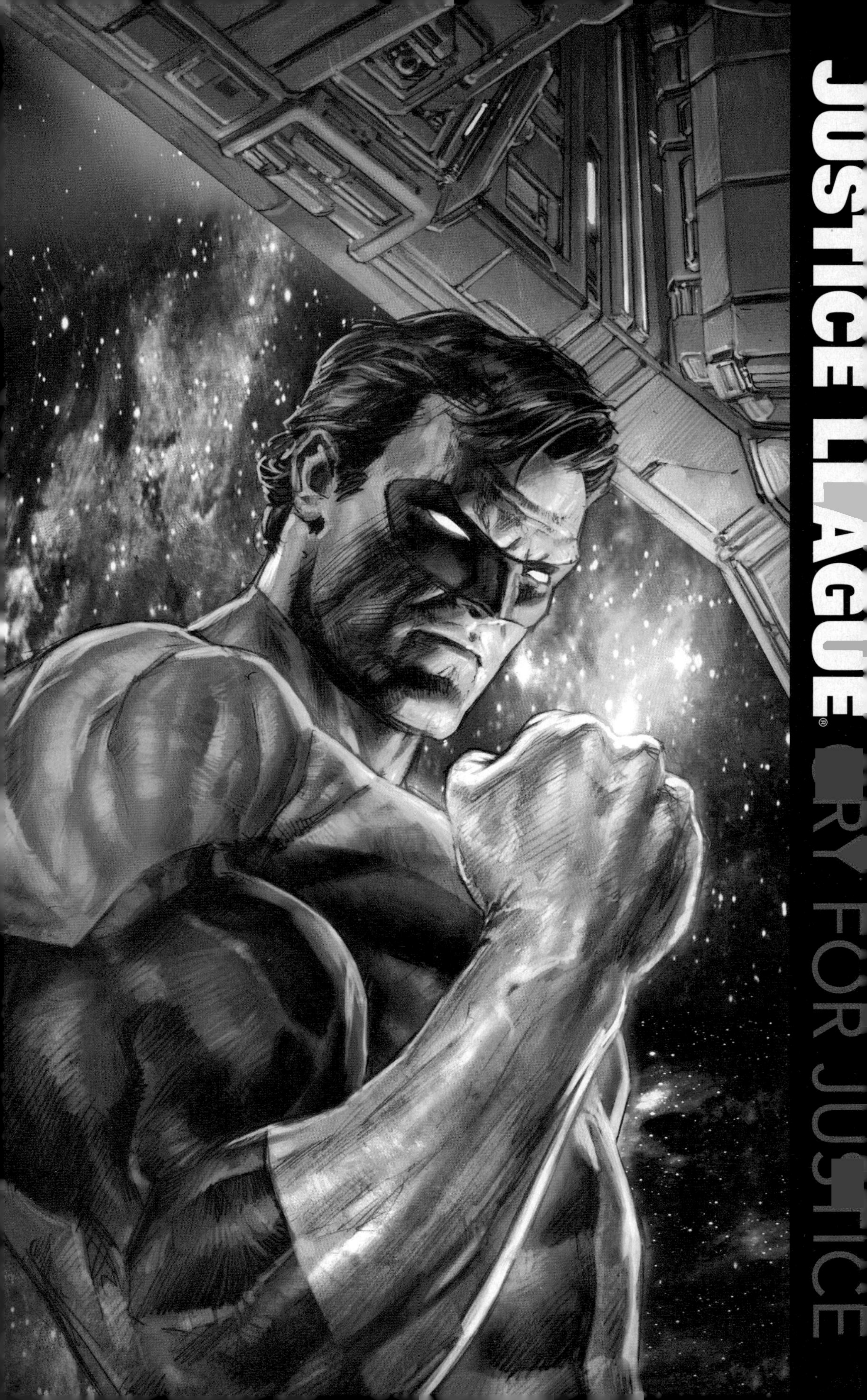
JUSTICE LEAGUE®
CRY FOR JUSTICE

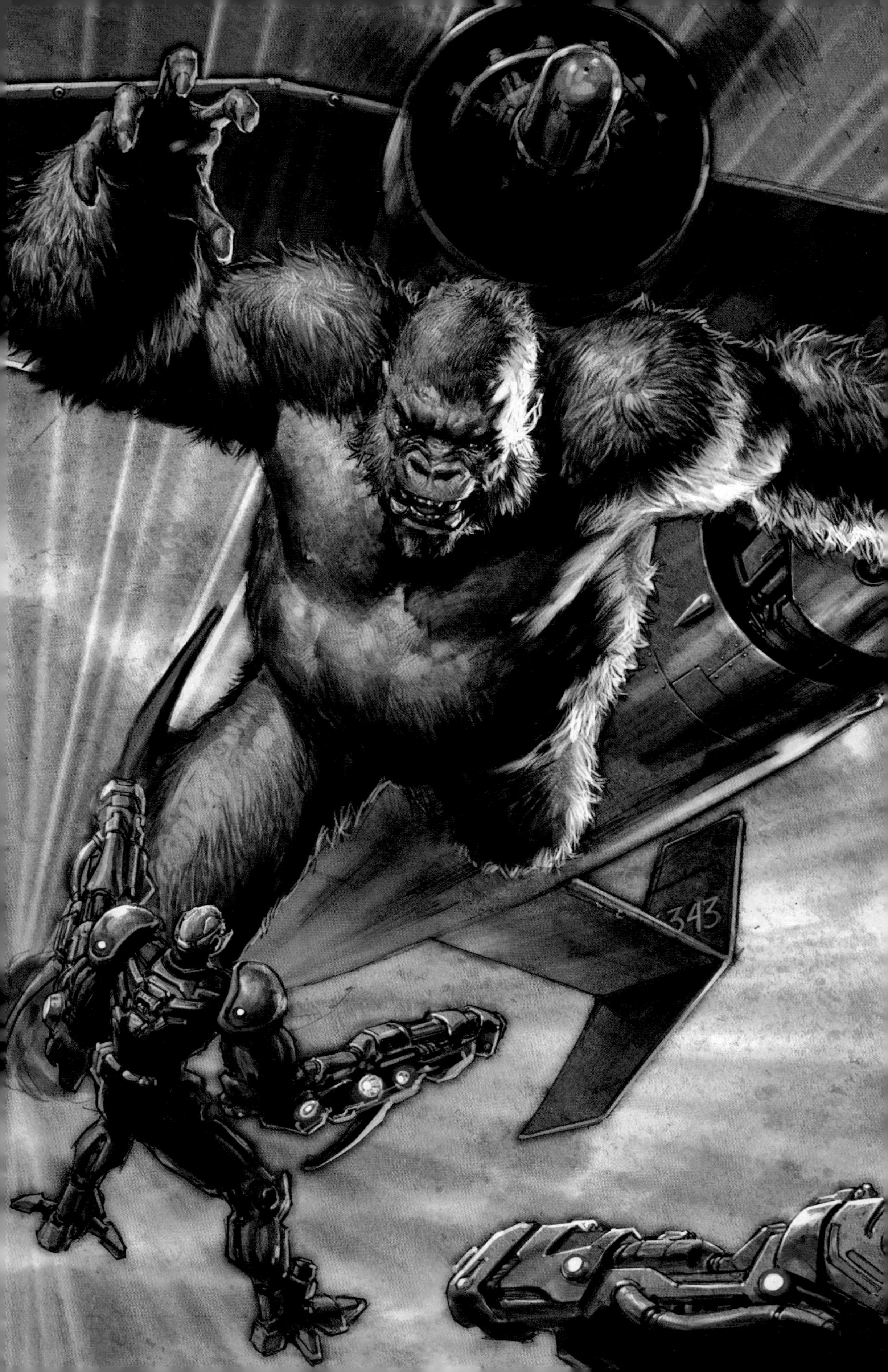
343

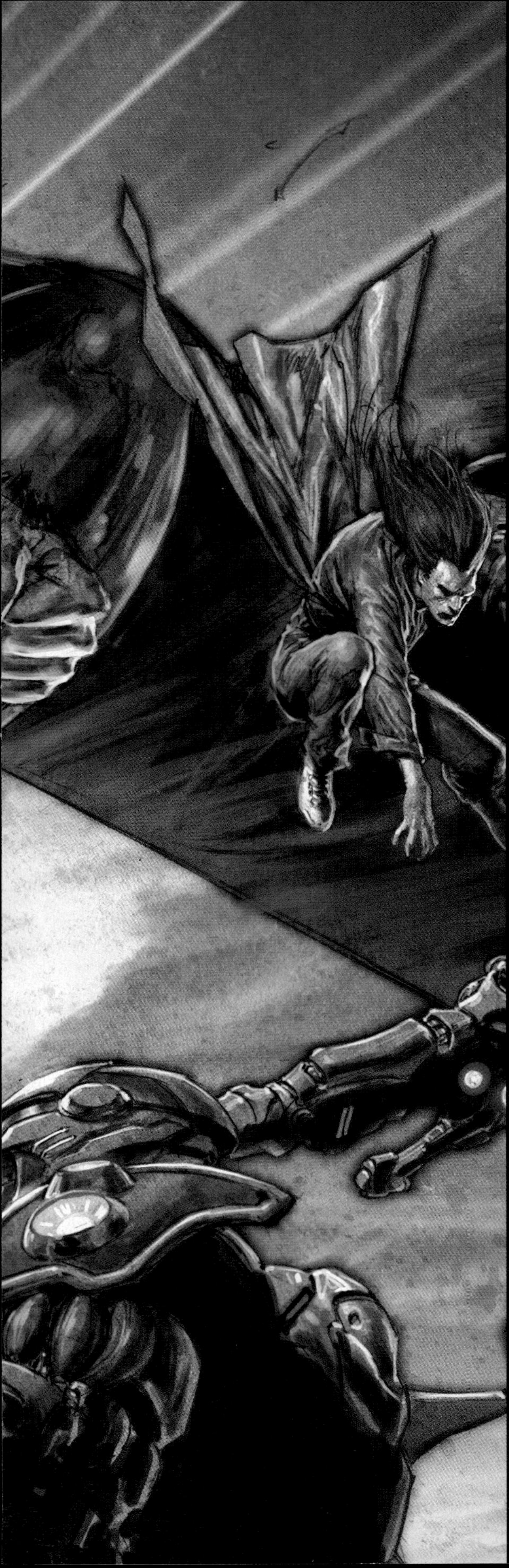

JUSTICE LEAGUE CRY FOR JUSTICE

CRY FOR JUSTICE

JAMES ROBINSON
Writer

MAURO CASCIOLI
Art: Parts One-Five, Seven

SCOTT CLARK
Art: Parts Five-Seven

IBRAIM ROBERSON
Additional Art: Part Seven

DAVID BEATTY
Additional Inks: Part Seven

MAURO CASCIOLI / SIYA OUM
GIOVANI KOSOSKI
Colorists

THE MAN WHO MURDERED PROMETHEUS

STERLING GATES
Writer

FEDERICO DALLOCCHIO
Art & Color

STEVE WANDS
Letterer

MAURO CASCIOLI
Original series covers

Prometheus created by
Grant Morrison

Eddie Berganza Editor-original series
Adam Schlagman Associate Editor-original series
Bob Harras Group Editor-Collected Editions
Sean Mackiewicz Editor
Robbin Brosterman Design Director-Books

DC COMICS
Diane Nelson President
Dan DiDio and Jim Lee Co-Publishers
Geoff Johns Chief Creative Officer
Patrick Caldon EVP-Finance and Administration
John Rood EVP-Sales, Marketing and Business Development
Amy Genkins SVP-Business and Legal Affairs
Steve Rotterdam SVP-Sales and Marketing
John Cunningham VP-Marketing
Terri Cunningham VP-Managing Editor
Alison Gill VP-Manufacturing
David Hyde VP-Publicity
Sue Pohja VP-Book Trade Sales
Alysse Soll VP-Advertising and Custom Publishing
Bob Wayne VP-Sales
Mark Chiarello Art Director

Cover by **Mauro Cascioli**

JUSTICE LEAGUE: CRY FOR JUSTICE
Published by DC Comics.

DC Comics, 1700 Broadway, New York, NY 10019
A Warner Bros. Entertainment Company
Printed by R.R. Donelley, Salem, VA, USA. 5/5/10. First printing.
ISBN: 978-1-4012-2567-4

SUSTAINABLE FORESTRY INITIATIVE
Certified Chain of Custody
Promoting Sustainable Forest Management
www.sfiprogram.org

Fiber used in this product line meets the sourcing requirements of the SFI program.
www.sfiprogram.org NFS-SPIC0C-C0001801

What a strange time it's been.

Since I first broached the idea of a second Justice League team to
Dan DiDio and now, as I type this introduction to the collection of the
seven issue miniseries that it subsequently became. It began so long ago.
Three years of stops and starts and changes/shifts to events with the DC
Universe. As I look back it's such a swirl, I'm not even sure where to begin.

**Here are random memories. Moments from the time spent creating
this work.**

Thought/memory 1 (these are in no chronological
order by the way)

My pitching the idea to Dan DiDio at San Diego
Comic-Con. The pair of us using the poster to
COUNTDOWN by Andy Kubert to pick out which
characters I'd feature. Dan asking me to include
Starman and to throw in one of the oddball
characters I'm (sort of) known for writing. I
decided then and there to instead include Mikaal
Tomas and Congorilla. I decided they would be
my "blue and the gold." Little did I realize
they'd be a part of the actual JLA as written
by me several years later.

Thought/memory 2
Me fearful this book was getting too dark. Tried
various ideas to lighten the tale, including a trip to
a parallel dimension in the past where anamorphic
versions of Tomahawk and his Rangers, all dogs and foxes, fought versions
of Lord Shilling and the Redcoats that were all felines. Not my greatest
idea.

(Still, this was the germ that led to me cameoing Tomahawk in
JUSTICE LEAGUE, for what that's worth.)

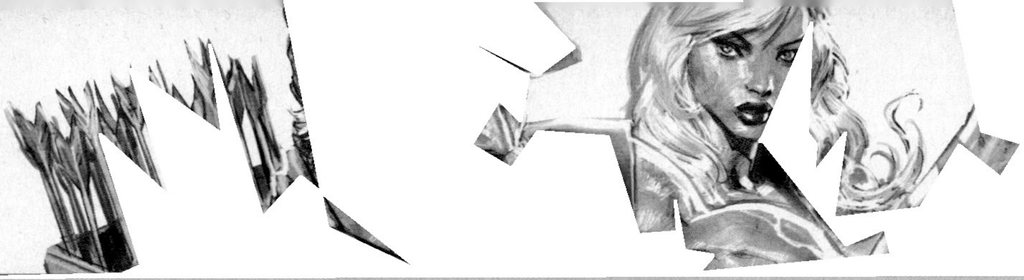

Thought/memory 3
Getting the call from Eddie Berganza, the series' editor, that to better aid stories/events unfolding in the DCU at that time, that it was preferred that CRY FOR JUSTICE be a finite series. I confess I was disappointed at the time, but soon saw it was for the best.

Thought/memory 3a
Deciding that if this was the case I'd begin to fold in more heroes, make it bigger and more of a singular event.

Thought/memory 4 (following on from 3)
That this is the first time I reference Darwin Jones in a comic in CFJ #5 (which I guess is now Chapter 5 of this volume). He's the mustachioed guy on the video wall of scientists. Why do I love Darwin Jones? Not sure. Maybe because he was DC's first science hero, appearing in STRANGE ADVENTURES #1, thereby predating Captain Comet (who first appeared in STRANGE ADVENTURES #9), who in turn predates J'onn J'onzz and therefore this making Darwin the first official DC Silver Age character. (I'm probably overlooking someone even more obscure and if so, please let me know.) Anyway, Darwin appeals to the DC geek in me.

Thought/memory 5 (following on from 4)
Beginning that feel/notion of sundry and varied characters/heroes also appearing, Jason Bard pops up early on. I've always loved this character. I loved his DETECTIVE COMICS backups back in the day, as written by his creator Frank Robbins, newspaper comic strip legend and creator of the wonderful Johnny Hazard adventure series that ran in papers across the country and indeed the world for four decades. (Note to all and sundry: if Googling the character for more info, make sure to only type his second name with one "z." Two "z"s will take you to a whole different kind of adventure.) Robbins was also the artist of Marvel's *Invaders* comics in the 1970s, and I've always been a sucker for his singular art style. I even liked the Shadow comics he did in the 1970s for DC, even though they followed the sublime work of Michael W. Kaluta, and as such seemed disconcerting to many readers at that time. However, with Bard's backups, although Robbins drew at least one that I remember (involving skydiving), other tales were drawn by Don Heck. As such, Robbins's skills as a writer alone shone through. I love P.I. comics anyway, but the way Robbins would show Bard, cool, calm, with his walking cane and limp, yet still tough when tough was needed, appealed to me as a kid. It was fun to write his backups myself in DETECTIVE COMICS when I wrote the "Face the Face" arc, and it was equally fun to show him here in this tale.

Thought/memory 6

Realizing after the fact how often I have people saying "justice" in the opening parts of the series.

Thought/memory 7

Realizing when I write scripts, I put in a lot of /s. Everything I describe is this/that or where/not or zebra/vacuum cleaner. My scripts and text pieces too are full of /s.

Thought/memory 8

When I got the word from DC what they wanted me to do to Roy Harper (which I'll refrain from revealing here for those who read this intro first and who haven't read the series in issue/episode form.) I was slightly leery, I'll be honest, but saw that it was perfectly apt for the dark path I'd allowed this tale to take already. And I truly think "I…I can't feel my fingers." is one of the best lines of dialogue I've ever written.

Thought/memory 9

Arguing successfully that an equally dark fate should not befall Mia/Speedy.

Thought/memory 10

The fun I had writing the text pieces for the individual issues. Taking time out of my day to muse, ponder and write about Ray Palmer's issues with women and the art of Mort Meskin. Digging into the past of Congo Bill and the history that I myself had already given to Mikaal Tomas, all of it unknowingly building/helping to shape how I'd handle those two characters as part of the JLA.

Thought/memory 11

The first time I saw the art by Mauro Cascioli for the series. Realizing what a beautiful book it would be. Seeing his unique layout sense with close-ups and panels and action merging and flowing one into the next in such a unique way, it really added another singular aspect to the art.

Thought/memory 12

Being unsure what working with Eddie Berganza would be like. Sure, I'd already worked with him on the TANGENT COMICS: GREEN LANTERN book, but that was a long time ago. And it was a one-time thing. This would be more long term. And with me coming back to comics after such a long time away, would we jell in the way that writer/editors do where together the work is all the better?

It was a slow build. Mainly my fault. I was newly back to comics and unfocused/distracted by things going on in my private life. However, Eddie and I quickly began a working relationship I'm very glad to be a part of. Working with him and Adam Schlagman, his associate editor, has been a real pleasure and something I continue to enjoy as we work on the adventures of the JLA in the ongoing book.

I really couldn't have gotten through this without them, so gentlemen, thank you for all your creative thinking and tenacity.

Thought/memory 13
In the course of doing this book, really looking at the work being done by other writers. Taking the time to really regard the genius of Geoff Johns, Grant Morrison, Mark Waid, Jeph Loeb, Brian Michael Bendis and so many other fantastic scribes currently working in comics.

Indeed, that is probably my happiest thought/memory. Really taking the time to stop and see all the fine work being done by others.

And on that slightly saccharine note…

I can honestly say that JUSTICE LEAGUE: CRY FOR JUSTICE was one of the weirdest, darkest tales I've ever written. I think it may be the darkest JLA story ever written, although others may beg to differ. Am I proud of that? Not proud, no. I merely state what I feel to be true. I certainly know this tale isn't to everyone's taste. I know some people are even angered by it. But it's a work I stand behind. I hope, reading it as one combined (and therefore quicker) read, you'll see what I was going for…the slower build, gaining momentum…the growing cast… the growing event.

And I thank you for your time reading it.

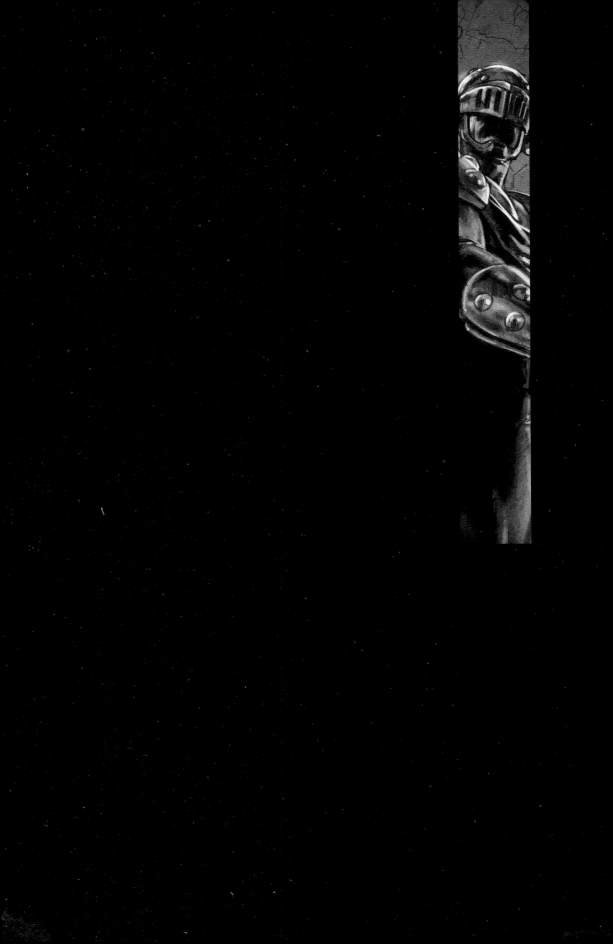

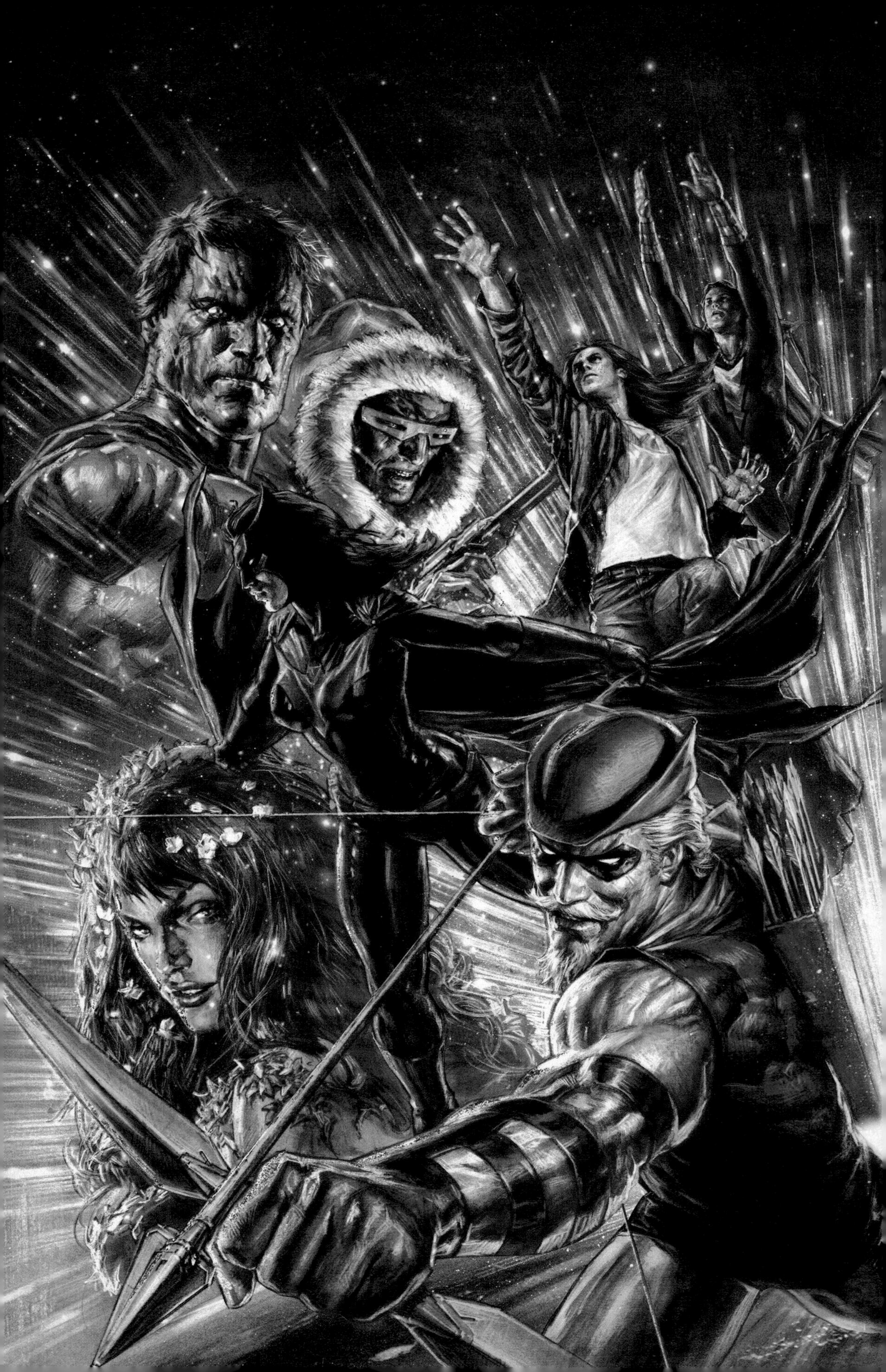

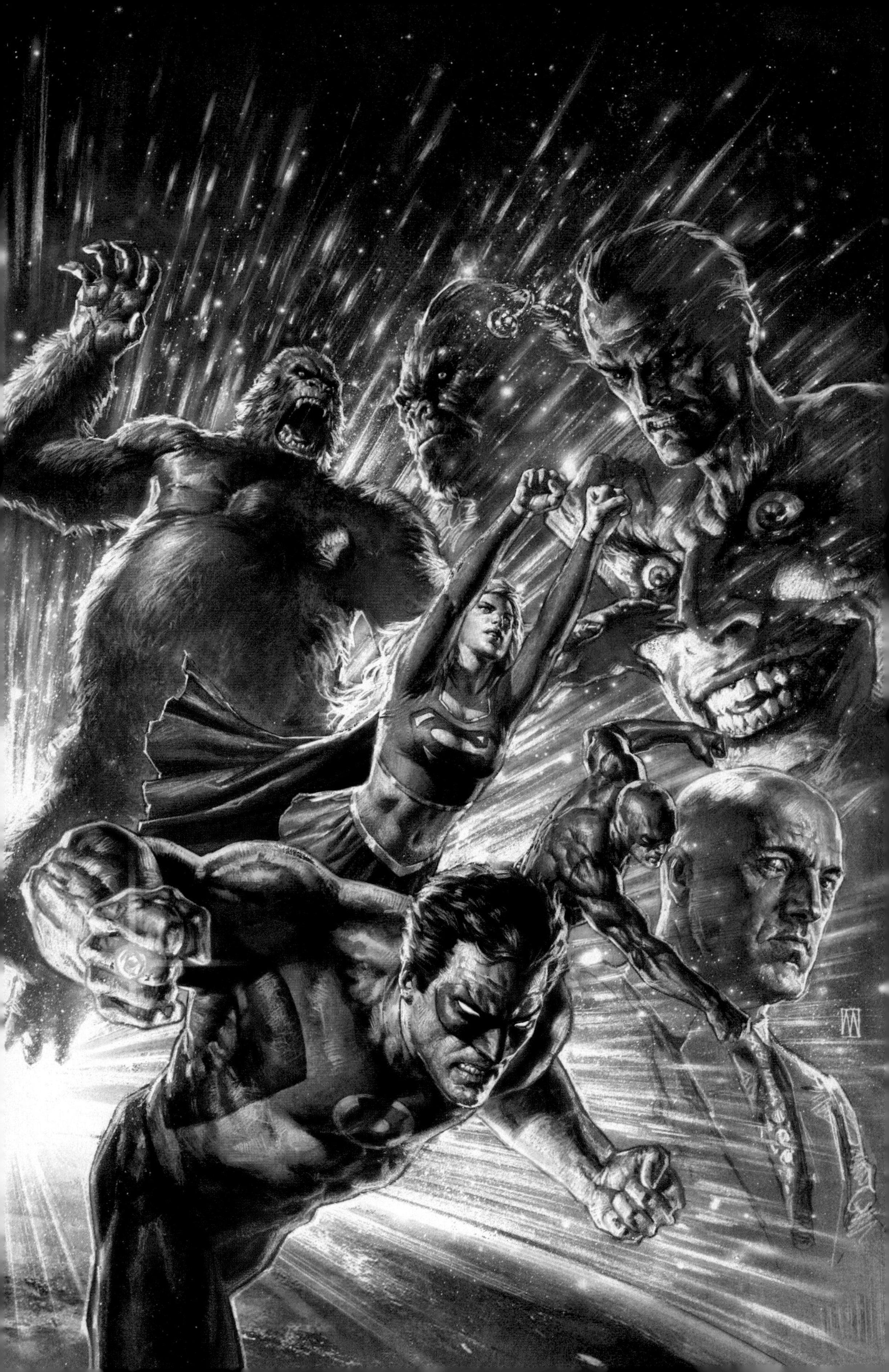

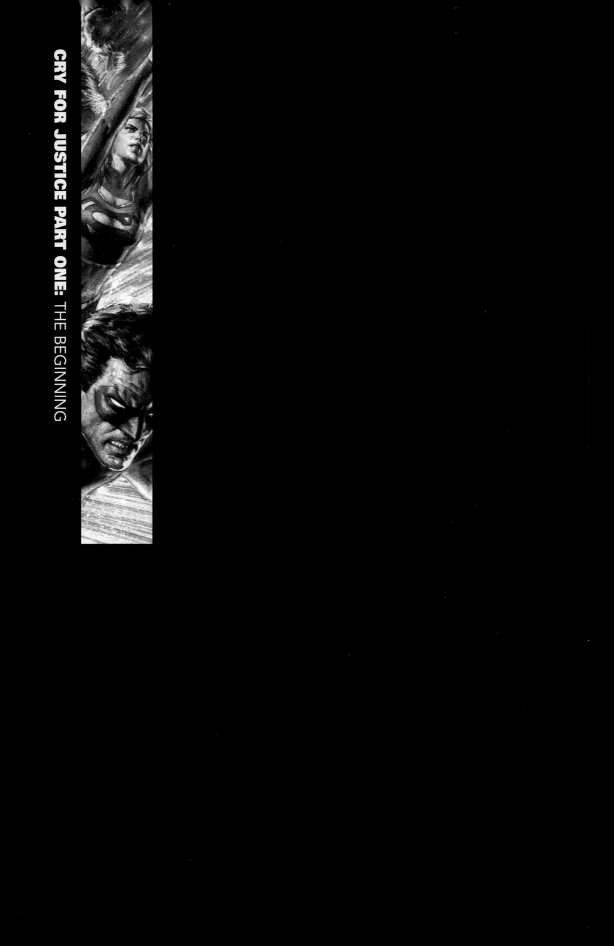

CRY FOR JUSTICE PART ONE: THE BEGINNING

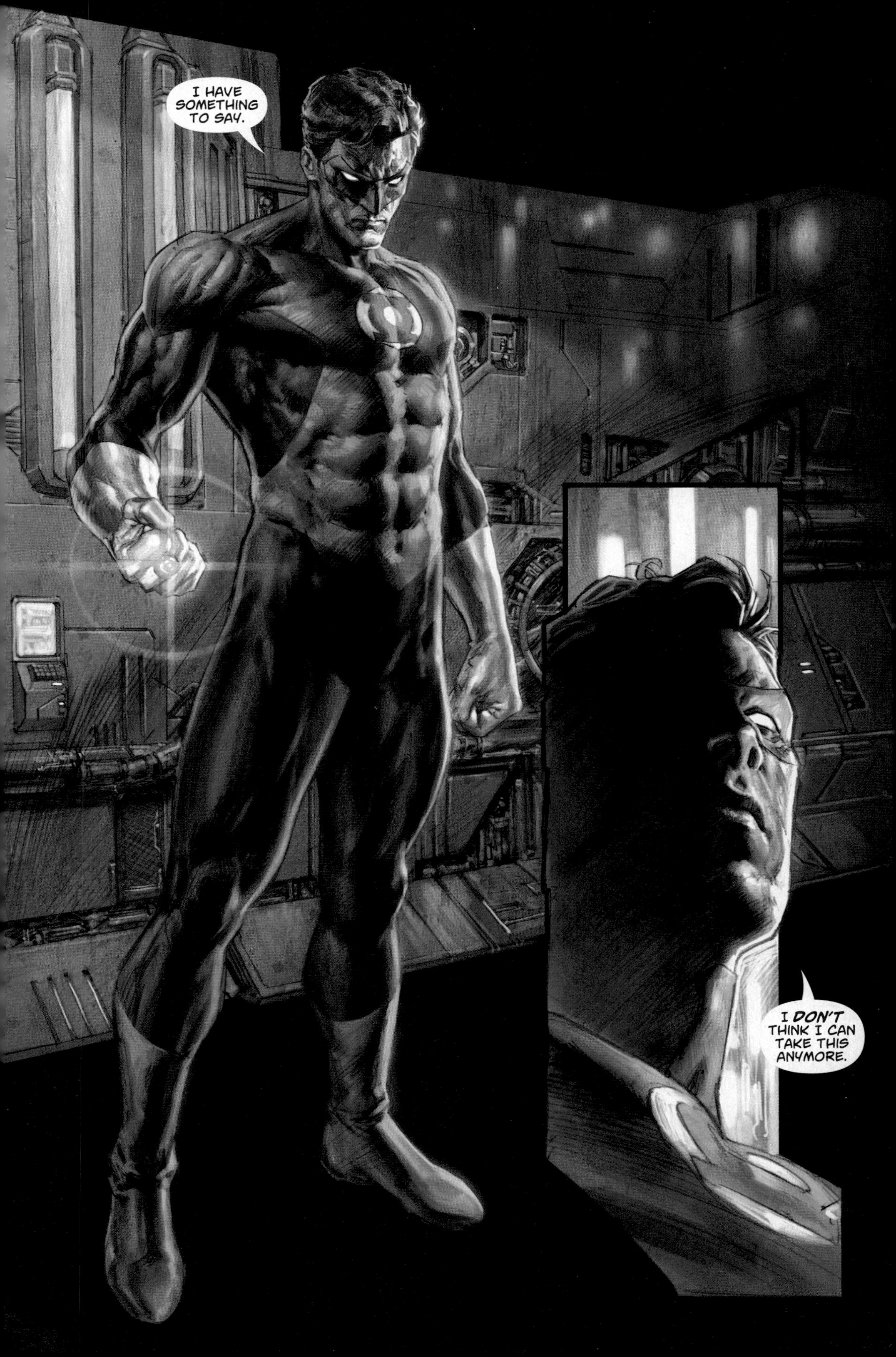
I HAVE SOMETHING TO SAY.
I DON'T THINK I CAN TAKE THIS ANYMORE.

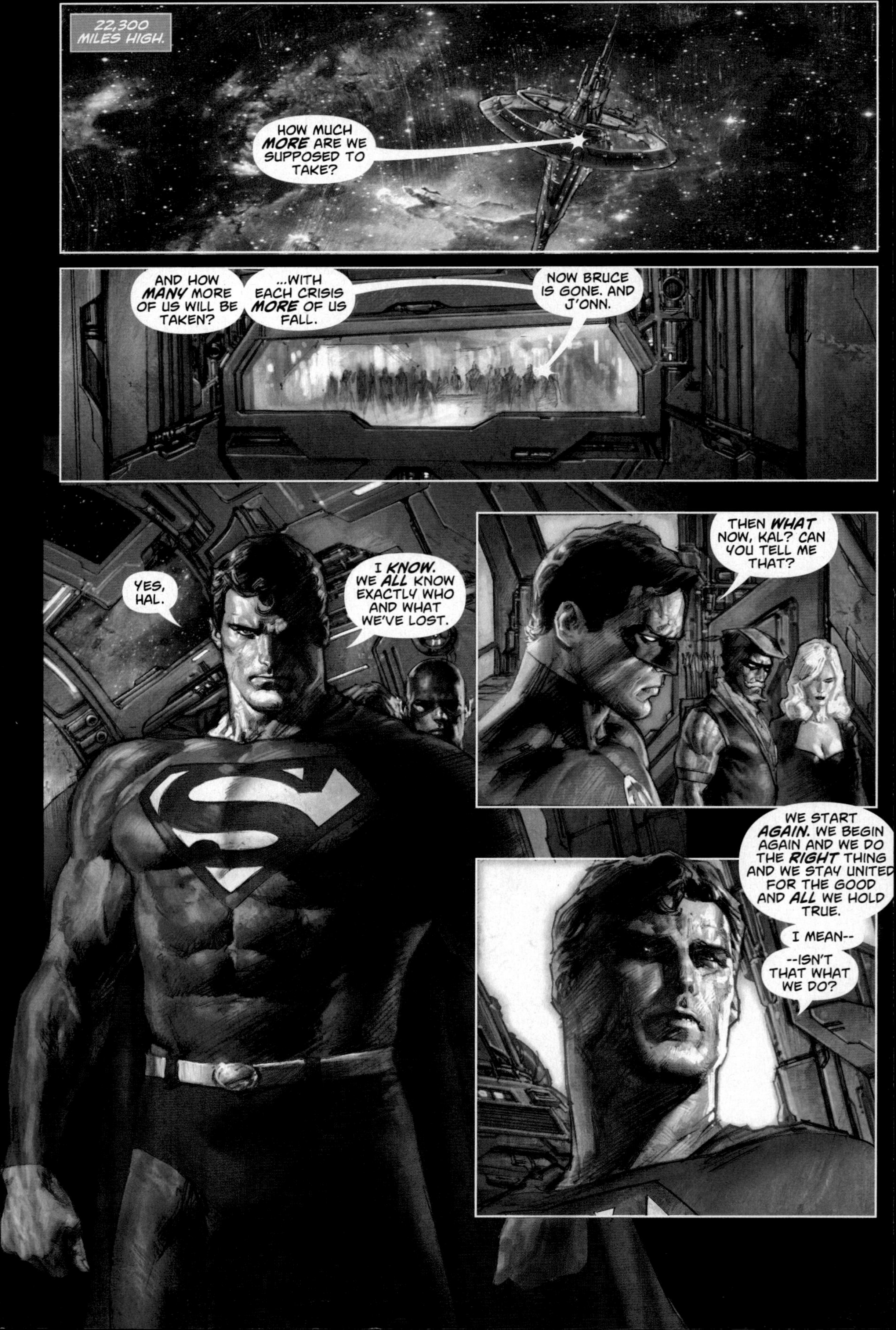

22,300 MILES HIGH.
HOW MUCH MORE ARE WE SUPPOSED TO TAKE?
AND HOW MANY MORE OF US WILL BE TAKEN?
...WITH EACH CRISIS MORE OF US FALL.
NOW BRUCE IS GONE. AND J'ONN.
YES, HAL.
I KNOW. WE ALL KNOW EXACTLY WHO AND WHAT WE'VE LOST.
THEN WHAT NOW, KAL? CAN YOU TELL ME THAT?
WE START AGAIN. WE BEGIN AGAIN AND WE DO THE RIGHT THING AND WE STAY UNITED FOR THE GOOD AND ALL WE HOLD TRUE.
I MEAN--
--ISN'T THAT WHAT WE DO?

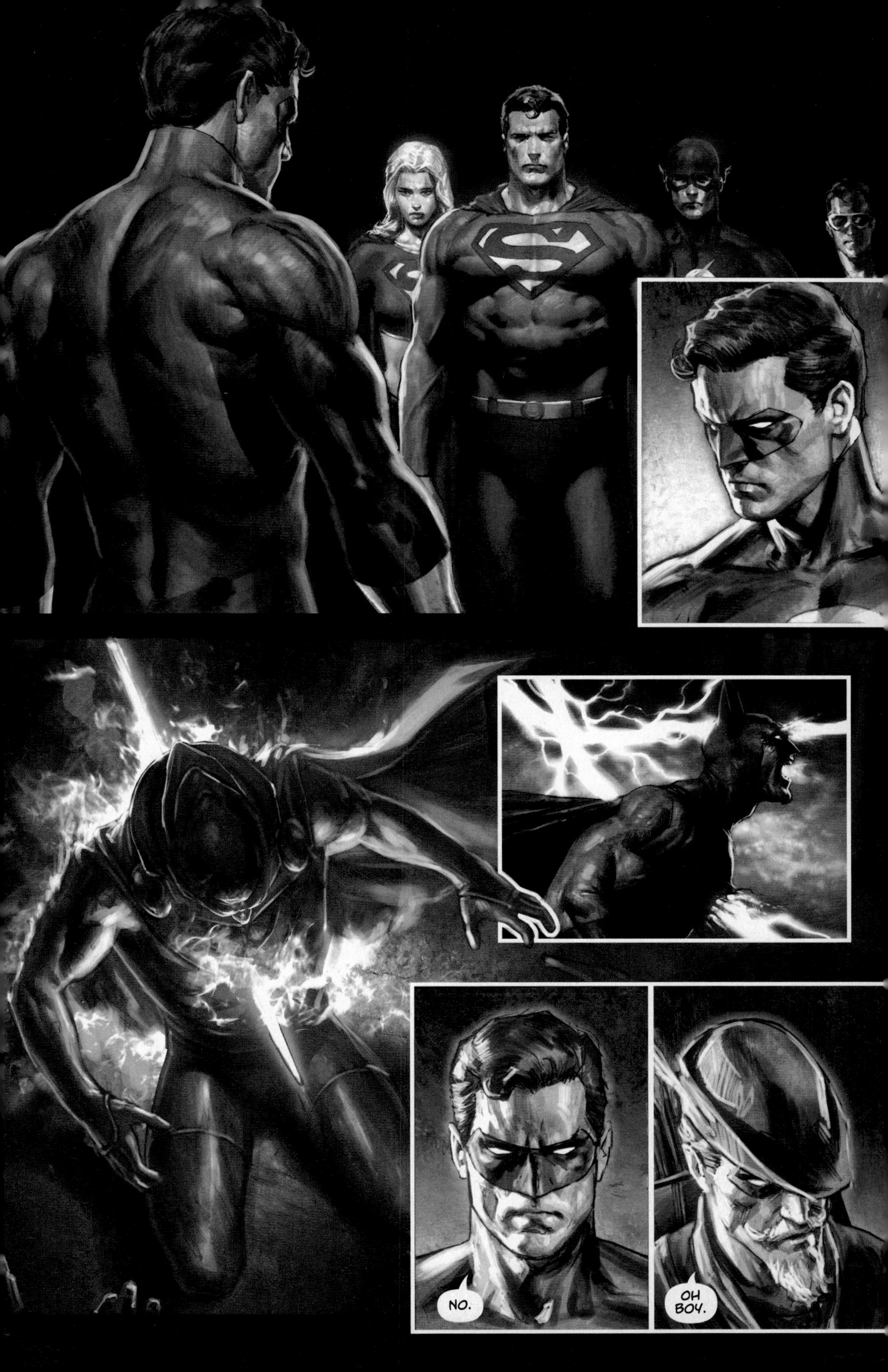
NO.
OH BOY.

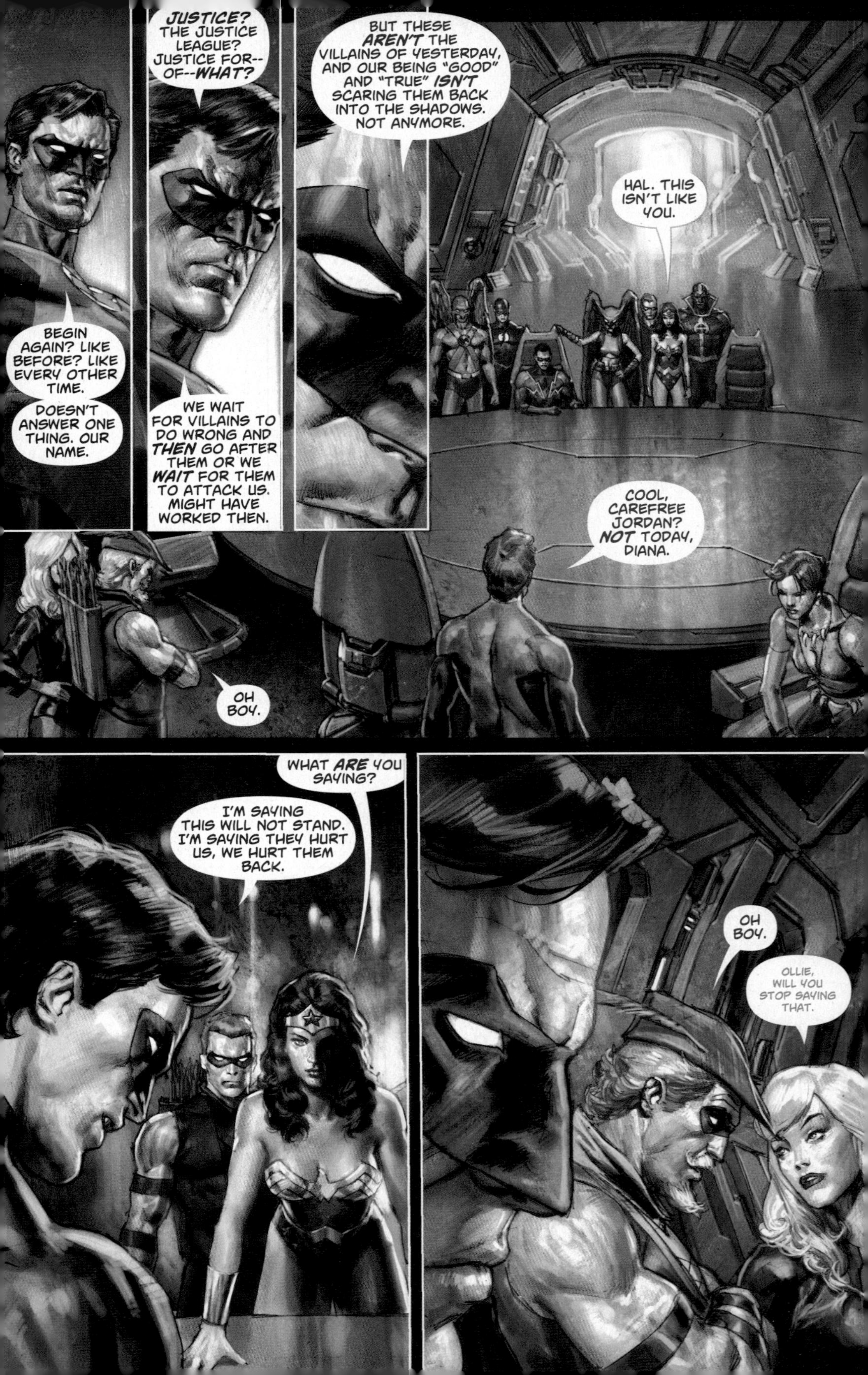
BEGIN AGAIN? LIKE BEFORE? LIKE EVERY OTHER TIME.
DOESN'T ANSWER ONE THING. OUR NAME.
JUSTICE? THE JUSTICE LEAGUE? JUSTICE FOR-- OF--WHAT?
WE WAIT FOR VILLAINS TO DO WRONG AND THEN GO AFTER THEM OR WE WAIT FOR THEM TO ATTACK US. MIGHT HAVE WORKED THEN.
BUT THESE AREN'T THE VILLAINS OF YESTERDAY, AND OUR BEING "GOOD" AND "TRUE" ISN'T SCARING THEM BACK INTO THE SHADOWS. NOT ANYMORE.
HAL. THIS ISN'T LIKE YOU.
COOL, CAREFREE JORDAN? NOT TODAY, DIANA.
OH BOY.
WHAT ARE YOU SAYING?
I'M SAYING THIS WILL NOT STAND. I'M SAYING THEY HURT US, WE HURT THEM BACK.
OH BOY.
OLLIE, WILL YOU STOP SAYING THAT.

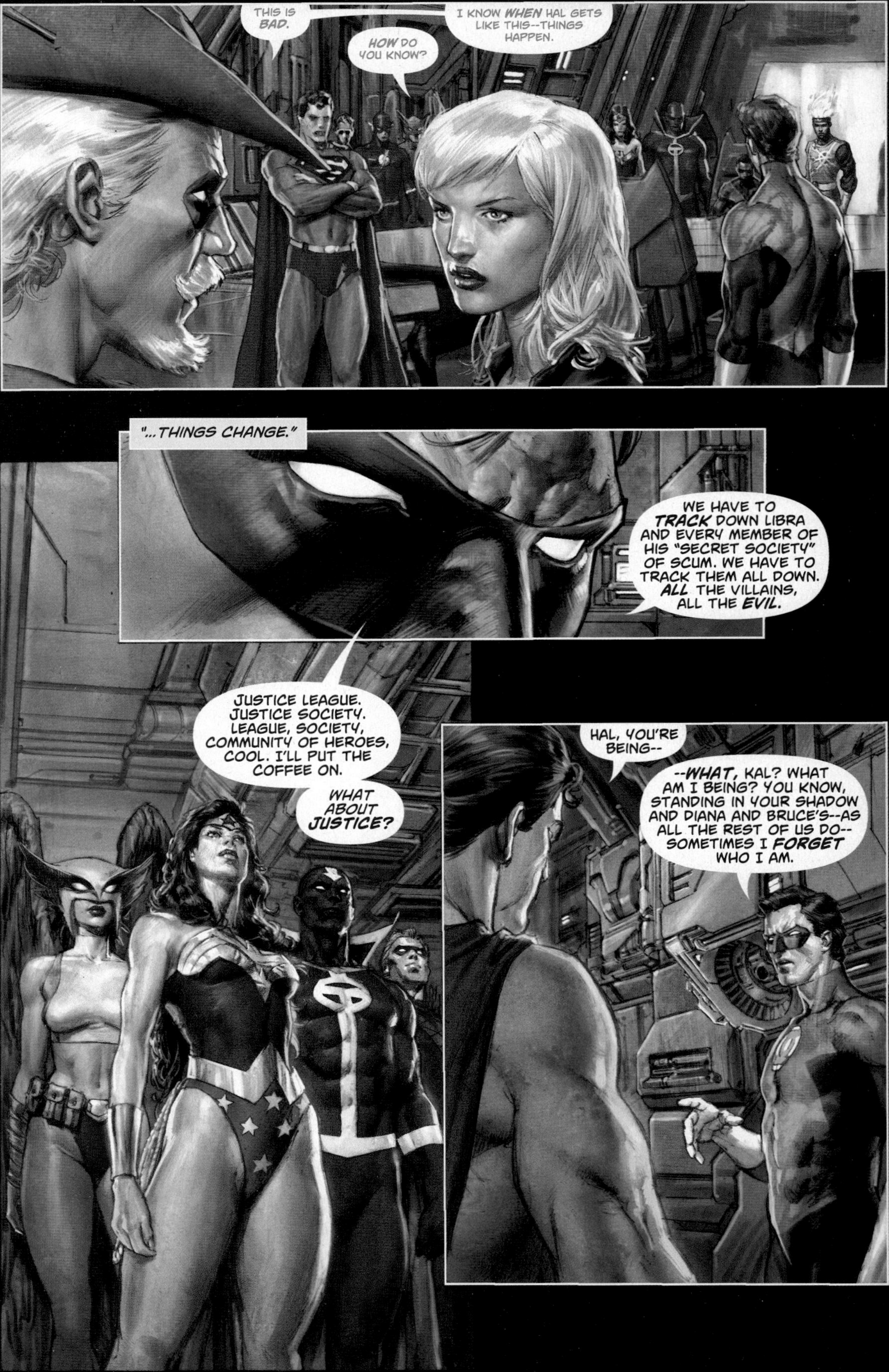
THIS IS BAD.
HOW DO YOU KNOW?
I KNOW WHEN HAL GETS LIKE THIS--THINGS HAPPEN.
"...THINGS CHANGE."
WE HAVE TO TRACK DOWN LIBRA AND EVERY MEMBER OF HIS "SECRET SOCIETY" OF SCUM. WE HAVE TO TRACK THEM ALL DOWN. ALL THE VILLAINS, ALL THE EVIL.
JUSTICE LEAGUE. JUSTICE SOCIETY. LEAGUE, SOCIETY, COMMUNITY OF HEROES, COOL. I'LL PUT THE COFFEE ON.
WHAT ABOUT JUSTICE?
HAL, YOU'RE BEING--
--WHAT, KAL? WHAT AM I BEING? YOU KNOW, STANDING IN YOUR SHADOW AND DIANA AND BRUCE'S--AS ALL THE REST OF US DO--SOMETIMES I FORGET WHO I AM.

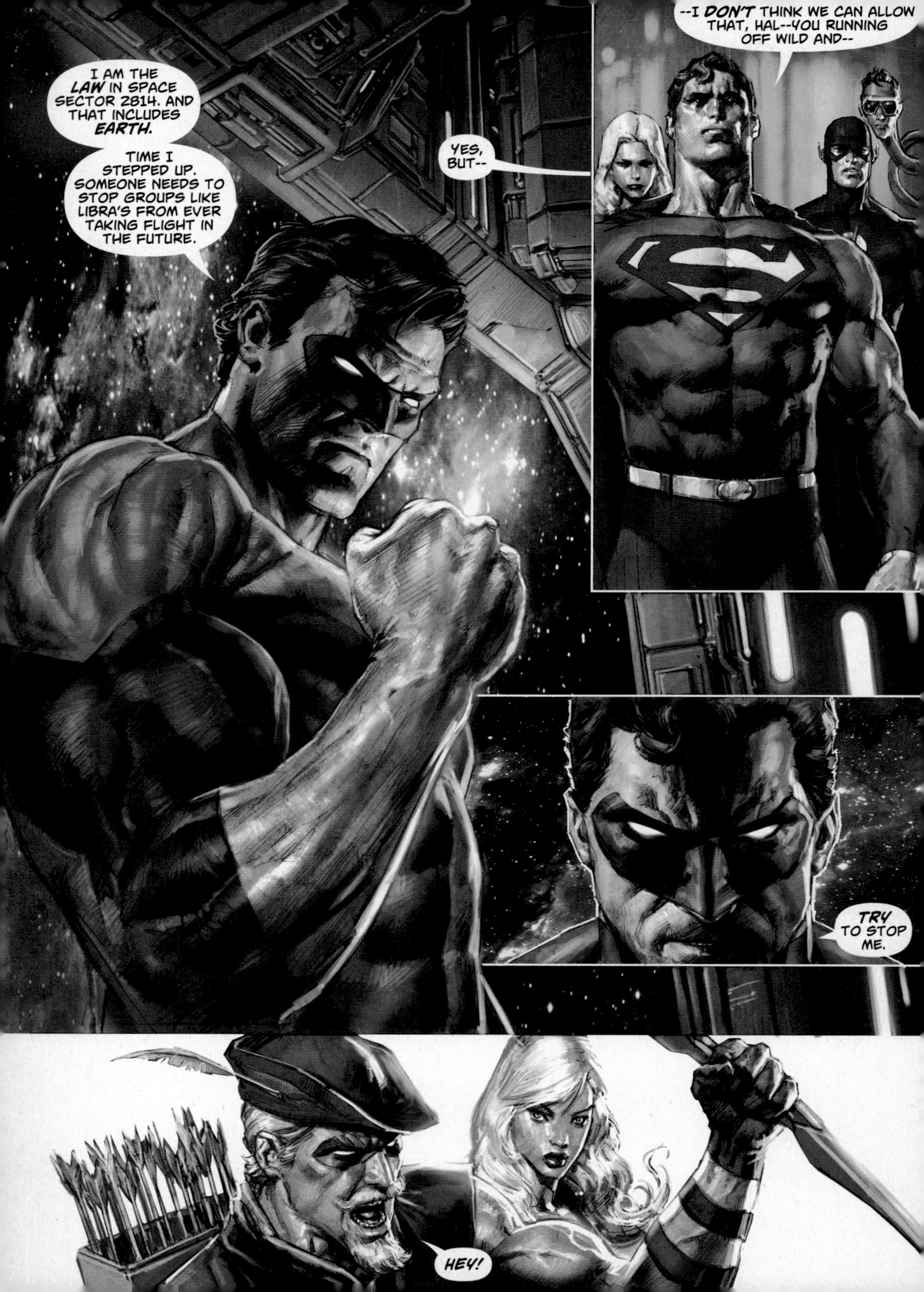
I AM THE LAW IN SPACE SECTOR 2814. AND THAT INCLUDES EARTH.
TIME I STEPPED UP. SOMEONE NEEDS TO STOP GROUPS LIKE LIBRA'S FROM EVER TAKING FLIGHT IN THE FUTURE.
YES, BUT--
--I DON'T THINK WE CAN ALLOW THAT, HAL--YOU RUNNING OFF WILD AND--
TRY TO STOP ME.
HEY!

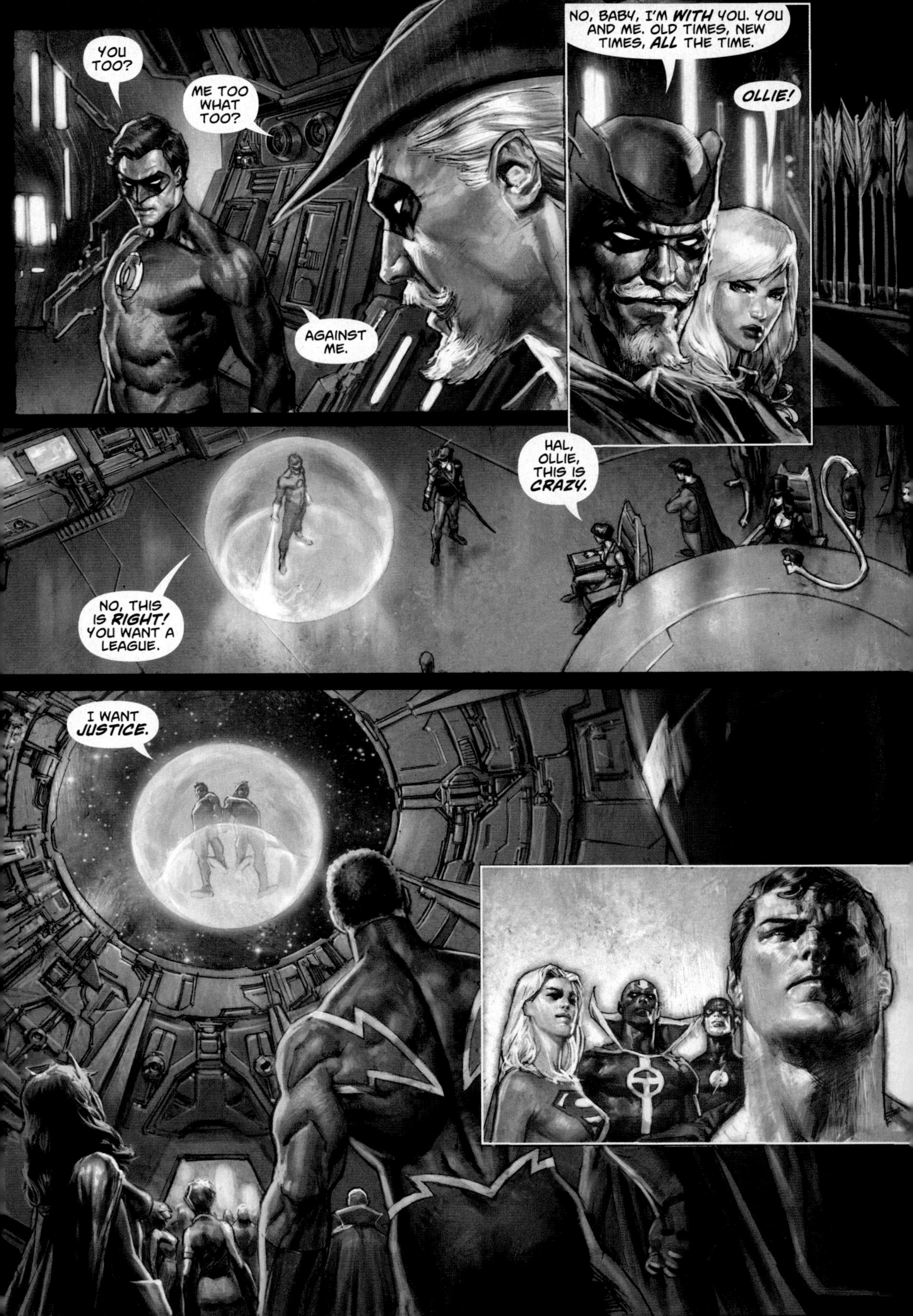
YOU TOO?
ME TOO WHAT TOO?
AGAINST ME.
NO, BABY, I'M WITH YOU. YOU AND ME. OLD TIMES, NEW TIMES, ALL THE TIME.
OLLIE!
HAL, OLLIE, THIS IS CRAZY.
NO, THIS IS RIGHT! YOU WANT A LEAGUE.
I WANT JUSTICE.

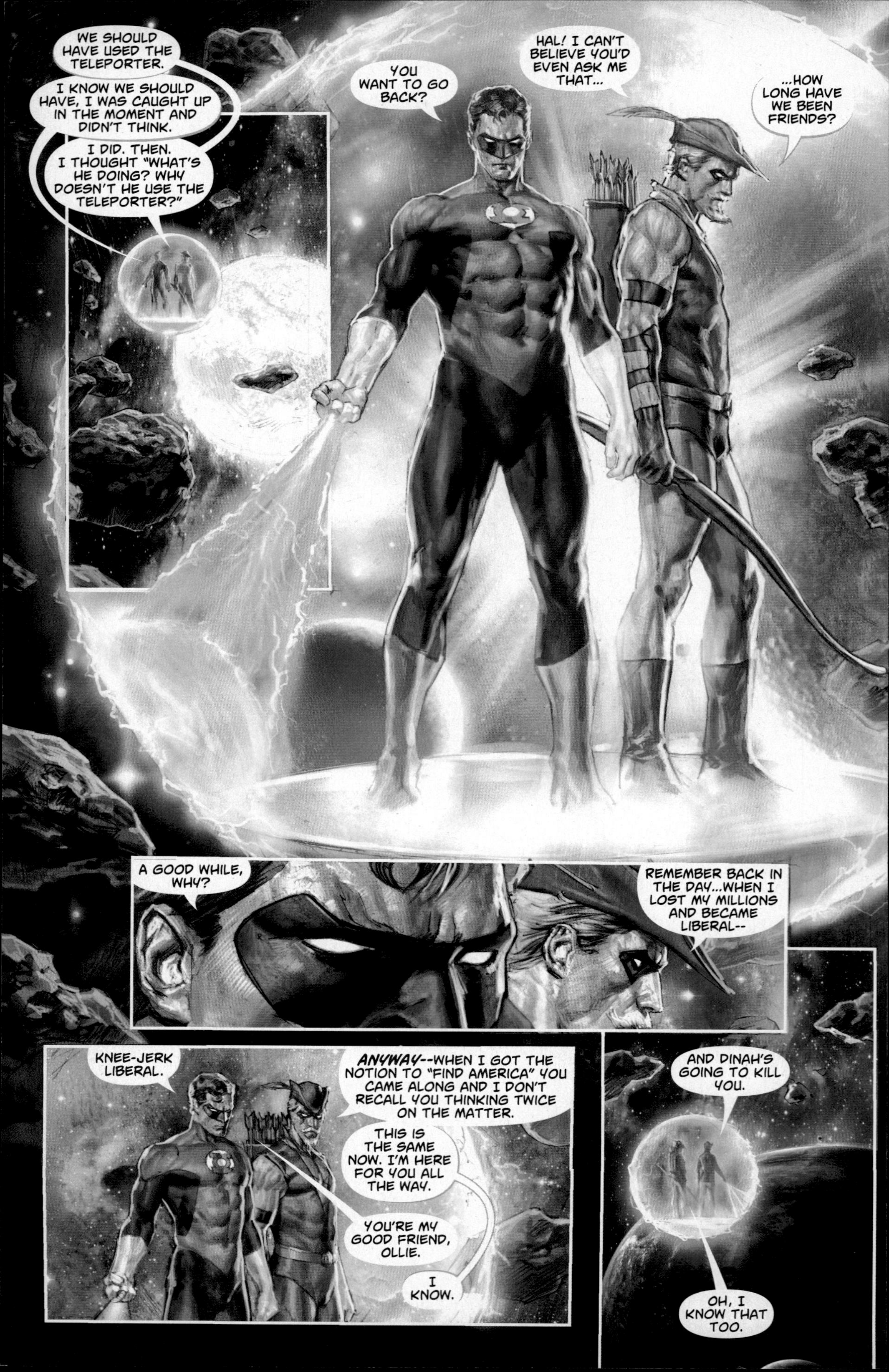
WE SHOULD HAVE USED THE TELEPORTER.
I KNOW WE SHOULD HAVE, I WAS CAUGHT UP IN THE MOMENT AND DIDN'T THINK.
I DID. THEN. I THOUGHT "WHAT'S HE DOING? WHY DOESN'T HE USE THE TELEPORTER?"
YOU WANT TO GO BACK?
HAL! I CAN'T BELIEVE YOU'D EVEN ASK ME THAT...
...HOW LONG HAVE WE BEEN FRIENDS?
A GOOD WHILE, WHY?
REMEMBER BACK IN THE DAY...WHEN I LOST MY MILLIONS AND BECAME LIBERAL--
KNEE-JERK LIBERAL.
ANYWAY--WHEN I GOT THE NOTION TO "FIND AMERICA" YOU CAME ALONG AND I DON'T RECALL YOU THINKING TWICE ON THE MATTER.
THIS IS THE SAME NOW. I'M HERE FOR YOU ALL THE WAY.
YOU'RE MY GOOD FRIEND, OLLIE.
I KNOW.
AND DINAH'S GOING TO KILL YOU.
OH, I KNOW THAT TOO.

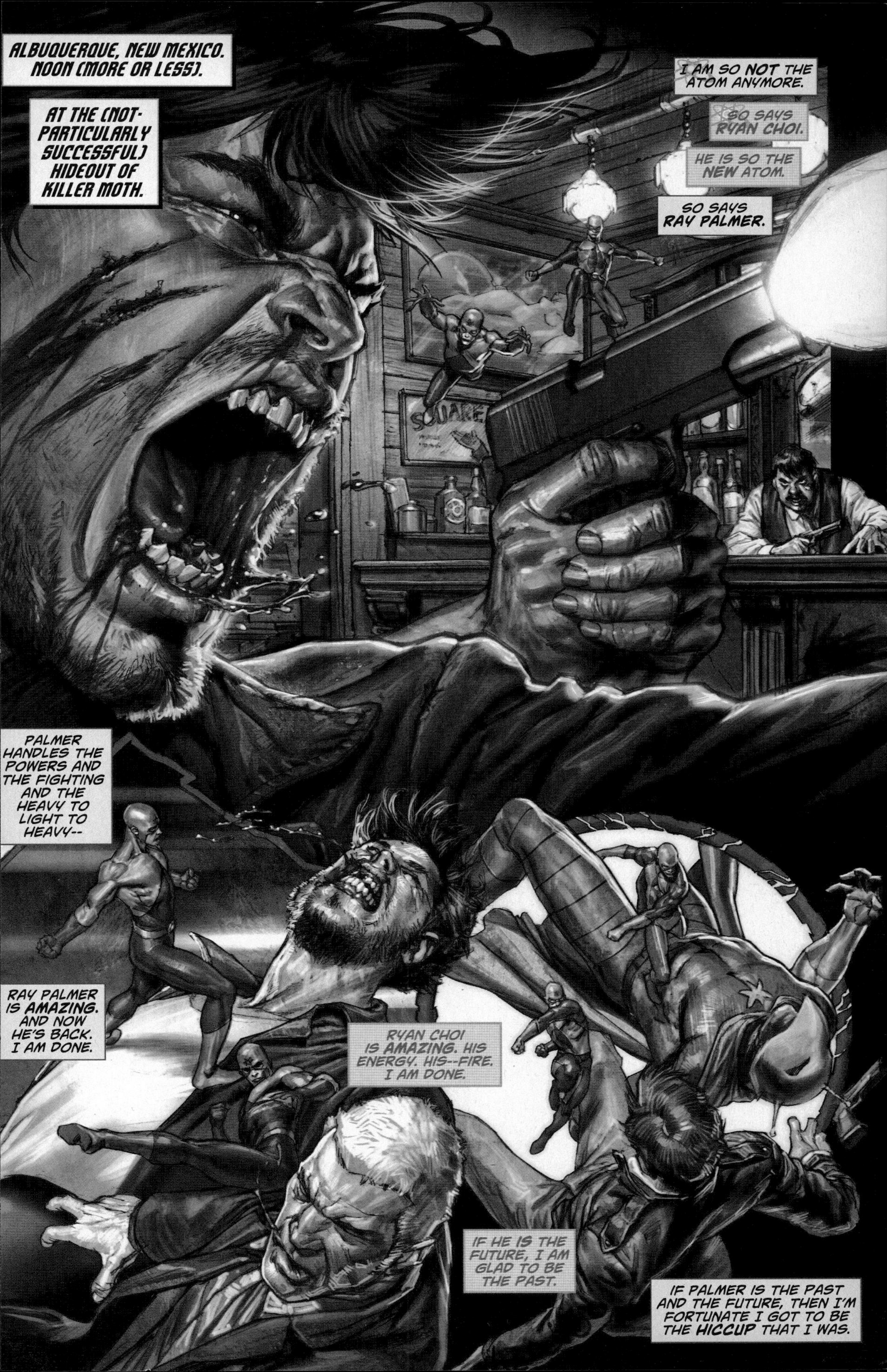
ALBUQUERQUE, NEW MEXICO. NOON (MORE OR LESS).
AT THE (NOT-PARTICULARLY SUCCESSFUL) HIDEOUT OF KILLER MOTH.
I AM SO NOT THE ATOM ANYMORE.
SO SAYS RYAN CHOI.
HE IS SO THE NEW ATOM.
SO SAYS RAY PALMER.
PALMER HANDLES THE POWERS AND THE FIGHTING AND THE HEAVY TO LIGHT TO HEAVY--
RAY PALMER IS AMAZING. AND NOW HE'S BACK. I AM DONE.
RYAN CHOI IS AMAZING. HIS ENERGY. HIS--FIRE. I AM DONE.
IF HE IS THE FUTURE, I AM GLAD TO BE THE PAST.
IF PALMER IS THE PAST AND THE FUTURE, THEN I'M FORTUNATE I GOT TO BE THE HICCUP THAT I WAS.

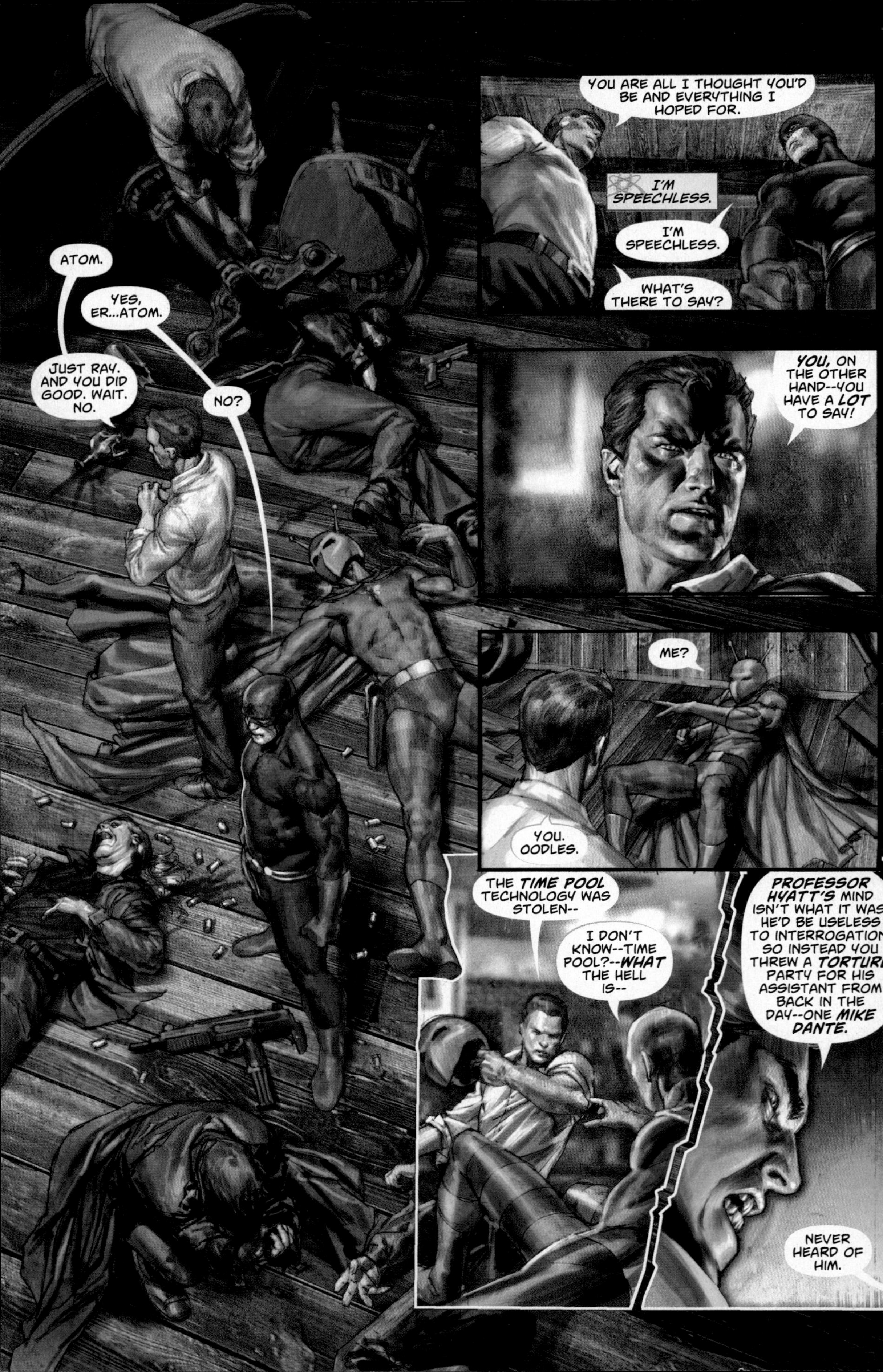
ATOM.
YES, ER...ATOM.
JUST RAY. AND YOU DID GOOD. WAIT. NO.
NO?
YOU ARE ALL I THOUGHT YOU'D BE AND EVERYTHING I HOPED FOR.
I'M SPEECHLESS.
I'M SPEECHLESS.
WHAT'S THERE TO SAY?
YOU, ON THE OTHER HAND--YOU HAVE A LOT TO SAY!
ME?
YOU. OODLES.
THE TIME POOL TECHNOLOGY WAS STOLEN--
I DON'T KNOW--TIME POOL?--WHAT THE HELL IS--
PROFESSOR HYATT'S MIND ISN'T WHAT IT WAS HE'D BE USELESS TO INTERROGATION SO INSTEAD YOU THREW A TORTURE PARTY FOR HIS ASSISTANT FROM BACK IN THE DAY--ONE MIKE DANTE.
NEVER HEARD OF HIM.

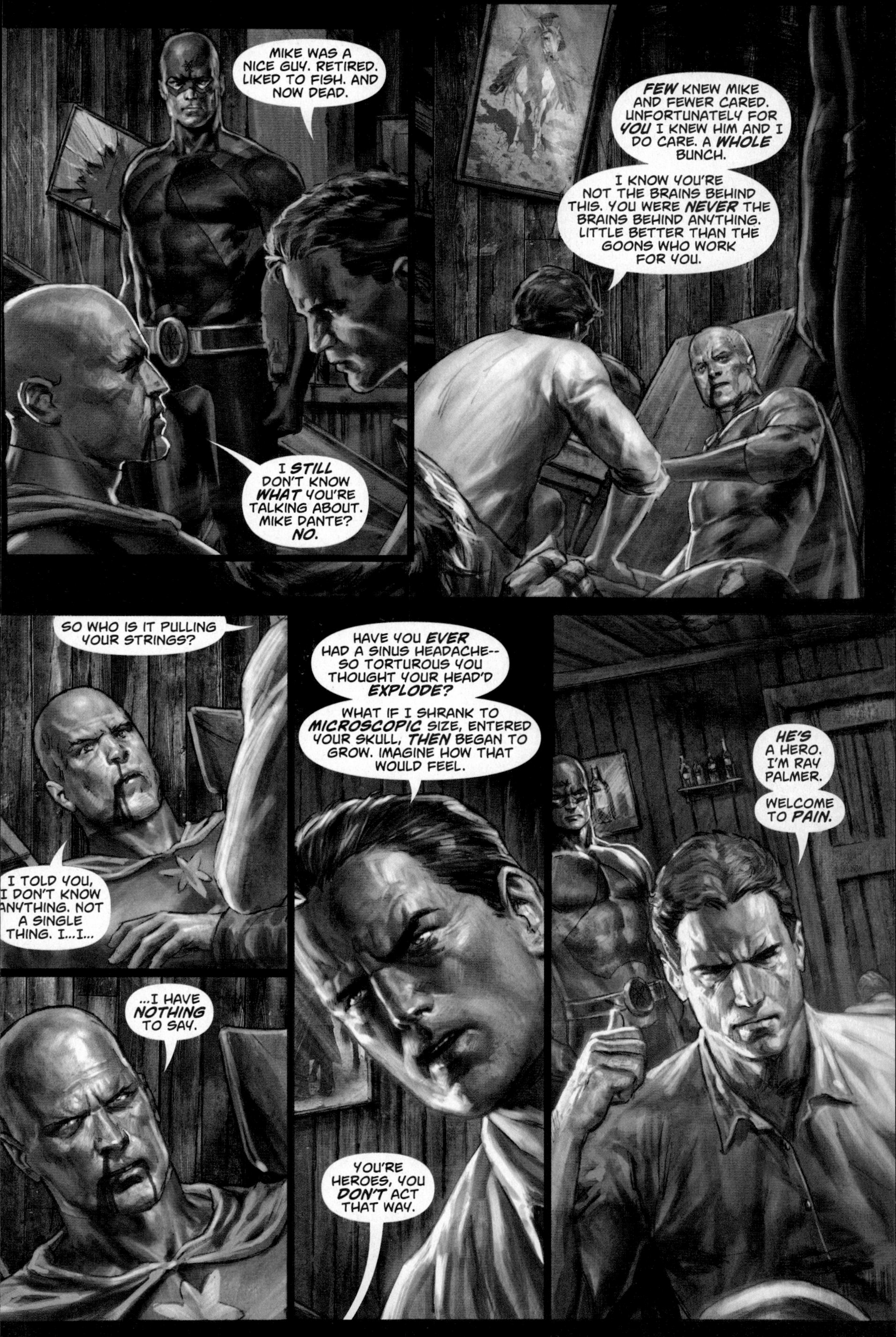
MIKE WAS A NICE GUY. RETIRED. LIKED TO FISH. AND NOW DEAD.
I STILL DON'T KNOW WHAT YOU'RE TALKING ABOUT. MIKE DANTE? NO.
FEW KNEW MIKE AND FEWER CARED. UNFORTUNATELY FOR YOU I KNEW HIM AND I DO CARE. A WHOLE BUNCH.
I KNOW YOU'RE NOT THE BRAINS BEHIND THIS. YOU WERE NEVER THE BRAINS BEHIND ANYTHING. LITTLE BETTER THAN THE GOONS WHO WORK FOR YOU.
SO WHO IS IT PULLING YOUR STRINGS?
I TOLD YOU, I DON'T KNOW ANYTHING. NOT A SINGLE THING. I...I...
...I HAVE NOTHING TO SAY.
HAVE YOU EVER HAD A SINUS HEADACHE-- SO TORTUROUS YOU THOUGHT YOUR HEAD'D EXPLODE?
WHAT IF I SHRANK TO MICROSCOPIC SIZE, ENTERED YOUR SKULL, THEN BEGAN TO GROW. IMAGINE HOW THAT WOULD FEEL.
YOU'RE HEROES, YOU DON'T ACT THAT WAY.
HE'S A HERO. I'M RAY PALMER.
WELCOME TO PAIN.

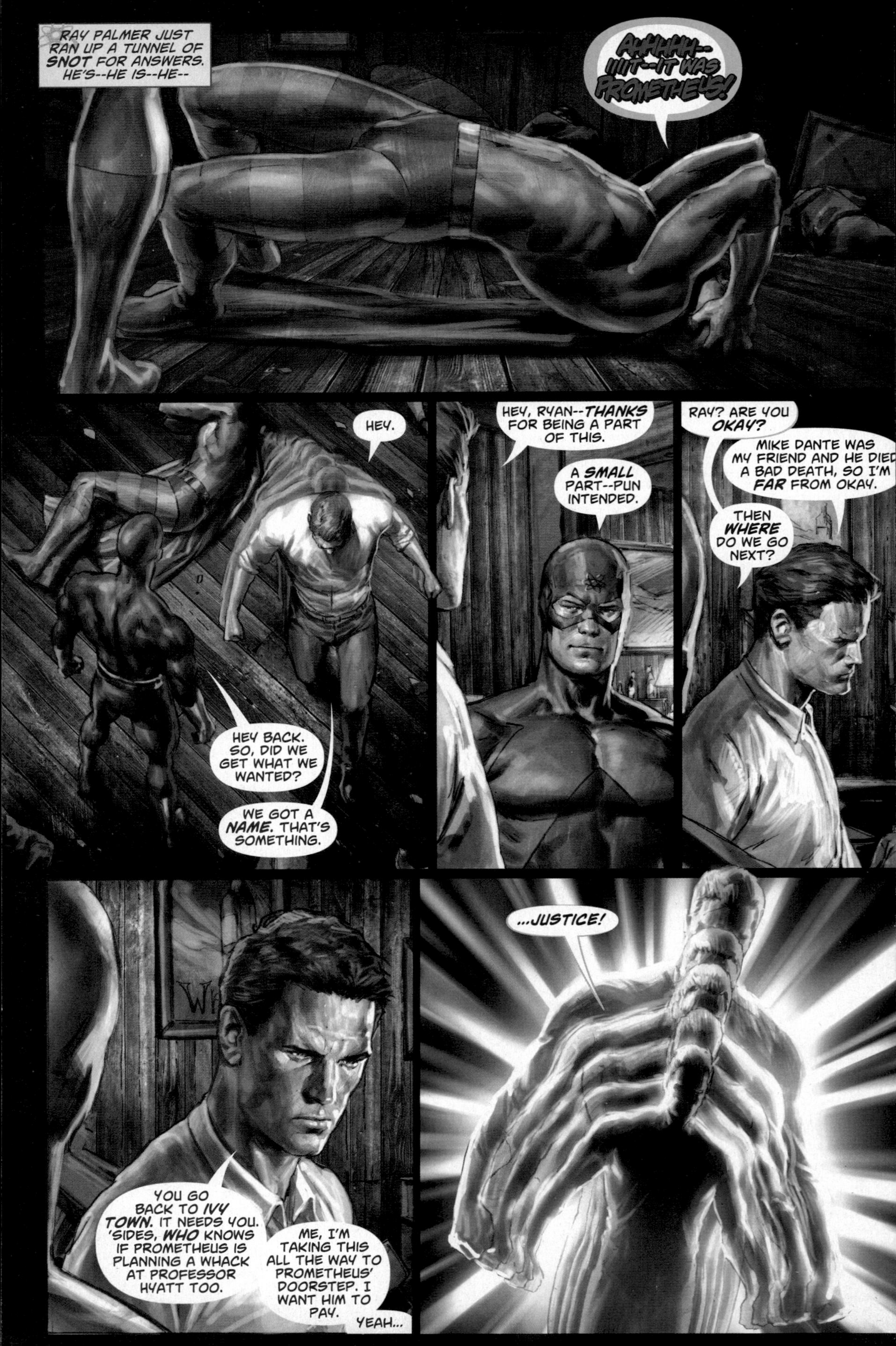
RAY PALMER JUST RAN UP A TUNNEL OF SNOT FOR ANSWERS. HE'S--HE IS--HE--
AHHHHH-- IIIIT--IT WAS PROMETHEUS!
HEY.
HEY BACK. SO, DID WE GET WHAT WE WANTED?
WE GOT A NAME. THAT'S SOMETHING.
HEY, RYAN--THANKS FOR BEING A PART OF THIS.
A SMALL PART--PUN INTENDED.
RAY? ARE YOU OKAY?
MIKE DANTE WAS MY FRIEND AND HE DIED A BAD DEATH, SO I'M FAR FROM OKAY.
THEN WHERE DO WE GO NEXT?
YOU GO BACK TO IVY TOWN. IT NEEDS YOU. 'SIDES, WHO KNOWS IF PROMETHEUS IS PLANNING A WHACK AT PROFESSOR HYATT TOO.
ME, I'M TAKING THIS ALL THE WAY TO PROMETHEUS' DOORSTEP. I WANT HIM TO PAY.
YEAH...
...JUSTICE!

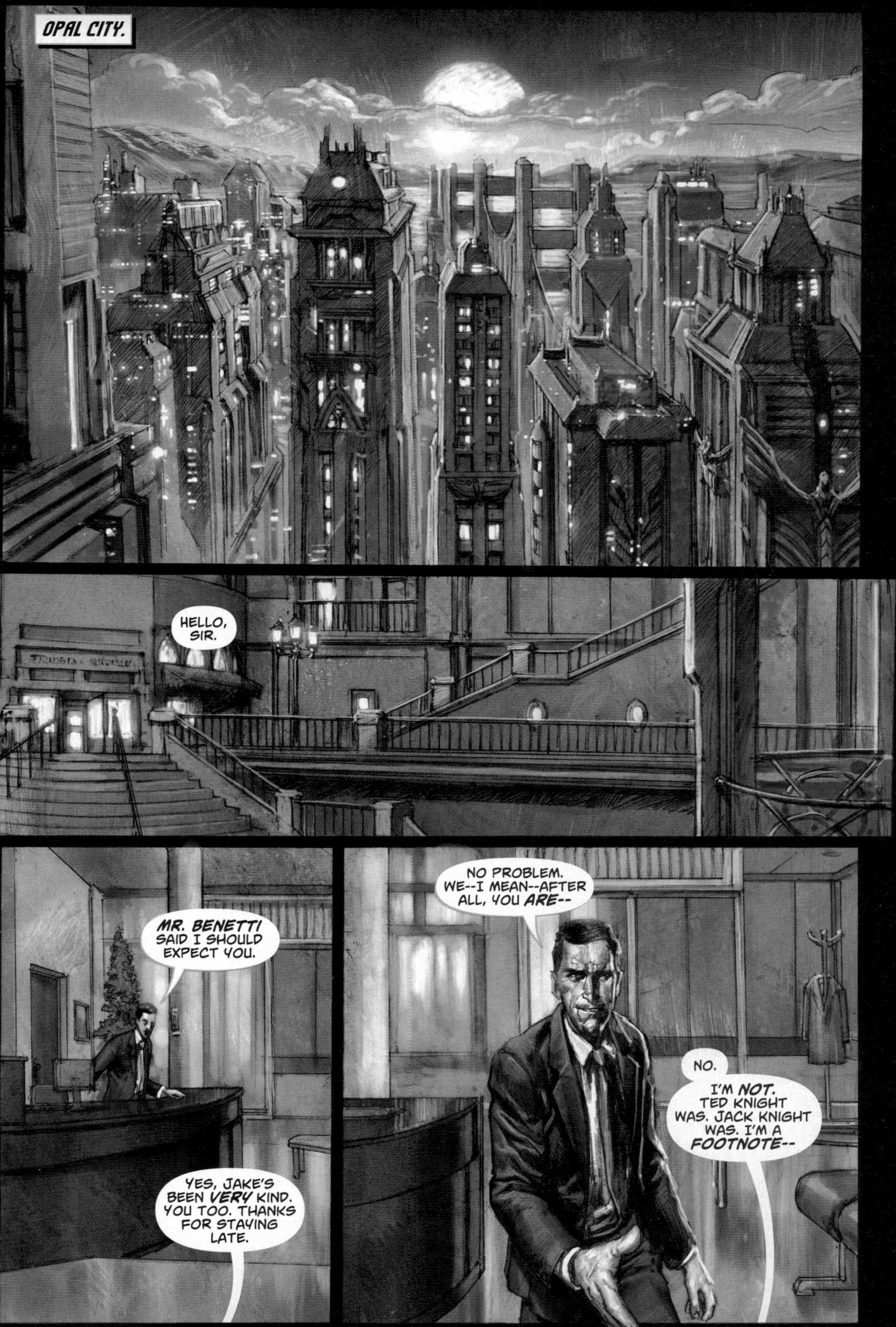
OPAL CITY.
HELLO, SIR.
MR. BENETTI SAID I SHOULD EXPECT YOU.
YES, JAKE'S BEEN VERY KIND. YOU TOO. THANKS FOR STAYING LATE.
NO PROBLEM. WE--I MEAN--AFTER ALL, YOU ARE--
NO.
I'M NOT. TED KNIGHT WAS. JACK KNIGHT WAS. I'M A FOOTNOTE--

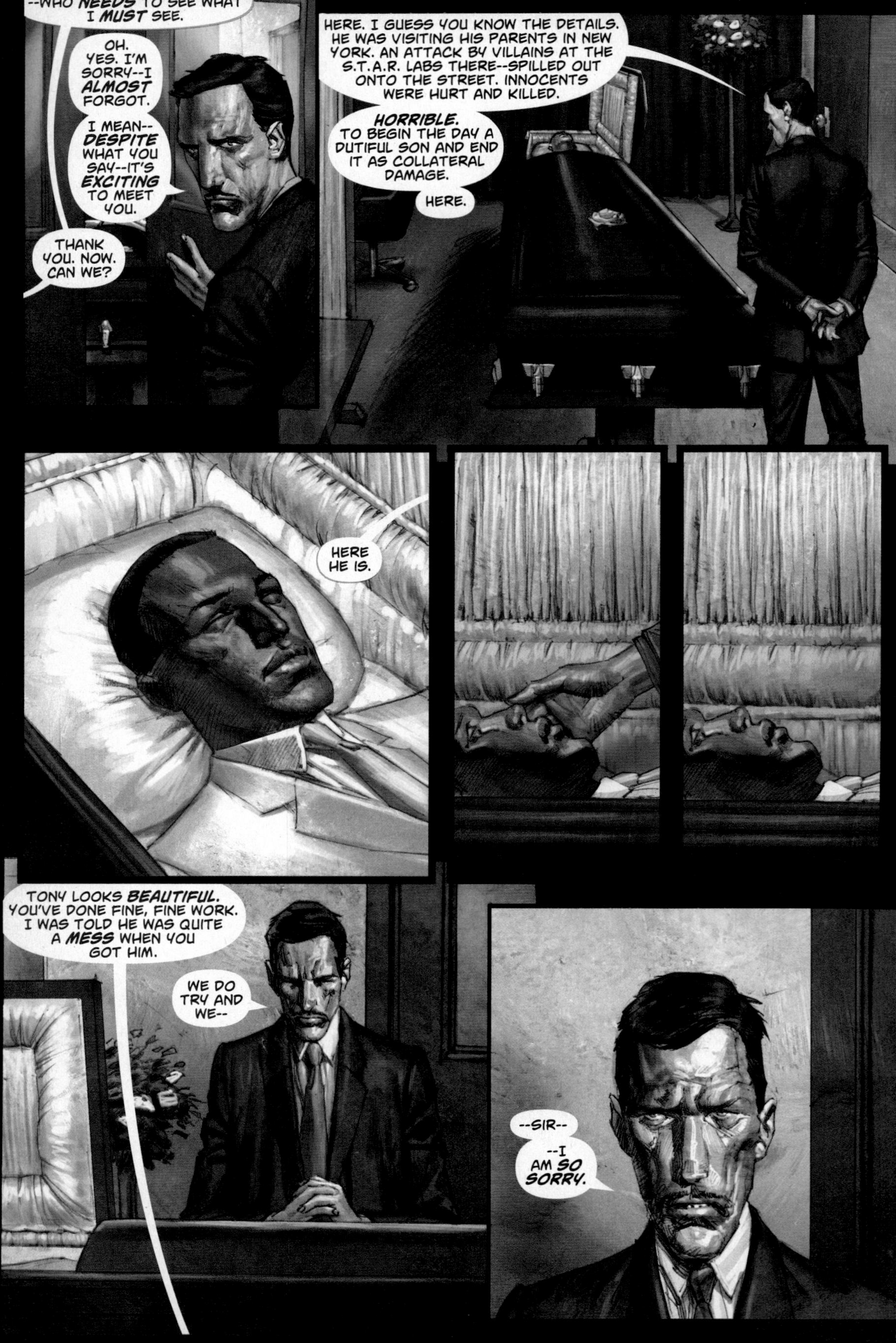
--WHO NEEDS TO SEE WHAT I MUST SEE.
OH. YES. I'M SORRY--I ALMOST FORGOT.
I MEAN--DESPITE WHAT YOU SAY--IT'S EXCITING TO MEET YOU.
THANK YOU. NOW. CAN WE?
HERE. I GUESS YOU KNOW THE DETAILS. HE WAS VISITING HIS PARENTS IN NEW YORK. AN ATTACK BY VILLAINS AT THE S.T.A.R. LABS THERE--SPILLED OUT ONTO THE STREET. INNOCENTS WERE HURT AND KILLED.
HORRIBLE. TO BEGIN THE DAY A DUTIFUL SON AND END IT AS COLLATERAL DAMAGE.
HERE.
HERE HE IS.
TONY LOOKS BEAUTIFUL. YOU'VE DONE FINE, FINE WORK. I WAS TOLD HE WAS QUITE A MESS WHEN YOU GOT HIM.
WE DO TRY AND WE--
--SIR--
--I AM SO SORRY.

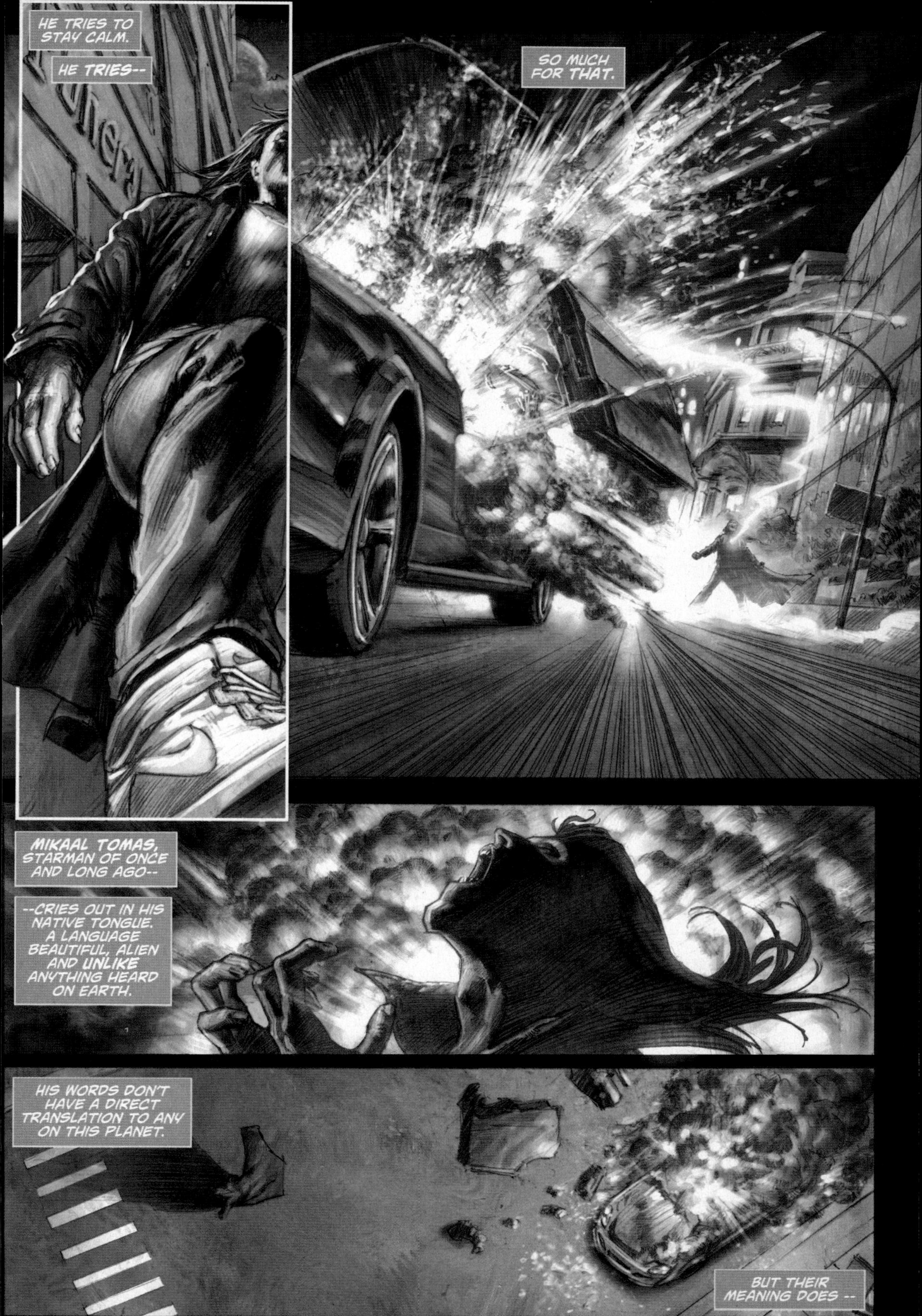
HE TRIES TO STAY CALM.
HE TRIES--
SO MUCH FOR THAT.
MIKAAL TOMAS, STARMAN OF ONCE AND LONG AGO--
--CRIES OUT IN HIS NATIVE TONGUE. A LANGUAGE BEAUTIFUL, ALIEN AND UNLIKE ANYTHING HEARD ON EARTH.
HIS WORDS DON'T HAVE A DIRECT TRANSLATION TO ANY ON THIS PLANET.
BUT THEIR MEANING DOES --

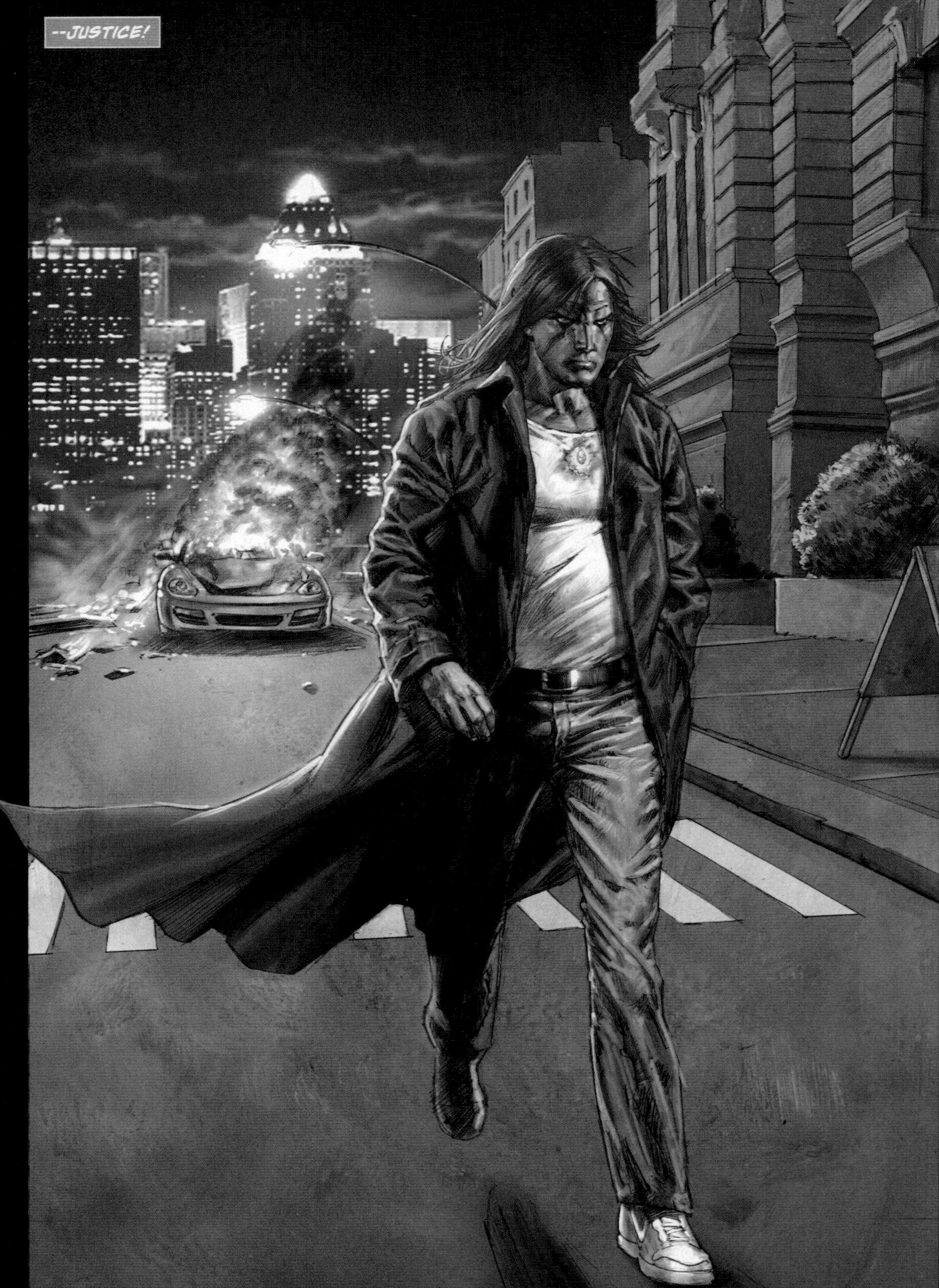
--JUSTICE!

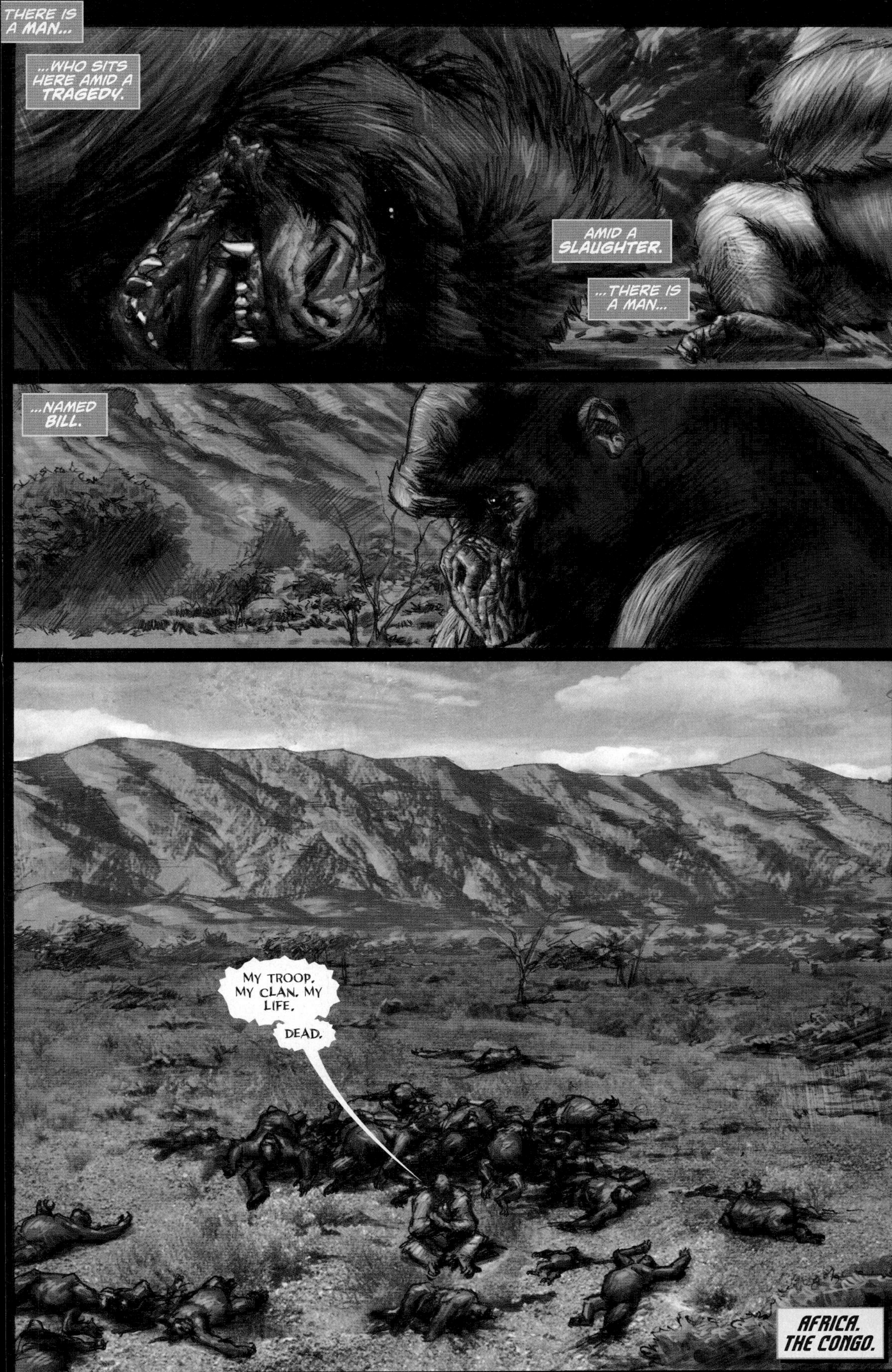
THERE IS A MAN...
...WHO SITS HERE AMID A TRAGEDY.
AMID A SLAUGHTER.
...THERE IS A MAN...
...NAMED BILL.
MY TROOP. MY CLAN. MY LIFE.
DEAD.
AFRICA. THE CONGO.

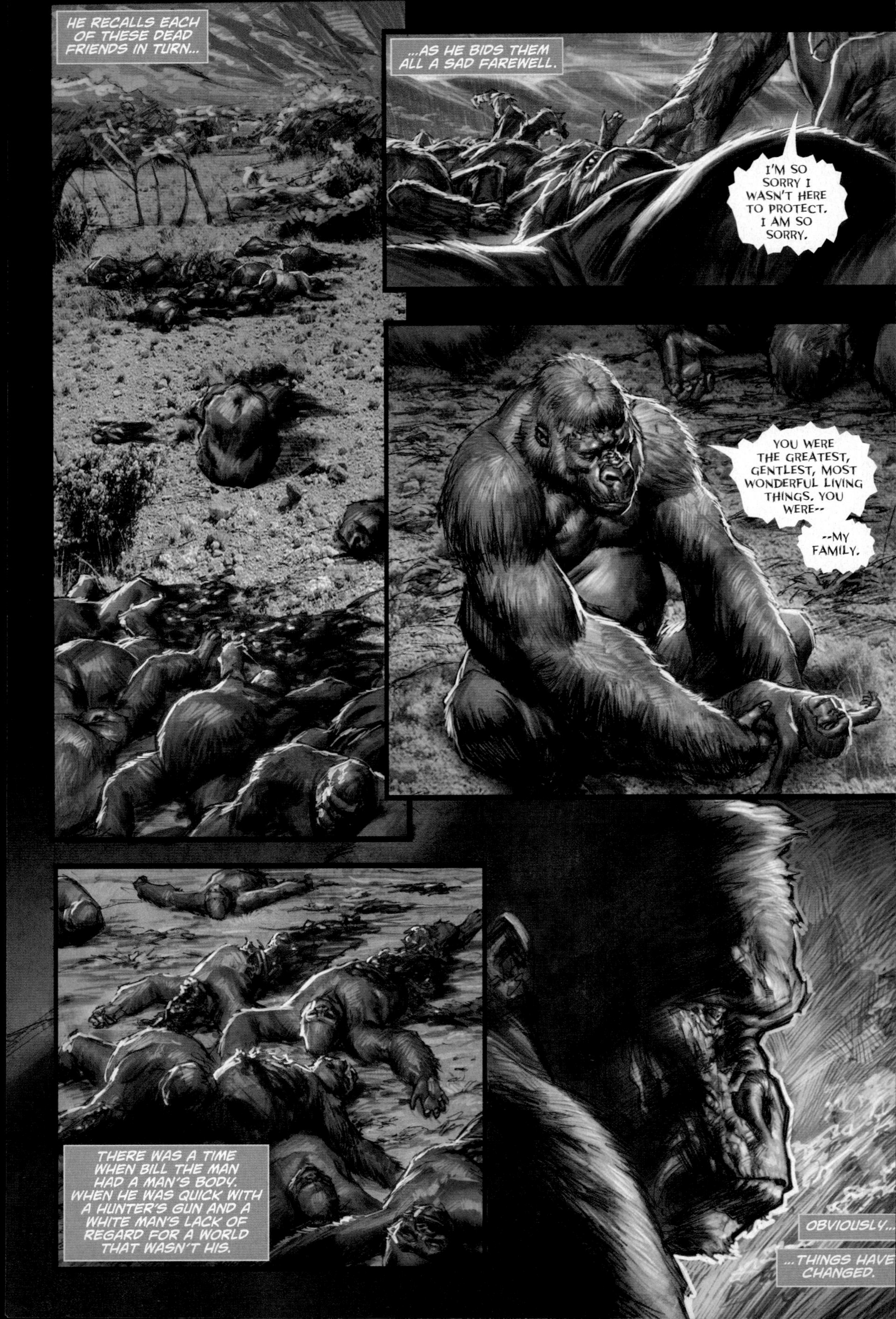
HE RECALLS EACH OF THESE DEAD FRIENDS IN TURN...
...AS HE BIDS THEM ALL A SAD FAREWELL.
I'M SO SORRY I WASN'T HERE TO PROTECT. I AM SO SORRY.
YOU WERE THE GREATEST, GENTLEST, MOST WONDERFUL LIVING THINGS. YOU WERE--
--MY FAMILY.
THERE WAS A TIME WHEN BILL THE MAN HAD A MAN'S BODY. WHEN HE WAS QUICK WITH A HUNTER'S GUN AND A WHITE MAN'S LACK OF REGARD FOR A WORLD THAT WASN'T HIS.
OBVIOUSLY...
...THINGS HAVE CHANGED.

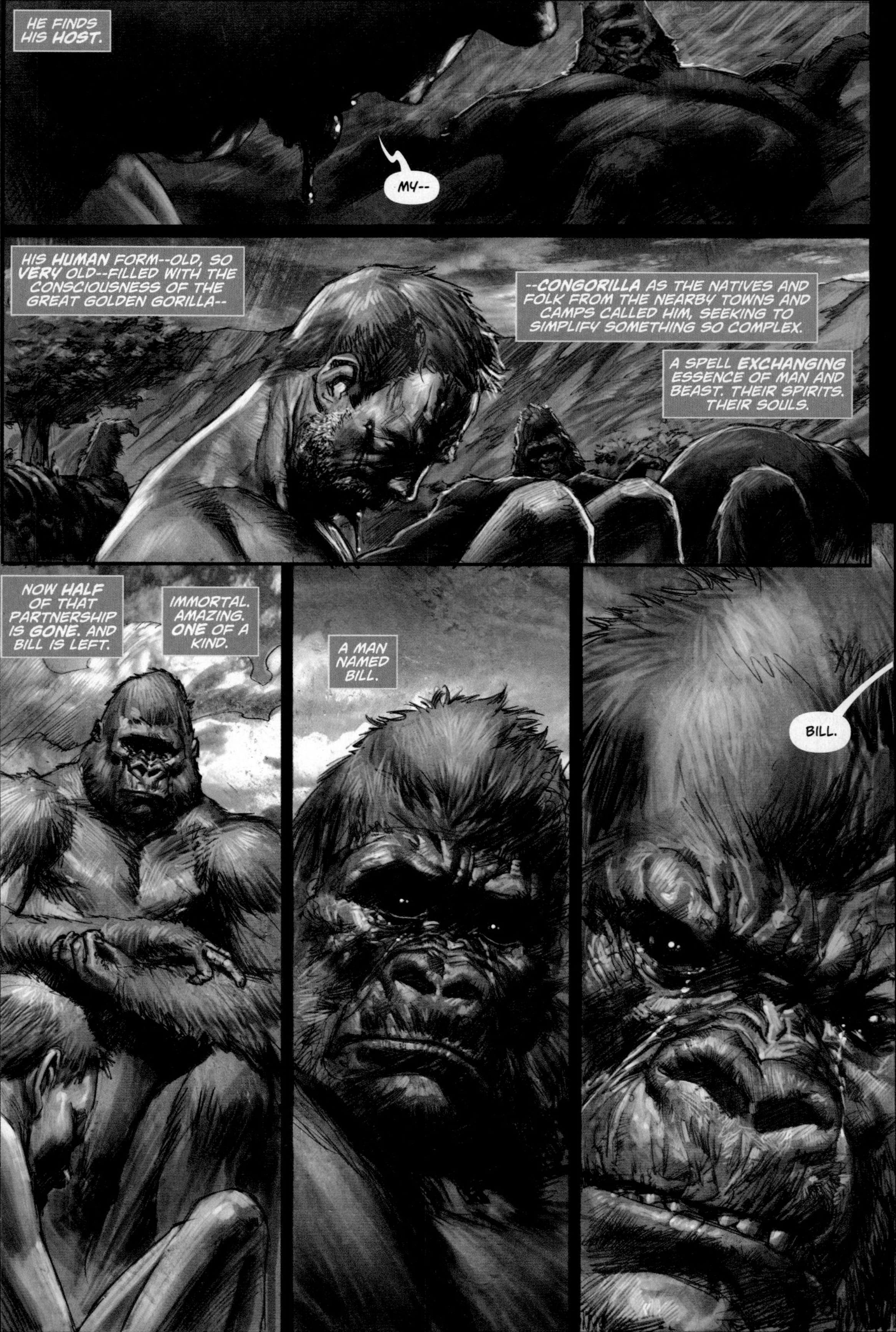
HE FINDS HIS HOST.
MY--
HIS HUMAN FORM--OLD, SO VERY OLD--FILLED WITH THE CONSCIOUSNESS OF THE GREAT GOLDEN GORILLA--
--CONGORILLA AS THE NATIVES AND FOLK FROM THE NEARBY TOWNS AND CAMPS CALLED HIM, SEEKING TO SIMPLIFY SOMETHING SO COMPLEX.
A SPELL EXCHANGING ESSENCE OF MAN AND BEAST. THEIR SPIRITS. THEIR SOULS.
NOW HALF OF THAT PARTNERSHIP IS GONE. AND BILL IS LEFT.
IMMORTAL. AMAZING. ONE OF A KIND.
A MAN NAMED BILL.
BILL.

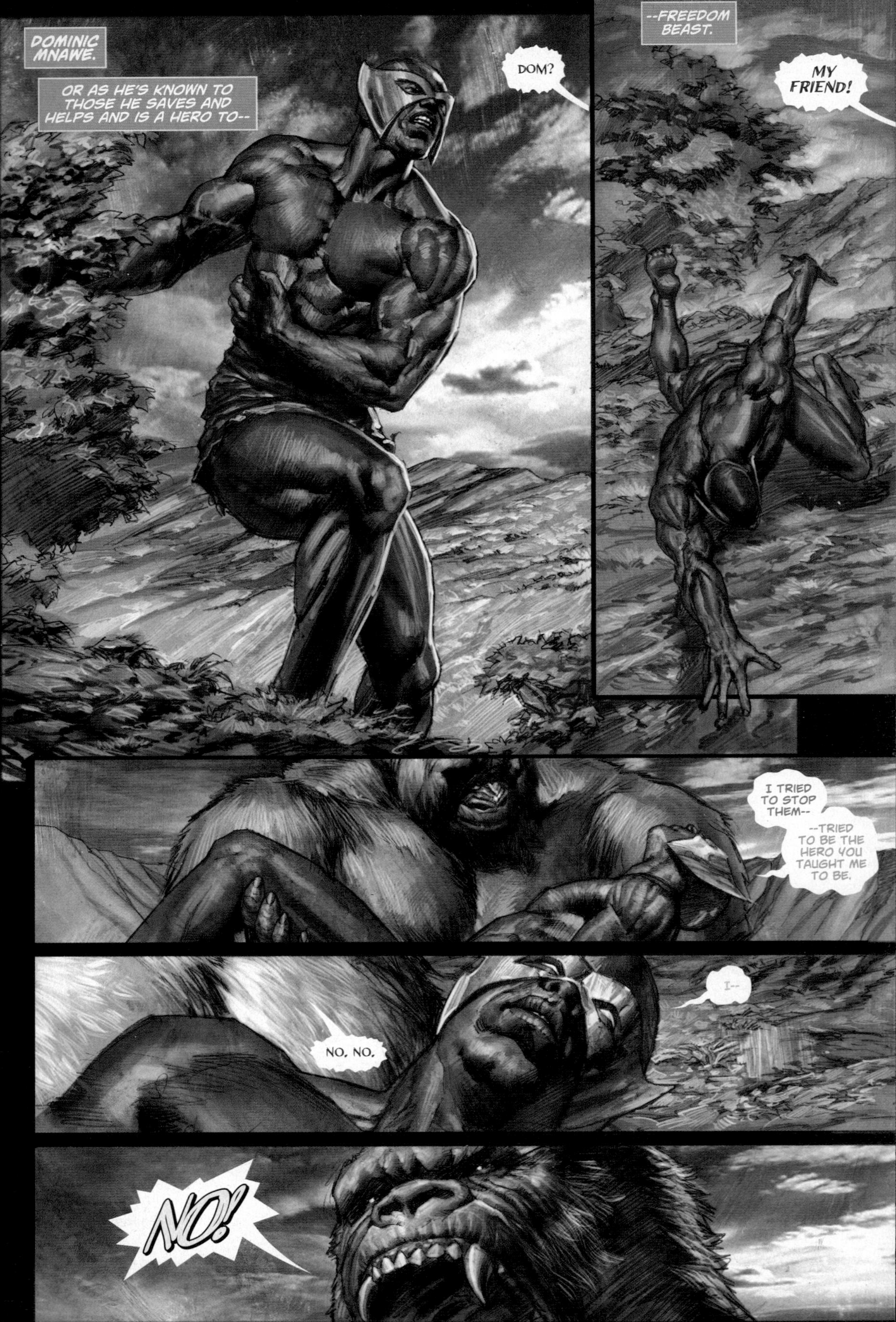
DOMINIC MNAWE.
OR AS HE'S KNOWN TO THOSE HE SAVES AND HELPS AND IS A HERO TO--
DOM?
--FREEDOM BEAST.
MY FRIEND!
I TRIED TO STOP THEM--
--TRIED TO BE THE HERO YOU TAUGHT ME TO BE.
I--
NO, NO.
NO!

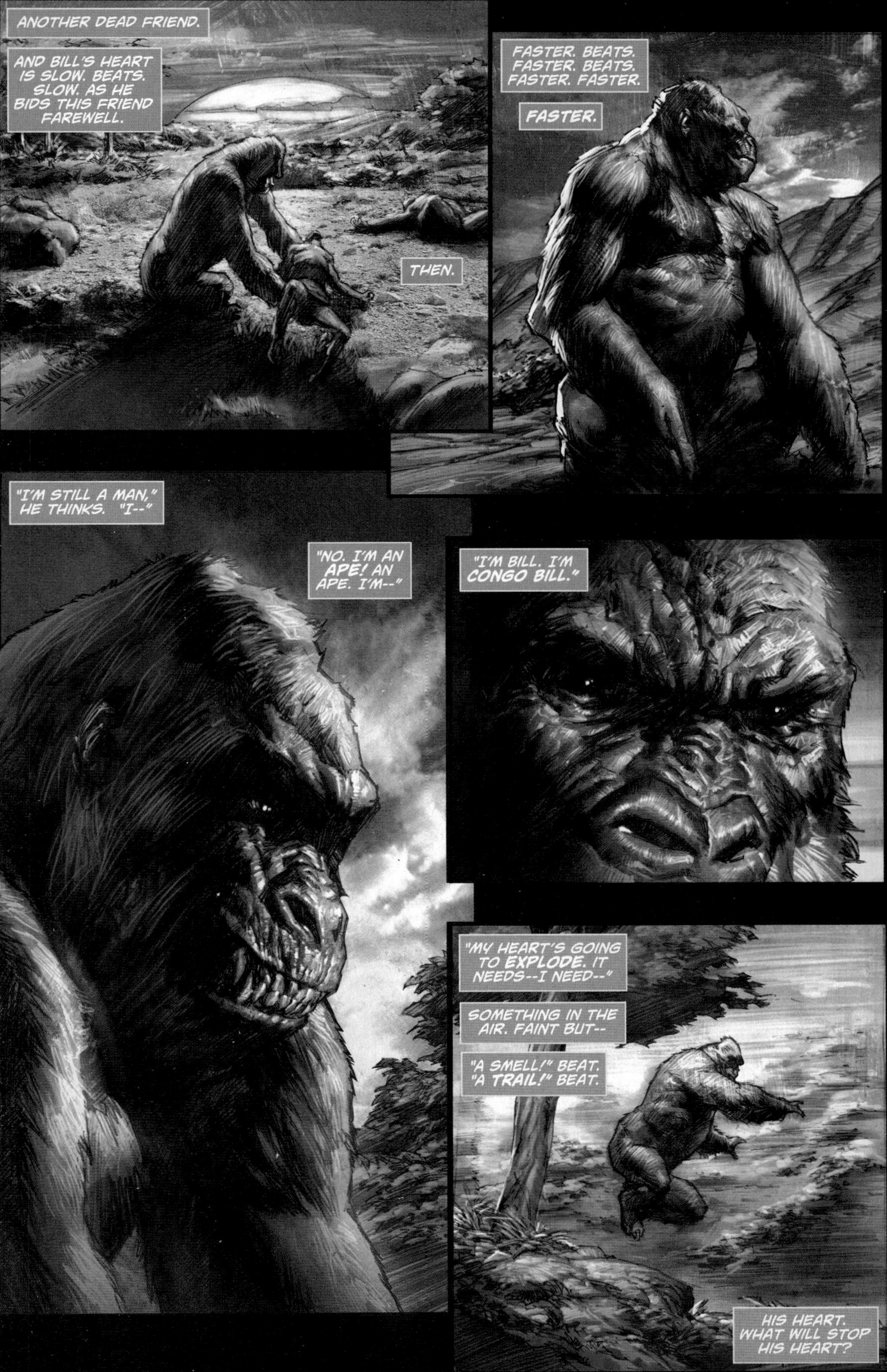
ANOTHER DEAD FRIEND.
AND BILL'S HEART IS SLOW. BEATS. SLOW. AS HE BIDS THIS FRIEND FAREWELL.
THEN.
FASTER. BEATS. FASTER. BEATS. FASTER. FASTER.
FASTER.
"I'M STILL A MAN," HE THINKS. "I--"
"NO. I'M AN APE! AN APE. I'M--"
"I'M BILL. I'M CONGO BILL."
"MY HEART'S GOING TO EXPLODE. IT NEEDS--I NEED--"
SOMETHING IN THE AIR. FAINT BUT--
"A SMELL!" BEAT. "A TRAIL!" BEAT.
HIS HEART. WHAT WILL STOP HIS HEART?

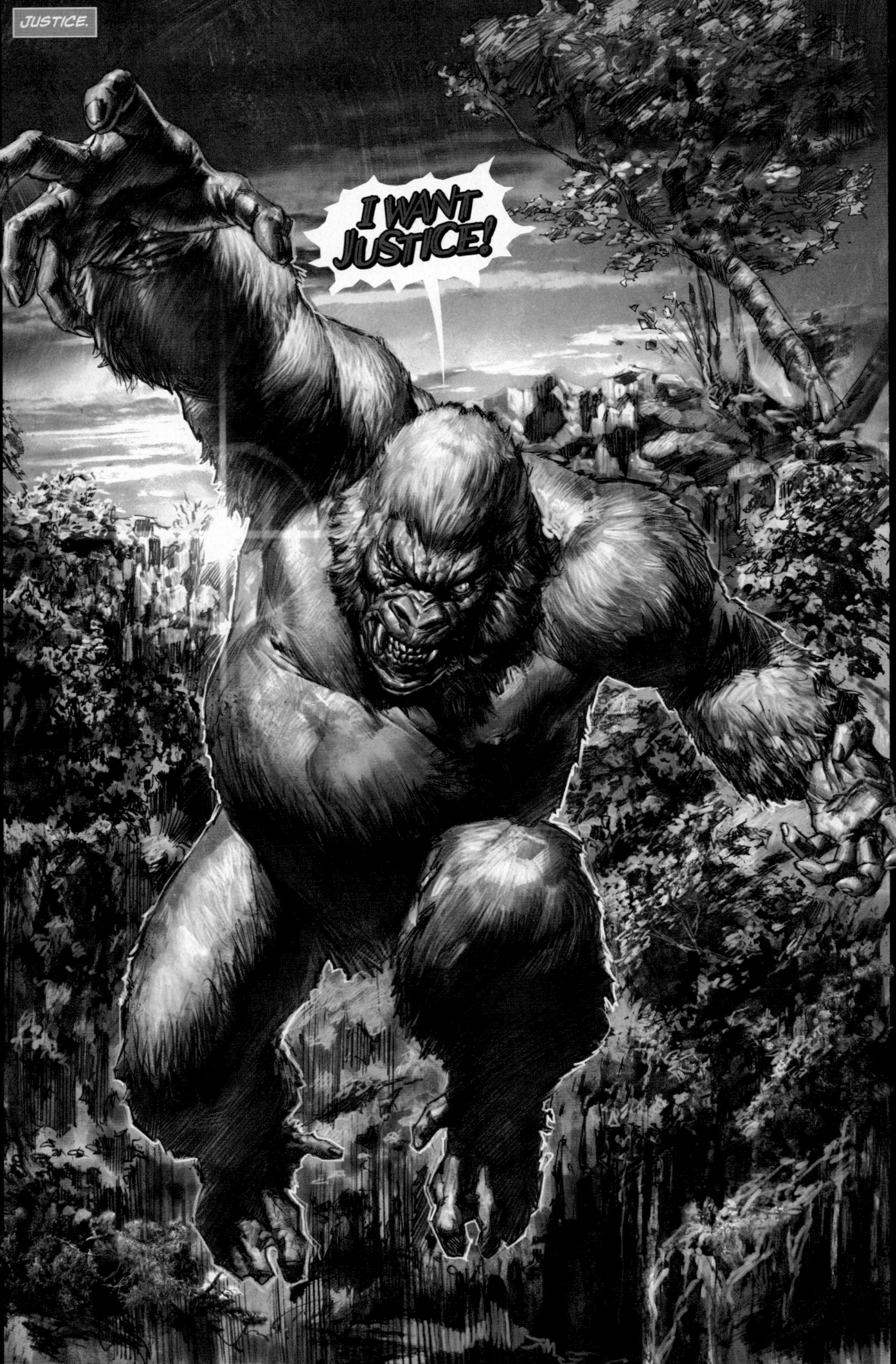
JUSTICE.
I WANT JUSTICE!

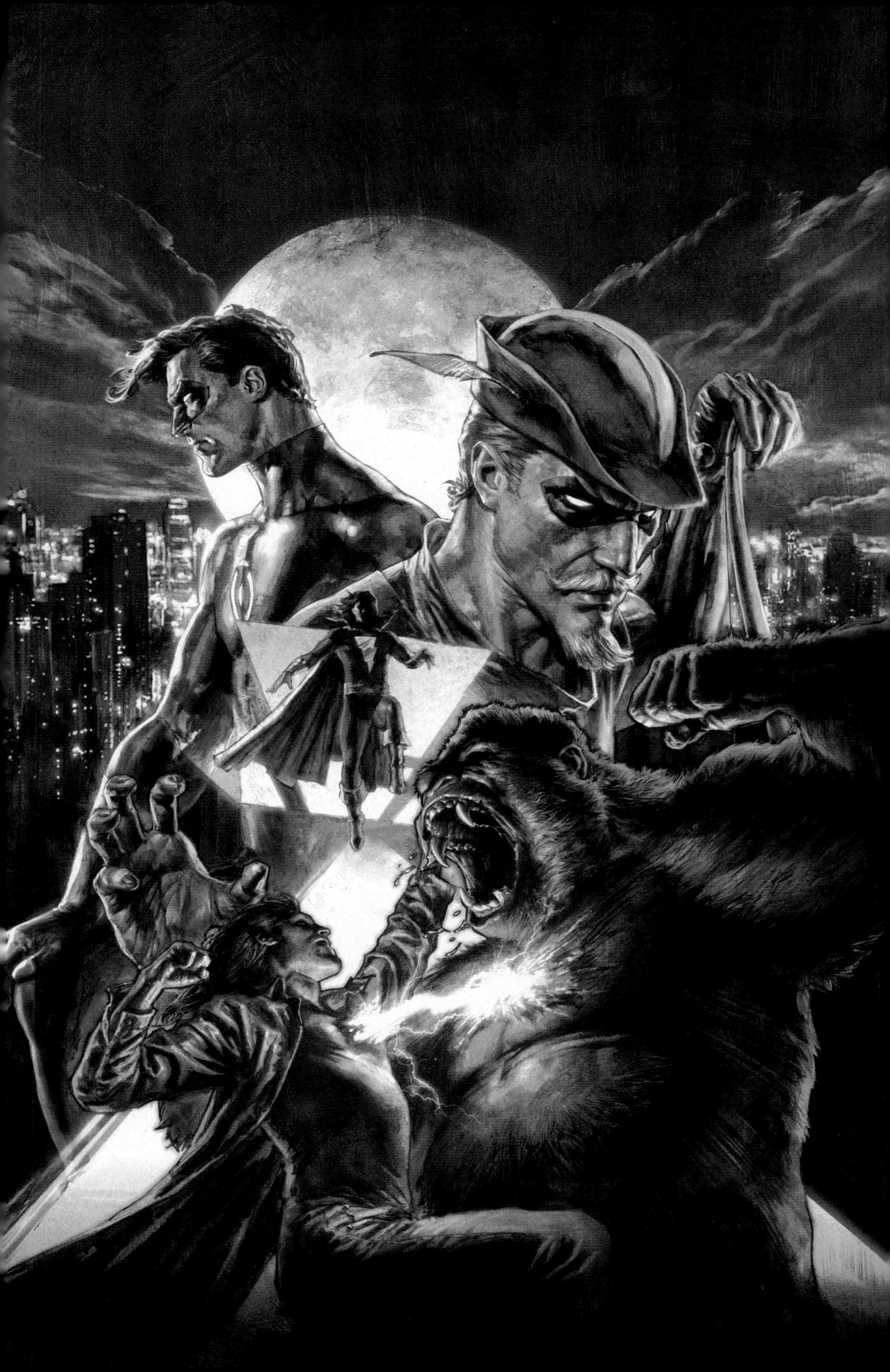

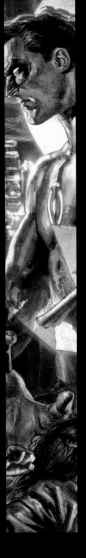

CRY FOR JUSTICE PART TWO: THE GATHERING

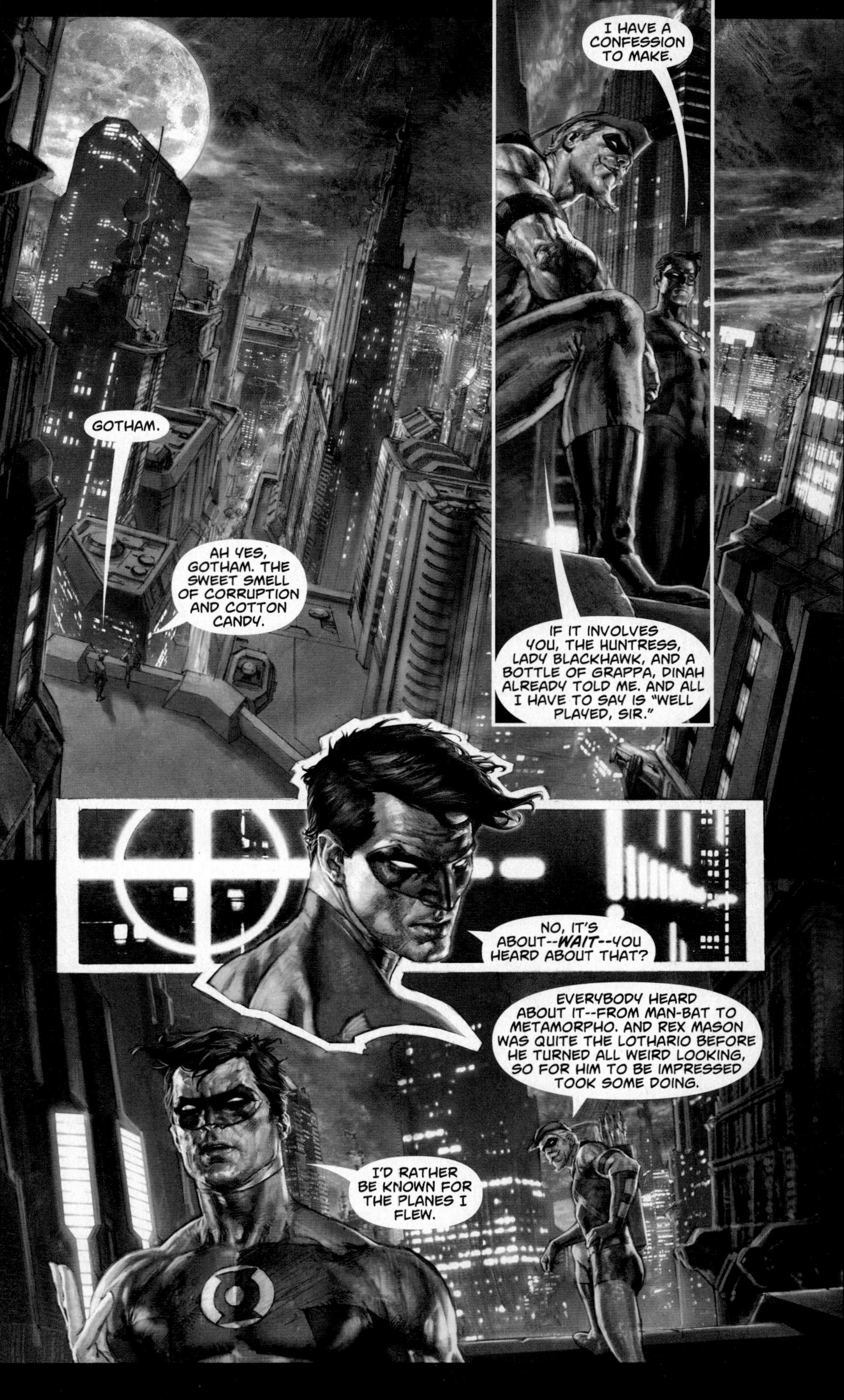

GOTHAM.
AH YES, GOTHAM. THE SWEET SMELL OF CORRUPTION AND COTTON CANDY.
I HAVE A CONFESSION TO MAKE.
IF IT INVOLVES YOU, THE HUNTRESS, LADY BLACKHAWK, AND A BOTTLE OF GRAPPA, DINAH ALREADY TOLD ME. AND ALL I HAVE TO SAY IS "WELL PLAYED, SIR."
NO, IT'S ABOUT--WAIT--YOU HEARD ABOUT THAT?
EVERYBODY HEARD ABOUT IT--FROM MAN-BAT TO METAMORPHO. AND REX MASON WAS QUITE THE LOTHARIO BEFORE HE TURNED ALL WEIRD LOOKING, SO FOR HIM TO BE IMPRESSED TOOK SOME DOING.
I'D RATHER BE KNOWN FOR THE PLANES I FLEW.

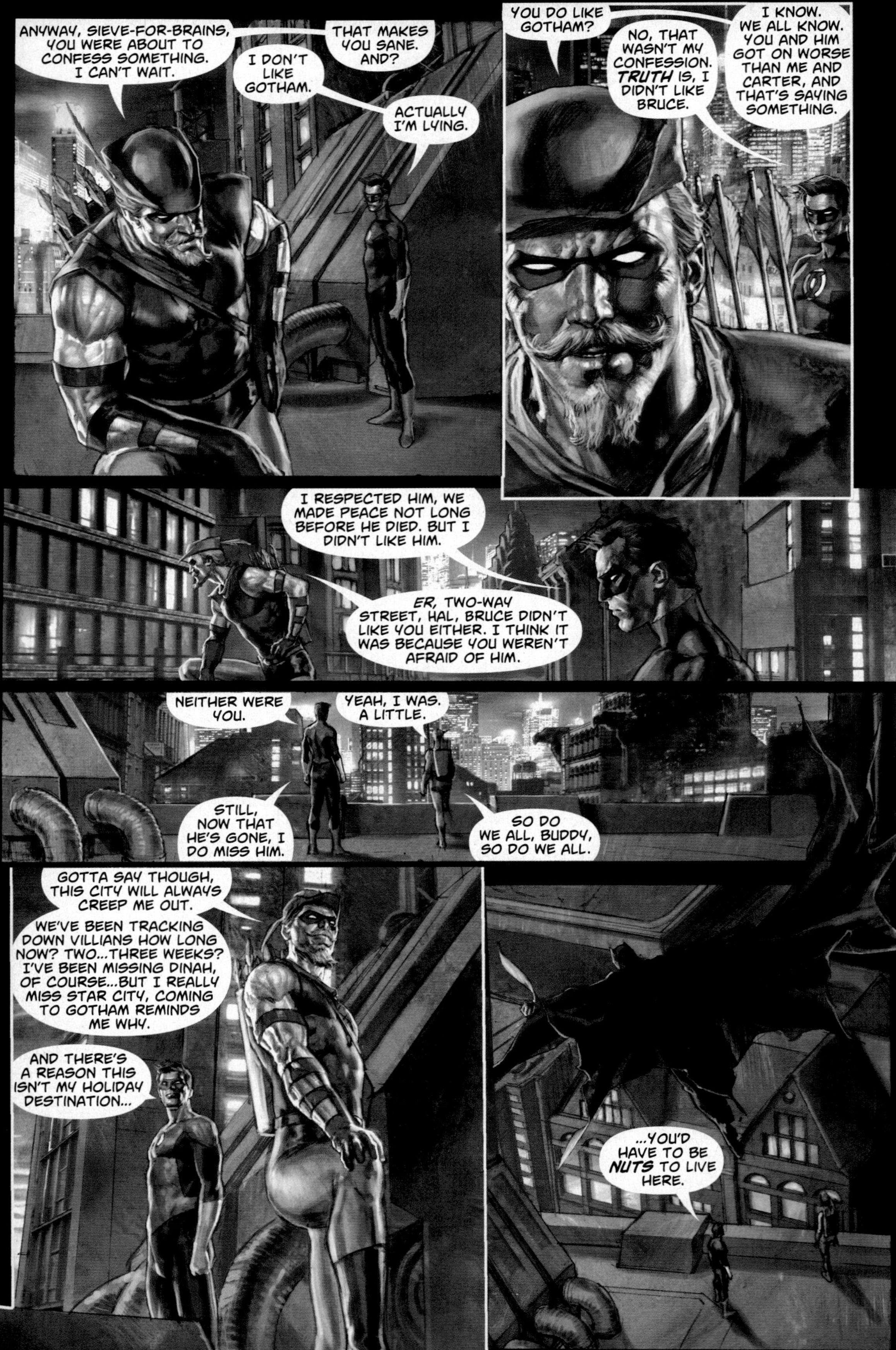

ANYWAY, SIEVE-FOR-BRAINS, YOU WERE ABOUT TO CONFESS SOMETHING. I CAN'T WAIT.
I DON'T LIKE GOTHAM.
THAT MAKES YOU SANE. AND?
ACTUALLY I'M LYING.
YOU DO LIKE GOTHAM?
NO, THAT WASN'T MY CONFESSION. TRUTH IS, I DIDN'T LIKE BRUCE.
I KNOW. WE ALL KNOW. YOU AND HIM GOT ON WORSE THAN ME AND CARTER, AND THAT'S SAYING SOMETHING.
I RESPECTED HIM, WE MADE PEACE NOT LONG BEFORE HE DIED. BUT I DIDN'T LIKE HIM.
ER, TWO-WAY STREET, HAL, BRUCE DIDN'T LIKE YOU EITHER. I THINK IT WAS BECAUSE YOU WEREN'T AFRAID OF HIM.
NEITHER WERE YOU.
YEAH, I WAS. A LITTLE.
STILL, NOW THAT HE'S GONE, I DO MISS HIM.
SO DO WE ALL, BUDDY, SO DO WE ALL.
GOTTA SAY THOUGH, THIS CITY WILL ALWAYS CREEP ME OUT.
WE'VE BEEN TRACKING DOWN VILLIANS HOW LONG NOW? TWO...THREE WEEKS? I'VE BEEN MISSING DINAH, OF COURSE...BUT I REALLY MISS STAR CITY, COMING TO GOTHAM REMINDS ME WHY.
AND THERE'S A REASON THIS ISN'T MY HOLIDAY DESTINATION...
...YOU'D HAVE TO BE NUTS TO LIVE HERE.

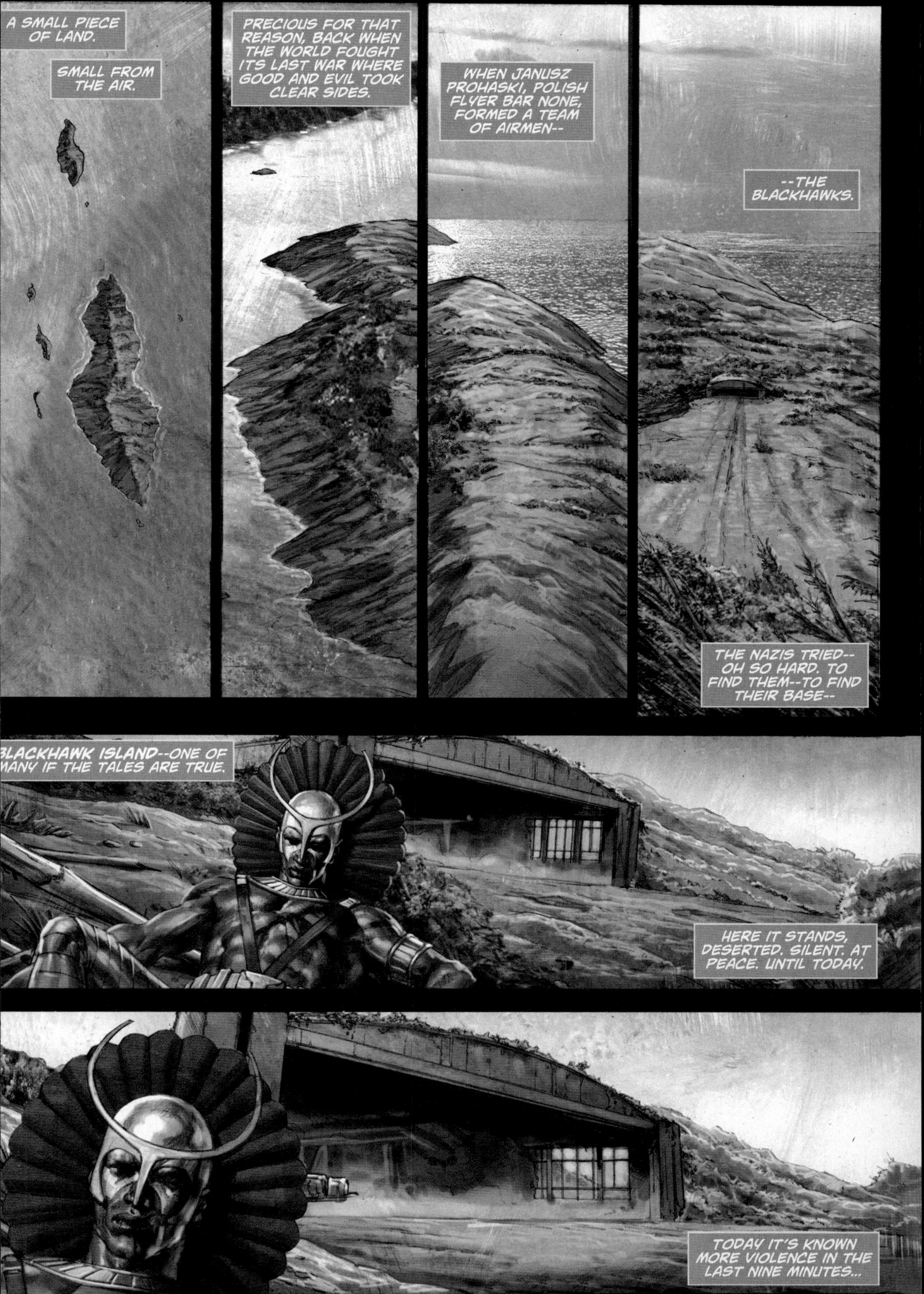
A SMALL PIECE OF LAND.
SMALL FROM THE AIR.
PRECIOUS FOR THAT REASON, BACK WHEN THE WORLD FOUGHT ITS LAST WAR WHERE GOOD AND EVIL TOOK CLEAR SIDES.
WHEN JANUSZ PROHASKI, POLISH FLYER BAR NONE, FORMED A TEAM OF AIRMEN--
--THE BLACKHAWKS.
THE NAZIS TRIED--OH SO HARD. TO FIND THEM--TO FIND THEIR BASE--
BLACKHAWK ISLAND--ONE OF MANY IF THE TALES ARE TRUE.
HERE IT STANDS, DESERTED. SILENT. AT PEACE. UNTIL TODAY.
TODAY IT'S KNOWN MORE VIOLENCE IN THE LAST NINE MINUTES...

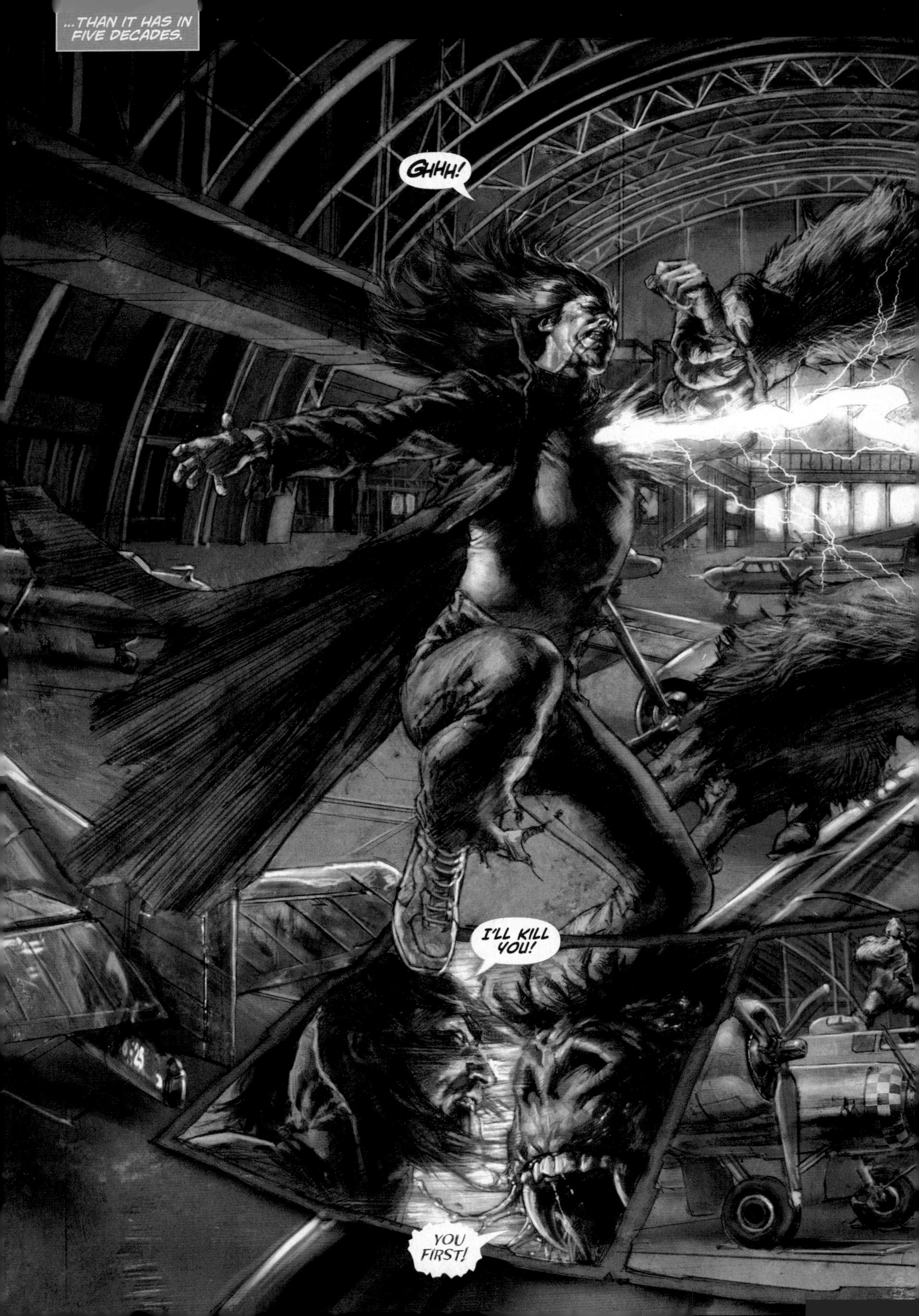
...THAN IT HAS IN FIVE DECADES.
GHHH!
I'LL KILL YOU!
YOU FIRST!

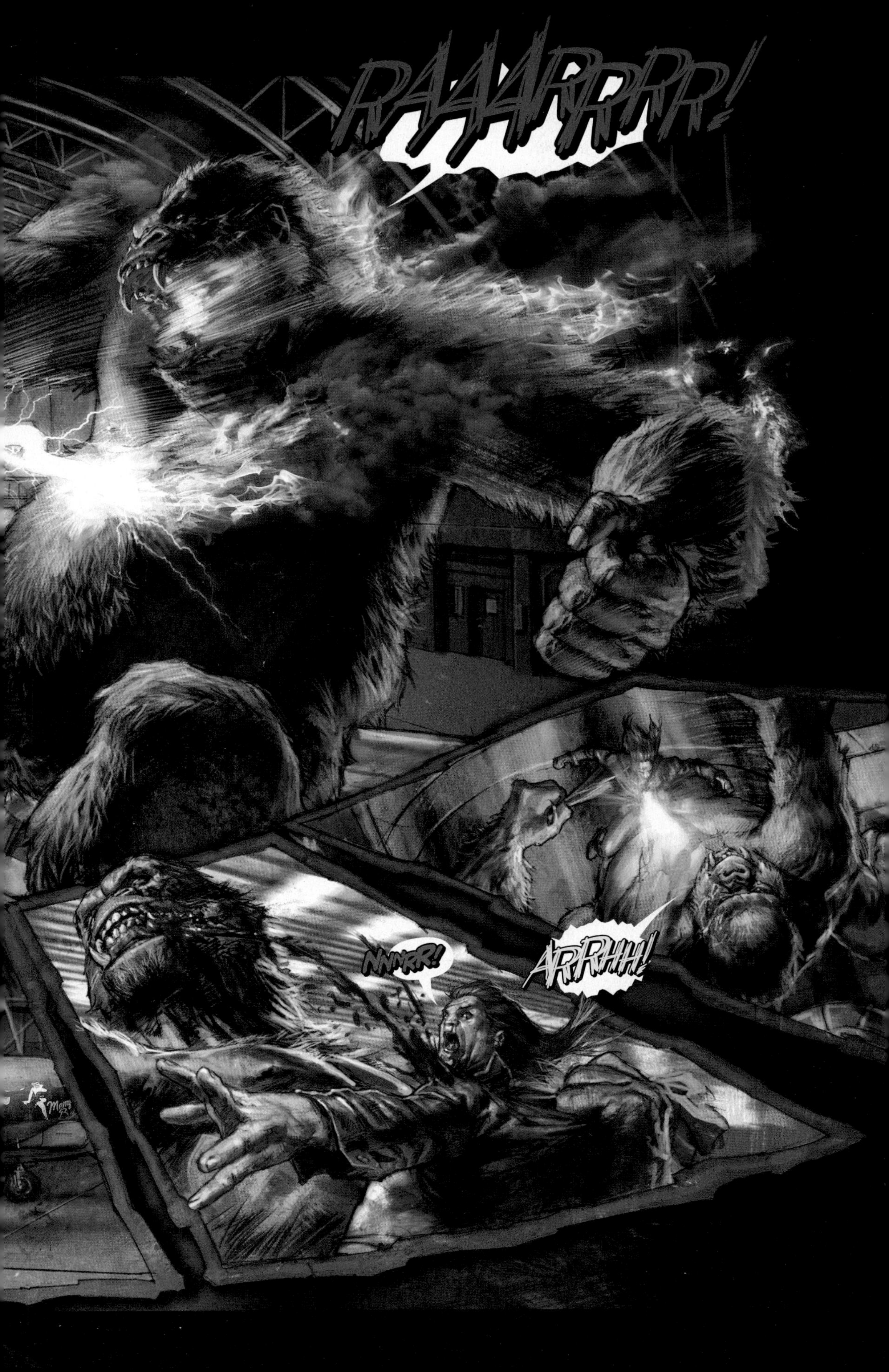
RAAARRRRR!
NNNRR!
ARRHH!

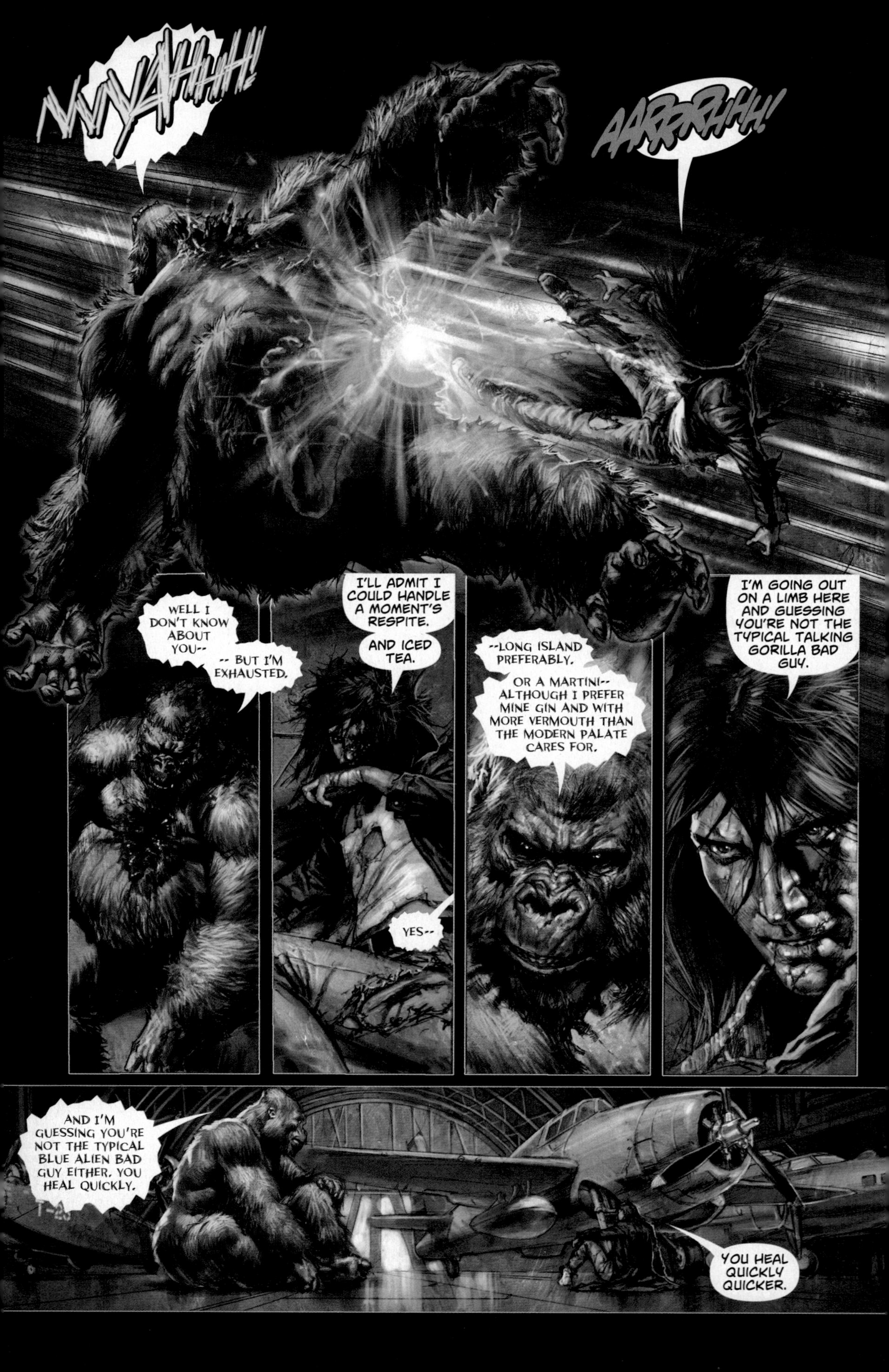
NWYAHHHH!
AARRRHHH!
WELL I DON'T KNOW ABOUT YOU--
-- BUT I'M EXHAUSTED.
I'LL ADMIT I COULD HANDLE A MOMENT'S RESPITE.
AND ICED TEA.
YES--
--LONG ISLAND PREFERABLY.
OR A MARTINI-- ALTHOUGH I PREFER MINE GIN AND WITH MORE VERMOUTH THAN THE MODERN PALATE CARES FOR.
I'M GOING OUT ON A LIMB HERE AND GUESSING YOU'RE NOT THE TYPICAL TALKING GORILLA BAD GUY.
AND I'M GUESSING YOU'RE NOT THE TYPICAL BLUE ALIEN BAD GUY EITHER. YOU HEAL QUICKLY.
YOU HEAL QUICKLY QUICKER.

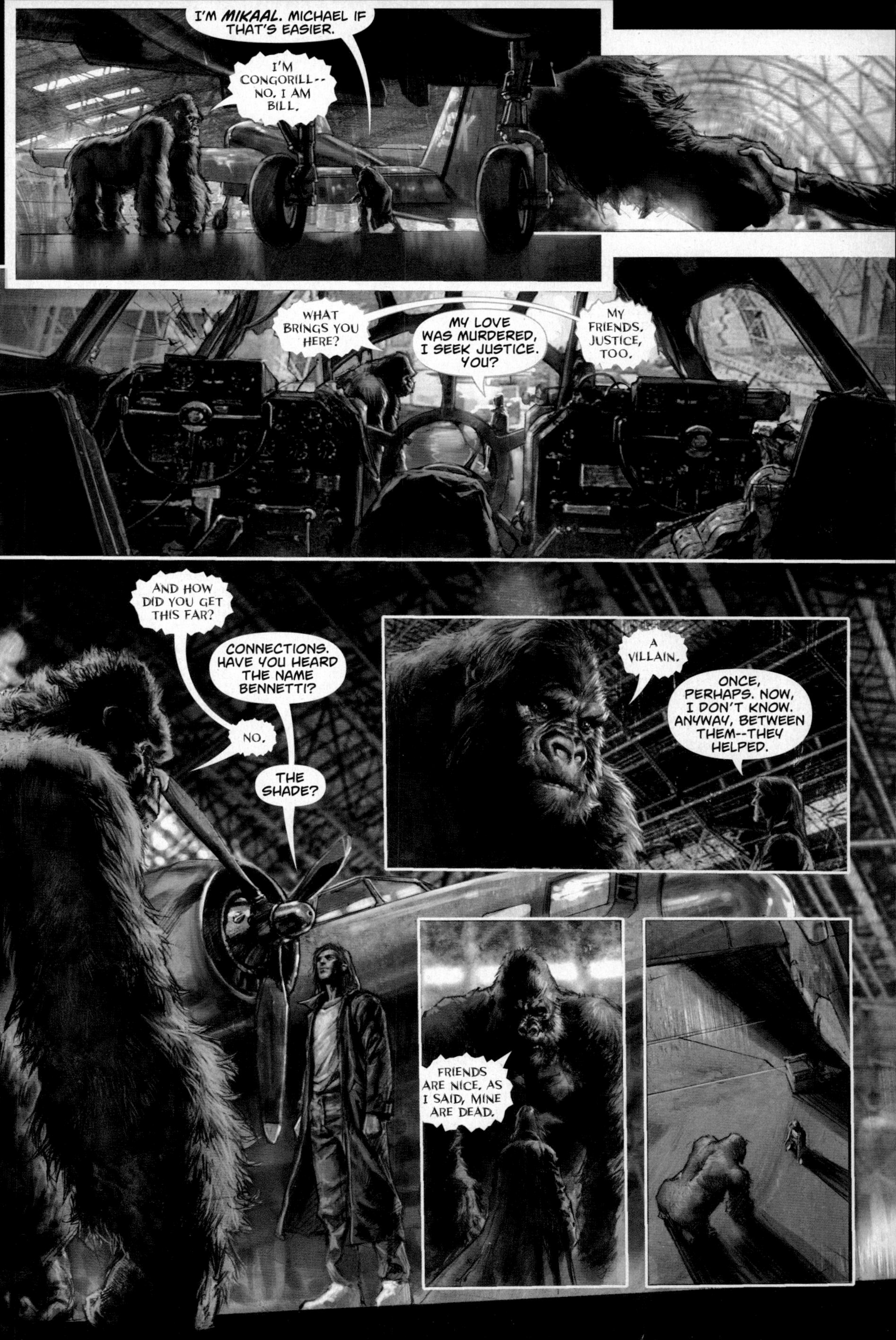
I'M MIKAAL. MICHAEL IF THAT'S EASIER.
I'M CONGORILL-- NO, I AM BILL.
WHAT BRINGS YOU HERE?
MY LOVE WAS MURDERED, I SEEK JUSTICE. YOU?
MY FRIENDS, JUSTICE, TOO.
AND HOW DID YOU GET THIS FAR?
CONNECTIONS. HAVE YOU HEARD THE NAME BENNETTI?
NO.
THE SHADE?
A VILLAIN.
ONCE, PERHAPS. NOW, I DON'T KNOW. ANYWAY, BETWEEN THEM--THEY HELPED.
FRIENDS ARE NICE, AS I SAID, MINE ARE DEAD.

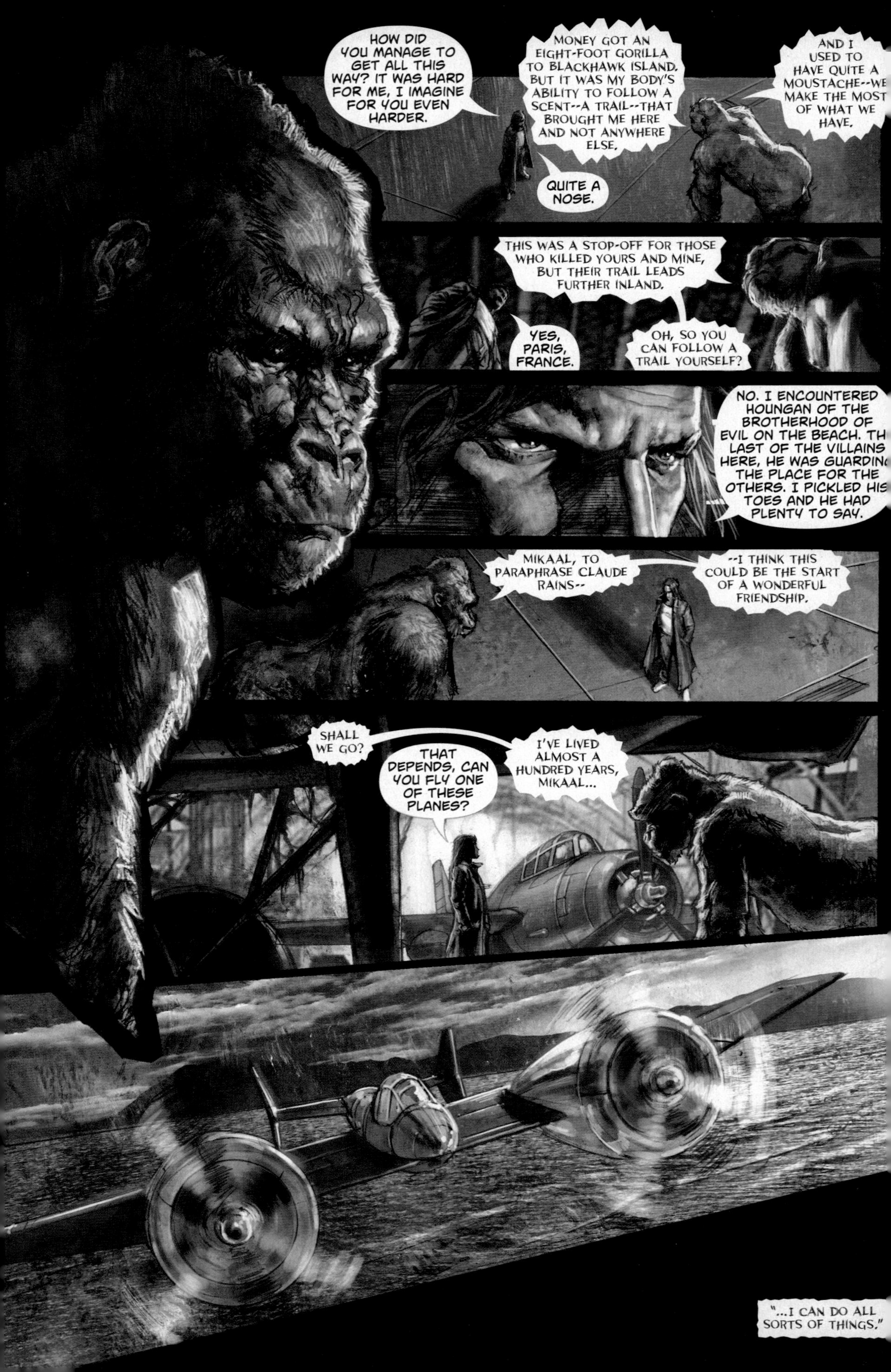
HOW DID YOU MANAGE TO GET ALL THIS WAY? IT WAS HARD FOR ME, I IMAGINE FOR YOU EVEN HARDER.
MONEY GOT AN EIGHT-FOOT GORILLA TO BLACKHAWK ISLAND. BUT IT WAS MY BODY'S ABILITY TO FOLLOW A SCENT--A TRAIL--THAT BROUGHT ME HERE AND NOT ANYWHERE ELSE.
QUITE A NOSE.
AND I USED TO HAVE QUITE A MOUSTACHE--WE MAKE THE MOST OF WHAT WE HAVE.
THIS WAS A STOP-OFF FOR THOSE WHO KILLED YOURS AND MINE, BUT THEIR TRAIL LEADS FURTHER INLAND.
YES, PARIS, FRANCE.
OH, SO YOU CAN FOLLOW A TRAIL YOURSELF?
NO. I ENCOUNTERED HOUNGAN OF THE BROTHERHOOD OF EVIL ON THE BEACH. TH LAST OF THE VILLAINS HERE, HE WAS GUARDIN THE PLACE FOR THE OTHERS. I PICKLED HIS TOES AND HE HAD PLENTY TO SAY.
MIKAAL, TO PARAPHRASE CLAUDE RAINS--
--I THINK THIS COULD BE THE START OF A WONDERFUL FRIENDSHIP.
SHALL WE GO?
THAT DEPENDS, CAN YOU FLY ONE OF THESE PLANES?
I'VE LIVED ALMOST A HUNDRED YEARS, MIKAAL...
"...I CAN DO ALL SORTS OF THINGS."

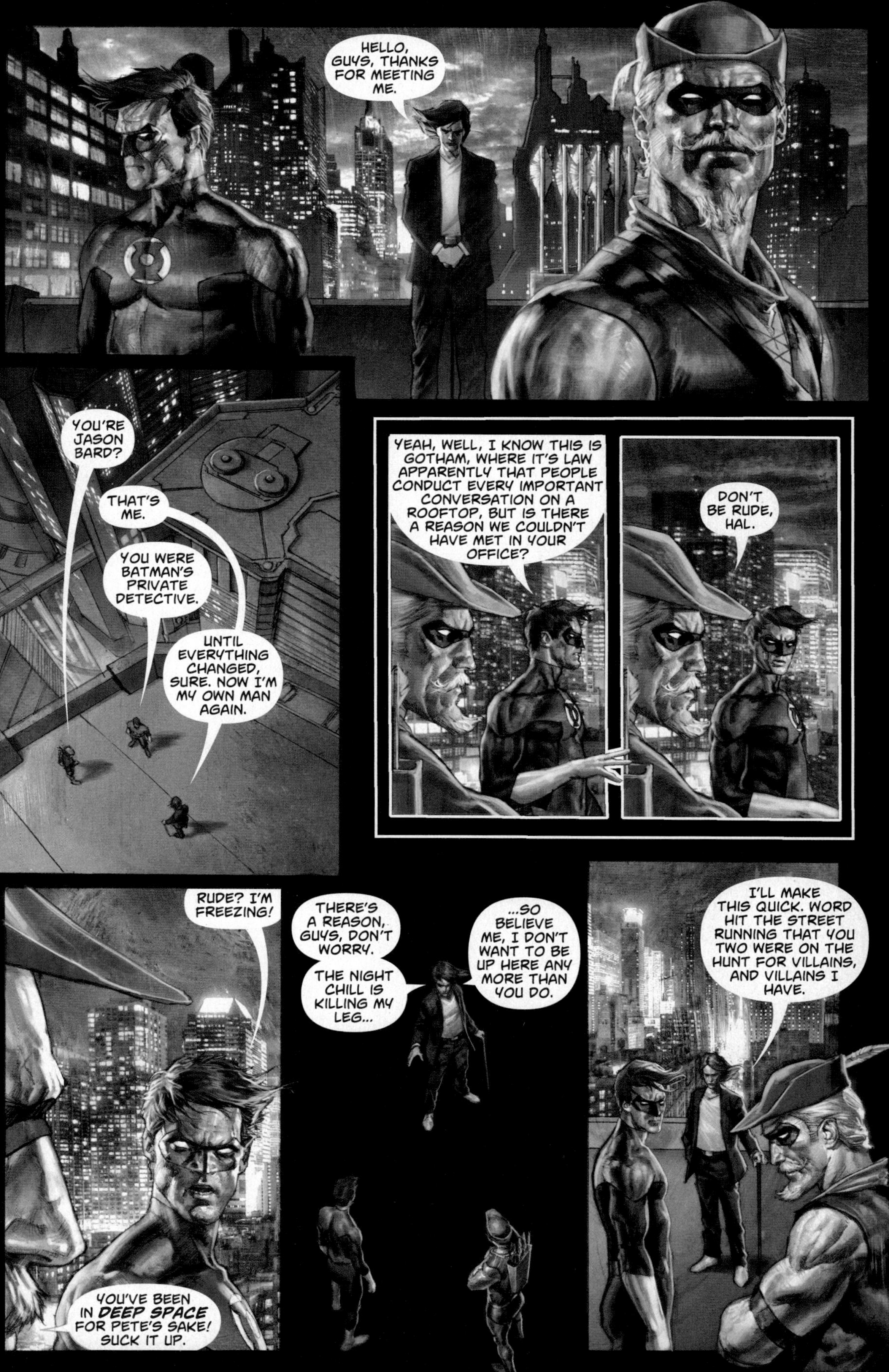
HELLO, GUYS, THANKS FOR MEETING ME.
YOU'RE JASON BARD?
THAT'S ME.
YOU WERE BATMAN'S PRIVATE DETECTIVE.
UNTIL EVERYTHING CHANGED, SURE. NOW I'M MY OWN MAN AGAIN.
YEAH, WELL, I KNOW THIS IS GOTHAM, WHERE IT'S LAW APPARENTLY THAT PEOPLE CONDUCT EVERY IMPORTANT CONVERSATION ON A ROOFTOP, BUT IS THERE A REASON WE COULDN'T HAVE MET IN YOUR OFFICE?
DON'T BE RUDE, HAL.
RUDE? I'M FREEZING!
YOU'VE BEEN IN DEEP SPACE FOR PETE'S SAKE! SUCK IT UP.
THERE'S A REASON, GUYS, DON'T WORRY.
THE NIGHT CHILL IS KILLING MY LEG...
...SO BELIEVE ME, I DON'T WANT TO BE UP HERE ANY MORE THAN YOU DO.
I'LL MAKE THIS QUICK. WORD HIT THE STREET RUNNING THAT YOU TWO WERE ON THE HUNT FOR VILLAINS, AND VILLAINS I HAVE.

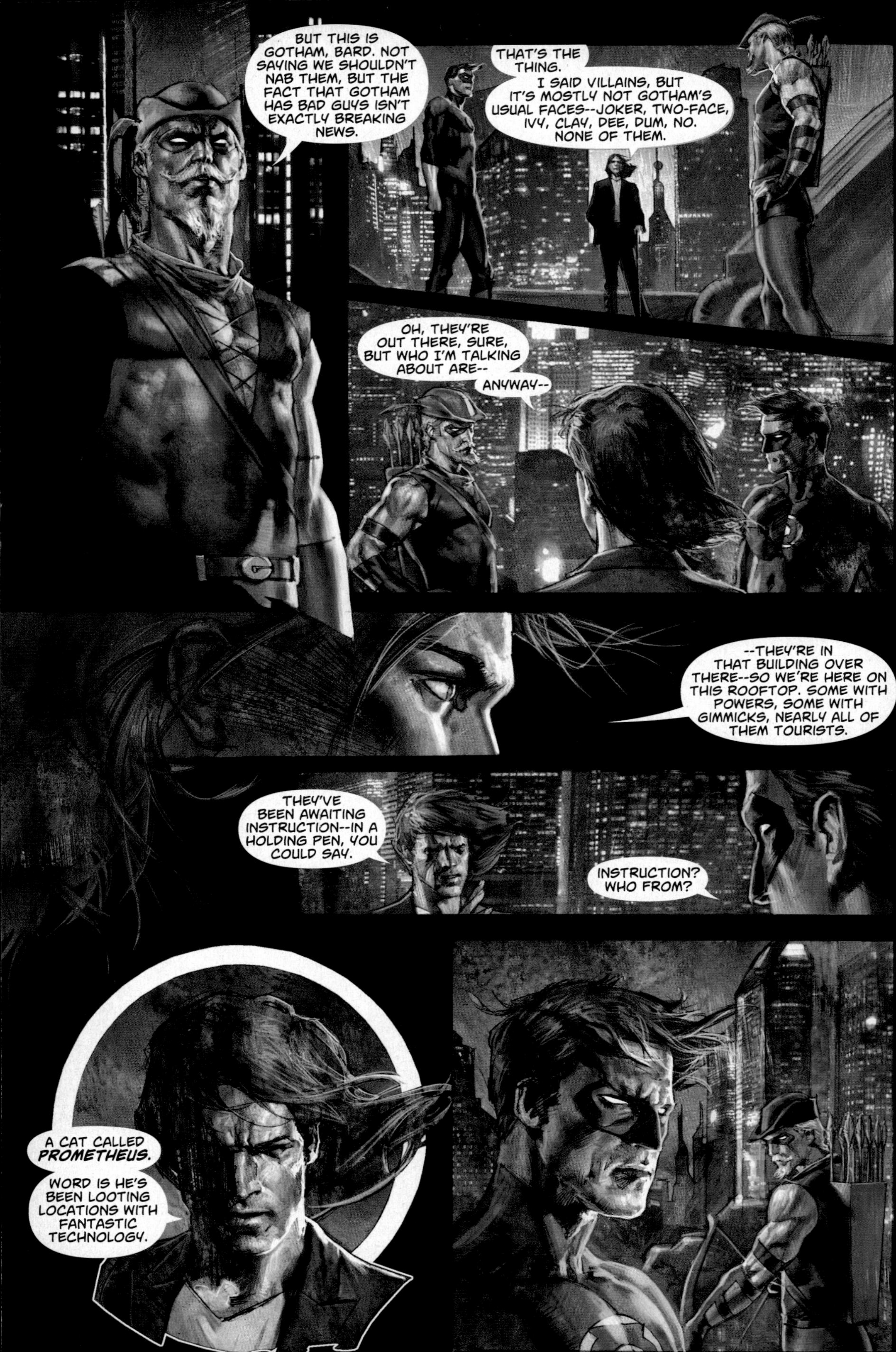
BUT THIS IS GOTHAM, BARD. NOT SAYING WE SHOULDN'T NAB THEM, BUT THE FACT THAT GOTHAM HAS BAD GUYS ISN'T EXACTLY BREAKING NEWS.
THAT'S THE THING.
I SAID VILLAINS, BUT IT'S MOSTLY NOT GOTHAM'S USUAL FACES--JOKER, TWO-FACE, IVY, CLAY, DEE, DUM, NO. NONE OF THEM.
OH, THEY'RE OUT THERE, SURE, BUT WHO I'M TALKING ABOUT ARE--
ANYWAY--
--THEY'RE IN THAT BUILDING OVER THERE--SO WE'RE HERE ON THIS ROOFTOP. SOME WITH POWERS, SOME WITH GIMMICKS, NEARLY ALL OF THEM TOURISTS.
THEY'VE BEEN AWAITING INSTRUCTION--IN A HOLDING PEN, YOU COULD SAY.
INSTRUCTION? WHO FROM?
A CAT CALLED ***PROMETHEUS***.
WORD IS HE'S BEEN LOOTING LOCATIONS WITH FANTASTIC TECHNOLOGY.

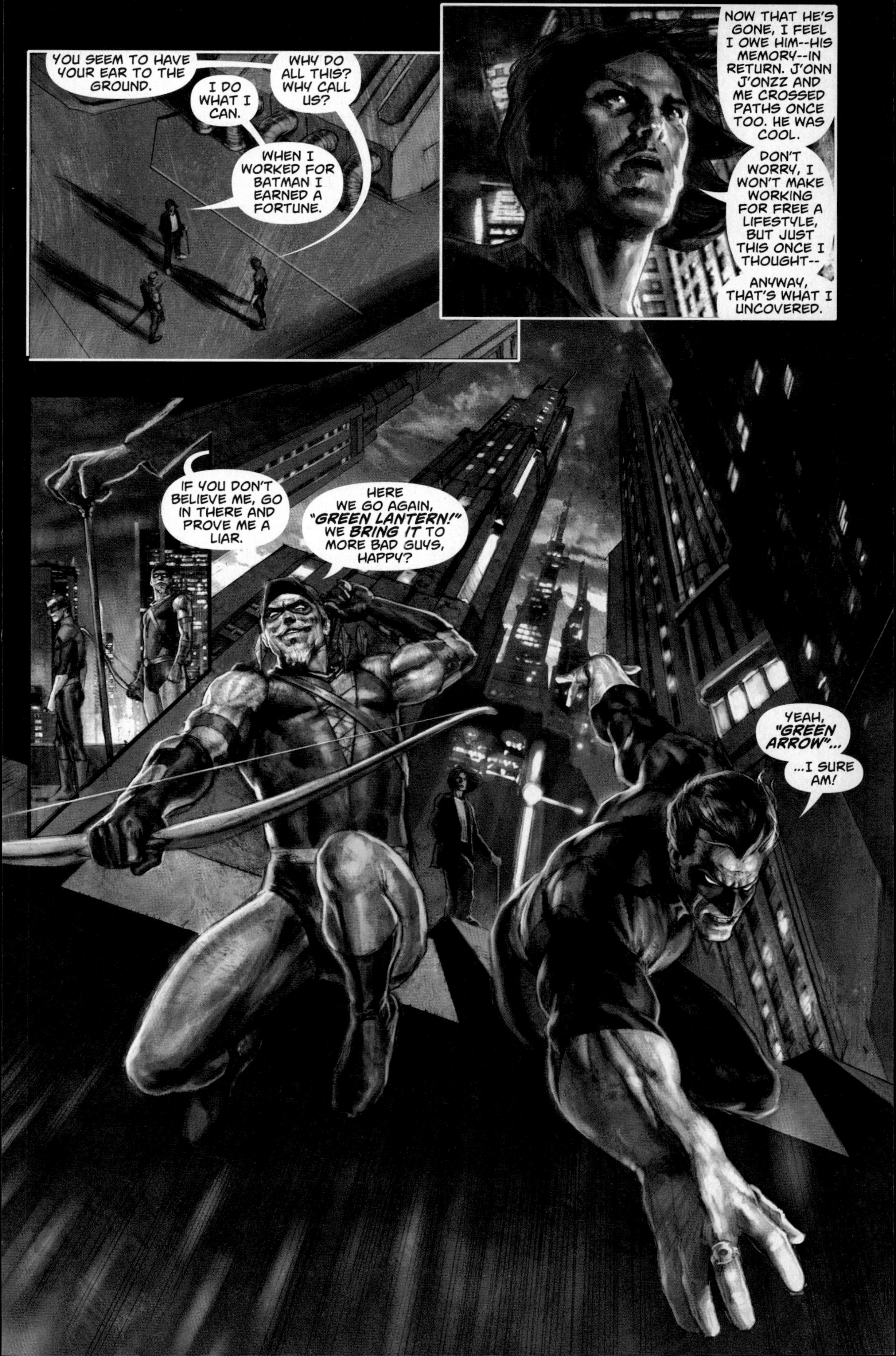
YOU SEEM TO HAVE YOUR EAR TO THE GROUND.
I DO WHAT I CAN.
WHY DO ALL THIS? WHY CALL US?
WHEN I WORKED FOR BATMAN I EARNED A FORTUNE.
NOW THAT HE'S GONE, I FEEL I OWE HIM--HIS MEMORY--IN RETURN. J'ONN J'ONZZ AND ME CROSSED PATHS ONCE TOO. HE WAS COOL.
DON'T WORRY, I WON'T MAKE WORKING FOR FREE A LIFESTYLE, BUT JUST THIS ONCE I THOUGHT--
ANYWAY, THAT'S WHAT I UNCOVERED.
IF YOU DON'T BELIEVE ME, GO IN THERE AND PROVE ME A LIAR.
HERE WE GO AGAIN, "GREEN LANTERN!" WE BRING IT TO MORE BAD GUYS, HAPPY?
YEAH, "GREEN ARROW"...
...I SURE AM!

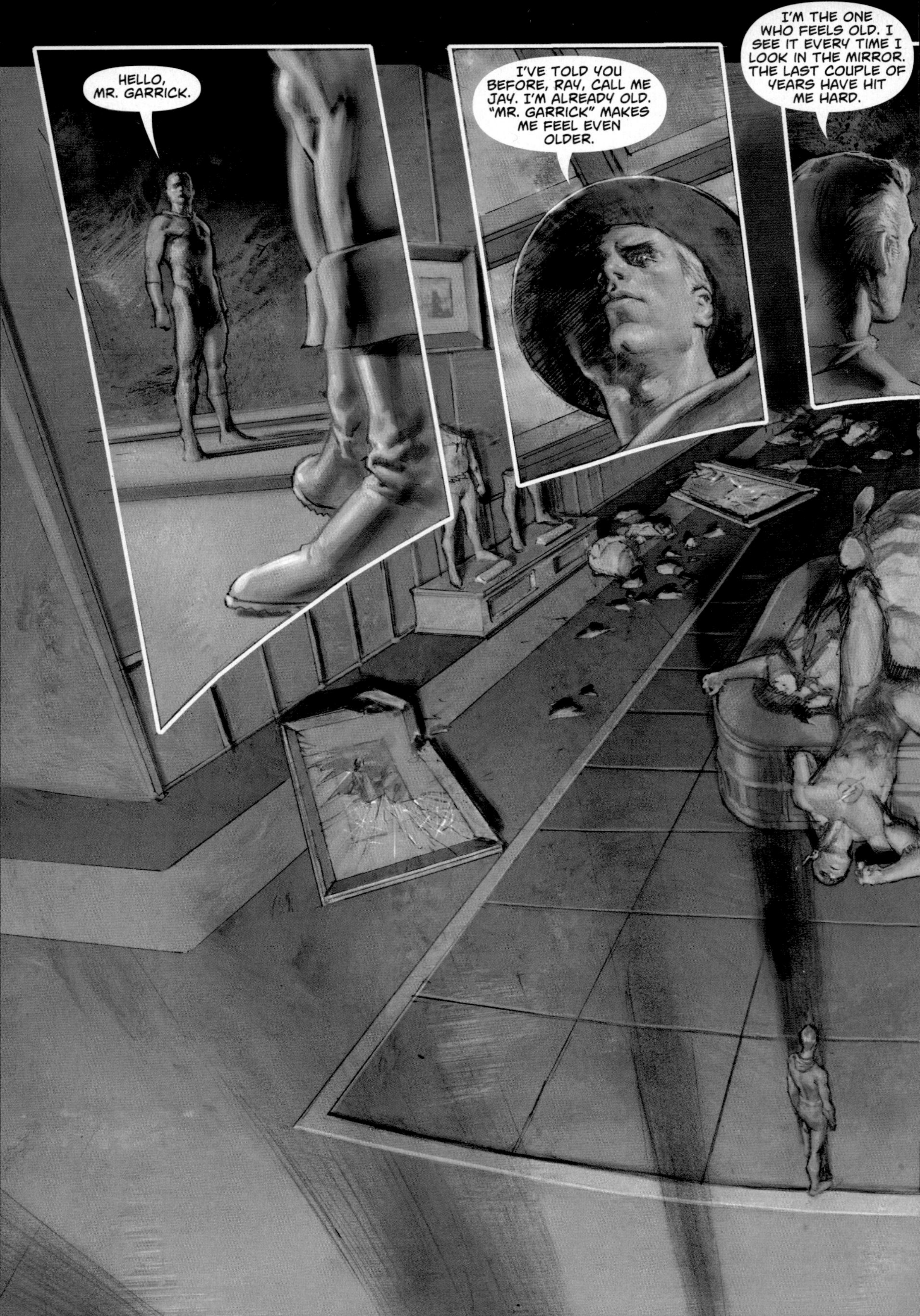
HELLO, MR. GARRICK.
I'VE TOLD YOU BEFORE, RAY, CALL ME JAY. I'M ALREADY OLD. "MR. GARRICK" MAKES ME FEEL EVEN OLDER.
I'M THE ONE WHO FEELS OLD. I SEE IT EVERY TIME I LOOK IN THE MIRROR. THE LAST COUPLE OF YEARS HAVE HIT ME HARD.

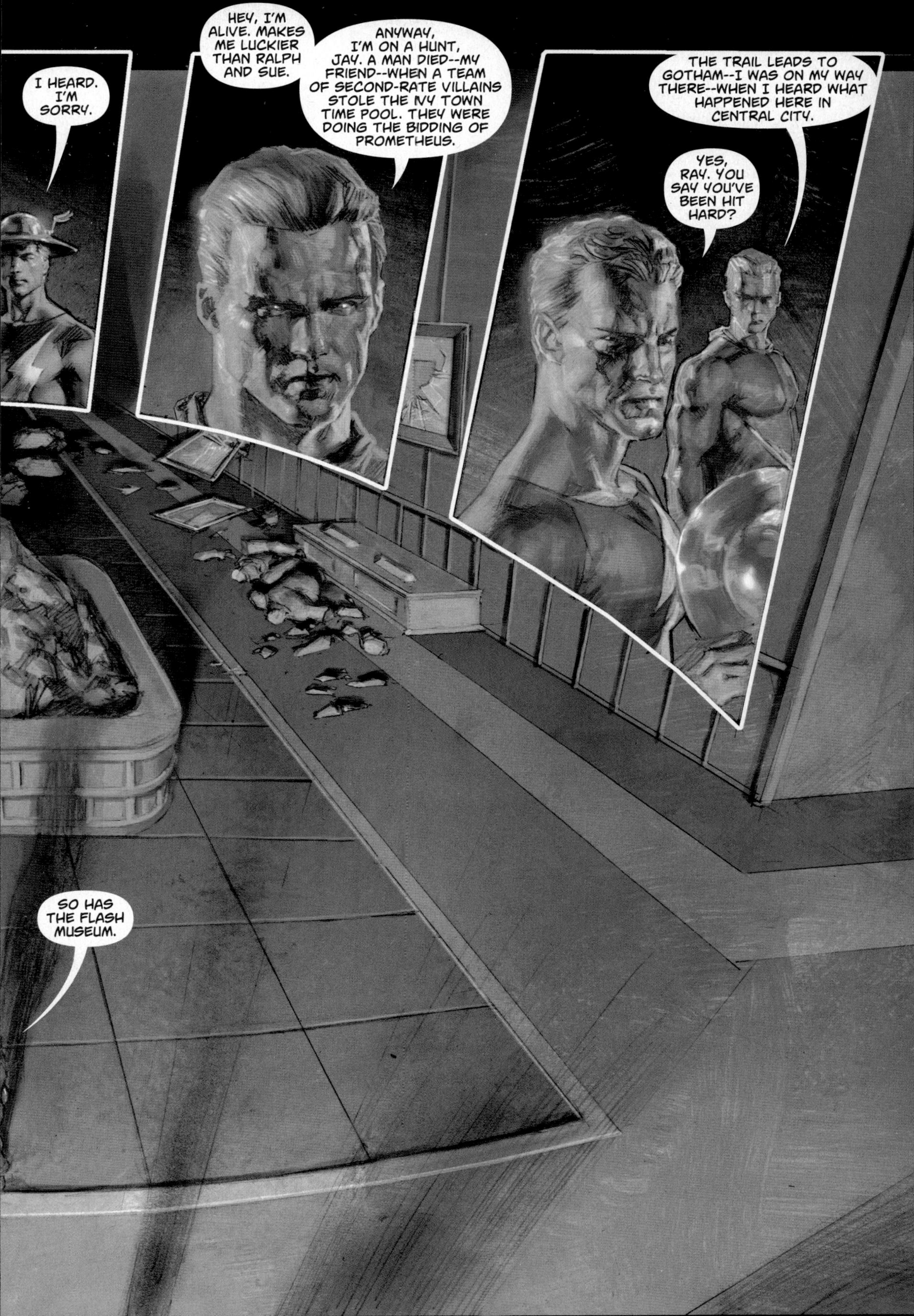

I HEARD. I'M SORRY.
HEY, I'M ALIVE. MAKES ME LUCKIER THAN RALPH AND SUE.
ANYWAY, I'M ON A HUNT, JAY. A MAN DIED--MY FRIEND--WHEN A TEAM OF SECOND-RATE VILLAINS STOLE THE IVY TOWN TIME POOL. THEY WERE DOING THE BIDDING OF PROMETHEUS.
THE TRAIL LEADS TO GOTHAM--I WAS ON MY WAY THERE--WHEN I HEARD WHAT HAPPENED HERE IN CENTRAL CITY.
YES, RAY. YOU SAY YOU'VE BEEN HIT HARD?
SO HAS THE FLASH MUSEUM.

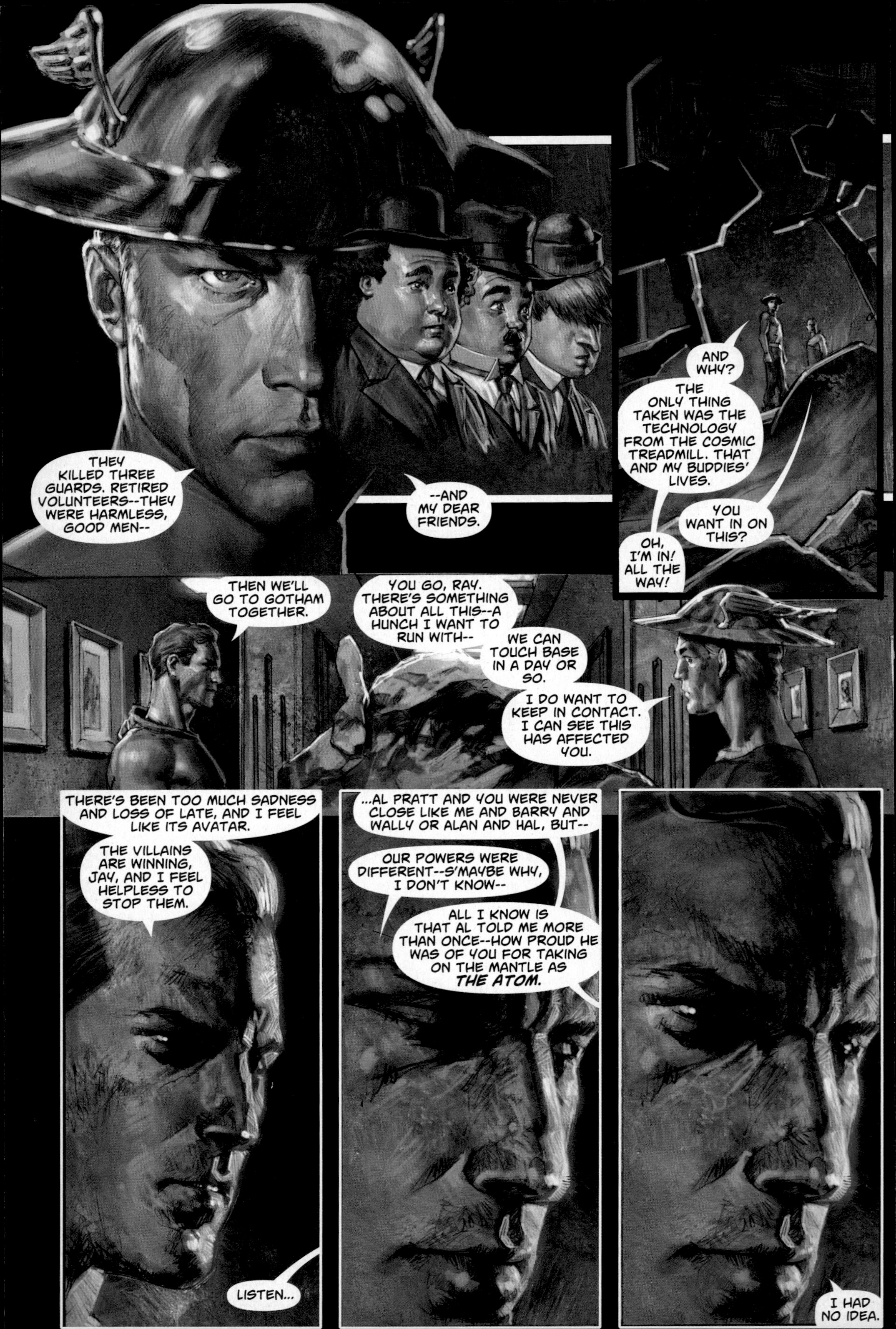
THEY KILLED THREE GUARDS. RETIRED VOLUNTEERS--THEY WERE HARMLESS, GOOD MEN--
--AND MY DEAR FRIENDS.
AND WHY?
THE ONLY THING TAKEN WAS THE TECHNOLOGY FROM THE COSMIC TREADMILL. THAT AND MY BUDDIES' LIVES.
YOU WANT IN ON THIS?
OH, I'M IN! ALL THE WAY!
THEN WE'LL GO TO GOTHAM TOGETHER.
YOU GO, RAY. THERE'S SOMETHING ABOUT ALL THIS--A HUNCH I WANT TO RUN WITH--
WE CAN TOUCH BASE IN A DAY OR SO.
I DO WANT TO KEEP IN CONTACT. I CAN SEE THIS HAS AFFECTED YOU.
THERE'S BEEN TOO MUCH SADNESS AND LOSS OF LATE, AND I FEEL LIKE ITS AVATAR.
THE VILLAINS ARE WINNING, JAY, AND I FEEL HELPLESS TO STOP THEM.
LISTEN...
...AL PRATT AND YOU WERE NEVER CLOSE LIKE ME AND BARRY AND WALLY OR ALAN AND HAL, BUT--
OUR POWERS WERE DIFFERENT--S'MAYBE WHY, I DON'T KNOW--
ALL I KNOW IS THAT AL TOLD ME MORE THAN ONCE--HOW PROUD HE WAS OF YOU FOR TAKING ON THE MANTLE AS THE ATOM.
I HAD NO IDEA.

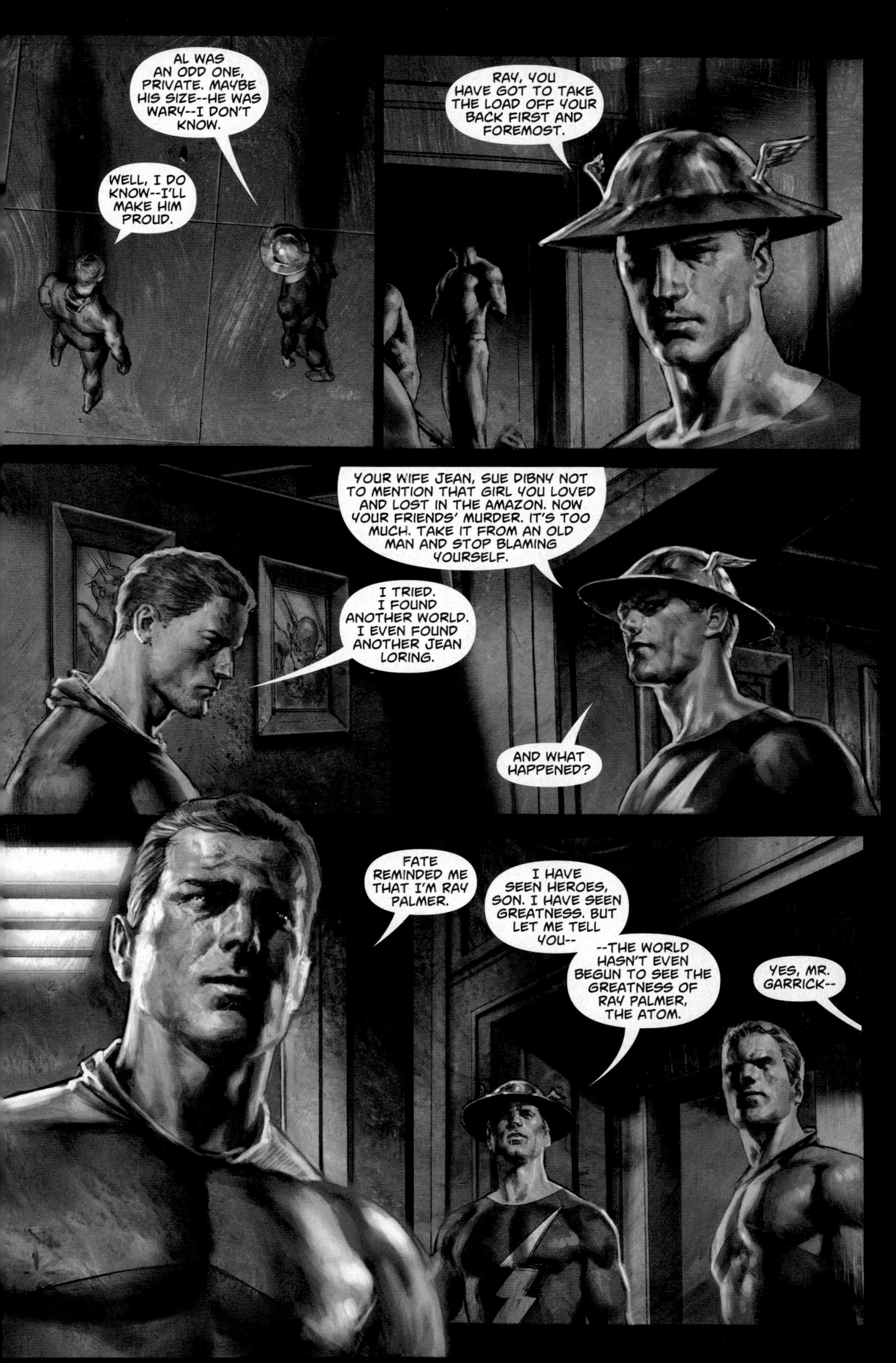
AL WAS AN ODD ONE, PRIVATE. MAYBE HIS SIZE--HE WAS WARY--I DON'T KNOW.
WELL, I DO KNOW--I'LL MAKE HIM PROUD.
RAY, YOU HAVE GOT TO TAKE THE LOAD OFF YOUR BACK FIRST AND FOREMOST.
YOUR WIFE JEAN, SUE DIBNY NOT TO MENTION THAT GIRL YOU LOVED AND LOST IN THE AMAZON. NOW YOUR FRIENDS' MURDER. IT'S TOO MUCH. TAKE IT FROM AN OLD MAN AND STOP BLAMING YOURSELF.
I TRIED. I FOUND ANOTHER WORLD. I EVEN FOUND ANOTHER JEAN LORING.
AND WHAT HAPPENED?
FATE REMINDED ME THAT I'M RAY PALMER.
I HAVE SEEN HEROES, SON. I HAVE SEEN GREATNESS. BUT LET ME TELL YOU--
--THE WORLD HASN'T EVEN BEGUN TO SEE THE GREATNESS OF RAY PALMER, THE ATOM.
YES, MR. GARRICK--

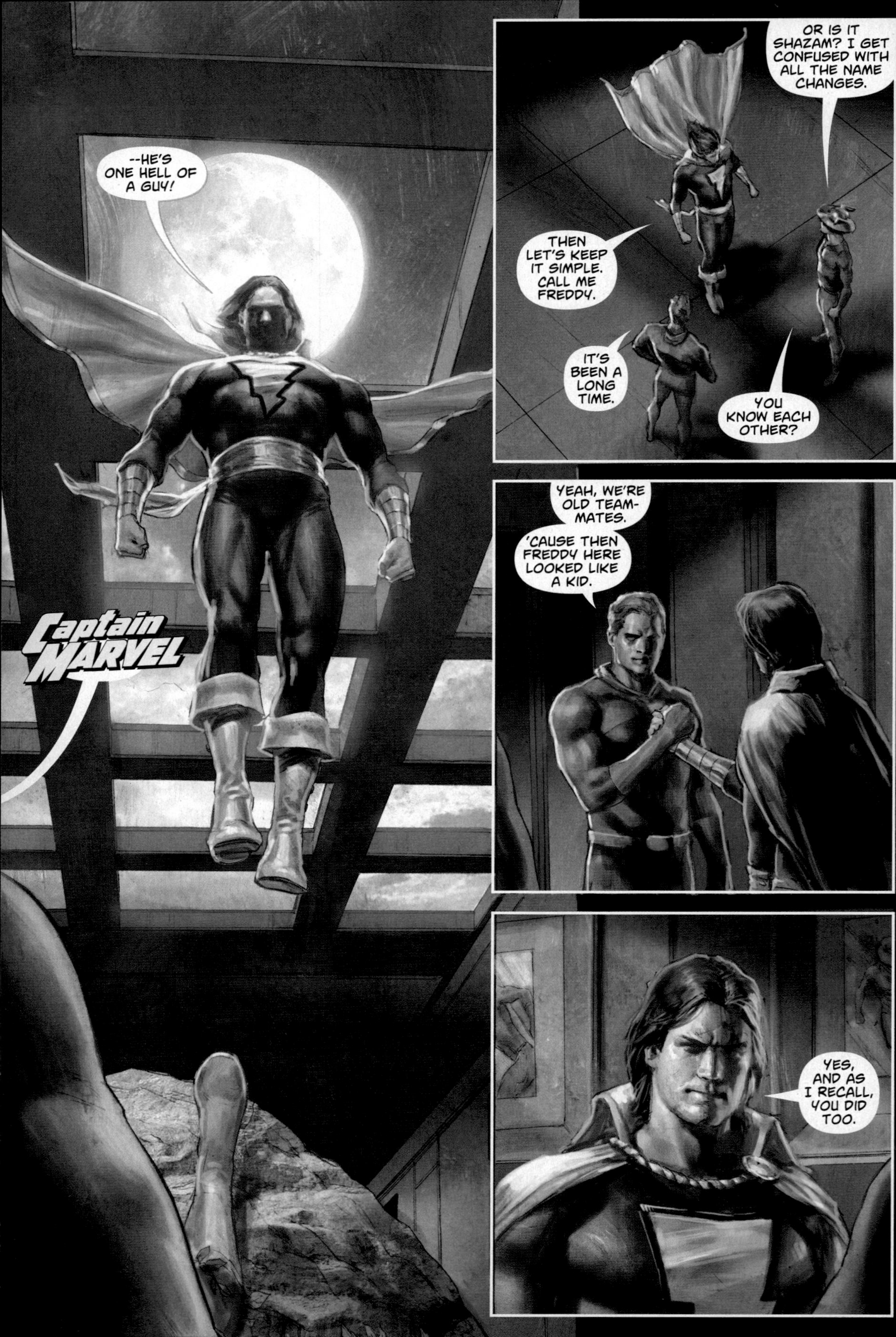
--HE'S ONE HELL OF A GUY!
Captain MARVEL
OR IS IT SHAZAM? I GET CONFUSED WITH ALL THE NAME CHANGES.
THEN LET'S KEEP IT SIMPLE. CALL ME FREDDY.
IT'S BEEN A LONG TIME.
YOU KNOW EACH OTHER?
YEAH, WE'RE OLD TEAM-MATES.
'CAUSE THEN FREDDY HERE LOOKED LIKE A KID.
YES, AND AS I RECALL, YOU DID TOO.

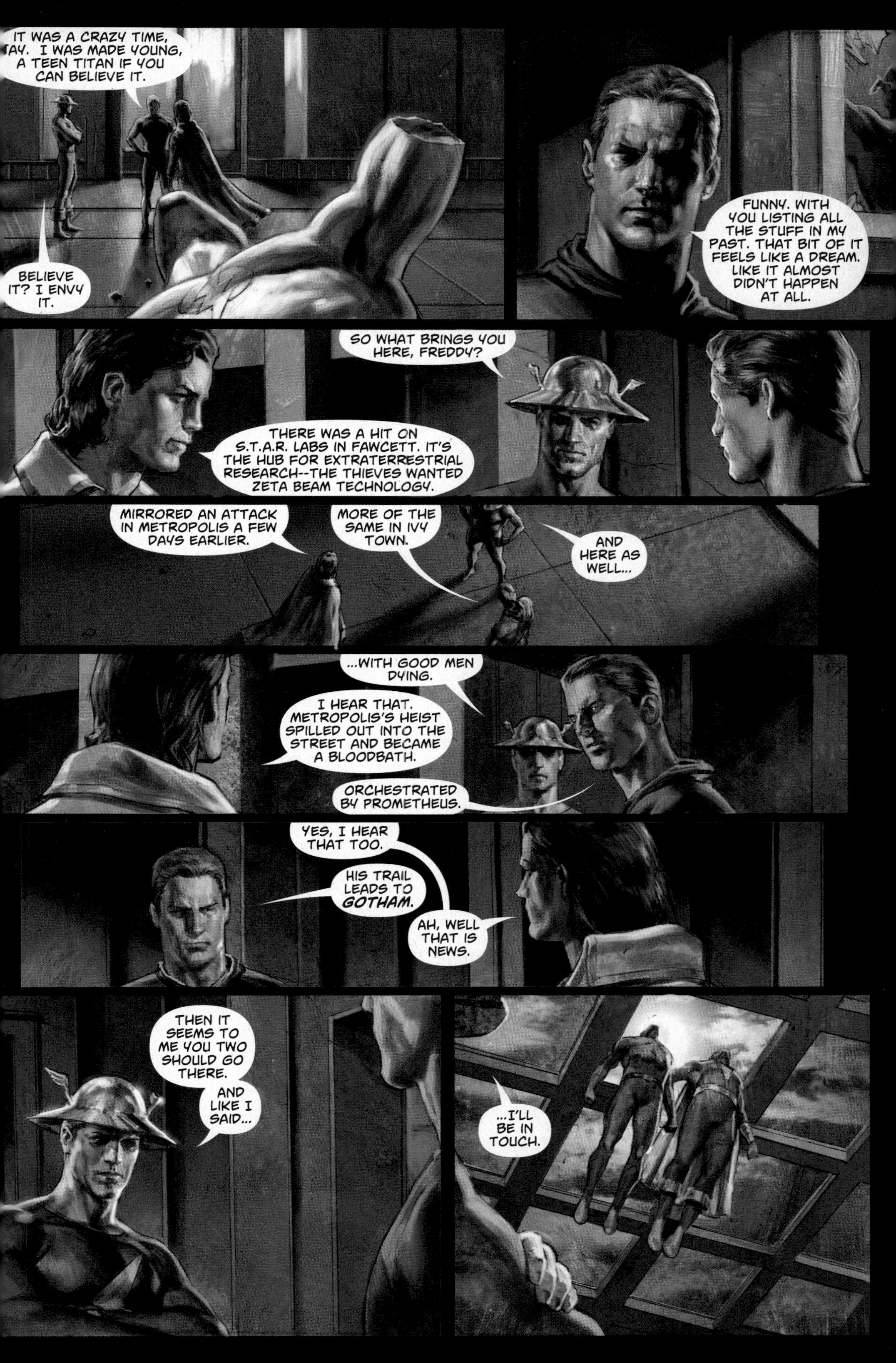
IT WAS A CRAZY TIME, JAY. I WAS MADE YOUNG, A TEEN TITAN IF YOU CAN BELIEVE IT.
BELIEVE IT? I ENVY IT.
FUNNY. WITH YOU LISTING ALL THE STUFF IN MY PAST. THAT BIT OF IT FEELS LIKE A DREAM. LIKE IT ALMOST DIDN'T HAPPEN AT ALL.
SO WHAT BRINGS YOU HERE, FREDDY?
THERE WAS A HIT ON S.T.A.R. LABS IN FAWCETT. IT'S THE HUB FOR EXTRATERRESTRIAL RESEARCH--THE THIEVES WANTED ZETA BEAM TECHNOLOGY.
MIRRORED AN ATTACK IN METROPOLIS A FEW DAYS EARLIER.
MORE OF THE SAME IN IVY TOWN.
AND HERE AS WELL...
...WITH GOOD MEN DYING.
I HEAR THAT. METROPOLIS'S HEIST SPILLED OUT INTO THE STREET AND BECAME A BLOODBATH.
ORCHESTRATED BY PROMETHEUS.
YES, I HEAR THAT TOO.
HIS TRAIL LEADS TO GOTHAM.
AH, WELL THAT IS NEWS.
THEN IT SEEMS TO ME YOU TWO SHOULD GO THERE.
AND LIKE I SAID...
...I'LL BE IN TOUCH.

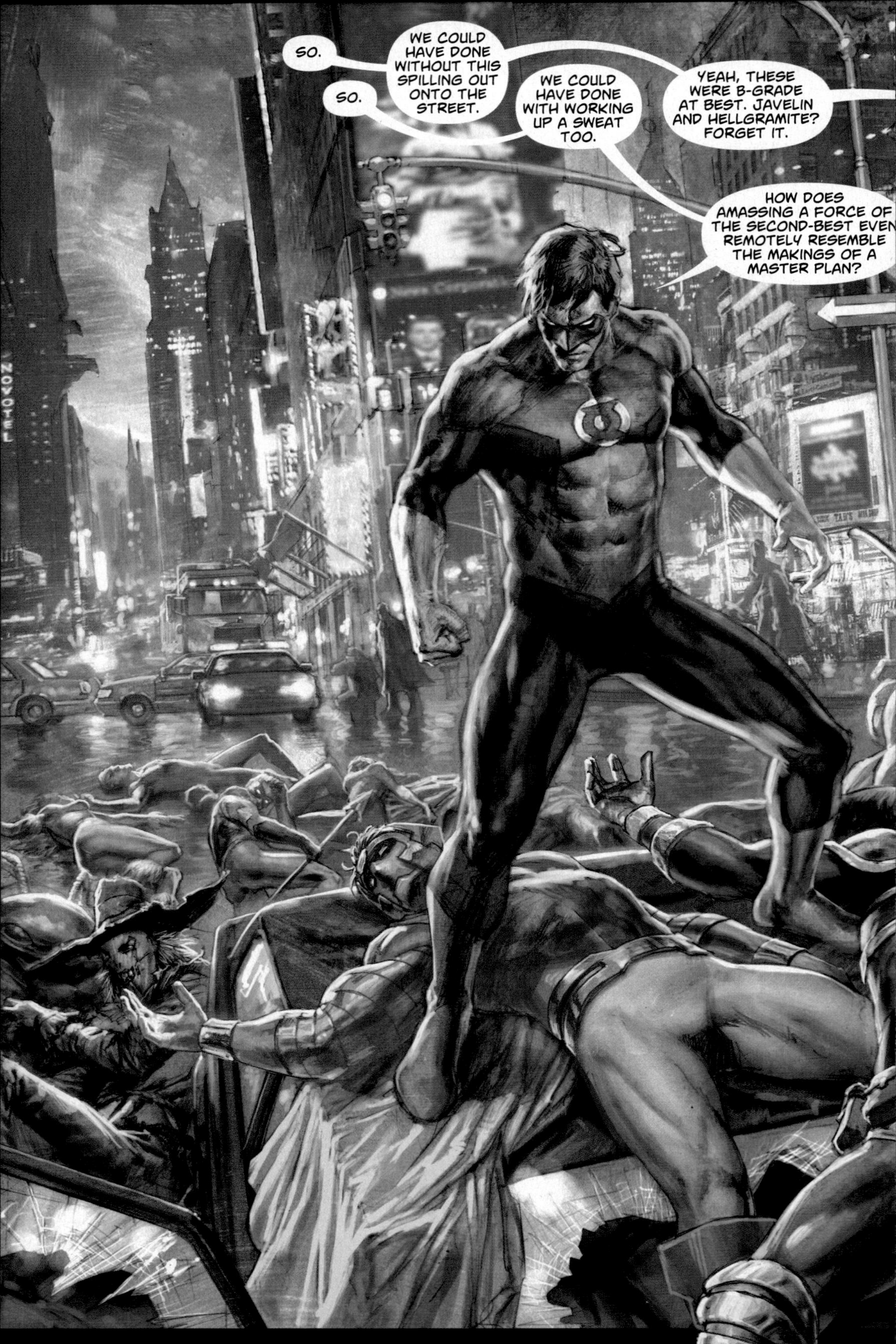
SO.
WE COULD HAVE DONE WITHOUT THIS SPILLING OUT ONTO THE STREET.
SO.
WE COULD HAVE DONE WITH WORKING UP A SWEAT TOO.
YEAH, THESE WERE B-GRADE AT BEST. JAVELIN AND HELLGRAMITE? FORGET IT.
HOW DOES AMASSING A FORCE OF THE SECOND-BEST EVEN REMOTELY RESEMBLE THE MAKINGS OF A MASTER PLAN?
NOVOTEL

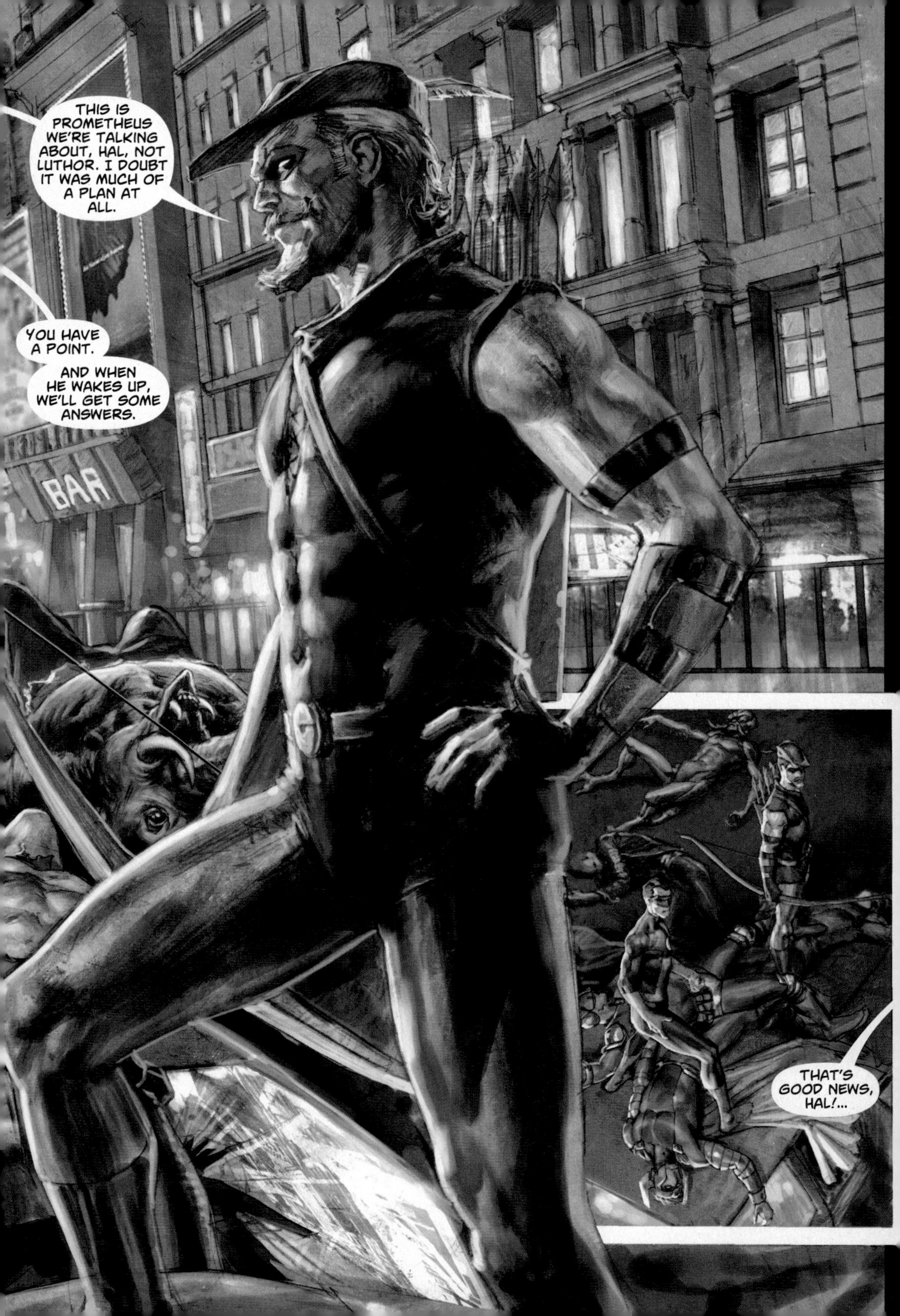
THIS IS PROMETHEUS WE'RE TALKING ABOUT, HAL, NOT LUTHOR. I DOUBT IT WAS MUCH OF A PLAN AT ALL.
YOU HAVE A POINT.
AND WHEN HE WAKES UP, WE'LL GET SOME ANSWERS.
BAR
THAT'S GOOD NEWS, HAL!...

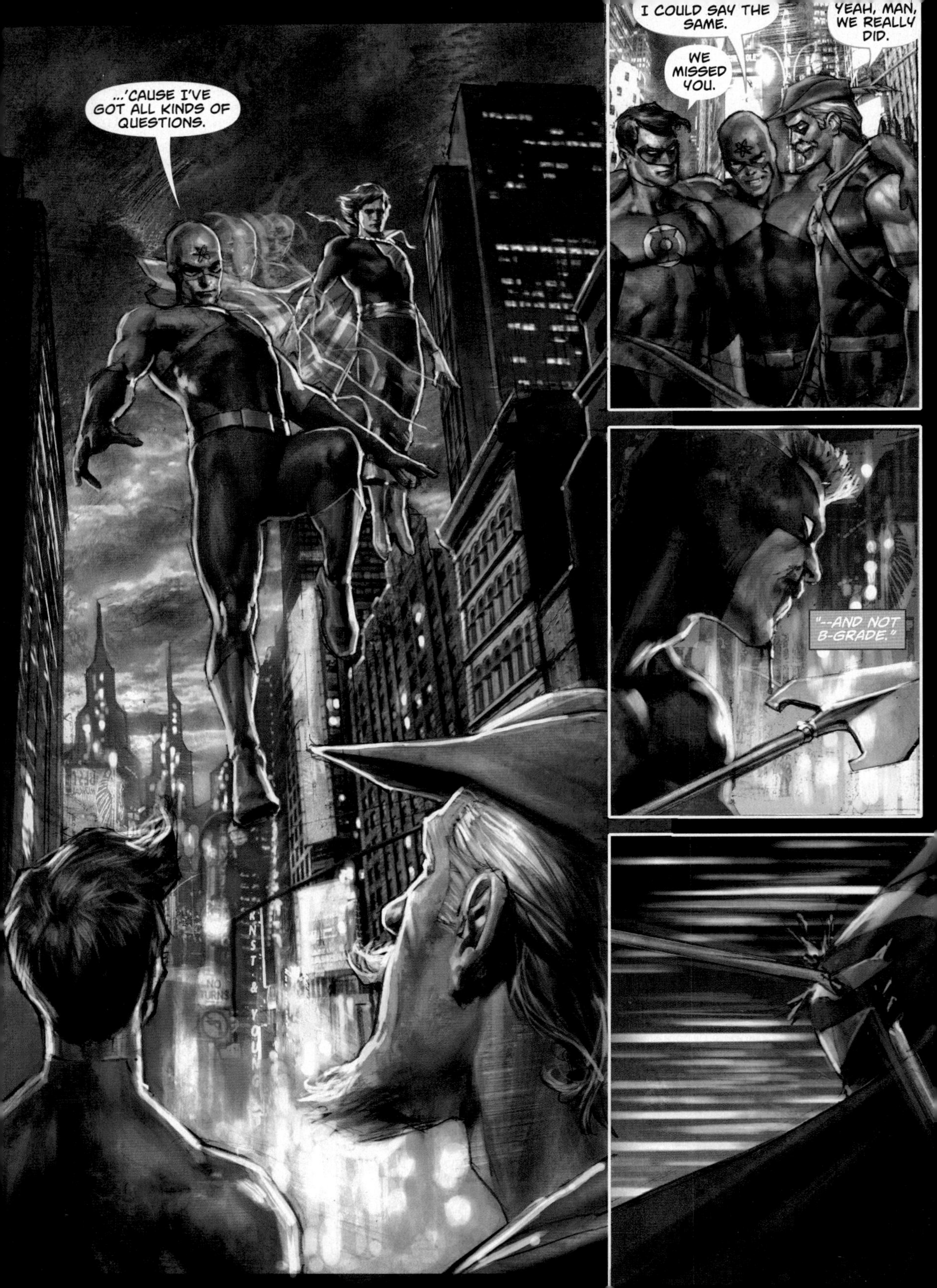
...'CAUSE I'VE GOT ALL KINDS OF QUESTIONS.
I COULD SAY THE SAME.
WE MISSED YOU.
YEAH, MAN, WE REALLY DID.
"--AND NOT B-GRADE."

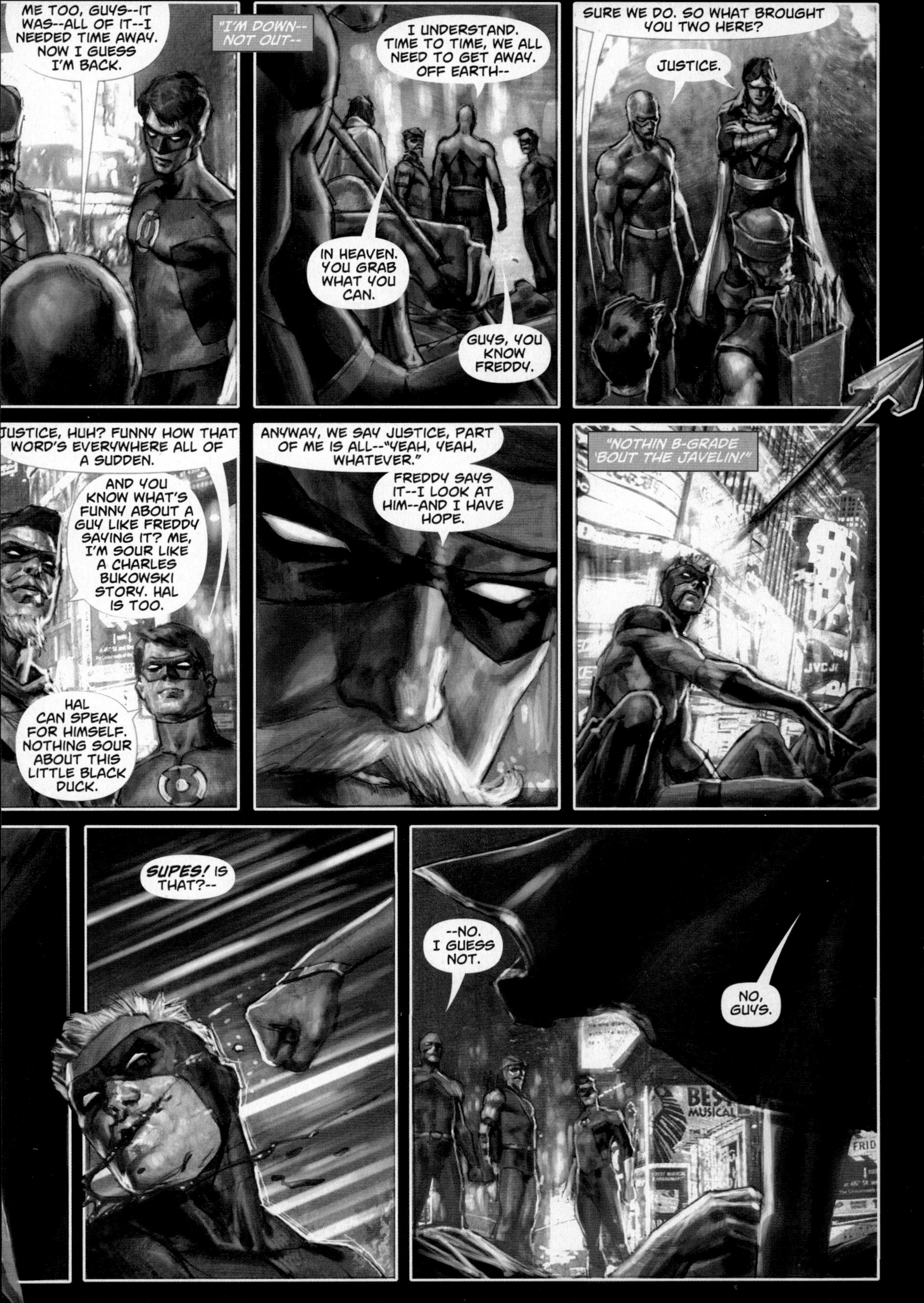
ME TOO, GUYS--IT WAS--ALL OF IT--I NEEDED TIME AWAY. NOW I GUESS I'M BACK.
"I'M DOWN-- NOT OUT--
I UNDERSTAND. TIME TO TIME, WE ALL NEED TO GET AWAY. OFF EARTH--
IN HEAVEN. YOU GRAB WHAT YOU CAN.
GUYS, YOU KNOW FREDDY.
SURE WE DO. SO WHAT BROUGHT YOU TWO HERE?
JUSTICE.
JUSTICE, HUH? FUNNY HOW THAT WORD'S EVERYWHERE ALL OF A SUDDEN.
AND YOU KNOW WHAT'S FUNNY ABOUT A GUY LIKE FREDDY SAYING IT? ME, I'M SOUR LIKE A CHARLES BUKOWSKI STORY. HAL IS TOO.
HAL CAN SPEAK FOR HIMSELF. NOTHING SOUR ABOUT THIS LITTLE BLACK DUCK.
ANYWAY, WE SAY JUSTICE, PART OF ME IS ALL--"YEAH, YEAH, WHATEVER."
FREDDY SAYS IT--I LOOK AT HIM--AND I HAVE HOPE.
"NOTHIN B-GRADE 'BOUT THE JAVELIN!"
SUPES! IS THAT?--
--NO. I GUESS NOT.
NO, GUYS.

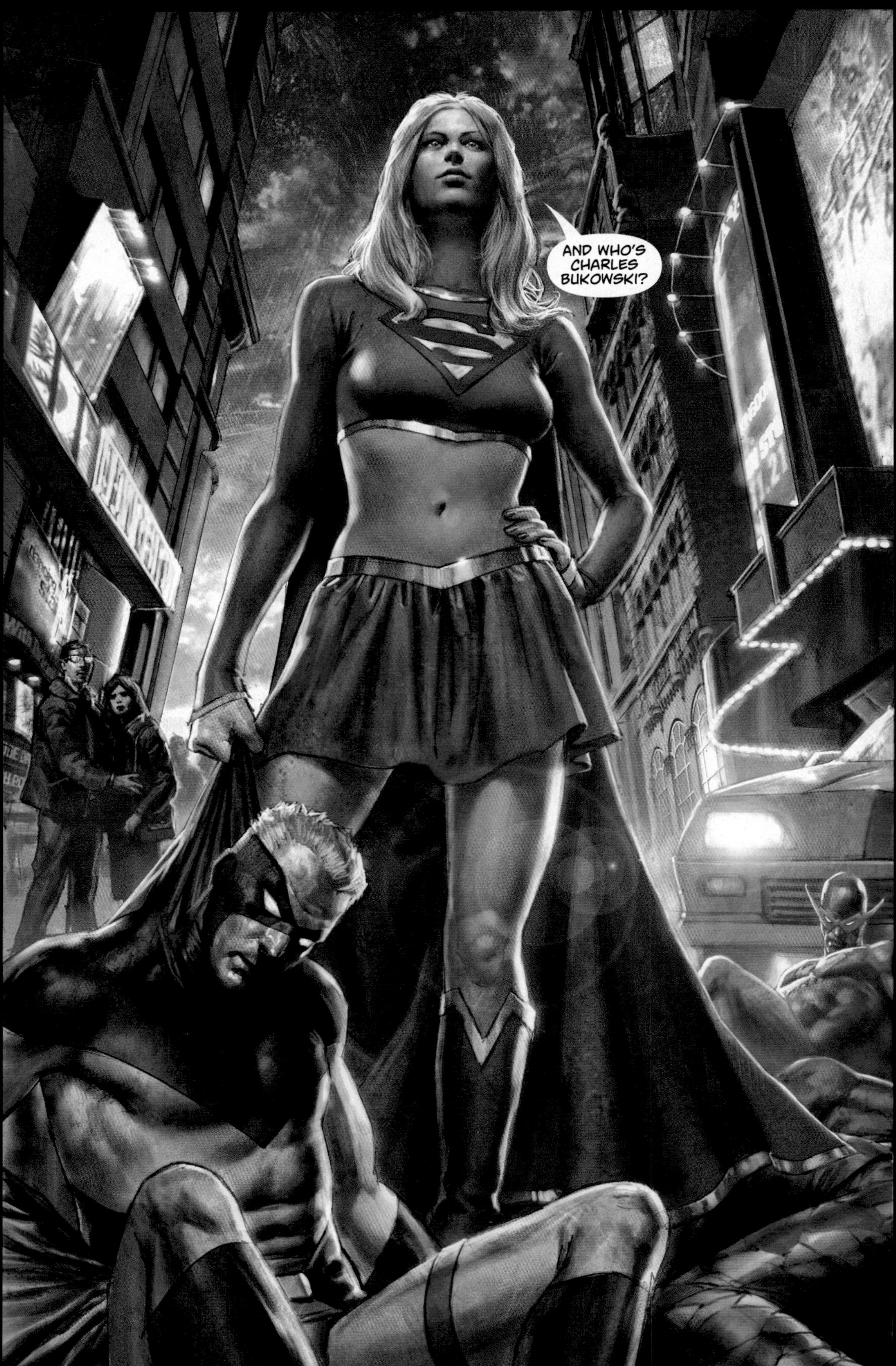
AND WHO'S CHARLES BUKOWSKI!?

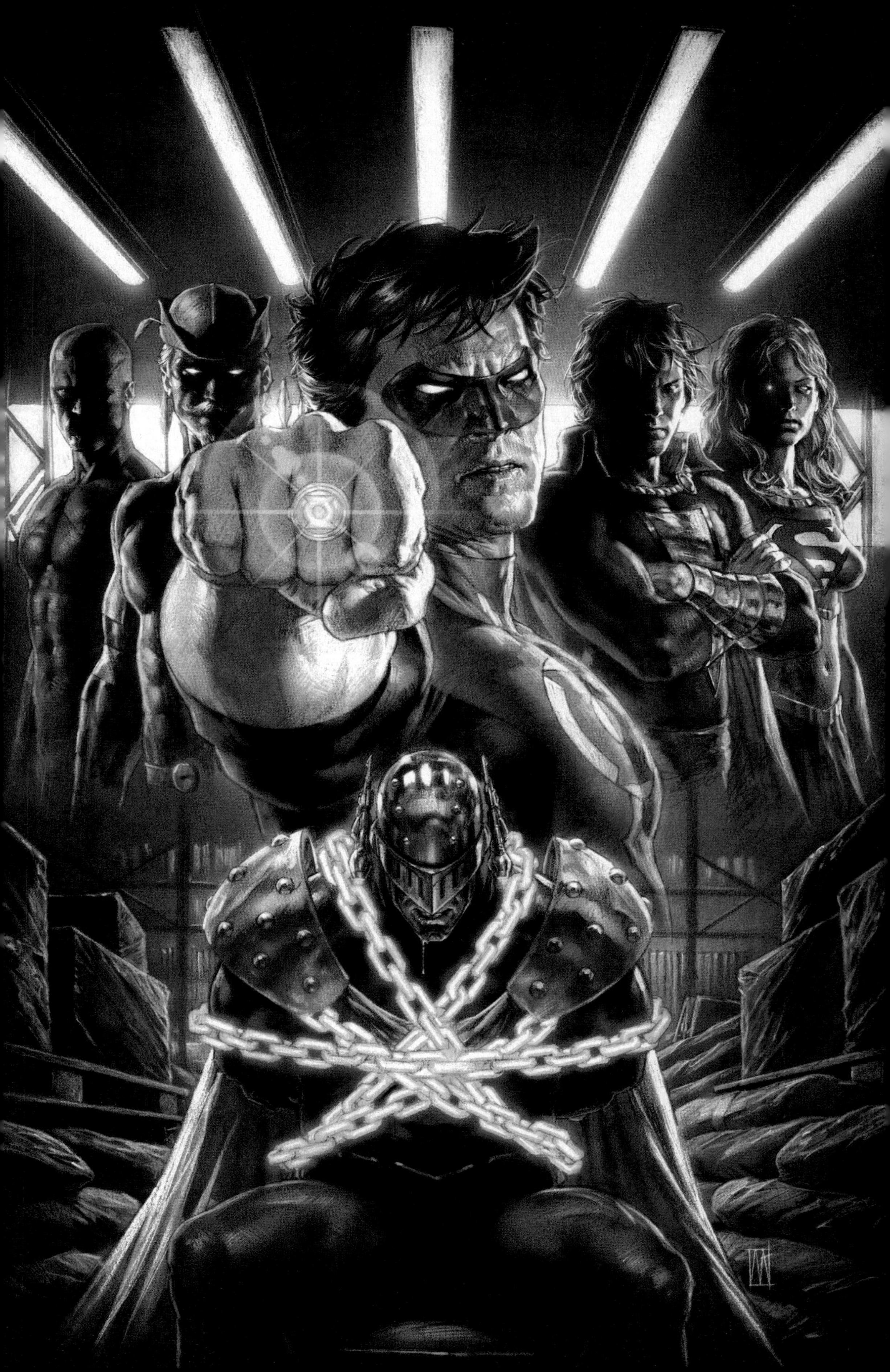

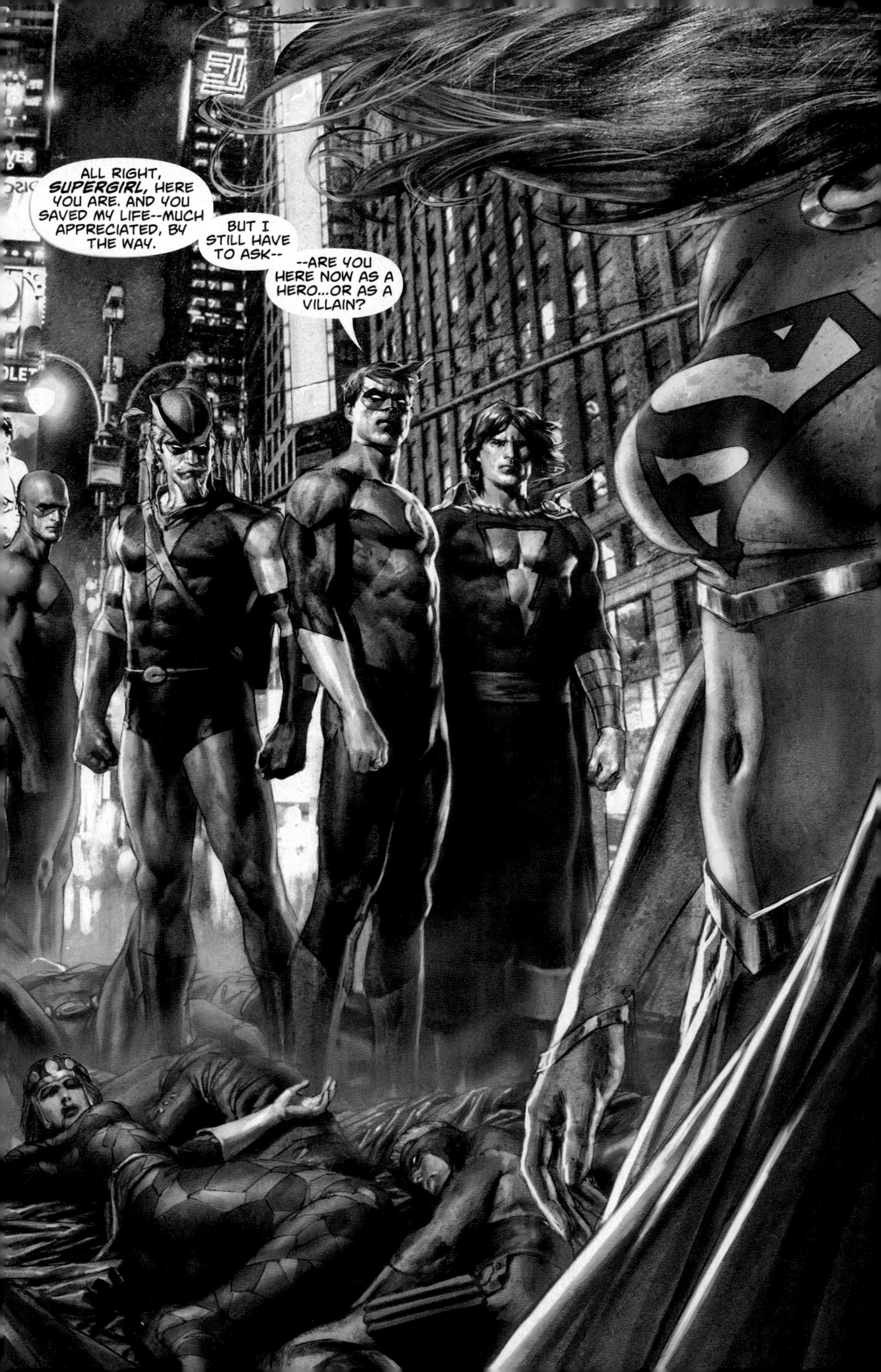
ALL RIGHT, SUPERGIRL, HERE YOU ARE. AND YOU SAVED MY LIFE--MUCH APPRECIATED, BY THE WAY.
BUT I STILL HAVE TO ASK--
--ARE YOU HERE NOW AS A HERO...OR AS A VILLAIN?

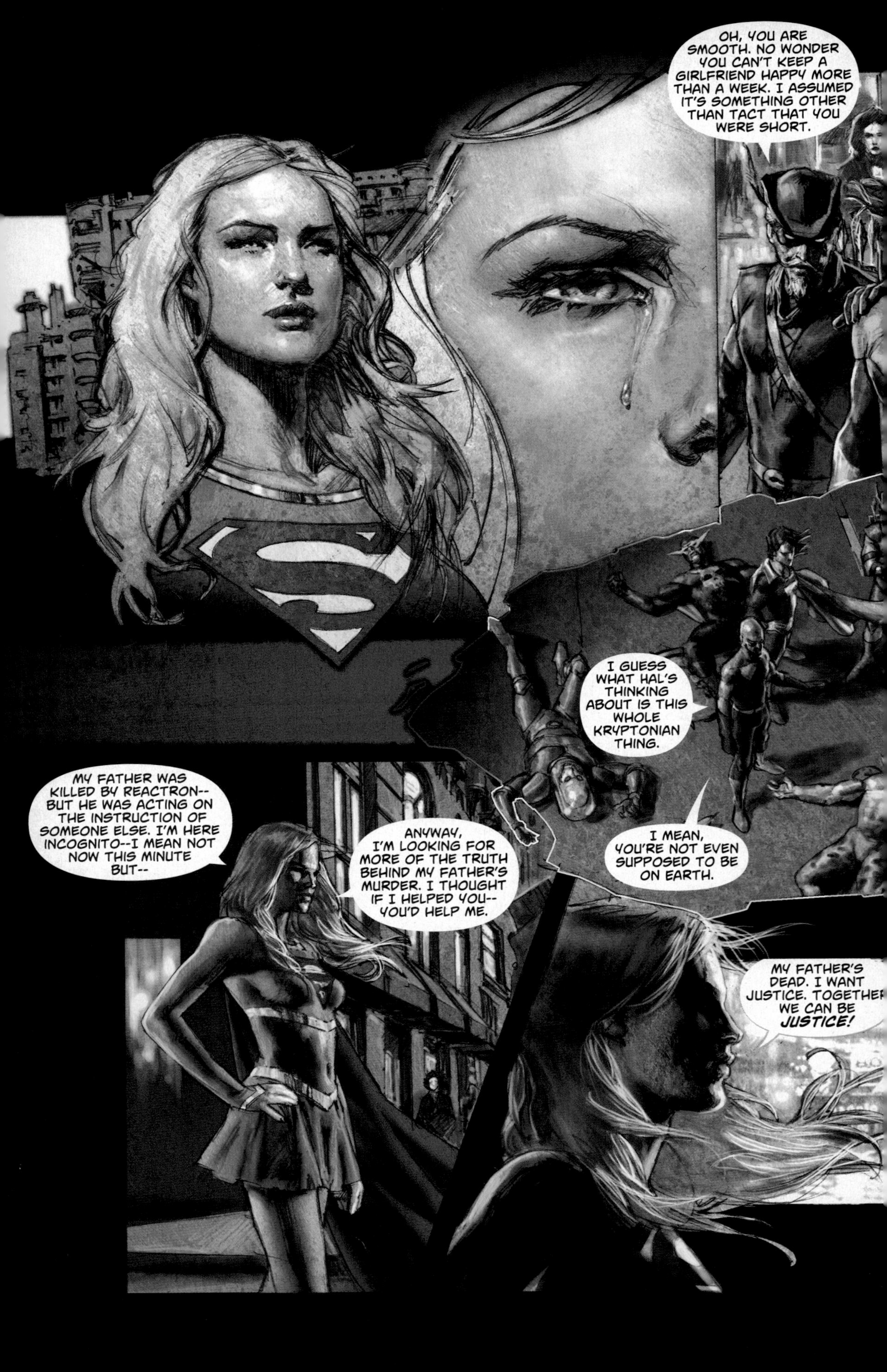
OH, YOU ARE SMOOTH. NO WONDER YOU CAN'T KEEP A GIRLFRIEND HAPPY MORE THAN A WEEK. I ASSUMED IT'S SOMETHING OTHER THAN TACT THAT YOU WERE SHORT.
I GUESS WHAT HAL'S THINKING ABOUT IS THIS WHOLE KRYPTONIAN THING.
I MEAN, YOU'RE NOT EVEN SUPPOSED TO BE ON EARTH.
MY FATHER WAS KILLED BY REACTRON-- BUT HE WAS ACTING ON THE INSTRUCTION OF SOMEONE ELSE. I'M HERE INCOGNITO--I MEAN NOT NOW THIS MINUTE BUT--
ANYWAY, I'M LOOKING FOR MORE OF THE TRUTH BEHIND MY FATHER'S MURDER. I THOUGHT IF I HELPED YOU-- YOU'D HELP ME.
MY FATHER'S DEAD. I WANT JUSTICE. TOGETHER WE CAN BE *JUSTICE!*

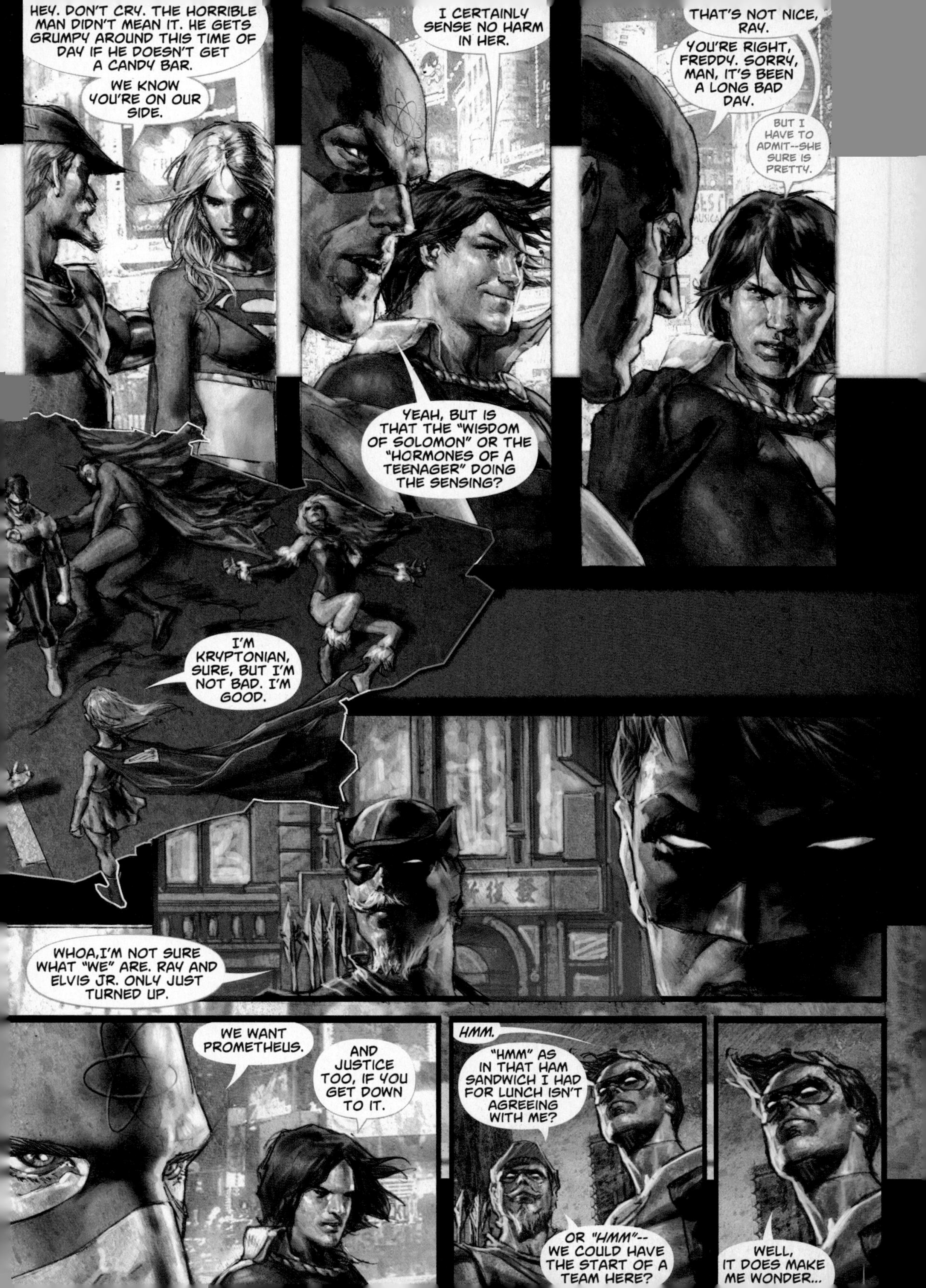

HEY. DON'T CRY. THE HORRIBLE MAN DIDN'T MEAN IT. HE GETS GRUMPY AROUND THIS TIME OF DAY IF HE DOESN'T GET A CANDY BAR.
WE KNOW YOU'RE ON OUR SIDE.
I CERTAINLY SENSE NO HARM IN HER.
YEAH, BUT IS THAT THE "WISDOM OF SOLOMON" OR THE "HORMONES OF A TEENAGER" DOING THE SENSING?
THAT'S NOT NICE, RAY.
YOU'RE RIGHT, FREDDY. SORRY, MAN, IT'S BEEN A LONG BAD DAY.
BUT I HAVE TO ADMIT--SHE SURE IS PRETTY.
I'M KRYPTONIAN, SURE, BUT I'M NOT BAD. I'M GOOD.
WHOA,I'M NOT SURE WHAT "WE" ARE. RAY AND ELVIS JR. ONLY JUST TURNED UP.
WE WANT PROMETHEUS.
AND JUSTICE TOO, IF YOU GET DOWN TO IT.
HMM.
"HMM" AS IN THAT HAM SANDWICH I HAD FOR LUNCH ISN'T AGREEING WITH ME?
OR "HMM"-- WE COULD HAVE THE START OF A TEAM HERE?
WELL, IT DOES MAKE ME WONDER.

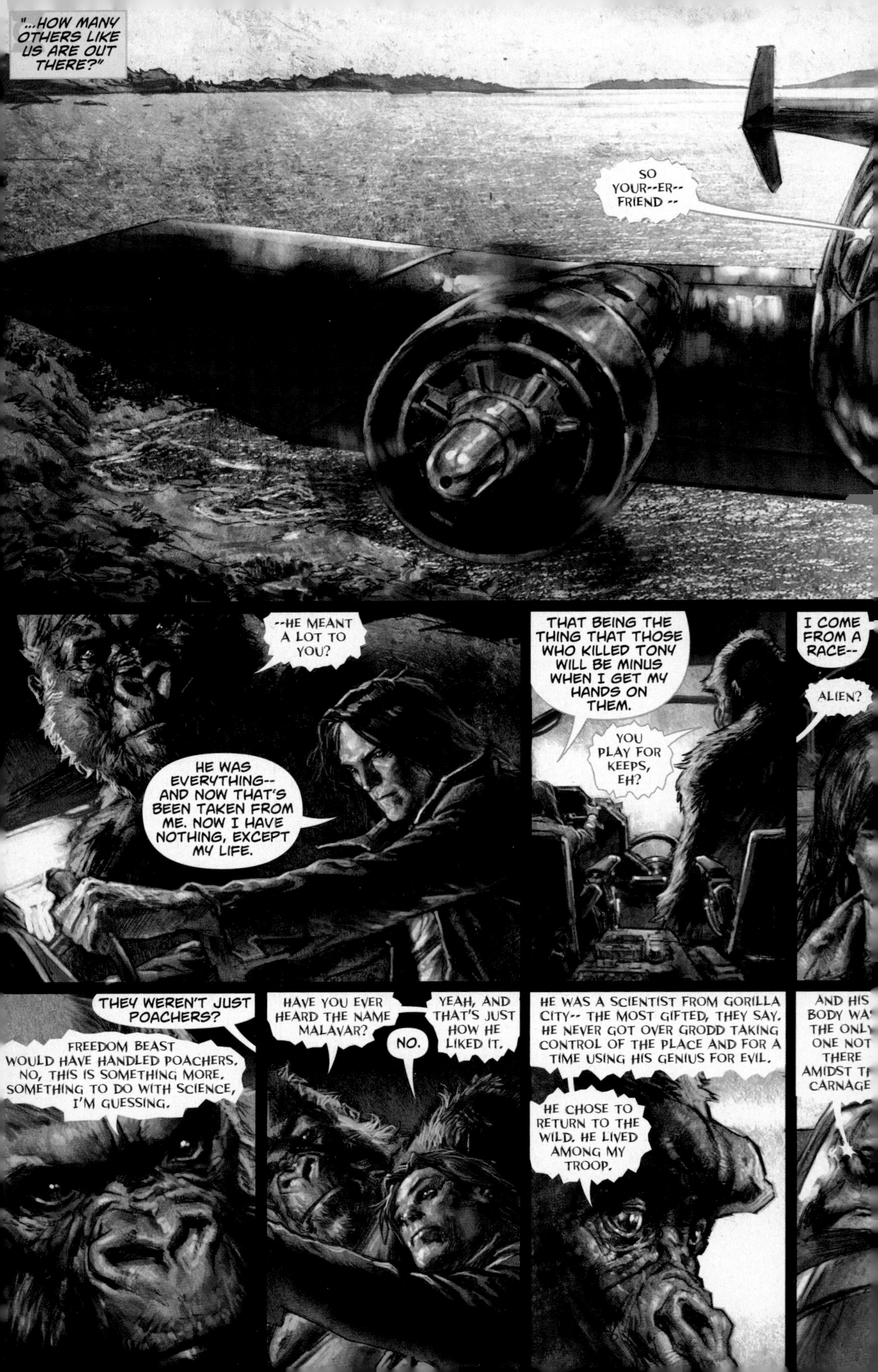
"...HOW MANY OTHERS LIKE US ARE OUT THERE?"
SO YOUR--ER-- FRIEND --
--HE MEANT A LOT TO YOU?
HE WAS EVERYTHING-- AND NOW THAT'S BEEN TAKEN FROM ME. NOW I HAVE NOTHING, EXCEPT MY LIFE.
THAT BEING THE THING THAT THOSE WHO KILLED TONY WILL BE MINUS WHEN I GET MY HANDS ON THEM.
YOU PLAY FOR KEEPS, EH?
I COME FROM A RACE--
ALIEN?
THEY WEREN'T JUST POACHERS?
FREEDOM BEAST WOULD HAVE HANDLED POACHERS. NO, THIS IS SOMETHING MORE. SOMETHING TO DO WITH SCIENCE, I'M GUESSING.
HAVE YOU EVER HEARD THE NAME MALAVAR?
NO.
YEAH, AND THAT'S JUST HOW HE LIKED IT.
HE WAS A SCIENTIST FROM GORILLA CITY-- THE MOST GIFTED, THEY SAY. HE NEVER GOT OVER GRODD TAKING CONTROL OF THE PLACE AND FOR A TIME USING HIS GENIUS FOR EVIL.
HE CHOSE TO RETURN TO THE WILD. HE LIVED AMONG MY TROOP.

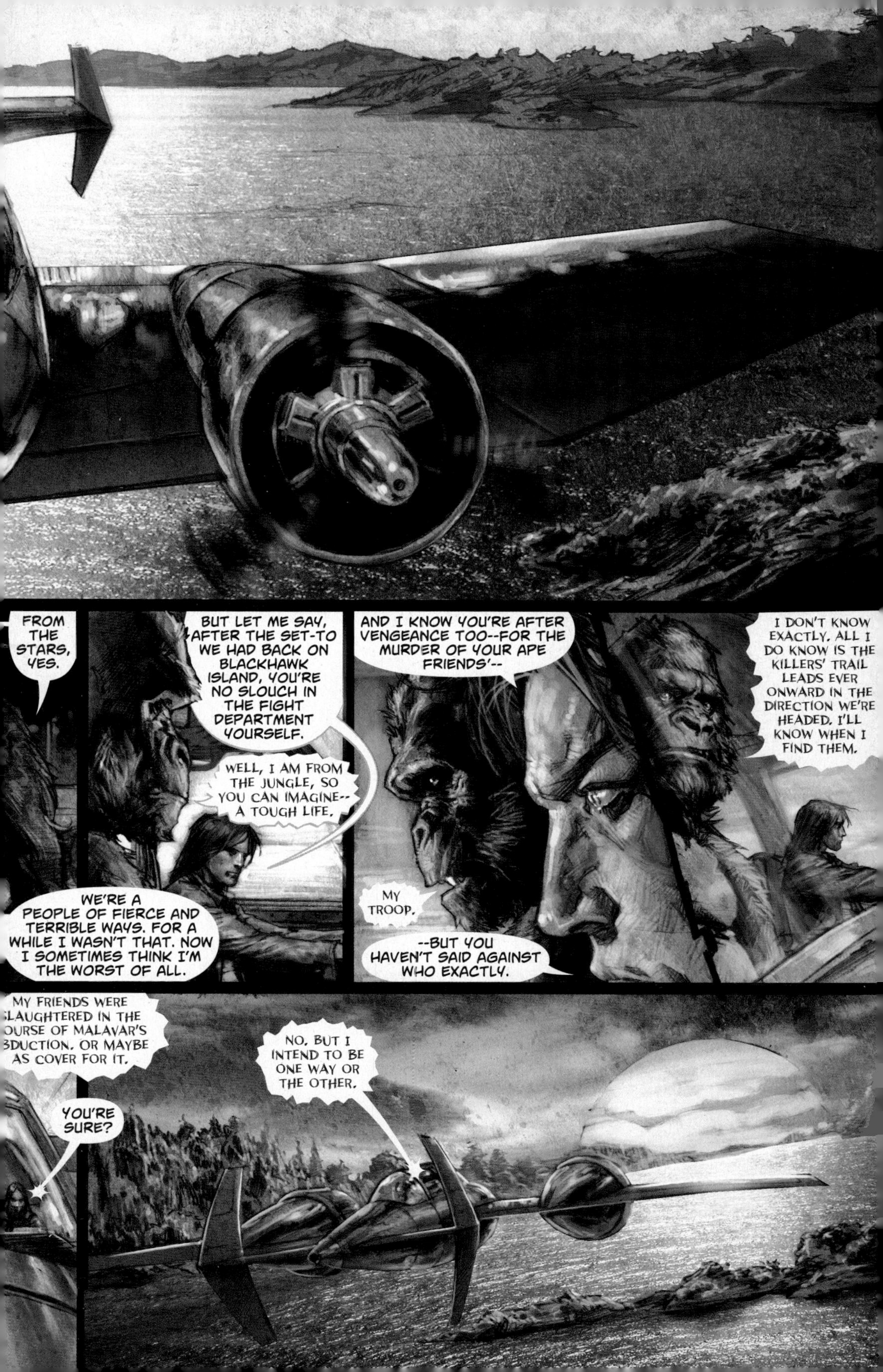
FROM THE STARS, YES.
BUT LET ME SAY, AFTER THE SET-TO WE HAD BACK ON BLACKHAWK ISLAND, YOU'RE NO SLOUCH IN THE FIGHT DEPARTMENT YOURSELF.
WELL, I AM FROM THE JUNGLE, SO YOU CAN IMAGINE-- A TOUGH LIFE.
WE'RE A PEOPLE OF FIERCE AND TERRIBLE WAYS. FOR A WHILE I WASN'T THAT. NOW I SOMETIMES THINK I'M THE WORST OF ALL.
AND I KNOW YOU'RE AFTER VENGEANCE TOO--FOR THE MURDER OF YOUR APE FRIENDS'--
MY TROOP.
--BUT YOU HAVEN'T SAID AGAINST WHO EXACTLY.
I DON'T KNOW EXACTLY. ALL I DO KNOW IS THE KILLERS' TRAIL LEADS EVER ONWARD IN THE DIRECTION WE'RE HEADED. I'LL KNOW WHEN I FIND THEM.
MY FRIENDS WERE LAUGHTERED IN THE OURSE OF MALAVAR'S BDUCTION. OR MAYBE AS COVER FOR IT.
YOU'RE SURE?
NO, BUT I INTEND TO BE ONE WAY OR THE OTHER.

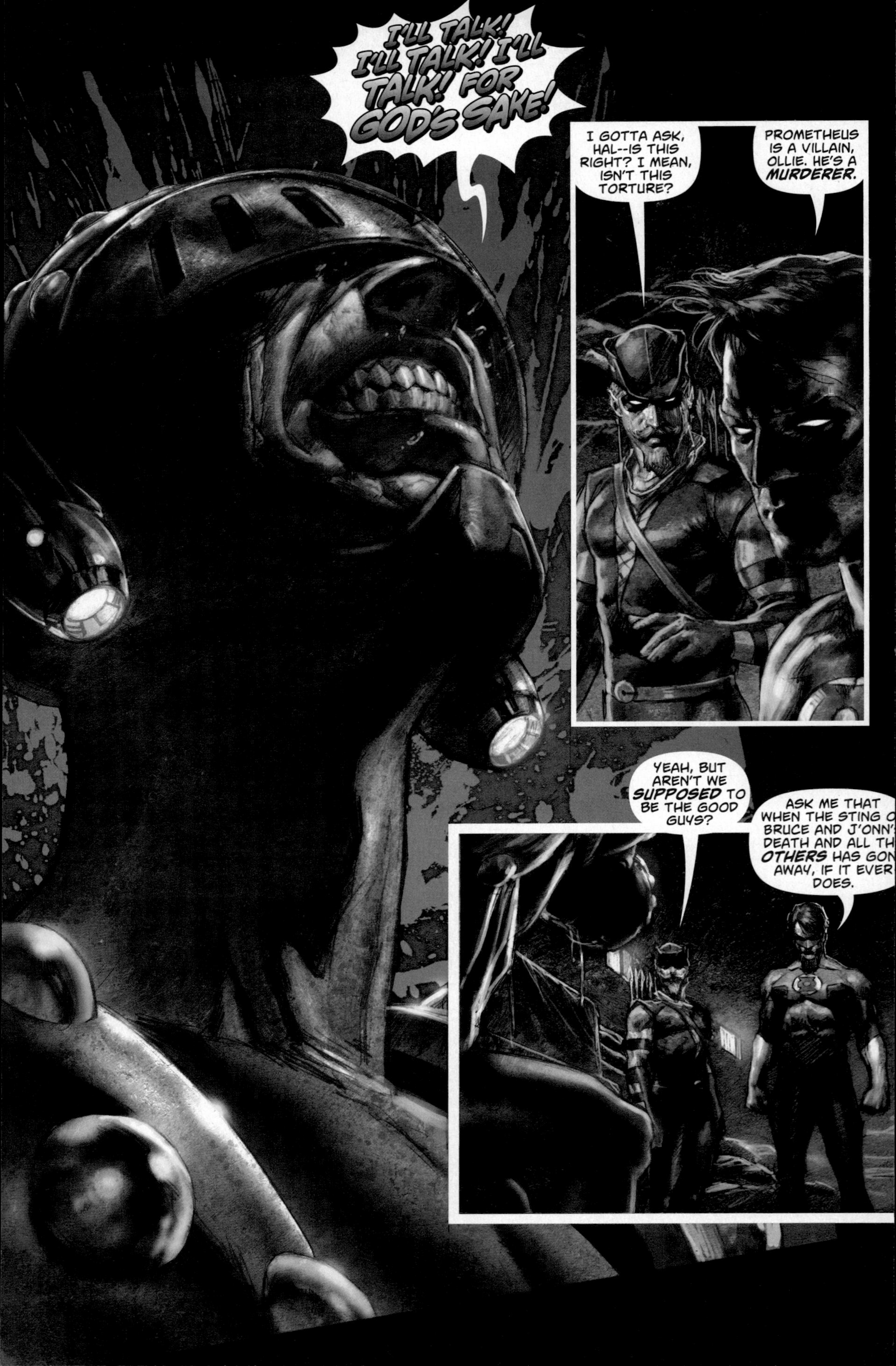
I'LL TALK! I'LL TALK! I'LL TALK! FOR GOD'S SAKE!
I GOTTA ASK, HAL--IS THIS RIGHT? I MEAN, ISN'T THIS TORTURE?
PROMETHEUS IS A VILLAIN, OLLIE. HE'S A MURDERER.
YEAH, BUT AREN'T WE SUPPOSED TO BE THE GOOD GUYS?
ASK ME THAT WHEN THE STING O BRUCE AND J'ONN' DEATH AND ALL TH OTHERS HAS GON AWAY, IF IT EVER DOES.

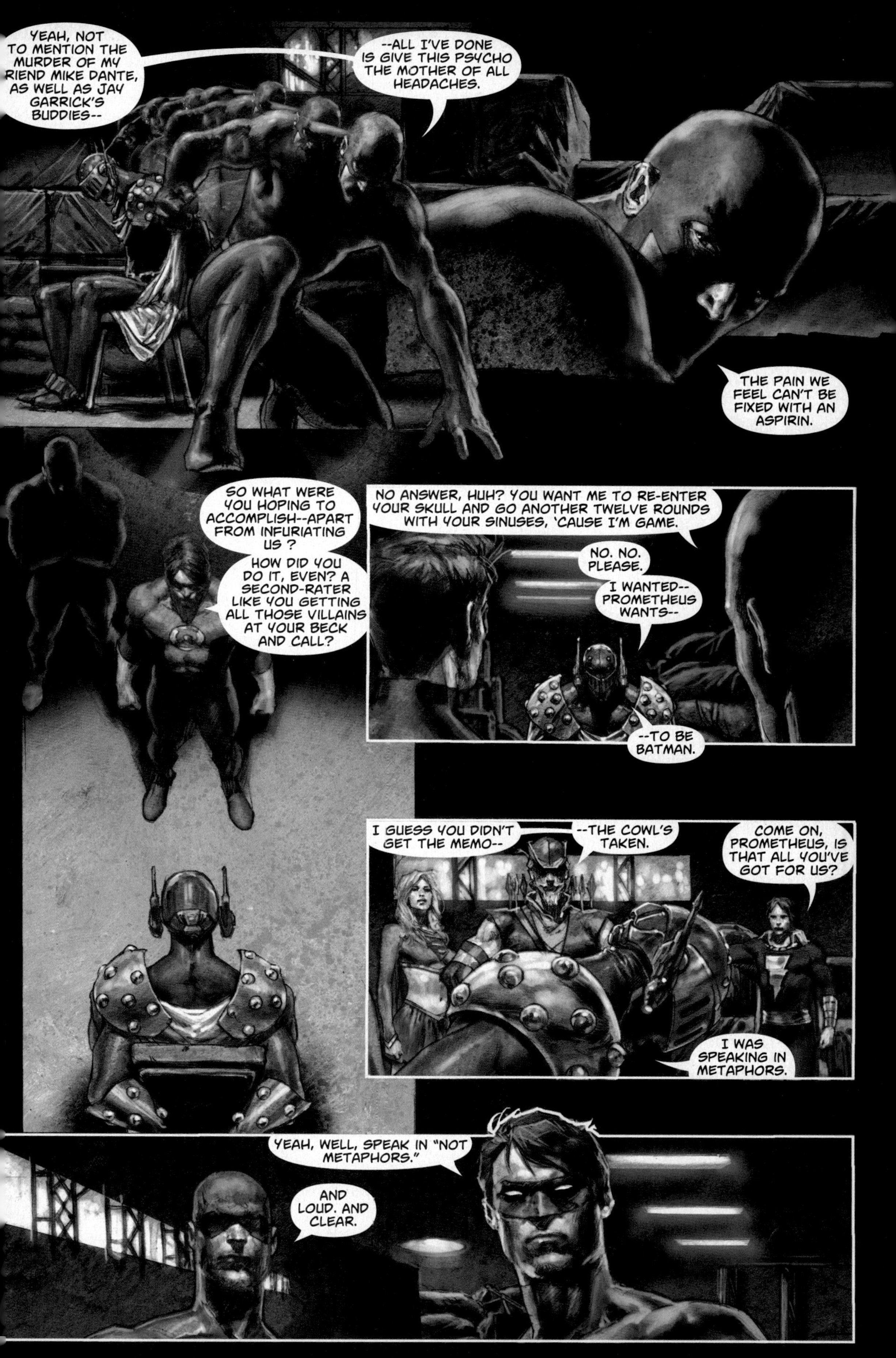
YEAH, NOT TO MENTION THE MURDER OF MY RIEND MIKE DANTE, AS WELL AS JAY GARRICK'S BUDDIES--
--ALL I'VE DONE IS GIVE THIS PSYCHO THE MOTHER OF ALL HEADACHES.
THE PAIN WE FEEL CAN'T BE FIXED WITH AN ASPIRIN.
SO WHAT WERE YOU HOPING TO ACCOMPLISH--APART FROM INFURIATING US ?
HOW DID YOU DO IT, EVEN? A SECOND-RATER LIKE YOU GETTING ALL THOSE VILLAINS AT YOUR BECK AND CALL?
NO ANSWER, HUH? YOU WANT ME TO RE-ENTER YOUR SKULL AND GO ANOTHER TWELVE ROUNDS WITH YOUR SINUSES, 'CAUSE I'M GAME.
NO. NO. PLEASE.
I WANTED-- PROMETHEUS WANTS--
--TO BE BATMAN.
I GUESS YOU DIDN'T GET THE MEMO--
--THE COWL'S TAKEN.
COME ON, PROMETHEUS, IS THAT ALL YOU'VE GOT FOR US?
I WAS SPEAKING IN METAPHORS.
YEAH, WELL, SPEAK IN "NOT METAPHORS."
AND LOUD. AND CLEAR.

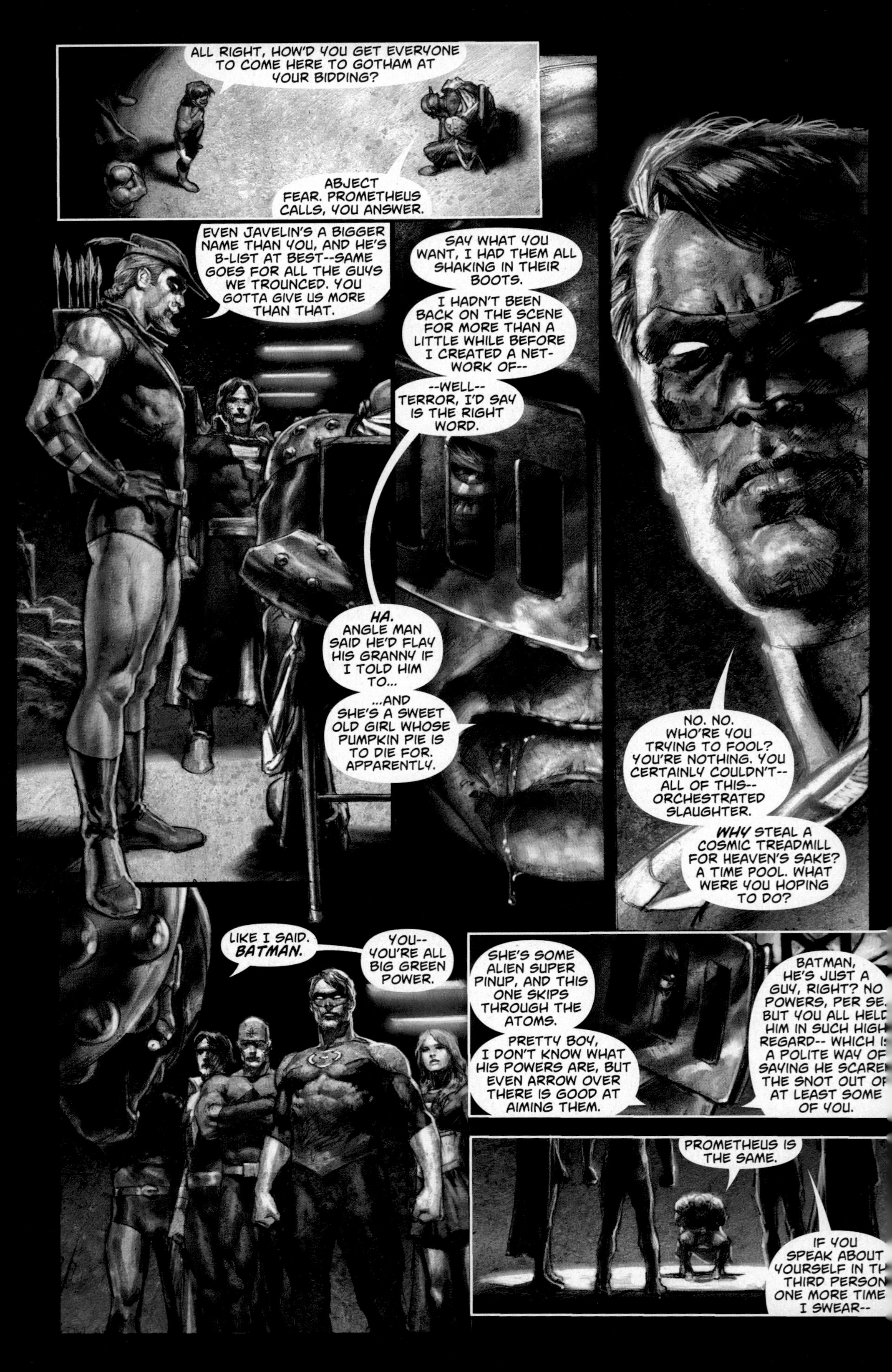
ALL RIGHT, HOW'D YOU GET EVERYONE TO COME HERE TO GOTHAM AT YOUR BIDDING?
ABJECT FEAR. PROMETHEUS CALLS, YOU ANSWER.
EVEN JAVELIN'S A BIGGER NAME THAN YOU, AND HE'S B-LIST AT BEST--SAME GOES FOR ALL THE GUYS WE TROUNCED. YOU GOTTA GIVE US MORE THAN THAT.
SAY WHAT YOU WANT, I HAD THEM ALL SHAKING IN THEIR BOOTS.
I HADN'T BEEN BACK ON THE SCENE FOR MORE THAN A LITTLE WHILE BEFORE I CREATED A NET-WORK OF--
--WELL-- TERROR, I'D SAY IS THE RIGHT WORD.
HA. ANGLE MAN SAID HE'D FLAY HIS GRANNY IF I TOLD HIM TO...
...AND SHE'S A SWEET OLD GIRL WHOSE PUMPKIN PIE IS TO DIE FOR. APPARENTLY.
NO. NO. WHO'RE YOU TRYING TO FOOL? YOU'RE NOTHING. YOU CERTAINLY COULDN'T-- ALL OF THIS-- ORCHESTRATED SLAUGHTER.
WHY STEAL A COSMIC TREADMILL FOR HEAVEN'S SAKE? A TIME POOL. WHAT WERE YOU HOPING TO DO?
LIKE I SAID. BATMAN.
YOU-- YOU'RE ALL BIG GREEN POWER.
SHE'S SOME ALIEN SUPER PINUP, AND THIS ONE SKIPS THROUGH THE ATOMS.
PRETTY BOY, I DON'T KNOW WHAT HIS POWERS ARE, BUT EVEN ARROW OVER THERE IS GOOD AT AIMING THEM.
BATMAN, HE'S JUST A GUY, RIGHT? NO POWERS, PER SE. BUT YOU ALL HELD HIM IN SUCH HIGH REGARD-- WHICH IS A POLITE WAY OF SAYING HE SCARED THE SNOT OUT OF AT LEAST SOME OF YOU.
PROMETHEUS IS THE SAME.
IF YOU SPEAK ABOUT YOURSELF IN TH THIRD PERSON ONE MORE TIME I SWEAR--

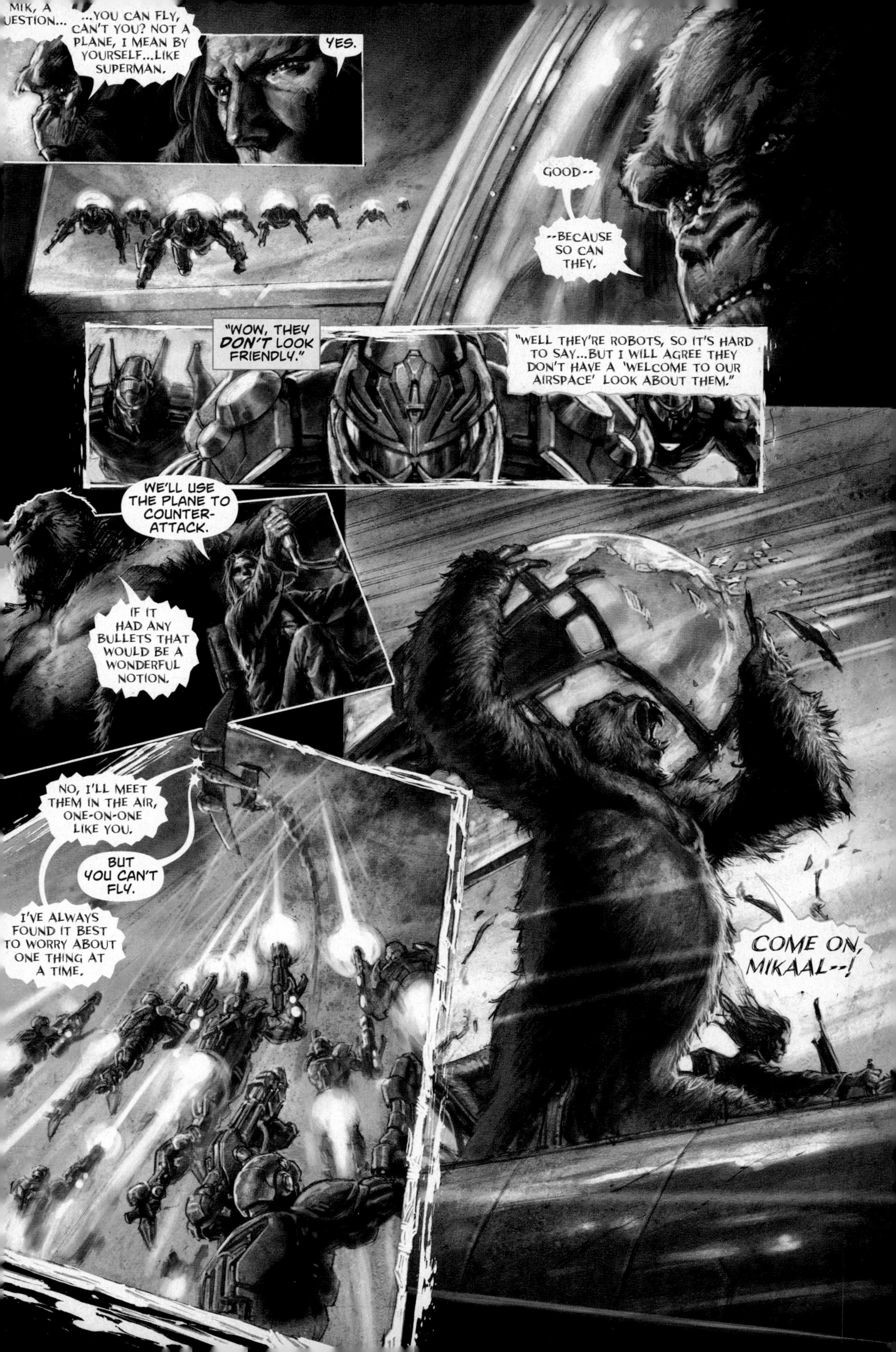
MIK, A
UESTION...
...YOU CAN FLY, CAN'T YOU? NOT A PLANE, I MEAN BY YOURSELF...LIKE SUPERMAN.
YES.
GOOD--
--BECAUSE SO CAN THEY.
"WOW, THEY DON'T LOOK FRIENDLY."
"WELL THEY'RE ROBOTS, SO IT'S HARD TO SAY...BUT I WILL AGREE THEY DON'T HAVE A 'WELCOME TO OUR AIRSPACE' LOOK ABOUT THEM."
WE'LL USE THE PLANE TO COUNTER-ATTACK.
IF IT HAD ANY BULLETS THAT WOULD BE A WONDERFUL NOTION.
NO, I'LL MEET THEM IN THE AIR, ONE-ON-ONE LIKE YOU.
BUT YOU CAN'T FLY.
I'VE ALWAYS FOUND IT BEST TO WORRY ABOUT ONE THING AT A TIME.
COME ON, MIKAAL--!

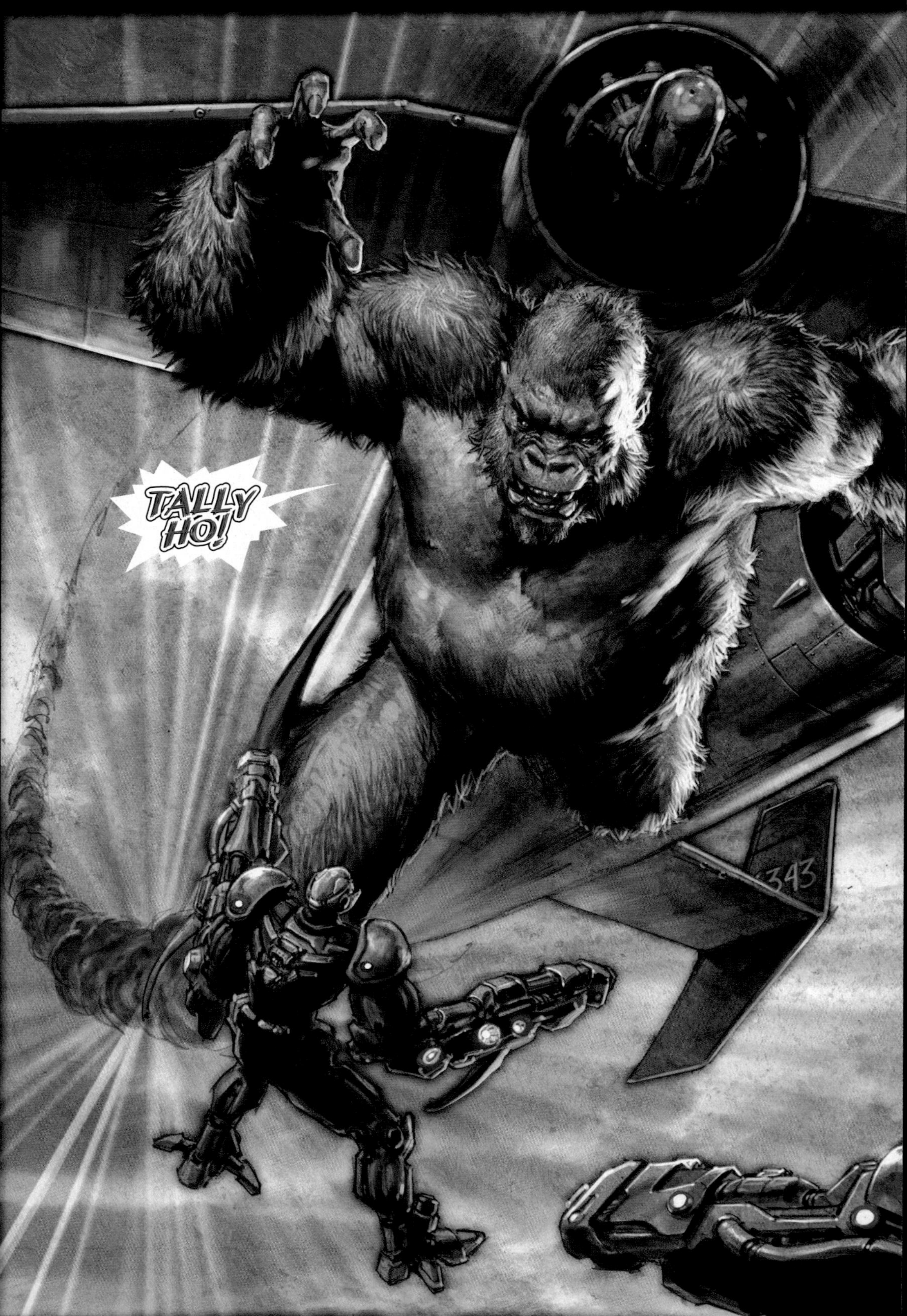
TALLY HO!
343

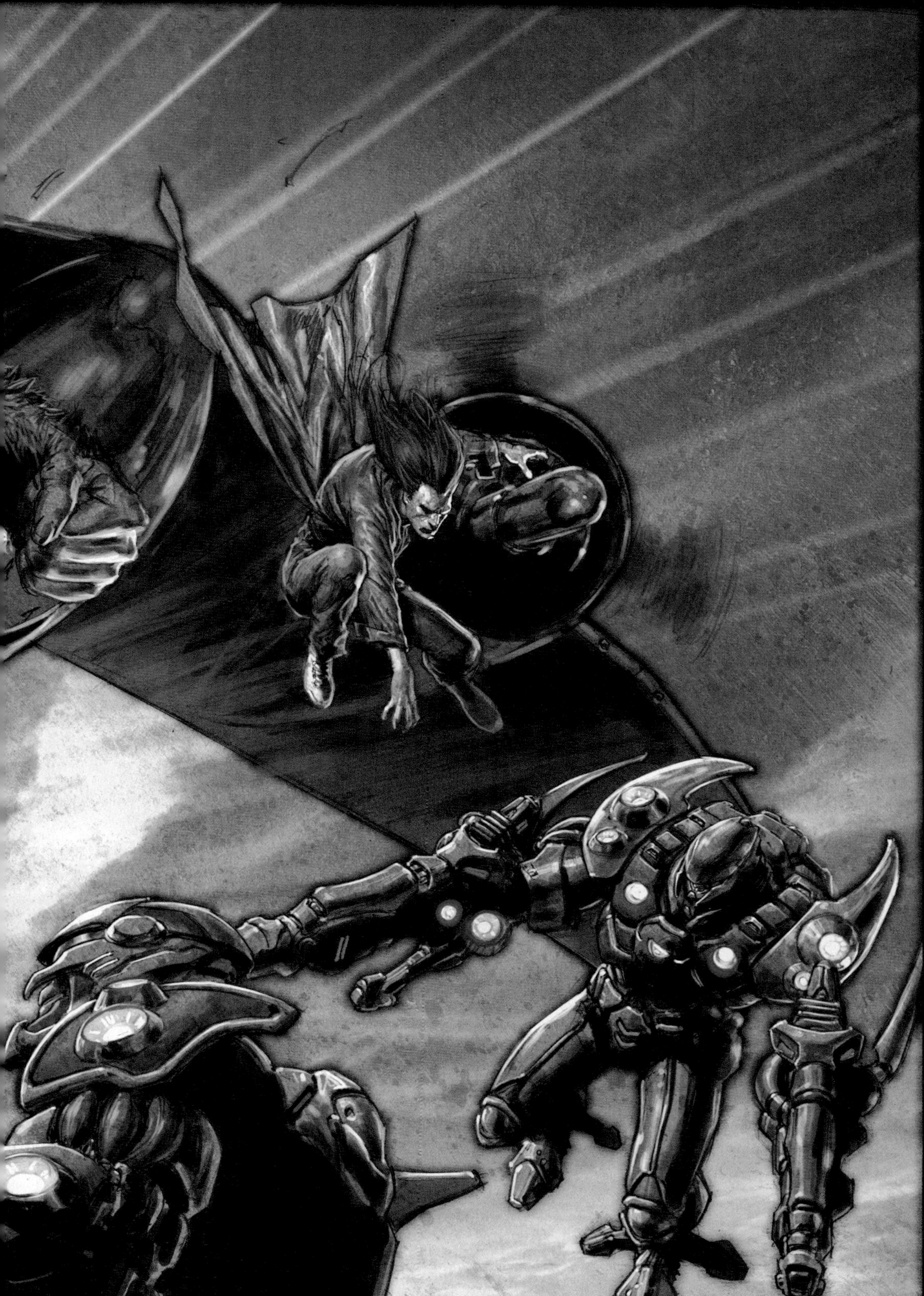

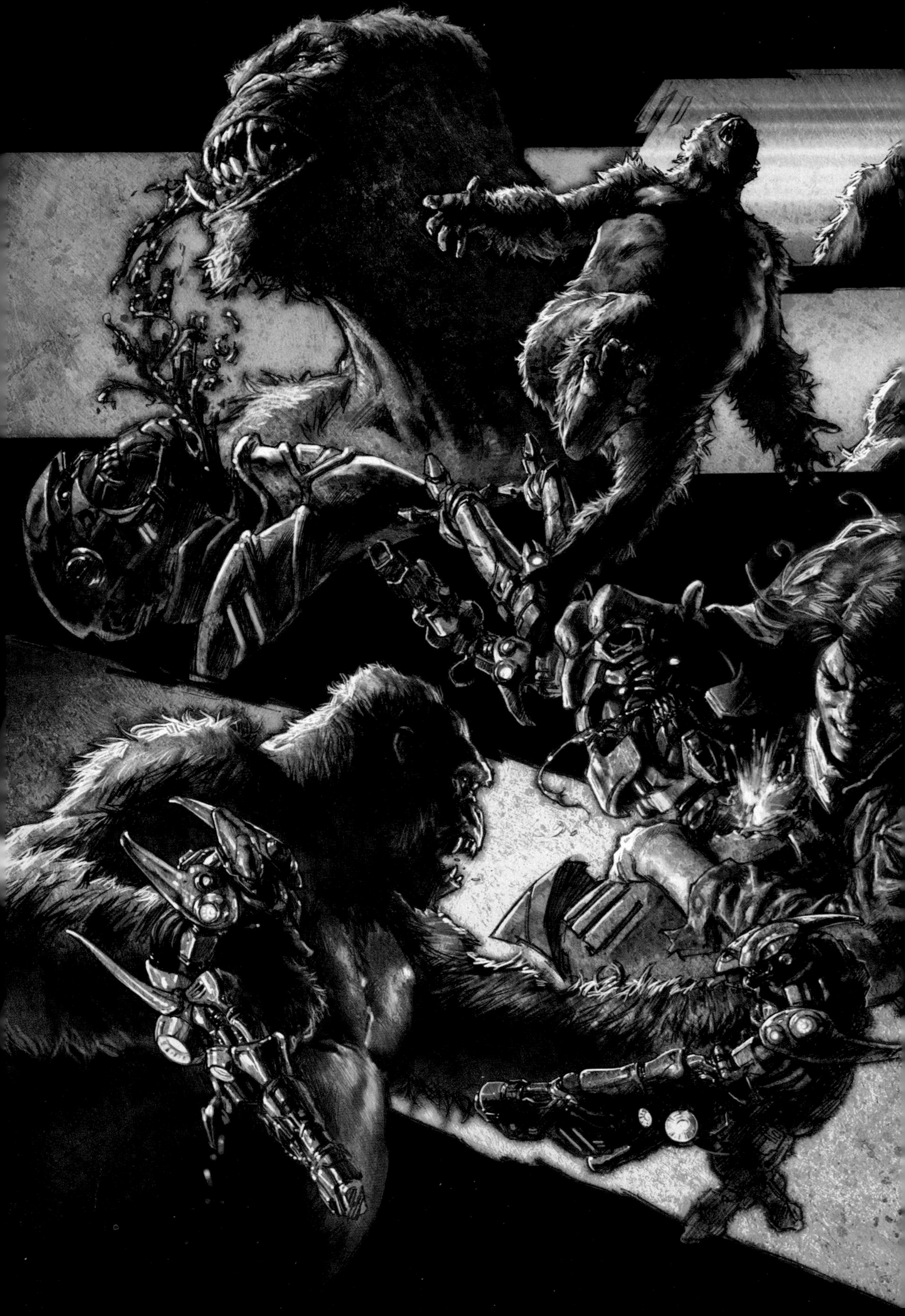

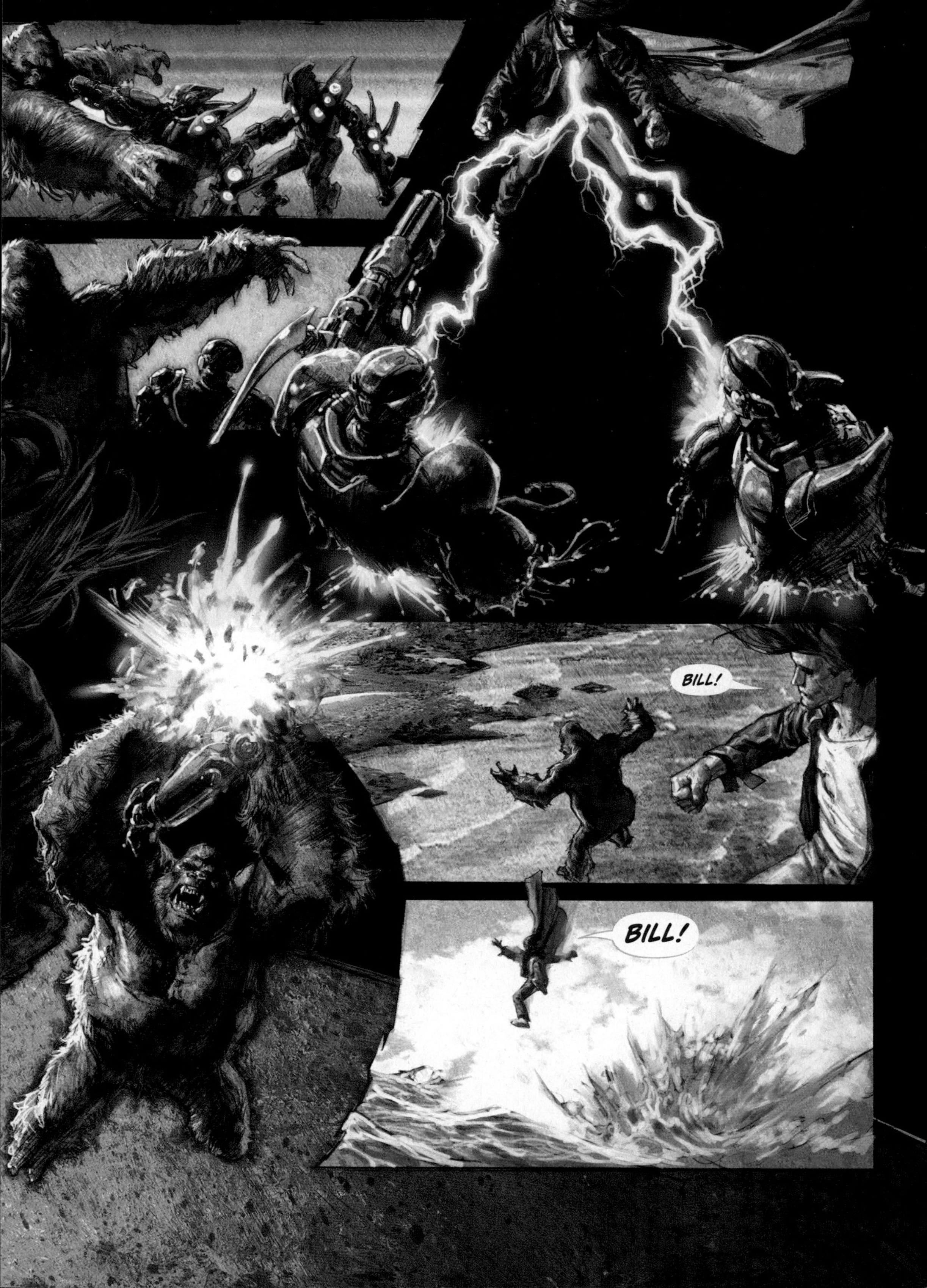
BILL!
BILL!

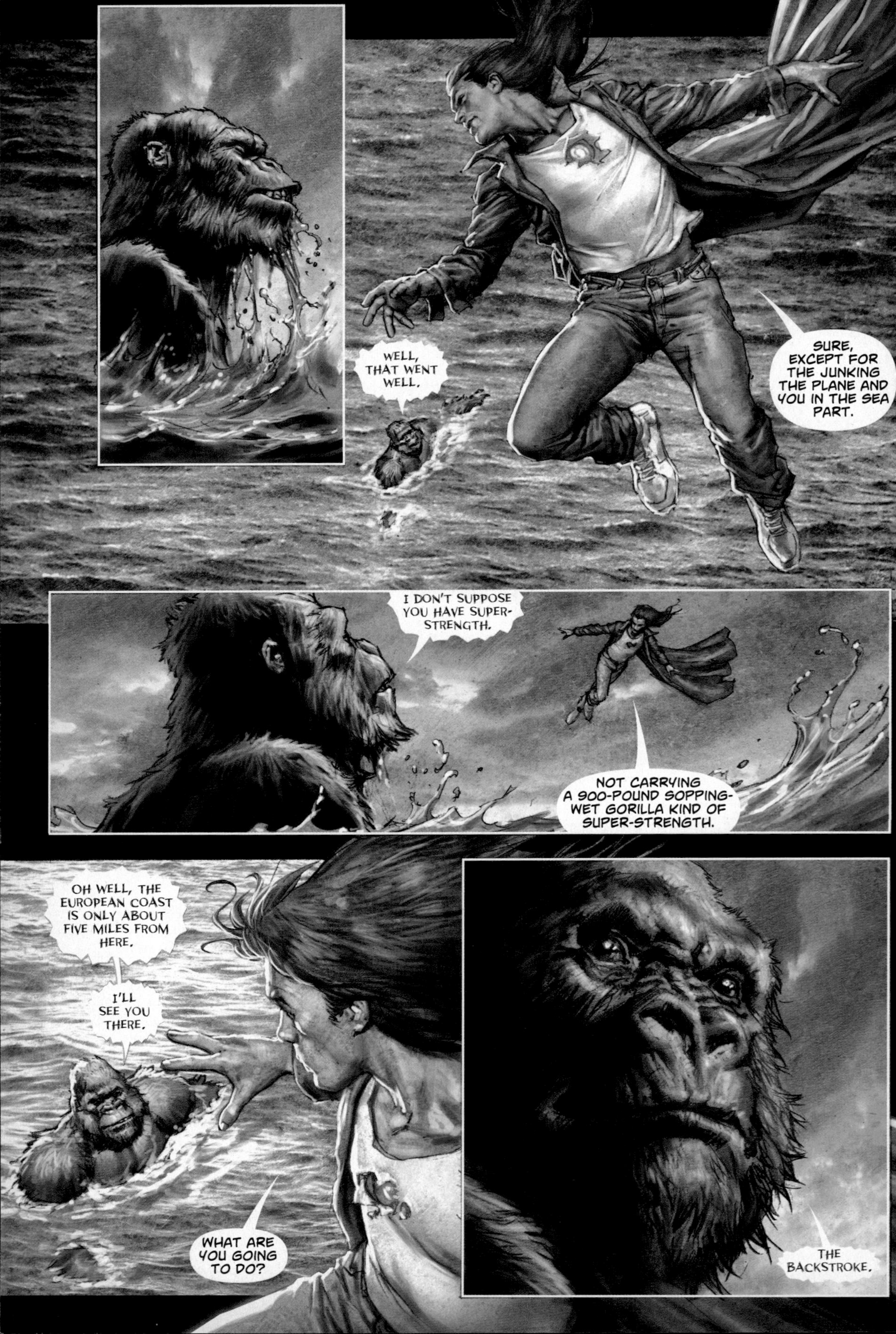
WELL, THAT WENT WELL.
SURE, EXCEPT FOR THE JUNKING THE PLANE AND YOU IN THE SEA PART.
I DON'T SUPPOSE YOU HAVE SUPER-STRENGTH.
NOT CARRYING A 900-POUND SOPPING-WET GORILLA KIND OF SUPER-STRENGTH.
OH WELL, THE EUROPEAN COAST IS ONLY ABOUT FIVE MILES FROM HERE.
I'LL SEE YOU THERE.
WHAT ARE YOU GOING TO DO?
THE BACKSTROKE.

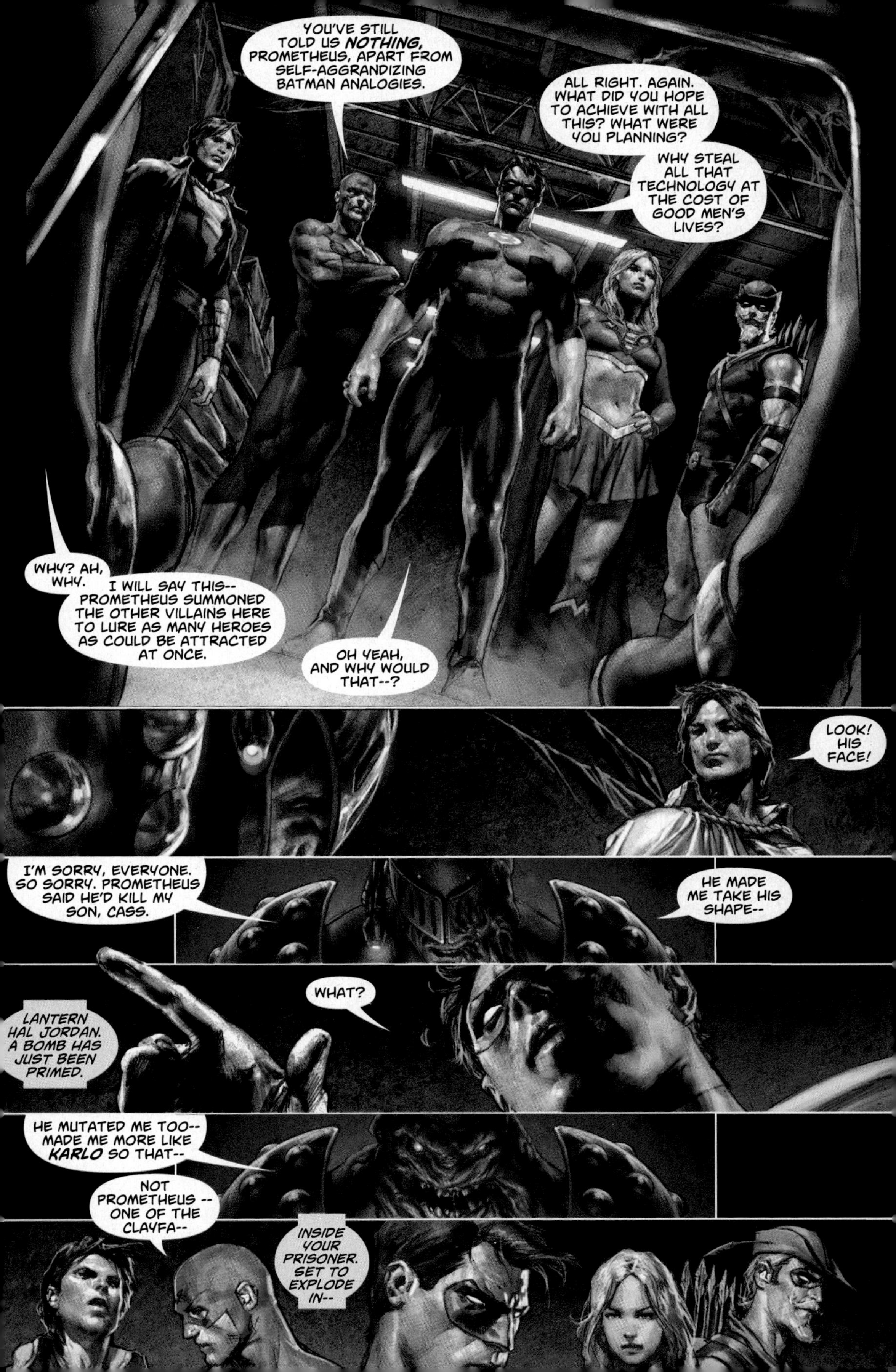
YOU'VE STILL TOLD US NOTHING, PROMETHEUS, APART FROM SELF-AGGRANDIZING BATMAN ANALOGIES.
ALL RIGHT. AGAIN. WHAT DID YOU HOPE TO ACHIEVE WITH ALL THIS? WHAT WERE YOU PLANNING?
WHY STEAL ALL THAT TECHNOLOGY AT THE COST OF GOOD MEN'S LIVES?
WHY? AH, WHY.
I WILL SAY THIS-- PROMETHEUS SUMMONED THE OTHER VILLAINS HERE TO LURE AS MANY HEROES AS COULD BE ATTRACTED AT ONCE.
OH YEAH, AND WHY WOULD THAT--?
LOOK! HIS FACE!
I'M SORRY, EVERYONE. SO SORRY. PROMETHEUS SAID HE'D KILL MY SON, CASS.
HE MADE ME TAKE HIS SHAPE--
WHAT?
LANTERN HAL JORDAN. A BOMB HAS JUST BEEN PRIMED.
HE MUTATED ME TOO-- MADE ME MORE LIKE KARLO SO THAT--
NOT PROMETHEUS -- ONE OF THE CLAYFA--
INSIDE YOUR PRISONER. SET TO EXPLODE IN--

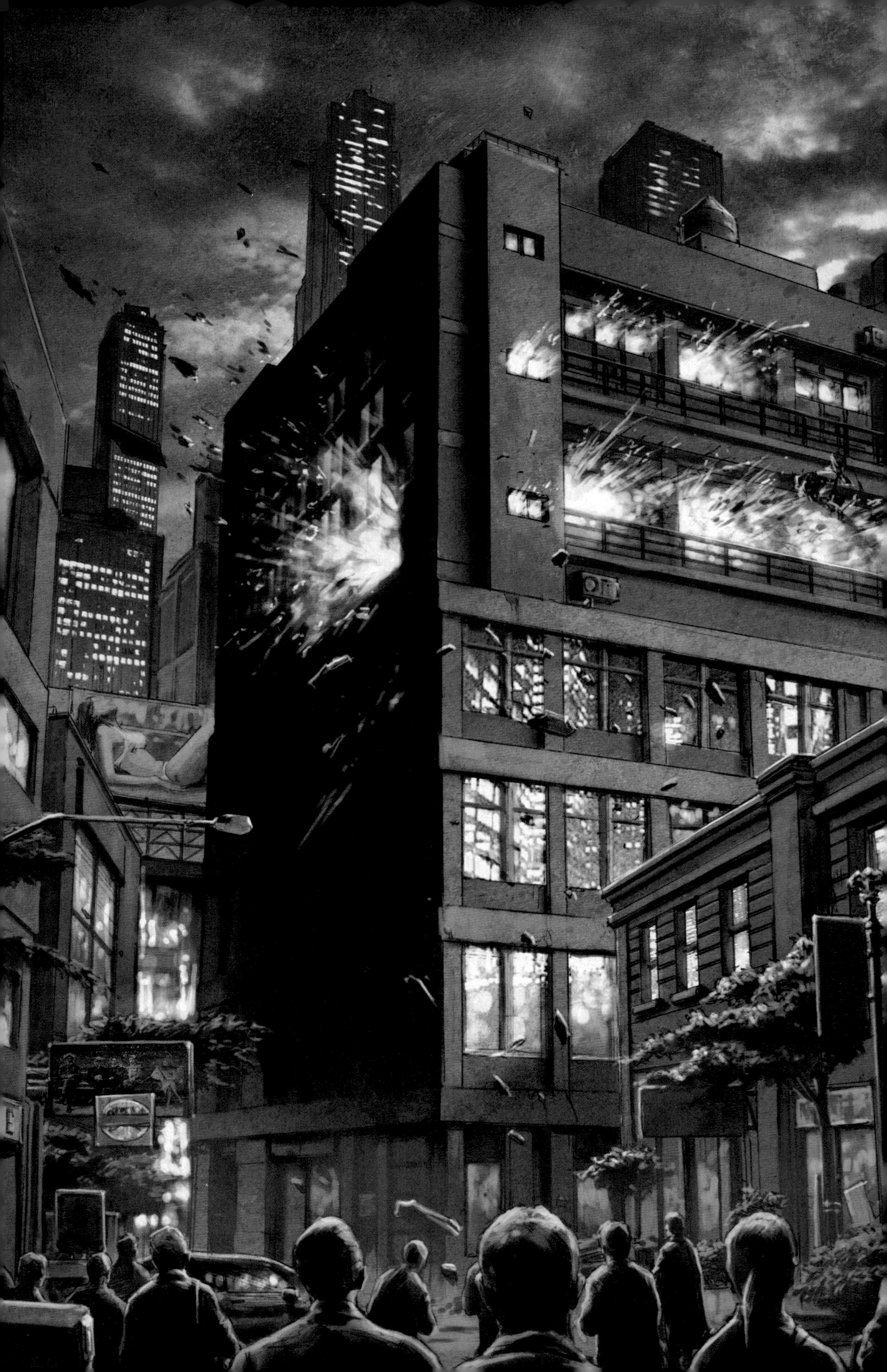

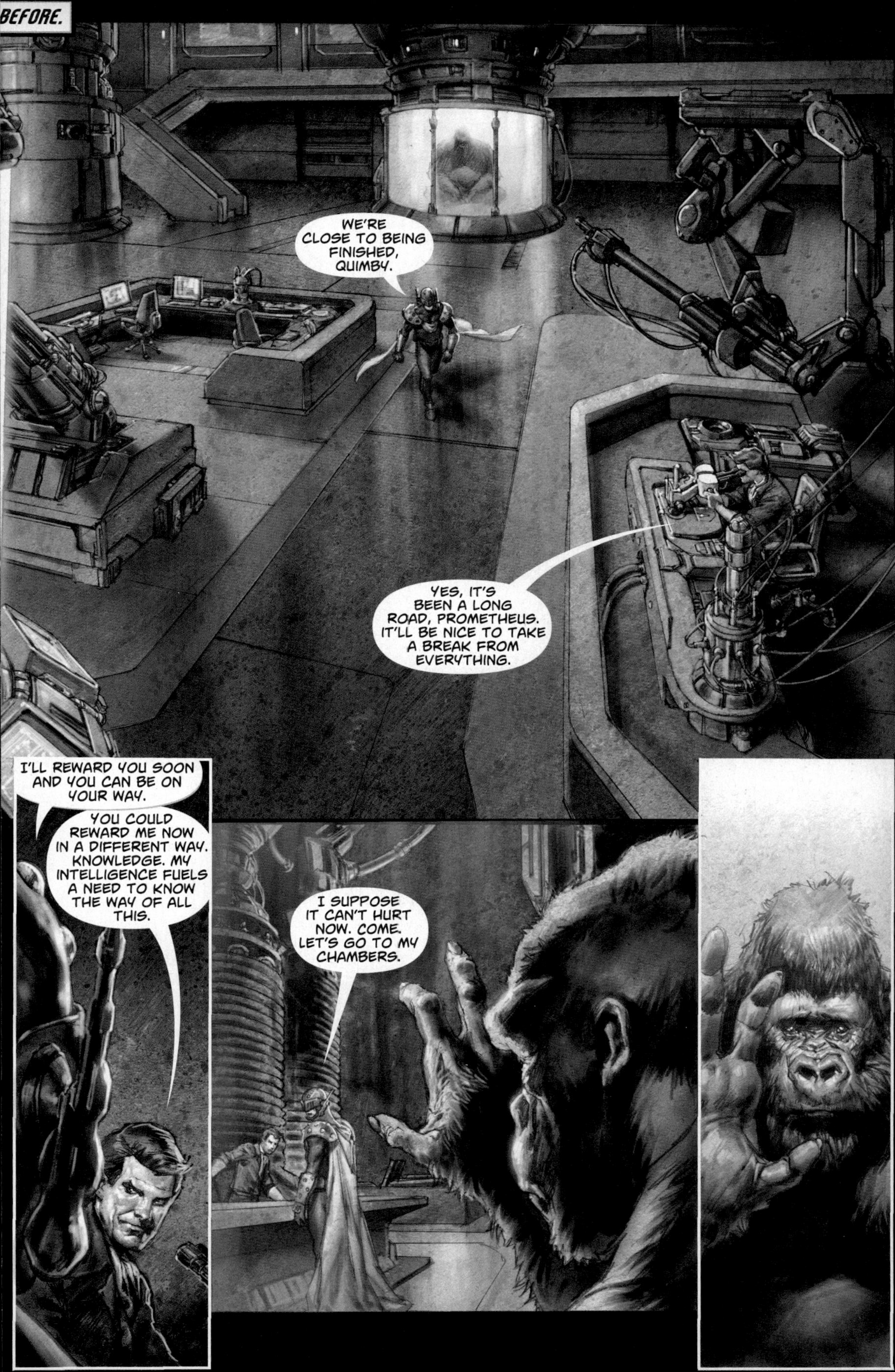
BEFORE.
WE'RE CLOSE TO BEING FINISHED, QUIMBY.
YES, IT'S BEEN A LONG ROAD, PROMETHEUS. IT'LL BE NICE TO TAKE A BREAK FROM EVERYTHING.
I'LL REWARD YOU SOON AND YOU CAN BE ON YOUR WAY.
YOU COULD REWARD ME NOW IN A DIFFERENT WAY. KNOWLEDGE. MY INTELLIGENCE FUELS A NEED TO KNOW THE WAY OF ALL THIS.
I SUPPOSE IT CAN'T HURT NOW. COME. LET'S GO TO MY CHAMBERS.

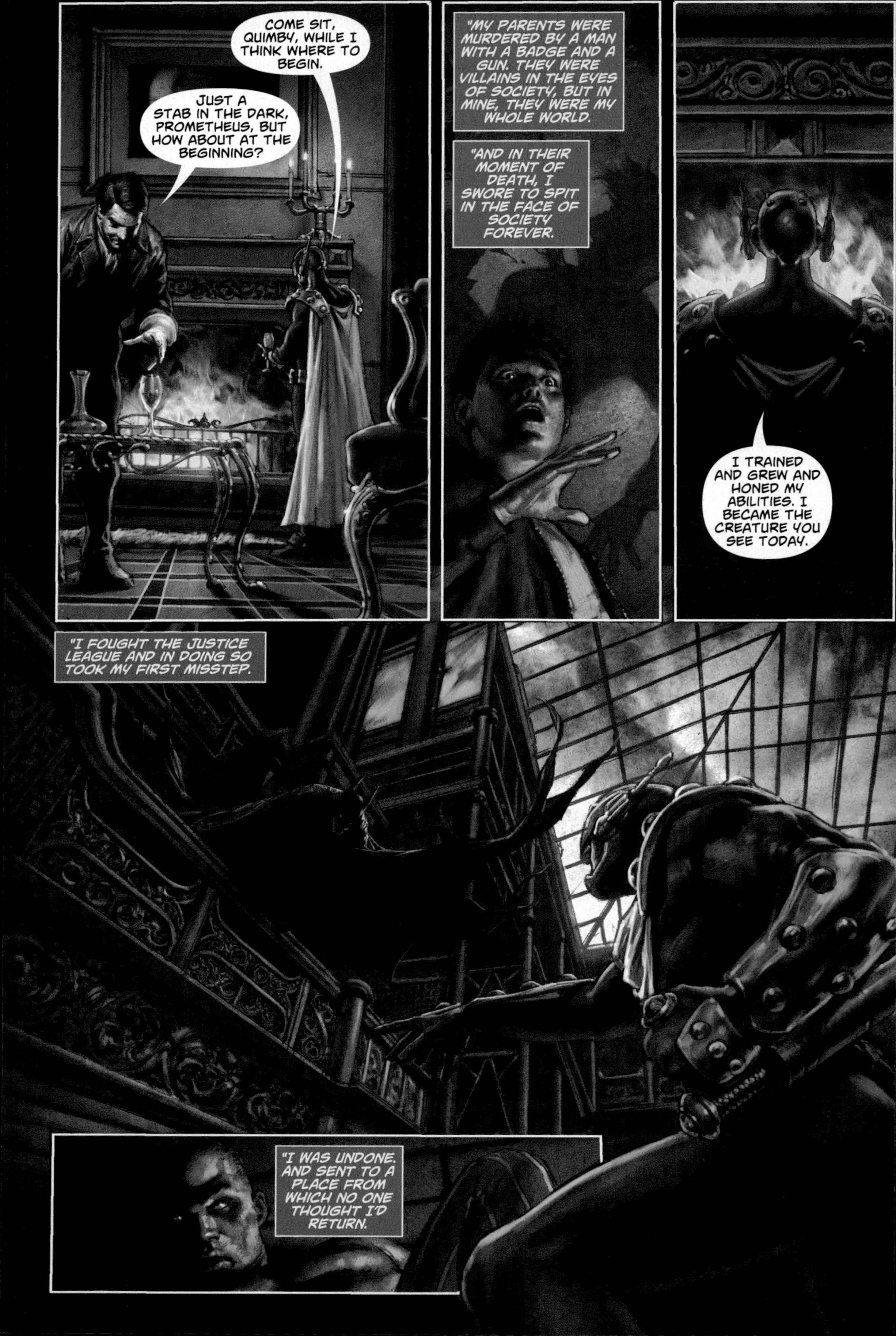
COME SIT, QUIMBY, WHILE I THINK WHERE TO BEGIN.
JUST A STAB IN THE DARK, PROMETHEUS, BUT HOW ABOUT AT THE BEGINNING?
"MY PARENTS WERE MURDERED BY A MAN WITH A BADGE AND A GUN. THEY WERE VILLAINS IN THE EYES OF SOCIETY, BUT IN MINE, THEY WERE MY WHOLE WORLD.
"AND IN THEIR MOMENT OF DEATH, I SWORE TO SPIT IN THE FACE OF SOCIETY FOREVER.
I TRAINED AND GREW AND HONED MY ABILITIES. I BECAME THE CREATURE YOU SEE TODAY.
"I FOUGHT THE JUSTICE LEAGUE AND IN DOING SO TOOK MY FIRST MISSTEP.
"I WAS UNDONE. AND SENT TO A PLACE FROM WHICH NO ONE THOUGHT I'D RETURN.

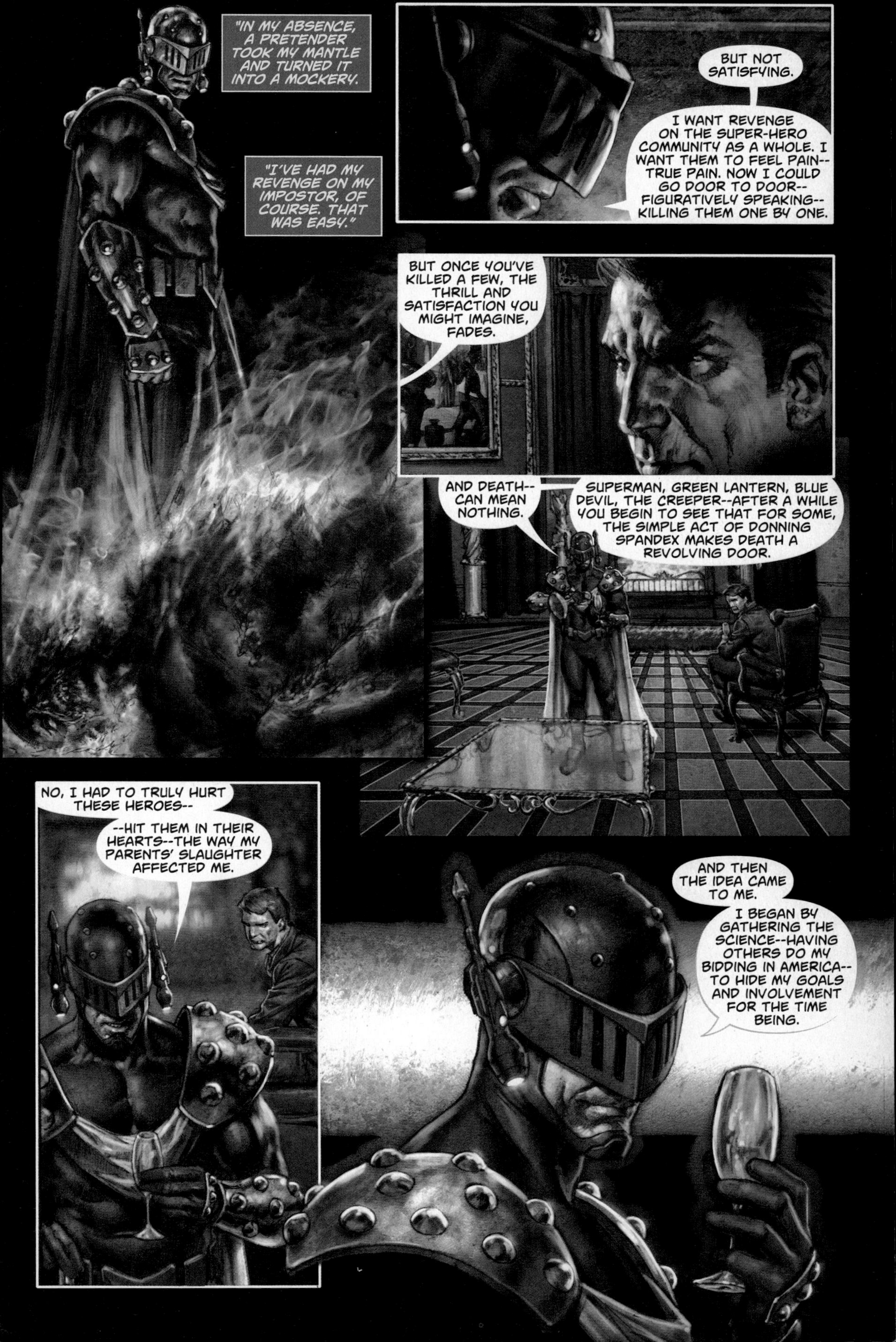
"IN MY ABSENCE, A PRETENDER TOOK MY MANTLE AND TURNED IT INTO A MOCKERY.
"I'VE HAD MY REVENGE ON MY IMPOSTOR, OF COURSE. THAT WAS EASY."
BUT NOT SATISFYING.
I WANT REVENGE ON THE SUPER-HERO COMMUNITY AS A WHOLE. I WANT THEM TO FEEL PAIN--TRUE PAIN. NOW I COULD GO DOOR TO DOOR--FIGURATIVELY SPEAKING--KILLING THEM ONE BY ONE.
BUT ONCE YOU'VE KILLED A FEW, THE THRILL AND SATISFACTION YOU MIGHT IMAGINE, FADES.
AND DEATH--CAN MEAN NOTHING.
SUPERMAN, GREEN LANTERN, BLUE DEVIL, THE CREEPER--AFTER A WHILE YOU BEGIN TO SEE THAT FOR SOME, THE SIMPLE ACT OF DONNING SPANDEX MAKES DEATH A REVOLVING DOOR.
NO, I HAD TO TRULY HURT THESE HEROES--
--HIT THEM IN THEIR HEARTS--THE WAY MY PARENTS' SLAUGHTER AFFECTED ME.
AND THEN THE IDEA CAME TO ME.
I BEGAN BY GATHERING THE SCIENCE--HAVING OTHERS DO MY BIDDING IN AMERICA--TO HIDE MY GOALS AND INVOLVEMENT FOR THE TIME BEING.

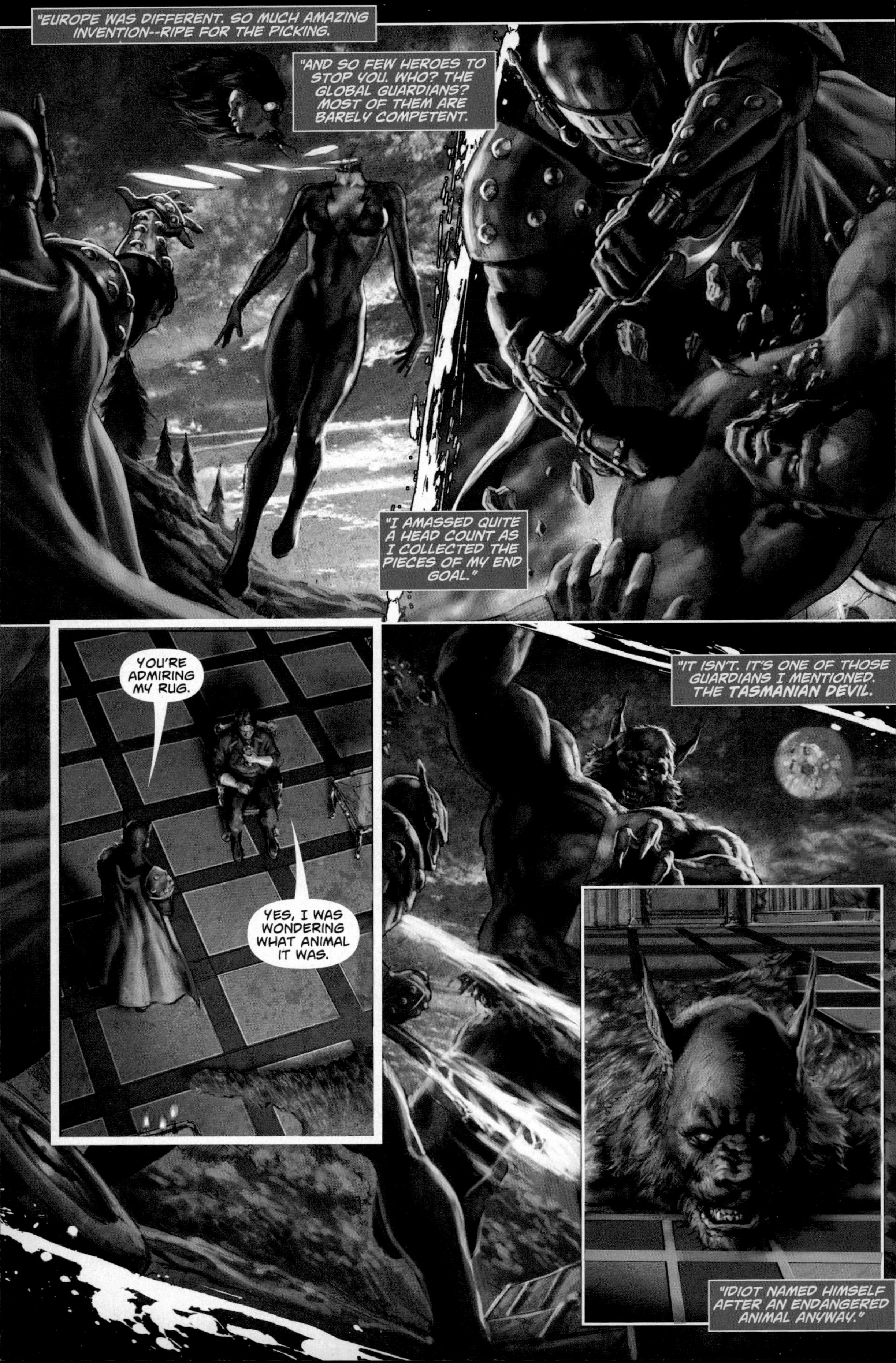
"EUROPE WAS DIFFERENT. SO MUCH AMAZING INVENTION--RIPE FOR THE PICKING.
"AND SO FEW HEROES TO STOP YOU. WHO? THE GLOBAL GUARDIANS? MOST OF THEM ARE BARELY COMPETENT.
"I AMASSED QUITE A HEAD COUNT AS I COLLECTED THE PIECES OF MY END GOAL."
YOU'RE ADMIRING MY RUG.
YES, I WAS WONDERING WHAT ANIMAL IT WAS.
"IT ISN'T. IT'S ONE OF THOSE GUARDIANS I MENTIONED. THE TASMANIAN DEVIL.
"IDIOT NAMED HIMSELF AFTER AN ENDANGERED ANIMAL ANYWAY."

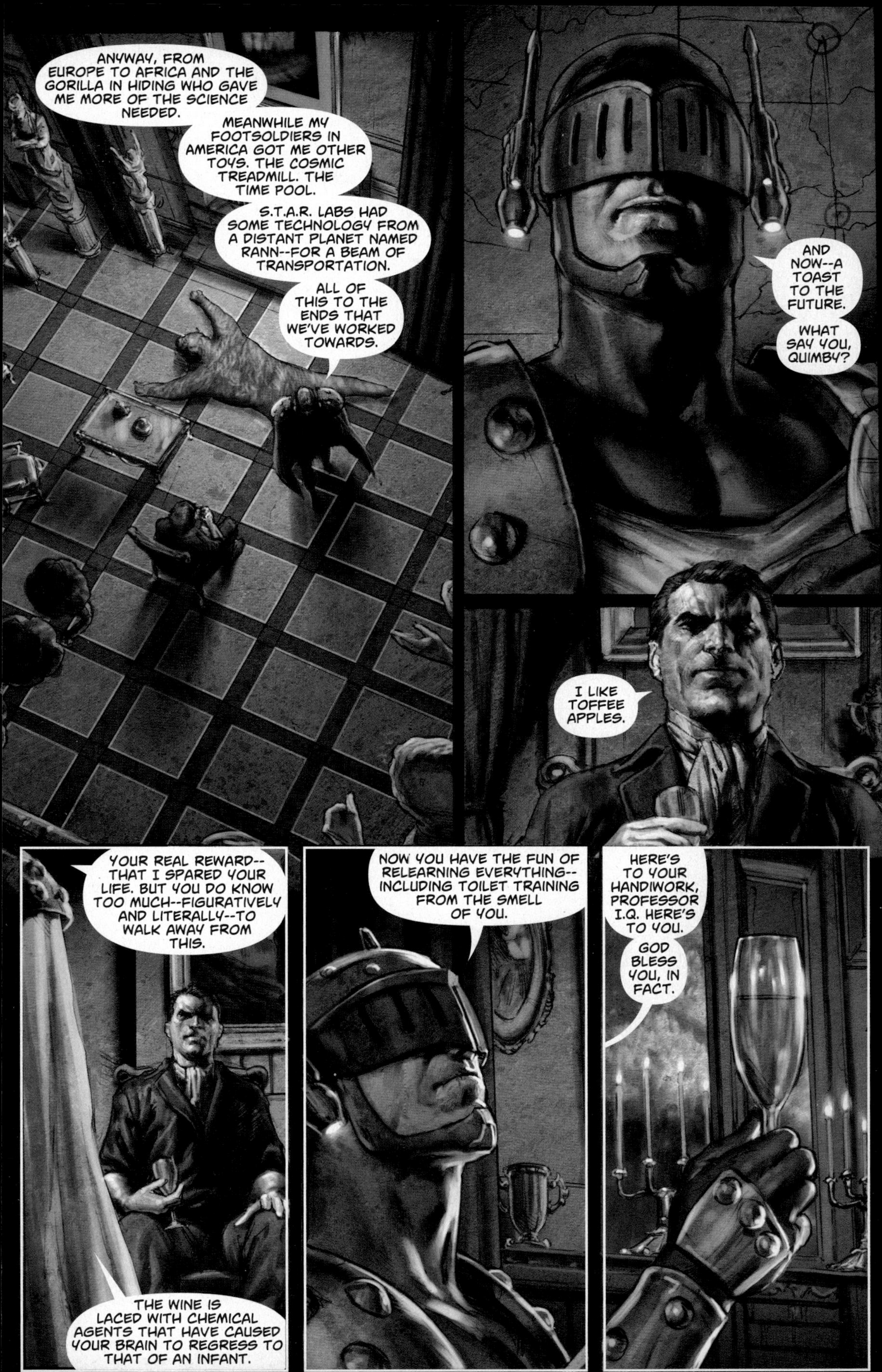
ANYWAY, FROM EUROPE TO AFRICA AND THE GORILLA IN HIDING WHO GAVE ME MORE OF THE SCIENCE NEEDED.
MEANWHILE MY FOOTSOLDIERS IN AMERICA GOT ME OTHER TOYS. THE COSMIC TREADMILL. THE TIME POOL.
S.T.A.R. LABS HAD SOME TECHNOLOGY FROM A DISTANT PLANET NAMED RANN--FOR A BEAM OF TRANSPORTATION.
ALL OF THIS TO THE ENDS THAT WE'VE WORKED TOWARDS.
AND NOW--A TOAST TO THE FUTURE.
WHAT SAY YOU, QUIMBY?
I LIKE TOFFEE APPLES.
YOUR REAL REWARD--THAT I SPARED YOUR LIFE. BUT YOU DO KNOW TOO MUCH--FIGURATIVELY AND LITERALLY--TO WALK AWAY FROM THIS.
THE WINE IS LACED WITH CHEMICAL AGENTS THAT HAVE CAUSED YOUR BRAIN TO REGRESS TO THAT OF AN INFANT.
NOW YOU HAVE THE FUN OF RELEARNING EVERYTHING--INCLUDING TOILET TRAINING FROM THE SMELL OF YOU.
HERE'S TO YOUR HANDIWORK, PROFESSOR I.Q. HERE'S TO YOU.
GOD BLESS YOU, IN FACT.

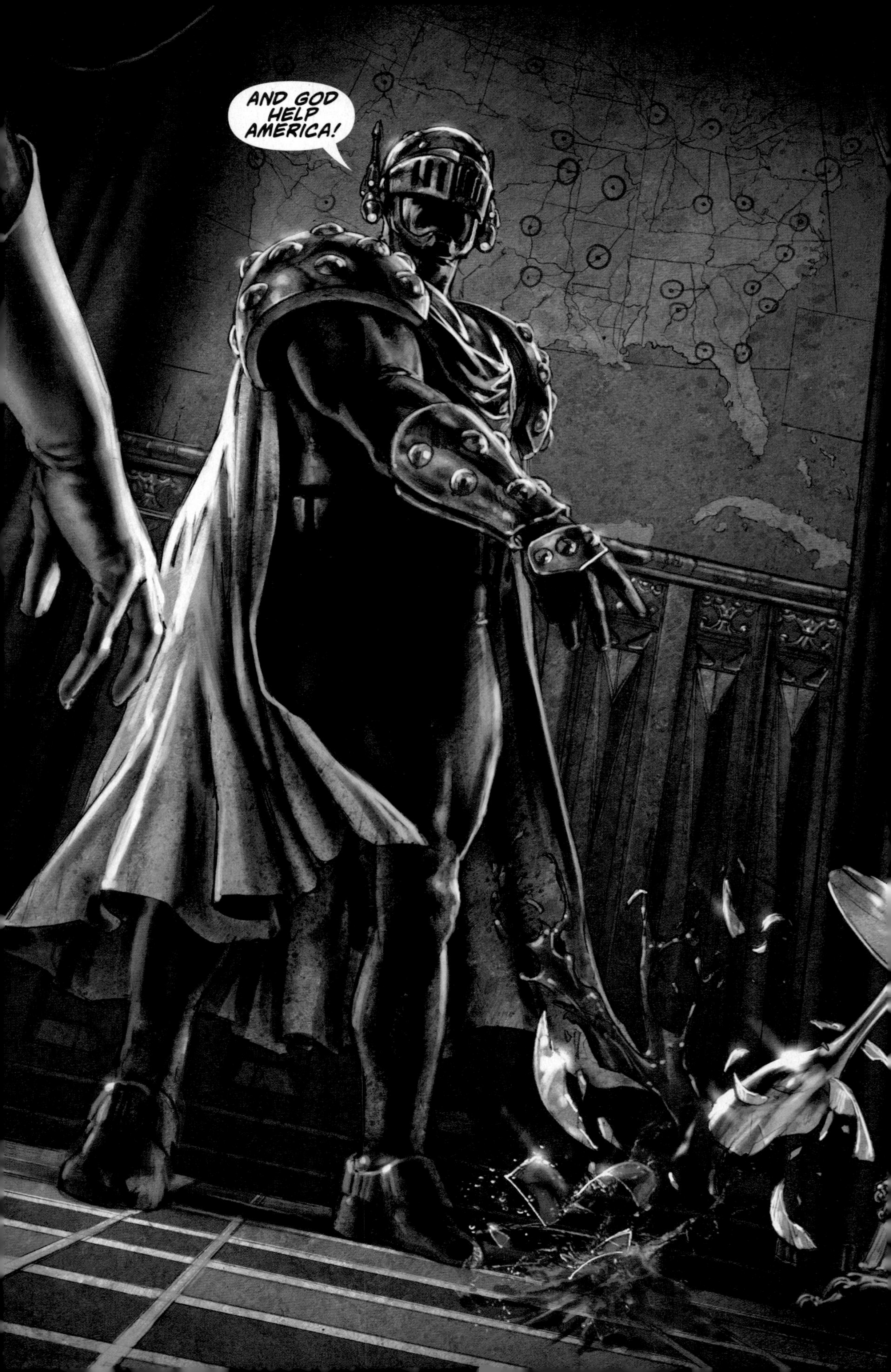
AND GOD HELP AMERICA!

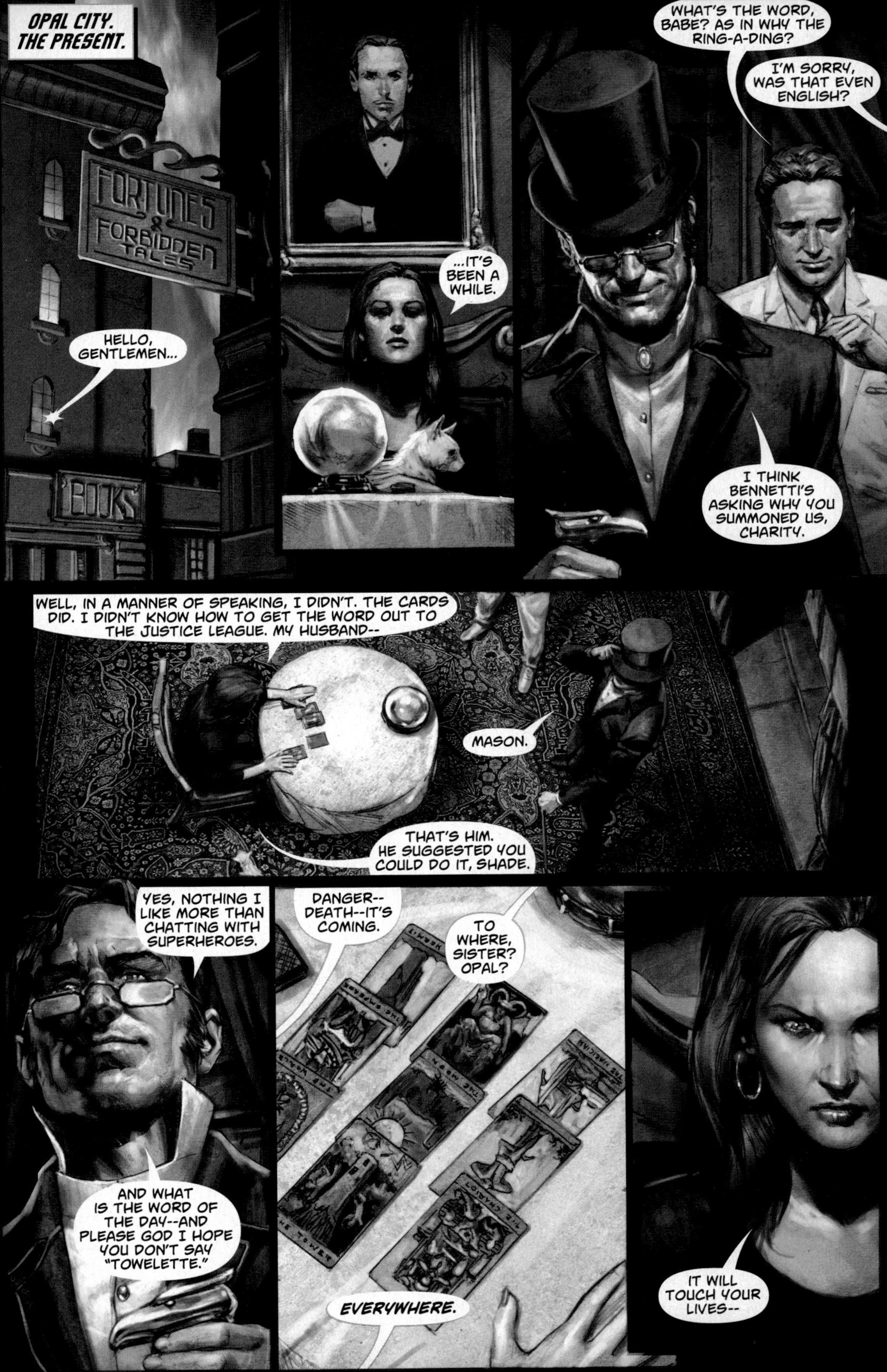
OPAL CITY. THE PRESENT.
FORTUNES & FORBIDDEN TALES
BOOKS
HELLO, GENTLEMEN...
...IT'S BEEN A WHILE.
WHAT'S THE WORD, BABE? AS IN WHY THE RING-A-DING?
I'M SORRY, WAS THAT EVEN ENGLISH?
I THINK BENNETTI'S ASKING WHY YOU SUMMONED US, CHARITY.
WELL, IN A MANNER OF SPEAKING, I DIDN'T. THE CARDS DID. I DIDN'T KNOW HOW TO GET THE WORD OUT TO THE JUSTICE LEAGUE. MY HUSBAND--
MASON.
THAT'S HIM. HE SUGGESTED YOU COULD DO IT, SHADE.
YES, NOTHING I LIKE MORE THAN CHATTING WITH SUPERHEROES.
AND WHAT IS THE WORD OF THE DAY--AND PLEASE GOD I HOPE YOU DON'T SAY "TOWELETTE."
DANGER--DEATH--IT'S COMING.
TO WHERE, SISTER? OPAL?
EVERYWHERE.
IT WILL TOUCH YOUR LIVES--

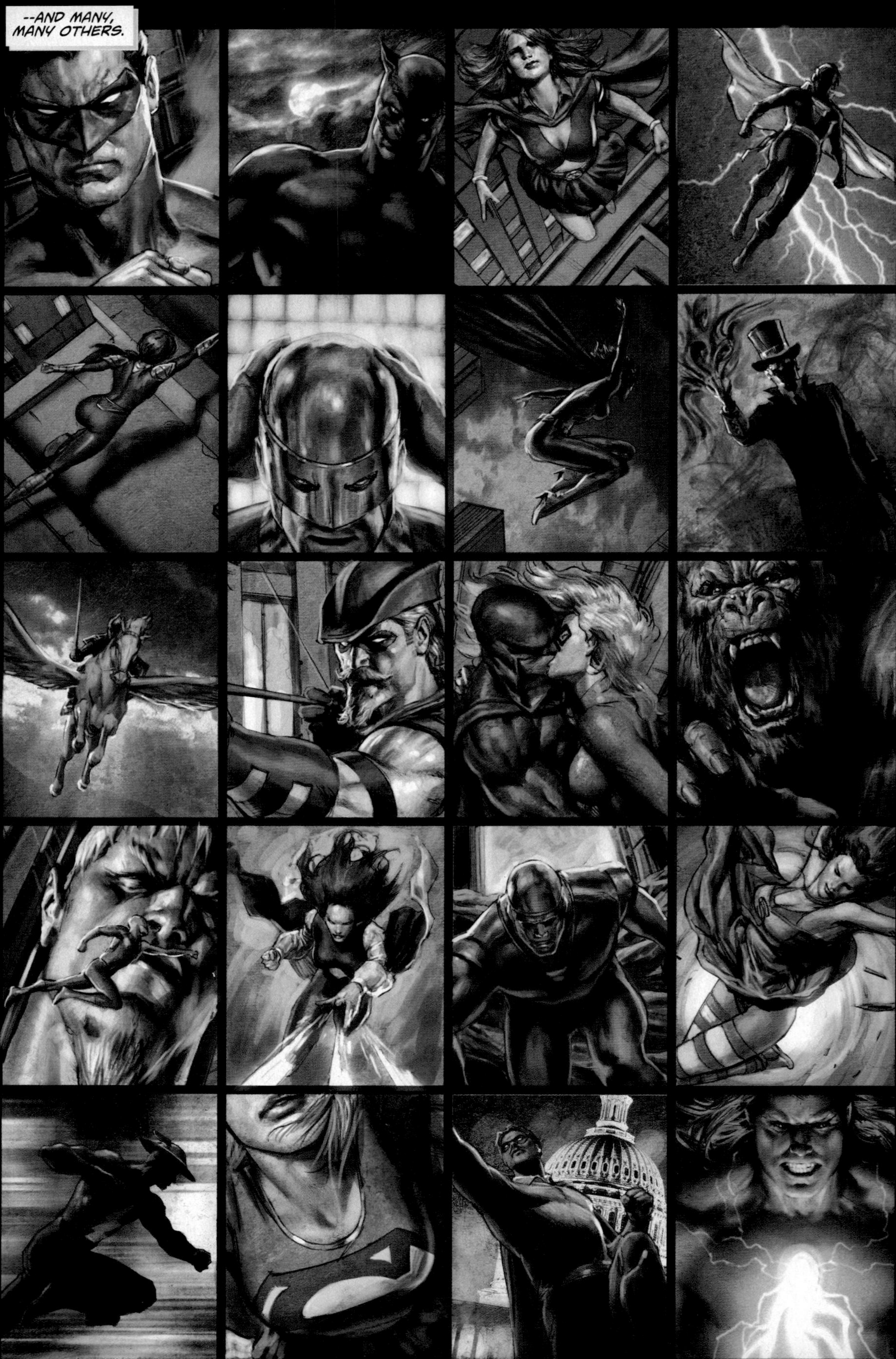
--AND MANY, MANY OTHERS.

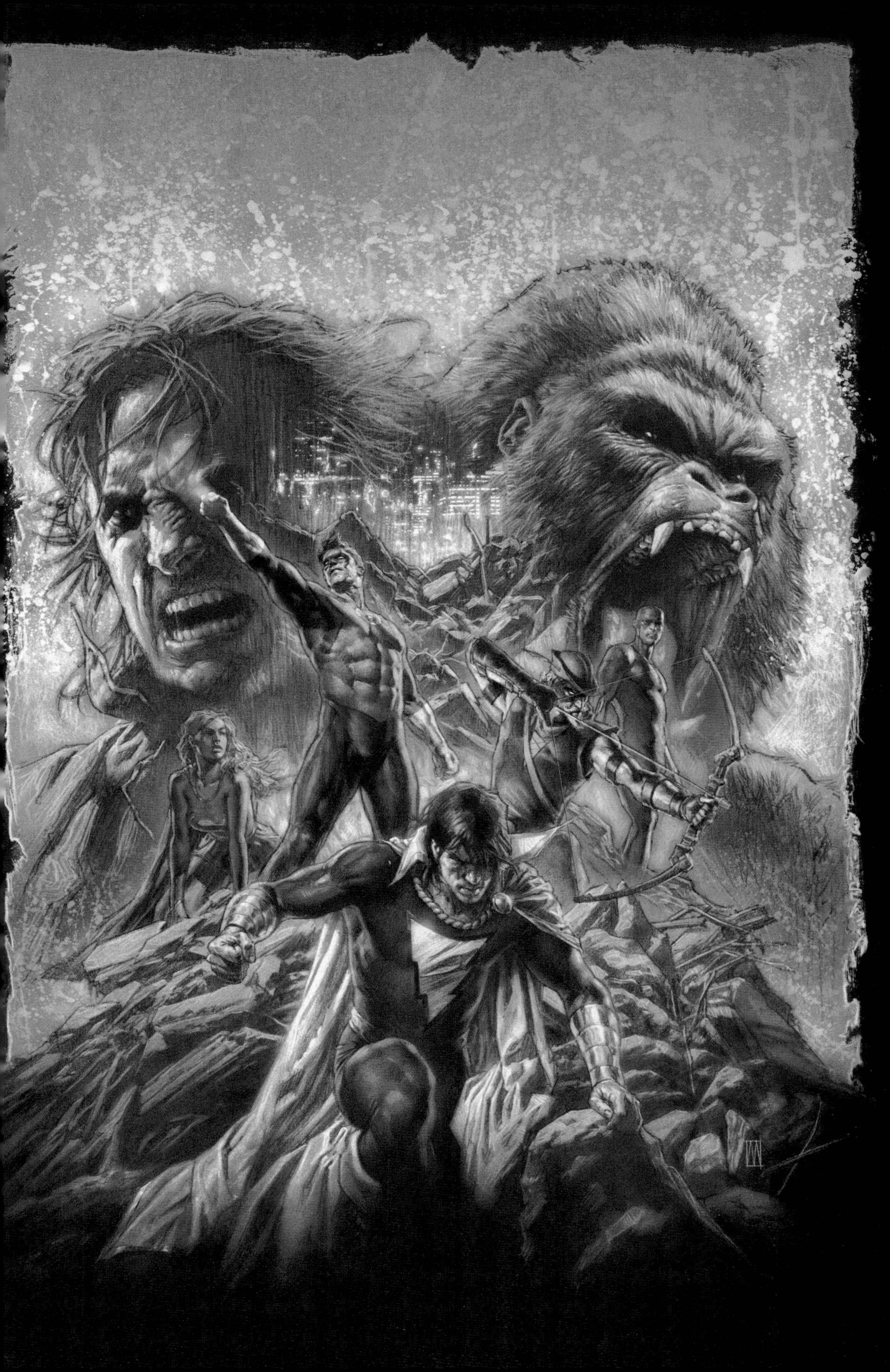

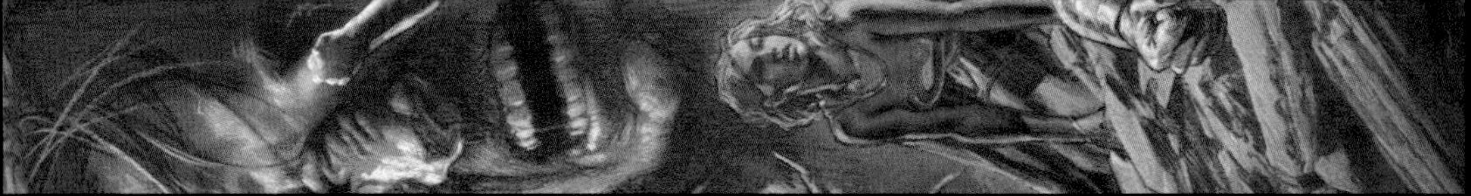

CRY FOR JUSTICE PART FOUR: THE FIX

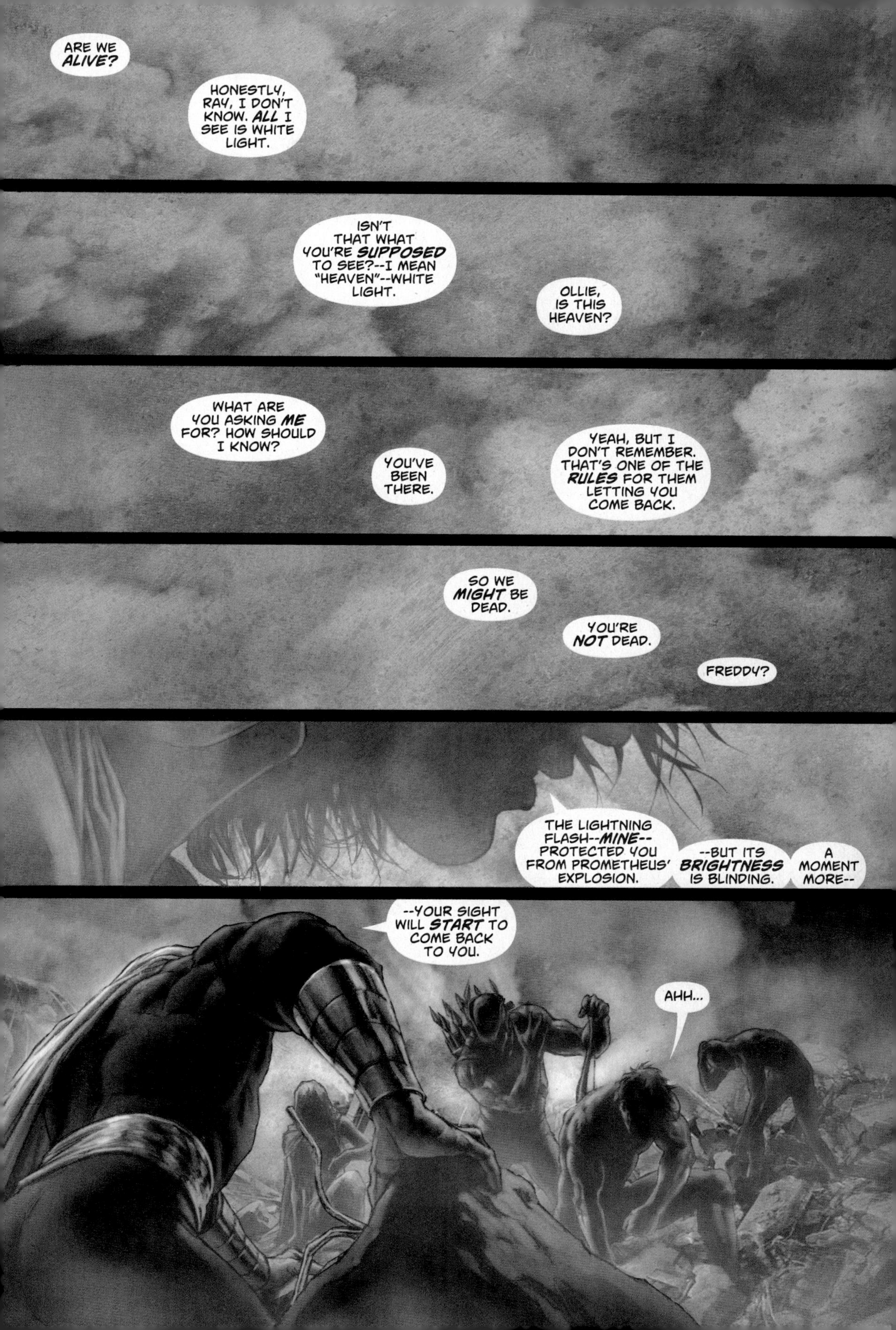

ARE WE *ALIVE?*
HONESTLY, RAY, I DON'T KNOW. *ALL* I SEE IS WHITE LIGHT.
ISN'T THAT WHAT YOU'RE *SUPPOSED* TO SEE?--I MEAN "HEAVEN"--WHITE LIGHT.
OLLIE, IS THIS HEAVEN?
WHAT ARE YOU ASKING *ME* FOR? HOW SHOULD I KNOW?
YOU'VE BEEN THERE.
YEAH, BUT I DON'T REMEMBER. THAT'S ONE OF THE *RULES* FOR THEM LETTING YOU COME BACK.
SO WE *MIGHT* BE DEAD.
YOU'RE *NOT* DEAD.
FREDDY?
THE LIGHTNING FLASH--*MINE*--PROTECTED YOU FROM PROMETHEUS' EXPLOSION.
--BUT ITS *BRIGHTNESS* IS BLINDING.
A MOMENT MORE--
--YOUR SIGHT WILL *START* TO COME BACK TO YOU.
AHH...

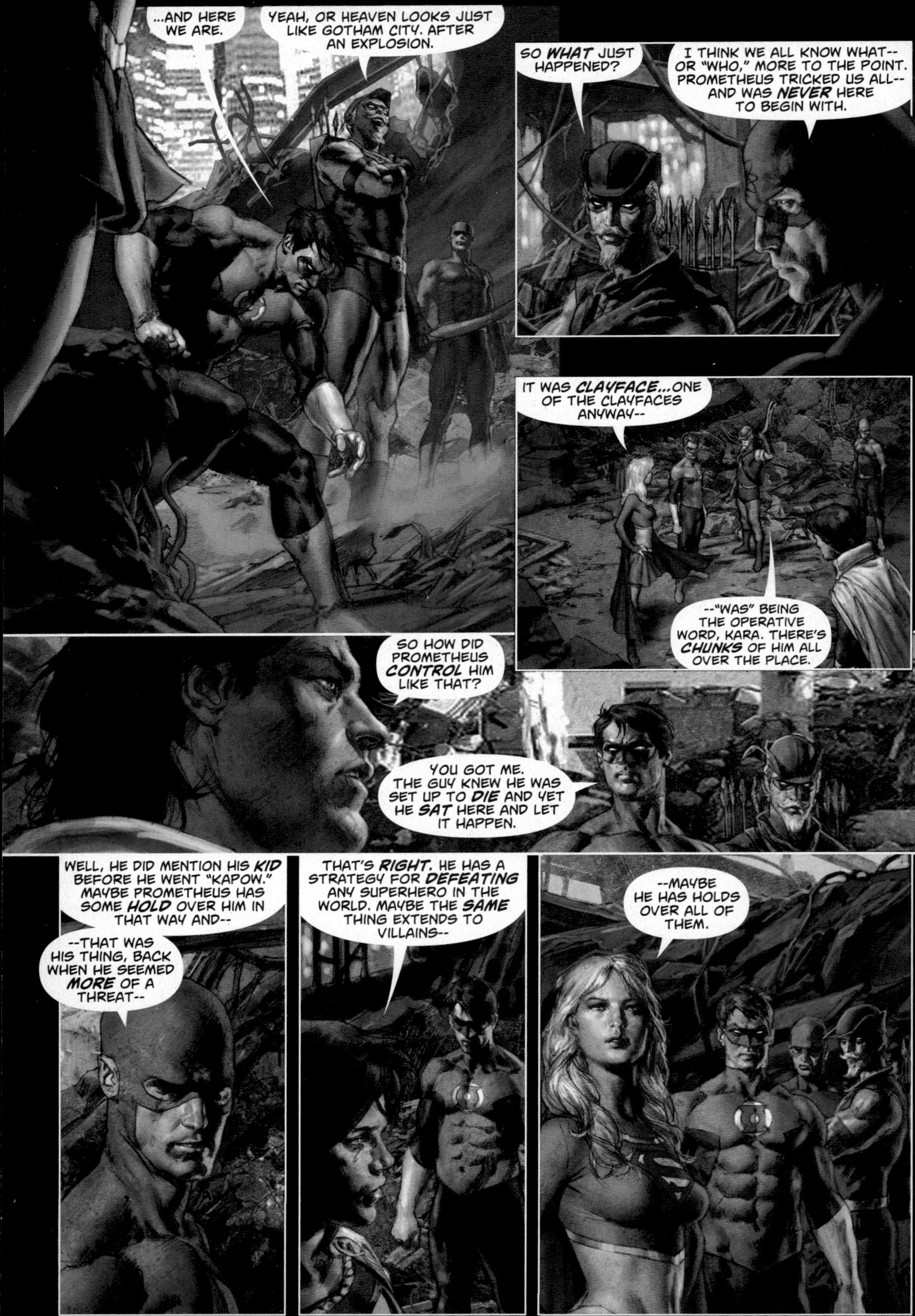
...AND HERE WE ARE.
YEAH, OR HEAVEN LOOKS JUST LIKE GOTHAM CITY. AFTER AN EXPLOSION.
SO WHAT JUST HAPPENED?
I THINK WE ALL KNOW WHAT-- OR "WHO," MORE TO THE POINT. PROMETHEUS TRICKED US ALL-- AND WAS NEVER HERE TO BEGIN WITH.
IT WAS CLAYFACE...ONE OF THE CLAYFACES ANYWAY--
--"WAS" BEING THE OPERATIVE WORD, KARA. THERE'S CHUNKS OF HIM ALL OVER THE PLACE.
SO HOW DID PROMETHEUS CONTROL HIM LIKE THAT?
YOU GOT ME. THE GUY KNEW HE WAS SET UP TO DIE AND YET HE SAT HERE AND LET IT HAPPEN.
WELL, HE DID MENTION HIS KID BEFORE HE WENT "KAPOW." MAYBE PROMETHEUS HAS SOME HOLD OVER HIM IN THAT WAY AND--
--THAT WAS HIS THING, BACK WHEN HE SEEMED MORE OF A THREAT--
THAT'S RIGHT. HE HAS A STRATEGY FOR DEFEATING ANY SUPERHERO IN THE WORLD. MAYBE THE SAME THING EXTENDS TO VILLAINS--
--MAYBE HE HAS HOLDS OVER ALL OF THEM.

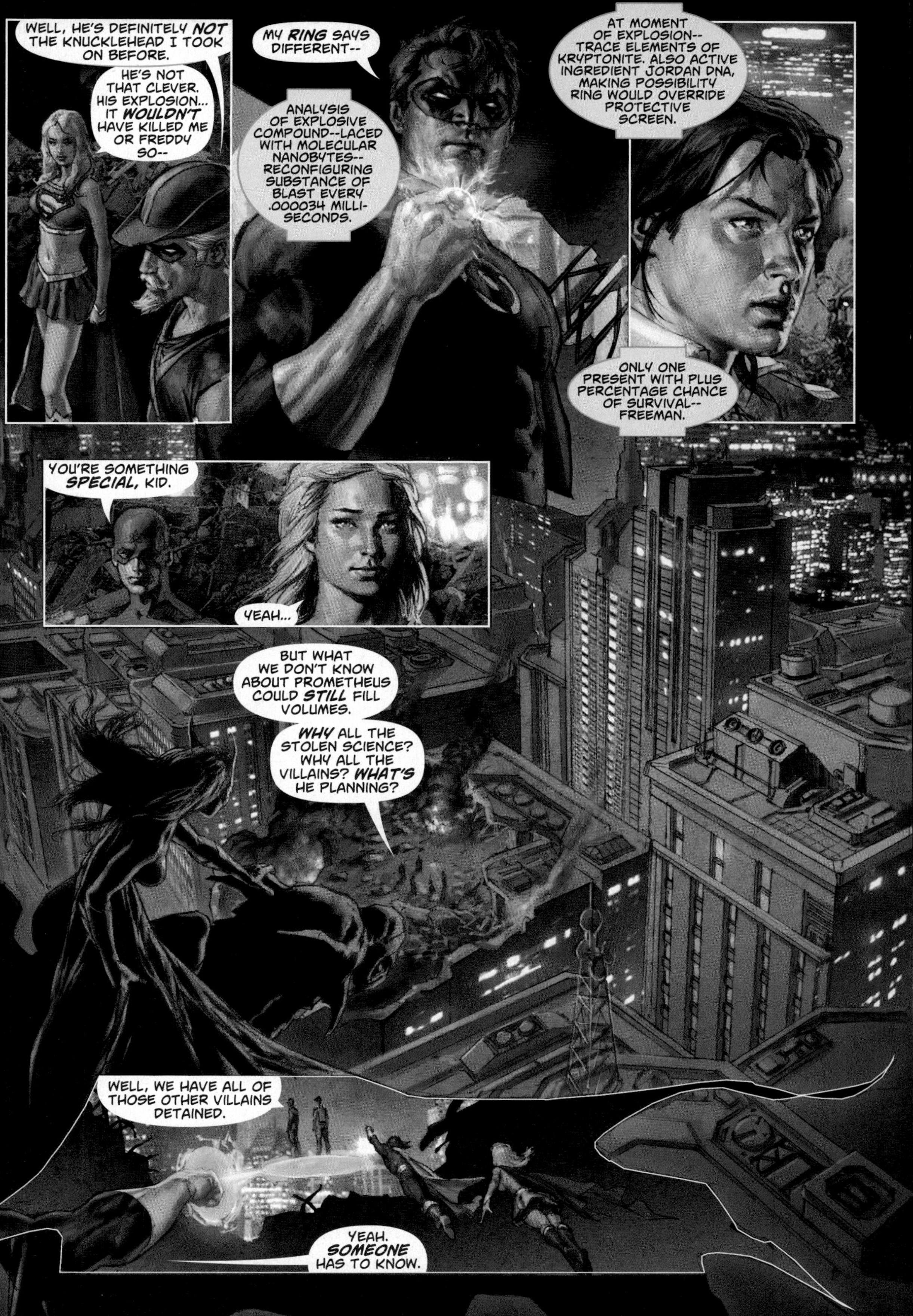
WELL, HE'S DEFINITELY NOT THE KNUCKLEHEAD I TOOK ON BEFORE.
HE'S NOT THAT CLEVER. HIS EXPLOSION... IT WOULDN'T HAVE KILLED ME OR FREDDY SO--
MY RING SAYS DIFFERENT--
ANALYSIS OF EXPLOSIVE COMPOUND--LACED WITH MOLECULAR NANOBYTES--RECONFIGURING SUBSTANCE OF BLAST EVERY .000034 MILLI-SECONDS.
AT MOMENT OF EXPLOSION--TRACE ELEMENTS OF KRYPTONITE. ALSO ACTIVE INGREDIENT JORDAN DNA, MAKING POSSIBILITY RING WOULD OVERRIDE PROTECTIVE SCREEN.
ONLY ONE PRESENT WITH PLUS PERCENTAGE CHANCE OF SURVIVAL--FREEMAN.
YOU'RE SOMETHING SPECIAL, KID.
YEAH...
BUT WHAT WE DON'T KNOW ABOUT PROMETHEUS COULD STILL FILL VOLUMES.
WHY ALL THE STOLEN SCIENCE? WHY ALL THE VILLAINS? WHAT'S HE PLANNING?
WELL, WE HAVE ALL OF THOSE OTHER VILLAINS DETAINED.
YEAH. SOMEONE HAS TO KNOW.

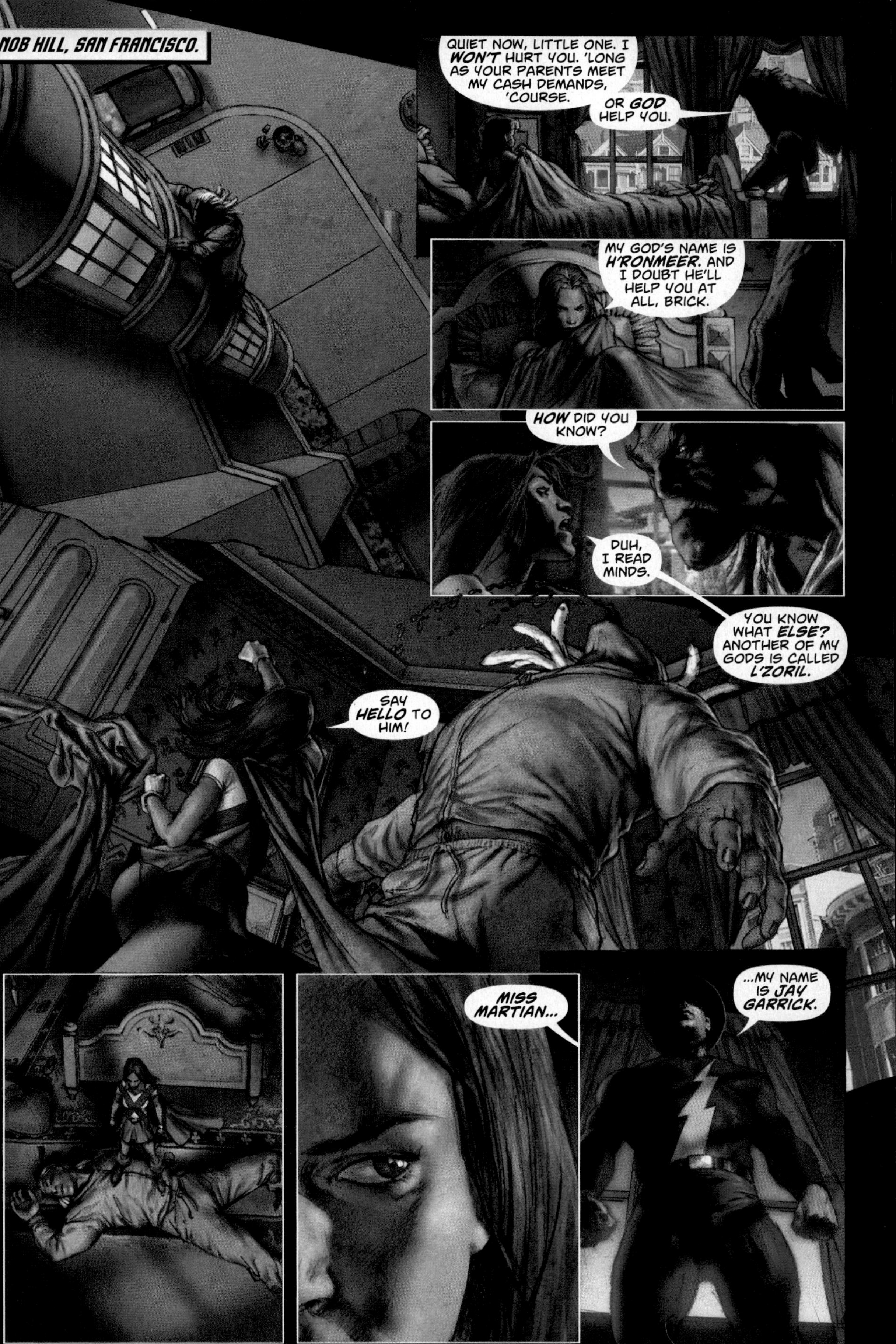
NOB HILL, SAN FRANCISCO.
QUIET NOW, LITTLE ONE. I WON'T HURT YOU. 'LONG AS YOUR PARENTS MEET MY CASH DEMANDS, 'COURSE.
OR GOD HELP YOU.
MY GOD'S NAME IS H'RONMEER. AND I DOUBT HE'LL HELP YOU AT ALL, BRICK.
HOW DID YOU KNOW?
DUH, I READ MINDS.
YOU KNOW WHAT ELSE? ANOTHER OF MY GODS IS CALLED L'ZORIL.
SAY HELLO TO HIM!
MISS MARTIAN...
...MY NAME IS JAY GARRICK.

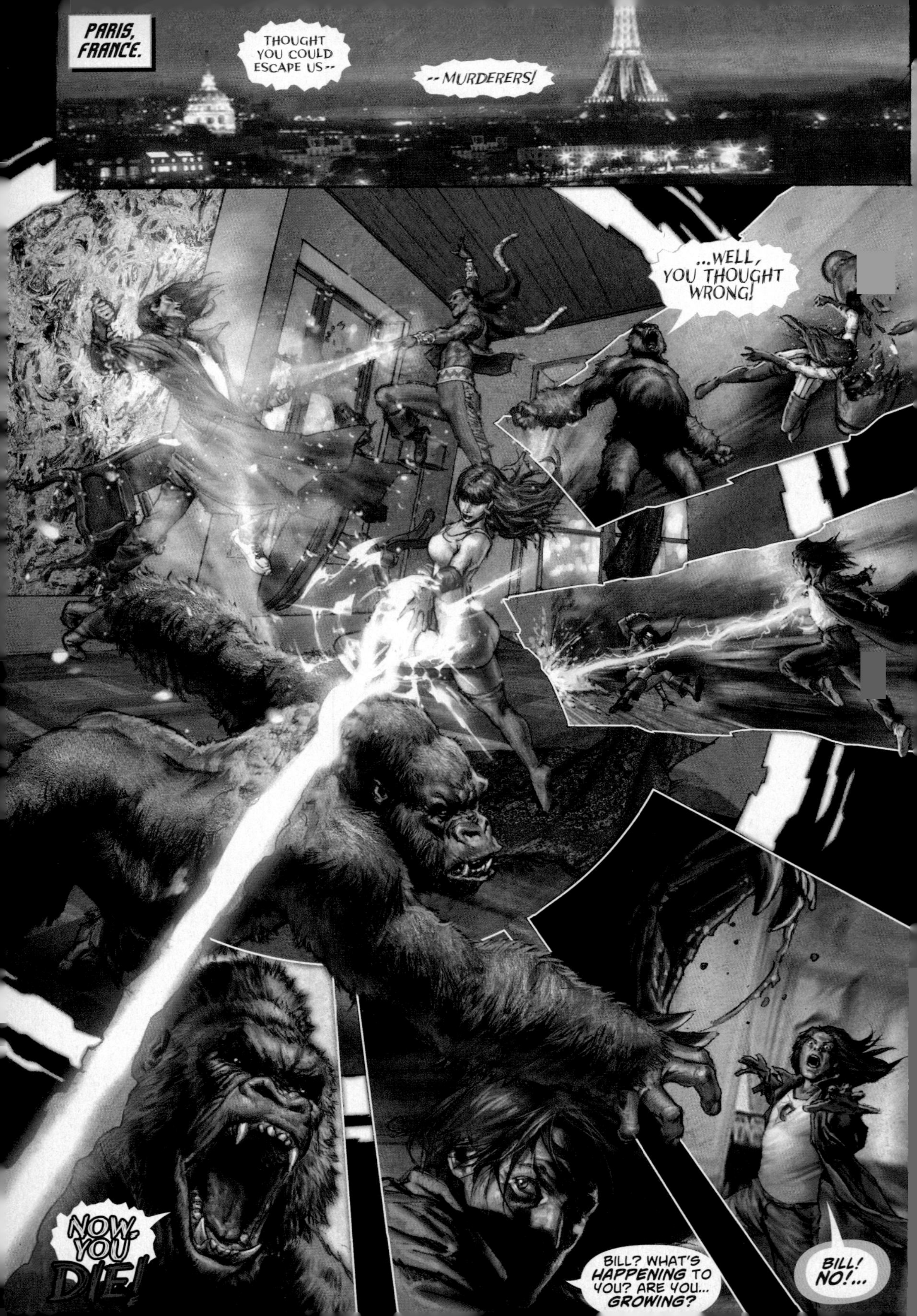
PARIS, FRANCE.
THOUGHT YOU COULD ESCAPE US--
--MURDERERS!
...WELL, YOU THOUGHT WRONG!
NOW, YOU DIE!
BILL? WHAT'S HAPPENING TO YOU? ARE YOU... GROWING?
BILL! NO!...

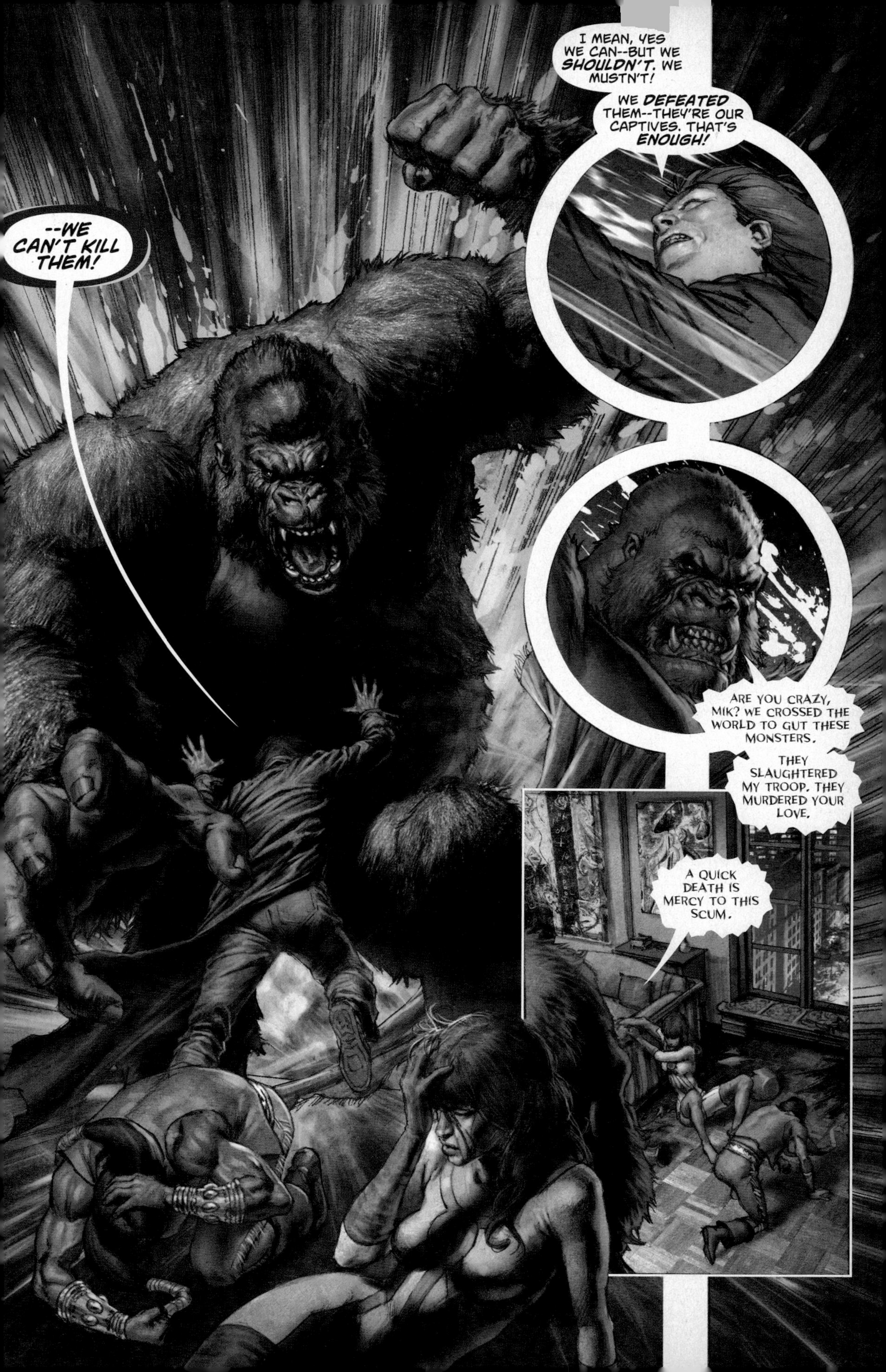
I MEAN, YES WE CAN--BUT WE *SHOULDN'T*. WE MUSTN'T!
WE *DEFEATED* THEM--THEY'RE OUR CAPTIVES. THAT'S *ENOUGH!*
--WE CAN'T KILL THEM!
ARE YOU CRAZY, MIK? WE CROSSED THE WORLD TO GUT THESE MONSTERS.
THEY SLAUGHTERED MY TROOP. THEY MURDERED YOUR LOVE.
A QUICK DEATH IS MERCY TO THIS SCUM.

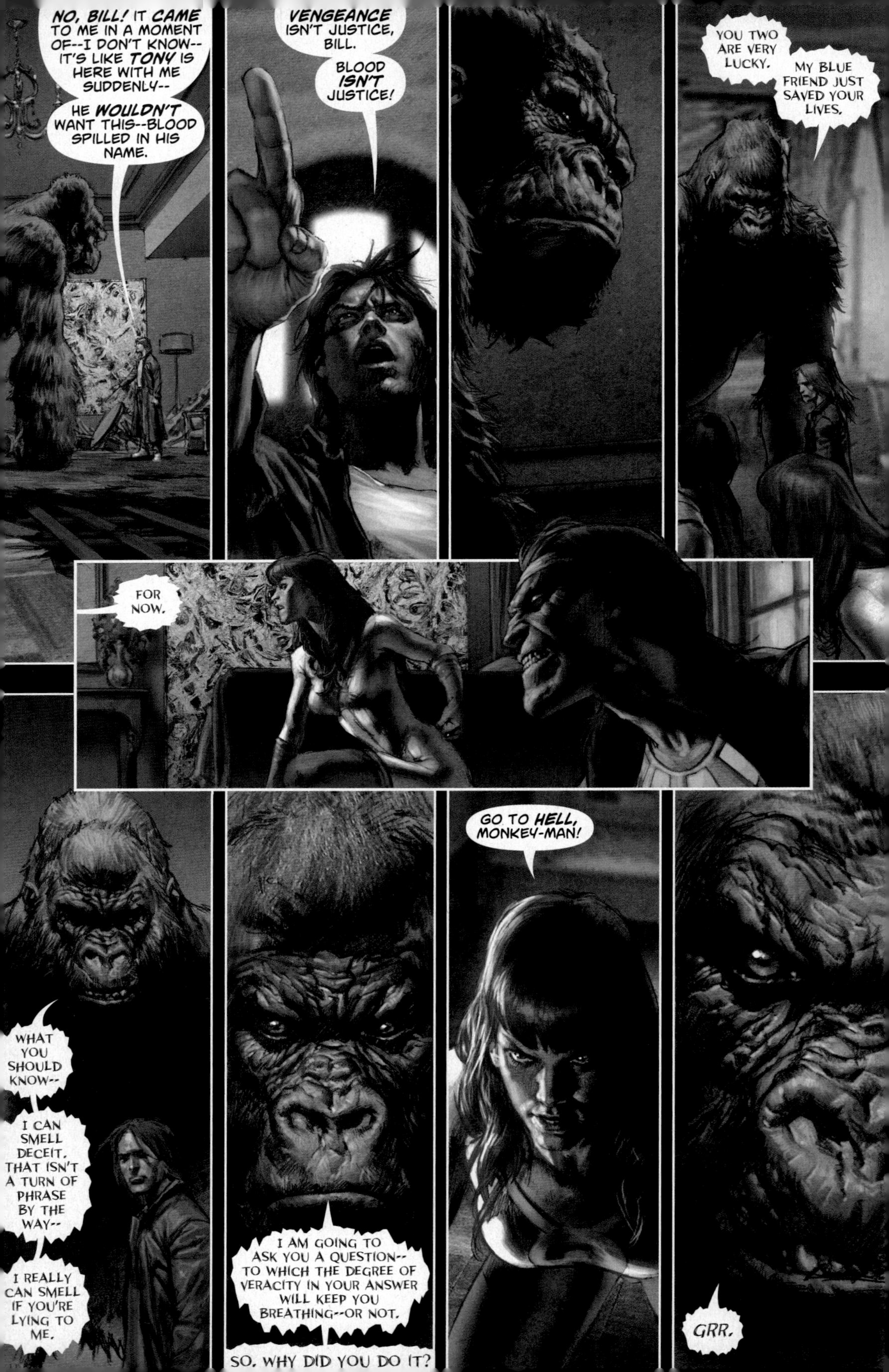

NO, BILL! IT CAME TO ME IN A MOMENT OF--I DON'T KNOW--IT'S LIKE TONY IS HERE WITH ME SUDDENLY--
HE WOULDN'T WANT THIS--BLOOD SPILLED IN HIS NAME.
VENGEANCE ISN'T JUSTICE, BILL.
BLOOD ISN'T JUSTICE!
YOU TWO ARE VERY LUCKY.
MY BLUE FRIEND JUST SAVED YOUR LIVES.
FOR NOW.
WHAT YOU SHOULD KNOW--
I CAN SMELL DECEIT. THAT ISN'T A TURN OF PHRASE BY THE WAY--
I REALLY CAN SMELL IF YOU'RE LYING TO ME.
I AM GOING TO ASK YOU A QUESTION--TO WHICH THE DEGREE OF VERACITY IN YOUR ANSWER WILL KEEP YOU BREATHING--OR NOT.
SO, WHY DID YOU DO IT?
GO TO HELL, MONKEY-MAN!
GRR.

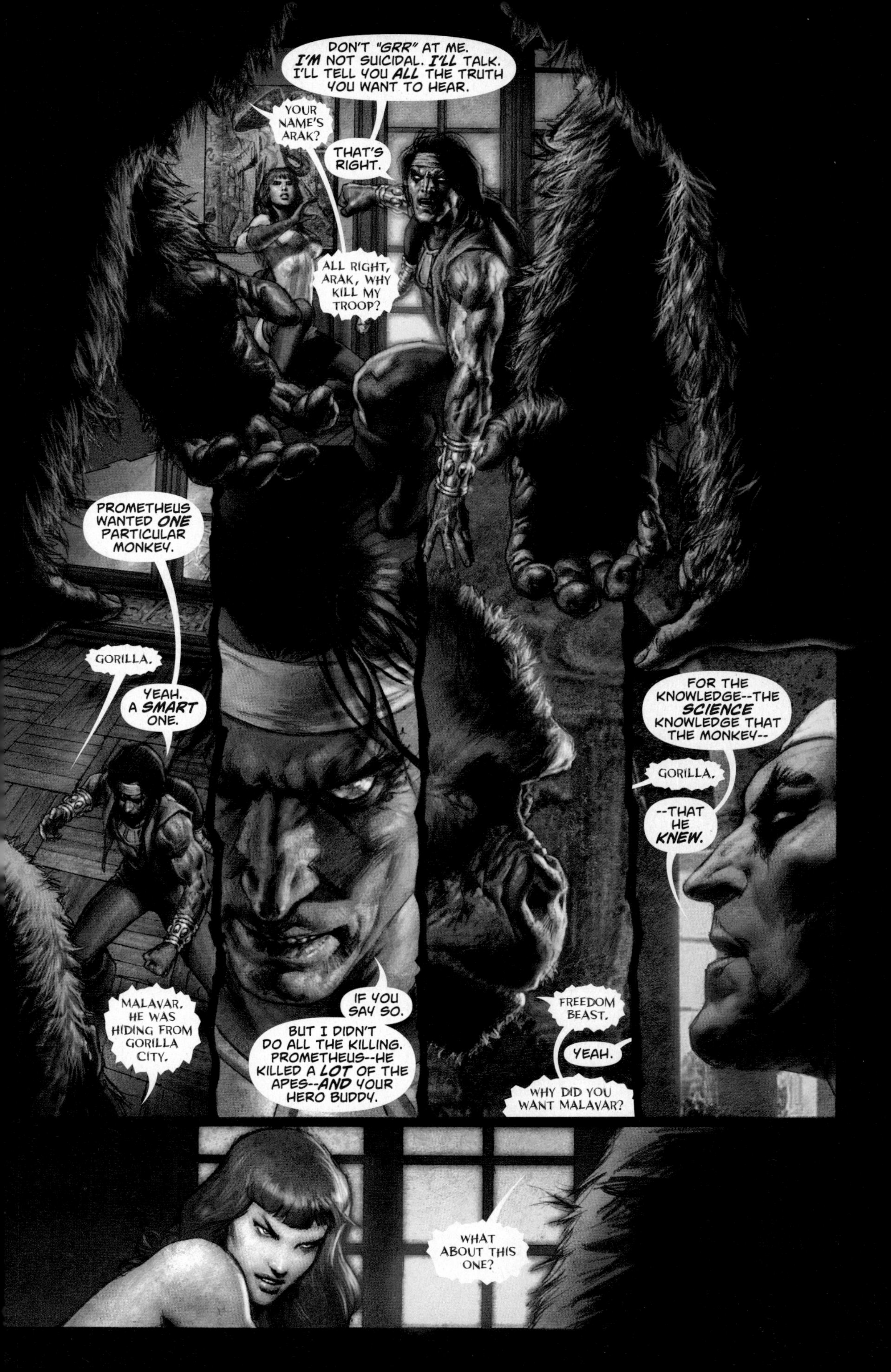
DON'T "GRR" AT ME. I'M NOT SUICIDAL. I'LL TALK. I'LL TELL YOU ALL THE TRUTH YOU WANT TO HEAR.
YOUR NAME'S ARAK?
THAT'S RIGHT.
ALL RIGHT, ARAK, WHY KILL MY TROOP?
PROMETHEUS WANTED ONE PARTICULAR MONKEY.
GORILLA.
YEAH. A SMART ONE.
MALAVAR. HE WAS HIDING FROM GORILLA CITY.
IF YOU SAY SO.
BUT I DIDN'T DO ALL THE KILLING. PROMETHEUS--HE KILLED A LOT OF THE APES--AND YOUR HERO BUDDY.
FREEDOM BEAST.
YEAH.
WHY DID YOU WANT MALAVAR?
FOR THE KNOWLEDGE--THE SCIENCE KNOWLEDGE THAT THE MONKEY--
GORILLA.
--THAT HE KNEW.
WHAT ABOUT THIS ONE?

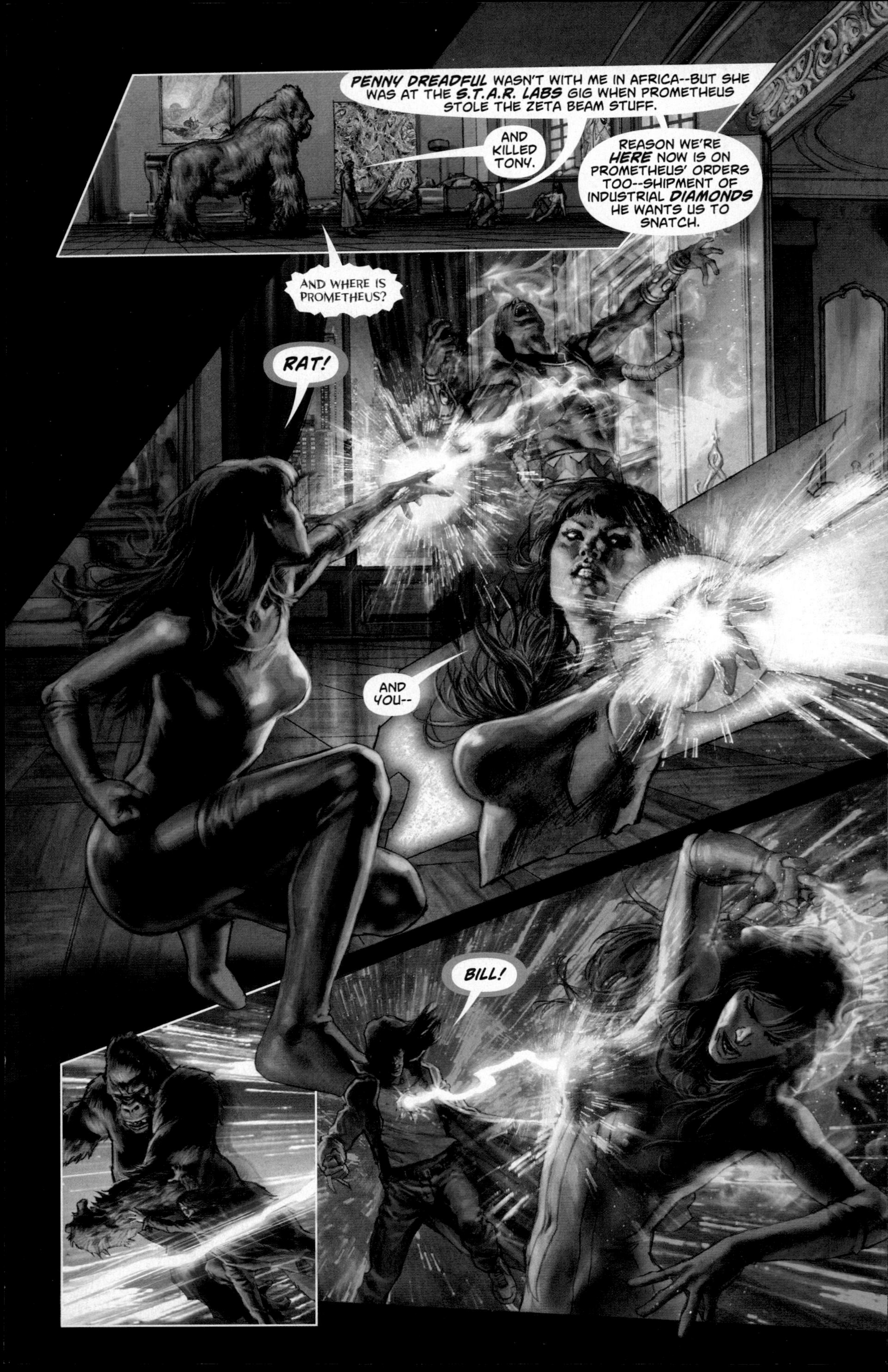
PENNY DREADFUL WASN'T WITH ME IN AFRICA--BUT SHE WAS AT THE S.T.A.R. LABS GIG WHEN PROMETHEUS STOLE THE ZETA BEAM STUFF.
AND KILLED TONY.
REASON WE'RE HERE NOW IS ON PROMETHEUS' ORDERS TOO--SHIPMENT OF INDUSTRIAL DIAMONDS HE WANTS US TO SNATCH.
AND WHERE IS PROMETHEUS?
RAT!
AND YOU--
BILL!

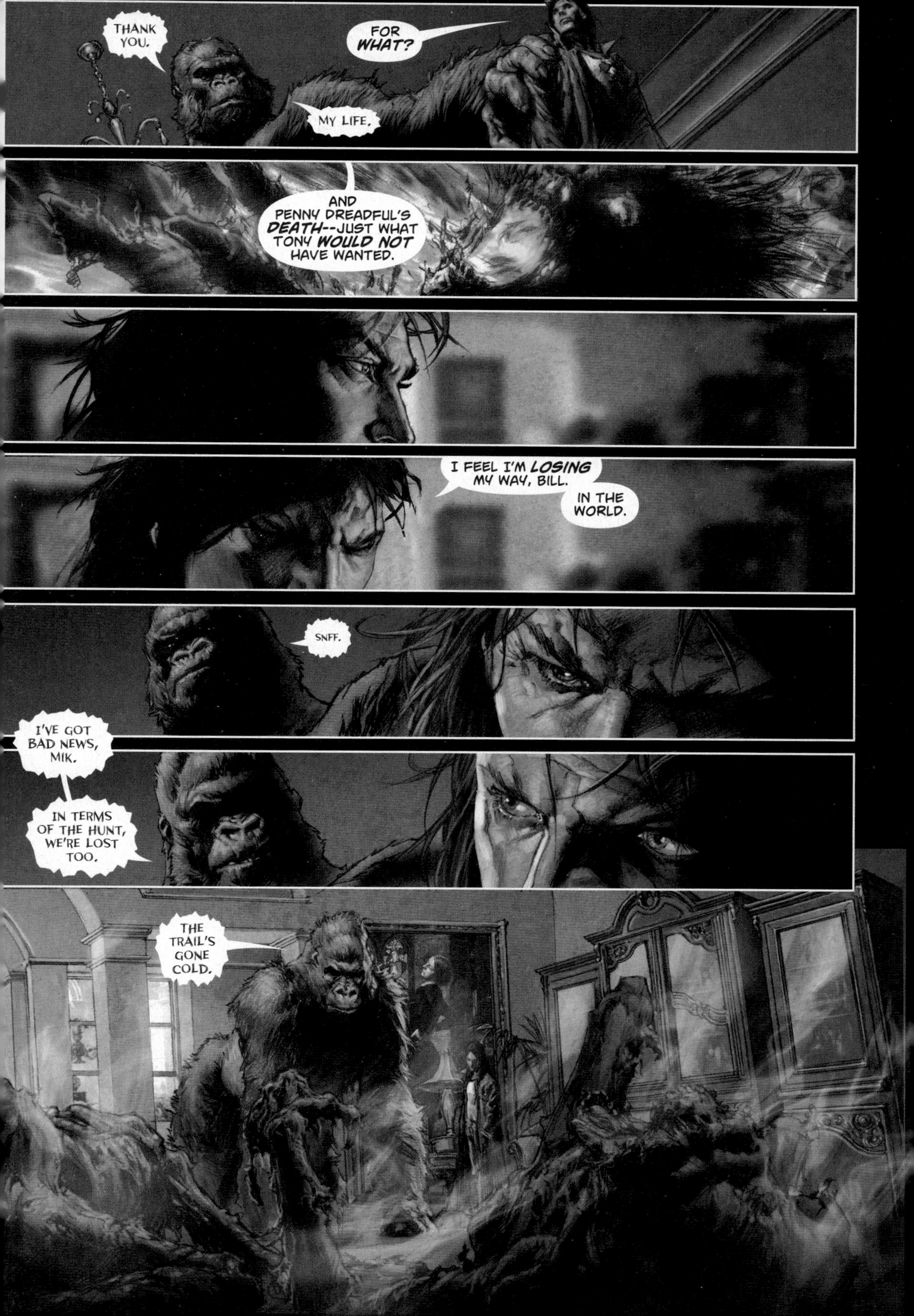

THANK YOU.
FOR *WHAT?*
MY LIFE.
AND PENNY DREADFUL'S *DEATH*--JUST WHAT TONY *WOULD NOT* HAVE WANTED.
I FEEL I'M *LOSING* MY WAY, BILL.
IN THE WORLD.
SNFF.
I'VE GOT BAD NEWS, MIK.
IN TERMS OF THE HUNT, WE'RE LOST TOO.
THE TRAIL'S GONE COLD.

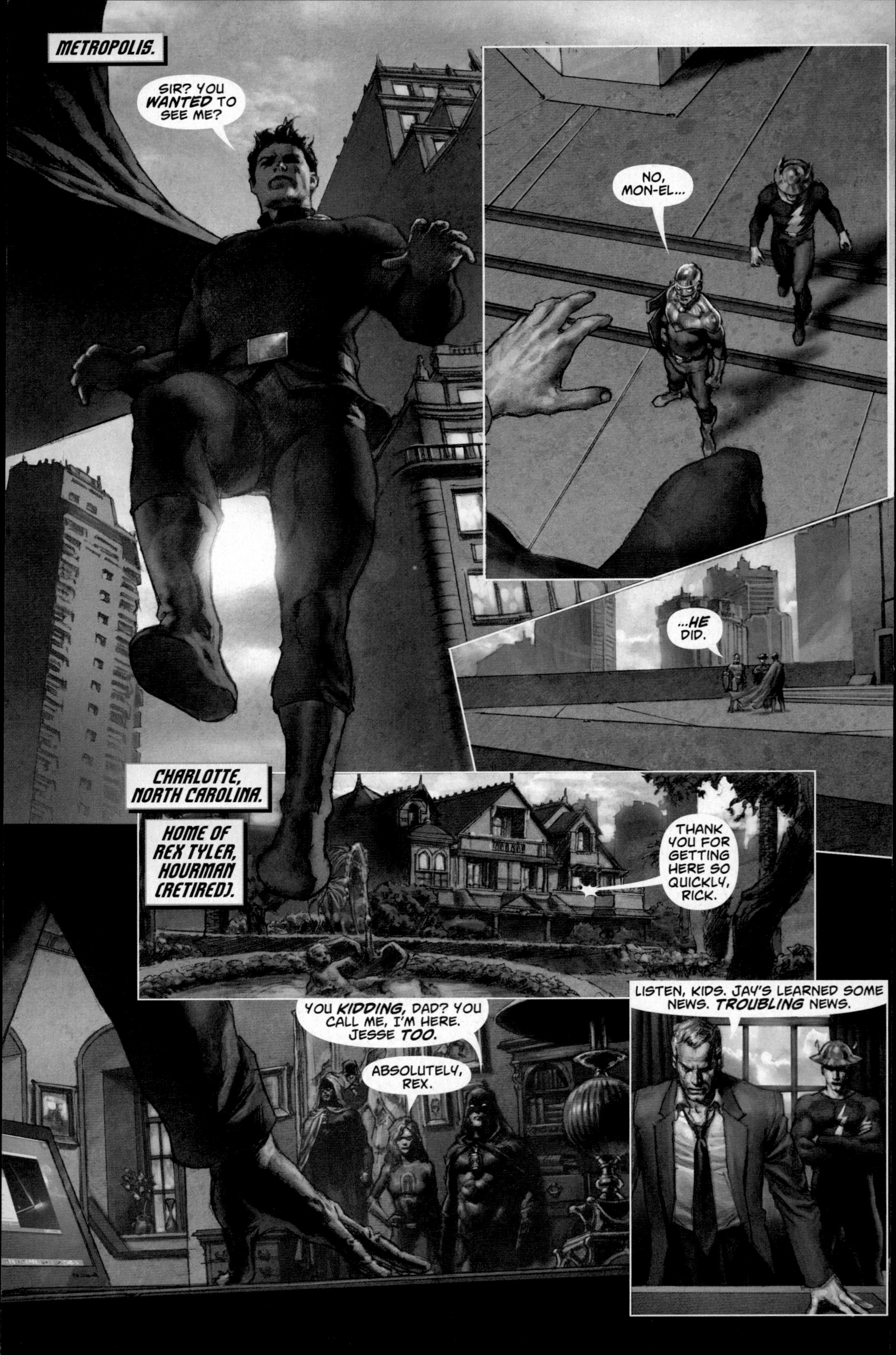
METROPOLIS.
SIR? YOU WANTED TO SEE ME?
NO, MON-EL...
...HE DID.
CHARLOTTE, NORTH CAROLINA.
HOME OF REX TYLER, HOURMAN (RETIRED).
THANK YOU FOR GETTING HERE SO QUICKLY, RICK.
YOU KIDDING, DAD? YOU CALL ME, I'M HERE. JESSE TOO.
ABSOLUTELY, REX.
LISTEN, KIDS. JAY'S LEARNED SOME NEWS. TROUBLING NEWS.

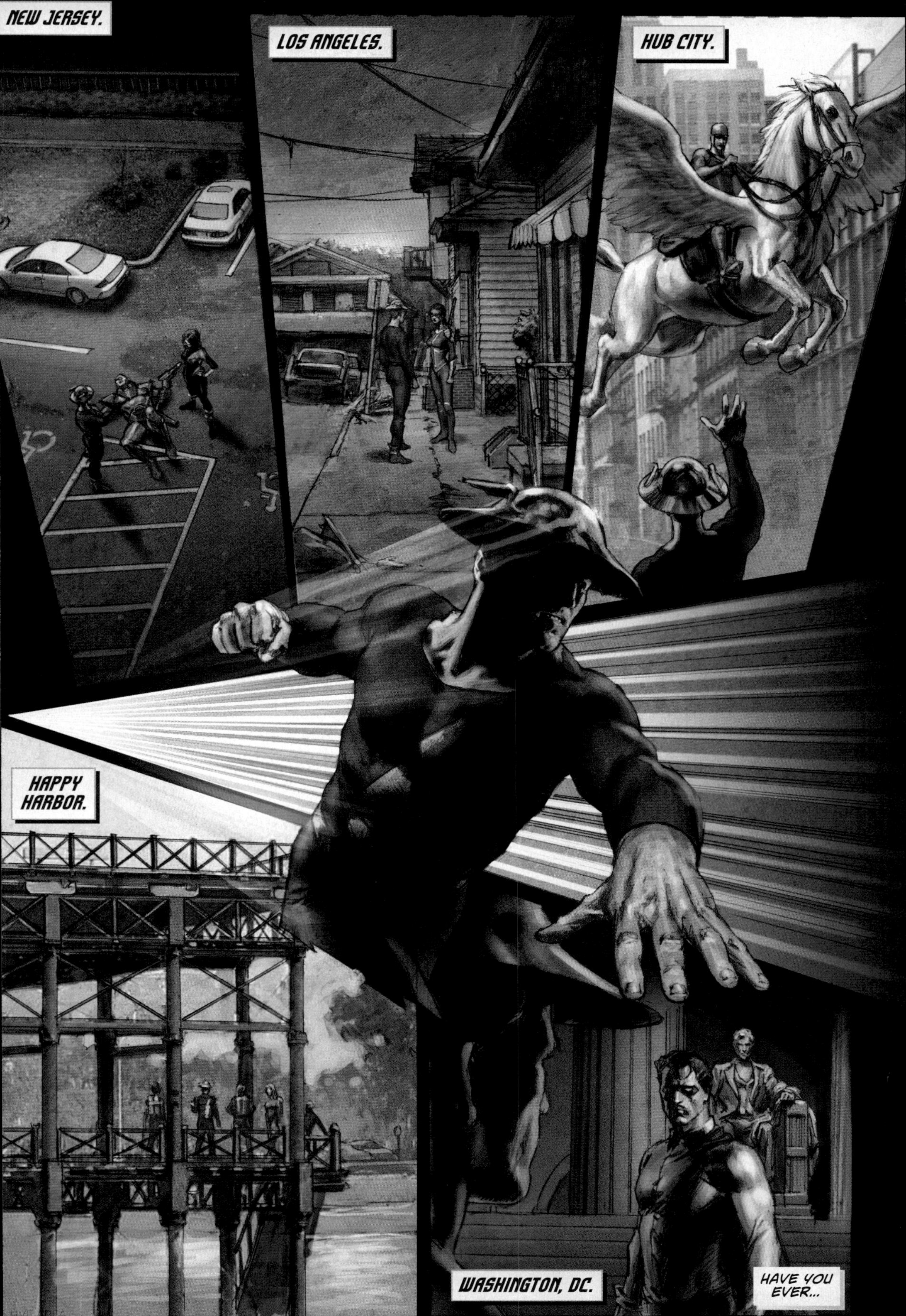
NEW JERSEY.
LOS ANGELES.
HUB CITY.
HAPPY HARBOR.
WASHINGTON, DC.
HAVE YOU EVER...

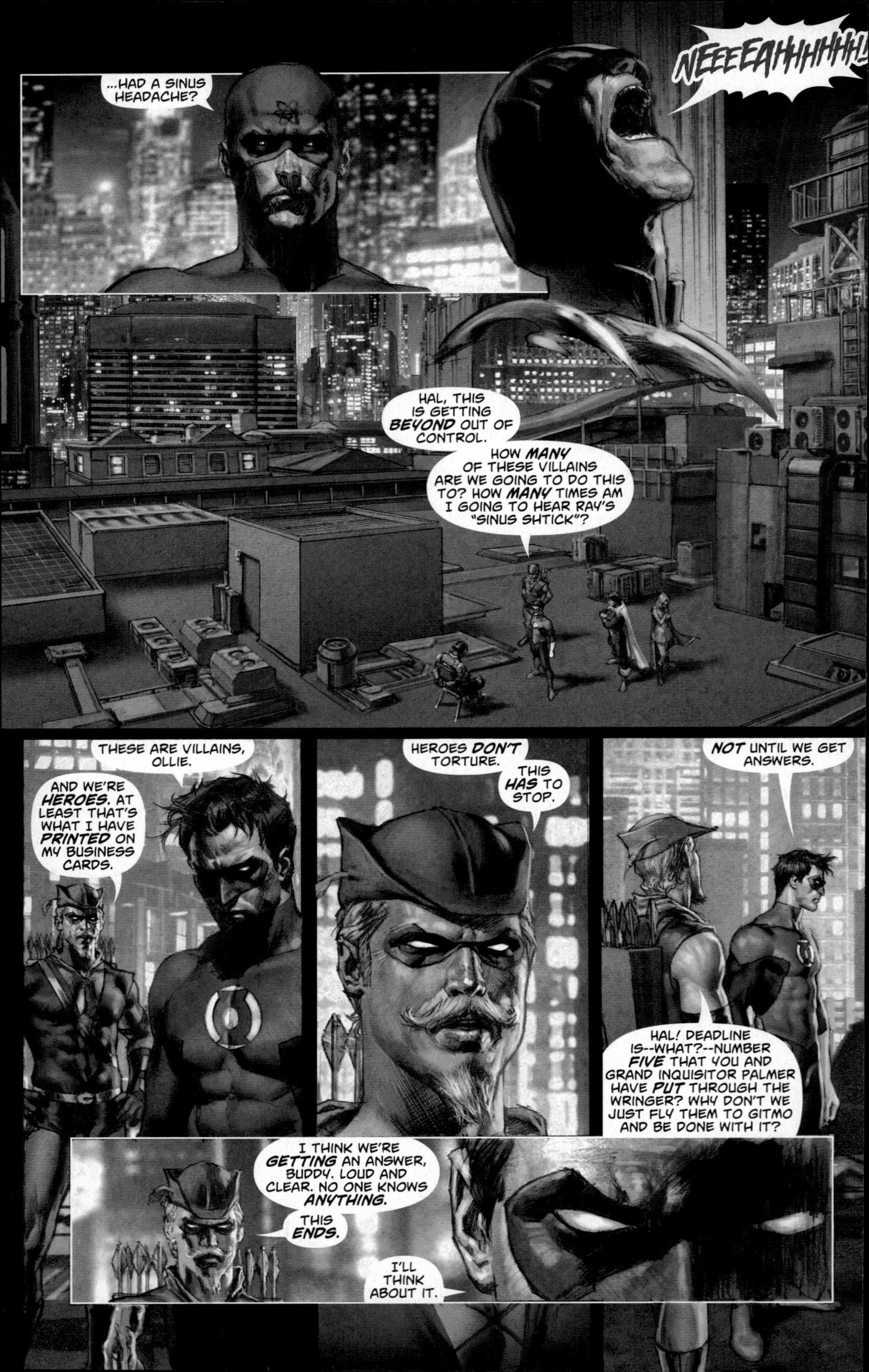
...HAD A SINUS HEADACHE?
NEEEEAHHHHH!
HAL, THIS IS GETTING BEYOND OUT OF CONTROL.
HOW MANY OF THESE VILLAINS ARE WE GOING TO DO THIS TO? HOW MANY TIMES AM I GOING TO HEAR RAY'S "SINUS SHTICK"?
THESE ARE VILLAINS, OLLIE.
AND WE'RE HEROES. AT LEAST THAT'S WHAT I HAVE PRINTED ON MY BUSINESS CARDS.
HEROES DON'T TORTURE.
THIS HAS TO STOP.
NOT UNTIL WE GET ANSWERS.
HAL! DEADLINE IS--WHAT?--NUMBER FIVE THAT YOU AND GRAND INQUISITOR PALMER HAVE PUT THROUGH THE WRINGER? WHY DON'T WE JUST FLY THEM TO GITMO AND BE DONE WITH IT?
I THINK WE'RE GETTING AN ANSWER, BUDDY. LOUD AND CLEAR. NO ONE KNOWS ANYTHING.
THIS ENDS.
I'LL THINK ABOUT IT.

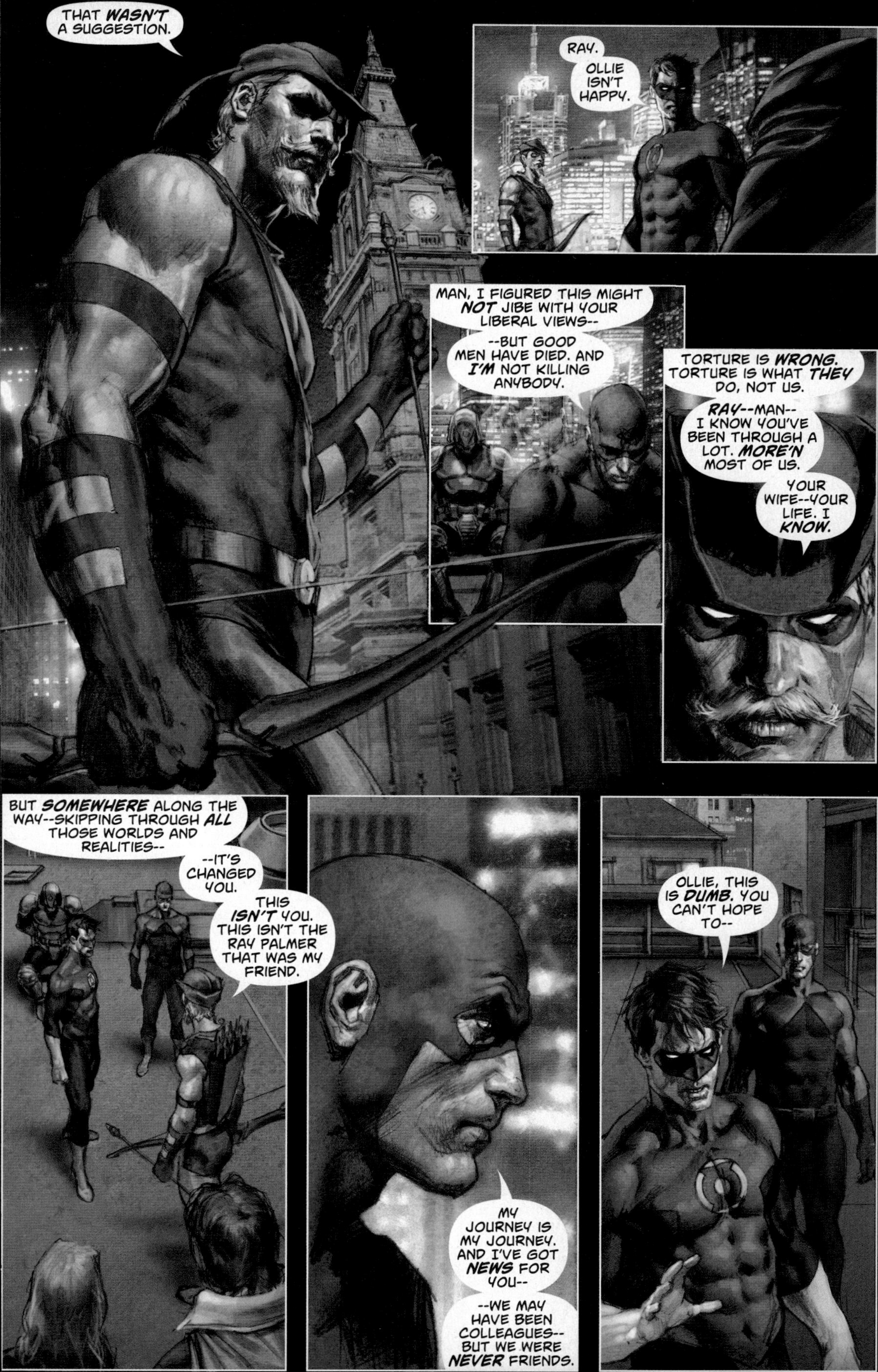
THAT WASN'T A SUGGESTION.
RAY.
OLLIE ISN'T HAPPY.
MAN, I FIGURED THIS MIGHT NOT JIBE WITH YOUR LIBERAL VIEWS--
--BUT GOOD MEN HAVE DIED. AND I'M NOT KILLING ANYBODY.
TORTURE IS WRONG. TORTURE IS WHAT THEY DO, NOT US.
RAY--MAN-- I KNOW YOU'VE BEEN THROUGH A LOT. MORE'N MOST OF US.
YOUR WIFE--YOUR LIFE. I KNOW.
BUT SOMEWHERE ALONG THE WAY--SKIPPING THROUGH ALL THOSE WORLDS AND REALITIES--
--IT'S CHANGED YOU.
THIS ISN'T YOU. THIS ISN'T THE RAY PALMER THAT WAS MY FRIEND.
MY JOURNEY IS MY JOURNEY. AND I'VE GOT NEWS FOR YOU--
--WE MAY HAVE BEEN COLLEAGUES-- BUT WE WERE NEVER FRIENDS.
OLLIE, THIS IS DUMB. YOU CAN'T HOPE TO--

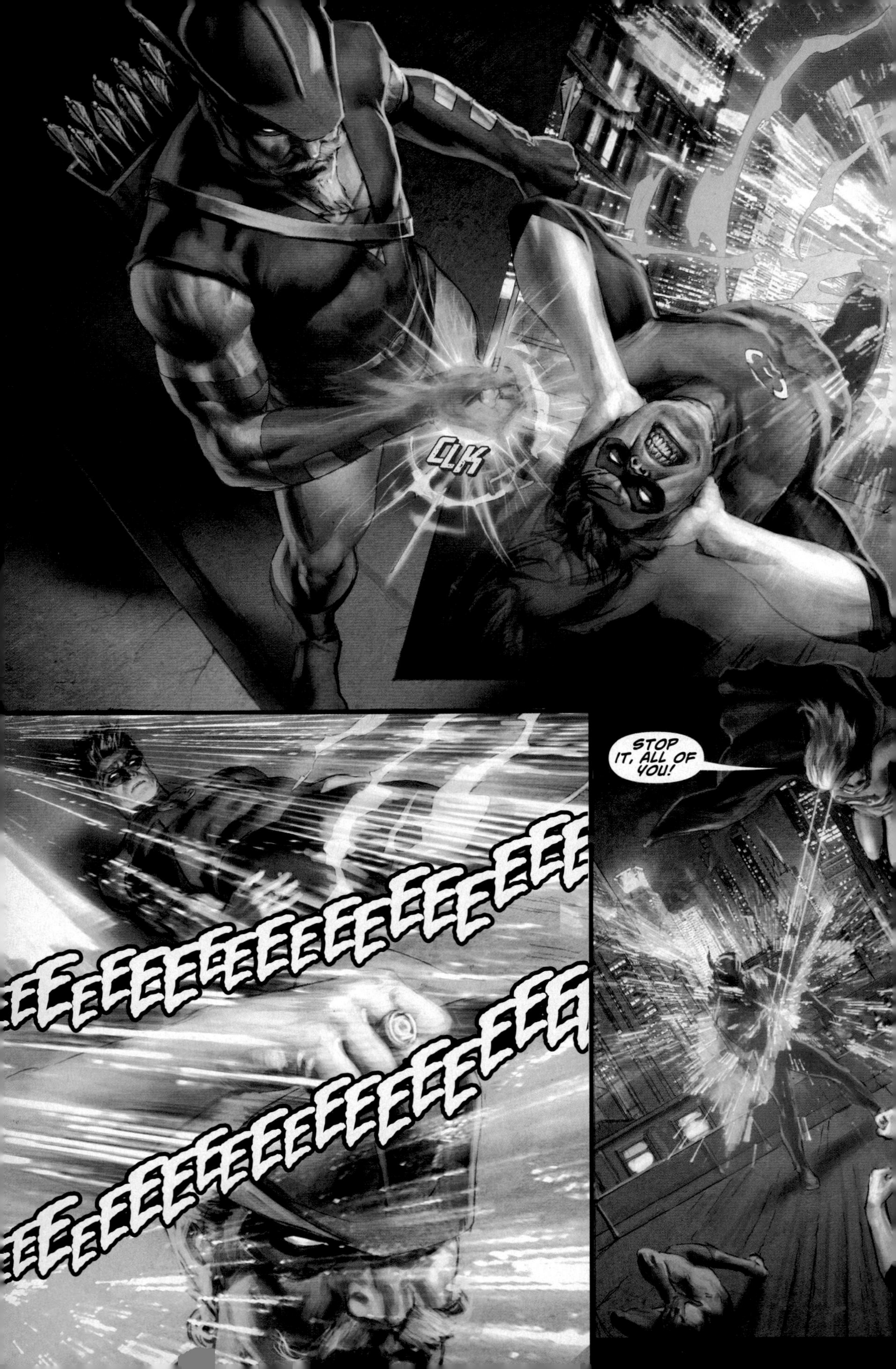
CLK
EEEEEEEEEEEEEEEEEEEE
EEEEEEEEEEEEEEEEEEEE
STOP IT, ALL OF YOU!

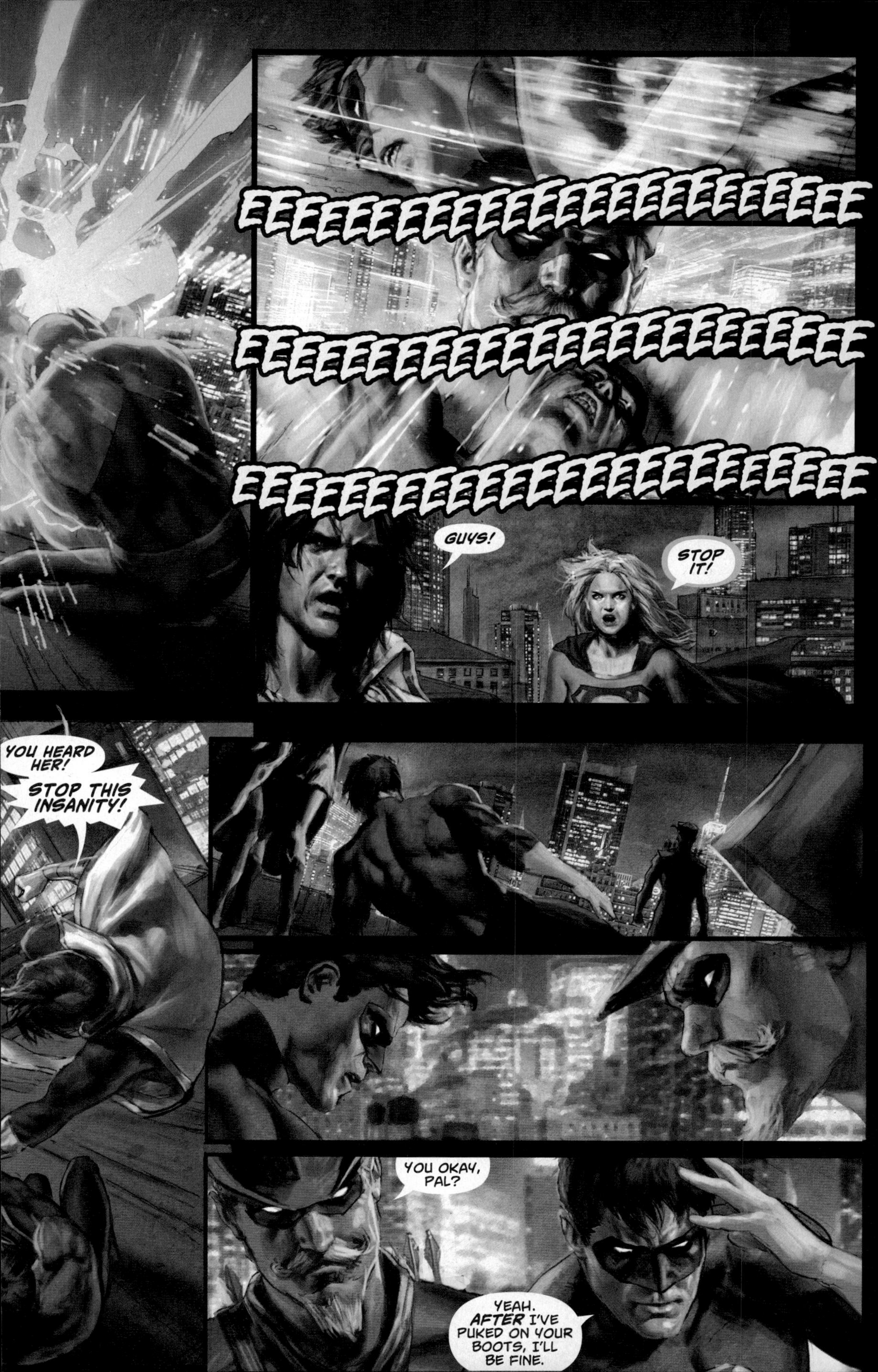
EEEEEEEEEEEEEEEEEEEEEEEEE
EEEEEEEEEEEEEEEEEEEEEEEEE
EEEEEEEEEEEEEEEEEEEEEEEEE
GUYS!
STOP IT!
YOU HEARD HER!
STOP THIS INSANITY!
YOU OKAY, PAL?
YEAH. AFTER I'VE PUKED ON YOUR BOOTS, I'LL BE FINE.

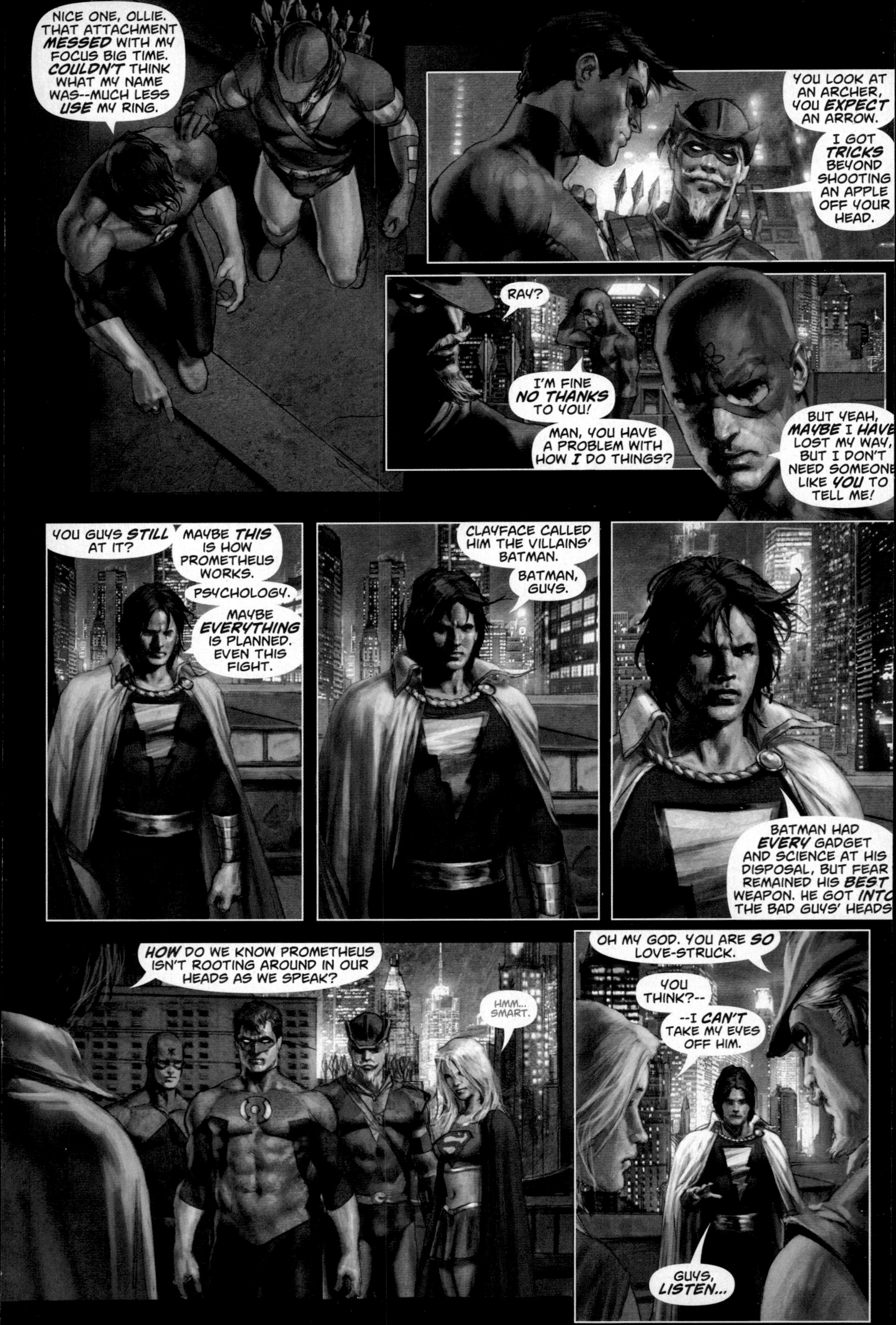
NICE ONE, OLLIE. THAT ATTACHMENT MESSED WITH MY FOCUS BIG TIME. COULDN'T THINK WHAT MY NAME WAS--MUCH LESS USE MY RING.
YOU LOOK AT AN ARCHER, YOU EXPECT AN ARROW.
I GOT TRICKS BEYOND SHOOTING AN APPLE OFF YOUR HEAD.
RAY?
I'M FINE NO THANKS TO YOU!
MAN, YOU HAVE A PROBLEM WITH HOW I DO THINGS?
BUT YEAH, MAYBE I HAVE LOST MY WAY, BUT I DON'T NEED SOMEONE LIKE YOU TO TELL ME!
YOU GUYS STILL AT IT?
MAYBE THIS IS HOW PROMETHEUS WORKS.
PSYCHOLOGY.
MAYBE EVERYTHING IS PLANNED. EVEN THIS FIGHT.
CLAYFACE CALLED HIM THE VILLAINS' BATMAN.
BATMAN, GUYS.
BATMAN HAD EVERY GADGET AND SCIENCE AT HIS DISPOSAL, BUT FEAR REMAINED HIS BEST WEAPON. HE GOT INTO THE BAD GUYS' HEADS.
HOW DO WE KNOW PROMETHEUS ISN'T ROOTING AROUND IN OUR HEADS AS WE SPEAK?
HMM... SMART.
OH MY GOD. YOU ARE SO LOVE-STRUCK.
YOU THINK?--
--I CAN'T TAKE MY EYES OFF HIM.
GUYS, LISTEN...

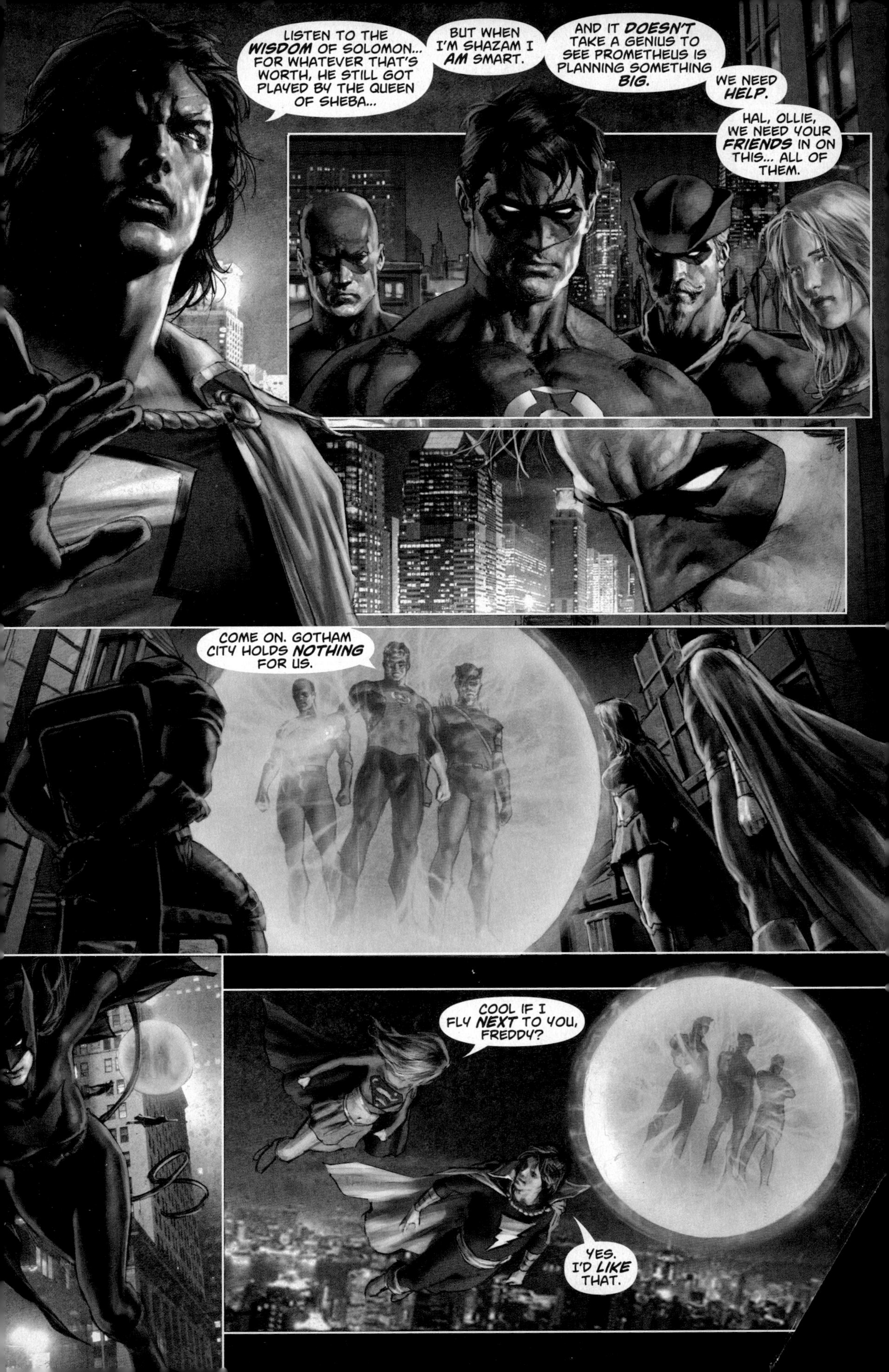
LISTEN TO THE WISDOM OF SOLOMON... FOR WHATEVER THAT'S WORTH, HE STILL GOT PLAYED BY THE QUEEN OF SHEBA...
BUT WHEN I'M SHAZAM I AM SMART.
AND IT DOESN'T TAKE A GENIUS TO SEE PROMETHEUS IS PLANNING SOMETHING BIG.
WE NEED HELP.
HAL, OLLIE, WE NEED YOUR FRIENDS IN ON THIS... ALL OF THEM.
COME ON. GOTHAM CITY HOLDS NOTHING FOR US.
COOL IF I FLY NEXT TO YOU, FREDDY?
YES. I'D LIKE THAT.

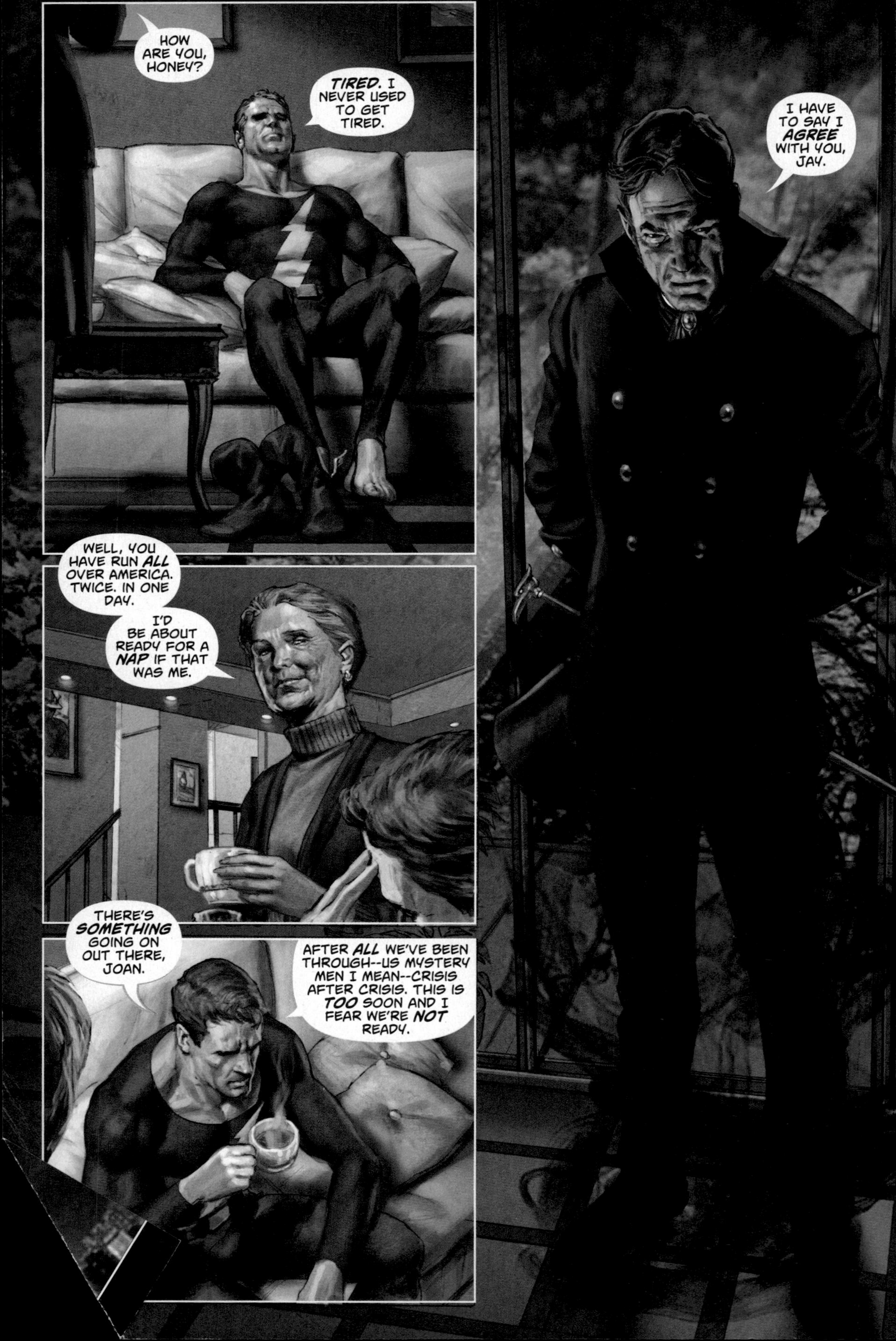
HOW ARE YOU, HONEY?
TIRED. I NEVER USED TO GET TIRED.
I HAVE TO SAY I AGREE WITH YOU, JAY.
WELL, YOU HAVE RUN ALL OVER AMERICA. TWICE. IN ONE DAY.
I'D BE ABOUT READY FOR A NAP IF THAT WAS ME.
THERE'S SOMETHING GOING ON OUT THERE, JOAN.
AFTER ALL WE'VE BEEN THROUGH--US MYSTERY MEN I MEAN--CRISIS AFTER CRISIS. THIS IS TOO SOON AND I FEAR WE'RE NOT READY.

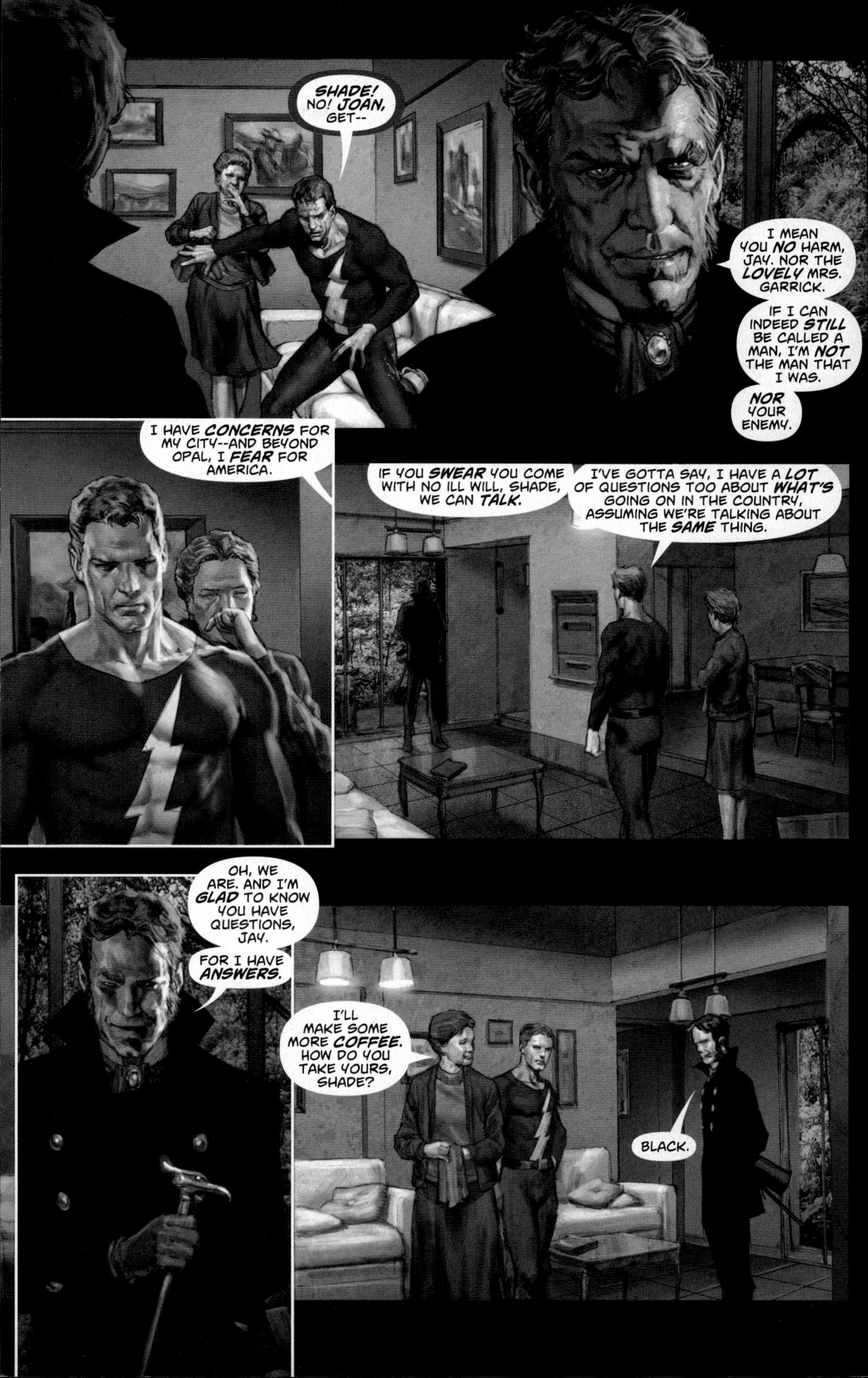
SHADE! NO! JOAN, GET--
I MEAN YOU NO HARM, JAY. NOR THE LOVELY MRS. GARRICK.
IF I CAN INDEED STILL BE CALLED A MAN, I'M NOT THE MAN THAT I WAS.
NOR YOUR ENEMY.
I HAVE CONCERNS FOR MY CITY--AND BEYOND OPAL, I FEAR FOR AMERICA.
IF YOU SWEAR YOU COME WITH NO ILL WILL, SHADE, WE CAN TALK.
I'VE GOTTA SAY, I HAVE A LOT OF QUESTIONS TOO ABOUT WHAT'S GOING ON IN THE COUNTRY, ASSUMING WE'RE TALKING ABOUT THE SAME THING.
OH, WE ARE. AND I'M GLAD TO KNOW YOU HAVE QUESTIONS, JAY.
FOR I HAVE ANSWERS.
I'LL MAKE SOME MORE COFFEE. HOW DO YOU TAKE YOURS, SHADE?
BLACK.

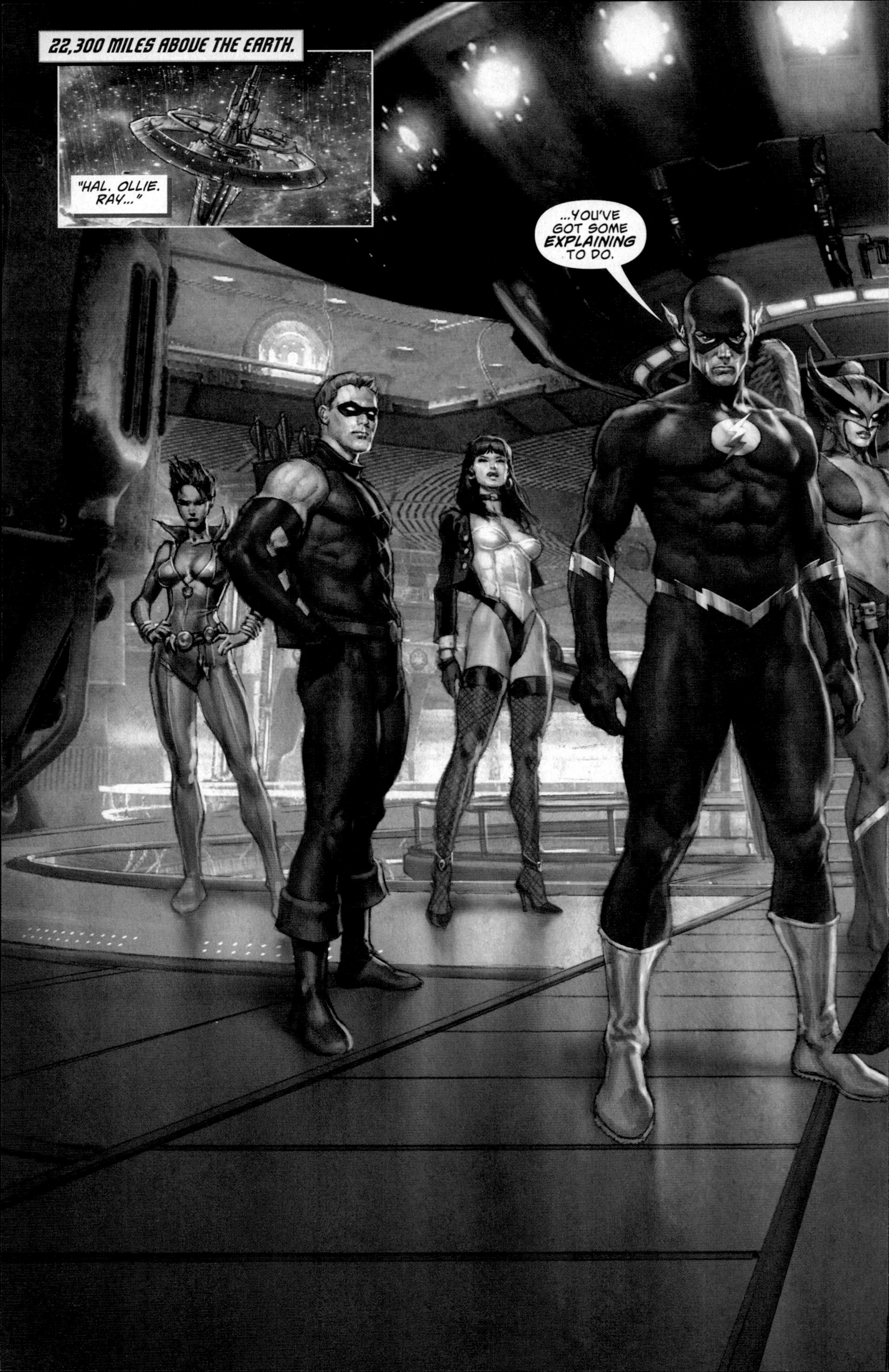
22,300 MILES ABOVE THE EARTH.
"HAL. OLLIE. RAY..."
...YOU'VE GOT SOME EXPLAINING TO DO.

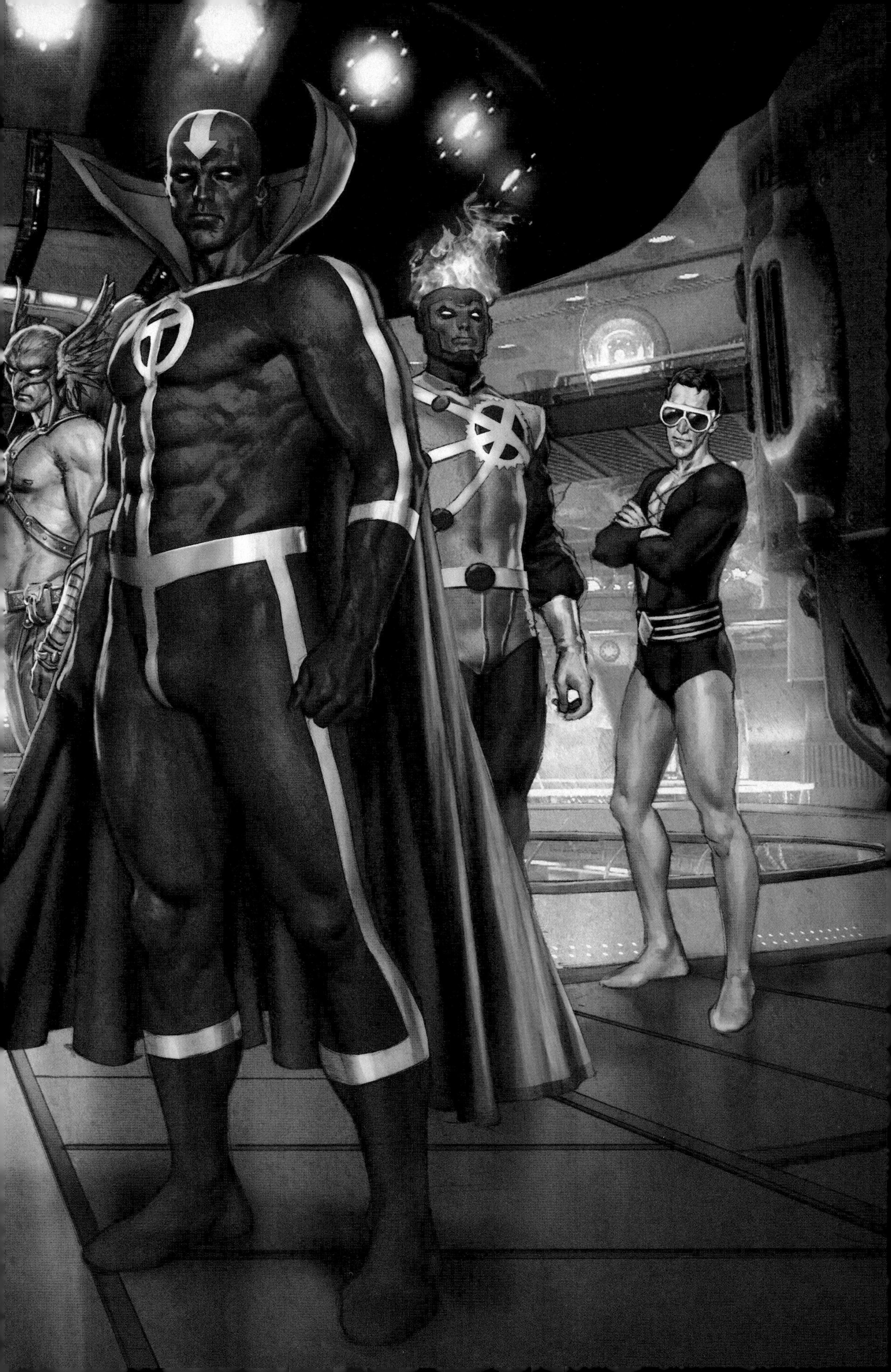

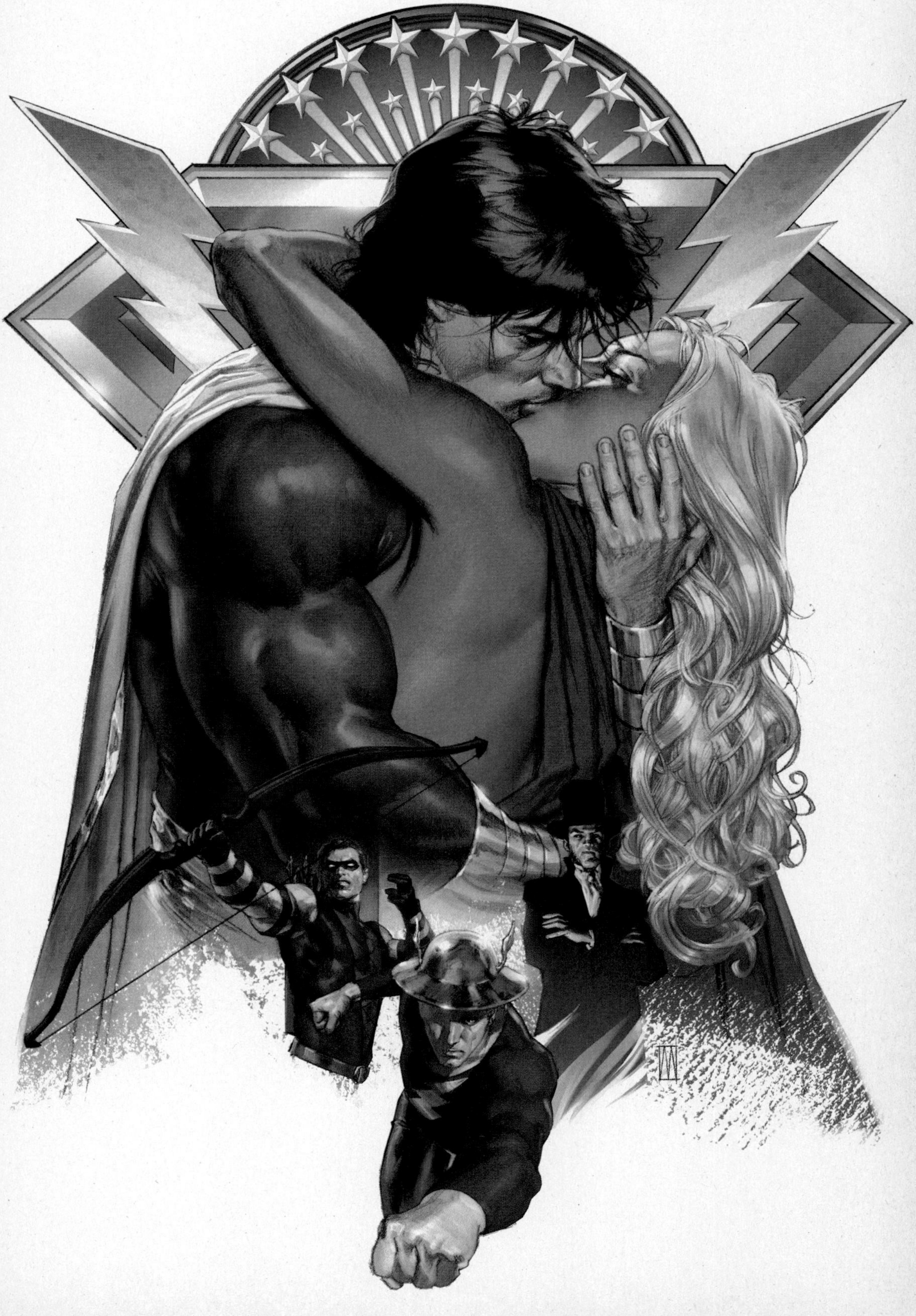

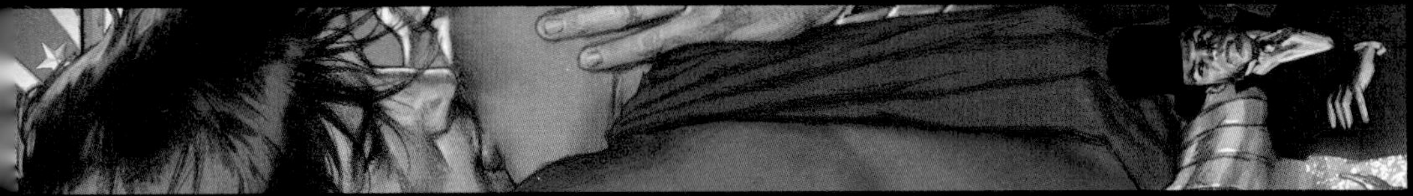

CRY FOR JUSTICE PART FIVE: THE LIE

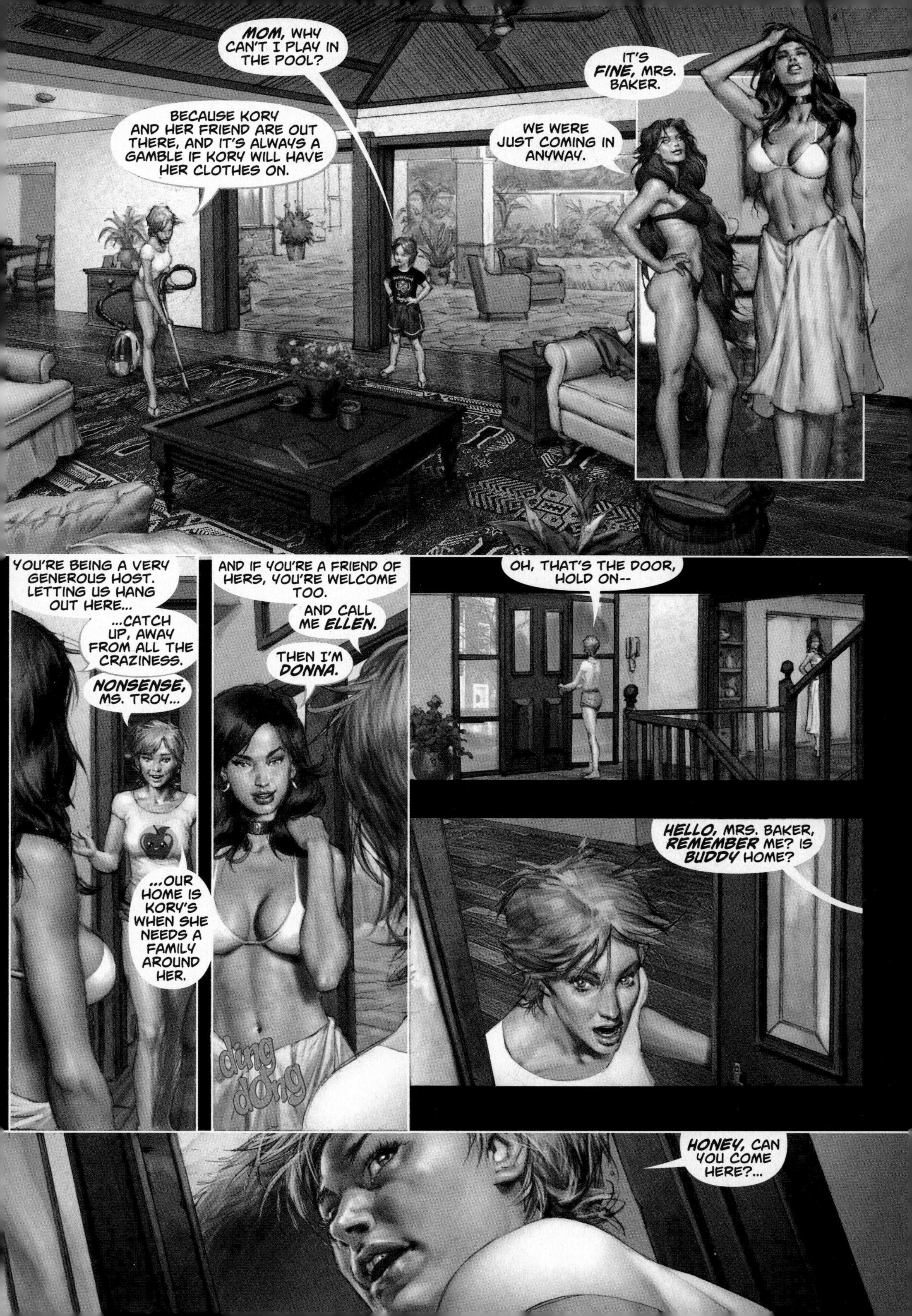
MOM, WHY CAN'T I PLAY IN THE POOL?
BECAUSE KORY AND HER FRIEND ARE OUT THERE, AND IT'S ALWAYS A GAMBLE IF KORY WILL HAVE HER CLOTHES ON.
IT'S FINE, MRS. BAKER.
WE WERE JUST COMING IN ANYWAY.
YOU'RE BEING A VERY GENEROUS HOST. LETTING US HANG OUT HERE...
...CATCH UP, AWAY FROM ALL THE CRAZINESS.
NONSENSE, MS. TROY...
...OUR HOME IS KORY'S WHEN SHE NEEDS A FAMILY AROUND HER.
AND IF YOU'RE A FRIEND OF HERS, YOU'RE WELCOME TOO.
AND CALL ME ELLEN.
THEN I'M DONNA.
ding dOng
OH, THAT'S THE DOOR, HOLD ON--
HELLO, MRS. BAKER, REMEMBER ME? IS BUDDY HOME?
HONEY, CAN YOU COME HERE?...

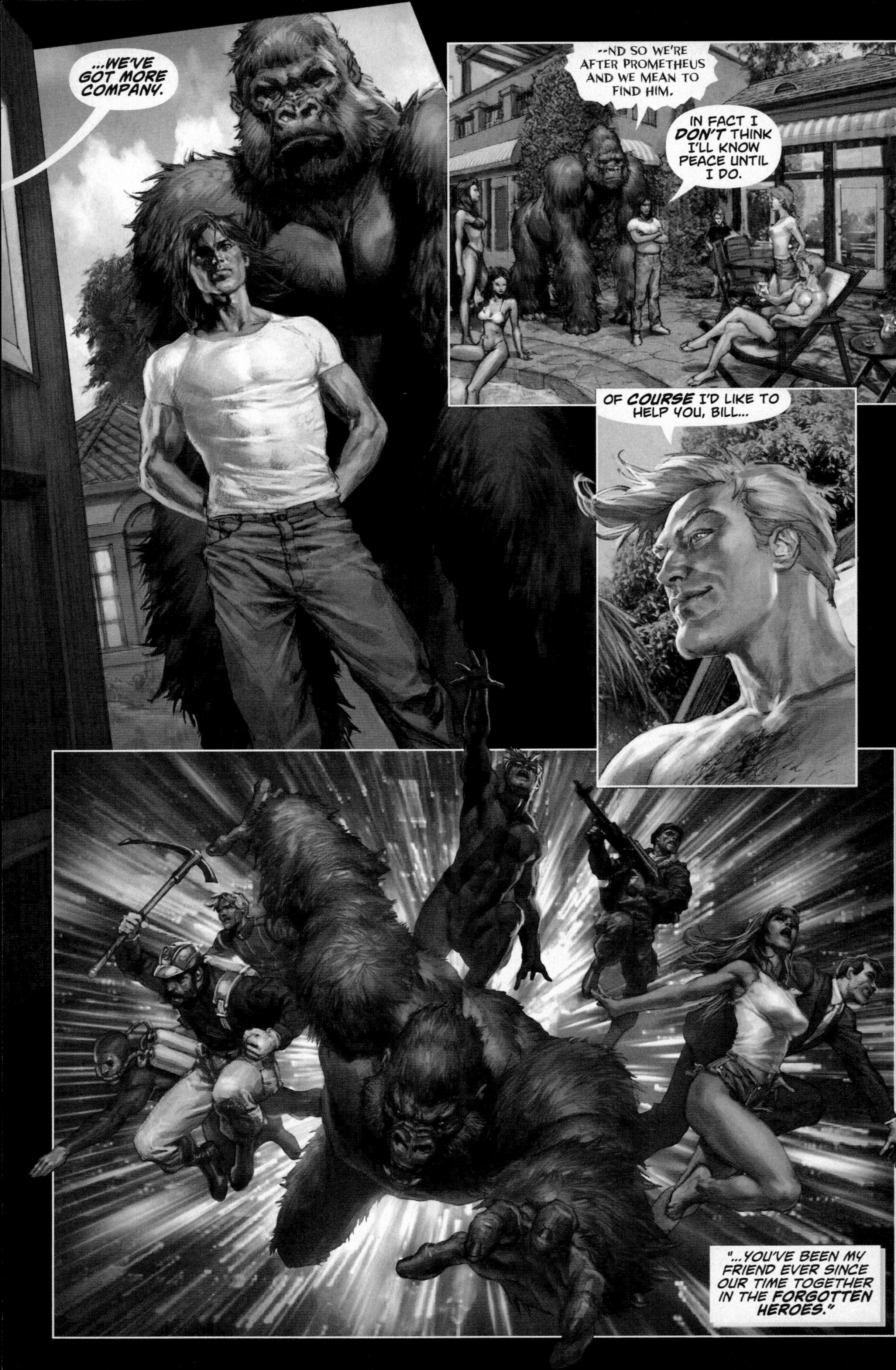
...WE'VE GOT MORE COMPANY.
--ND SO WE'RE AFTER PROMETHEUS AND WE MEAN TO FIND HIM.
IN FACT I DON'T THINK I'LL KNOW PEACE UNTIL I DO.
OF COURSE I'D LIKE TO HELP YOU, BILL...
"...YOU'VE BEEN MY FRIEND EVER SINCE OUR TIME TOGETHER IN THE FORGOTTEN HEROES."

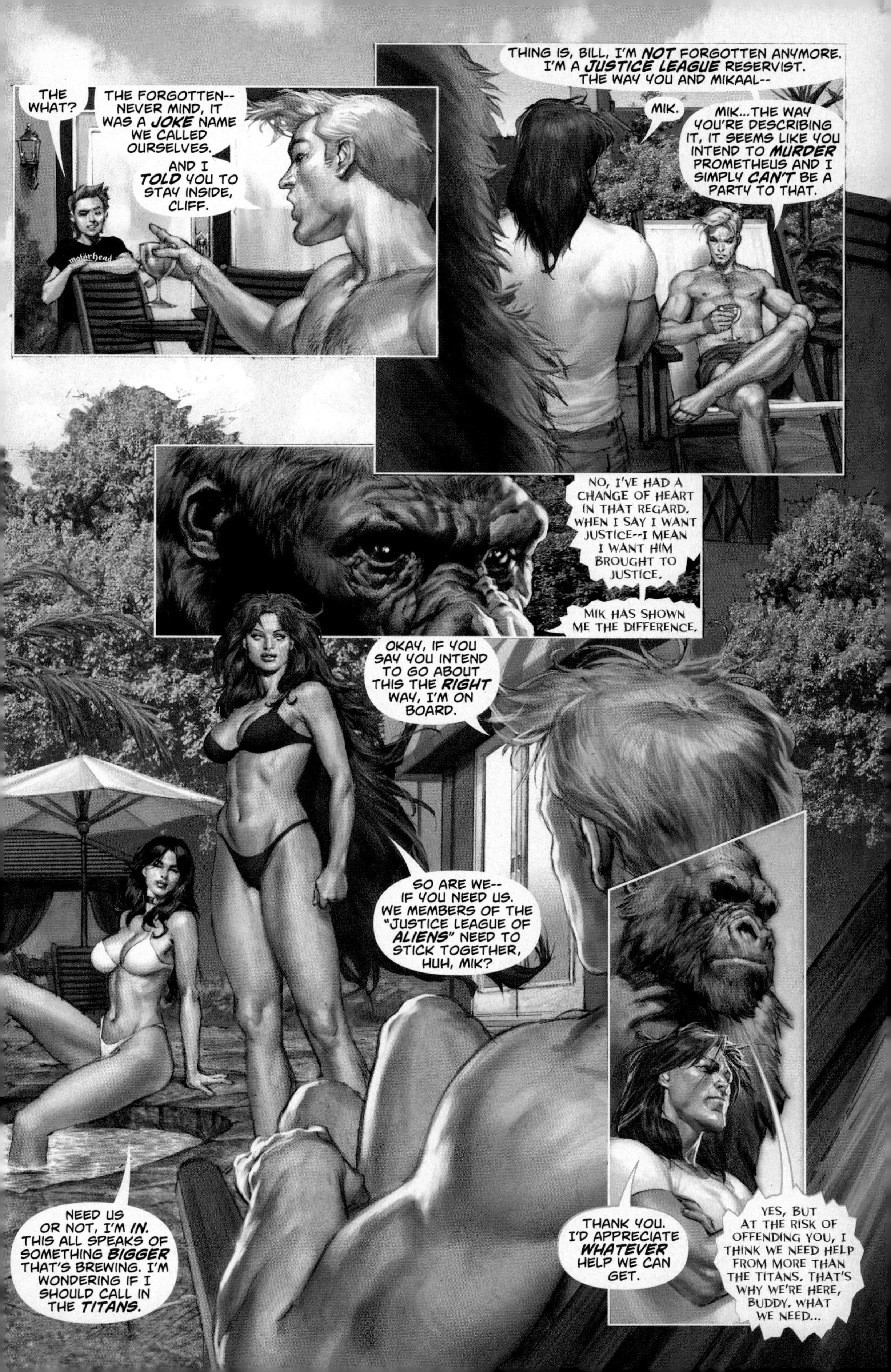
THE WHAT?
THE FORGOTTEN-- NEVER MIND, IT WAS A JOKE NAME WE CALLED OURSELVES.
AND I TOLD YOU TO STAY INSIDE, CLIFF.
motörhead
THING IS, BILL, I'M NOT FORGOTTEN ANYMORE. I'M A JUSTICE LEAGUE RESERVIST. THE WAY YOU AND MIKAAL--
MIK.
MIK...THE WAY YOU'RE DESCRIBING IT, IT SEEMS LIKE YOU INTEND TO MURDER PROMETHEUS AND I SIMPLY CAN'T BE A PARTY TO THAT.
NO, I'VE HAD A CHANGE OF HEART IN THAT REGARD. WHEN I SAY I WANT JUSTICE--I MEAN I WANT HIM BROUGHT TO JUSTICE.
MIK HAS SHOWN ME THE DIFFERENCE.
OKAY, IF YOU SAY YOU INTEND TO GO ABOUT THIS THE RIGHT WAY, I'M ON BOARD.
SO ARE WE-- IF YOU NEED US. WE MEMBERS OF THE "JUSTICE LEAGUE OF ALIENS" NEED TO STICK TOGETHER, HUH, MIK?
NEED US OR NOT, I'M IN. THIS ALL SPEAKS OF SOMETHING BIGGER THAT'S BREWING. I'M WONDERING IF I SHOULD CALL IN THE TITANS.
THANK YOU. I'D APPRECIATE WHATEVER HELP WE CAN GET.
YES, BUT AT THE RISK OF OFFENDING YOU, I THINK WE NEED HELP FROM MORE THAN THE TITANS. THAT'S WHY WE'RE HERE, BUDDY. WHAT WE NEED...

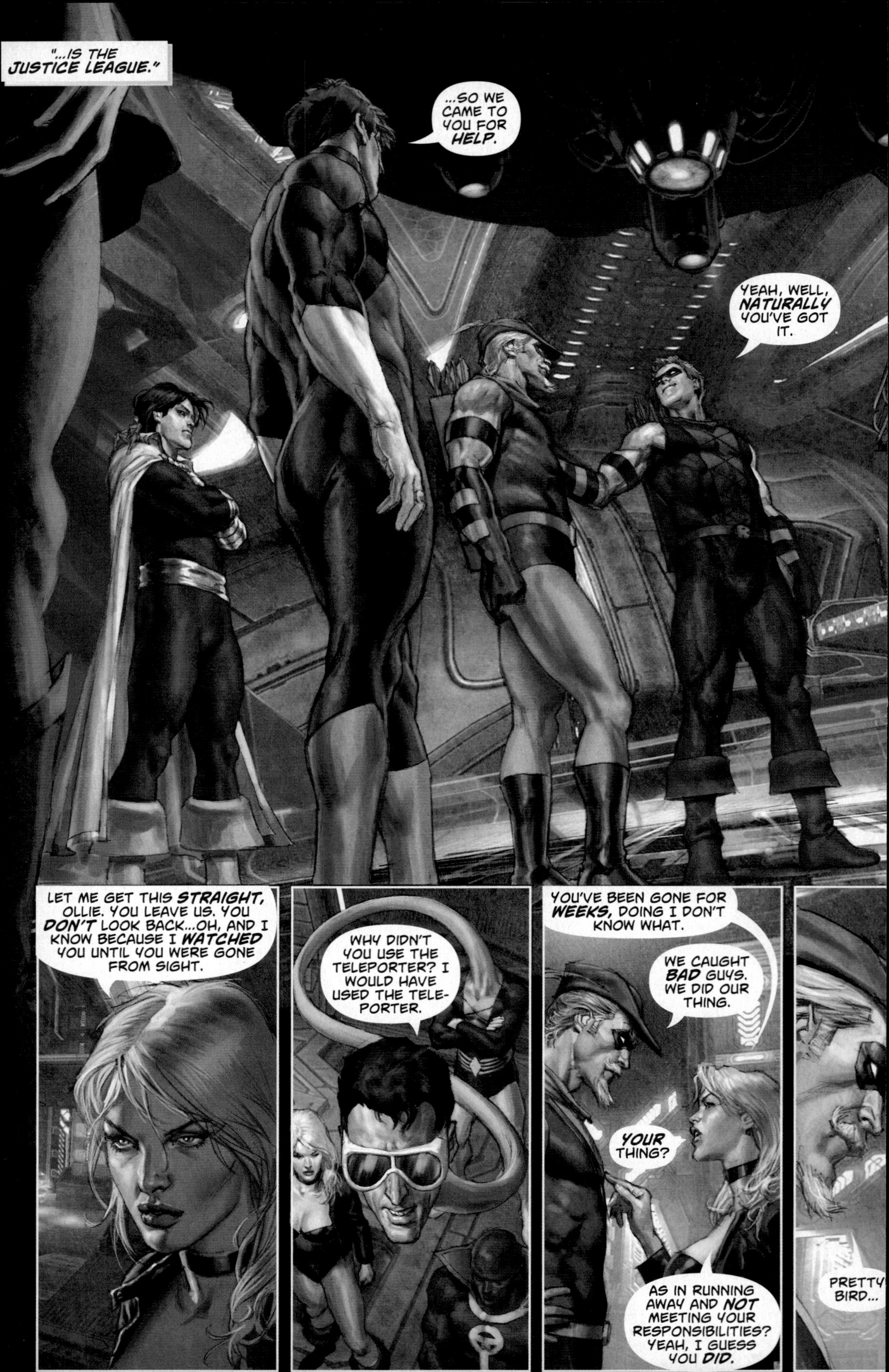
"...IS THE JUSTICE LEAGUE."
...SO WE CAME TO YOU FOR HELP.
YEAH, WELL, NATURALLY YOU'VE GOT IT.
LET ME GET THIS STRAIGHT, OLLIE. YOU LEAVE US. YOU DON'T LOOK BACK...OH, AND I KNOW BECAUSE I WATCHED YOU UNTIL YOU WERE GONE FROM SIGHT.
WHY DIDN'T YOU USE THE TELEPORTER? I WOULD HAVE USED THE TELEPORTER.
YOU'VE BEEN GONE FOR WEEKS, DOING I DON'T KNOW WHAT.
WE CAUGHT BAD GUYS. WE DID OUR THING.
YOUR THING?
AS IN RUNNING AWAY AND NOT MEETING YOUR RESPONSIBILITIES? YEAH, I GUESS YOU DID.
PRETTY BIRD...

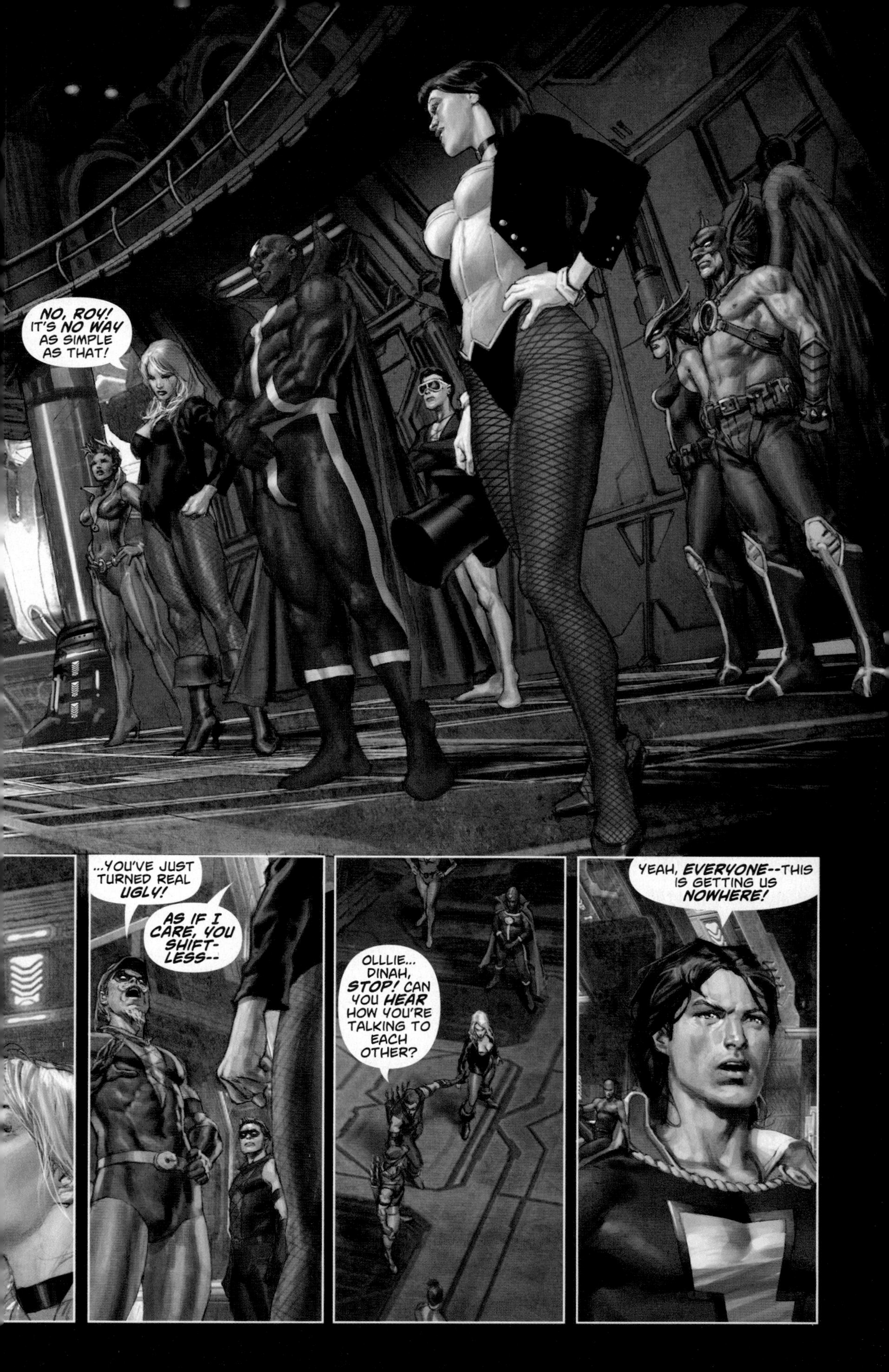
NO, ROY! IT'S NO WAY AS SIMPLE AS THAT!
...YOU'VE JUST TURNED REAL UGLY!
AS IF I CARE, YOU SHIFT-LESS--
OLLLIE... DINAH, STOP! CAN YOU HEAR HOW YOU'RE TALKING TO EACH OTHER?
YEAH, EVERYONE--THIS IS GETTING US NOWHERE!

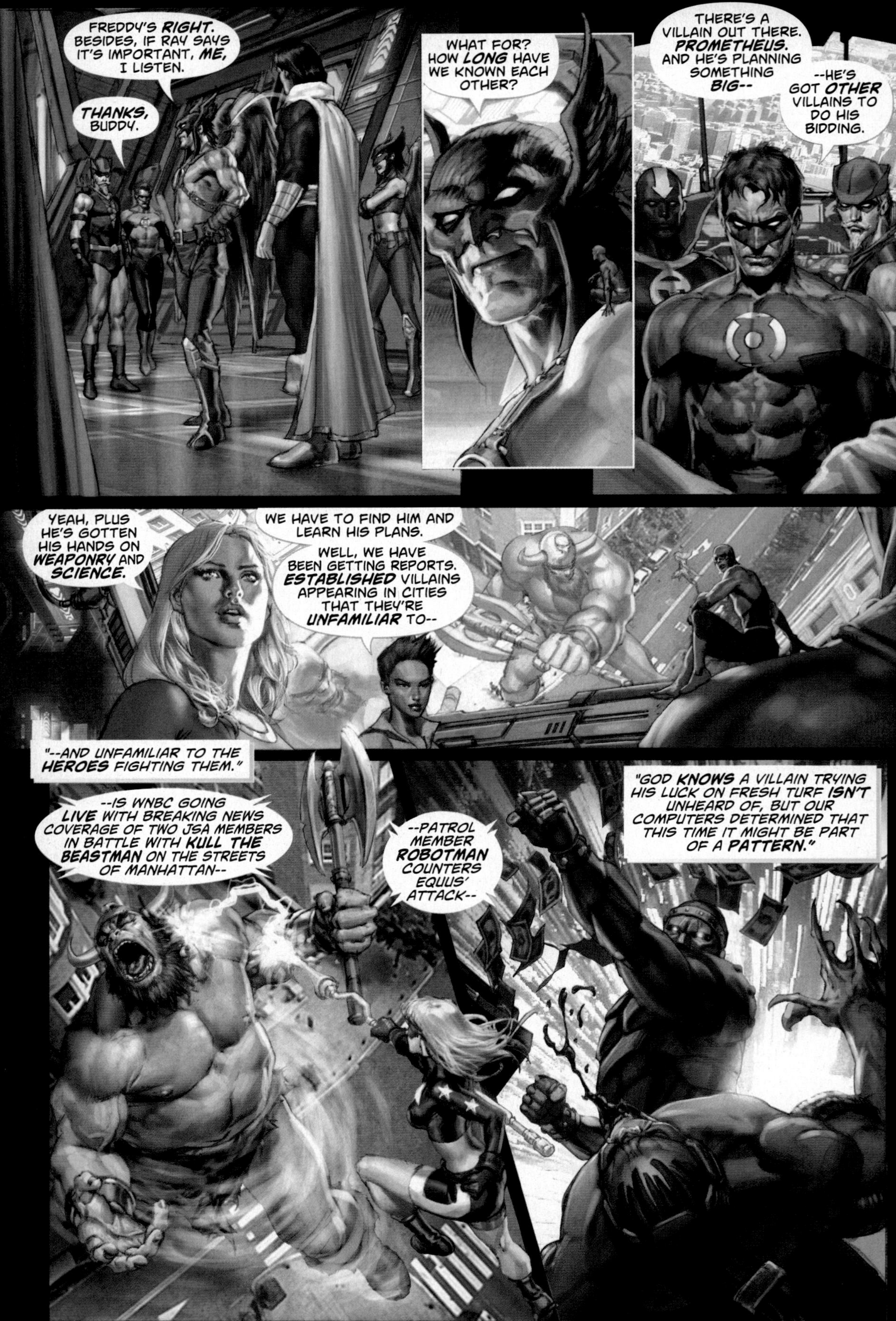
FREDDY'S RIGHT. BESIDES, IF RAY SAYS IT'S IMPORTANT, ME, I LISTEN.
THANKS, BUDDY.
WHAT FOR? HOW LONG HAVE WE KNOWN EACH OTHER?
THERE'S A VILLAIN OUT THERE. PROMETHEUS. AND HE'S PLANNING SOMETHING BIG--
--HE'S GOT OTHER VILLAINS TO DO HIS BIDDING.
YEAH, PLUS HE'S GOTTEN HIS HANDS ON WEAPONRY AND SCIENCE.
WE HAVE TO FIND HIM AND LEARN HIS PLANS.
WELL, WE HAVE BEEN GETTING REPORTS. ESTABLISHED VILLAINS APPEARING IN CITIES THAT THEY'RE UNFAMILIAR TO--
"--AND UNFAMILIAR TO THE HEROES FIGHTING THEM."
--IS WNBC GOING LIVE WITH BREAKING NEWS COVERAGE OF TWO JSA MEMBERS IN BATTLE WITH KULL THE BEASTMAN ON THE STREETS OF MANHATTAN--
--PATROL MEMBER ROBOTMAN COUNTERS EQUUS' ATTACK--
"GOD KNOWS A VILLAIN TRYING HIS LUCK ON FRESH TURF ISN'T UNHEARD OF, BUT OUR COMPUTERS DETERMINED THAT THIS TIME IT MIGHT BE PART OF A PATTERN."

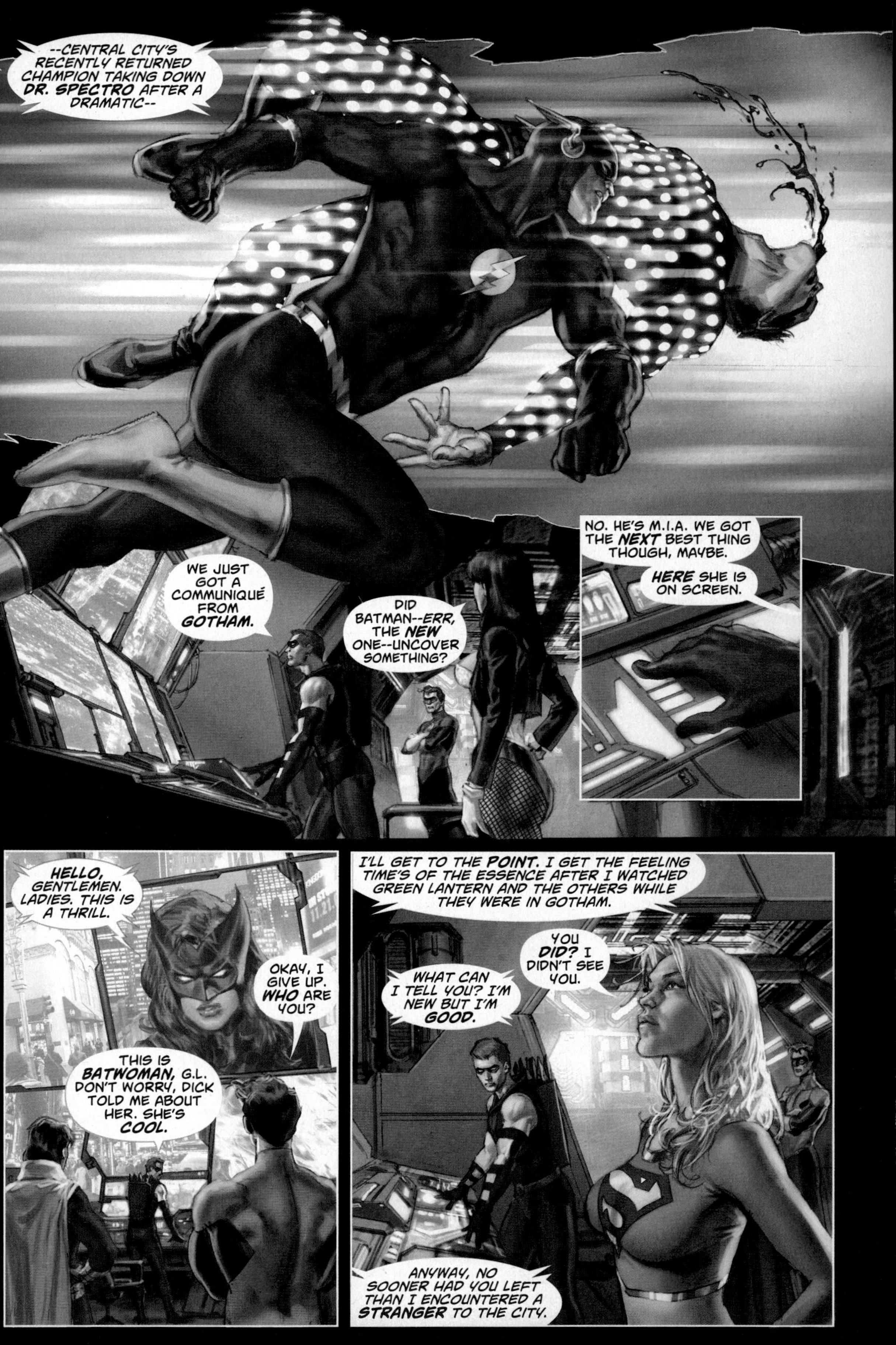
--CENTRAL CITY'S RECENTLY RETURNED CHAMPION TAKING DOWN DR. SPECTRO AFTER A DRAMATIC--
WE JUST GOT A COMMUNIQUÉ FROM GOTHAM.
DID BATMAN--ERR, THE NEW ONE--UNCOVER SOMETHING?
NO. HE'S M.I.A. WE GOT THE NEXT BEST THING THOUGH, MAYBE.
HERE SHE IS ON SCREEN.
HELLO, GENTLEMEN. LADIES. THIS IS A THRILL.
OKAY, I GIVE UP. WHO ARE YOU?
THIS IS BATWOMAN, G.L. DON'T WORRY, DICK TOLD ME ABOUT HER. SHE'S COOL.
I'LL GET TO THE POINT. I GET THE FEELING TIME'S OF THE ESSENCE AFTER I WATCHED GREEN LANTERN AND THE OTHERS WHILE THEY WERE IN GOTHAM.
YOU DID? I DIDN'T SEE YOU.
WHAT CAN I TELL YOU? I'M NEW BUT I'M GOOD.
ANYWAY, NO SOONER HAD YOU LEFT THAN I ENCOUNTERED A STRANGER TO THE CITY.

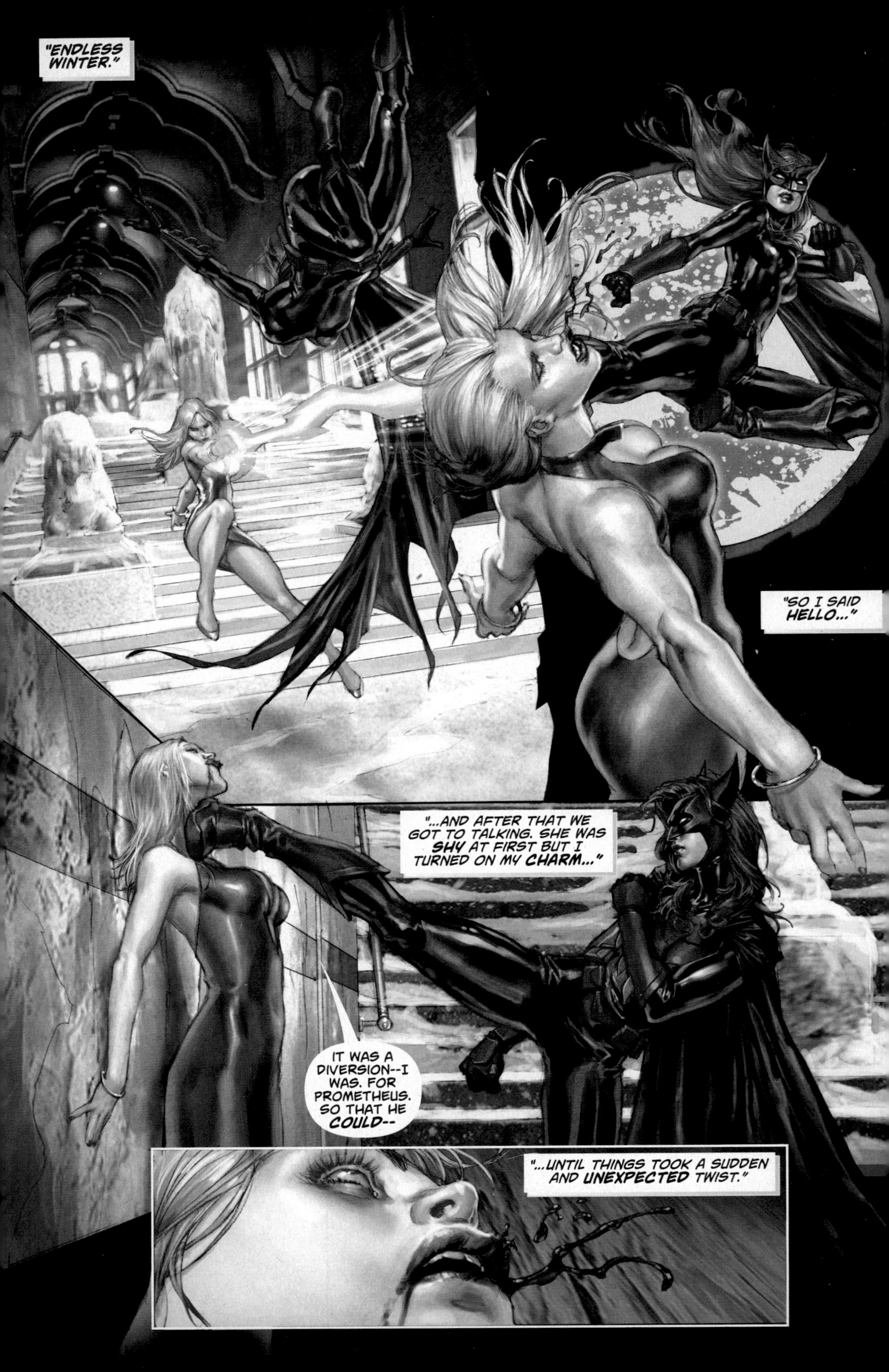
"ENDLESS WINTER."
"SO I SAID HELLO..."
"...AND AFTER THAT WE GOT TO TALKING. SHE WAS SHY AT FIRST BUT I TURNED ON MY CHARM..."
IT WAS A DIVERSION--I WAS. FOR PROMETHEUS. SO THAT HE COULD--
"...UNTIL THINGS TOOK A SUDDEN AND UNEXPECTED TWIST."

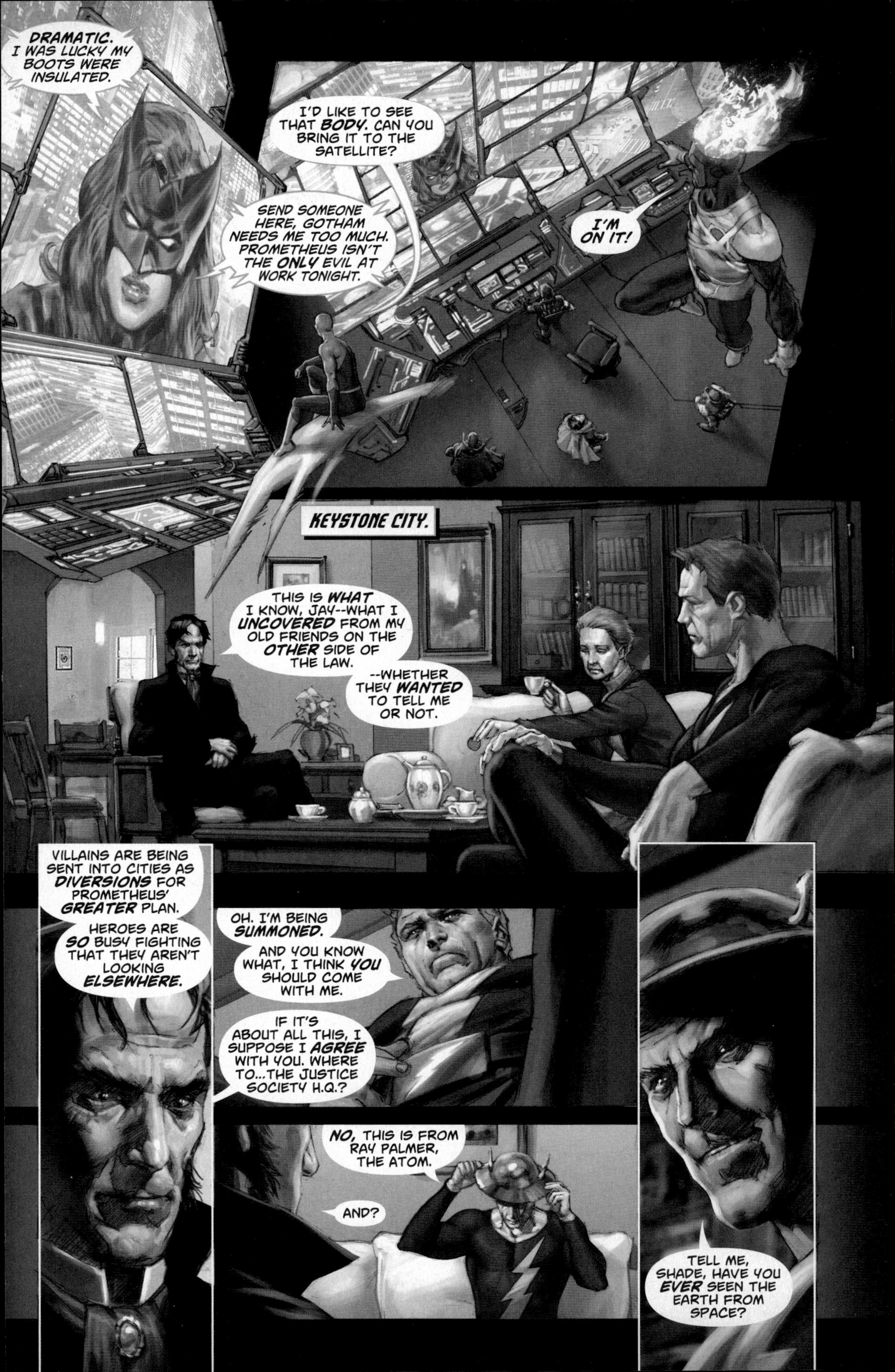
DRAMATIC. I WAS LUCKY MY BOOTS WERE INSULATED.
I'D LIKE TO SEE THAT BODY. CAN YOU BRING IT TO THE SATELLITE?
SEND SOMEONE HERE, GOTHAM NEEDS ME TOO MUCH. PROMETHEUS ISN'T THE ONLY EVIL AT WORK TONIGHT.
I'M ON IT!
KEYSTONE CITY.
THIS IS WHAT I KNOW, JAY--WHAT I UNCOVERED FROM MY OLD FRIENDS ON THE OTHER SIDE OF THE LAW.
--WHETHER THEY WANTED TO TELL ME OR NOT.
VILLAINS ARE BEING SENT INTO CITIES AS DIVERSIONS FOR PROMETHEUS' GREATER PLAN.
HEROES ARE SO BUSY FIGHTING THAT THEY AREN'T LOOKING ELSEWHERE.
OH. I'M BEING SUMMONED.
AND YOU KNOW WHAT, I THINK YOU SHOULD COME WITH ME.
IF IT'S ABOUT ALL THIS, I SUPPOSE I AGREE WITH YOU. WHERE TO...THE JUSTICE SOCIETY H.Q.?
NO, THIS IS FROM RAY PALMER, THE ATOM.
AND?
TELL ME, SHADE, HAVE YOU EVER SEEN THE EARTH FROM SPACE?

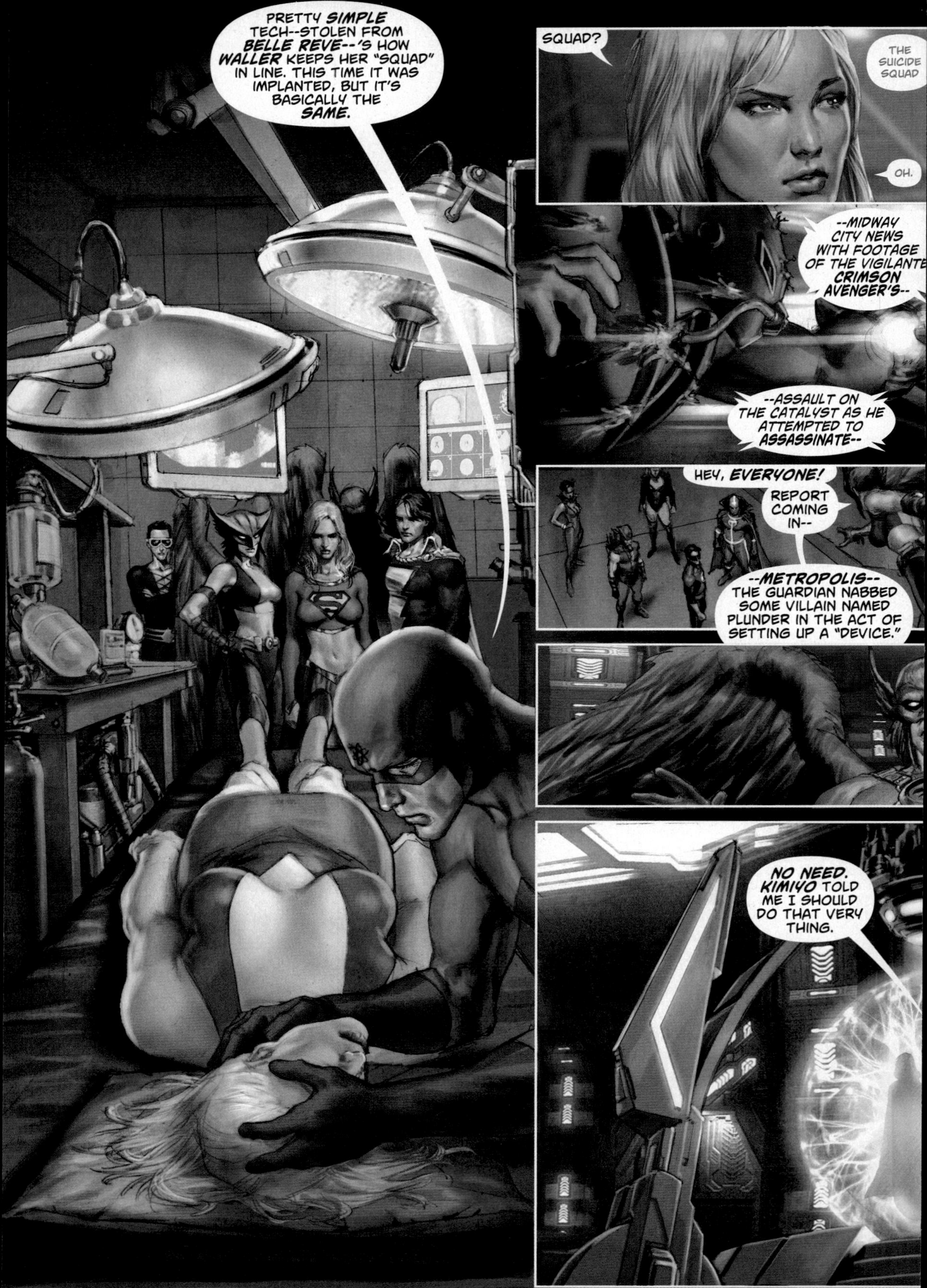
PRETTY SIMPLE TECH--STOLEN FROM BELLE REVE--'S HOW WALLER KEEPS HER "SQUAD" IN LINE. THIS TIME IT WAS IMPLANTED, BUT IT'S BASICALLY THE SAME.
SQUAD?
THE SUICIDE SQUAD
OH.
--MIDWAY CITY NEWS WITH FOOTAGE OF THE VIGILANTE CRIMSON AVENGER'S--
--ASSAULT ON THE CATALYST AS HE ATTEMPTED TO ASSASSINATE--
HEY, EVERYONE!
REPORT COMING IN--
--METROPOLIS-- THE GUARDIAN NABBED SOME VILLAIN NAMED PLUNDER IN THE ACT OF SETTING UP A "DEVICE."
NO NEED. KIMIYO TOLD ME I SHOULD DO THAT VERY THING.

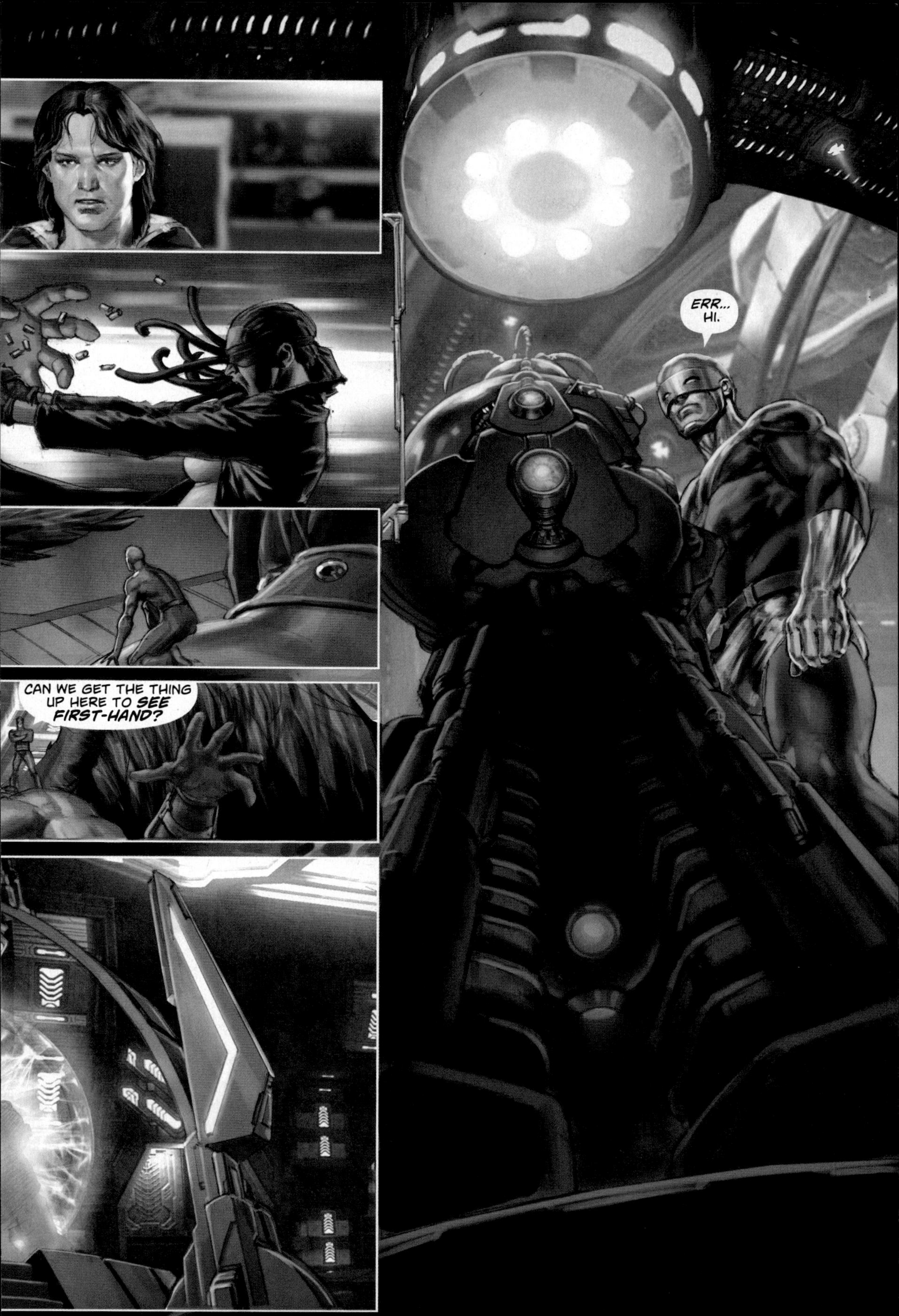
CAN WE GET THE THING UP HERE TO SEE FIRST-HAND?
ERR... HI.

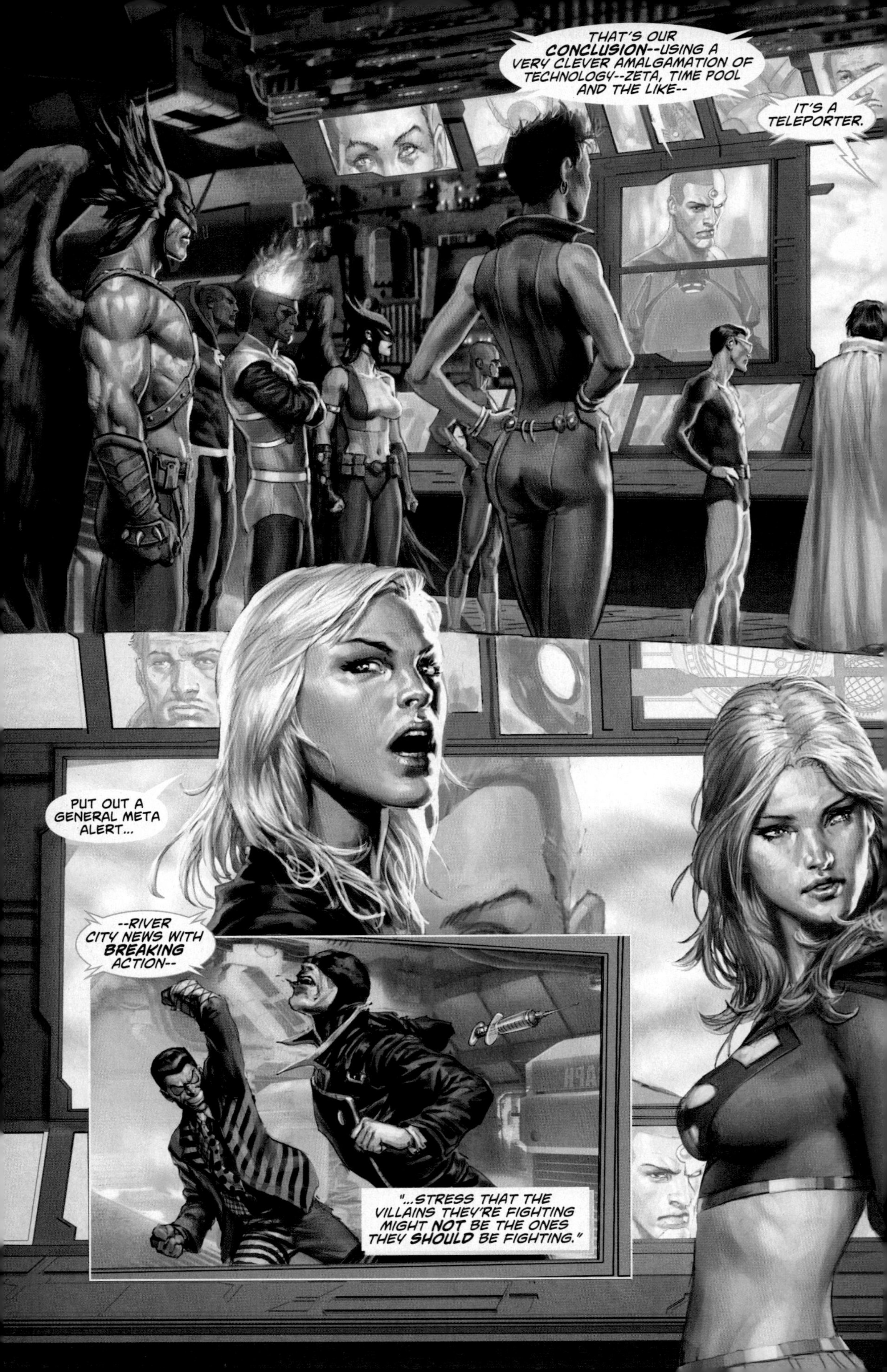
THAT'S OUR CONCLUSION--USING A VERY CLEVER AMALGAMATION OF TECHNOLOGY--ZETA, TIME POOL AND THE LIKE--
IT'S A TELEPORTER.
PUT OUT A GENERAL META ALERT...
--RIVER CITY NEWS WITH BREAKING ACTION--
"...STRESS THAT THE VILLAINS THEY'RE FIGHTING MIGHT NOT BE THE ONES THEY SHOULD BE FIGHTING."

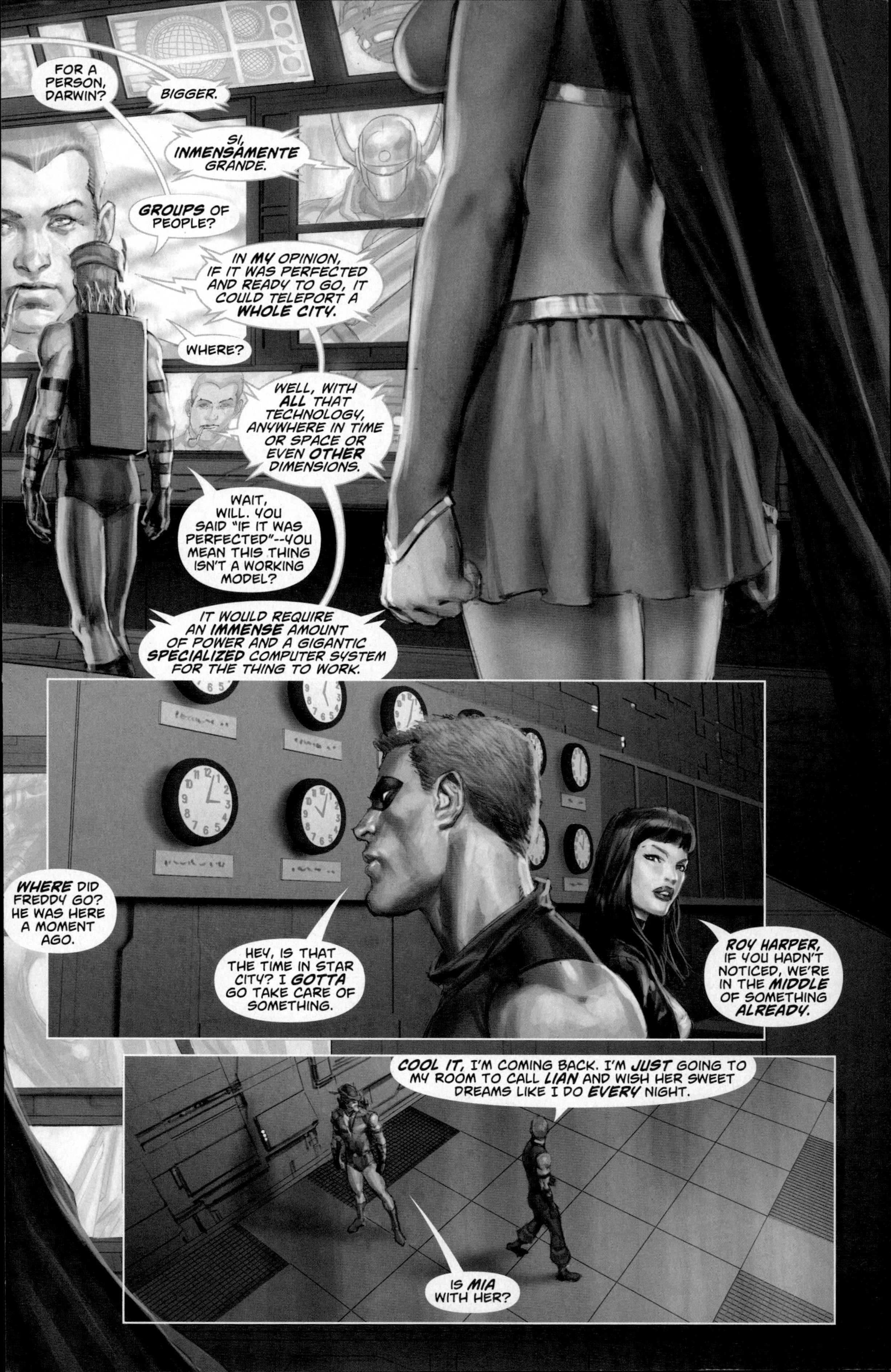
FOR A PERSON, DARWIN?
BIGGER.
SI, INMENSAMENTE GRANDE.
GROUPS OF PEOPLE?
IN MY OPINION, IF IT WAS PERFECTED AND READY TO GO, IT COULD TELEPORT A WHOLE CITY.
WHERE?
WELL, WITH ALL THAT TECHNOLOGY, ANYWHERE IN TIME OR SPACE OR EVEN OTHER DIMENSIONS.
WAIT, WILL. YOU SAID "IF IT WAS PERFECTED"--YOU MEAN THIS THING ISN'T A WORKING MODEL?
IT WOULD REQUIRE AN IMMENSE AMOUNT OF POWER AND A GIGANTIC SPECIALIZED COMPUTER SYSTEM FOR THE THING TO WORK.
WHERE DID FREDDY GO? HE WAS HERE A MOMENT AGO.
HEY, IS THAT THE TIME IN STAR CITY? I GOTTA GO TAKE CARE OF SOMETHING.
ROY HARPER, IF YOU HADN'T NOTICED, WE'RE IN THE MIDDLE OF SOMETHING ALREADY.
COOL IT, I'M COMING BACK. I'M JUST GOING TO MY ROOM TO CALL LIAN AND WISH HER SWEET DREAMS LIKE I DO EVERY NIGHT.
IS MIA WITH HER?

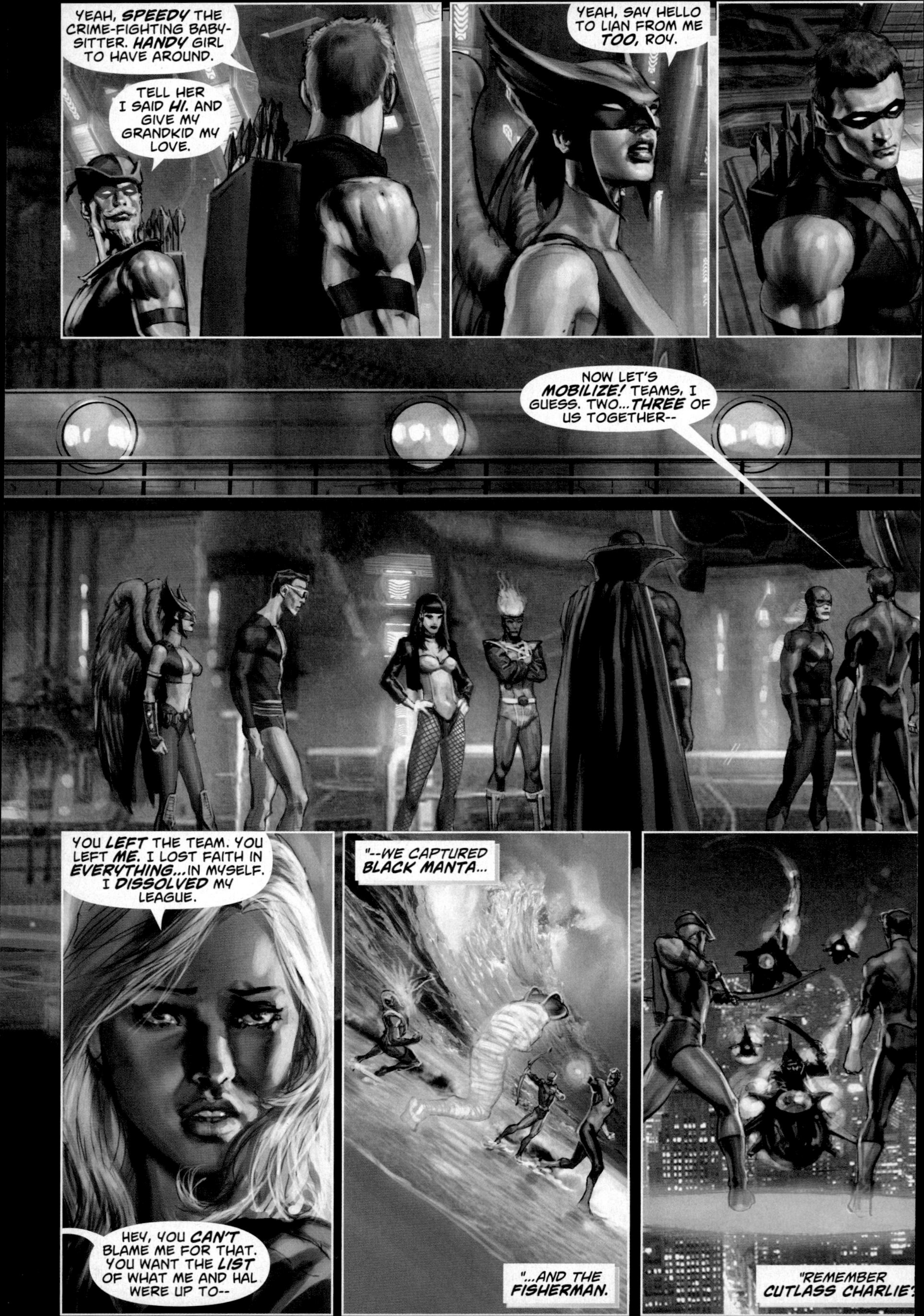
YEAH, SPEEDY THE CRIME-FIGHTING BABY-SITTER. HANDY GIRL TO HAVE AROUND.
TELL HER I SAID HI. AND GIVE MY GRANDKID MY LOVE.
YEAH, SAY HELLO TO LIAN FROM ME TOO, ROY.
NOW LET'S MOBILIZE! TEAMS, I GUESS. TWO...THREE OF US TOGETHER--
YOU LEFT THE TEAM. YOU LEFT ME. I LOST FAITH IN EVERYTHING...IN MYSELF. I DISSOLVED MY LEAGUE.
HEY, YOU CAN'T BLAME ME FOR THAT. YOU WANT THE LIST OF WHAT ME AND HAL WERE UP TO--
"--WE CAPTURED BLACK MANTA...
"...AND THE FISHERMAN.
"REMEMBER CUTLASS CHARLIE?

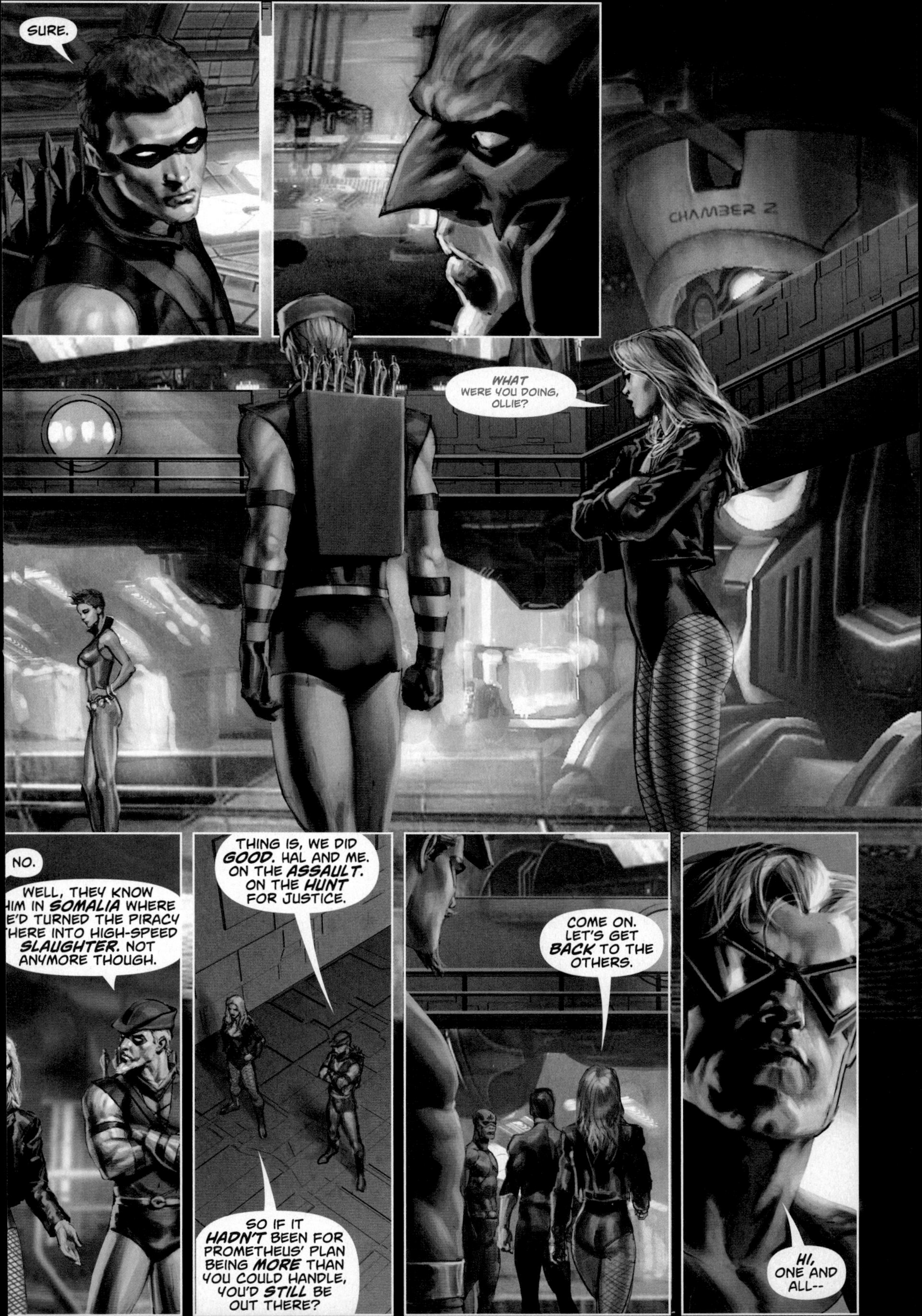
SURE.
CHAMBER 2
WHAT WERE YOU DOING, OLLIE?
NO.
WELL, THEY KNOW HIM IN SOMALIA WHERE HE'D TURNED THE PIRACY THERE INTO HIGH-SPEED SLAUGHTER. NOT ANYMORE THOUGH.
THING IS, WE DID GOOD. HAL AND ME. ON THE ASSAULT. ON THE HUNT FOR JUSTICE.
SO IF IT HADN'T BEEN FOR PROMETHEUS' PLAN BEING MORE THAN YOU COULD HANDLE, YOU'D STILL BE OUT THERE?
COME ON. LET'S GET BACK TO THE OTHERS.
HI, ONE AND ALL--

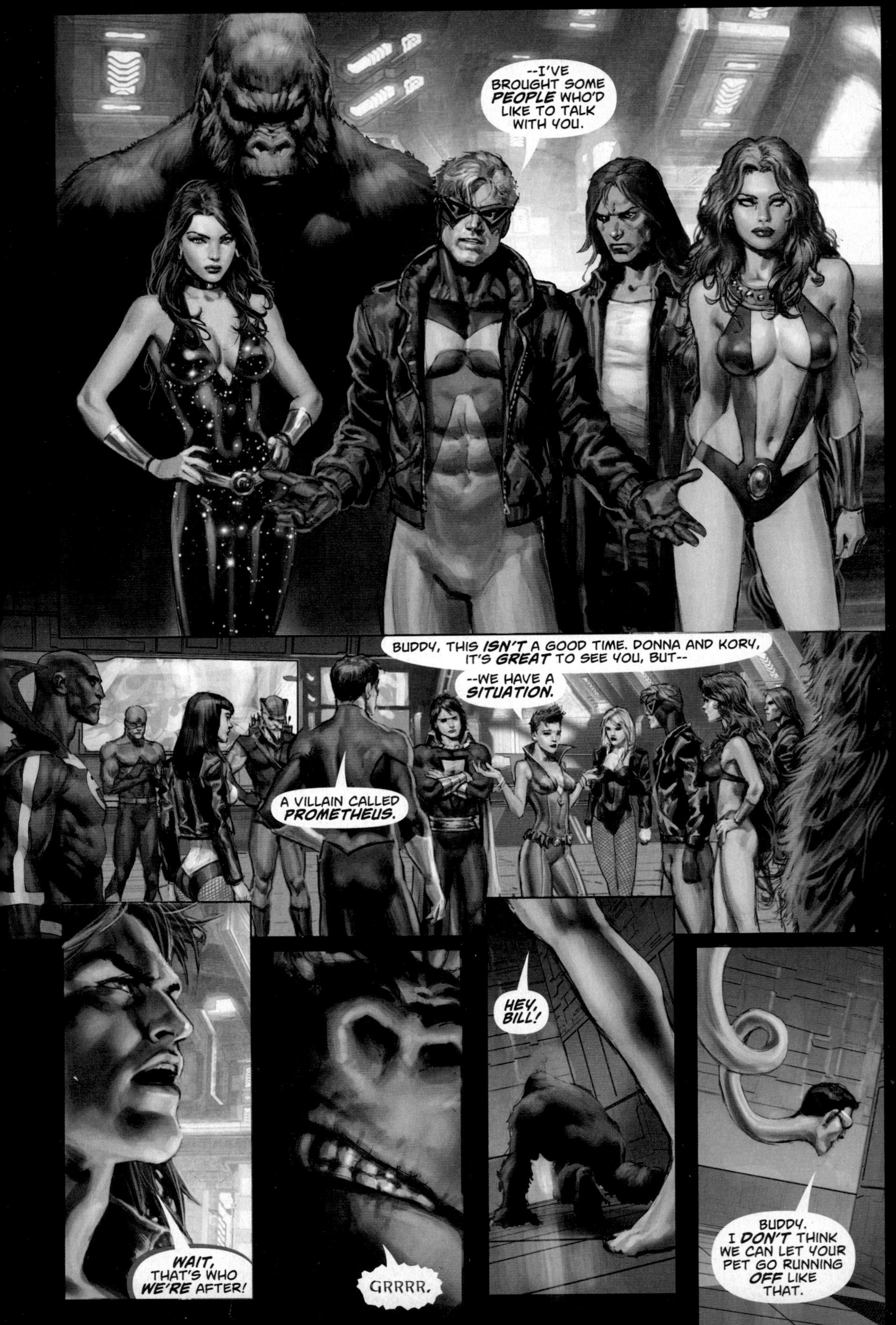
--I'VE BROUGHT SOME PEOPLE WHO'D LIKE TO TALK WITH YOU.
BUDDY, THIS ISN'T A GOOD TIME. DONNA AND KORY, IT'S GREAT TO SEE YOU, BUT--
--WE HAVE A SITUATION.
A VILLAIN CALLED PROMETHEUS.
WAIT, THAT'S WHO WE'RE AFTER!
GRRRR.
HEY, BILL!
BUDDY. I DON'T THINK WE CAN LET YOUR PET GO RUNNING OFF LIKE THAT.

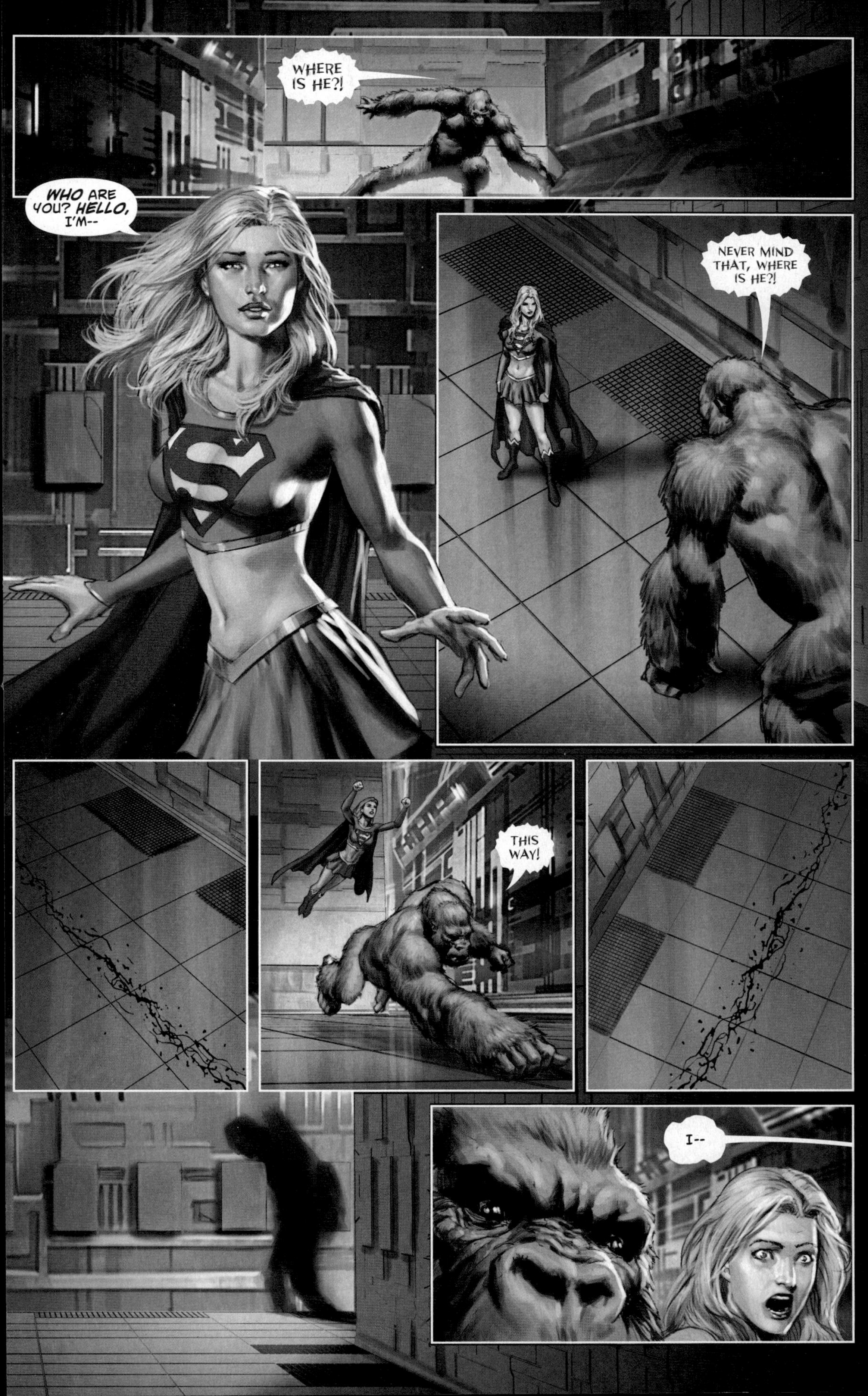
WHERE IS HE?!
WHO ARE YOU? HELLO, I'M--
NEVER MIND THAT, WHERE IS HE?!
THIS WAY!
I--

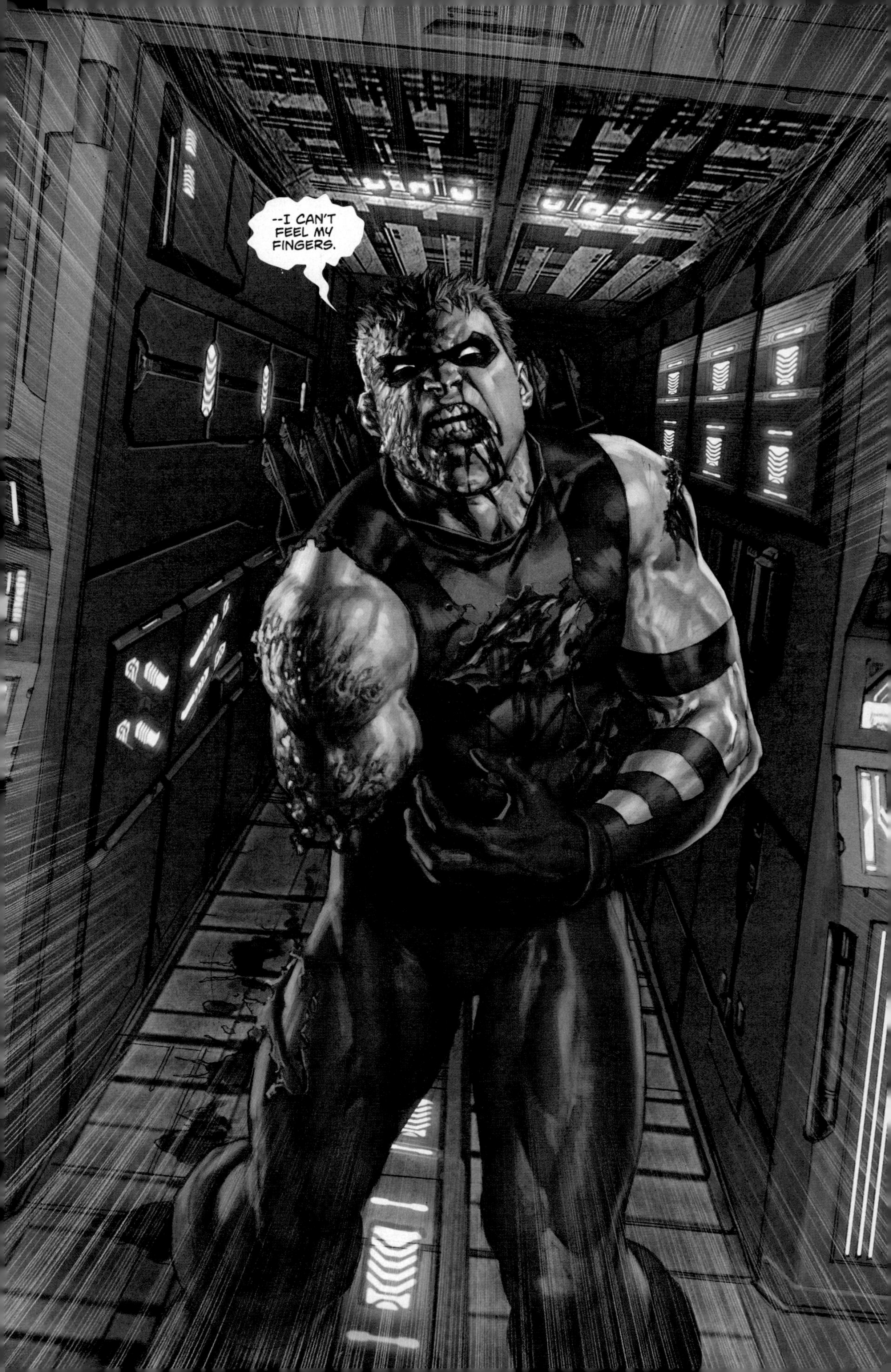
--I CAN'T FEEL MY FINGERS.

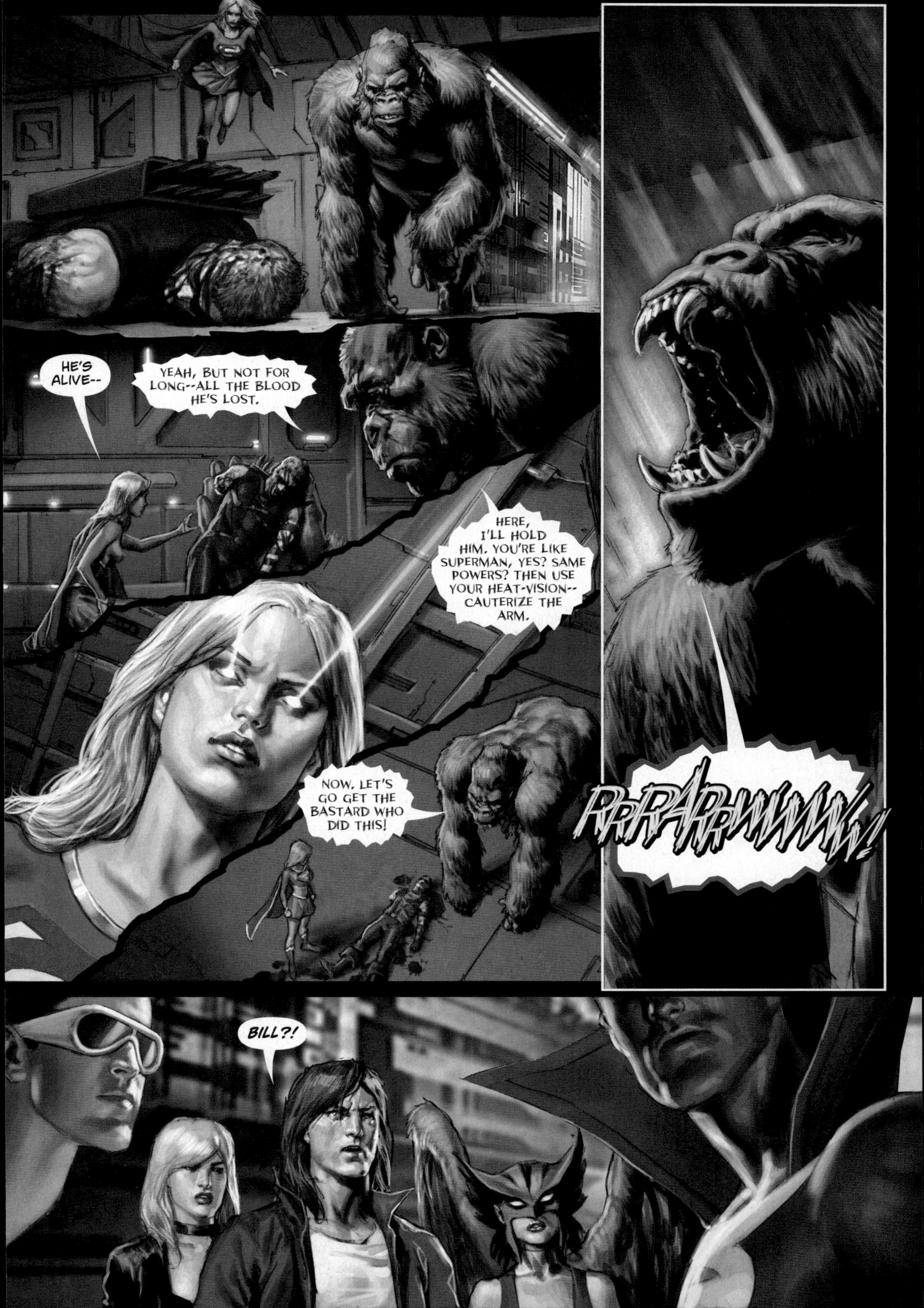
HE'S ALIVE--
YEAH, BUT NOT FOR LONG--ALL THE BLOOD HE'S LOST.
HERE, I'LL HOLD HIM. YOU'RE LIKE SUPERMAN, YES? SAME POWERS? THEN USE YOUR HEAT-VISION--CAUTERIZE THE ARM.
NOW, LET'S GO GET THE BASTARD WHO DID THIS!
RRRRARRRWWWWW!
BILL?!

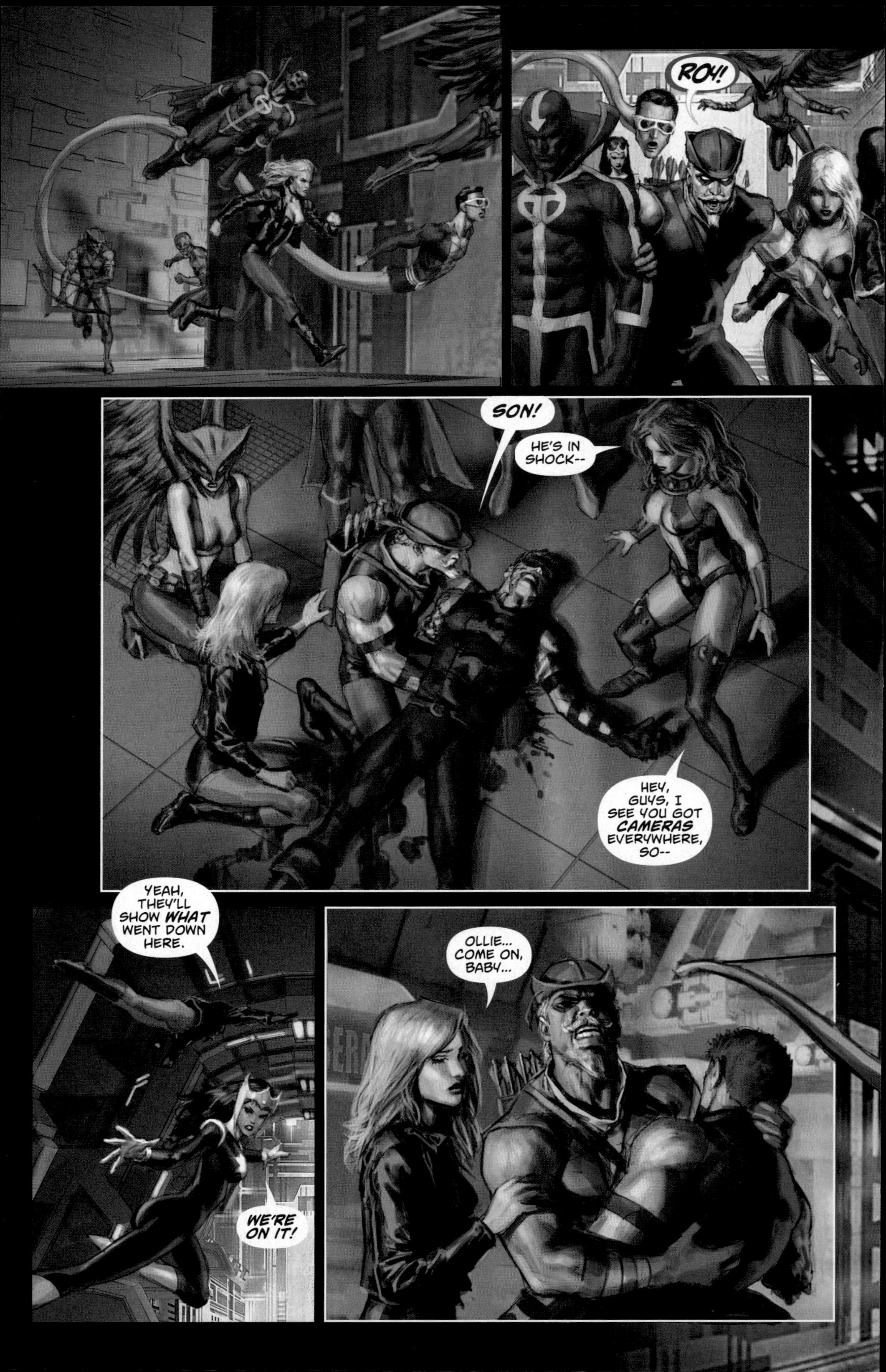
ROY!
SON!
HE'S IN SHOCK--
HEY, GUYS, I SEE YOU GOT CAMERAS EVERYWHERE, SO--
YEAH, THEY'LL SHOW WHAT WENT DOWN HERE.
WE'RE ON IT!
OLLIE... COME ON, BABY...

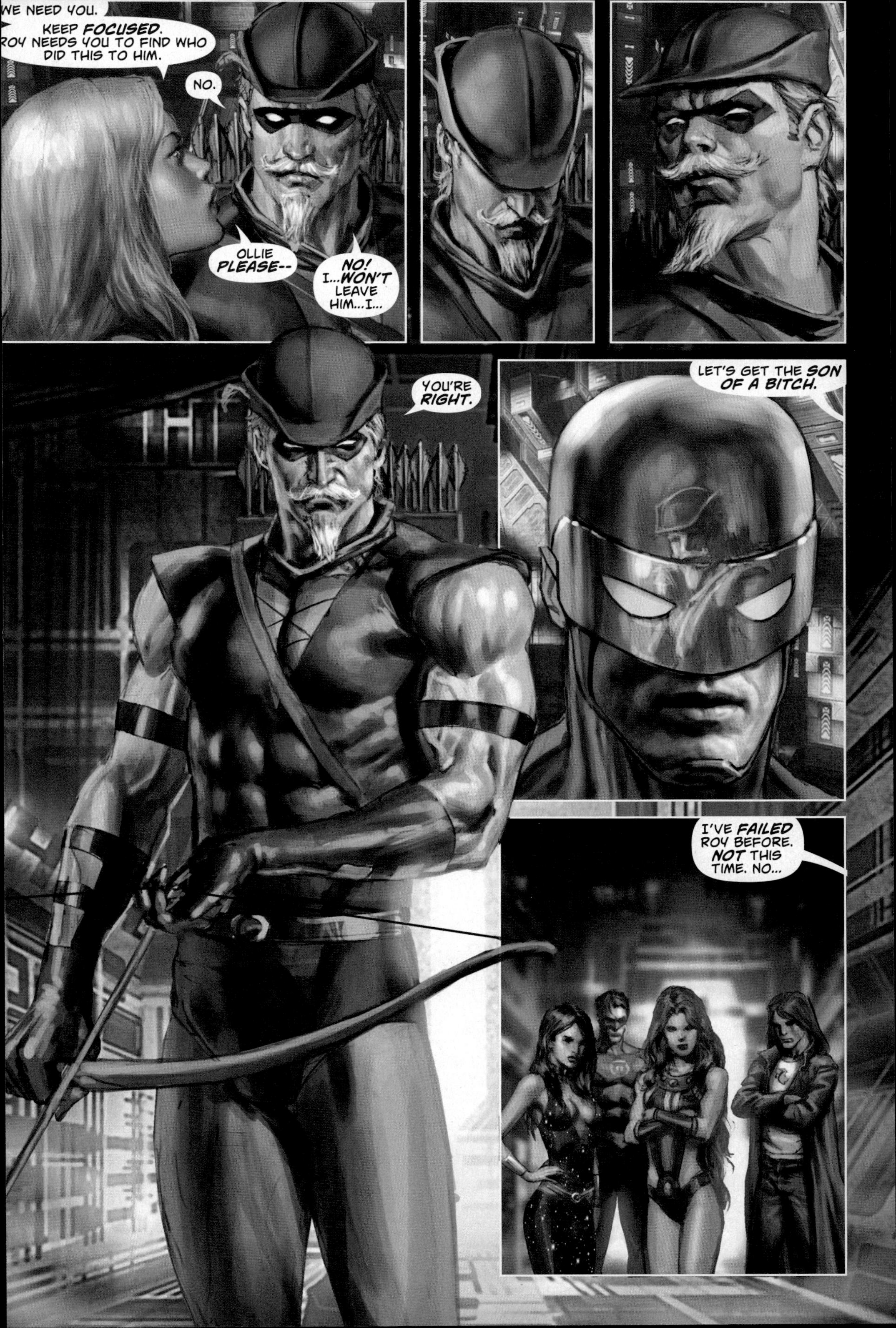
WE NEED YOU.
KEEP FOCUSED. ROY NEEDS YOU TO FIND WHO DID THIS TO HIM.
NO.
OLLIE PLEASE--
NO! I...WON'T LEAVE HIM...I...
YOU'RE RIGHT.
LET'S GET THE SON OF A BITCH.
I'VE FAILED ROY BEFORE. NOT THIS TIME. NO...

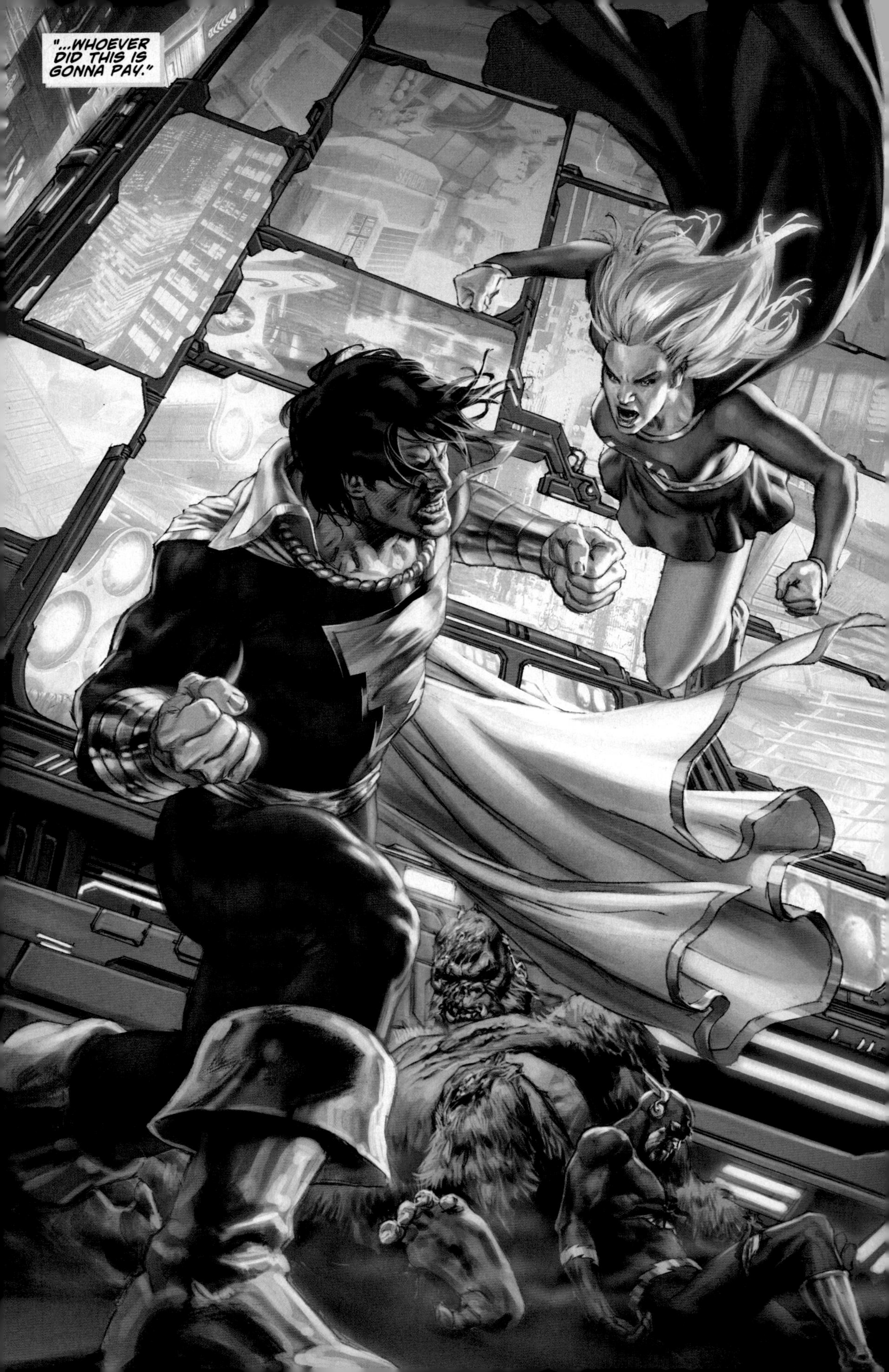
"...WHOEVER DID THIS IS GONNA PAY."

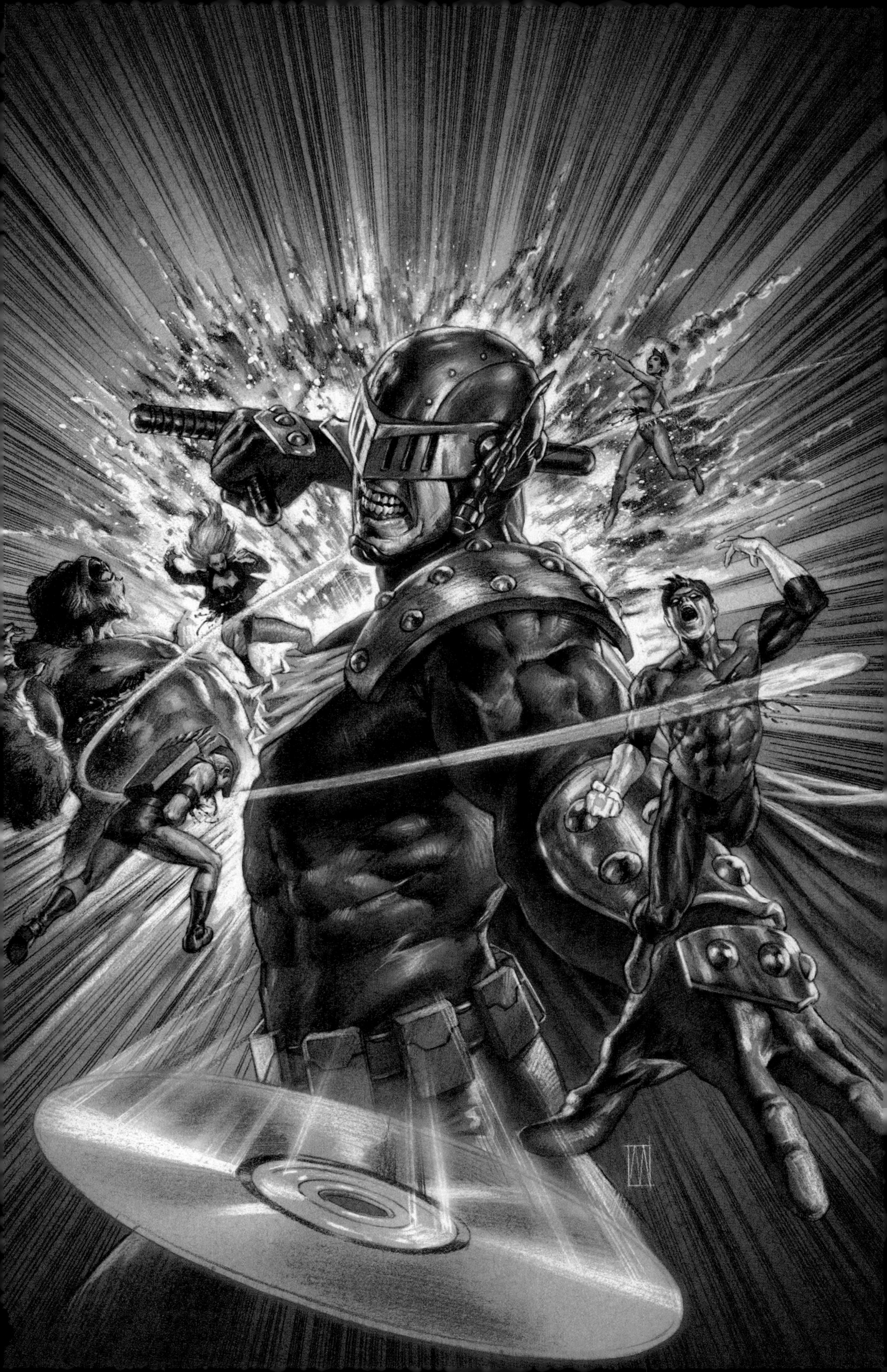

CRY FOR JUSTICE PART SIX: THE GAME

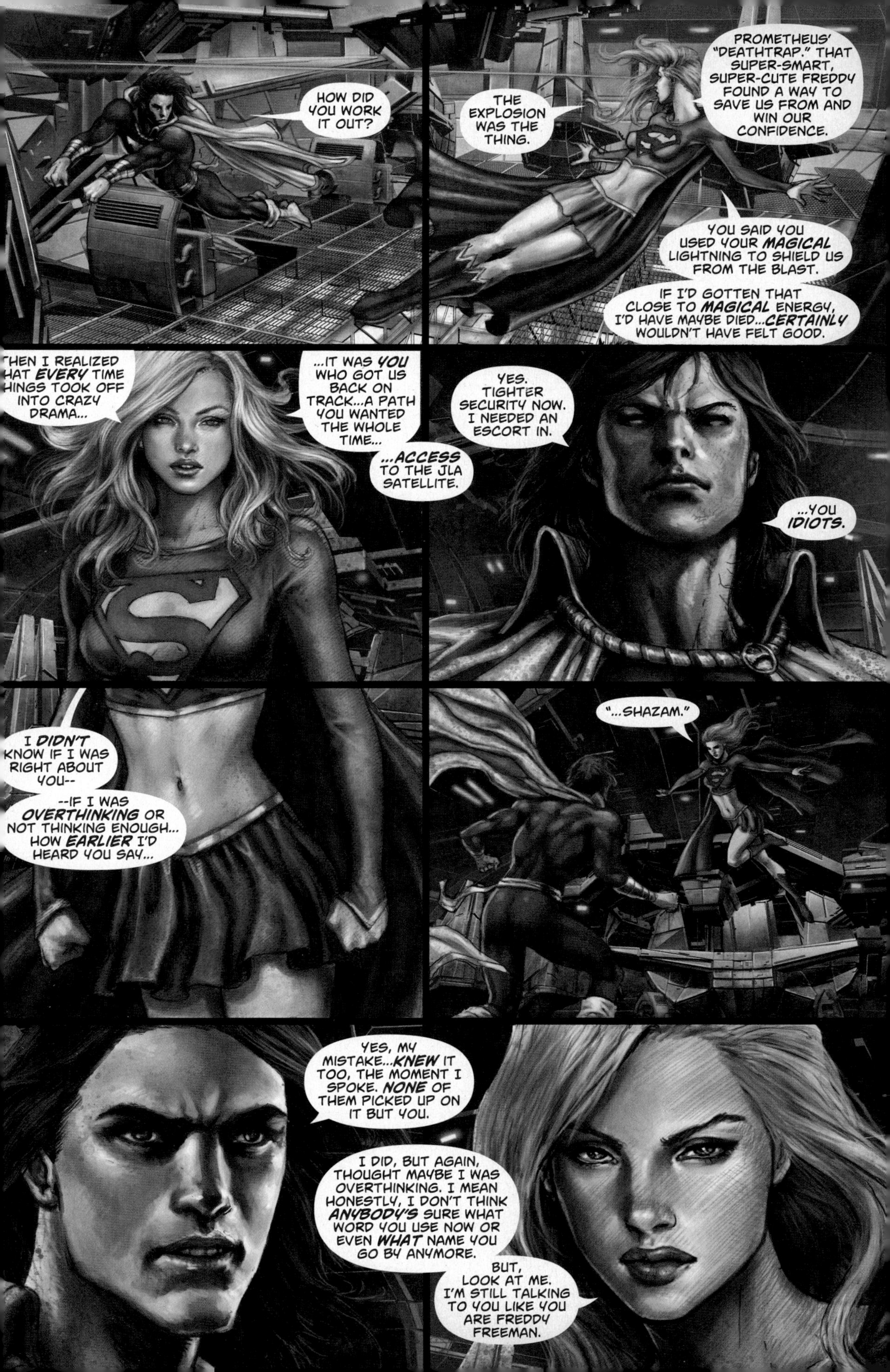

HOW DID YOU WORK IT OUT?
THE EXPLOSION WAS THE THING.
PROMETHEUS' "DEATHTRAP." THAT SUPER-SMART, SUPER-CUTE FREDDY FOUND A WAY TO SAVE US FROM AND WIN OUR CONFIDENCE.
YOU SAID YOU USED YOUR MAGICAL LIGHTNING TO SHIELD US FROM THE BLAST.
IF I'D GOTTEN THAT CLOSE TO MAGICAL ENERGY, I'D HAVE MAYBE DIED...CERTAINLY WOULDN'T HAVE FELT GOOD.
THEN I REALIZED THAT EVERY TIME THINGS TOOK OFF INTO CRAZY DRAMA...
...IT WAS YOU WHO GOT US BACK ON TRACK...A PATH YOU WANTED THE WHOLE TIME...
...ACCESS TO THE JLA SATELLITE.
YES. TIGHTER SECURITY NOW. I NEEDED AN ESCORT IN.
...YOU IDIOTS.
I DIDN'T KNOW IF I WAS RIGHT ABOUT YOU--
--IF I WAS OVERTHINKING OR NOT THINKING ENOUGH... HOW EARLIER I'D HEARD YOU SAY...
"...SHAZAM."
YES, MY MISTAKE...KNEW IT TOO, THE MOMENT I SPOKE. NONE OF THEM PICKED UP ON IT BUT YOU.
I DID, BUT AGAIN, THOUGHT MAYBE I WAS OVERTHINKING. I MEAN HONESTLY, I DON'T THINK ANYBODY'S SURE WHAT WORD YOU USE NOW OR EVEN WHAT NAME YOU GO BY ANYMORE.
BUT, LOOK AT ME. I'M STILL TALKING TO YOU LIKE YOU ARE FREDDY FREEMAN.

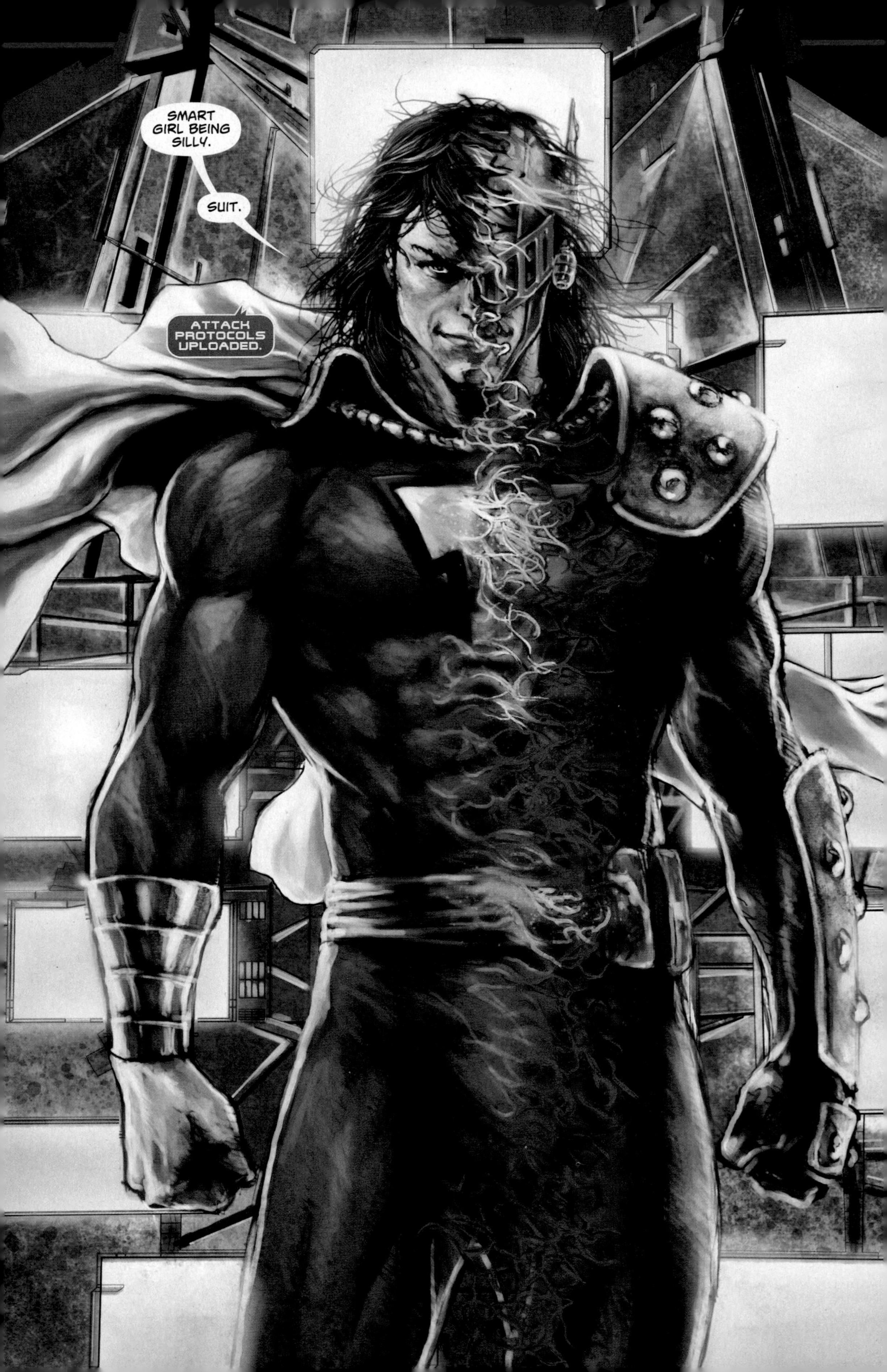
SMART GIRL BEING SILLY.
SUIT.
ATTACK PROTOCOLS UPLOADED.

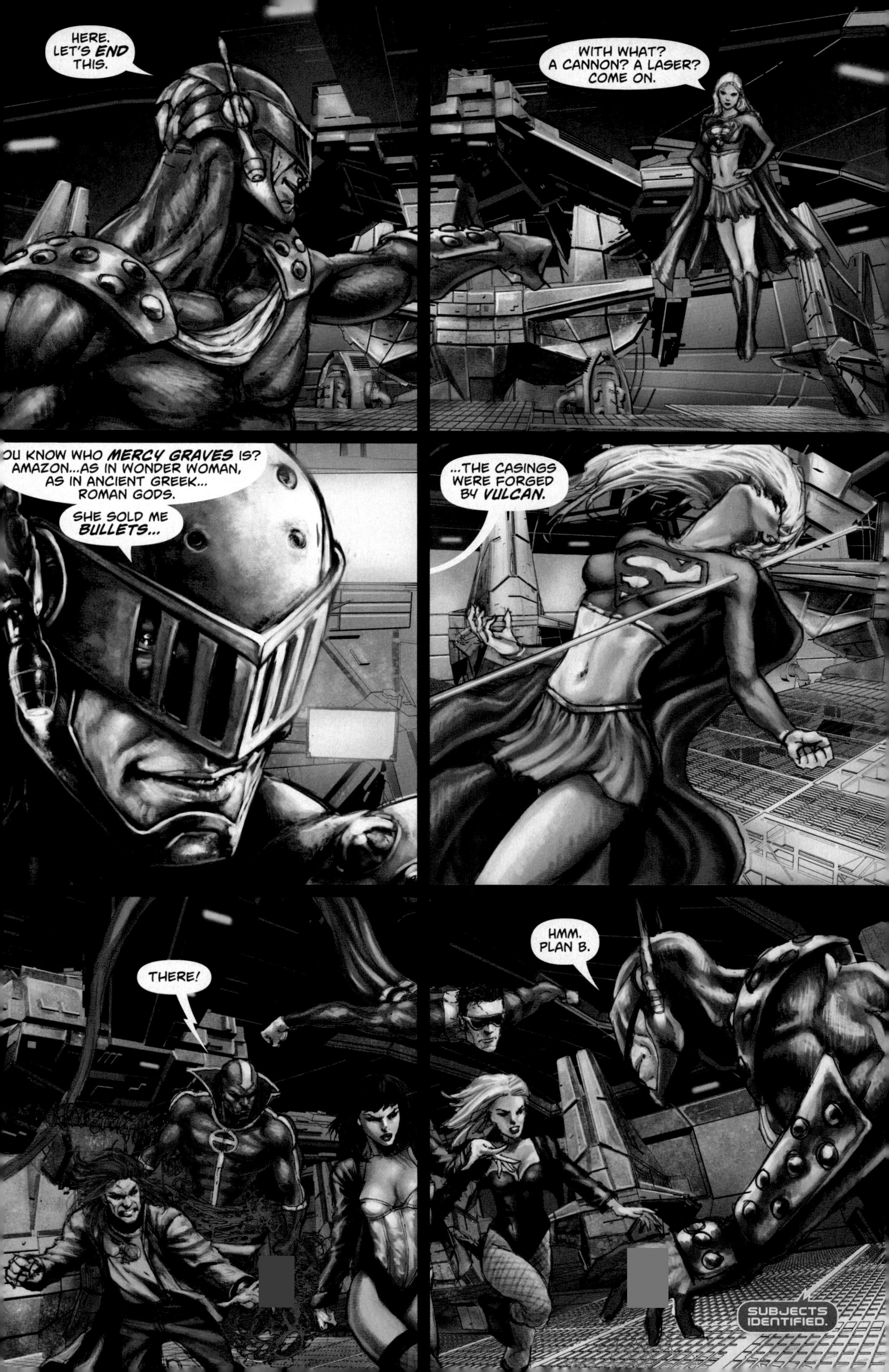
HERE. LET'S END THIS.
WITH WHAT? A CANNON? A LASER? COME ON.
OU KNOW WHO MERCY GRAVES IS? AMAZON...AS IN WONDER WOMAN, AS IN ANCIENT GREEK... ROMAN GODS.
SHE SOLD ME BULLETS...
...THE CASINGS WERE FORGED BY VULCAN.
THERE!
HMM. PLAN B.
SUBJECTS IDENTIFIED.

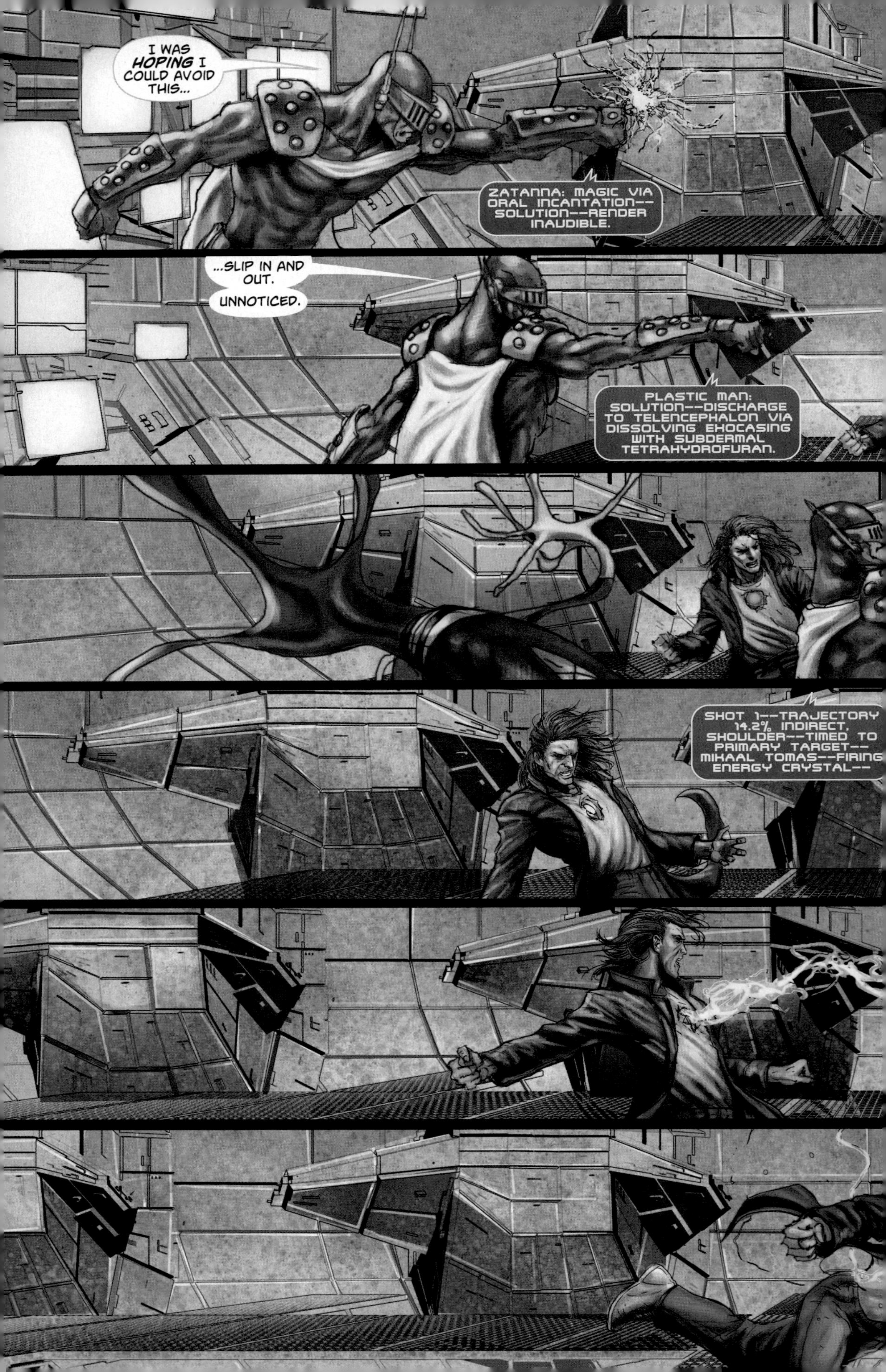
I WAS HOPING I COULD AVOID THIS...
ZATANNA: MAGIC VIA ORAL INCANTATION--SOLUTION--RENDER INAUDIBLE.
...SLIP IN AND OUT.
UNNOTICED.
PLASTIC MAN: SOLUTION--DISCHARGE TO TELENCEPHALON VIA DISSOLVING EXOCASING WITH SUBDERMAL TETRAHYDROFURAN.
SHOT 1--TRAJECTORY 14.2% INDIRECT, SHOULDER--TIMED TO PRIMARY TARGET--MIKAAL TOMAS--FIRING ENERGY CRYSTAL--

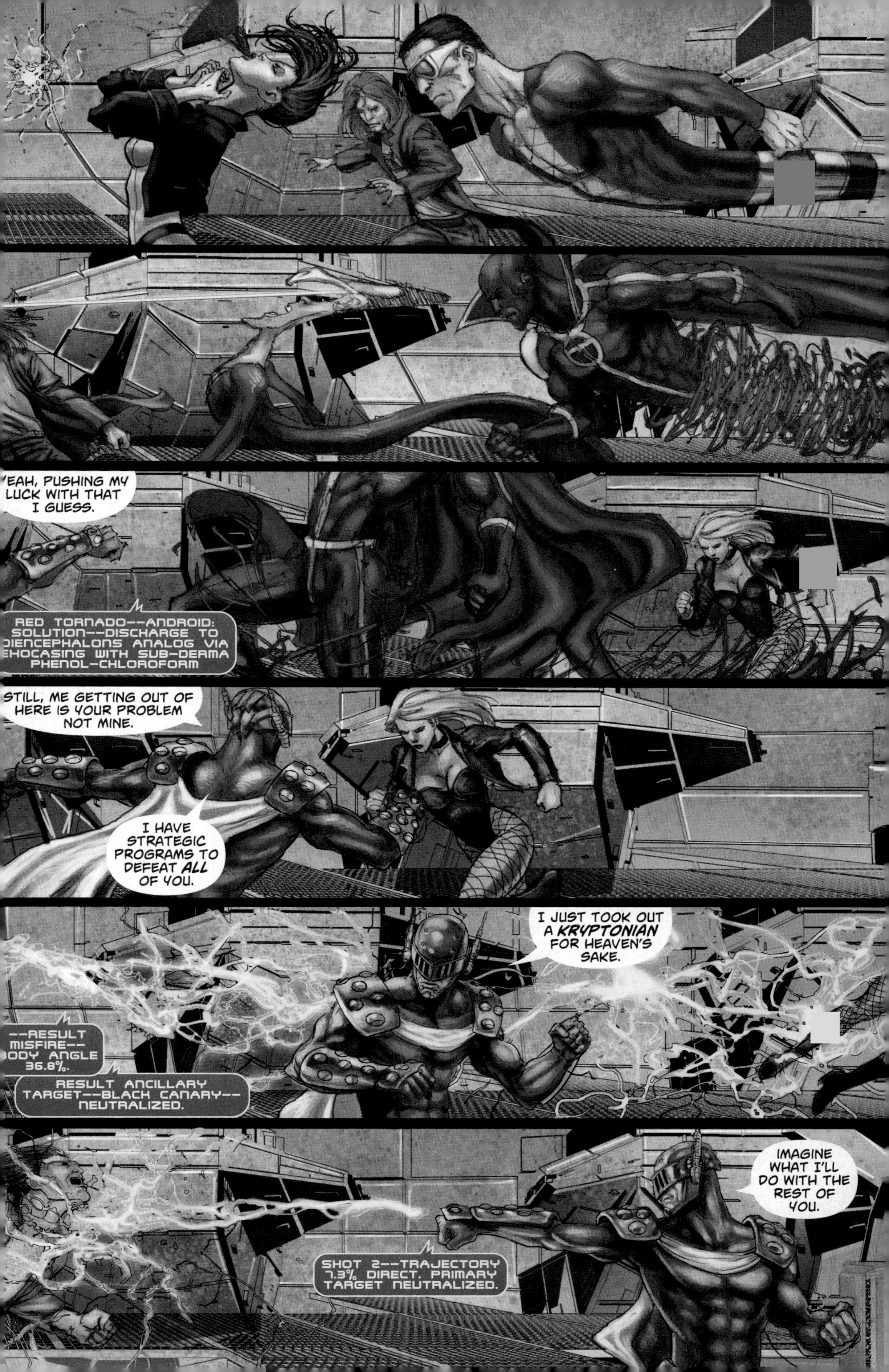
YEAH, PUSHING MY LUCK WITH THAT I GUESS.
RED TORNADO--ANDROID: SOLUTION--DISCHARGE TO DIENCEPHALONS ANALOG VIA EHOCASING WITH SUB-DERMA PHENOL-CHLOROFORM
STILL, ME GETTING OUT OF HERE IS YOUR PROBLEM NOT MINE.
I HAVE STRATEGIC PROGRAMS TO DEFEAT ALL OF YOU.
I JUST TOOK OUT A KRYPTONIAN FOR HEAVEN'S SAKE.
--RESULT MISFIRE--BODY ANGLE 36.8%.
RESULT ANCILLARY TARGET--BLACK CANARY--NEUTRALIZED.
IMAGINE WHAT I'LL DO WITH THE REST OF YOU.
SHOT 2--TRAJECTORY 7.3% DIRECT. PRIMARY TARGET NEUTRALIZED.

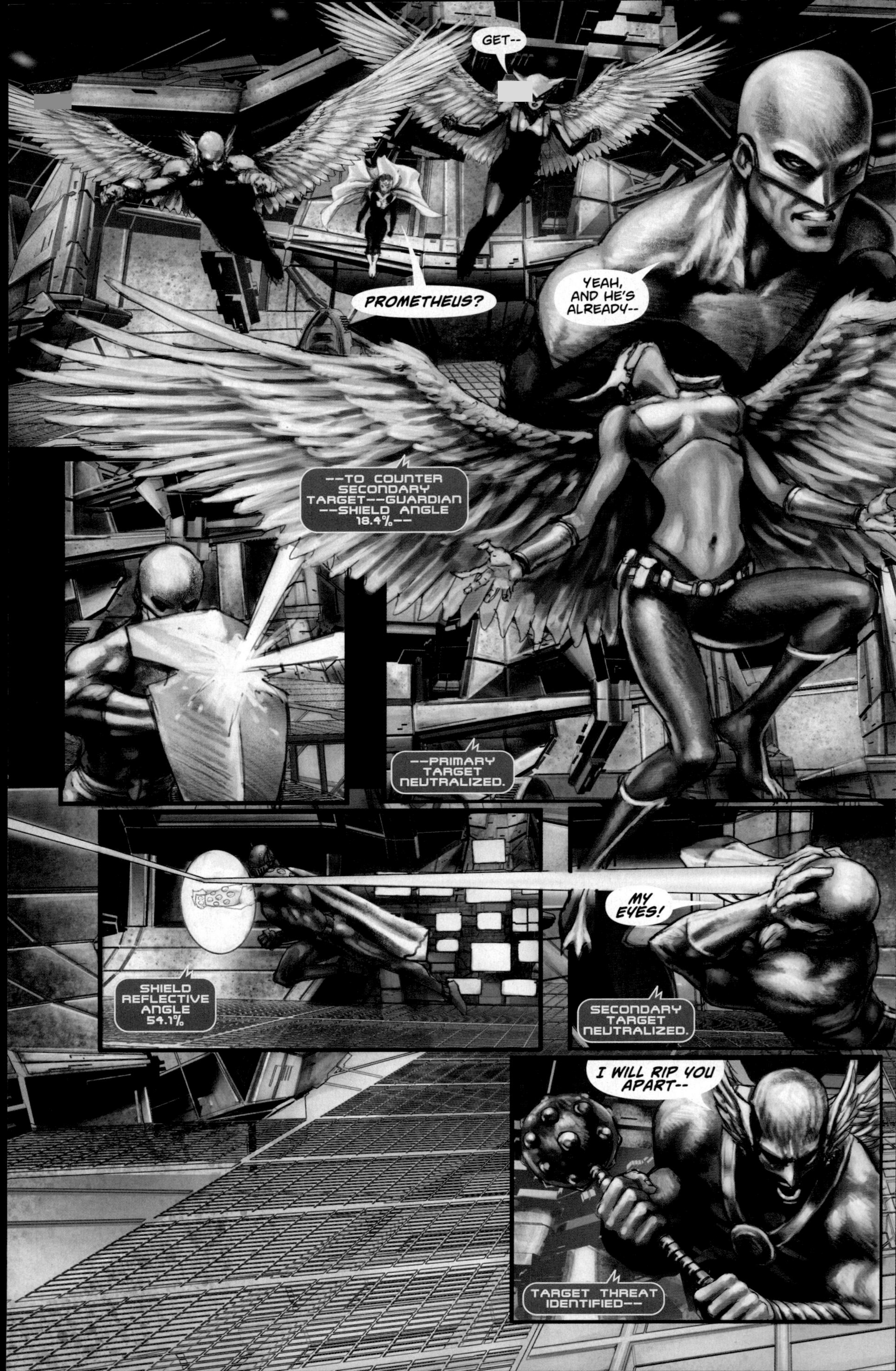
GET--
PROMETHEUS?
YEAH, AND HE'S ALREADY--
--TO COUNTER SECONDARY TARGET--GUARDIAN --SHIELD ANGLE 18.4%--
--PRIMARY TARGET NEUTRALIZED.
SHIELD REFLECTIVE ANGLE 54.1%
MY EYES!
SECONDARY TARGET NEUTRALIZED.
I WILL RIP YOU APART--
TARGET THREAT IDENTIFIED--

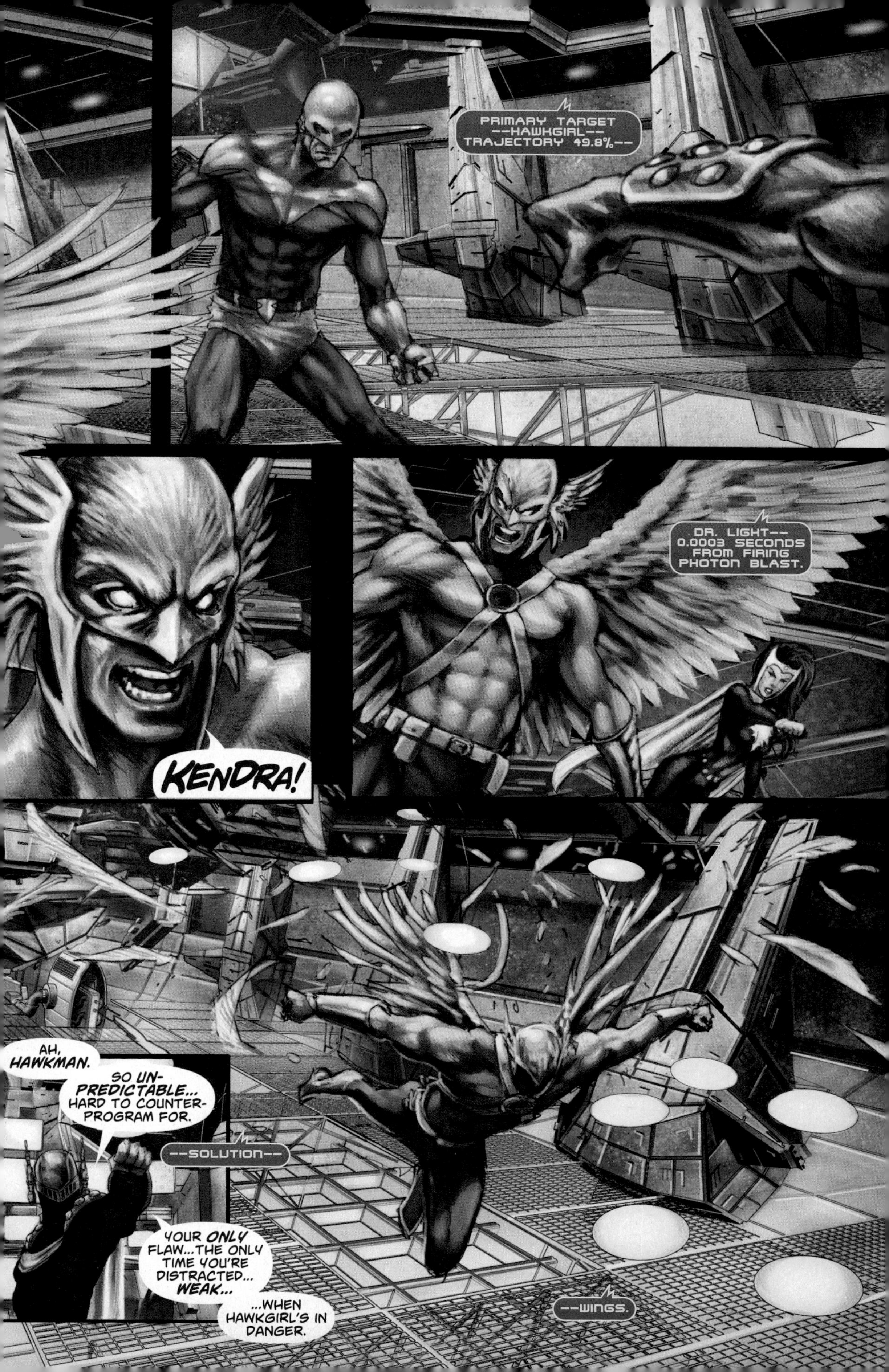
PRIMARY TARGET
--HAWKGIRL--
TRAJECTORY 49.8%--
KENDRA!
DR. LIGHT--
0.0003 SECONDS
FROM FIRING
PHOTON BLAST.
AH, HAWKMAN.
SO UN-PREDICTABLE... HARD TO COUNTER-PROGRAM FOR.
--SOLUTION--
YOUR ONLY FLAW...THE ONLY TIME YOU'RE DISTRACTED... WEAK...
...WHEN HAWKGIRL'S IN DANGER.
--WINGS.

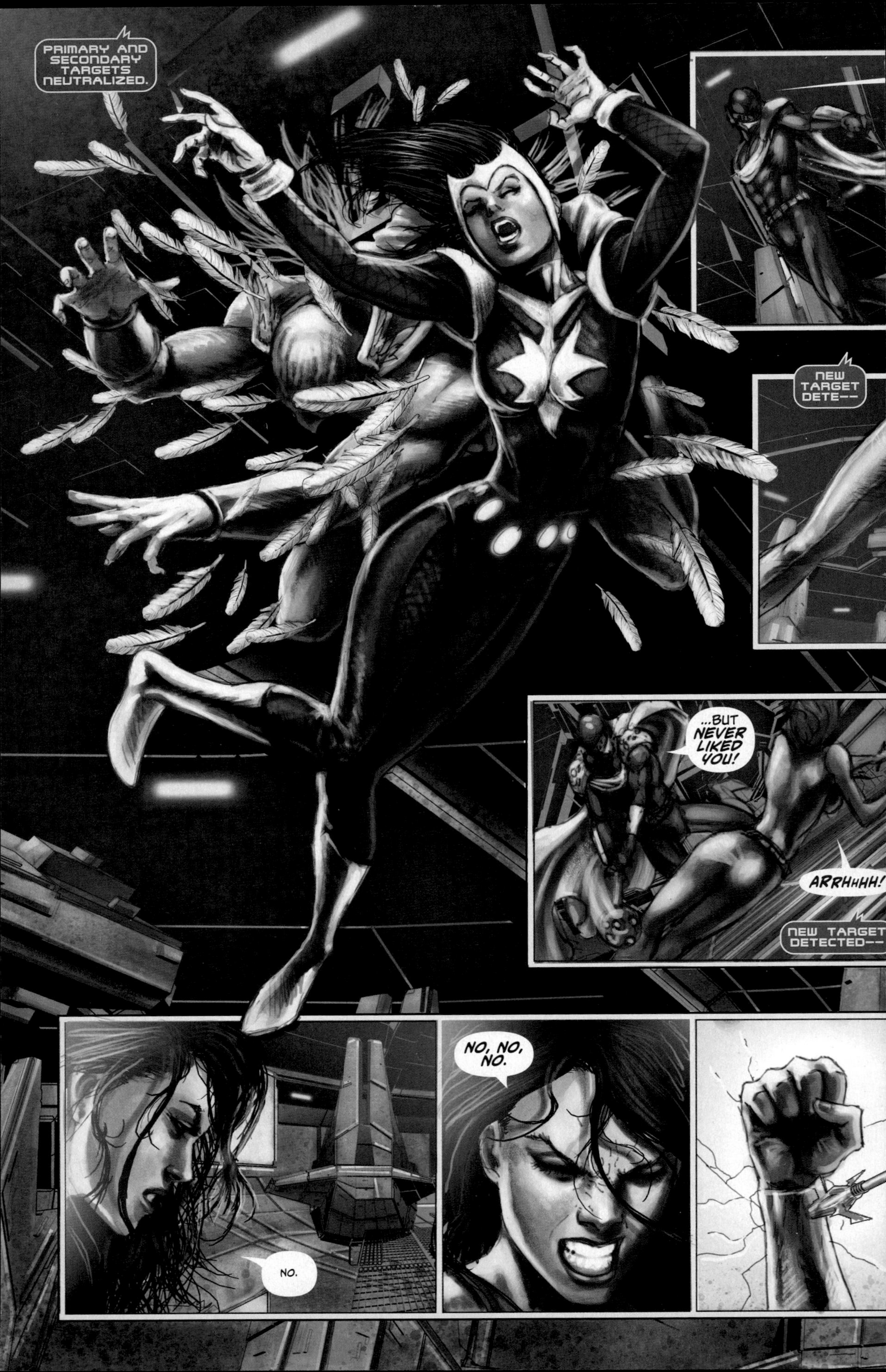
PRIMARY AND SECONDARY TARGETS NEUTRALIZED.
NEW TARGET DETE--
...BUT NEVER LIKED YOU!
ARRHHHH!
NEW TARGET DETECTED--
NO.
NO, NO, NO.

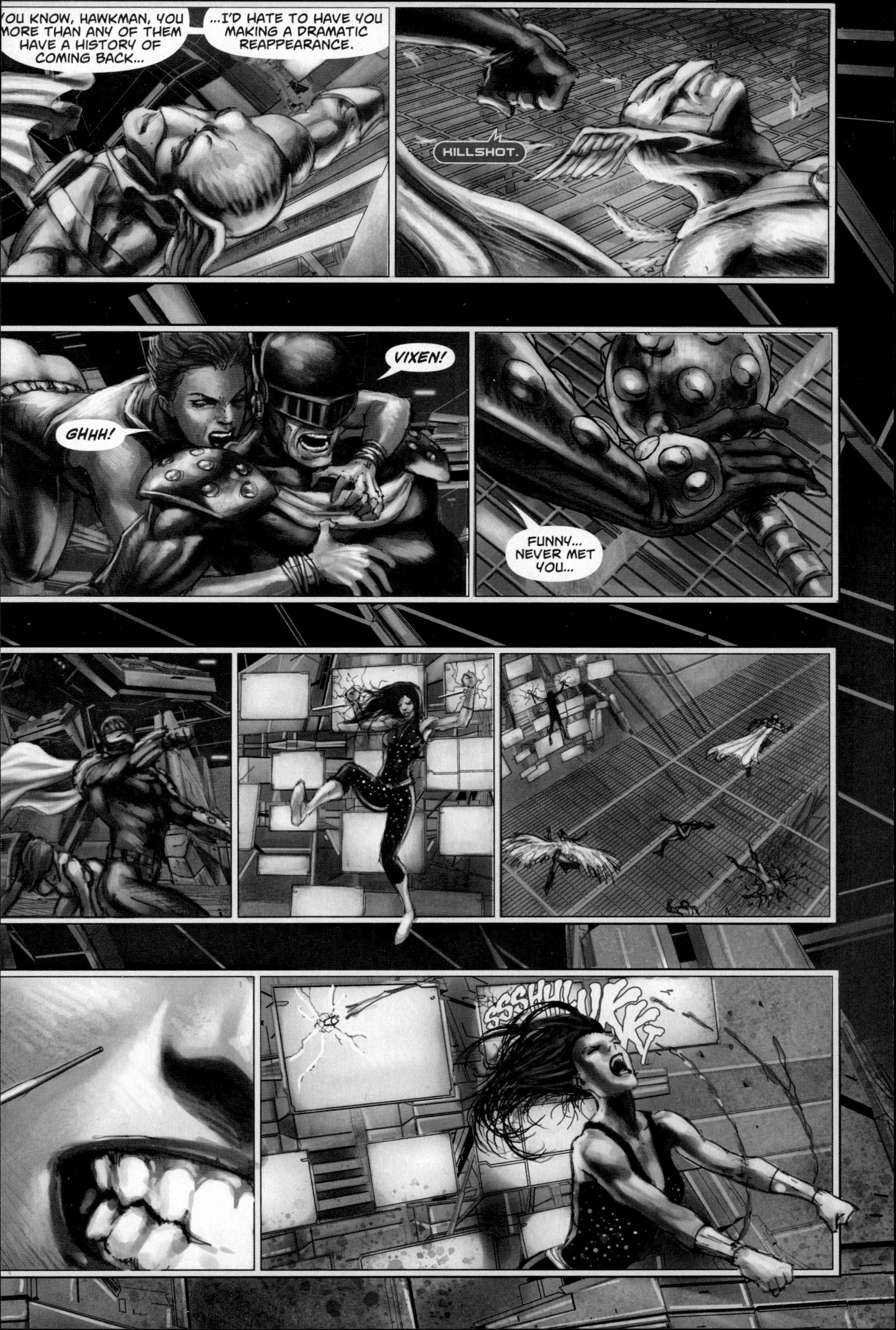
YOU KNOW, HAWKMAN, YOU MORE THAN ANY OF THEM HAVE A HISTORY OF COMING BACK...
...I'D HATE TO HAVE YOU MAKING A DRAMATIC REAPPEARANCE.
KILLSHOT.
VIXEN!
GHHH!
FUNNY... NEVER MET YOU...
SSSHULUKK

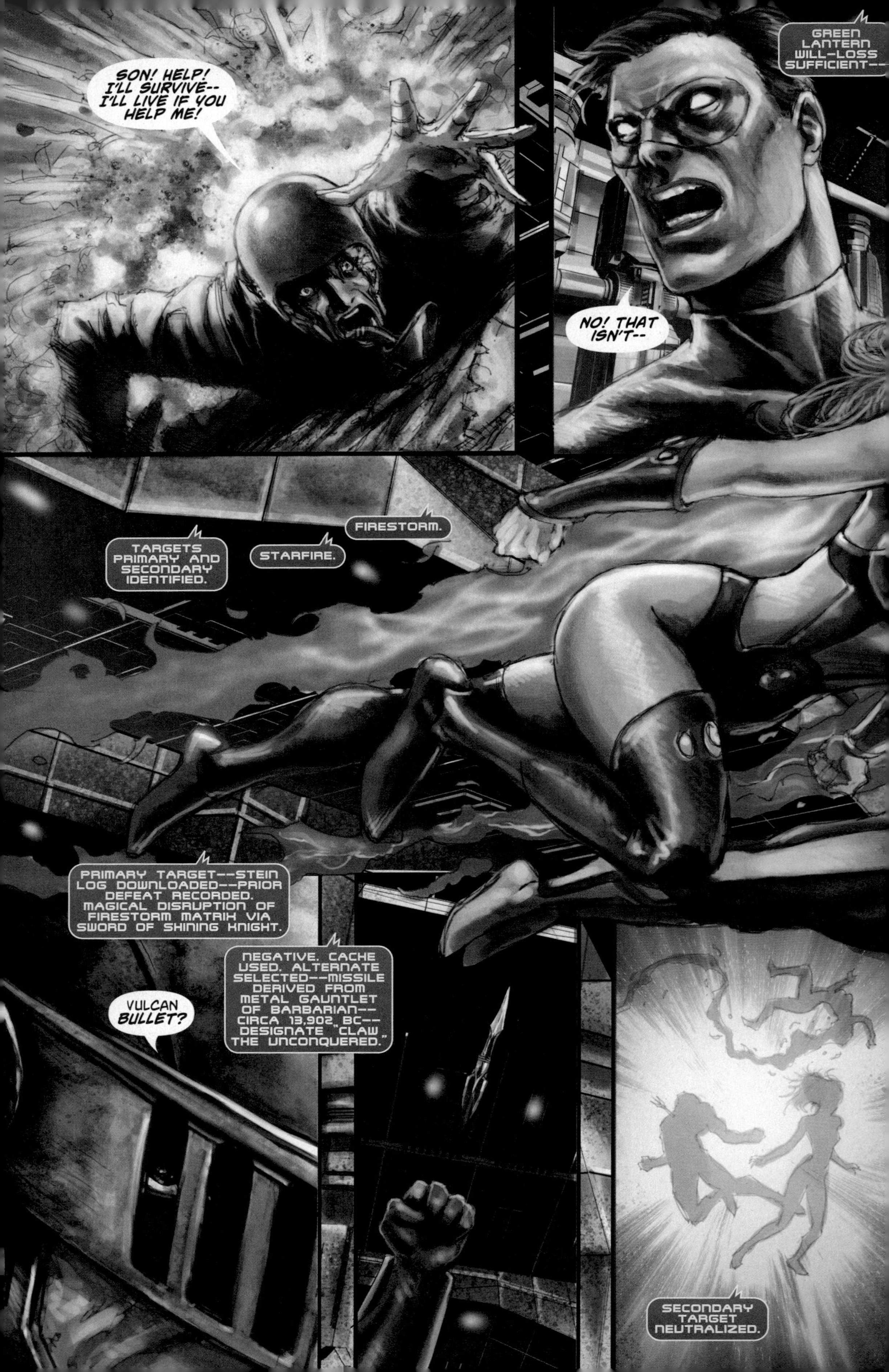
SON! HELP! I'LL SURVIVE-- I'LL LIVE IF YOU HELP ME!
GREEN LANTERN WILL-LOSS SUFFICIENT--
NO! THAT ISN'T--
TARGETS PRIMARY AND SECONDARY IDENTIFIED.
STARFIRE.
FIRESTORM.
PRIMARY TARGET--STEIN LOG DOWNLOADED--PRIOR DEFEAT RECORDED. MAGICAL DISRUPTION OF FIRESTORM MATRIX VIA SWORD OF SHINING KNIGHT.
VULCAN BULLET?
NEGATIVE. CACHE USED. ALTERNATE SELECTED--MISSILE DERIVED FROM METAL GAUNTLET OF BARBARIAN-- CIRCA 13,902 BC-- DESIGNATE "CLAW THE UNCONQUERED."
SECONDARY TARGET NEUTRALIZED.

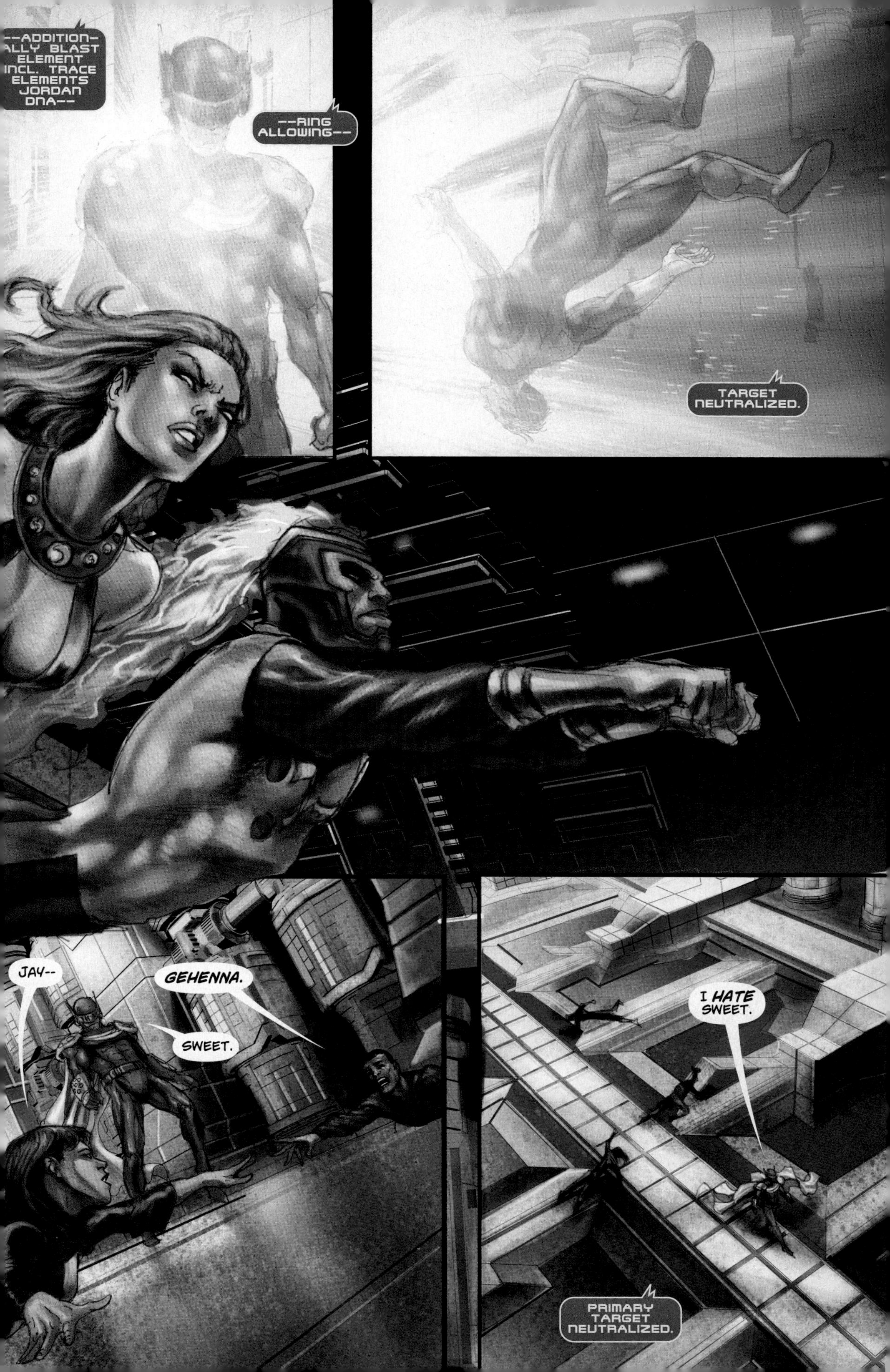

--ADDITION-ALLY BLAST ELEMENT INCL. TRACE ELEMENTS JORDAN DNA--
--RING ALLOWING--
TARGET NEUTRALIZED.
JAY--
GEHENNA.
SWEET.
I HATE SWEET.
PRIMARY TARGET NEUTRALIZED.

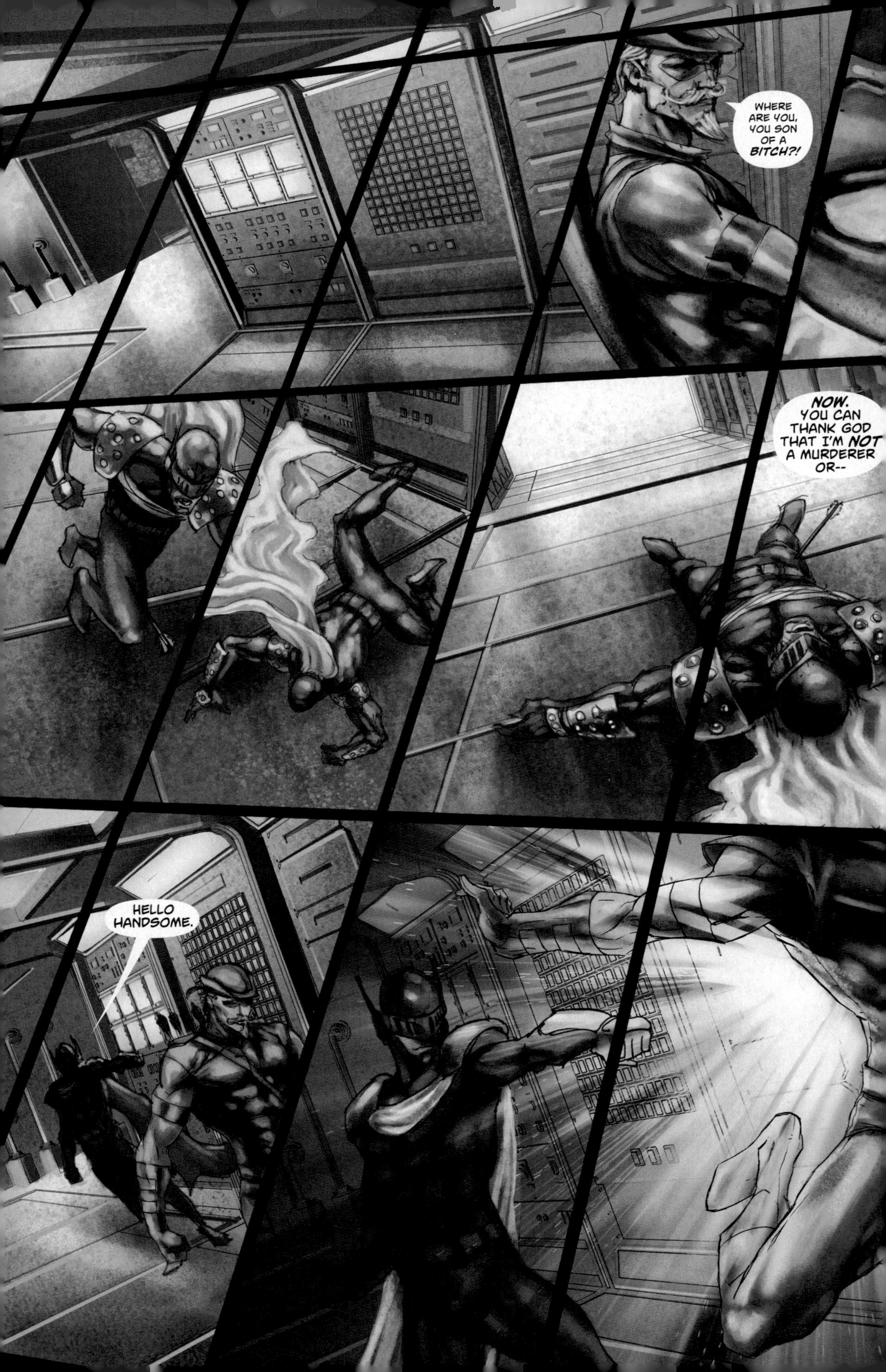
WHERE ARE YOU, YOU SON OF A BITCH?!
NOW. YOU CAN THANK GOD THAT I'M NOT A MURDERER OR--
HELLO HANDSOME.

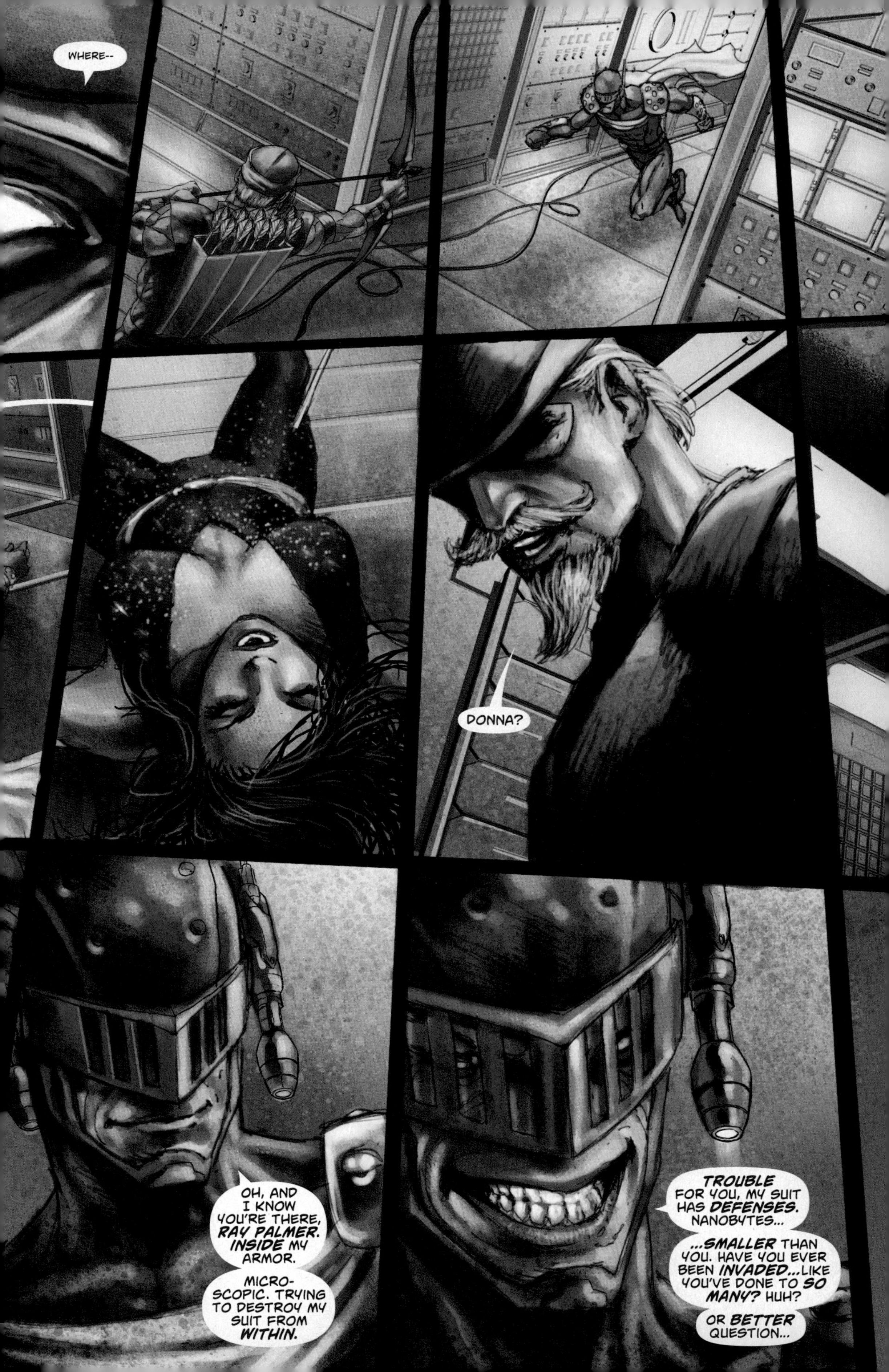
WHERE--
DONNA?
OH, AND I KNOW YOU'RE THERE, RAY PALMER. INSIDE MY ARMOR.
MICRO-SCOPIC. TRYING TO DESTROY MY SUIT FROM WITHIN.
TROUBLE FOR YOU, MY SUIT HAS DEFENSES. NANOBYTES...
...SMALLER THAN YOU. HAVE YOU EVER BEEN INVADED...LIKE YOU'VE DONE TO SO MANY? HUH?
OR BETTER QUESTION...

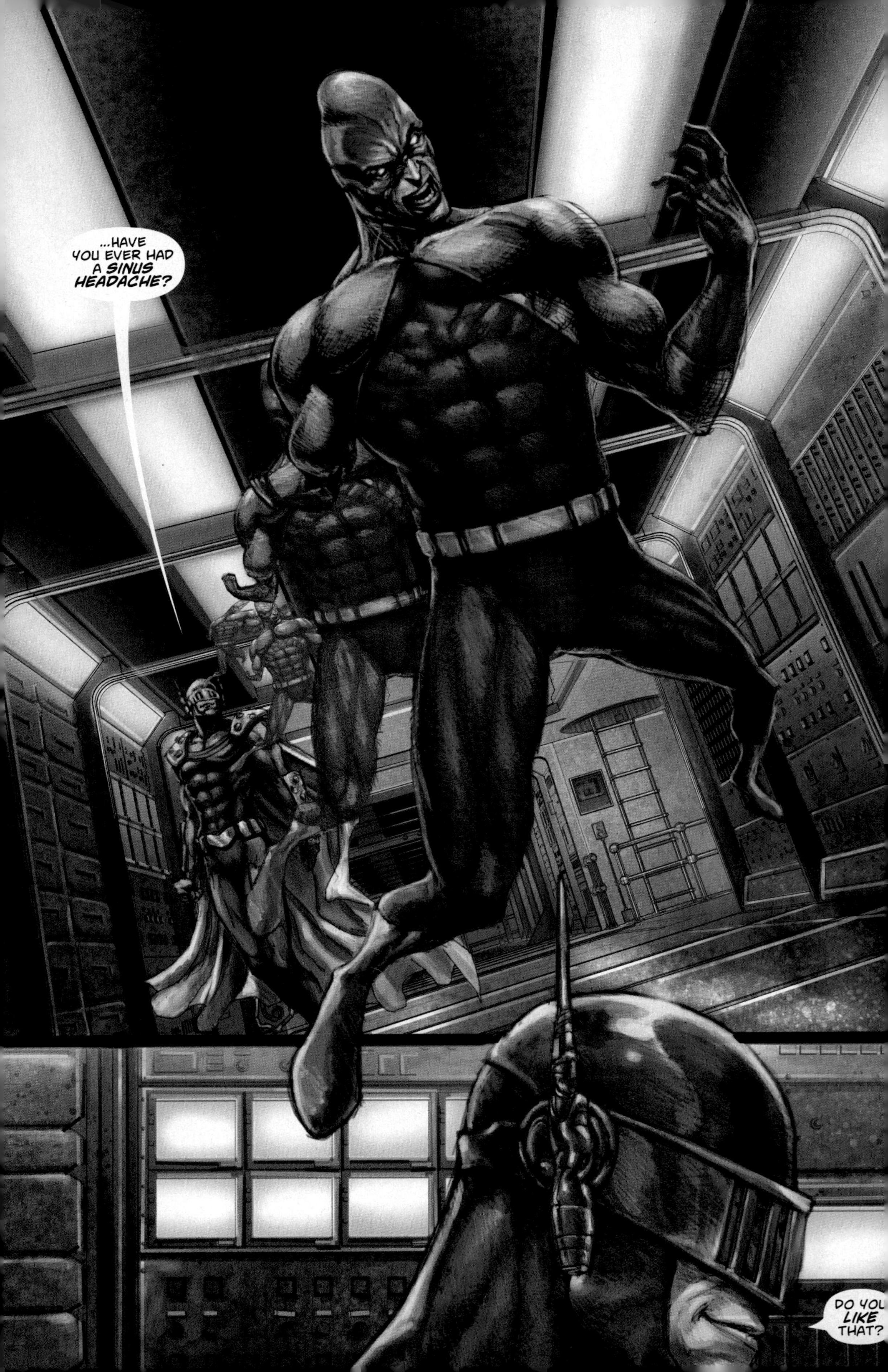
...HAVE YOU EVER HAD A SINUS HEADACHE?
DO YOU LIKE THAT?

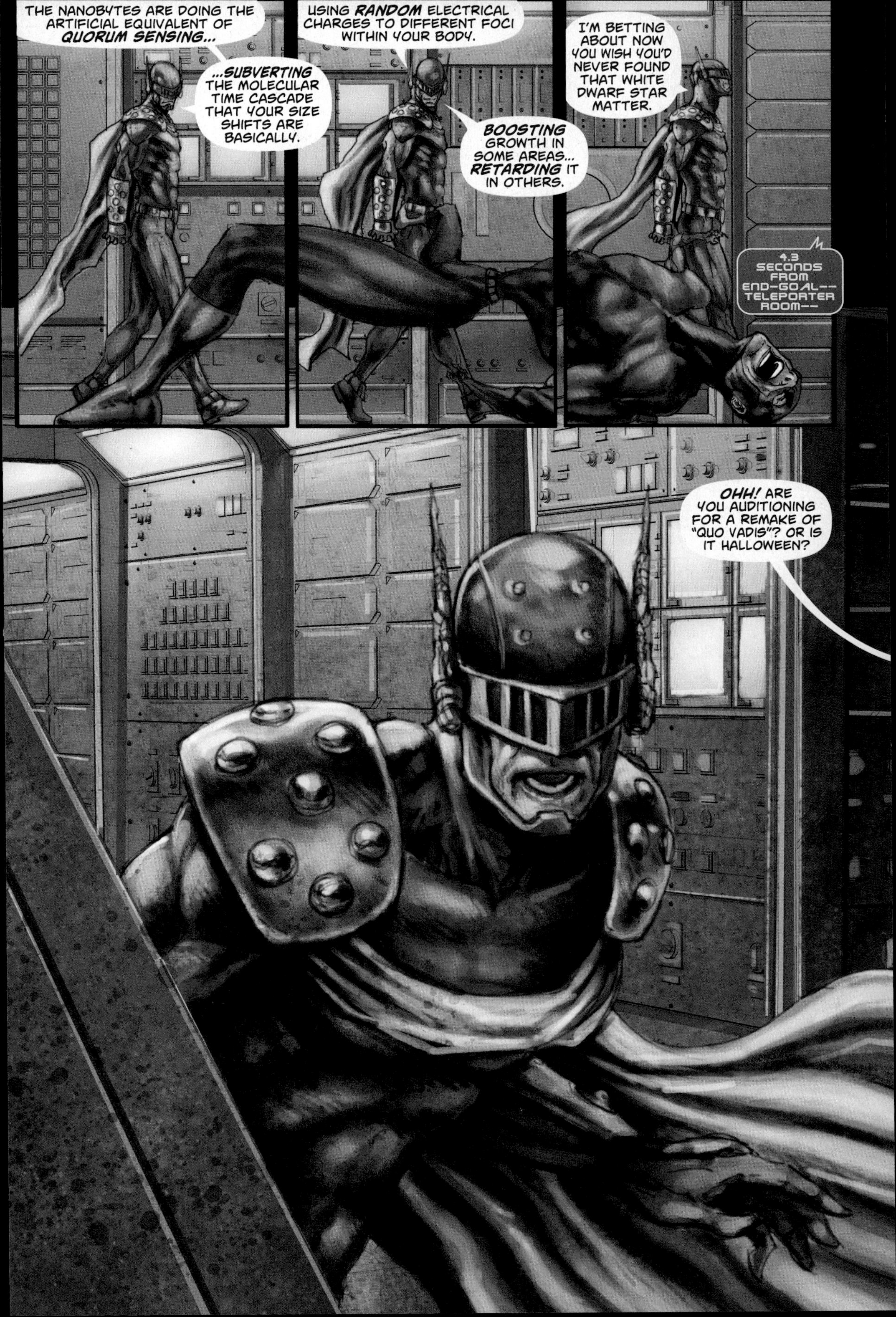
THE NANOBYTES ARE DOING THE ARTIFICIAL EQUIVALENT OF QUORUM SENSING...
...SUBVERTING THE MOLECULAR TIME CASCADE THAT YOUR SIZE SHIFTS ARE BASICALLY.
USING RANDOM ELECTRICAL CHARGES TO DIFFERENT FOCI WITHIN YOUR BODY.
BOOSTING GROWTH IN SOME AREAS... RETARDING IT IN OTHERS.
I'M BETTING ABOUT NOW YOU WISH YOU'D NEVER FOUND THAT WHITE DWARF STAR MATTER.
4.3 SECONDS FROM END-GOAL-- TELEPORTER ROOM--
OHH! ARE YOU AUDITIONING FOR A REMAKE OF "QUO VADIS"? OR IS IT HALLOWEEN?

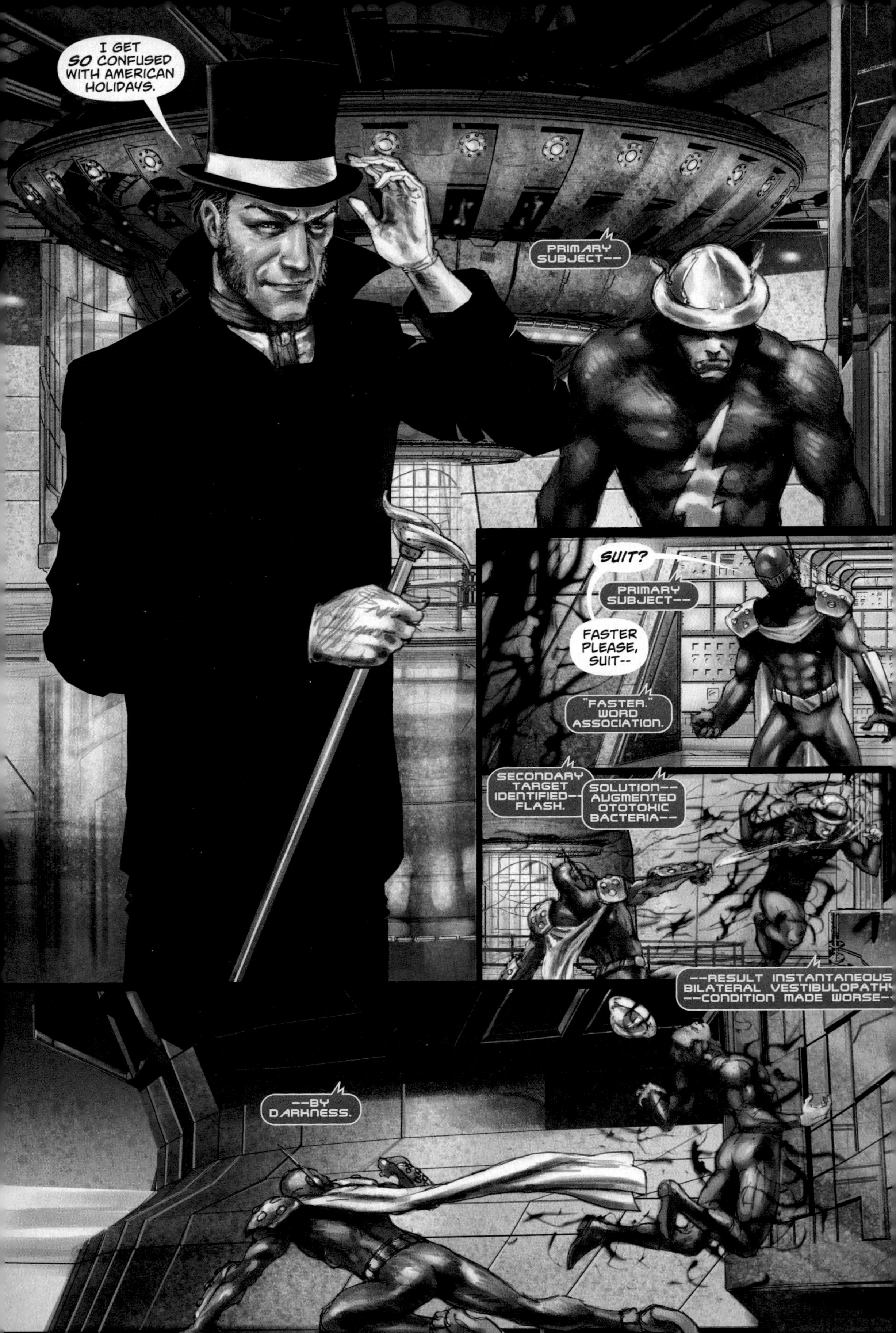
I GET SO CONFUSED WITH AMERICAN HOLIDAYS.
PRIMARY SUBJECT--
SUIT?
PRIMARY SUBJECT--
FASTER PLEASE, SUIT--
"FASTER." WORD ASSOCIATION.
SECONDARY TARGET IDENTIFIED-- FLASH.
SOLUTION-- AUGMENTED OTOTOXIC BACTERIA--
--RESULT INSTANTANEOUS BILATERAL VESTIBULOPATHY --CONDITION MADE WORSE--
--BY DARKNESS.

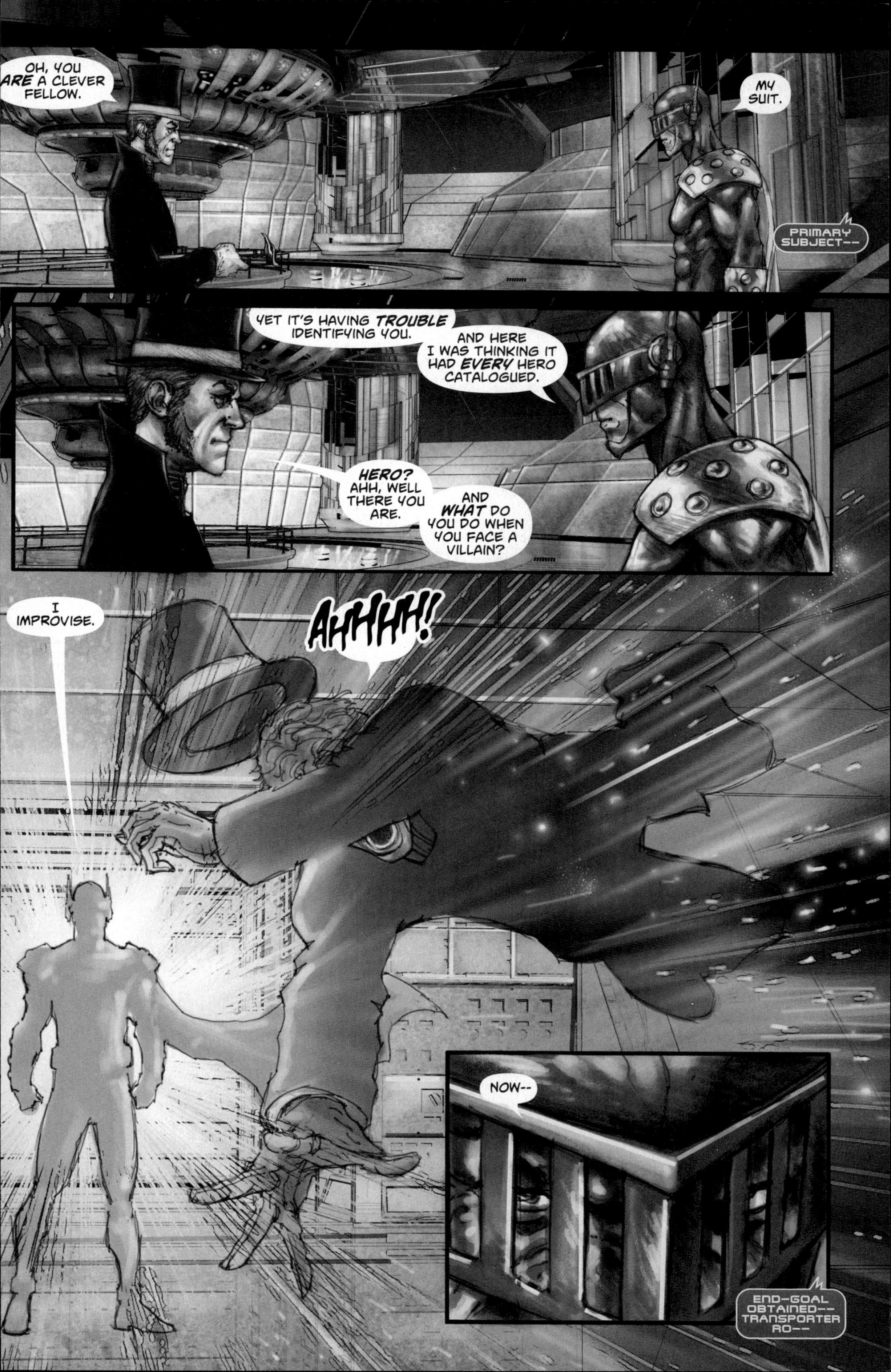

OH, YOU ARE A CLEVER FELLOW.
MY SUIT.
PRIMARY SUBJECT--
YET IT'S HAVING TROUBLE IDENTIFYING YOU.
AND HERE I WAS THINKING IT HAD EVERY HERO CATALOGUED.
HERO? AHH, WELL THERE YOU ARE.
AND WHAT DO YOU DO WHEN YOU FACE A VILLAIN?
I IMPROVISE.
AHHHH!
NOW--
END-GOAL OBTAINED-- TRANSPORTER RO--

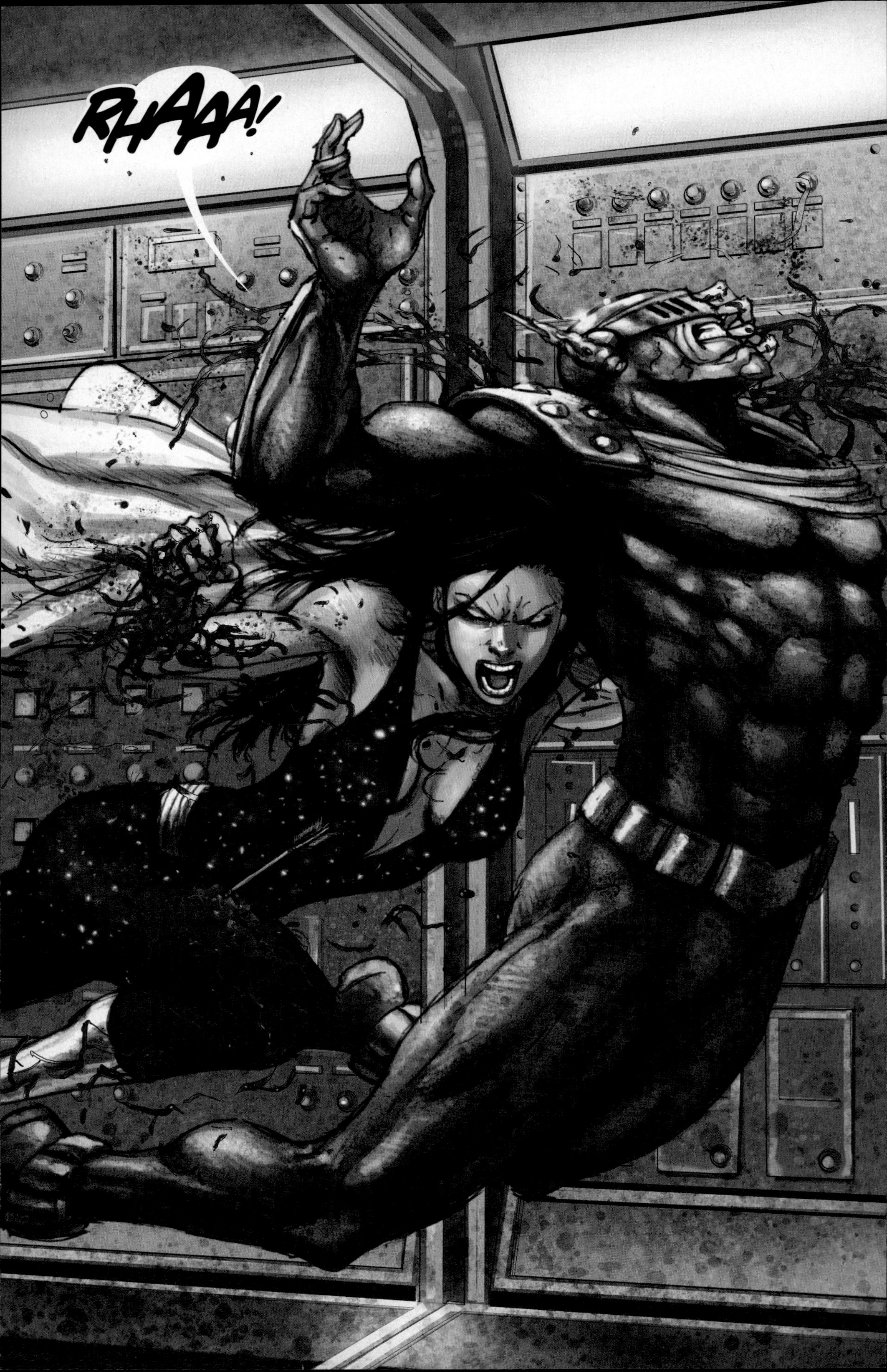
RHAAA!

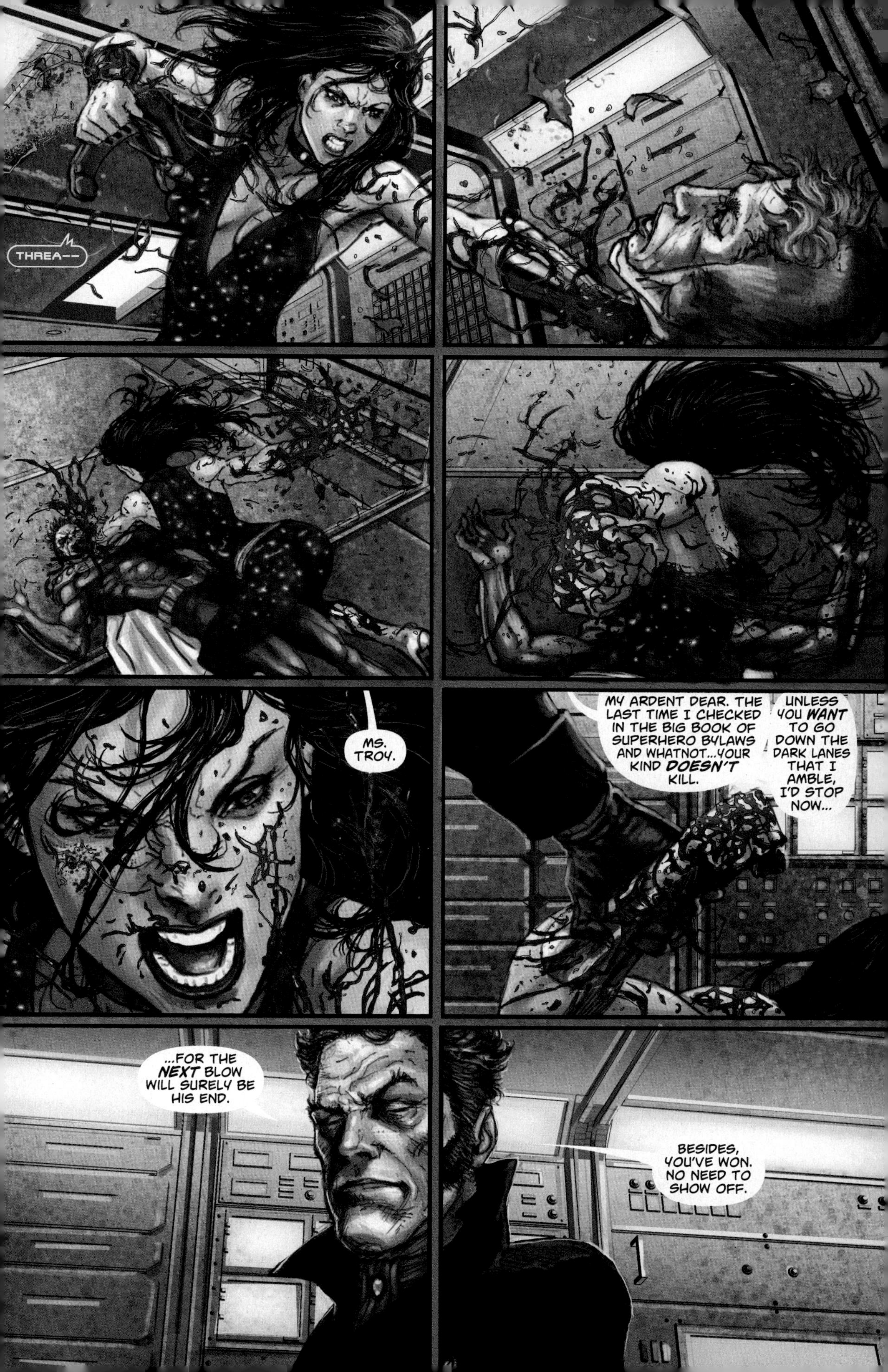
THREA--
MS. TROY.
MY ARDENT DEAR. THE LAST TIME I CHECKED IN THE BIG BOOK OF SUPERHERO BYLAWS AND WHATNOT...YOUR KIND DOESN'T KILL.
UNLESS YOU WANT TO GO DOWN THE DARK LANES THAT I AMBLE, I'D STOP NOW...
...FOR THE NEXT BLOW WILL SURELY BE HIS END.
BESIDES, YOU'VE WON. NO NEED TO SHOW OFF.

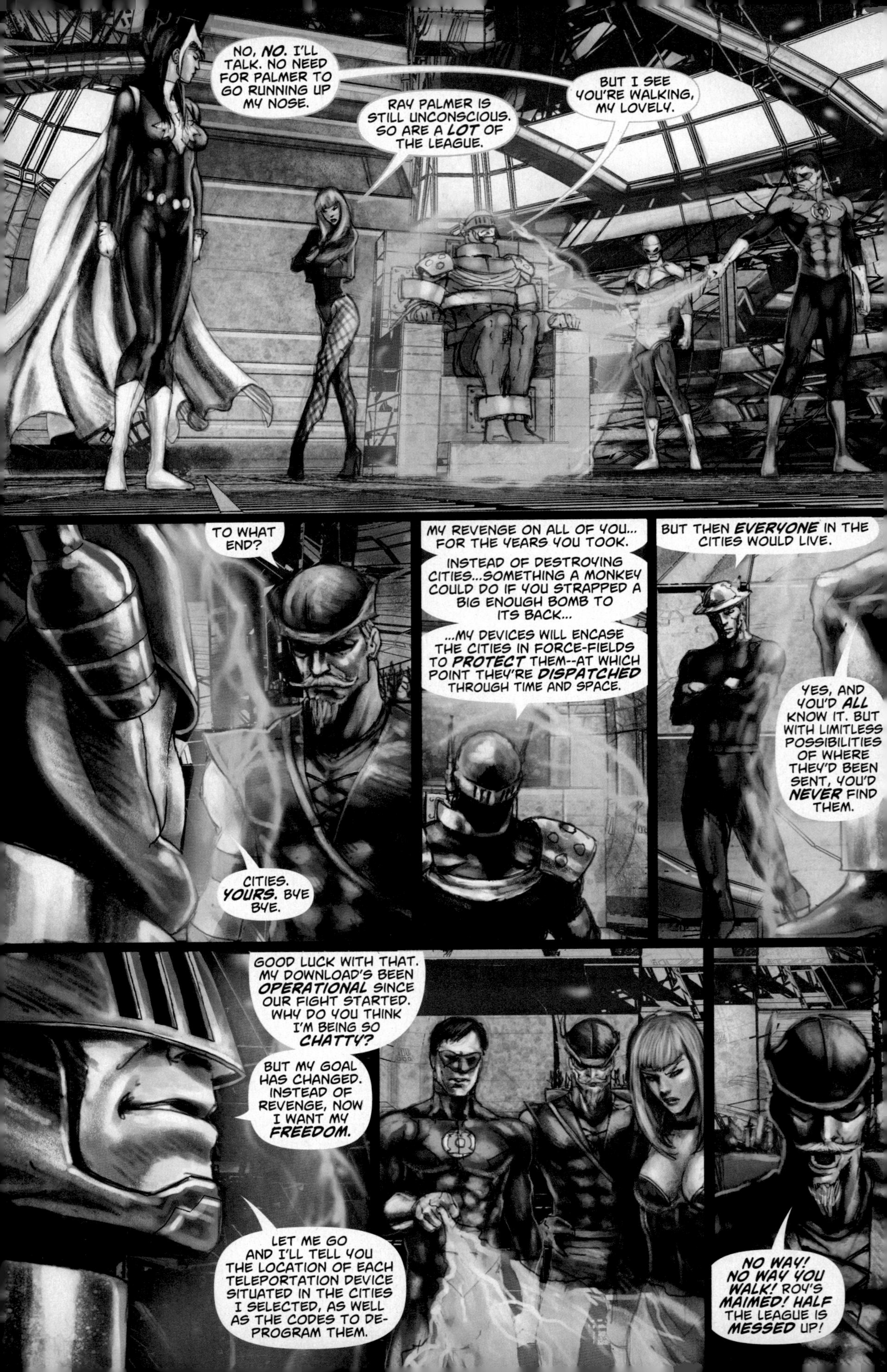

NO, **NO.** I'LL TALK. NO NEED FOR PALMER TO GO RUNNING UP MY NOSE.
RAY PALMER IS STILL UNCONSCIOUS. SO ARE A **LOT** OF THE LEAGUE.
BUT I SEE YOU'RE WALKING, MY LOVELY.
TO WHAT END?
CITIES. **YOURS.** BYE BYE.
MY REVENGE ON ALL OF YOU... FOR THE YEARS YOU TOOK.
INSTEAD OF DESTROYING CITIES...SOMETHING A MONKEY COULD DO IF YOU STRAPPED A BIG ENOUGH BOMB TO ITS BACK...
...MY DEVICES WILL ENCASE THE CITIES IN FORCE-FIELDS TO **PROTECT** THEM--AT WHICH POINT THEY'RE **DISPATCHED** THROUGH TIME AND SPACE.
BUT THEN **EVERYONE** IN THE CITIES WOULD LIVE.
YES, AND YOU'D **ALL** KNOW IT. BUT WITH LIMITLESS POSSIBILITIES OF WHERE THEY'D BEEN SENT, YOU'D **NEVER** FIND THEM.
GOOD LUCK WITH THAT. MY DOWNLOAD'S BEEN **OPERATIONAL** SINCE OUR FIGHT STARTED. WHY DO YOU THINK I'M BEING SO **CHATTY?**
BUT MY GOAL HAS CHANGED. INSTEAD OF REVENGE, NOW I WANT MY **FREEDOM.**
LET ME GO AND I'LL TELL YOU THE LOCATION OF EACH TELEPORTATION DEVICE SITUATED IN THE CITIES I SELECTED, AS WELL AS THE CODES TO DE-PROGRAM THEM.
NO WAY! NO WAY YOU WALK! ROY'S **MAIMED! HALF** THE LEAGUE IS **MESSED** UP!

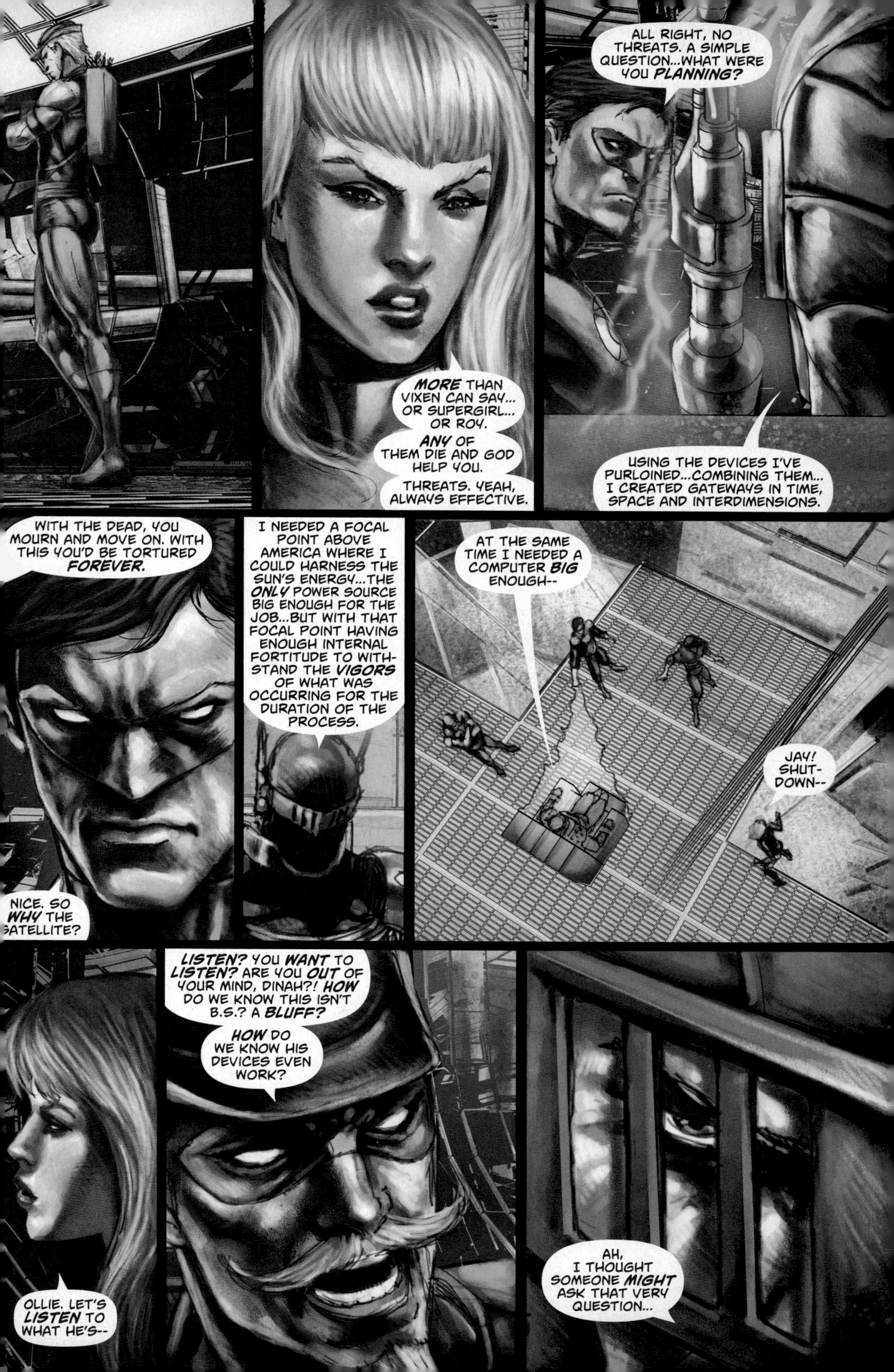
MORE THAN VIXEN CAN SAY... OR SUPERGIRL... OR ROY.
ANY OF THEM DIE AND GOD HELP YOU.
THREATS. YEAH, ALWAYS EFFECTIVE.
ALL RIGHT, NO THREATS. A SIMPLE QUESTION...WHAT WERE YOU PLANNING?
USING THE DEVICES I'VE PURLOINED...COMBINING THEM... I CREATED GATEWAYS IN TIME, SPACE AND INTERDIMENSIONS.
WITH THE DEAD, YOU MOURN AND MOVE ON. WITH THIS YOU'D BE TORTURED FOREVER.
NICE. SO WHY THE SATELLITE?
I NEEDED A FOCAL POINT ABOVE AMERICA WHERE I COULD HARNESS THE SUN'S ENERGY...THE ONLY POWER SOURCE BIG ENOUGH FOR THE JOB...BUT WITH THAT FOCAL POINT HAVING ENOUGH INTERNAL FORTITUDE TO WITH-STAND THE VIGORS OF WHAT WAS OCCURRING FOR THE DURATION OF THE PROCESS.
AT THE SAME TIME I NEEDED A COMPUTER BIG ENOUGH--
JAY! SHUT-DOWN--
OLLIE. LET'S LISTEN TO WHAT HE'S--
LISTEN? YOU WANT TO LISTEN? ARE YOU OUT OF YOUR MIND, DINAH?! HOW DO WE KNOW THIS ISN'T B.S.? A BLUFF?
HOW DO WE KNOW HIS DEVICES EVEN WORK?
AH, I THOUGHT SOMEONE MIGHT ASK THAT VERY QUESTION...

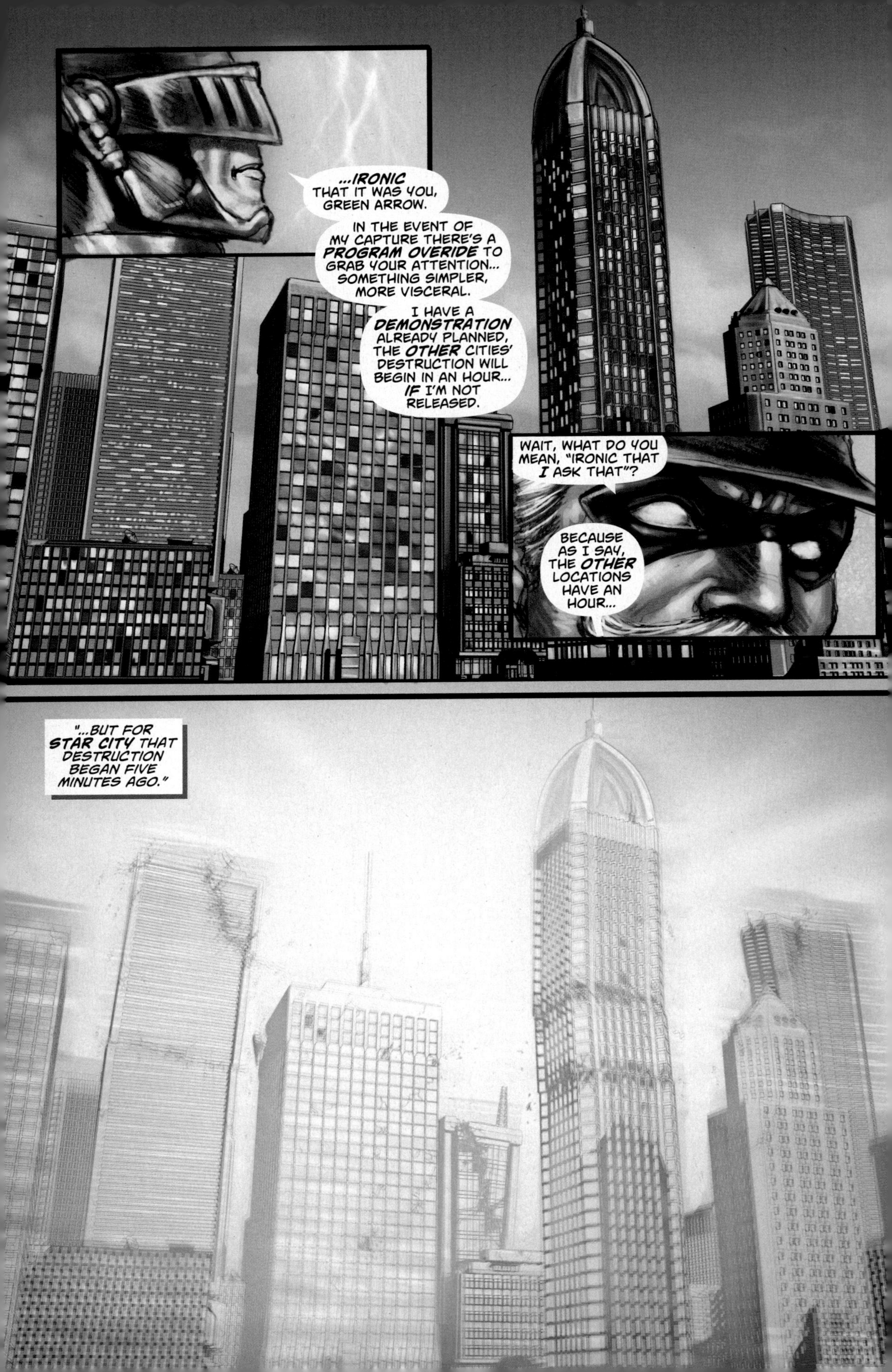

...IRONIC THAT IT WAS YOU, GREEN ARROW.
IN THE EVENT OF MY CAPTURE THERE'S A PROGRAM OVERIDE TO GRAB YOUR ATTENTION... SOMETHING SIMPLER, MORE VISCERAL.
I HAVE A DEMONSTRATION ALREADY PLANNED, THE OTHER CITIES' DESTRUCTION WILL BEGIN IN AN HOUR... IF I'M NOT RELEASED.
WAIT, WHAT DO YOU MEAN, "IRONIC THAT I ASK THAT"?
BECAUSE AS I SAY, THE OTHER LOCATIONS HAVE AN HOUR...
"...BUT FOR STAR CITY THAT DESTRUCTION BEGAN FIVE MINUTES AGO."

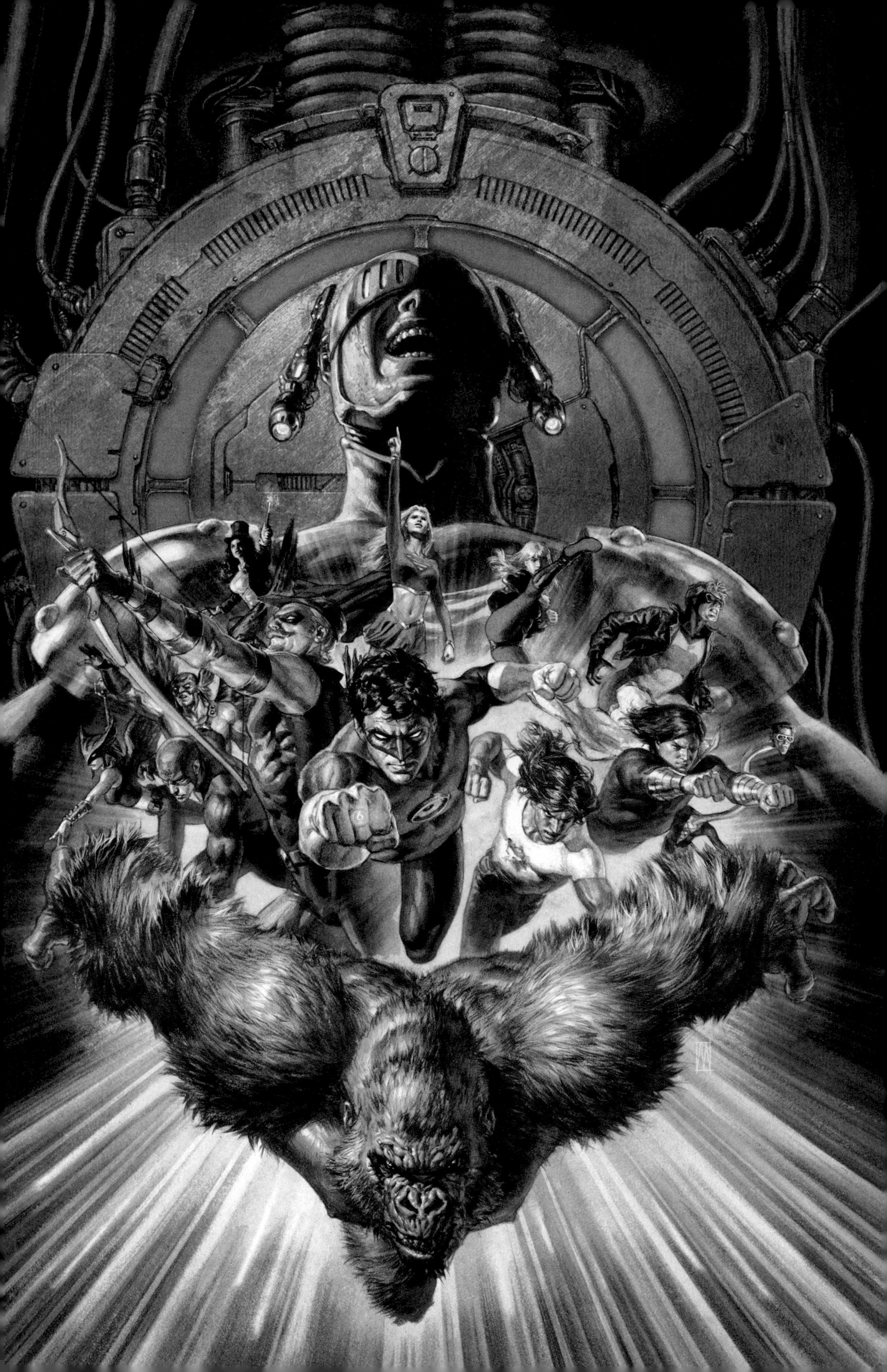

CRY FOR JUSTICE PART SEVEN: JUSTICE

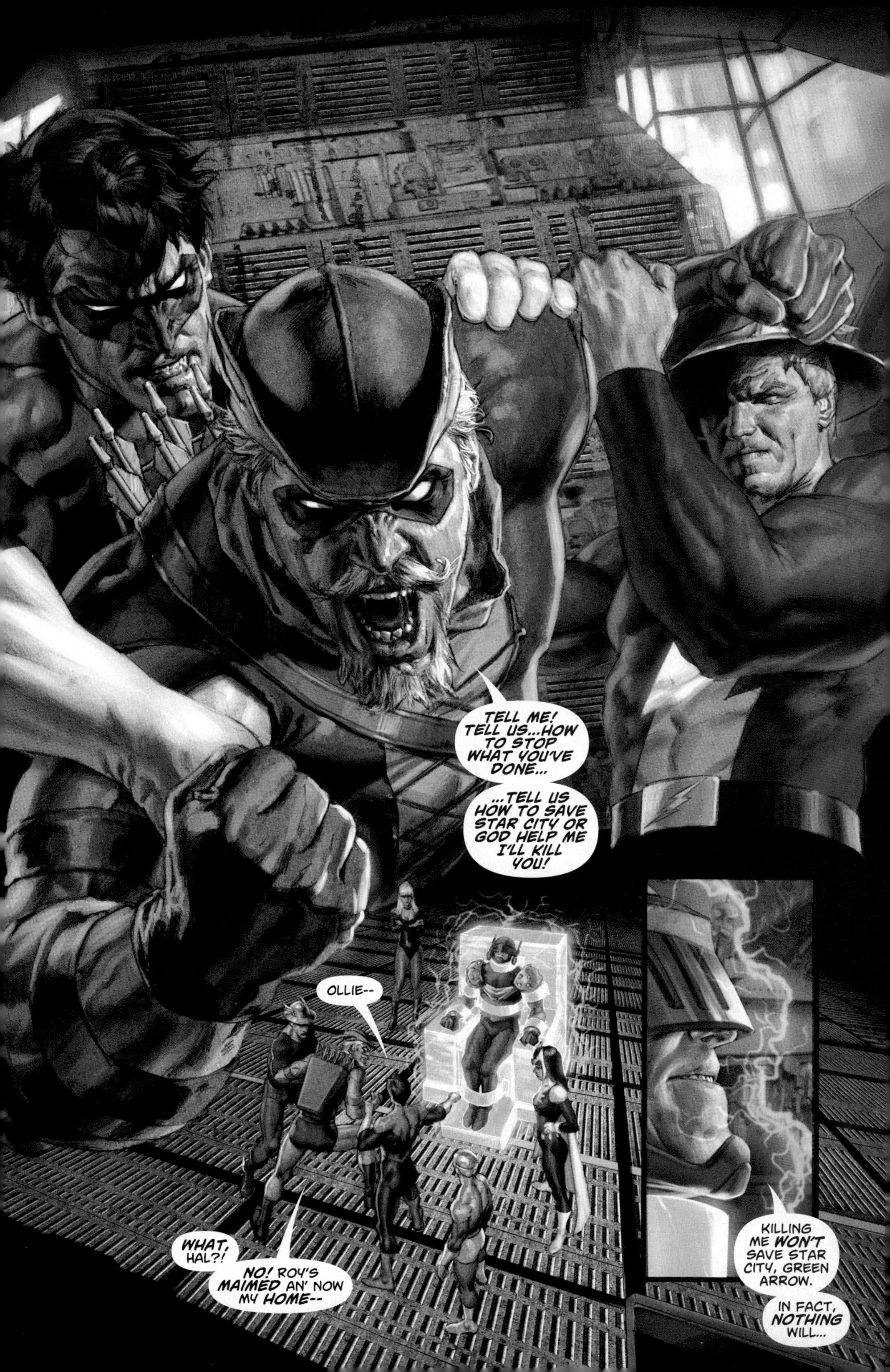

TELL ME! TELL US...HOW TO STOP WHAT YOU'VE DONE...
...TELL US HOW TO SAVE STAR CITY OR GOD HELP ME I'LL KILL YOU!
OLLIE--
WHAT, HAL?!
NO! ROY'S MAIMED AN' NOW MY HOME--
KILLING ME WON'T SAVE STAR CITY, GREEN ARROW.
IN FACT, NOTHING WILL...

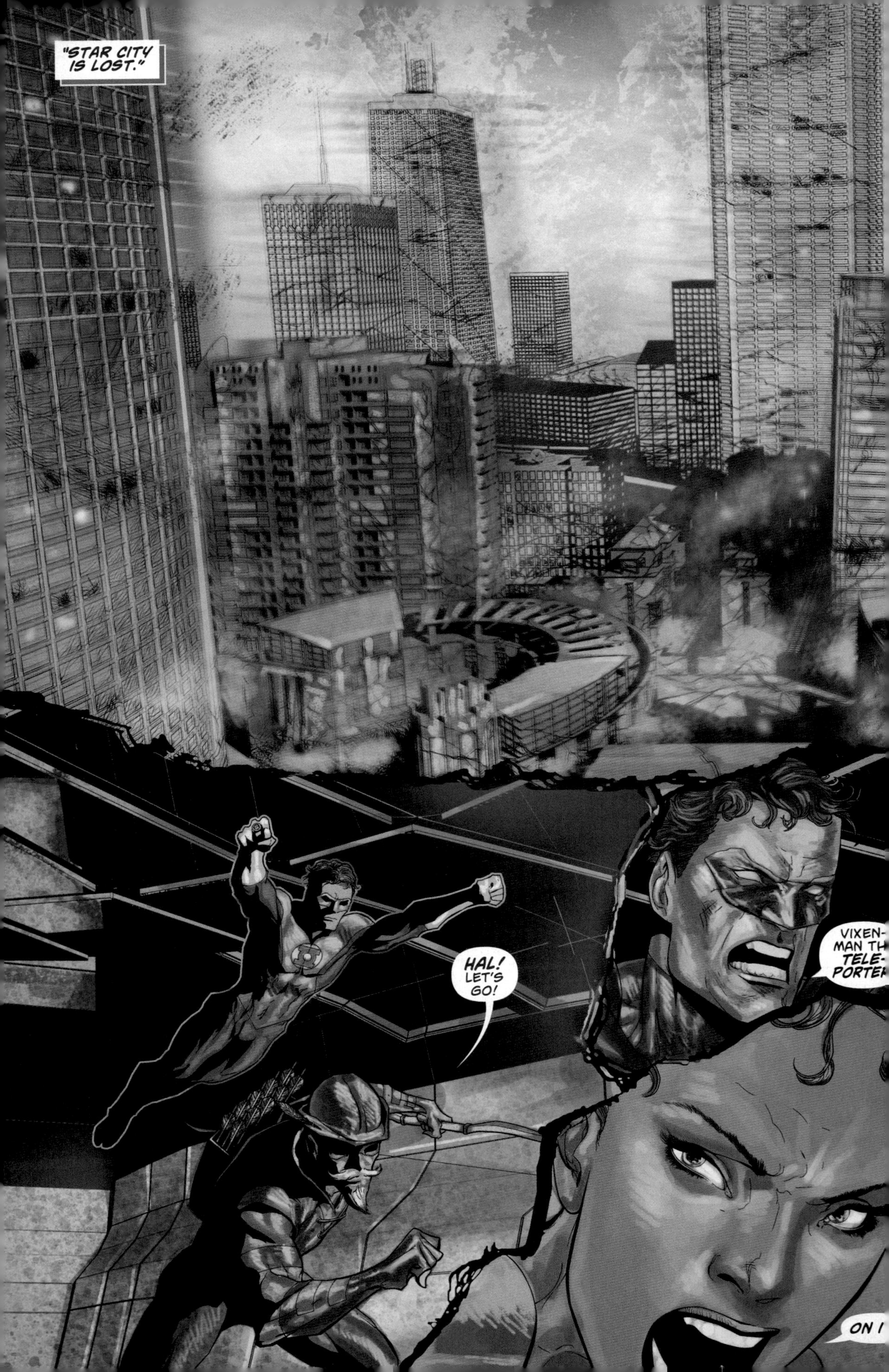
"STAR CITY IS LOST."
HAL! LET'S GO!
VIXEN-
MAN TH
TELE-
PORTER
ON I

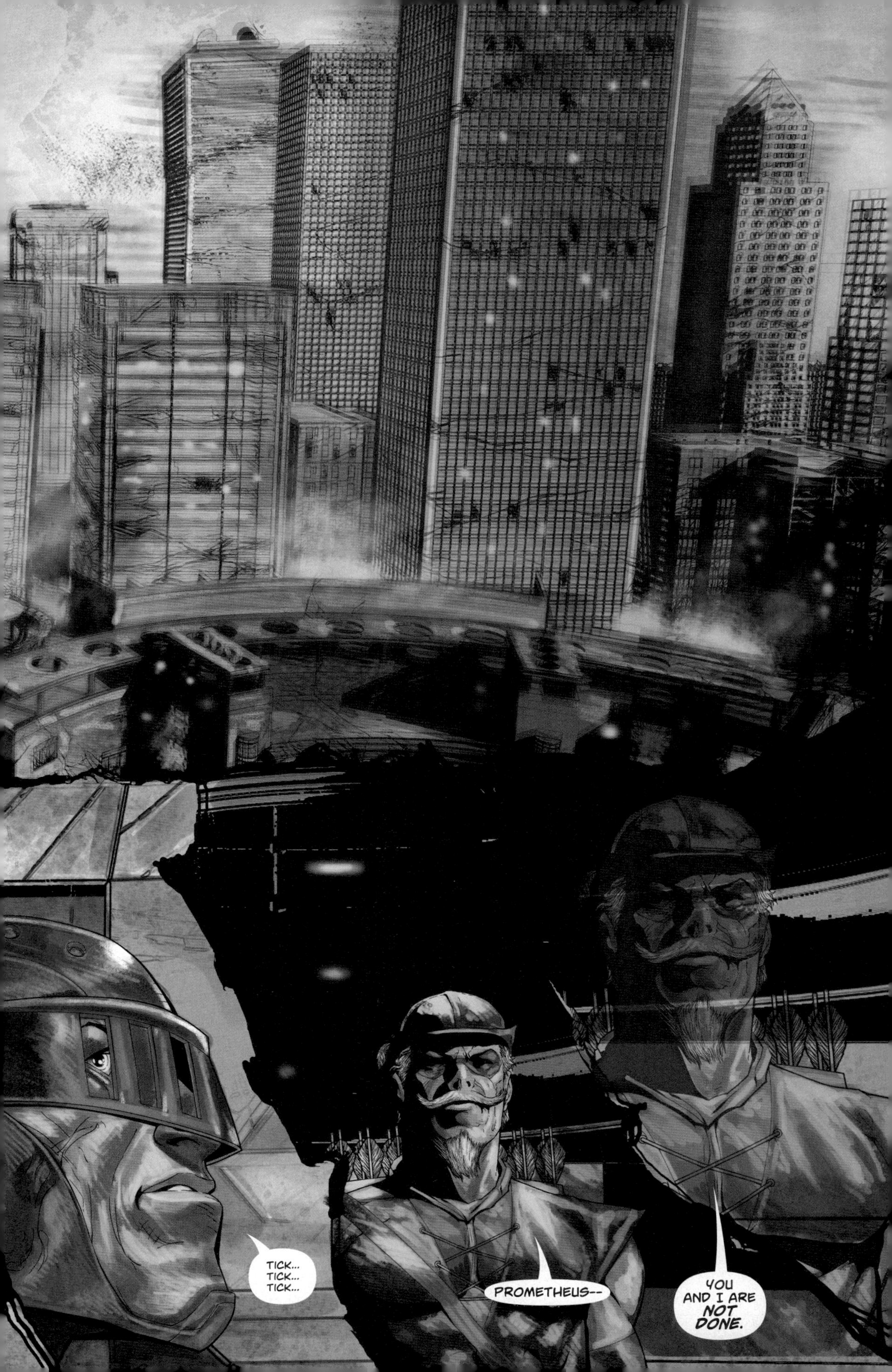
TICK...
TICK...
TICK...
PROMETHEUS--
YOU AND I ARE NOT DONE.

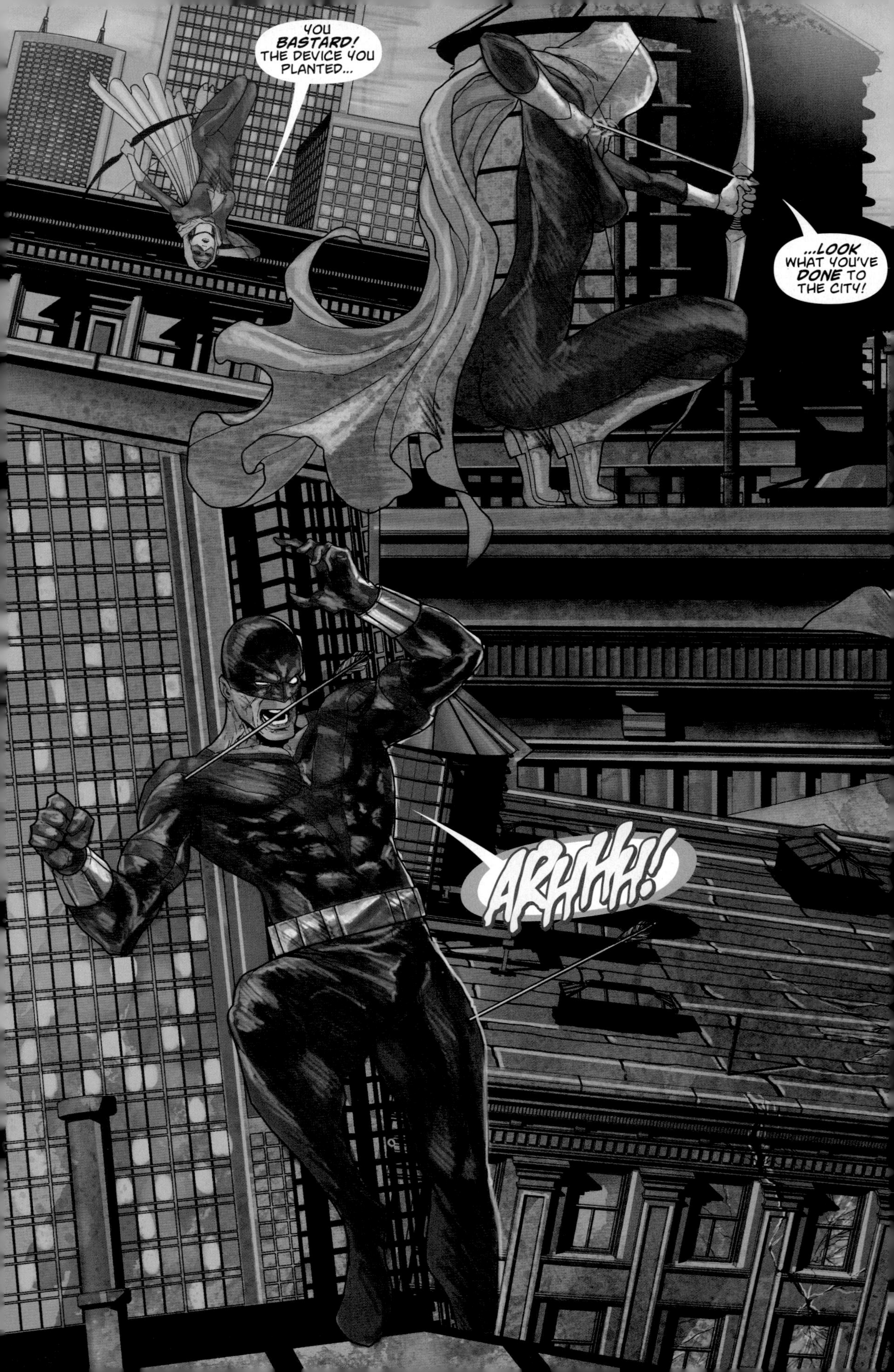
YOU **BASTARD!** THE DEVICE YOU PLANTED...
...**LOOK** WHAT YOU'VE **DONE** TO THE CITY!
ARHHH!!

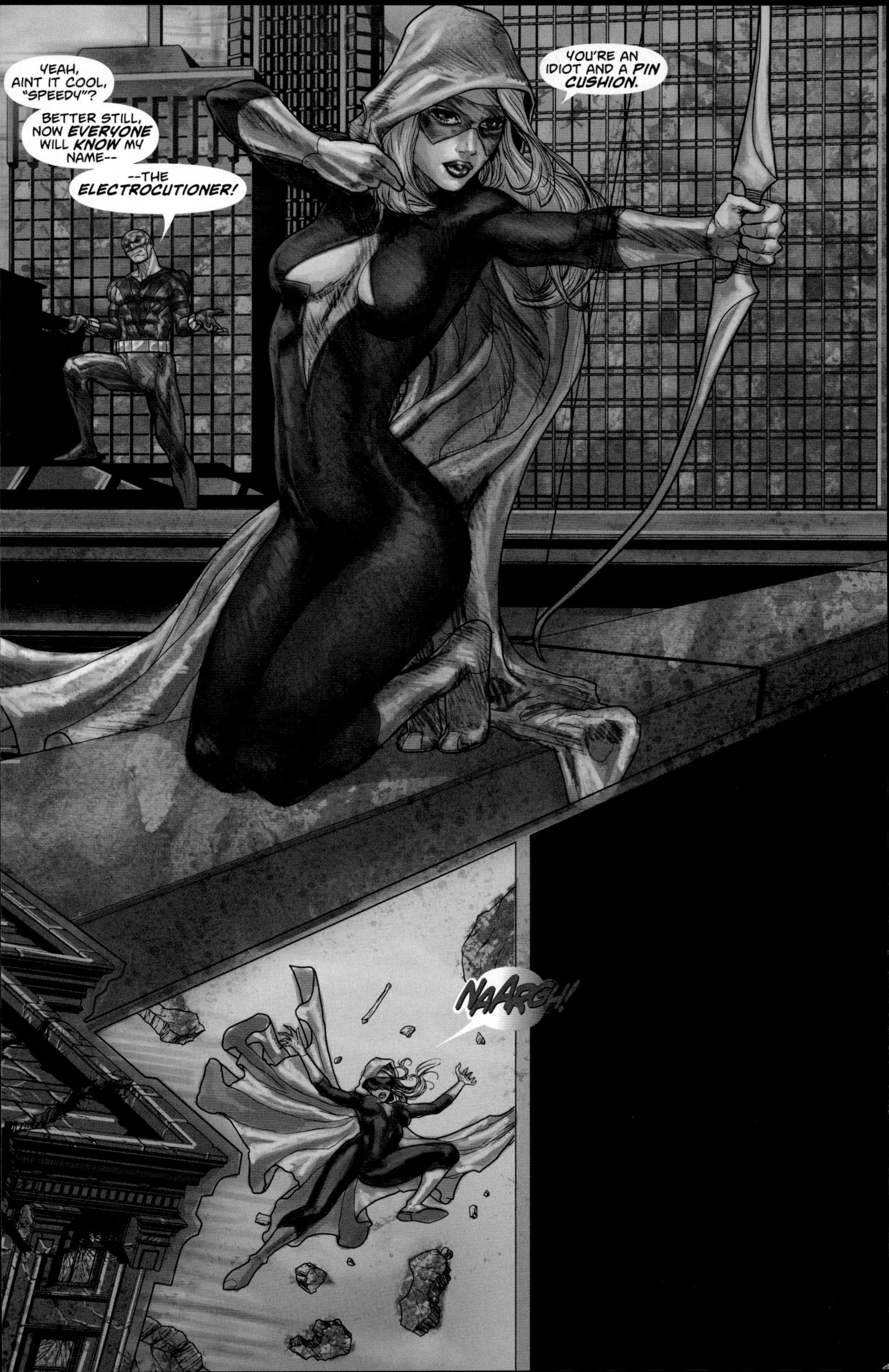
YEAH, AINT IT COOL, "SPEEDY"?
BETTER STILL, NOW EVERYONE WILL KNOW MY NAME--
--THE ELECTROCUTIONER!
YOU'RE AN IDIOT AND A PIN CUSHION.
NAARGH!

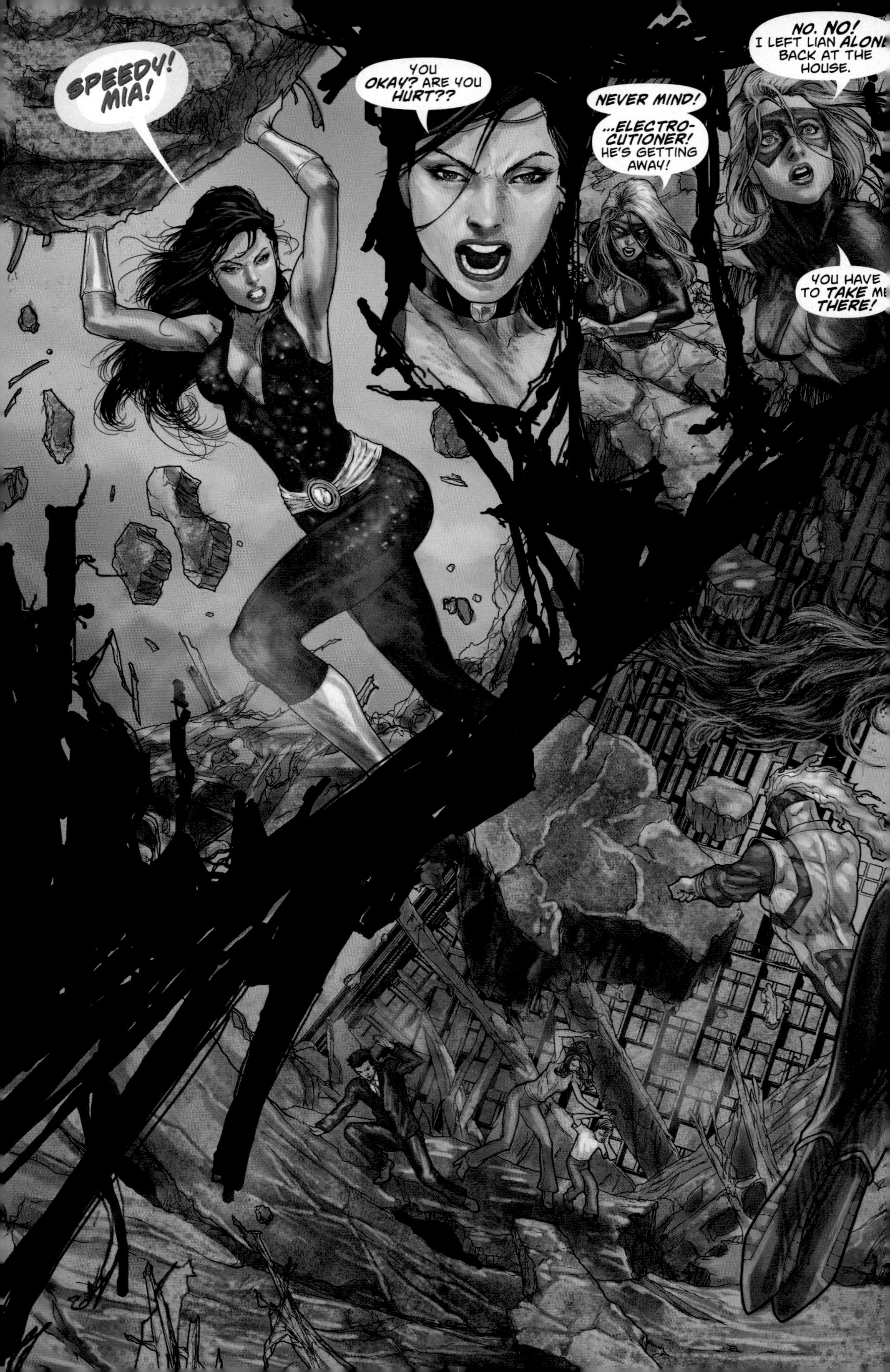
SPEEDY! MIA!
YOU OKAY? ARE YOU HURT??
NEVER MIND!
...ELECTRO-CUTIONER! HE'S GETTING AWAY!
NO. NO! I LEFT LIAN ALONE BACK AT THE HOUSE.
YOU HAVE TO TAKE ME THERE!

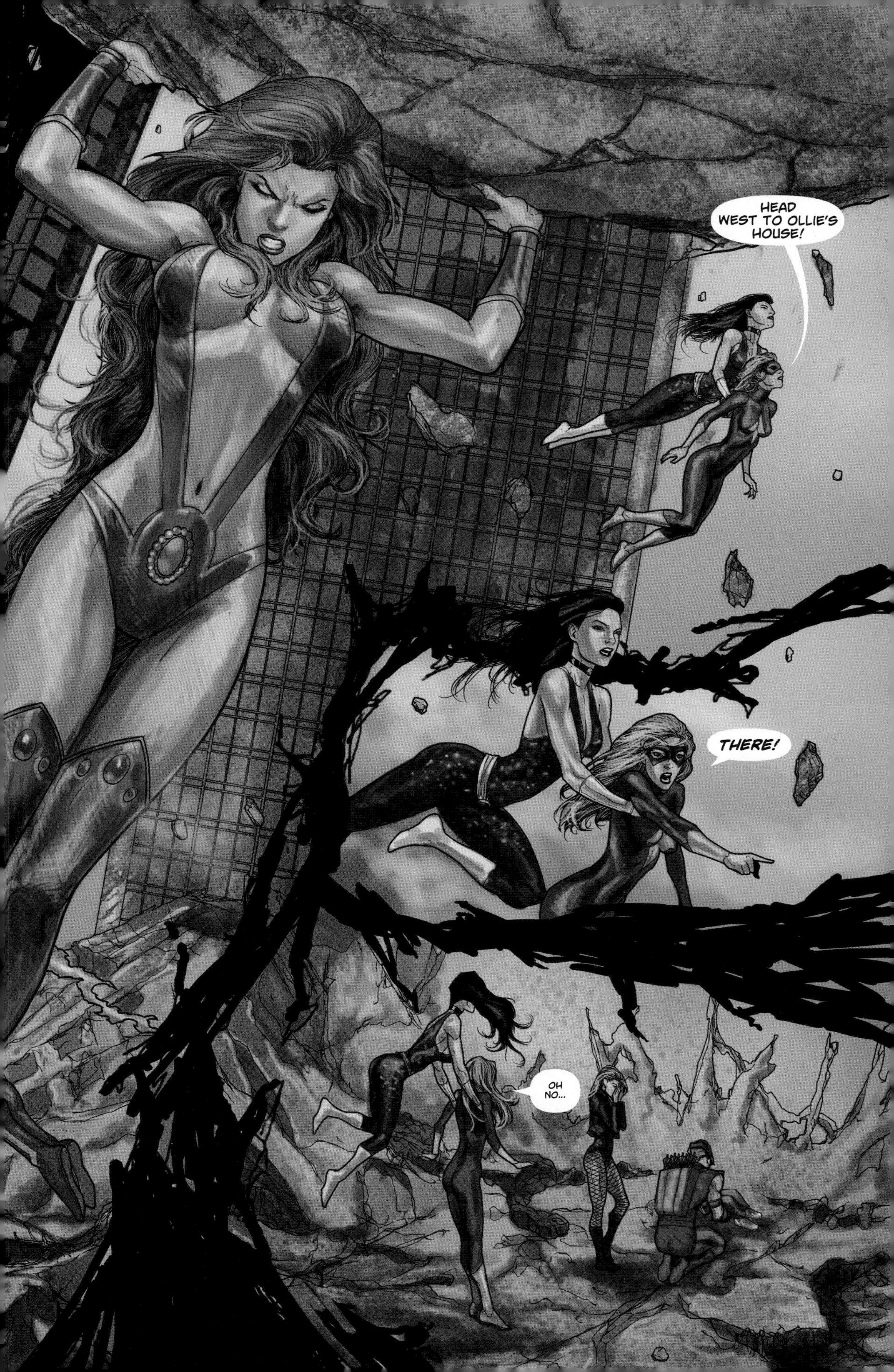
HEAD WEST TO OLLIE'S HOUSE!
THERE!
OH NO...

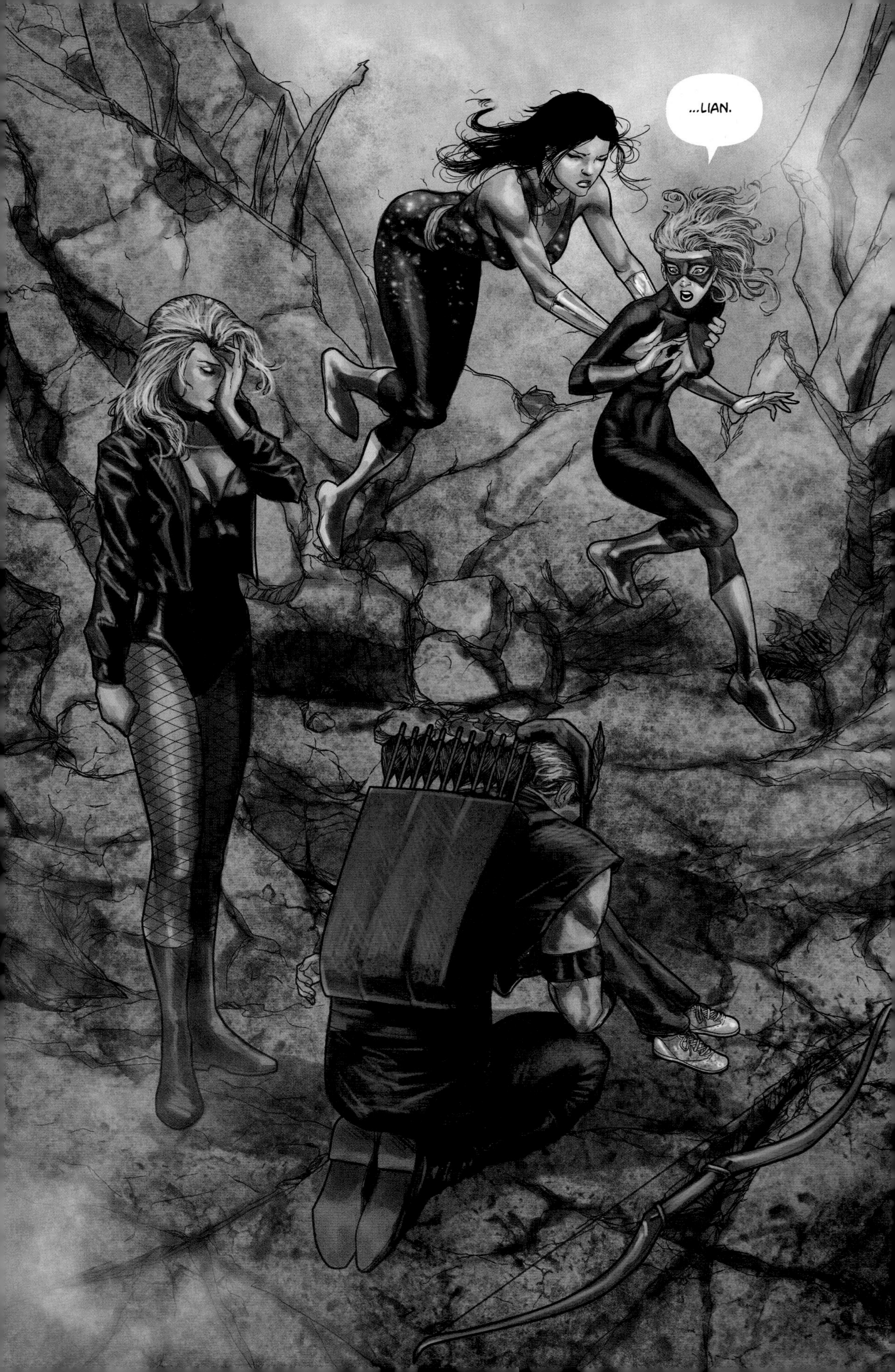
...LIAN.

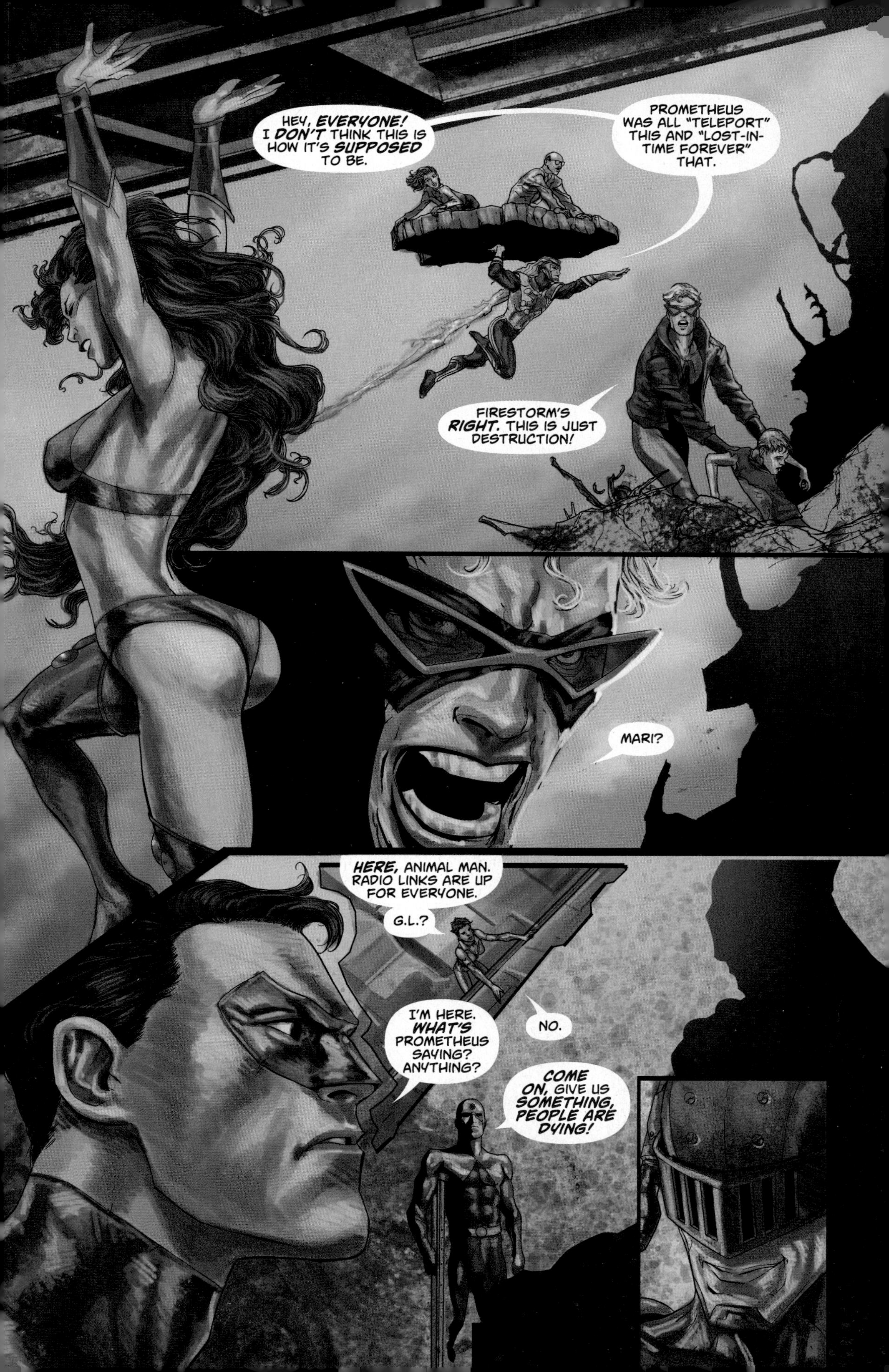
HEY, EVERYONE! I DON'T THINK THIS IS HOW IT'S SUPPOSED TO BE.
PROMETHEUS WAS ALL "TELEPORT" THIS AND "LOST-IN-TIME FOREVER" THAT.
FIRESTORM'S RIGHT. THIS IS JUST DESTRUCTION!
MARI?
HERE, ANIMAL MAN. RADIO LINKS ARE UP FOR EVERYONE.
G.L.?
I'M HERE. WHAT'S PROMETHEUS SAYING? ANYTHING?
NO.
COME ON, GIVE US SOMETHING, PEOPLE ARE DYING!

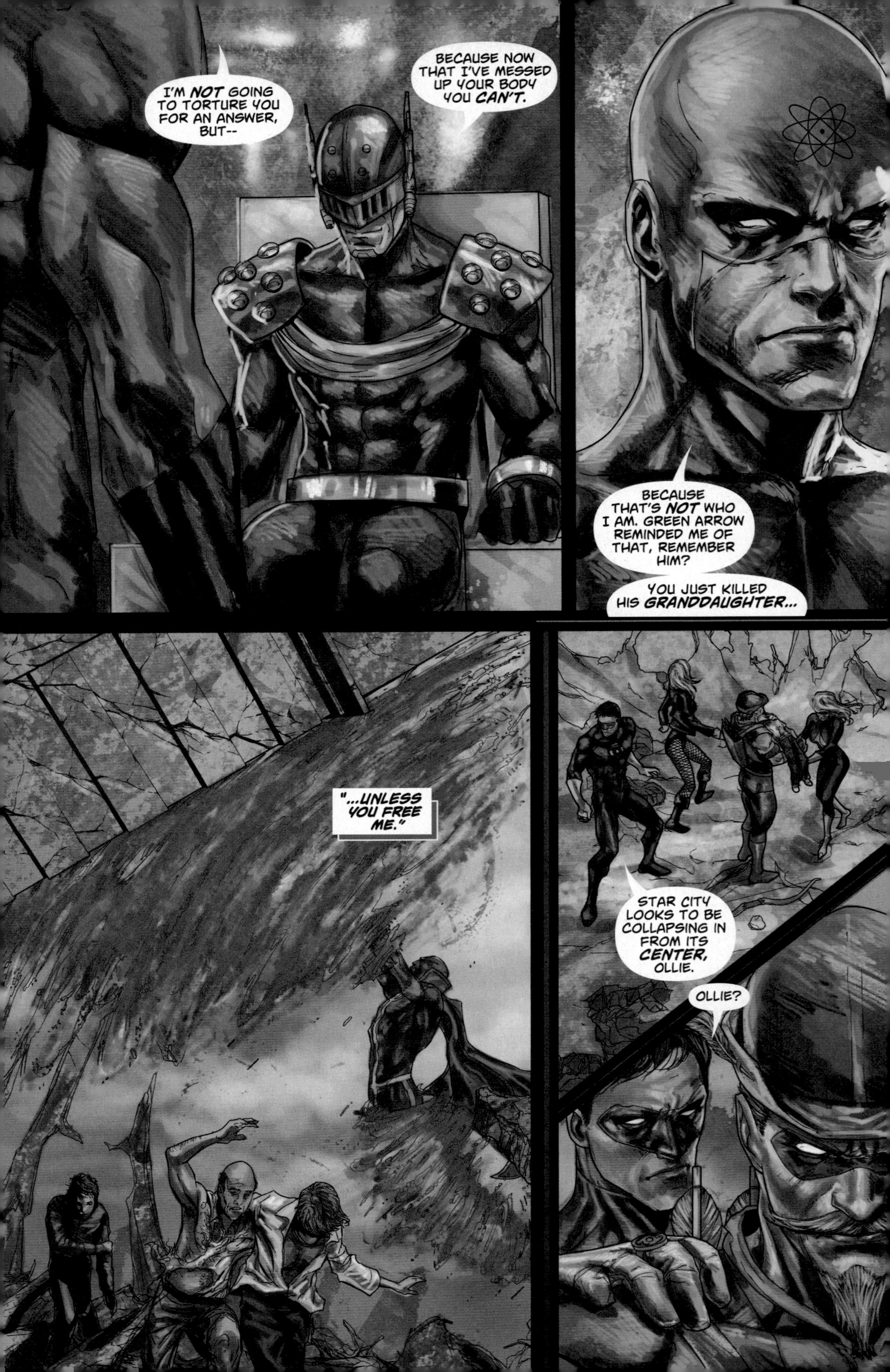
I'M NOT GOING TO TORTURE YOU FOR AN ANSWER, BUT--
BECAUSE NOW THAT I'VE MESSED UP YOUR BODY YOU CAN'T.
BECAUSE THAT'S NOT WHO I AM. GREEN ARROW REMINDED ME OF THAT, REMEMBER HIM?
YOU JUST KILLED HIS GRANDDAUGHTER...
"...UNLESS YOU FREE ME."
STAR CITY LOOKS TO BE COLLAPSING IN FROM ITS CENTER, OLLIE.
OLLIE?

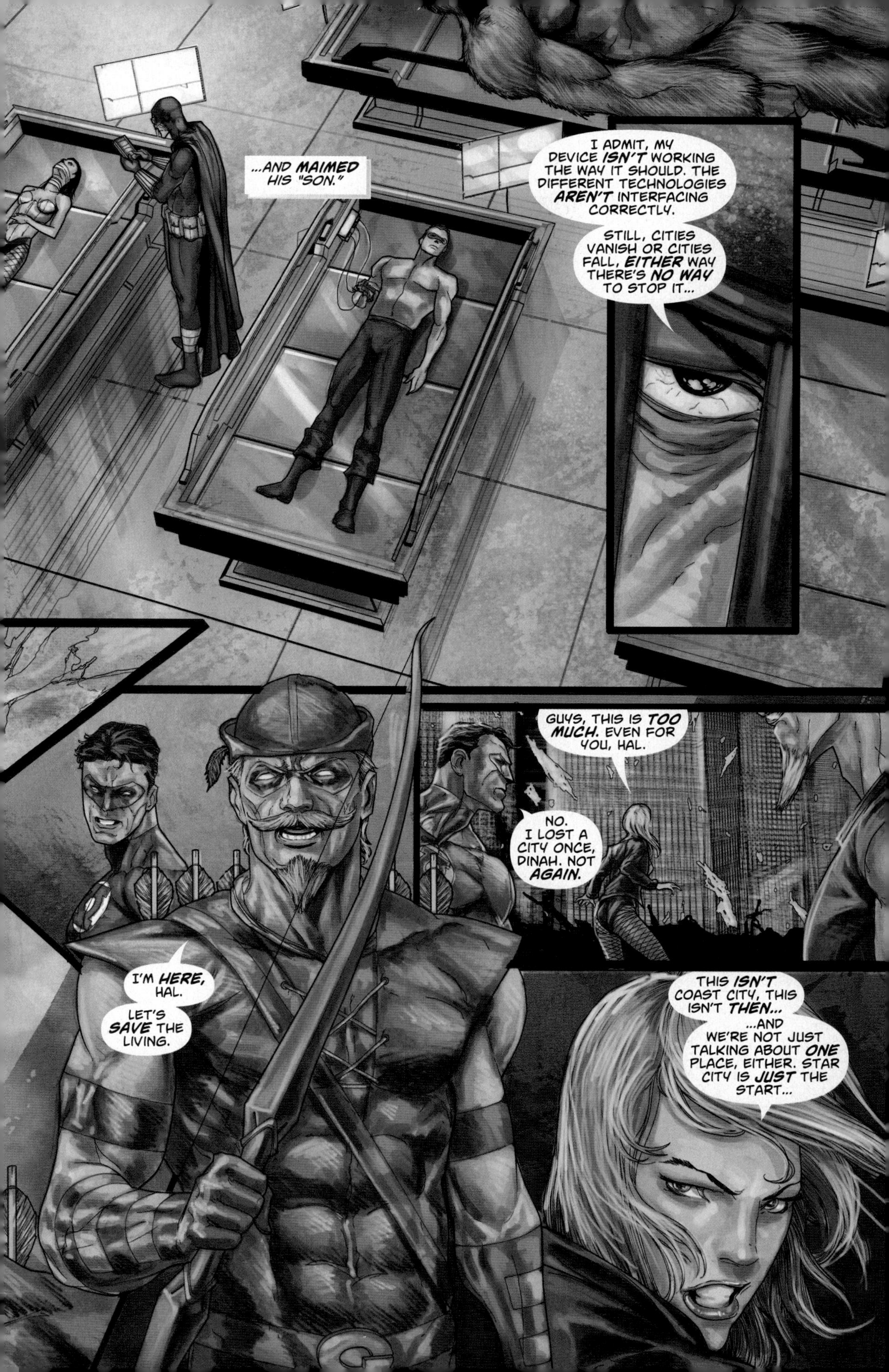
...AND MAIMED HIS "SON."
I ADMIT, MY DEVICE ISN'T WORKING THE WAY IT SHOULD. THE DIFFERENT TECHNOLOGIES AREN'T INTERFACING CORRECTLY.
STILL, CITIES VANISH OR CITIES FALL, EITHER WAY THERE'S NO WAY TO STOP IT...
GUYS, THIS IS TOO MUCH. EVEN FOR YOU, HAL.
NO. I LOST A CITY ONCE, DINAH. NOT AGAIN.
I'M HERE, HAL.
LET'S SAVE THE LIVING.
THIS ISN'T COAST CITY, THIS ISN'T THEN...
...AND WE'RE NOT JUST TALKING ABOUT ONE PLACE, EITHER. STAR CITY IS JUST THE START...

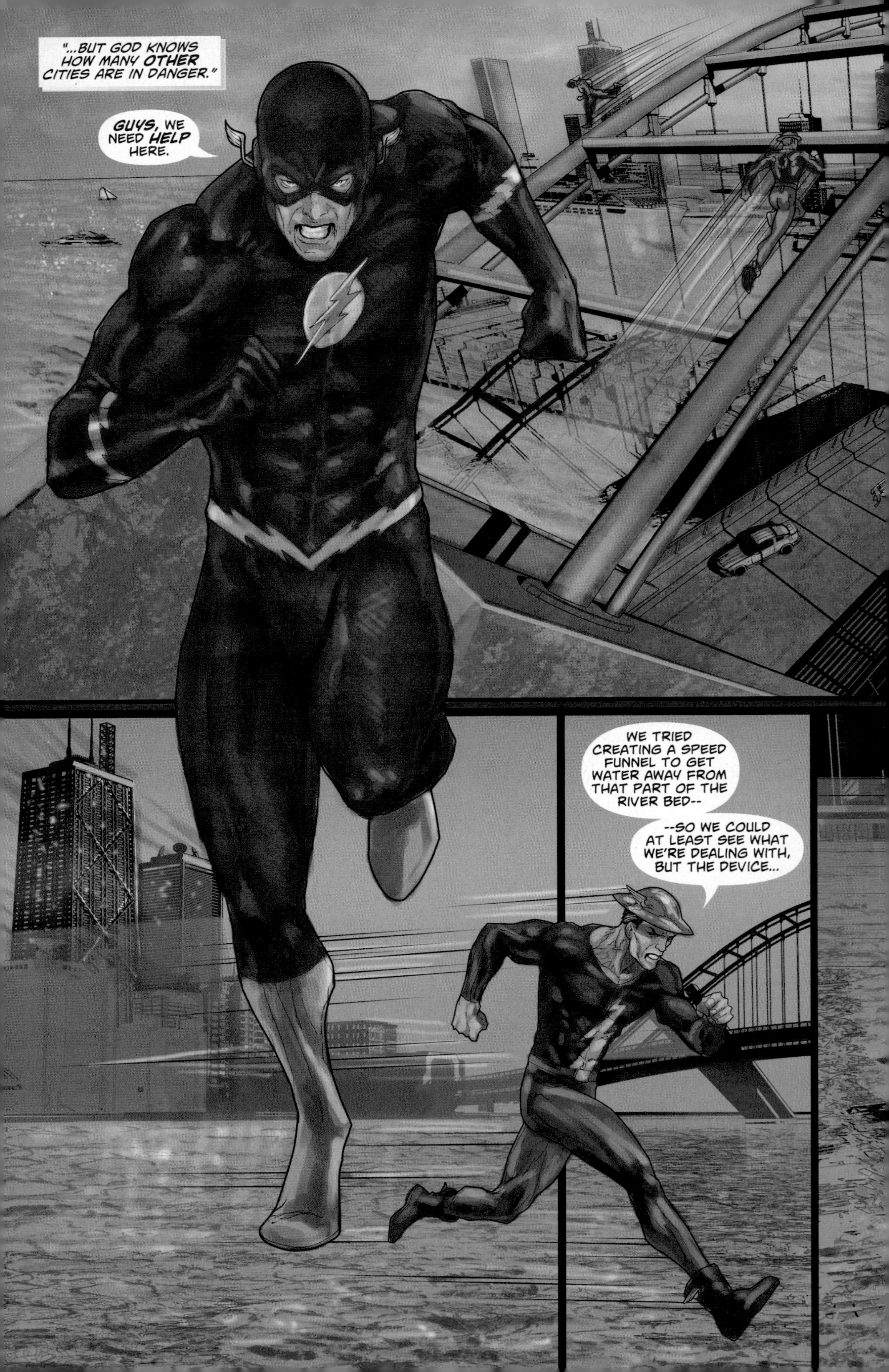
"...BUT GOD KNOWS HOW MANY OTHER CITIES ARE IN DANGER."
GUYS, WE NEED HELP HERE.
WE TRIED CREATING A SPEED FUNNEL TO GET WATER AWAY FROM THAT PART OF THE RIVER BED--
--SO WE COULD AT LEAST SEE WHAT WE'RE DEALING WITH, BUT THE DEVICE...

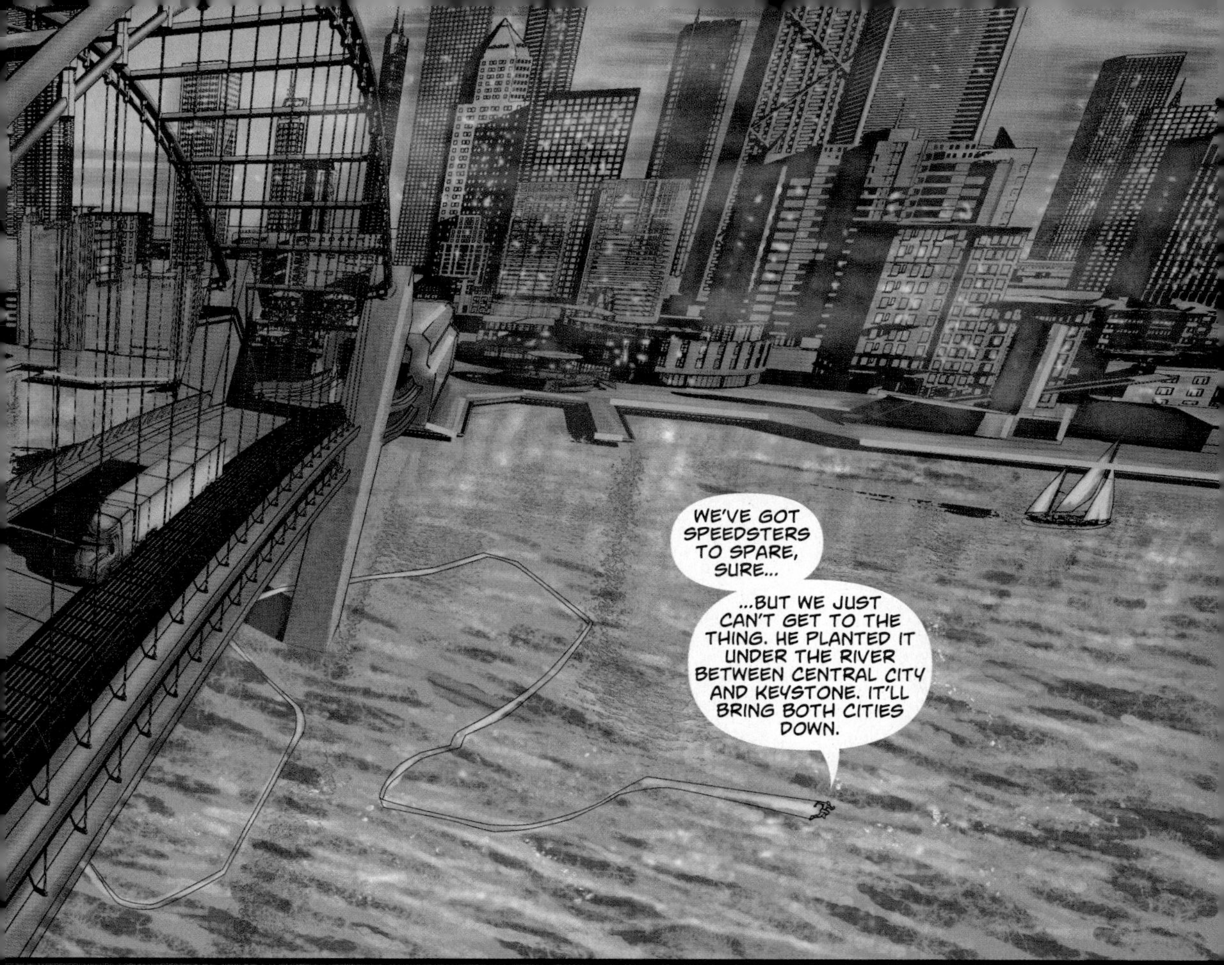
WE'VE GOT SPEEDSTERS TO SPARE, SURE...
...BUT WE JUST CAN'T GET TO THE THING. HE PLANTED IT UNDER THE RIVER BETWEEN CENTRAL CITY AND KEYSTONE. IT'LL BRING BOTH CITIES DOWN.

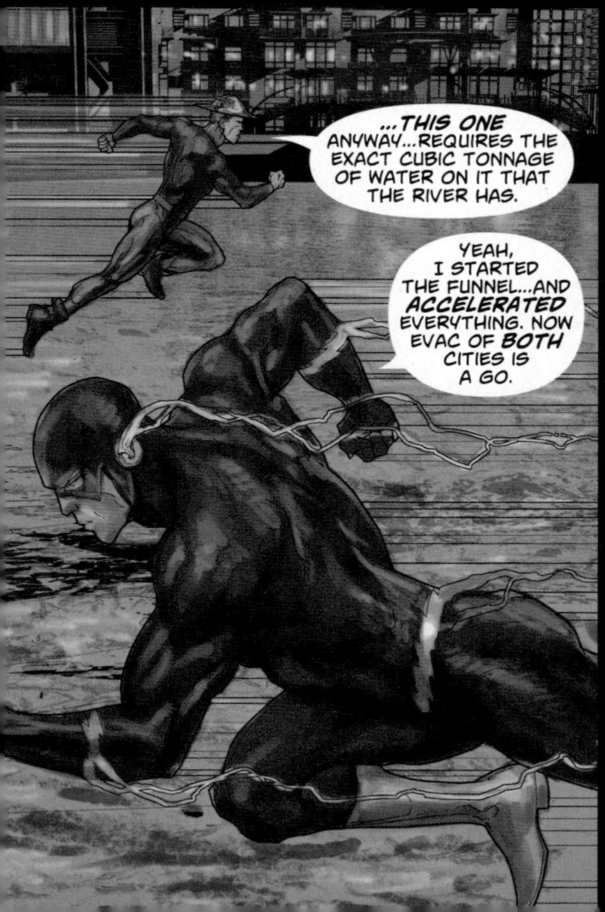
...THIS ONE ANYWAY...REQUIRES THE EXACT CUBIC TONNAGE OF WATER ON IT THAT THE RIVER HAS.
YEAH, I STARTED THE FUNNEL...AND ACCELERATED EVERYTHING. NOW EVAC OF BOTH CITIES IS A GO.

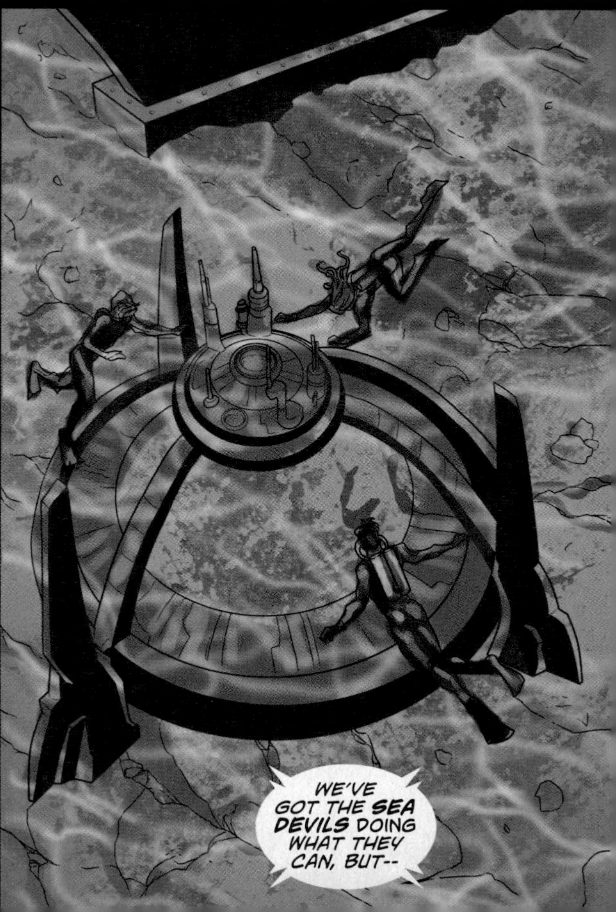
WE'VE GOT THE SEA DEVILS DOING WHAT THEY CAN, BUT--

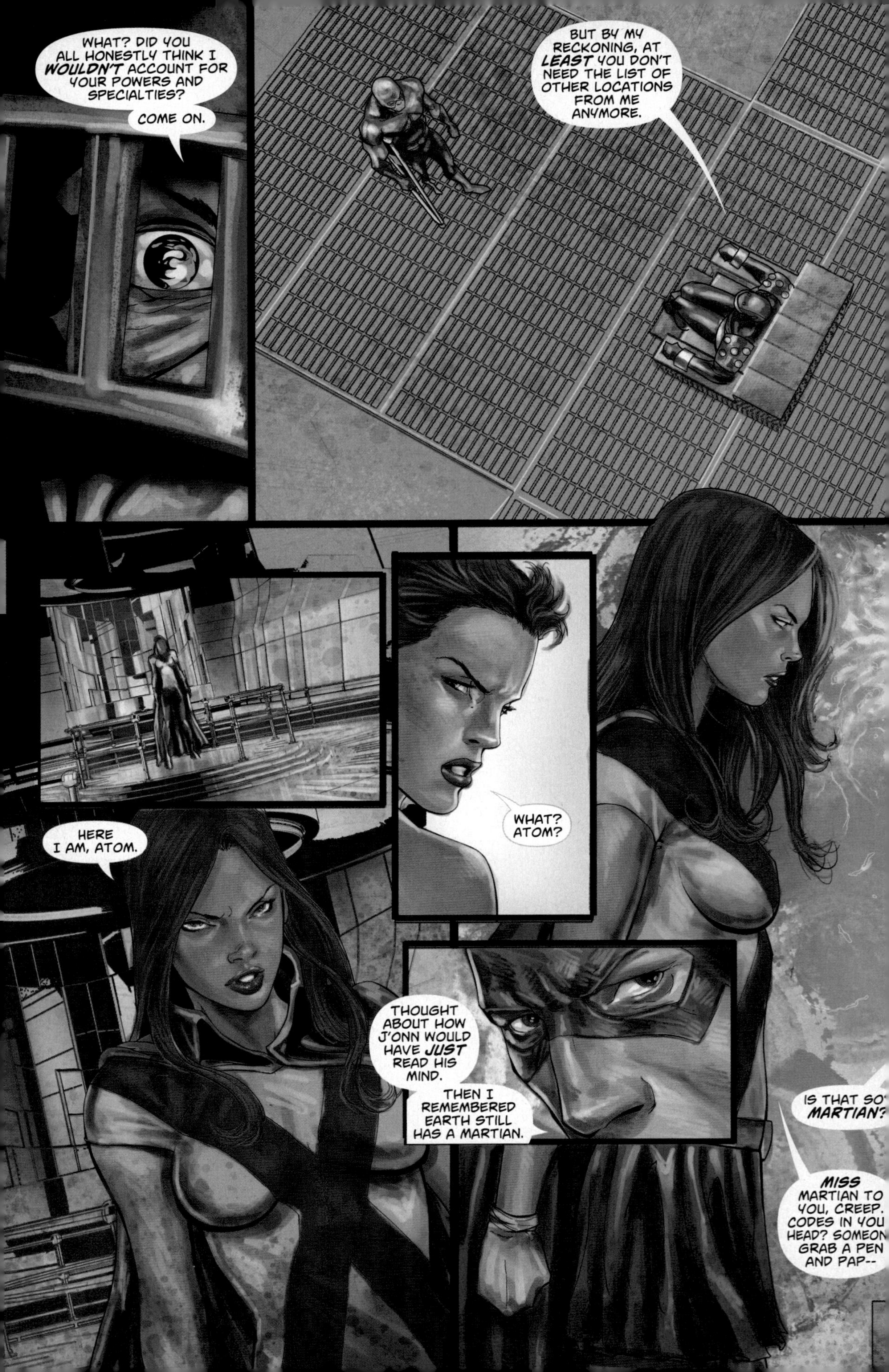
WHAT? DID YOU ALL HONESTLY THINK I WOULDN'T ACCOUNT FOR YOUR POWERS AND SPECIALTIES?
COME ON.
BUT BY MY RECKONING, AT LEAST YOU DON'T NEED THE LIST OF OTHER LOCATIONS FROM ME ANYMORE.
WHAT? ATOM?
HERE I AM, ATOM.
THOUGHT ABOUT HOW J'ONN WOULD HAVE JUST READ HIS MIND.
THEN I REMEMBERED EARTH STILL HAS A MARTIAN.
IS THAT SO MARTIAN?
MISS MARTIAN TO YOU, CREEP. CODES IN YOU HEAD? SOMEON GRAB A PEN AND PAP--

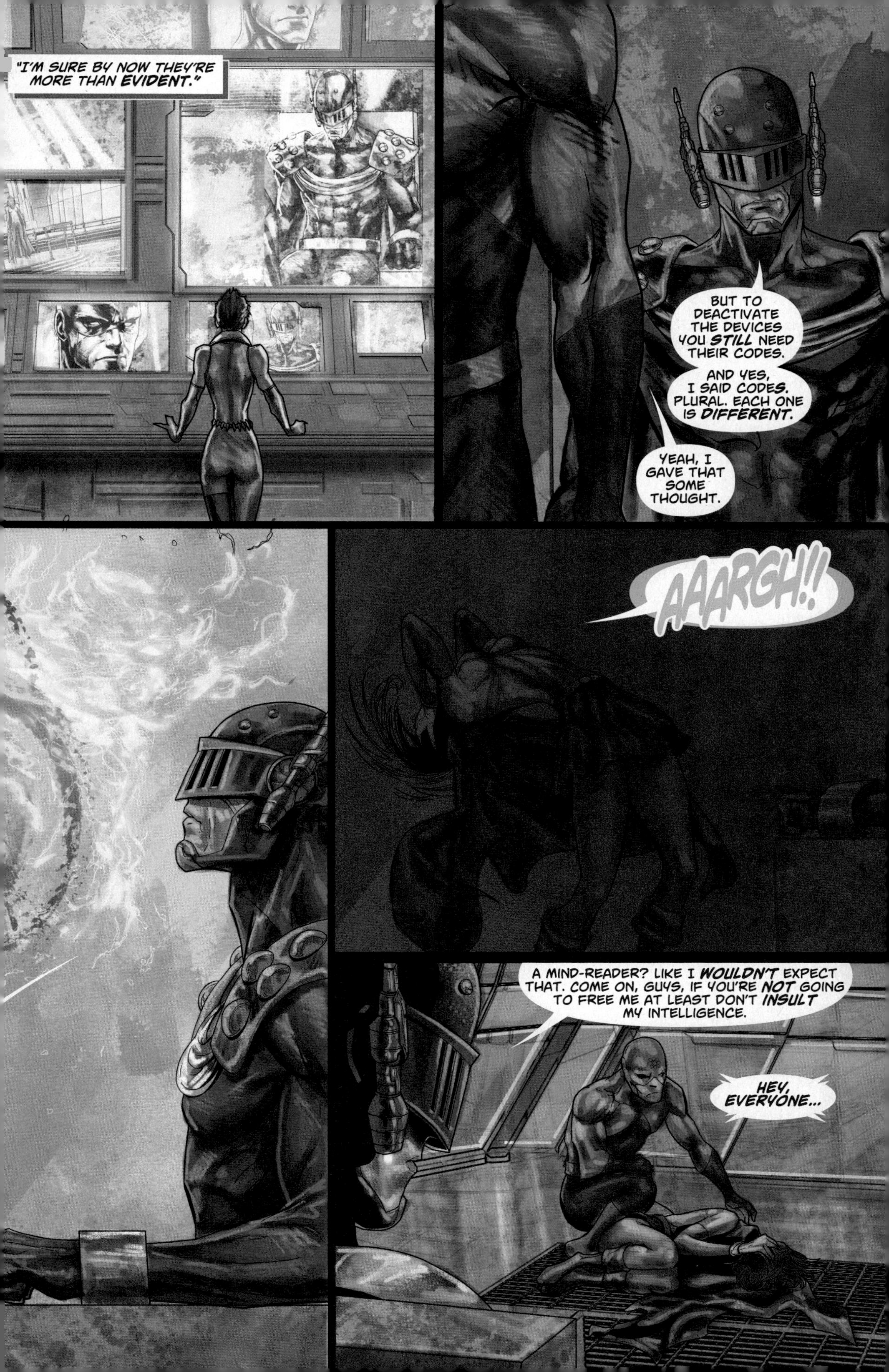
"I'M SURE BY NOW THEY'RE MORE THAN EVIDENT."
BUT TO DEACTIVATE THE DEVICES YOU STILL NEED THEIR CODES.
AND YES, I SAID CODES. PLURAL. EACH ONE IS DIFFERENT.
YEAH, I GAVE THAT SOME THOUGHT.
AAARGH!!
A MIND-READER? LIKE I WOULDN'T EXPECT THAT. COME ON, GUYS, IF YOU'RE NOT GOING TO FREE ME AT LEAST DON'T INSULT MY INTELLIGENCE.
HEY, EVERYONE...

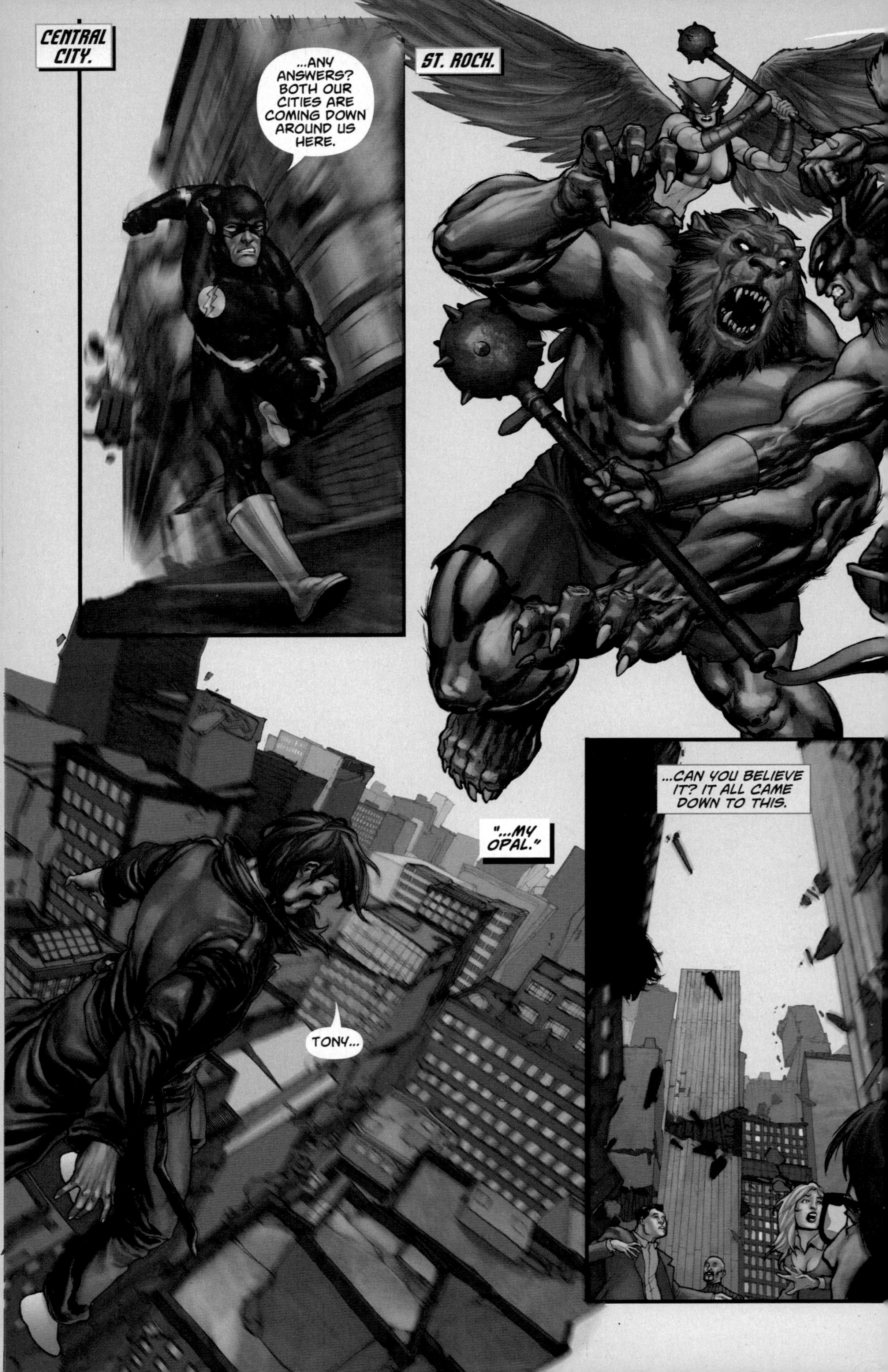
CENTRAL CITY.
...ANY ANSWERS? BOTH OUR CITIES ARE COMING DOWN AROUND US HERE.
ST. ROCH.
"...MY OPAL."
TONY...
...CAN YOU BELIEVE IT? IT ALL CAME DOWN TO THIS.

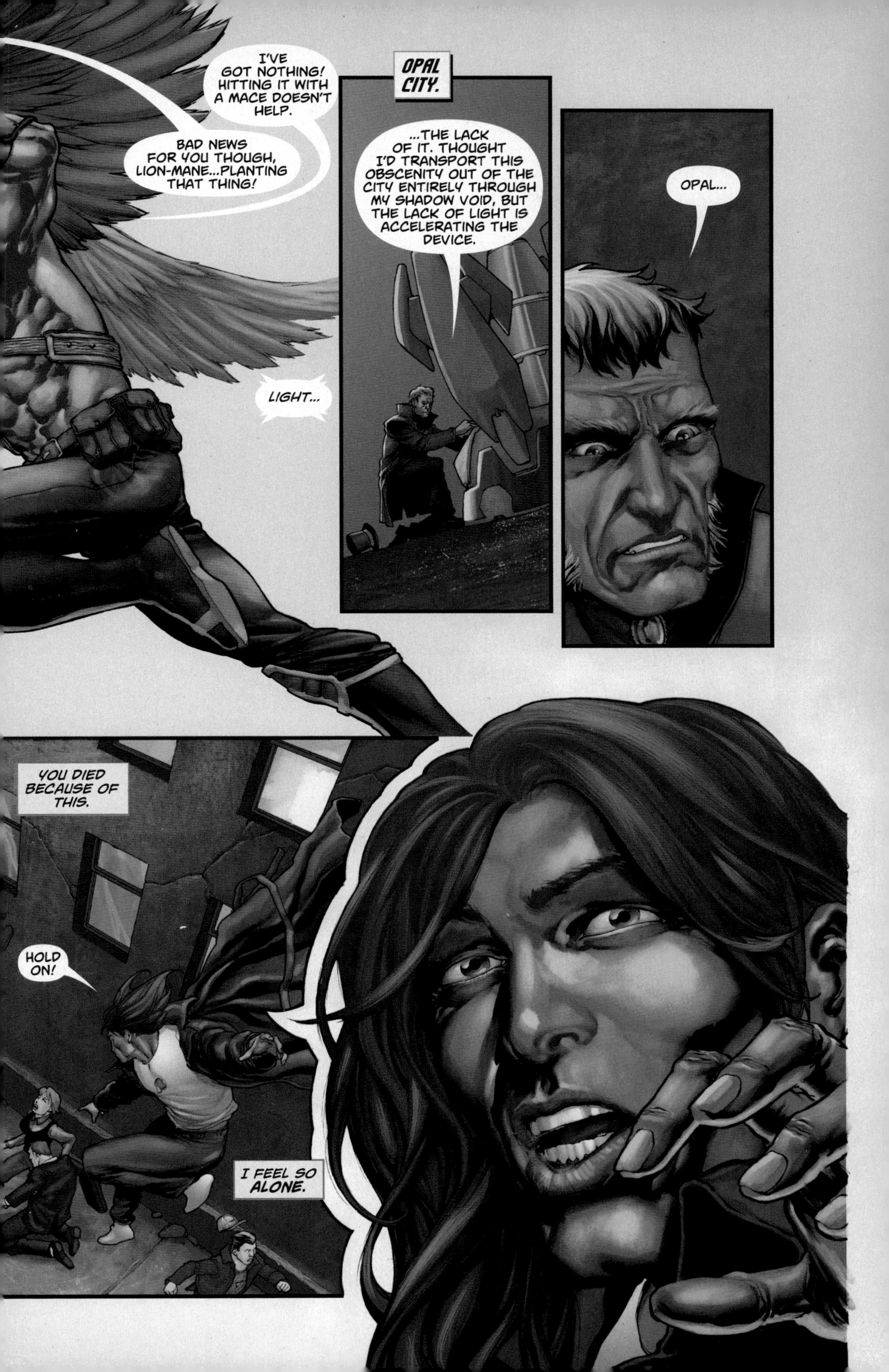
I'VE GOT NOTHING! HITTING IT WITH A MACE DOESN'T HELP.
BAD NEWS FOR YOU THOUGH, LION-MANE...PLANTING THAT THING!
LIGHT...
OPAL CITY.
...THE LACK OF IT. THOUGHT I'D TRANSPORT THIS OBSCENITY OUT OF THE CITY ENTIRELY THROUGH MY SHADOW VOID, BUT THE LACK OF LIGHT IS ACCELERATING THE DEVICE.
OPAL...
YOU DIED BECAUSE OF THIS.
HOLD ON!
I FEEL SO ALONE.

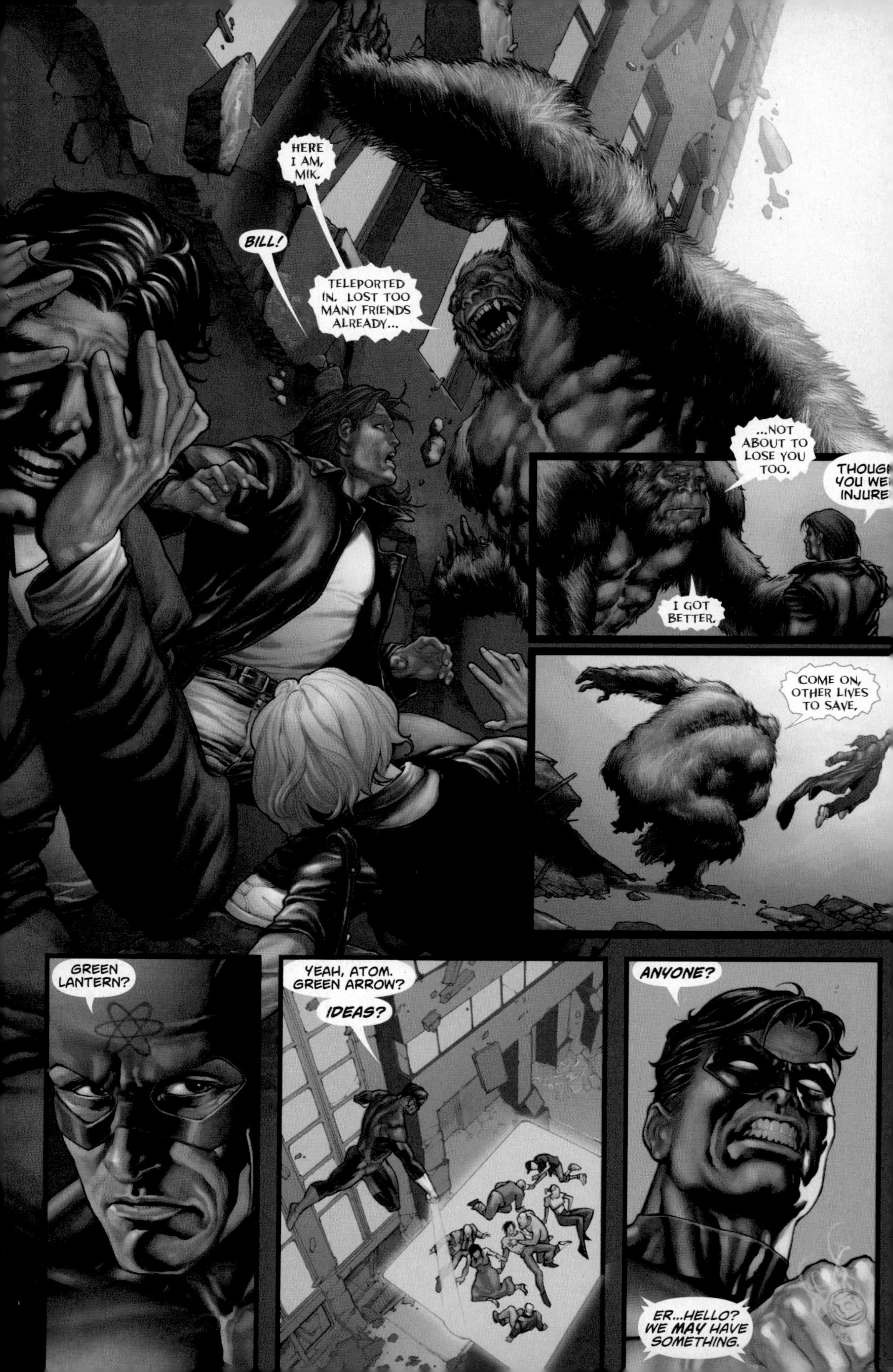
HERE I AM, MIK.
BILL!
TELEPORTED IN. LOST TOO MANY FRIENDS ALREADY...
...NOT ABOUT TO LOSE YOU TOO.
THOUG YOU WE INJURE
I GOT BETTER.
COME ON, OTHER LIVES TO SAVE.
GREEN LANTERN?
YEAH, ATOM. GREEN ARROW?
IDEAS?
ANYONE?
ER...HELLO? WE MAY HAVE SOMETHING.

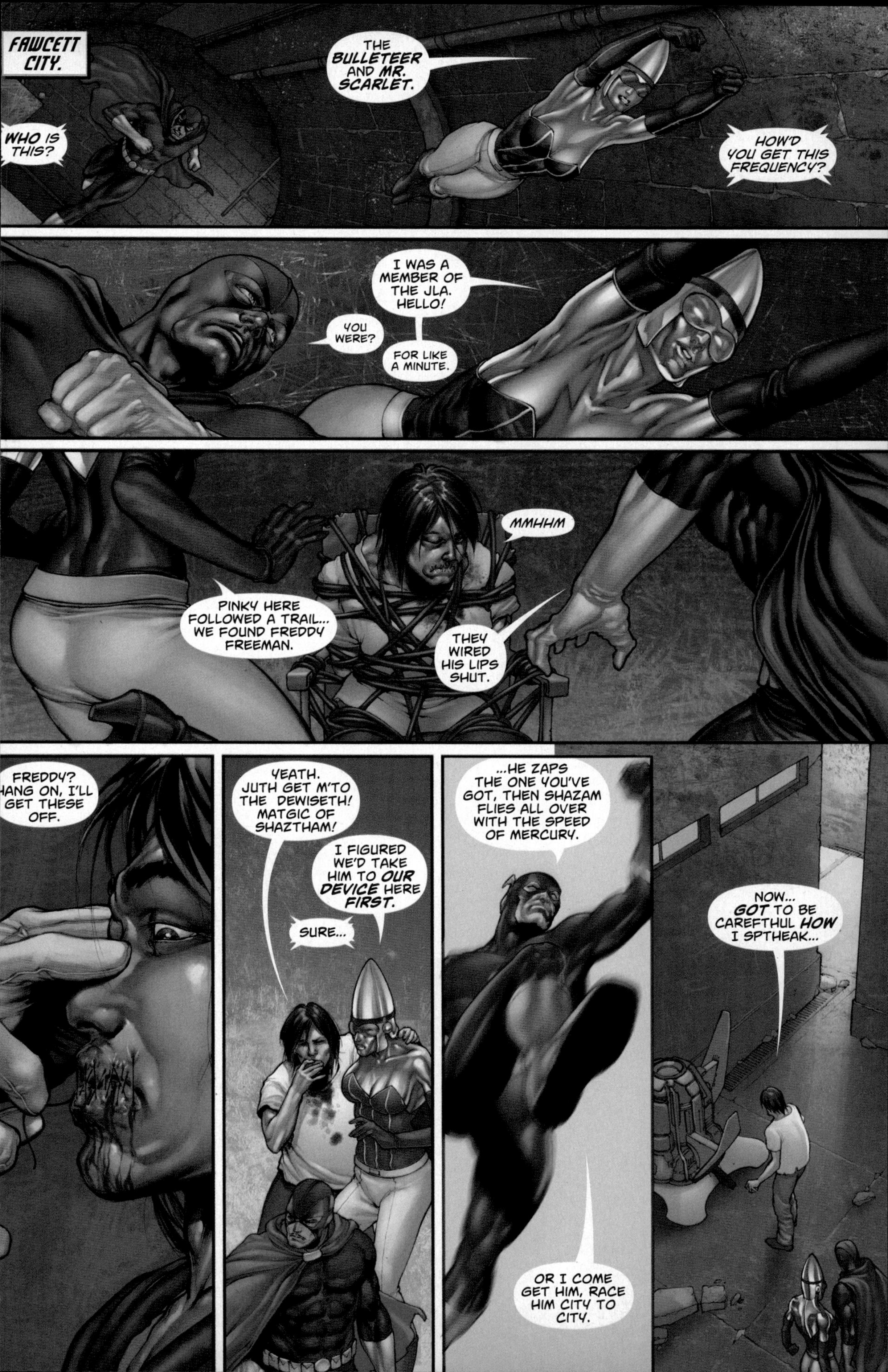
FAWCETT CITY.
WHO IS THIS?
THE BULLETEER AND MR. SCARLET.
HOW'D YOU GET THIS FREQUENCY?
I WAS A MEMBER OF THE JLA. HELLO!
YOU WERE?
FOR LIKE A MINUTE.
MMHHM
PINKY HERE FOLLOWED A TRAIL... WE FOUND FREDDY FREEMAN.
THEY WIRED HIS LIPS SHUT.
FREDDY? HANG ON, I'LL GET THESE OFF.
YEATH. JUTH GET M'TO THE DEWISETH! MATGIC OF SHAZTHAM!
I FIGURED WE'D TAKE HIM TO OUR DEVICE HERE FIRST.
SURE...
...HE ZAPS THE ONE YOU'VE GOT, THEN SHAZAM FLIES ALL OVER WITH THE SPEED OF MERCURY.
OR I COME GET HIM, RACE HIM CITY TO CITY.
NOW... GOT TO BE CAREFTHUL HOW I SPTHEAK...

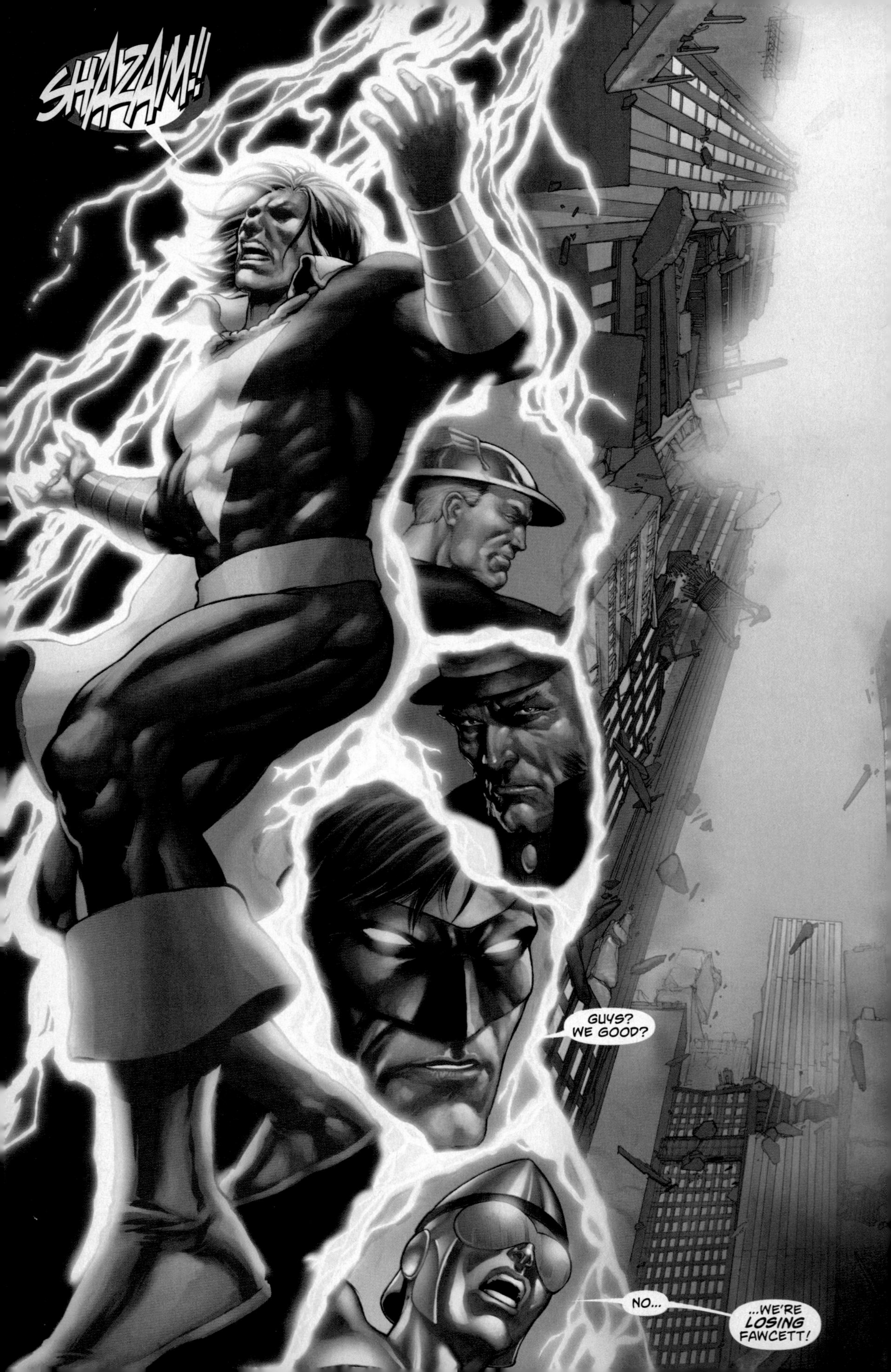
SHAZAM!!
GUYS? WE GOOD?
NO...
...WE'RE LOSING FAWCETT!

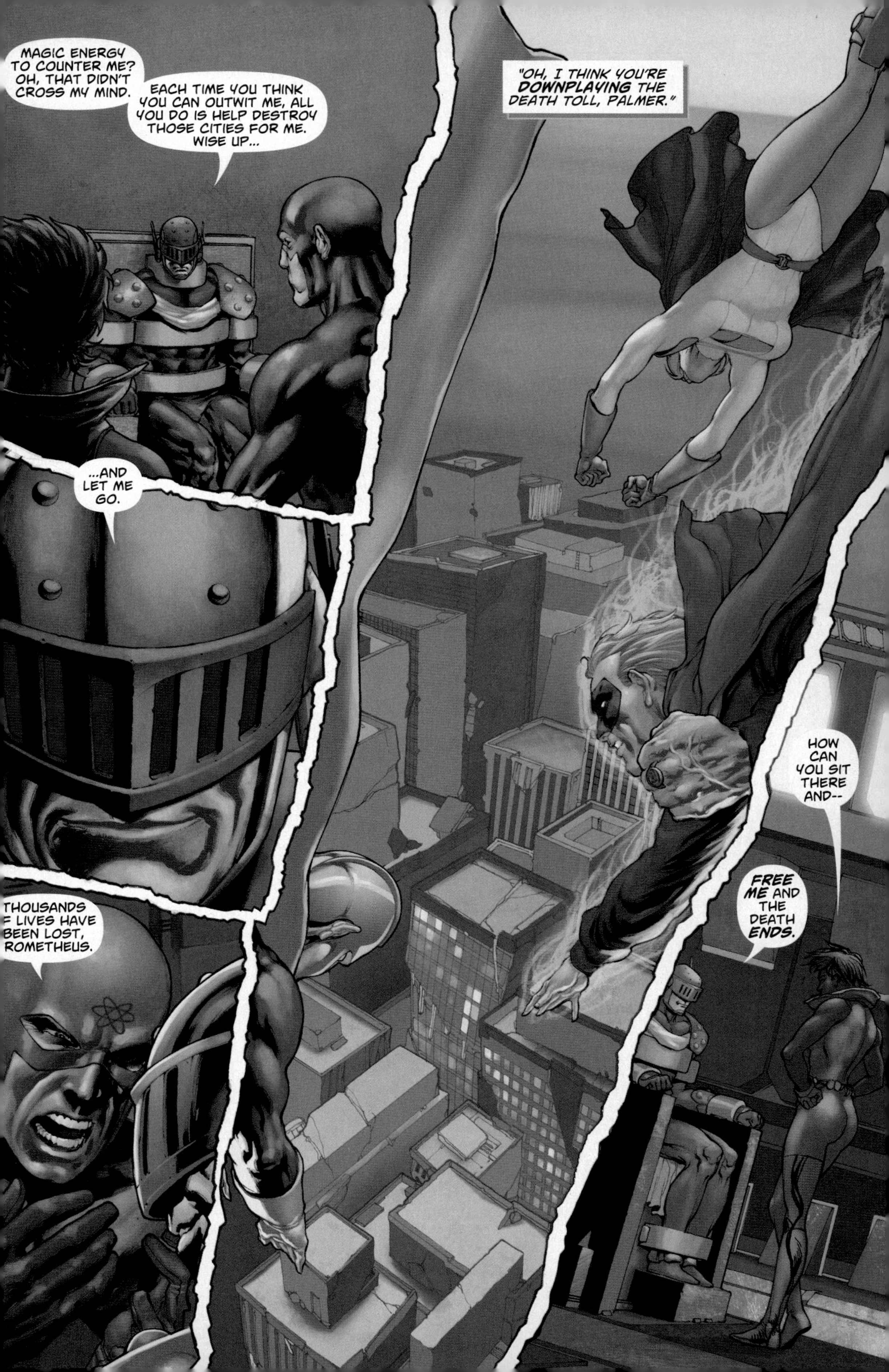
MAGIC ENERGY TO COUNTER ME? OH, THAT DIDN'T CROSS MY MIND.
EACH TIME YOU THINK YOU CAN OUTWIT ME, ALL YOU DO IS HELP DESTROY THOSE CITIES FOR ME. WISE UP...
...AND LET ME GO.
THOUSANDS F LIVES HAVE BEEN LOST, ROMETHEUS.
"OH, I THINK YOU'RE DOWNPLAYING THE DEATH TOLL, PALMER."
HOW CAN YOU SIT THERE AND--
FREE ME AND THE DEATH ENDS.

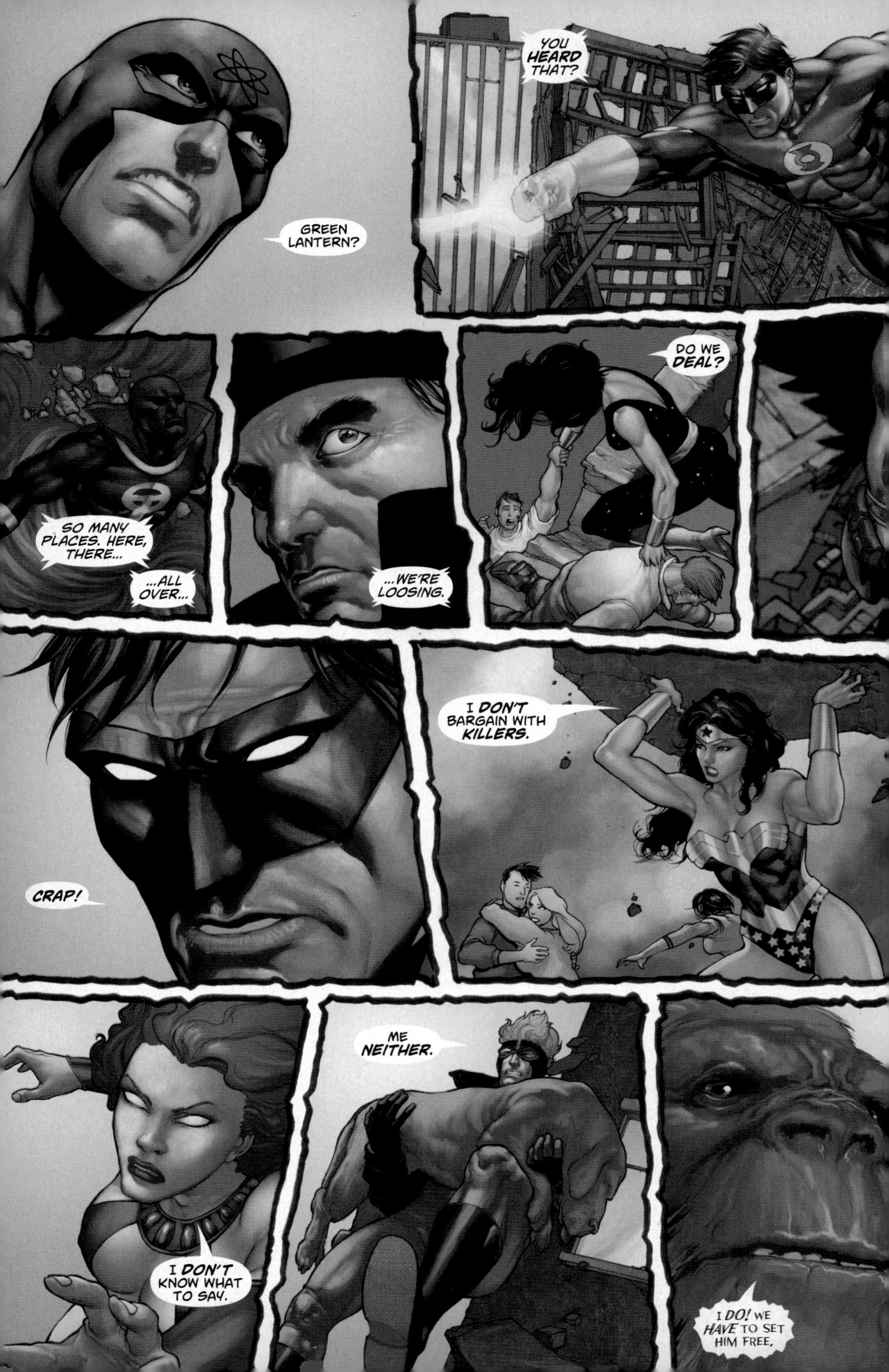
GREEN LANTERN?
YOU HEARD THAT?
SO MANY PLACES. HERE, THERE...
...ALL OVER...
...WE'RE LOOSING.
DO WE DEAL?
CRAP!
I DON'T BARGAIN WITH KILLERS.
I DON'T KNOW WHAT TO SAY.
ME NEITHER.
I DO! WE HAVE TO SET HIM FREE.

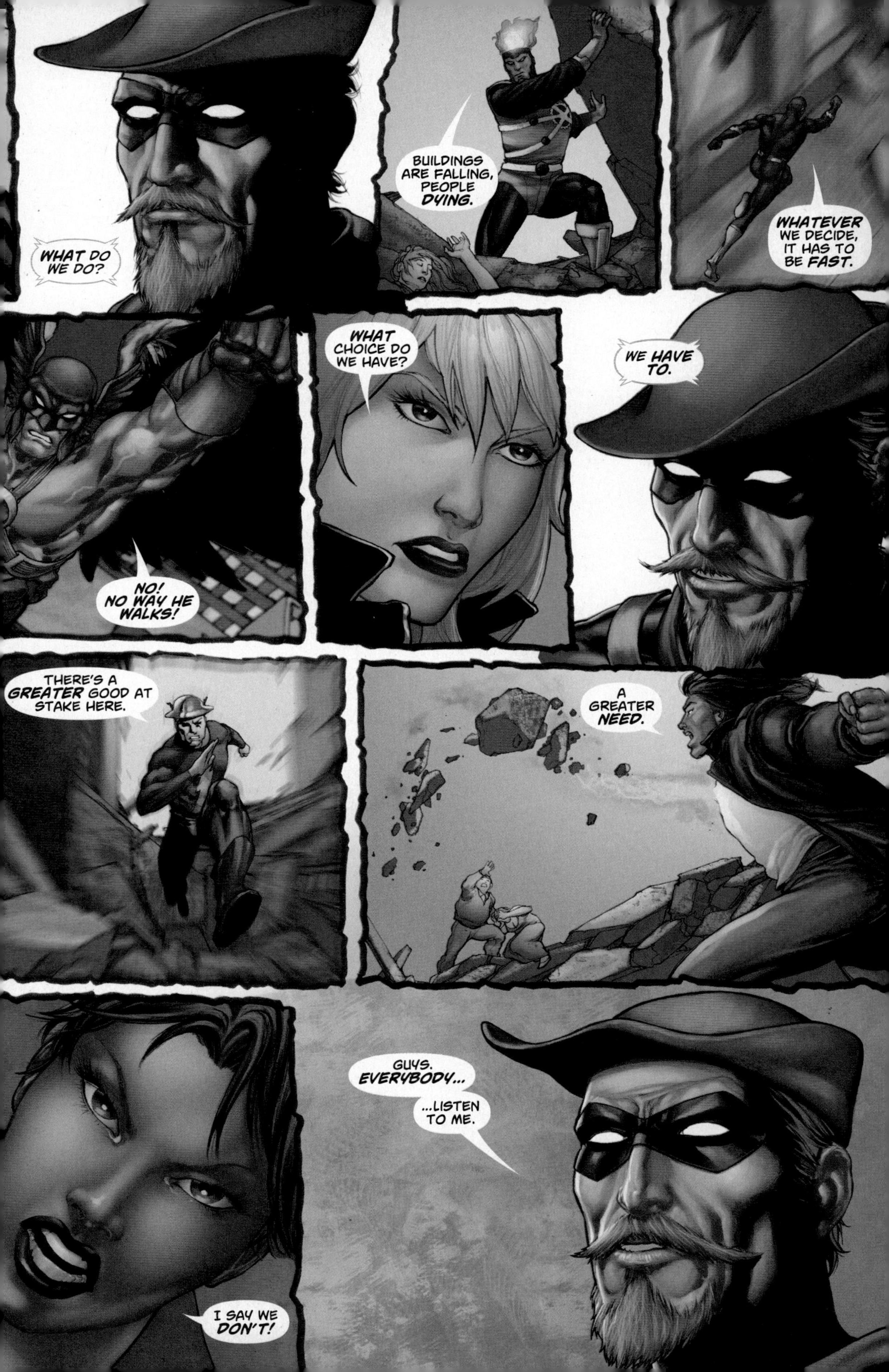
WHAT DO WE DO?
BUILDINGS ARE FALLING, PEOPLE DYING.
WHATEVER WE DECIDE, IT HAS TO BE FAST.
NO! NO WAY HE WALKS!
WHAT CHOICE DO WE HAVE?
WE HAVE TO.
THERE'S A GREATER GOOD AT STAKE HERE.
A GREATER NEED.
I SAY WE DON'T!
GUYS. EVERYBODY...
...LISTEN TO ME.

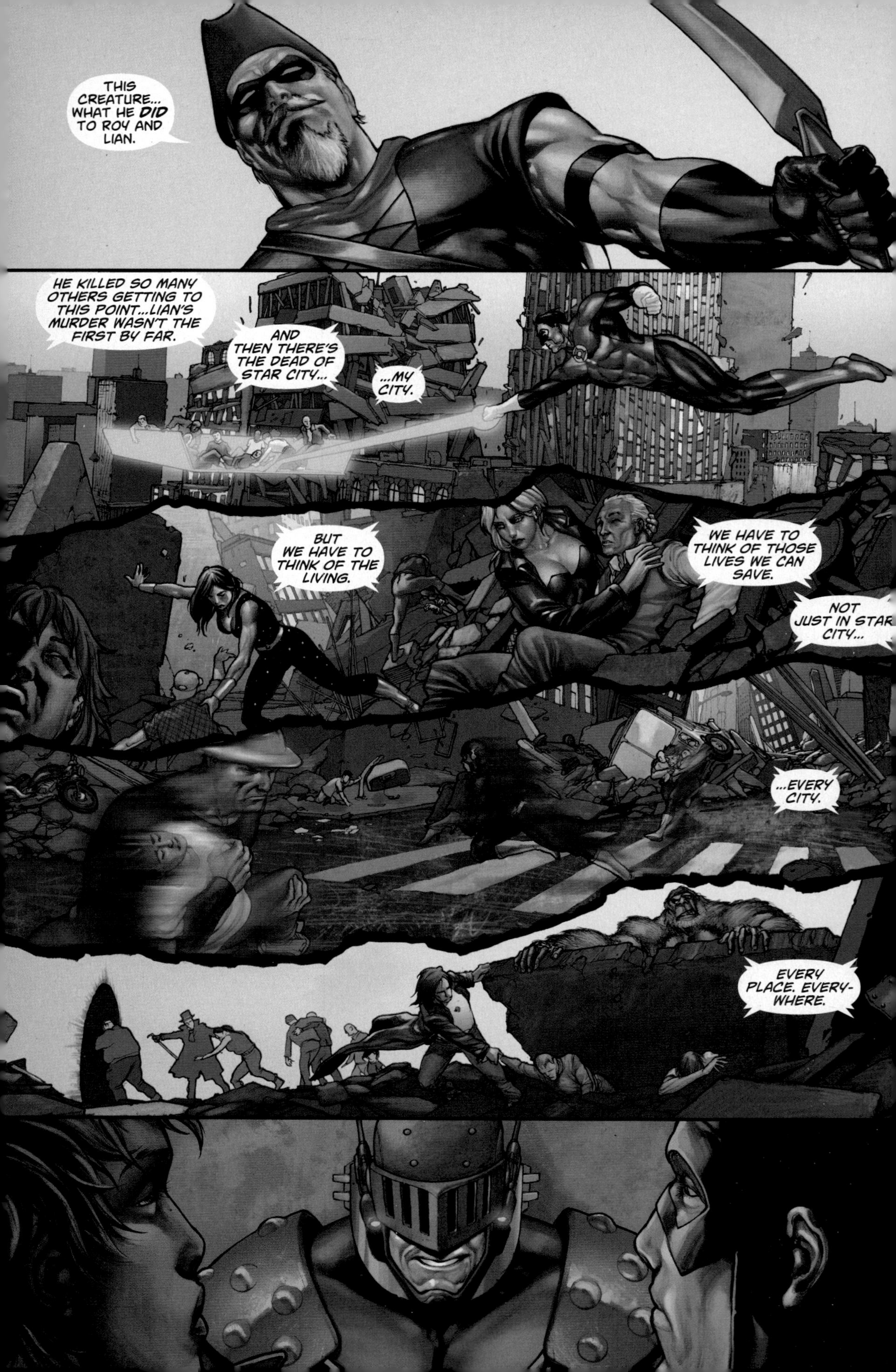
THIS CREATURE... WHAT HE DID TO ROY AND LIAN.
HE KILLED SO MANY OTHERS GETTING TO THIS POINT...LIAN'S MURDER WASN'T THE FIRST BY FAR.
AND THEN THERE'S THE DEAD OF STAR CITY...
...MY CITY.
BUT WE HAVE TO THINK OF THE LIVING.
WE HAVE TO THINK OF THOSE LIVES WE CAN SAVE.
NOT JUST IN STAR CITY...
...EVERY CITY.
EVERY PLACE. EVERY-WHERE.

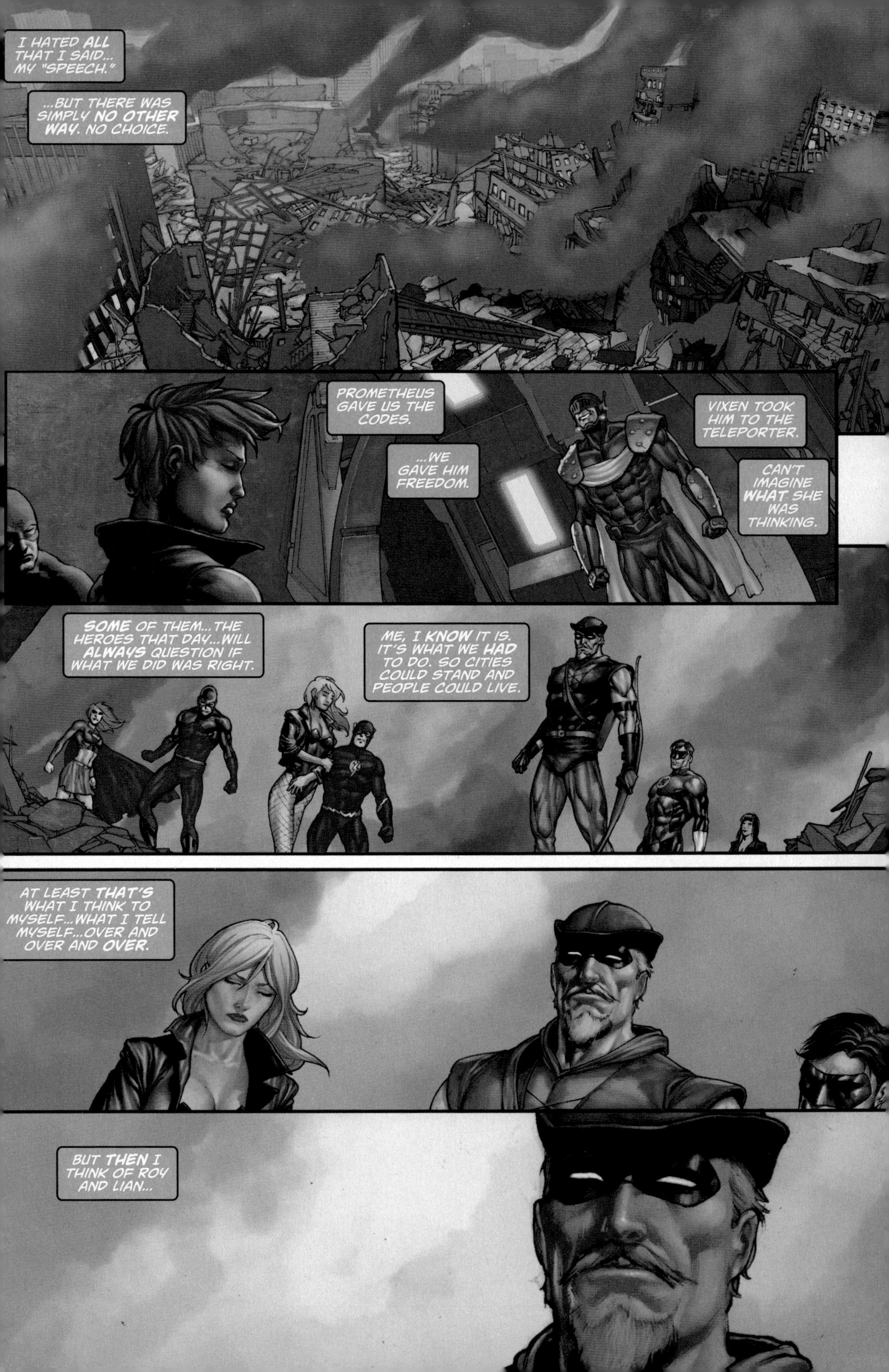

I HATED ALL THAT I SAID... MY "SPEECH."
...BUT THERE WAS SIMPLY NO OTHER WAY. NO CHOICE.
PROMETHEUS GAVE US THE CODES.
...WE GAVE HIM FREEDOM.
VIXEN TOOK HIM TO THE TELEPORTER.
CAN'T IMAGINE WHAT SHE WAS THINKING.
SOME OF THEM...THE HEROES THAT DAY...WILL ALWAYS QUESTION IF WHAT WE DID WAS RIGHT.
ME, I KNOW IT IS. IT'S WHAT WE HAD TO DO. SO CITIES COULD STAND AND PEOPLE COULD LIVE.
AT LEAST THAT'S WHAT I THINK TO MYSELF...WHAT I TELL MYSELF...OVER AND OVER AND OVER.
BUT THEN I THINK OF ROY AND LIAN...

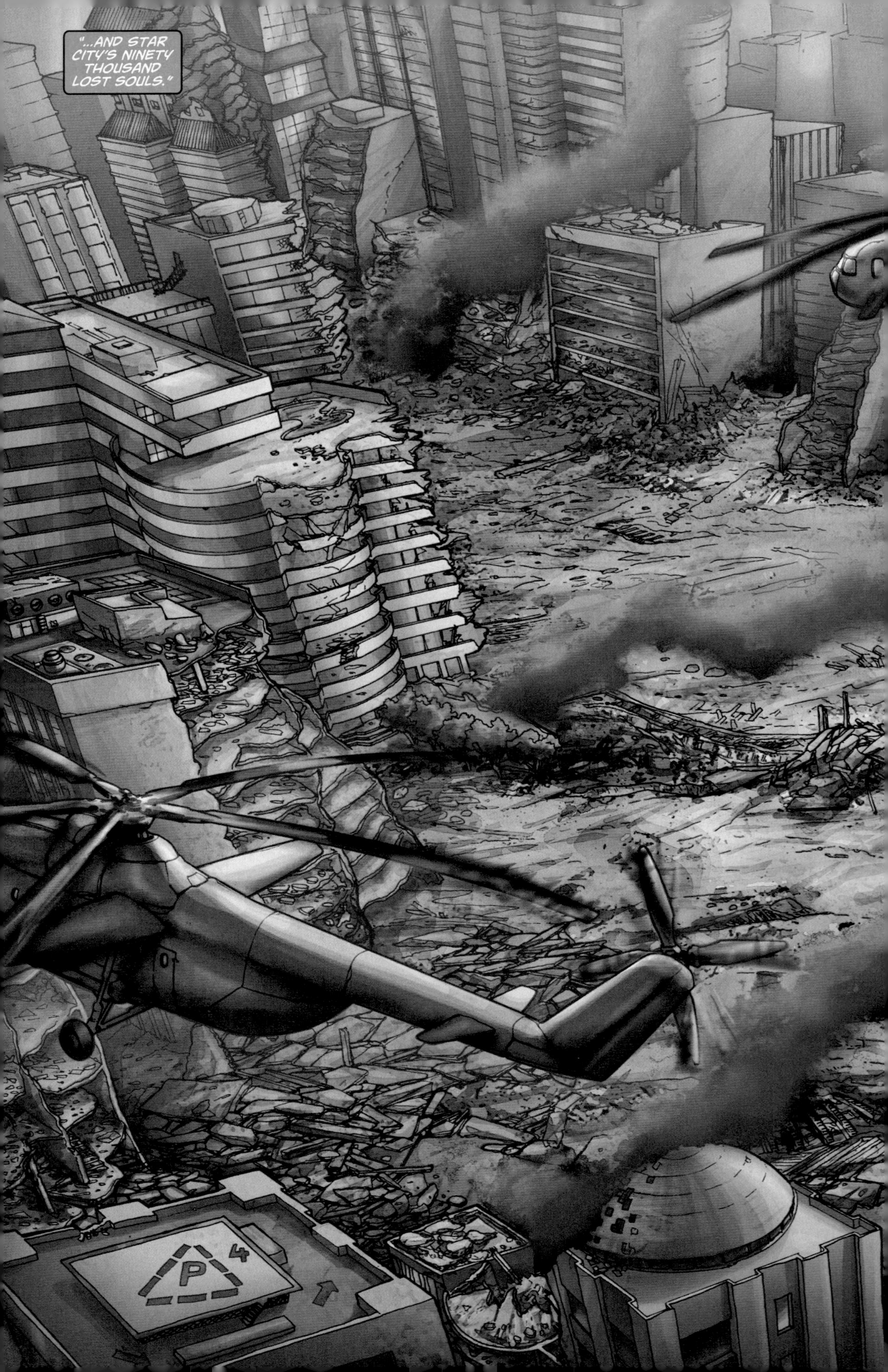
"...AND STAR CITY'S NINETY THOUSAND LOST SOULS."

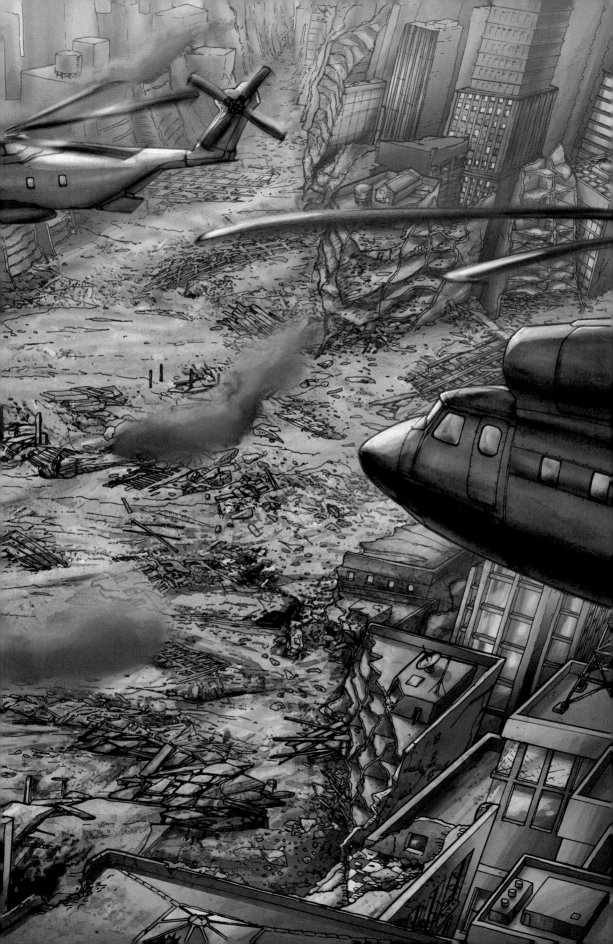

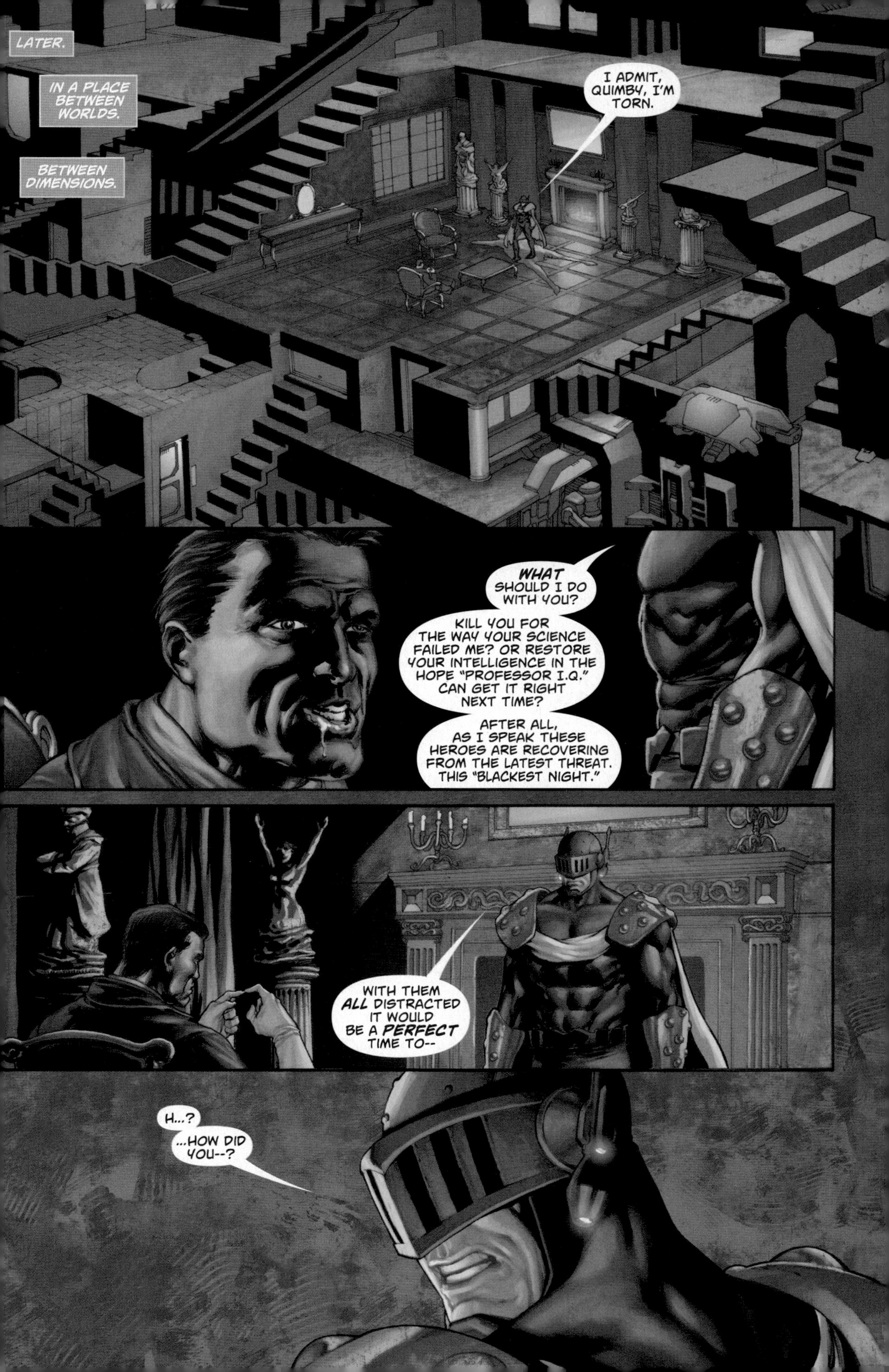
LATER.
IN A PLACE BETWEEN WORLDS.
BETWEEN DIMENSIONS.
I ADMIT, QUIMBY, I'M TORN.
WHAT SHOULD I DO WITH YOU?
KILL YOU FOR THE WAY YOUR SCIENCE FAILED ME? OR RESTORE YOUR INTELLIGENCE IN THE HOPE "PROFESSOR I.Q." CAN GET IT RIGHT NEXT TIME?
AFTER ALL, AS I SPEAK THESE HEROES ARE RECOVERING FROM THE LATEST THREAT. THIS "BLACKEST NIGHT."
WITH THEM ALL DISTRACTED IT WOULD BE A PERFECT TIME TO--
H...?
...HOW DID YOU--?

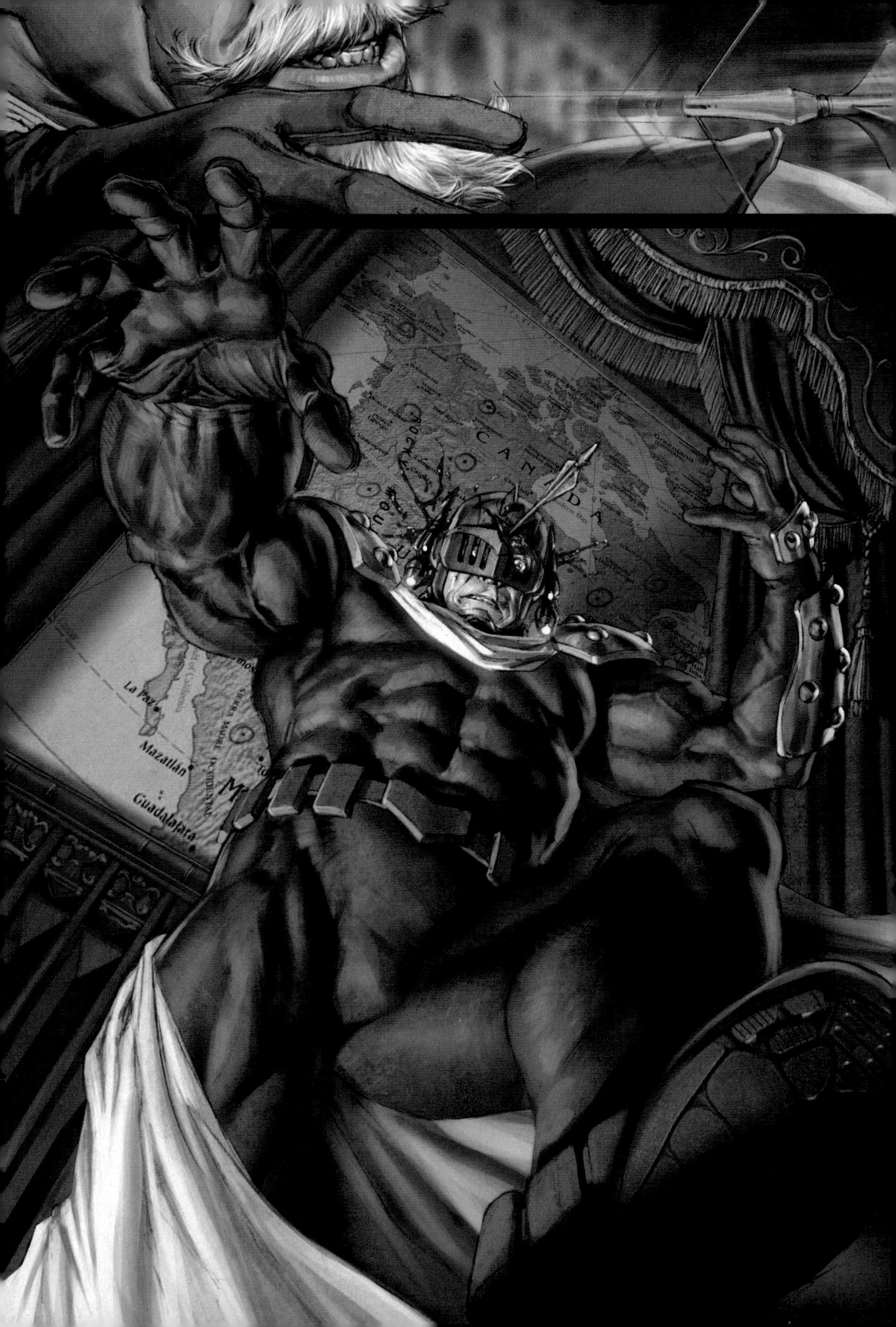
La Paz
Mazatlán
Guadalajara

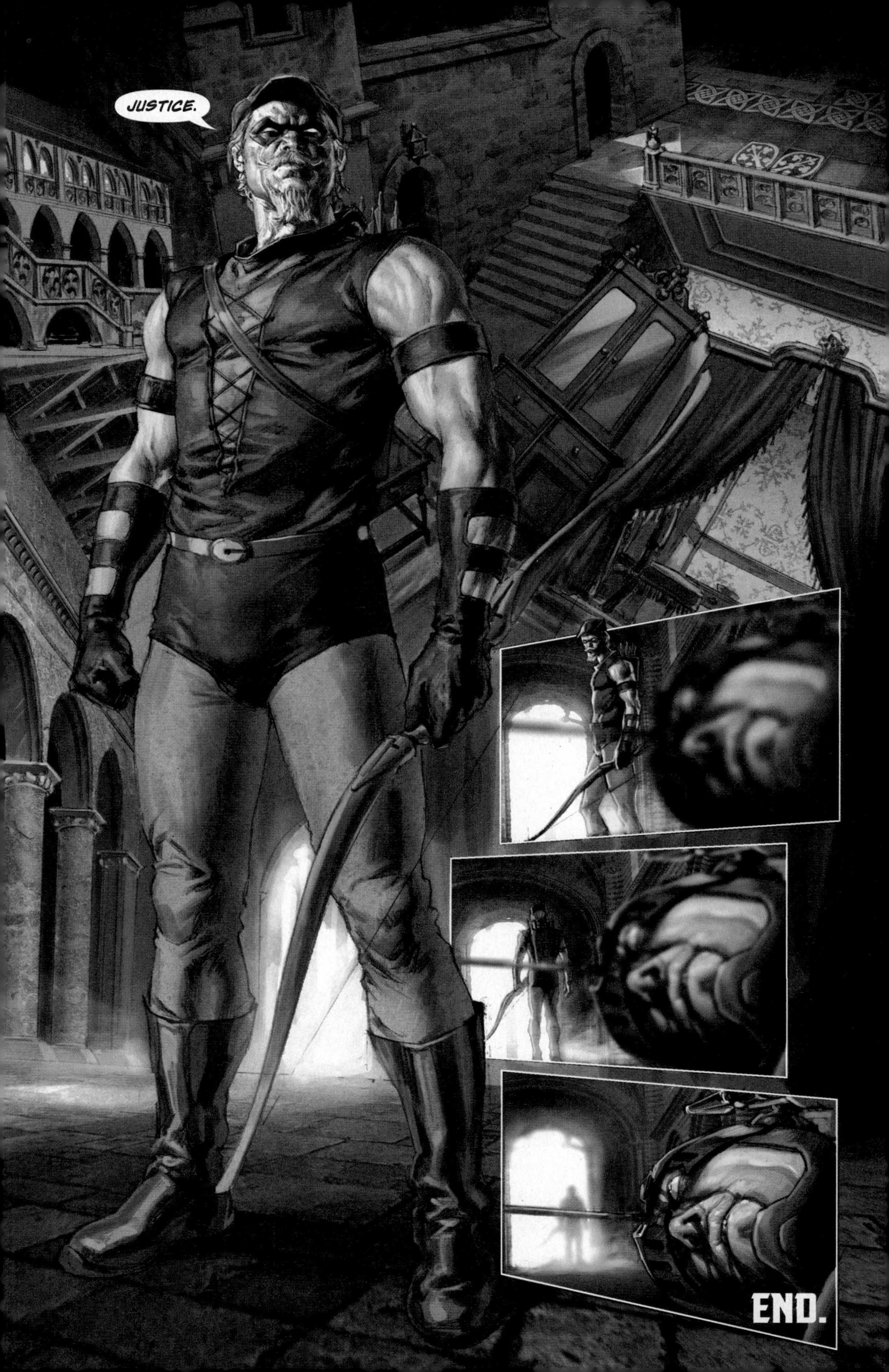
JUSTICE.
END.

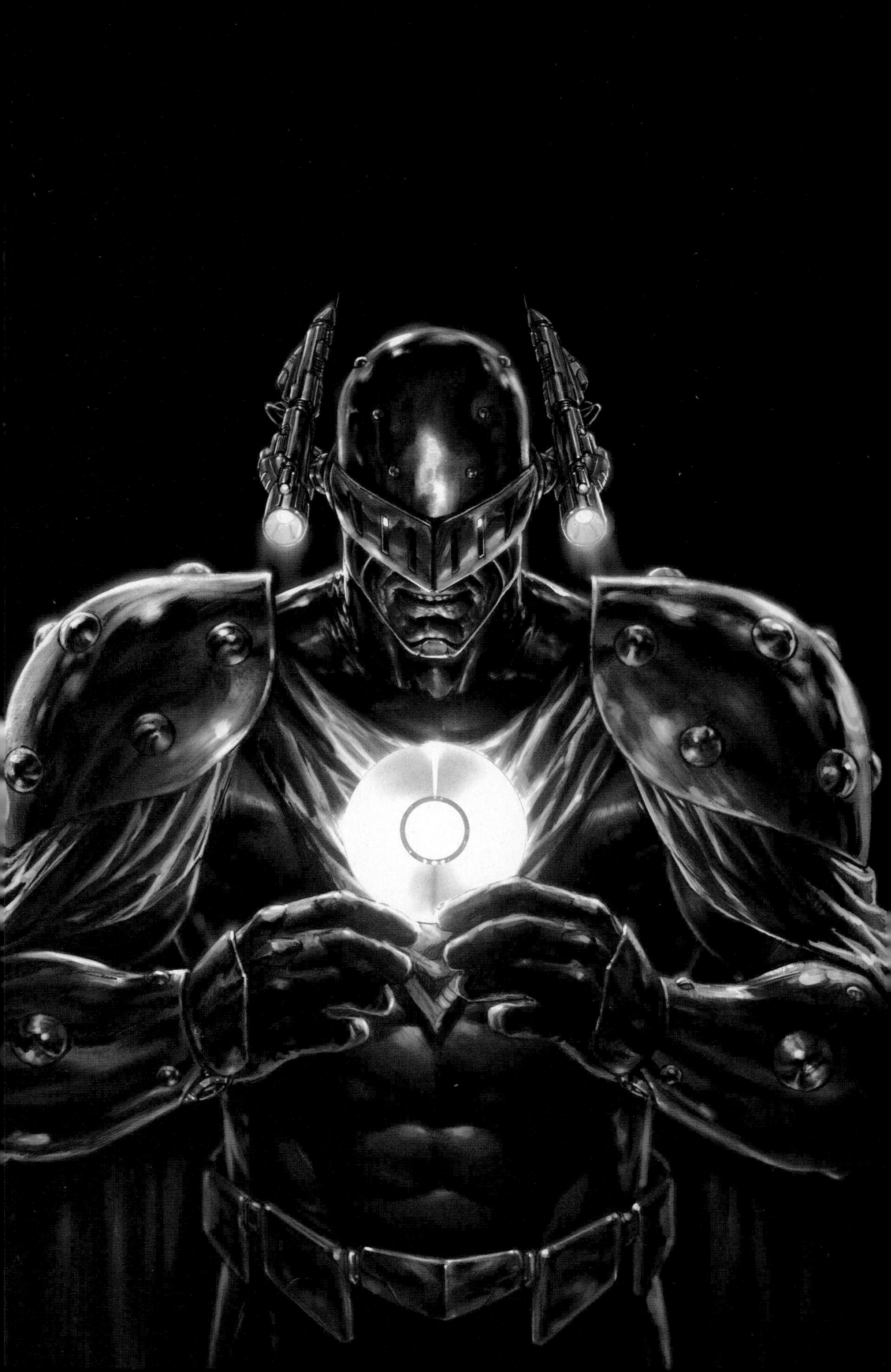

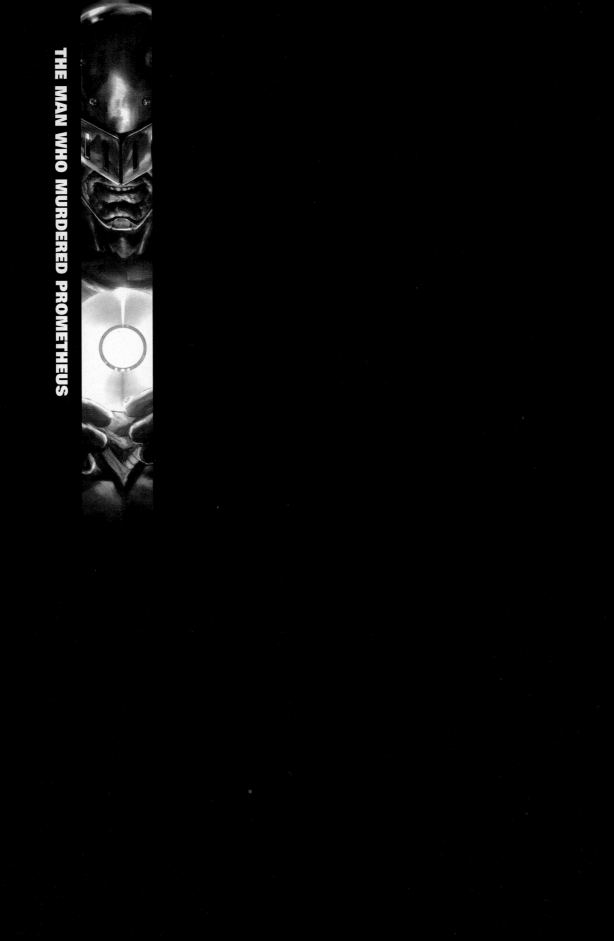

THE MAN WHO MURDERED PROMETHEUS

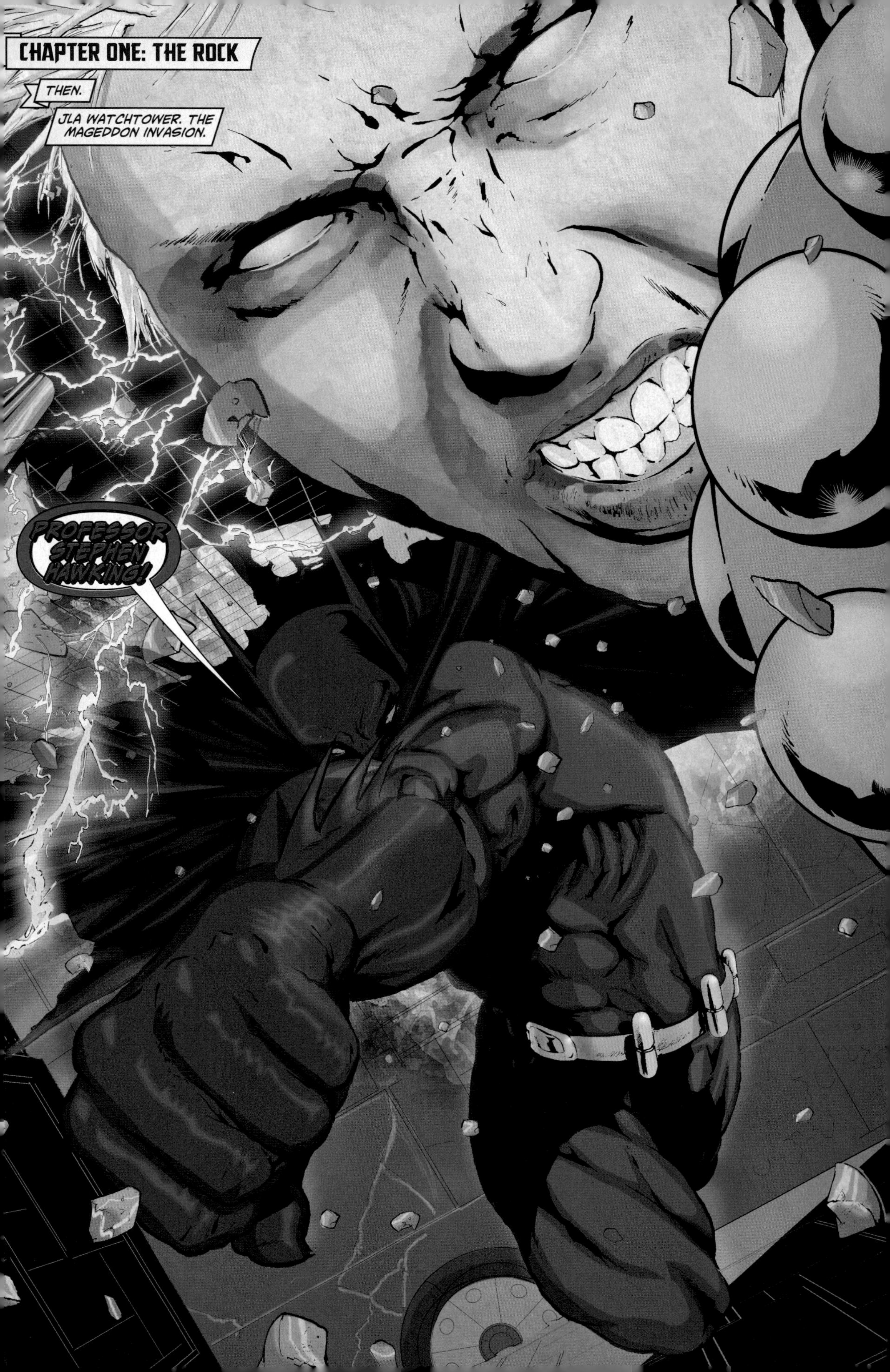
CHAPTER ONE: THE ROCK
THEN.
JLA WATCHTOWER. THE MAGEDDON INVASION.
PROFESSOR STEPHEN HAWKING!

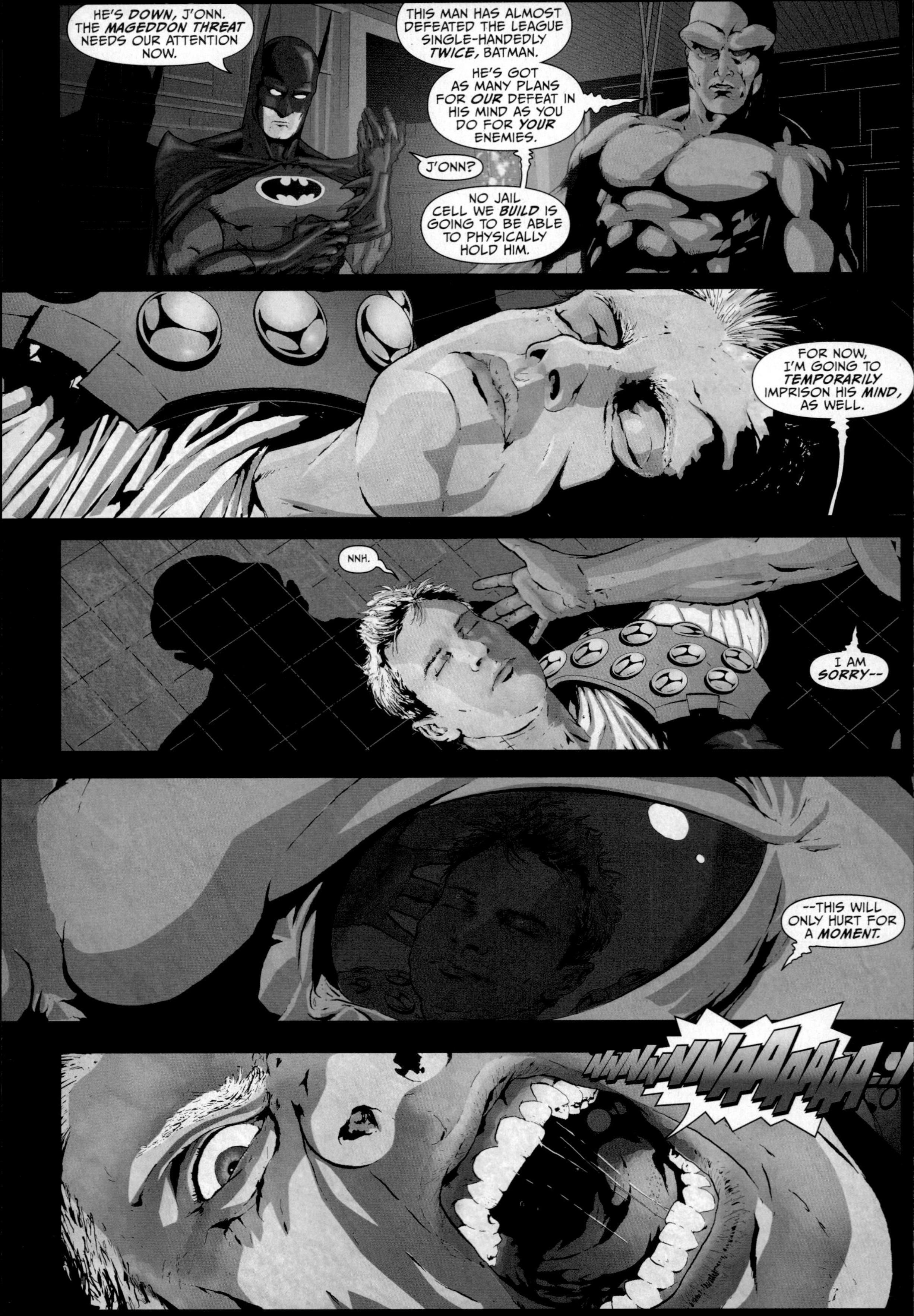

HE'S DOWN, J'ONN. THE MAGEDDON THREAT NEEDS OUR ATTENTION NOW.
THIS MAN HAS ALMOST DEFEATED THE LEAGUE SINGLE-HANDEDLY TWICE, BATMAN.
HE'S GOT AS MANY PLANS FOR OUR DEFEAT IN HIS MIND AS YOU DO FOR YOUR ENEMIES.
J'ONN?
NO JAIL CELL WE BUILD IS GOING TO BE ABLE TO PHYSICALLY HOLD HIM.
FOR NOW, I'M GOING TO TEMPORARILY IMPRISON HIS MIND, AS WELL.
NNH.
I AM SORRY--
--THIS WILL ONLY HURT FOR A MOMENT.
NNNNNNAAAAAA-!

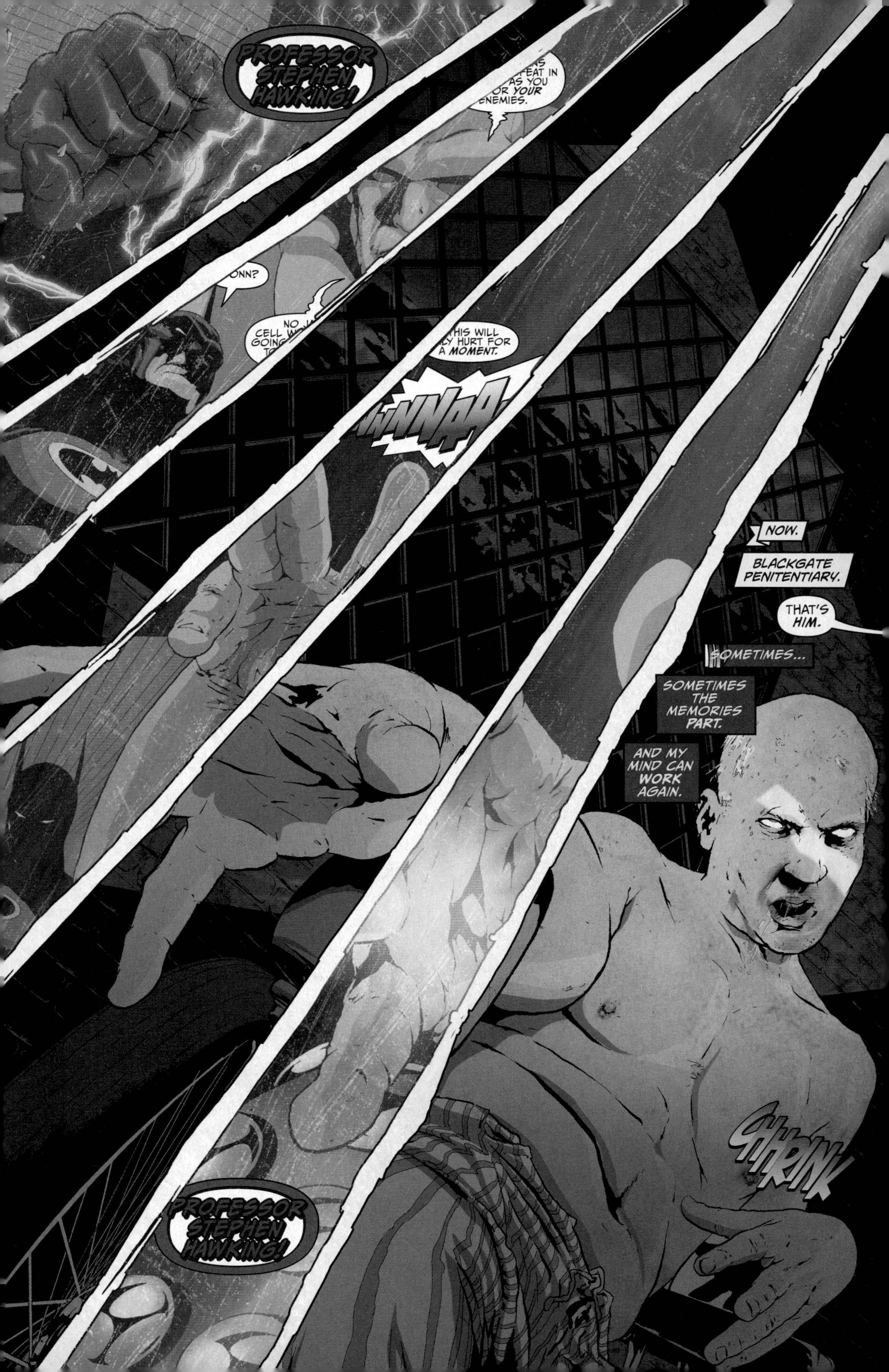
PROFESSOR STEPHEN HAWKING!
FEAT IN AS YOU OR YOUR ENEMIES.
ONN?
NO CELL GOING
THIS WILL HURT FOR A MOMENT.
NNNAA
NOW.
BLACKGATE PENITENTIARY.
THAT'S HIM.
SOMETIMES...
SOMETIMES THE MEMORIES PART.
AND MY MIND CAN WORK AGAIN.
CHRINK
PROFESSOR STEPHEN HAWKING!

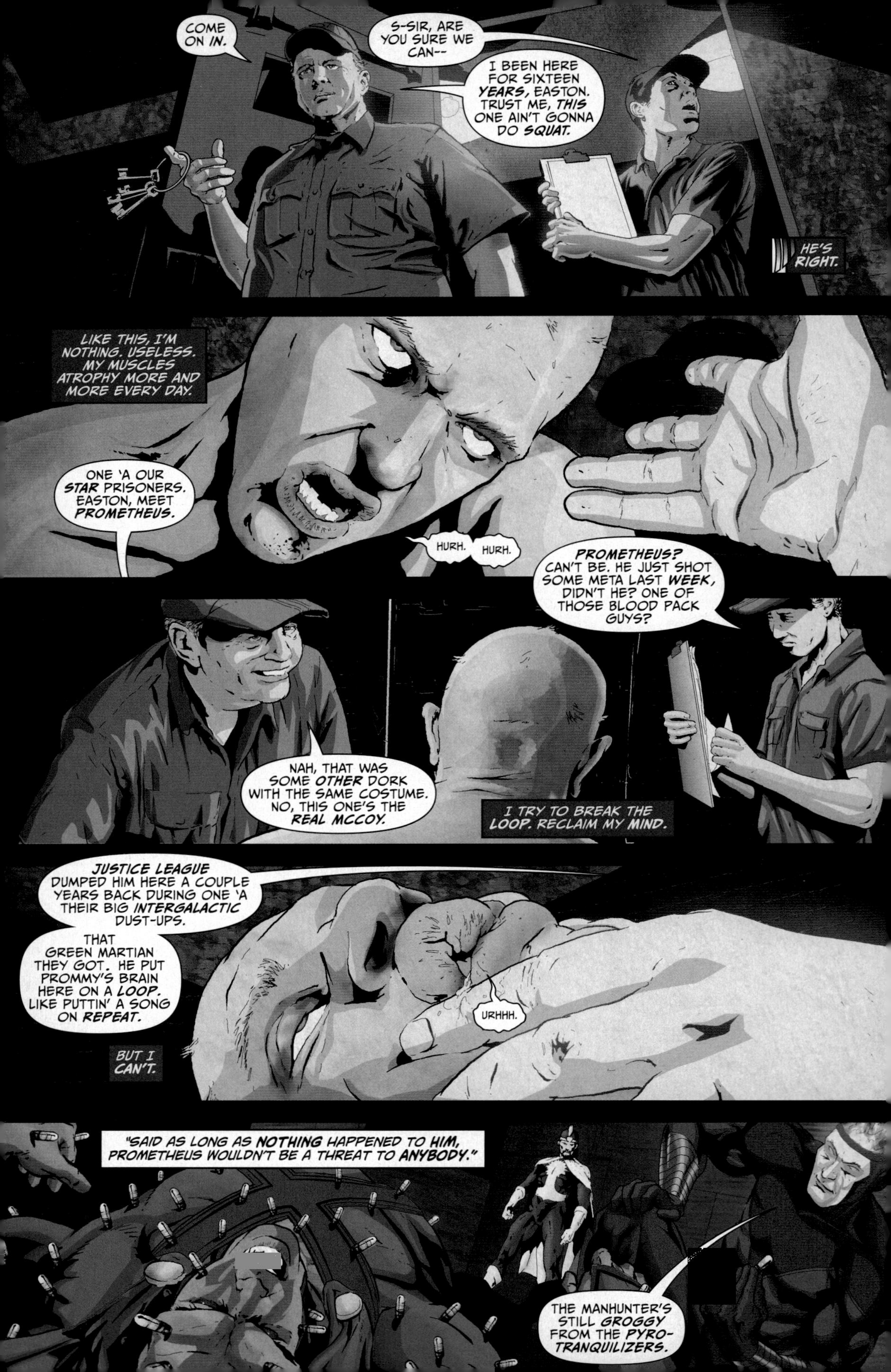
COME ON IN.
S-SIR, ARE YOU SURE WE CAN--
I BEEN HERE FOR SIXTEEN YEARS, EASTON. TRUST ME, THIS ONE AIN'T GONNA DO SQUAT.
HE'S RIGHT.
LIKE THIS, I'M NOTHING. USELESS. MY MUSCLES ATROPHY MORE AND MORE EVERY DAY.
ONE 'A OUR STAR PRISONERS. EASTON, MEET PROMETHEUS.
HURH.
HURH.
PROMETHEUS? CAN'T BE. HE JUST SHOT SOME META LAST WEEK, DIDN'T HE? ONE OF THOSE BLOOD PACK GUYS?
NAH, THAT WAS SOME OTHER DORK WITH THE SAME COSTUME. NO, THIS ONE'S THE REAL MCCOY.
I TRY TO BREAK THE LOOP. RECLAIM MY MIND.
JUSTICE LEAGUE DUMPED HIM HERE A COUPLE YEARS BACK DURING ONE 'A THEIR BIG INTERGALACTIC DUST-UPS.
THAT GREEN MARTIAN THEY GOT. HE PUT PROMMY'S BRAIN HERE ON A LOOP. LIKE PUTTIN' A SONG ON REPEAT.
URHHH.
BUT I CAN'T.
"SAID AS LONG AS NOTHING HAPPENED TO HIM, PROMETHEUS WOULDN'T BE A THREAT TO ANYBODY."
THE MANHUNTER'S STILL GROGGY FROM THE PYRO-TRANQUILIZERS.

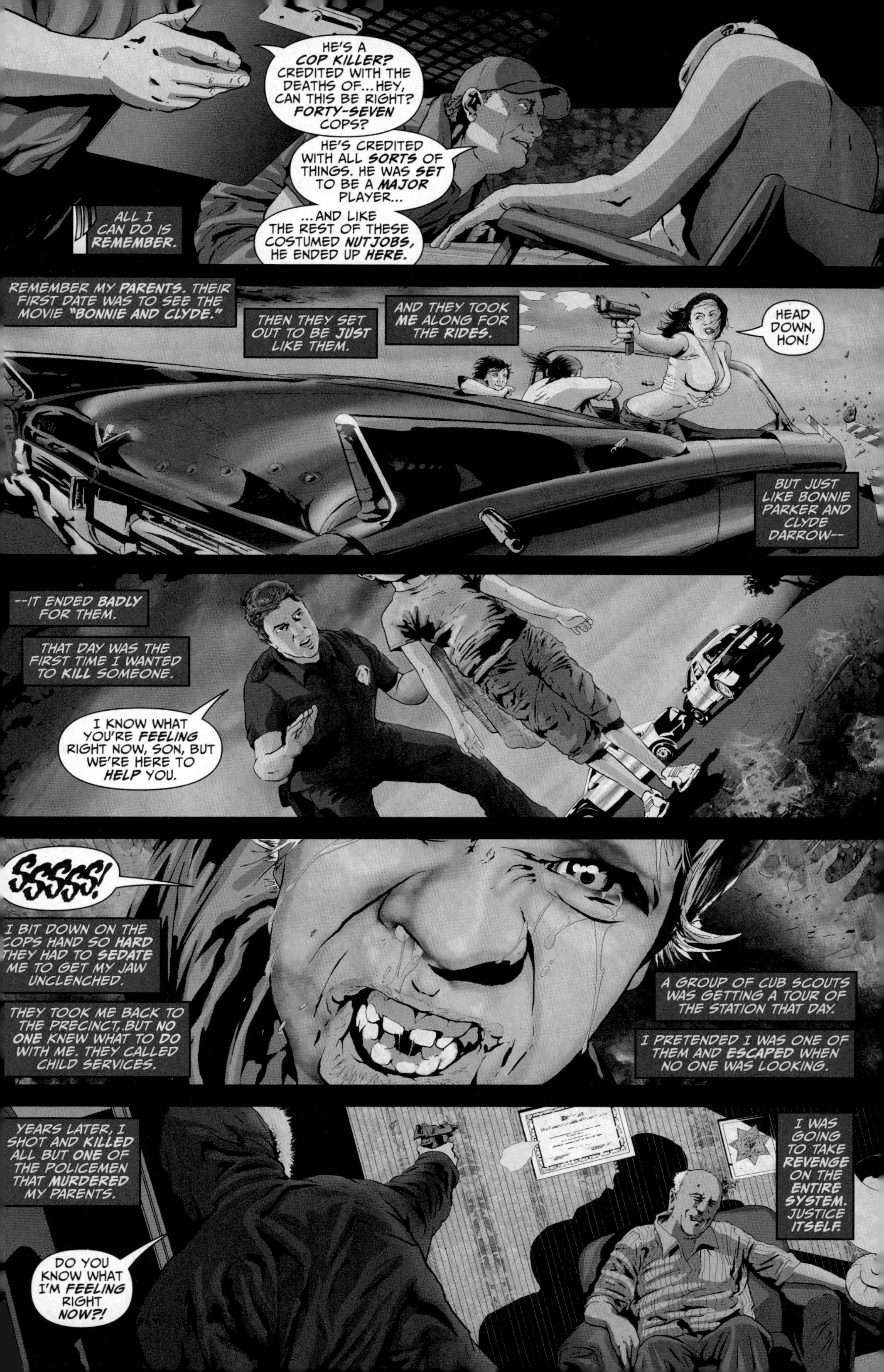
HE'S A COP KILLER? CREDITED WITH THE DEATHS OF... HEY, CAN THIS BE RIGHT? FORTY-SEVEN COPS?
HE'S CREDITED WITH ALL SORTS OF THINGS. HE WAS SET TO BE A MAJOR PLAYER...
ALL I CAN DO IS REMEMBER.
...AND LIKE THE REST OF THESE COSTUMED NUTJOBS, HE ENDED UP HERE.
REMEMBER MY PARENTS. THEIR FIRST DATE WAS TO SEE THE MOVIE "BONNIE AND CLYDE."
THEN THEY SET OUT TO BE JUST LIKE THEM.
AND THEY TOOK ME ALONG FOR THE RIDES.
HEAD DOWN, HON!
BUT JUST LIKE BONNIE PARKER AND CLYDE DARROW--
--IT ENDED BADLY FOR THEM.
THAT DAY WAS THE FIRST TIME I WANTED TO KILL SOMEONE.
I KNOW WHAT YOU'RE FEELING RIGHT NOW, SON, BUT WE'RE HERE TO HELP YOU.
SSSSS!
I BIT DOWN ON THE COPS HAND SO HARD THEY HAD TO SEDATE ME TO GET MY JAW UNCLENCHED.
THEY TOOK ME BACK TO THE PRECINCT, BUT NO ONE KNEW WHAT TO DO WITH ME. THEY CALLED CHILD SERVICES.
A GROUP OF CUB SCOUTS WAS GETTING A TOUR OF THE STATION THAT DAY.
I PRETENDED I WAS ONE OF THEM AND ESCAPED WHEN NO ONE WAS LOOKING.
YEARS LATER, I SHOT AND KILLED ALL BUT ONE OF THE POLICEMEN THAT MURDERED MY PARENTS.
I WAS GOING TO TAKE REVENGE ON THE ENTIRE SYSTEM. JUSTICE ITSELF.
DO YOU KNOW WHAT I'M FEELING RIGHT NOW?!

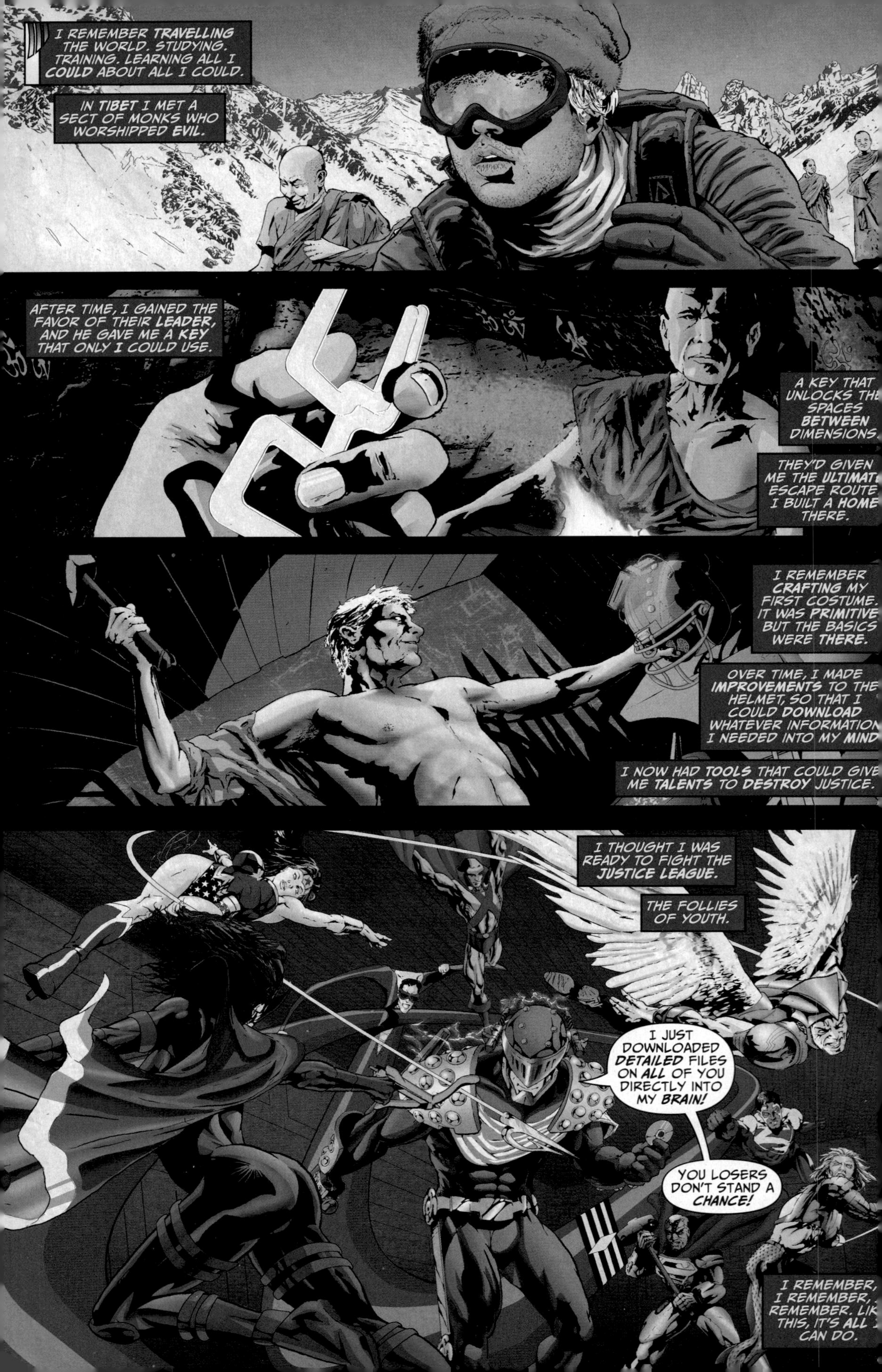
I REMEMBER TRAVELLING THE WORLD. STUDYING. TRAINING. LEARNING ALL I COULD ABOUT ALL I COULD.
IN TIBET I MET A SECT OF MONKS WHO WORSHIPPED EVIL.
AFTER TIME, I GAINED THE FAVOR OF THEIR LEADER, AND HE GAVE ME A KEY THAT ONLY I COULD USE.
A KEY THAT UNLOCKS THE SPACES BETWEEN DIMENSIONS.
THEY'D GIVEN ME THE ULTIMATE ESCAPE ROUTE. I BUILT A HOME THERE.
I REMEMBER CRAFTING MY FIRST COSTUME. IT WAS PRIMITIVE BUT THE BASICS WERE THERE.
OVER TIME, I MADE IMPROVEMENTS TO THE HELMET, SO THAT I COULD DOWNLOAD WHATEVER INFORMATION I NEEDED INTO MY MIND.
I NOW HAD TOOLS THAT COULD GIVE ME TALENTS TO DESTROY JUSTICE.
I THOUGHT I WAS READY TO FIGHT THE JUSTICE LEAGUE.
THE FOLLIES OF YOUTH.
I JUST DOWNLOADED DETAILED FILES ON ALL OF YOU DIRECTLY INTO MY BRAIN!
YOU LOSERS DON'T STAND A CHANCE!
I REMEMBER, I REMEMBER, I REMEMBER. LIKE THIS, IT'S ALL I CAN DO.

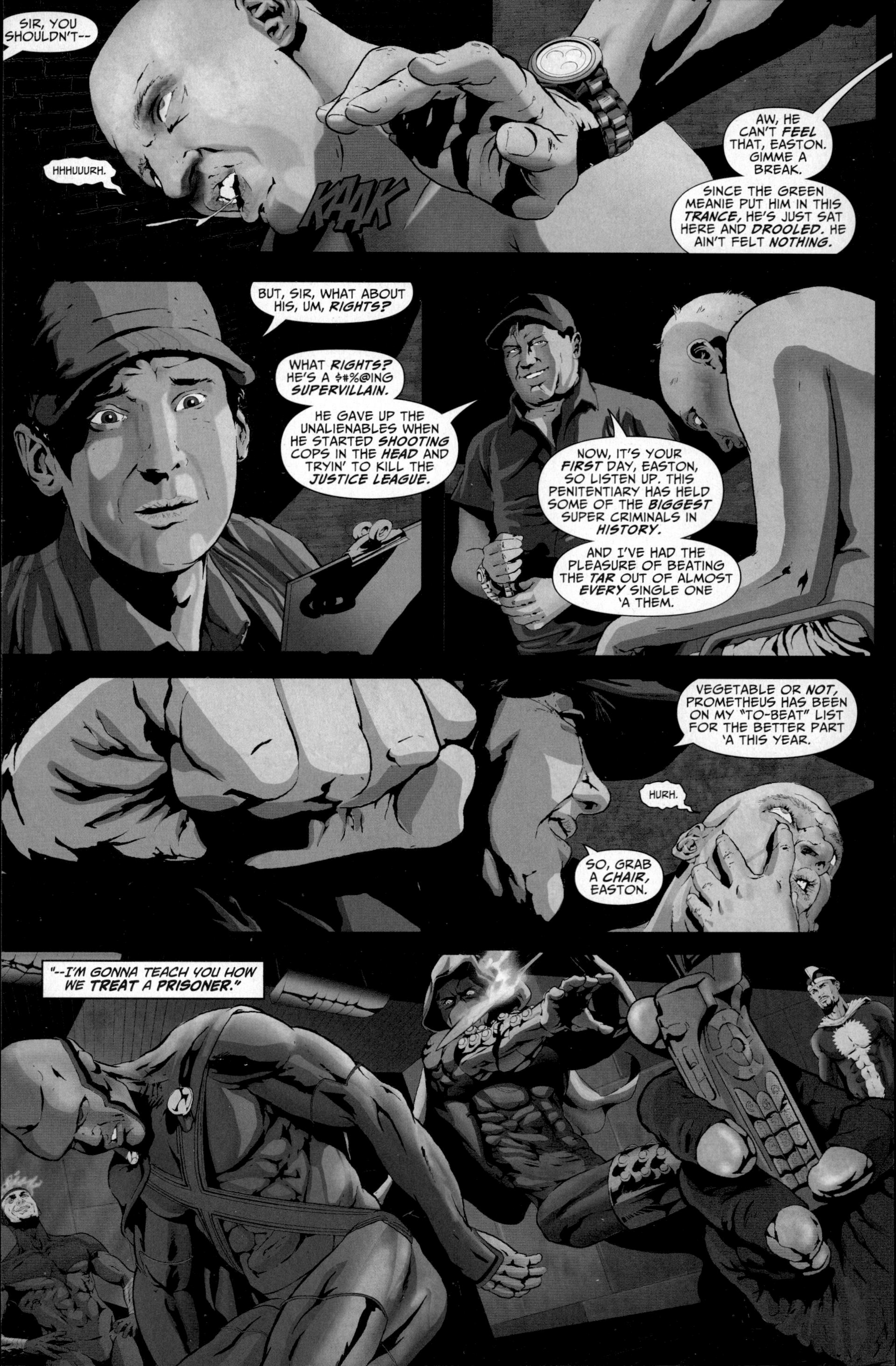
SIR, YOU SHOULDN'T--
HHHUUURH.
KAAK
AW, HE CAN'T FEEL THAT, EASTON. GIMME A BREAK.
SINCE THE GREEN MEANIE PUT HIM IN THIS TRANCE, HE'S JUST SAT HERE AND DROOLED. HE AIN'T FELT NOTHING.
BUT, SIR, WHAT ABOUT HIS, UM, RIGHTS?
WHAT RIGHTS? HE'S A $#%@ING SUPERVILLAIN.
HE GAVE UP THE UNALIENABLES WHEN HE STARTED SHOOTING COPS IN THE HEAD AND TRYIN' TO KILL THE JUSTICE LEAGUE.
NOW, IT'S YOUR FIRST DAY, EASTON, SO LISTEN UP. THIS PENITENTIARY HAS HELD SOME OF THE BIGGEST SUPER CRIMINALS IN HISTORY.
AND I'VE HAD THE PLEASURE OF HAD BEATING THE TAR OUT OF ALMOST EVERY SINGLE ONE 'A THEM.
VEGETABLE OR NOT, PROMETHEUS HAS BEEN ON MY "TO-BEAT" LIST FOR THE BETTER PART 'A THIS YEAR.
HURH.
SO, GRAB A CHAIR, EASTON.
"--I'M GONNA TEACH YOU HOW WE TREAT A PRISONER."

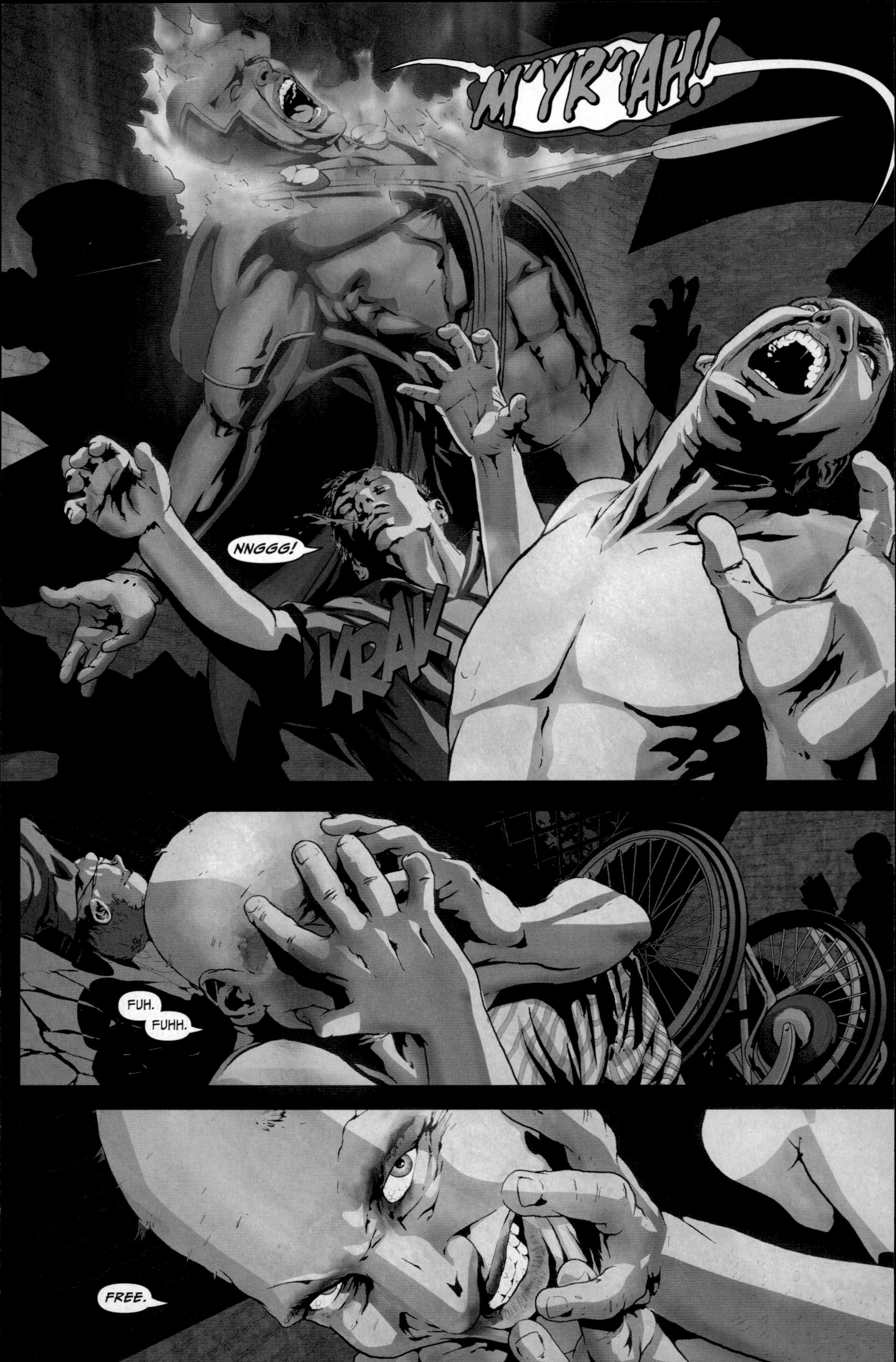
M'YR'IAH!
NNGGG!
KRAK
FUH.
FUHH.
FREE.

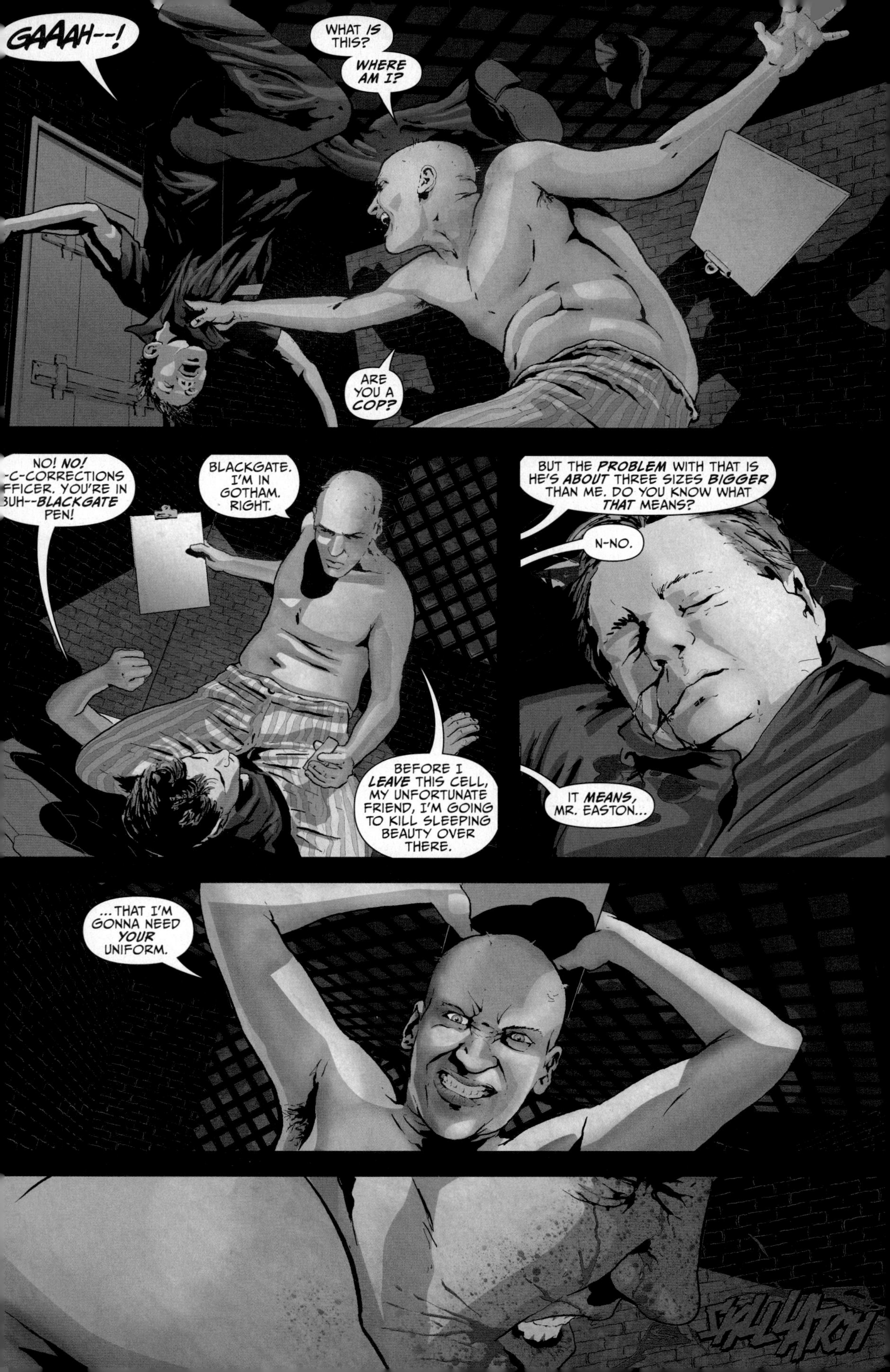
GAAAH--!
WHAT IS THIS? WHERE AM I?
ARE YOU A COP?
NO! NO! -C-CORRECTIONS FFICER. YOU'RE IN BUH--BLACKGATE PEN!
BLACKGATE. I'M IN GOTHAM. RIGHT.
BEFORE I LEAVE THIS CELL, MY UNFORTUNATE FRIEND, I'M GOING TO KILL SLEEPING BEAUTY OVER THERE.
BUT THE PROBLEM WITH THAT IS HE'S ABOUT THREE SIZES BIGGER THAN ME. DO YOU KNOW WHAT THAT MEANS?
N-NO.
IT MEANS, MR. EASTON...
...THAT I'M GONNA NEED YOUR UNIFORM.

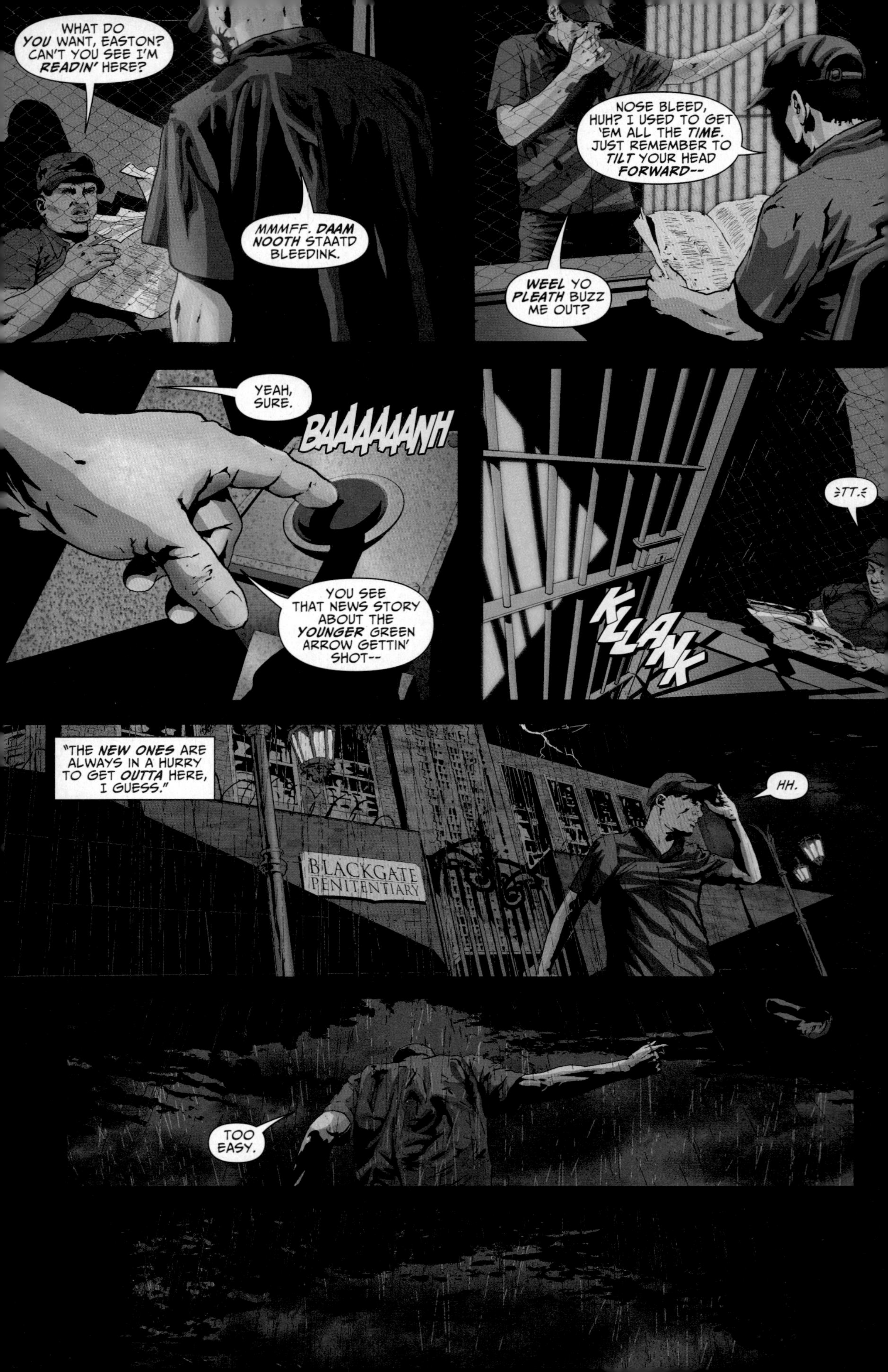
WHAT DO YOU WANT, EASTON? CAN'T YOU SEE I'M READIN' HERE?
MMMFF. DAAM NOOTH STAATD BLEEDINK.
NOSE BLEED, HUH? I USED TO GET 'EM ALL THE TIME. JUST REMEMBER TO TILT YOUR HEAD FORWARD--
WEEL YO PLEATH BUZZ ME OUT?
YEAH, SURE.
BAAAAAANH
YOU SEE THAT NEWS STORY ABOUT THE YOUNGER GREEN ARROW GETTIN' SHOT--
KLLANK
TT.
"THE NEW ONES ARE ALWAYS IN A HURRY TO GET OUTTA HERE, I GUESS."
BLACKGATE PENITENTIARY
HH.
TOO EASY.

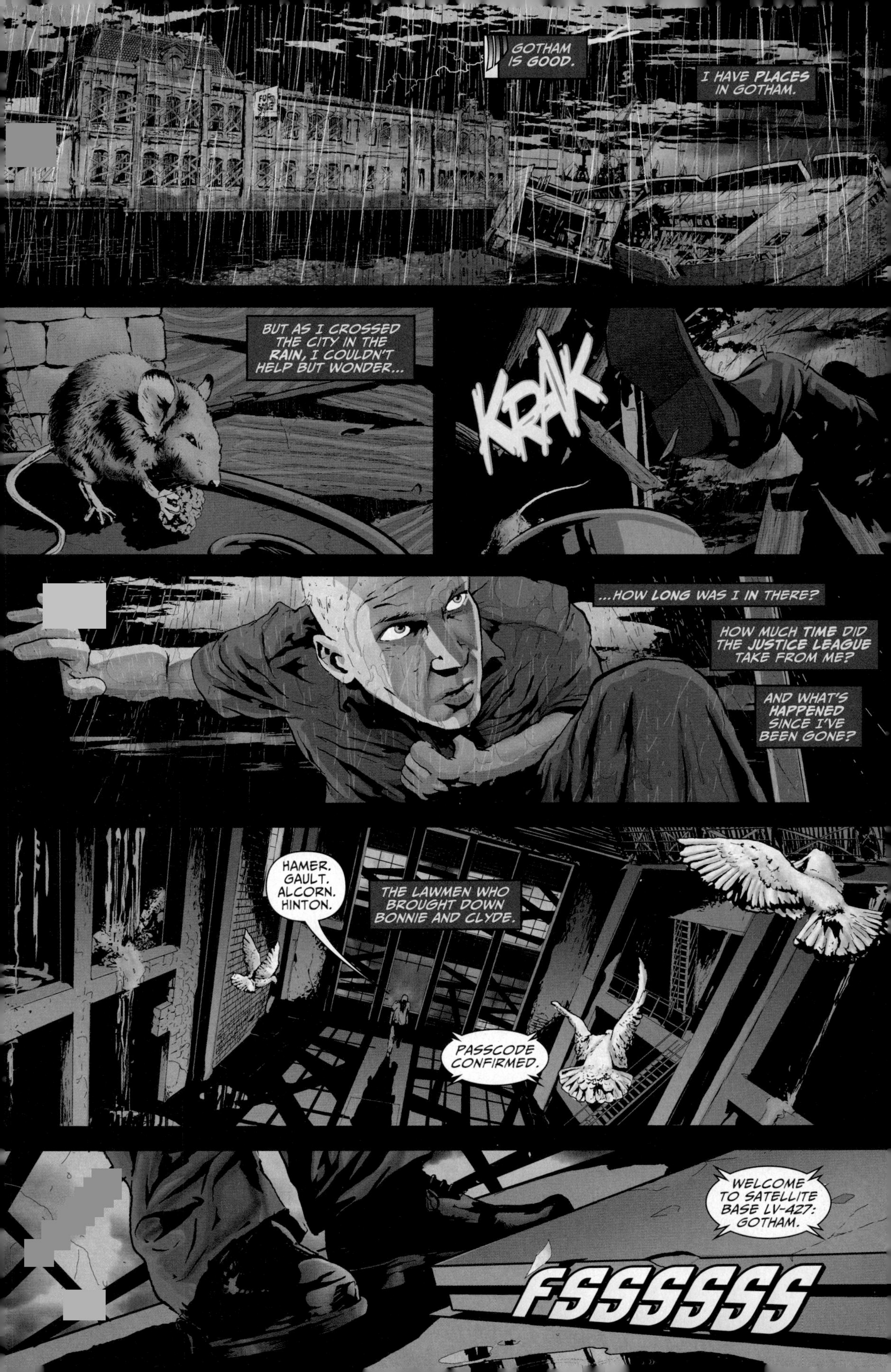
GOTHAM IS GOOD.
I HAVE PLACES IN GOTHAM.
FOR SALE
BUT AS I CROSSED THE CITY IN THE RAIN, I COULDN'T HELP BUT WONDER...
KRAK
...HOW LONG WAS I IN THERE?
HOW MUCH TIME DID THE JUSTICE LEAGUE TAKE FROM ME?
AND WHAT'S HAPPENED SINCE I'VE BEEN GONE?
HAMER. GAULT. ALCORN. HINTON.
THE LAWMEN WHO BROUGHT DOWN BONNIE AND CLYDE.
PASSCODE CONFIRMED.
WELCOME TO SATELLITE BASE LV-427: GOTHAM.
FSSSSSS

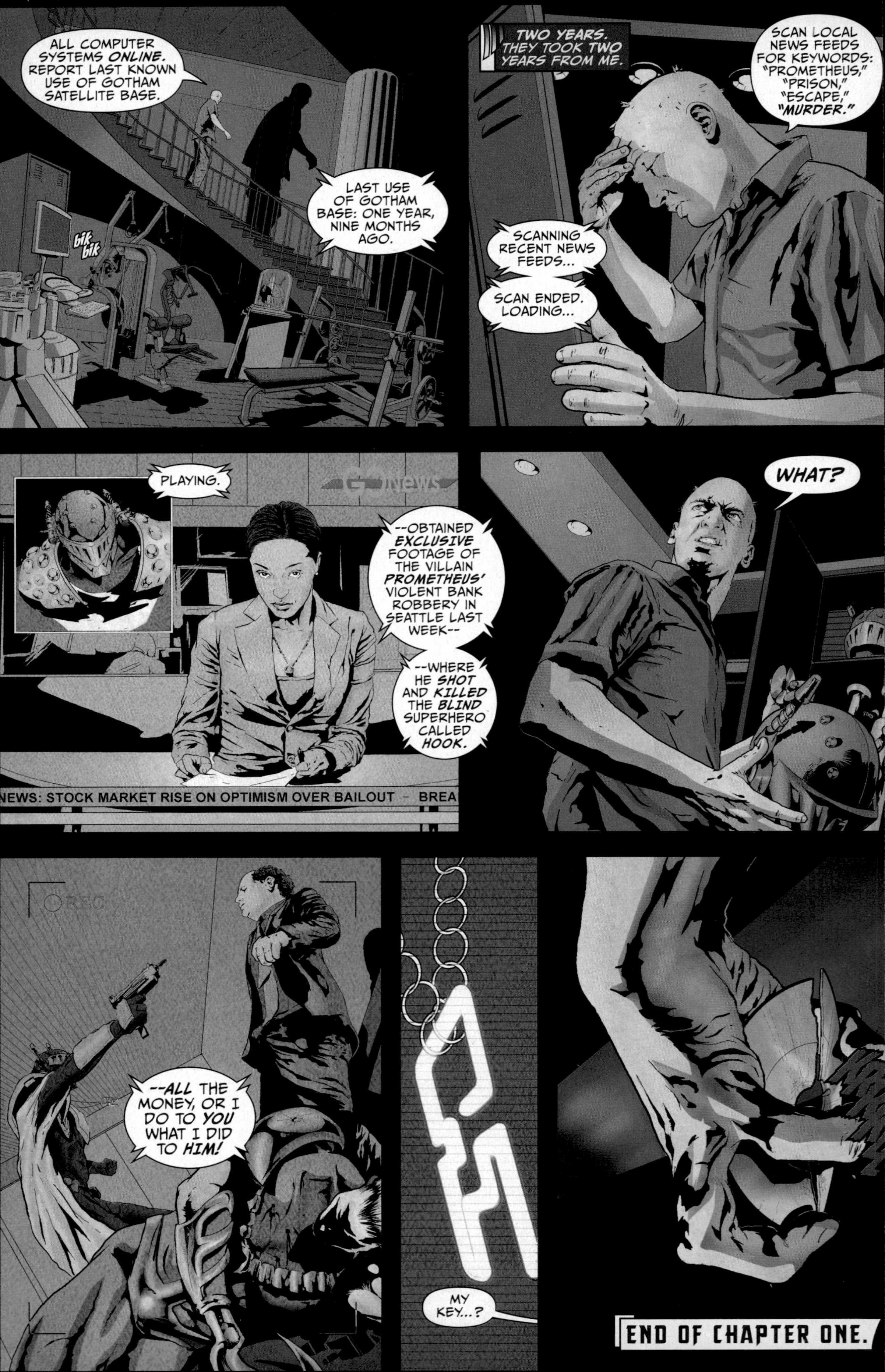
ALL COMPUTER SYSTEMS ONLINE. REPORT LAST KNOWN USE OF GOTHAM SATELLITE BASE.
bik bik
LAST USE OF GOTHAM BASE: ONE YEAR, NINE MONTHS AGO.
TWO YEARS. THEY TOOK TWO YEARS FROM ME.
SCAN LOCAL NEWS FEEDS FOR KEYWORDS: "PROMETHEUS," "PRISON," "ESCAPE," "MURDER."
SCANNING RECENT NEWS FEEDS...
SCAN ENDED. LOADING...
PLAYING.
GC News
--OBTAINED EXCLUSIVE FOOTAGE OF THE VILLAIN PROMETHEUS' VIOLENT BANK ROBBERY IN SEATTLE LAST WEEK--
--WHERE HE SHOT AND KILLED THE BLIND SUPERHERO CALLED HOOK.
NEWS: STOCK MARKET RISE ON OPTIMISM OVER BAILOUT - BREA
WHAT?
REC
--ALL THE MONEY, OR I DO TO YOU WHAT I DID TO HIM!
MY KEY...?
END OF CHAPTER ONE.

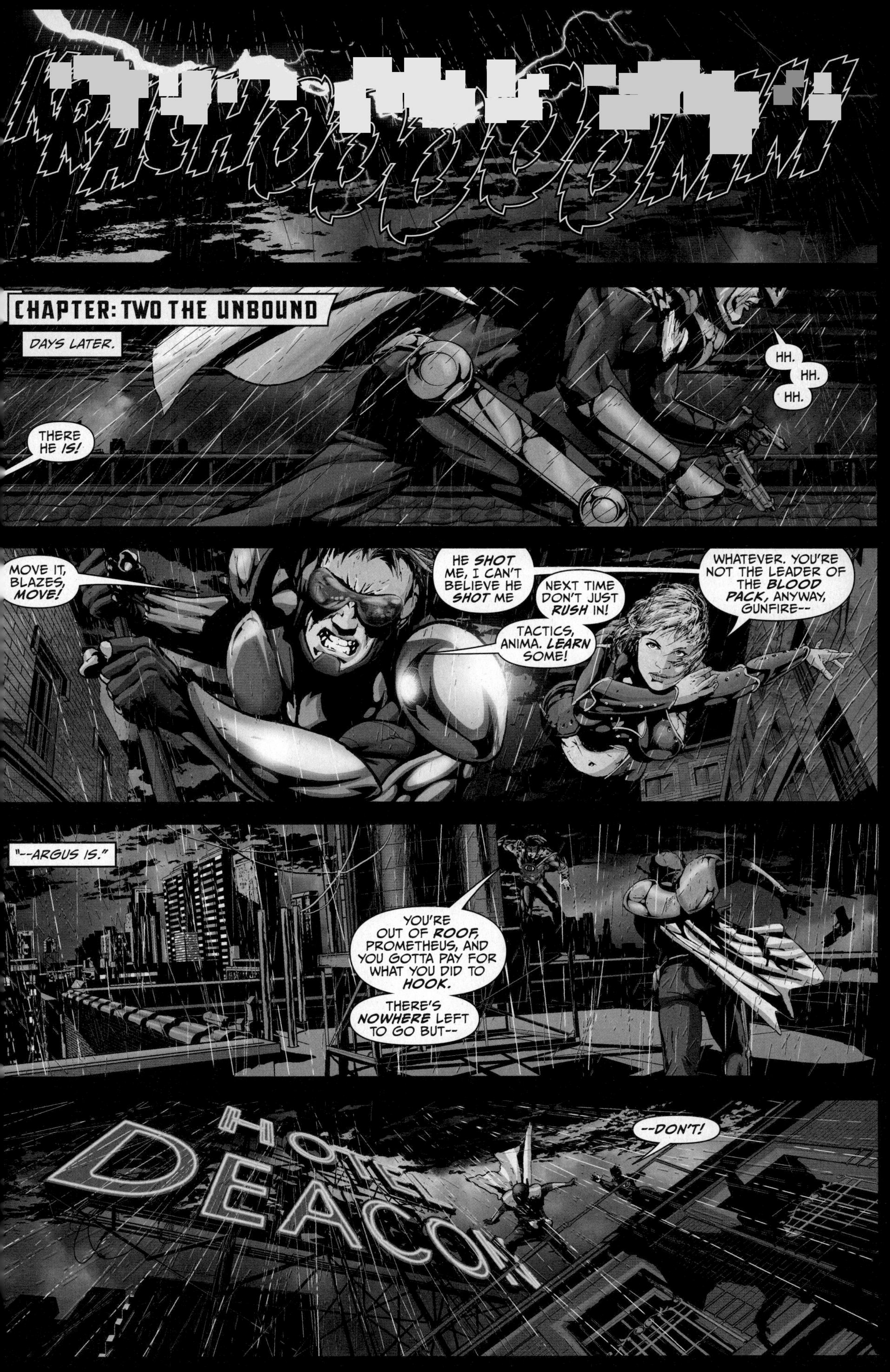
CHAPTER: TWO THE UNBOUND
DAYS LATER.
HH.
HH.
HH.
THERE HE IS!
MOVE IT, BLAZES, MOVE!
HE SHOT ME, I CAN'T BELIEVE HE SHOT ME
NEXT TIME DON'T JUST RUSH IN!
TACTICS, ANIMA. LEARN SOME!
WHATEVER. YOU'RE NOT THE LEADER OF THE BLOOD PACK, ANYWAY, GUNFIRE--
"--ARGUS IS."
YOU'RE OUT OF ROOF, PROMETHEUS, AND YOU GOTTA PAY FOR WHAT YOU DID TO HOOK.
THERE'S NOWHERE LEFT TO GO BUT--
DEACON
--DON'T!

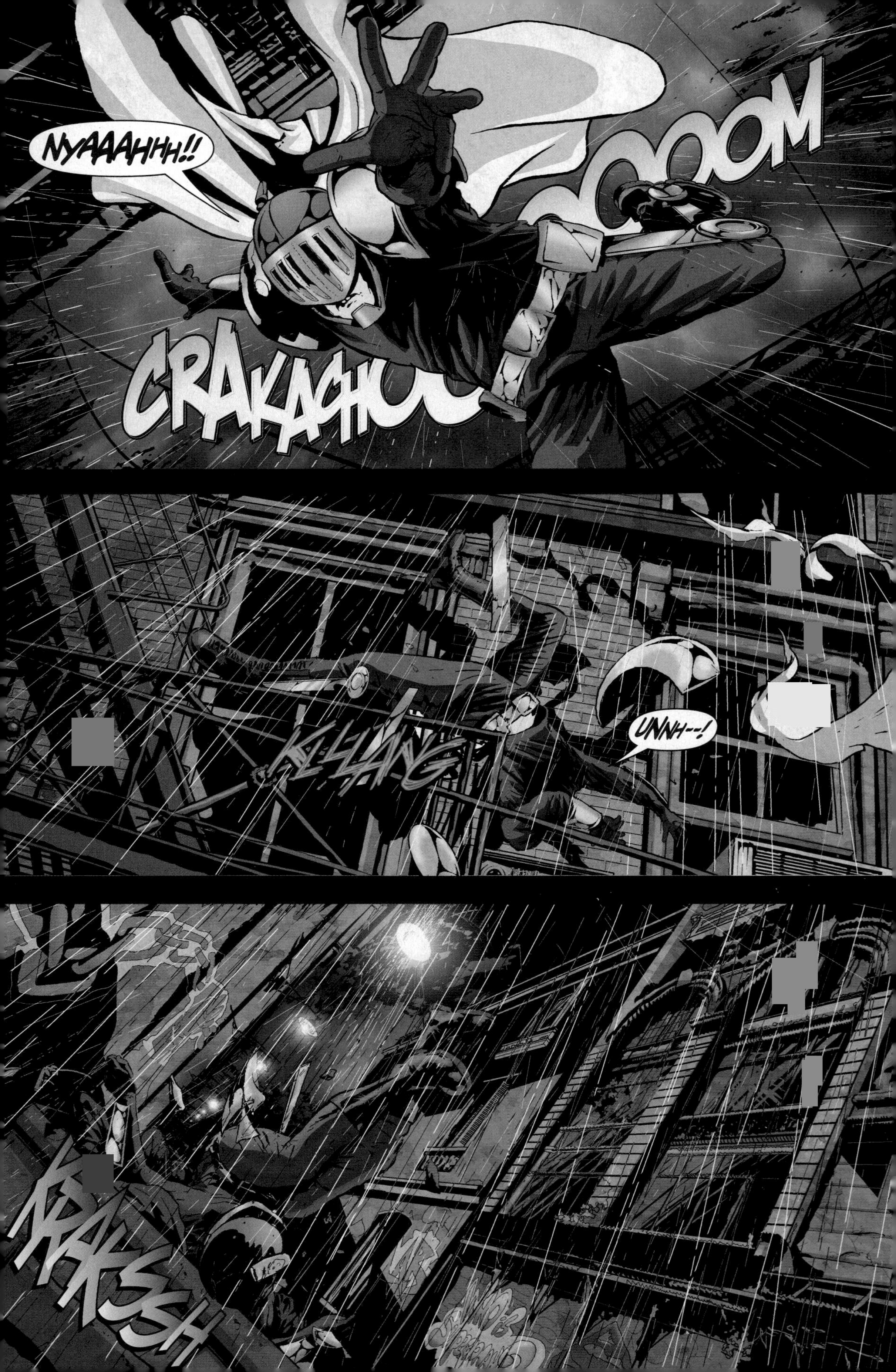
NYAAAHHH!!
CRAKACHOO
OOOOM
KLLANG
UNNH--!
KRAKSSH

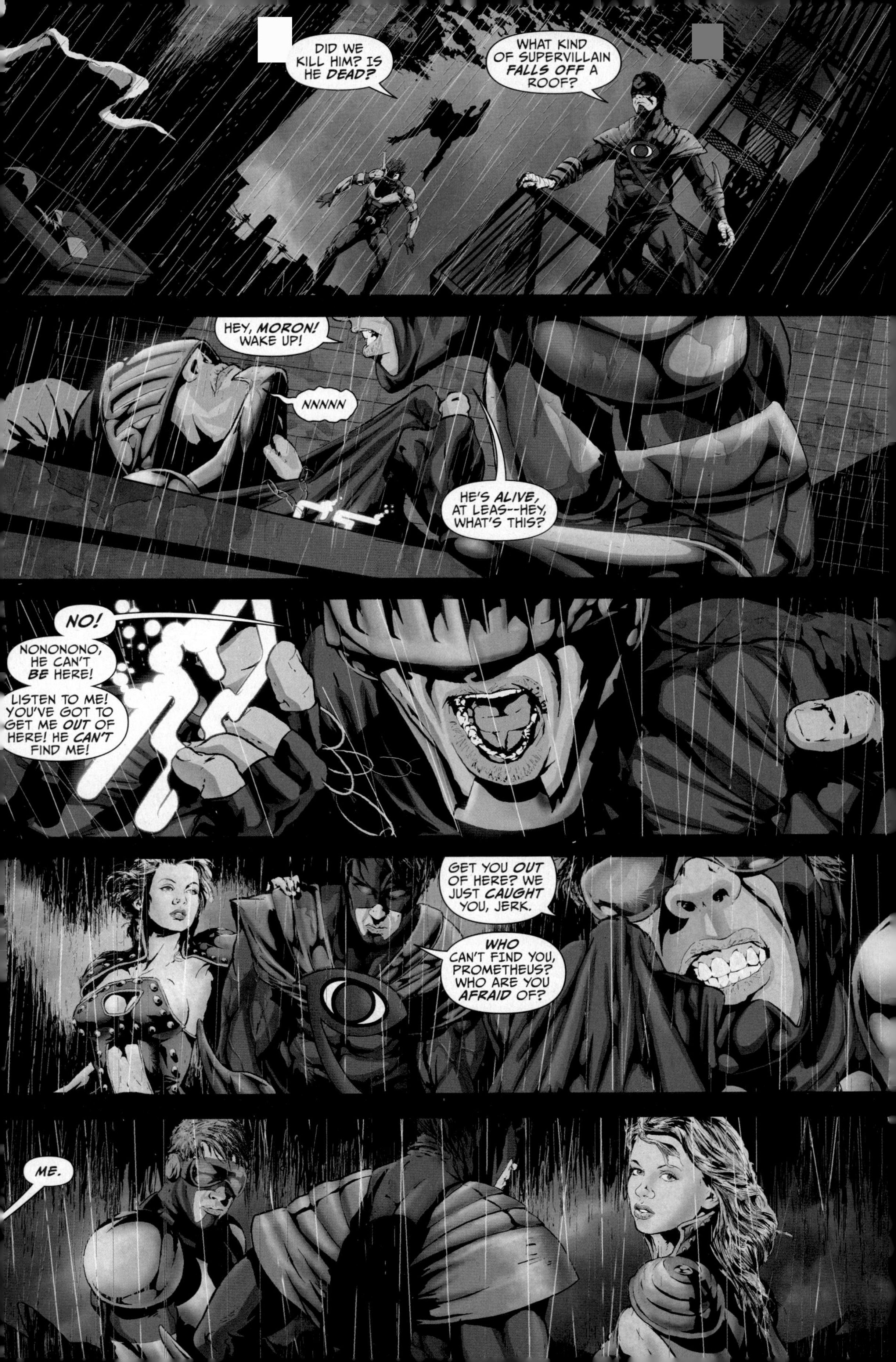

DID WE KILL HIM? IS HE DEAD?
WHAT KIND OF SUPERVILLAIN FALLS OFF A ROOF?
HEY, MORON! WAKE UP!
NNNNN
HE'S ALIVE, AT LEAS--HEY, WHAT'S THIS?
NO!
NONONONO, HE CAN'T BE HERE!
LISTEN TO ME! YOU'VE GOT TO GET ME OUT OF HERE! HE CAN'T FIND ME!
GET YOU OUT OF HERE? WE JUST CAUGHT YOU, JERK.
WHO CAN'T FIND YOU, PROMETHEUS? WHO ARE YOU AFRAID OF?
ME.

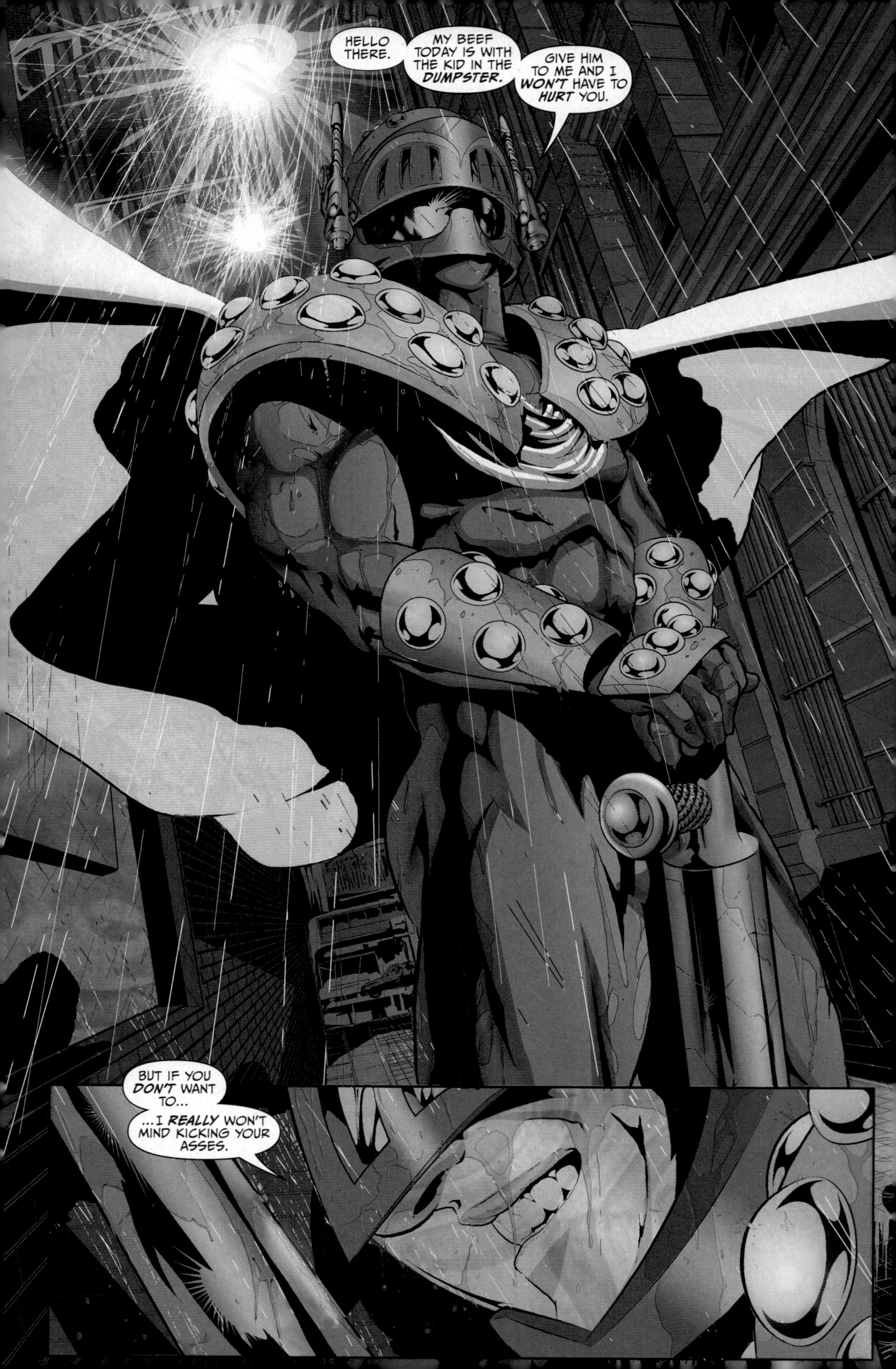
HELLO THERE.
MY BEEF TODAY IS WITH THE KID IN THE *DUMPSTER.*
GIVE HIM TO ME AND I *WON'T* HAVE TO *HURT* YOU.
BUT IF YOU *DON'T* WANT TO...
...I *REALLY* WON'T MIND KICKING YOUR ASSES.

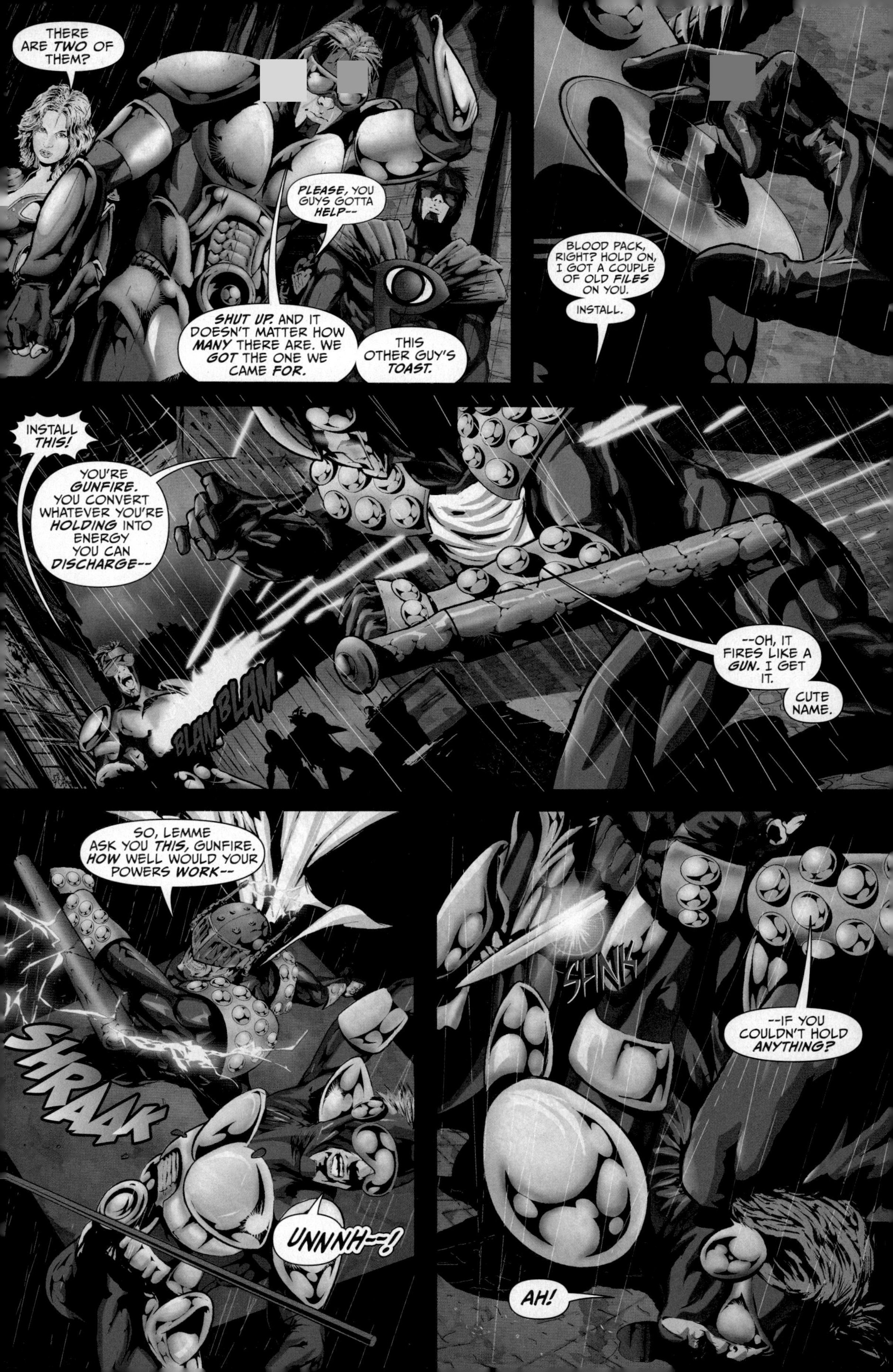
THERE ARE *TWO* OF THEM?
PLEASE, YOU GUYS GOTTA *HELP*--
SHUT UP. AND IT DOESN'T MATTER HOW *MANY* THERE ARE. WE *GOT* THE ONE WE CAME *FOR.*
THIS OTHER GUY'S *TOAST.*
BLOOD PACK, RIGHT? HOLD ON, I GOT A COUPLE OF OLD *FILES* ON YOU.
INSTALL.
INSTALL *THIS!*
YOU'RE *GUNFIRE*. YOU CONVERT WHATEVER YOU'RE *HOLDING* INTO ENERGY YOU CAN *DISCHARGE*--
BLAM BLAM
--OH, IT FIRES LIKE A *GUN*. I GET IT.
CUTE NAME.
SO, LEMME ASK YOU *THIS*, GUNFIRE. *HOW* WELL WOULD YOUR POWERS *WORK*--
SHRAAK
UNNNH--!
SHNK
--IF YOU COULDN'T HOLD *ANYTHING?*
AH!

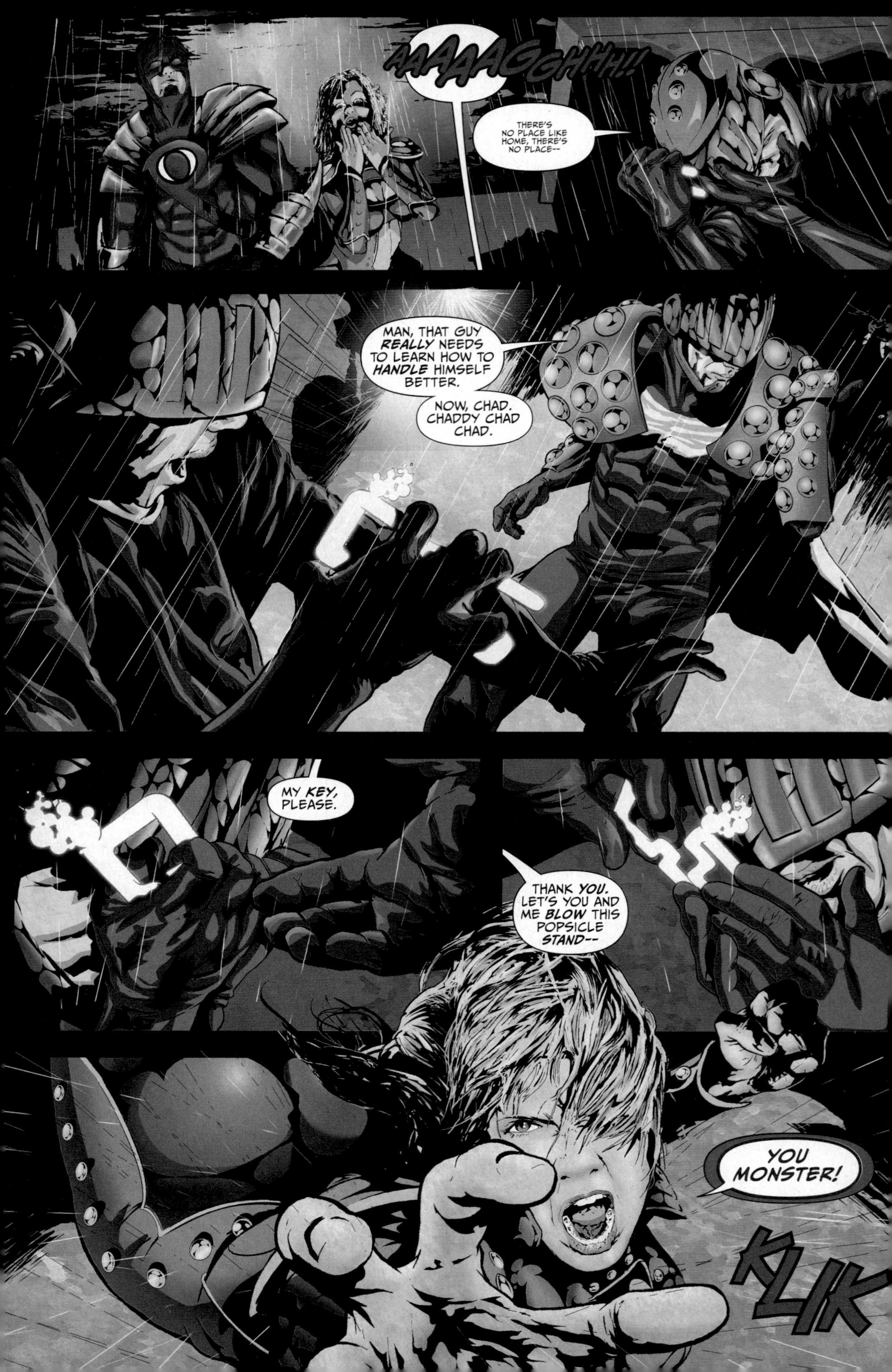
AAAAAAGGHHHH!!
THERE'S NO PLACE LIKE HOME, THERE'S NO PLACE--
MAN, THAT GUY REALLY NEEDS TO LEARN HOW TO HANDLE HIMSELF BETTER.
NOW, CHAD. CHADDY CHAD CHAD.
MY KEY, PLEASE.
THANK YOU. LET'S YOU AND ME BLOW THIS POPSICLE STAND--
YOU MONSTER!
KLIK

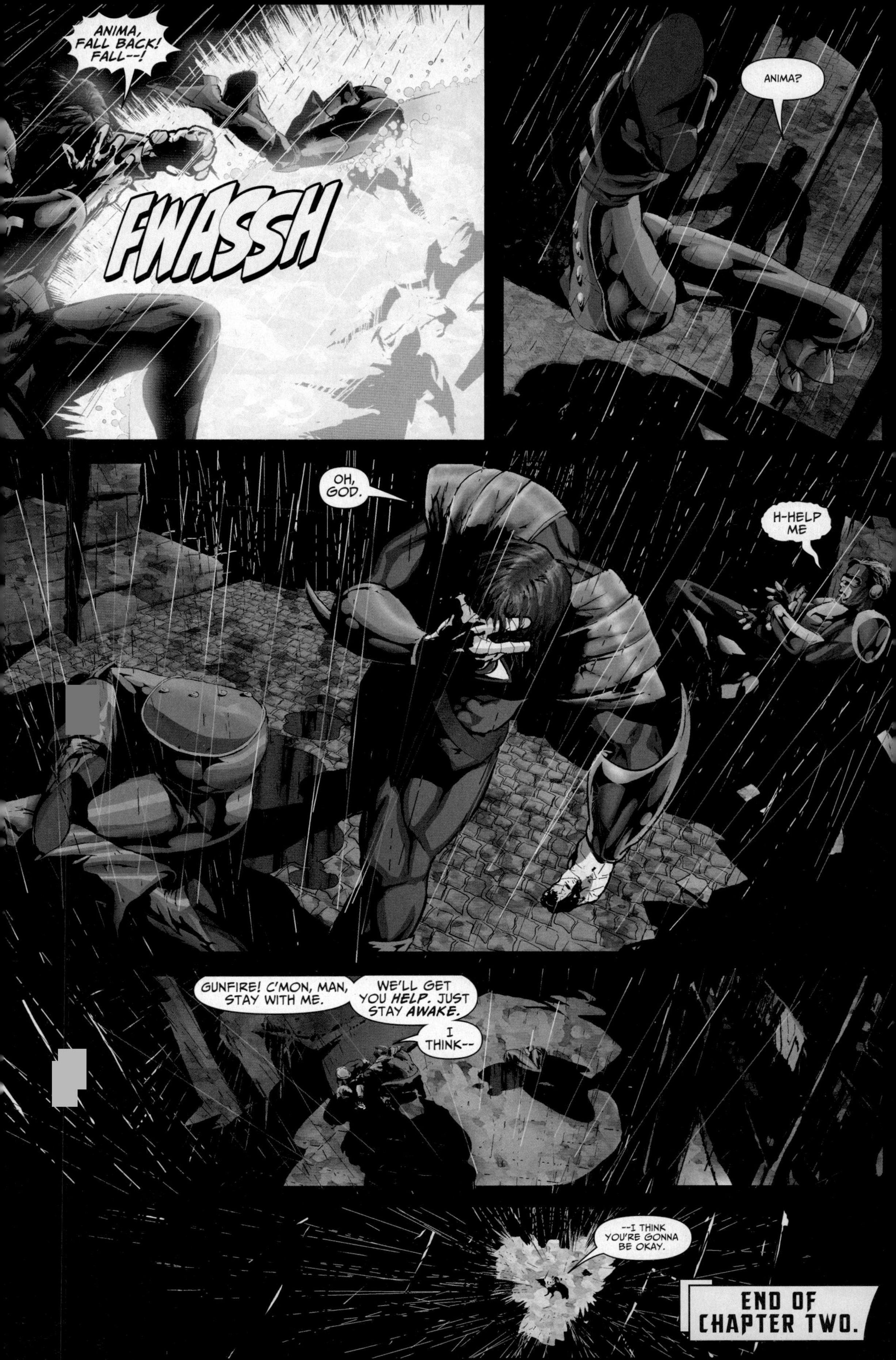
ANIMA, FALL BACK! FALL--!
FWASSH
ANIMA?
OH, GOD.
H-HELP ME
GUNFIRE! C'MON, MAN, STAY WITH ME.
WE'LL GET YOU HELP. JUST STAY AWAKE.
I THINK--
--I THINK YOU'RE GONNA BE OKAY.
END OF CHAPTER TWO.

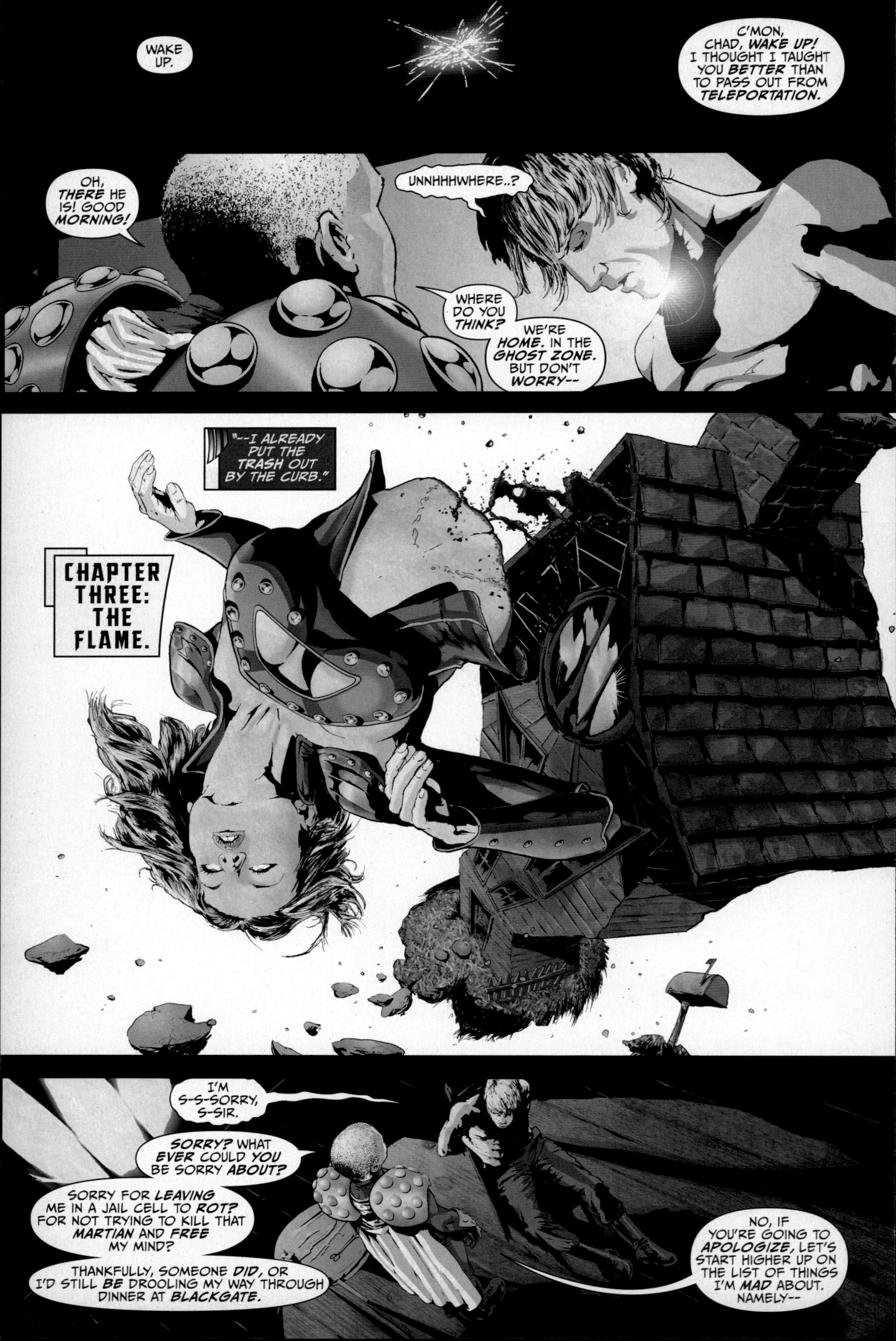

WAKE UP.
C'MON, CHAD, WAKE UP! I THOUGHT I TAUGHT YOU BETTER THAN TO PASS OUT FROM TELEPORTATION.
OH, THERE HE IS! GOOD MORNING!
UNNHHHWHERE..?
WHERE DO YOU THINK?
WE'RE HOME. IN THE GHOST ZONE. BUT DON'T WORRY--
"--I ALREADY PUT THE TRASH OUT BY THE CURB."
CHAPTER THREE: THE FLAME.
I'M S-S-SORRY, S-SIR.
SORRY? WHAT EVER COULD YOU BE SORRY ABOUT?
SORRY FOR LEAVING ME IN A JAIL CELL TO ROT? FOR NOT TRYING TO KILL THAT MARTIAN AND FREE MY MIND?
THANKFULLY, SOMEONE DID, OR I'D STILL BE DROOLING MY WAY THROUGH DINNER AT BLACKGATE.
NO, IF YOU'RE GOING TO APOLOGIZE, LET'S START HIGHER UP ON THE LIST OF THINGS I'M MAD ABOUT. NAMELY--

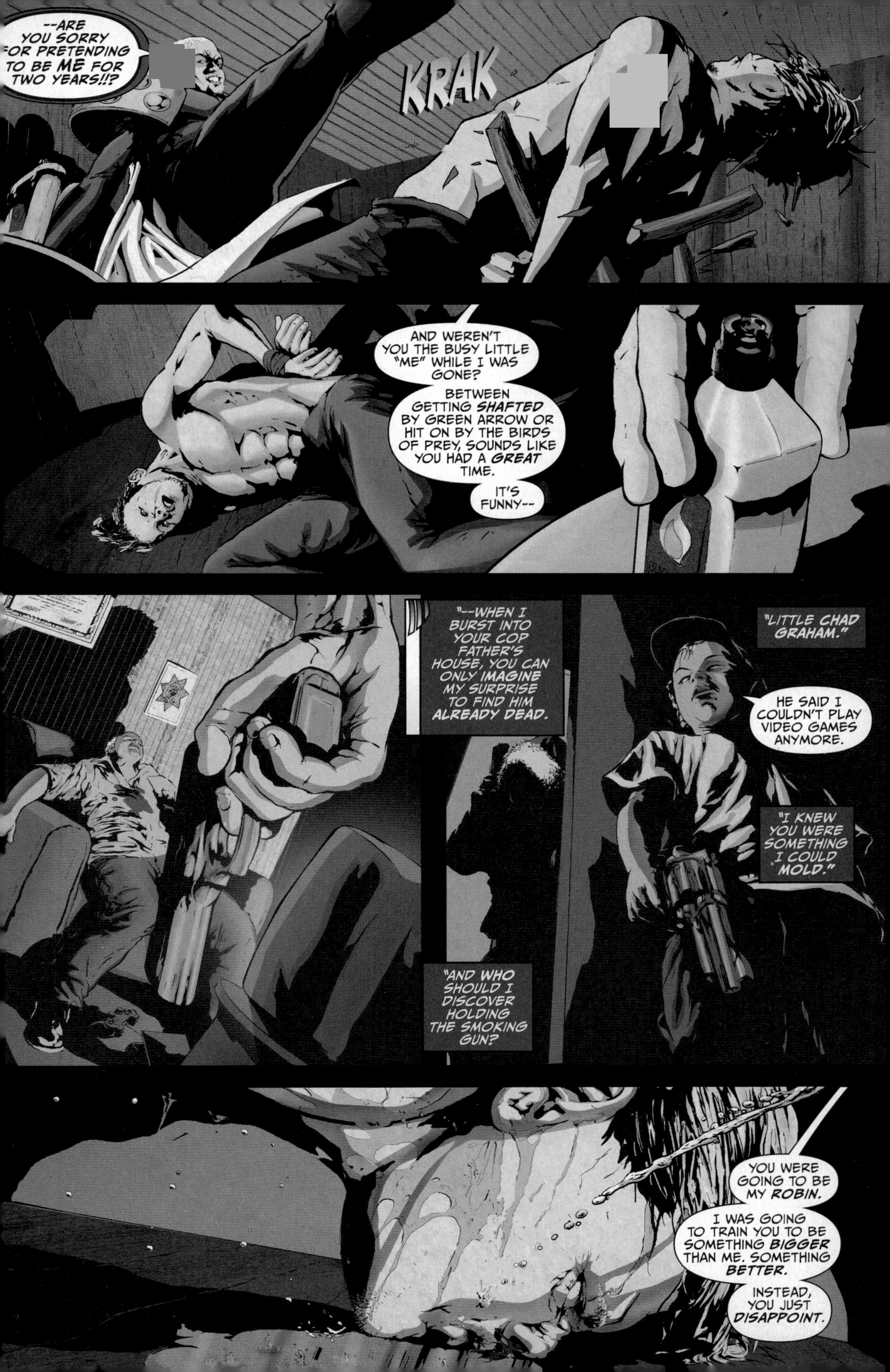
--ARE YOU SORRY FOR PRETENDING TO BE ME FOR TWO YEARS!!?
KRAK
AND WEREN'T YOU THE BUSY LITTLE "ME" WHILE I WAS GONE?
BETWEEN GETTING SHAFTED BY GREEN ARROW OR HIT ON BY THE BIRDS OF PREY, SOUNDS LIKE YOU HAD A GREAT TIME.
IT'S FUNNY--
"--WHEN I BURST INTO YOUR COP FATHER'S HOUSE, YOU CAN ONLY IMAGINE MY SURPRISE TO FIND HIM ALREADY DEAD.
"AND WHO SHOULD I DISCOVER HOLDING THE SMOKING GUN?
"LITTLE CHAD GRAHAM."
HE SAID I COULDN'T PLAY VIDEO GAMES ANYMORE.
"I KNEW YOU WERE SOMETHING I COULD MOLD."
YOU WERE GOING TO BE MY ROBIN.
I WAS GOING TO TRAIN YOU TO BE SOMETHING BIGGER THAN ME. SOMETHING BETTER.
INSTEAD, YOU JUST DISAPPOINT.

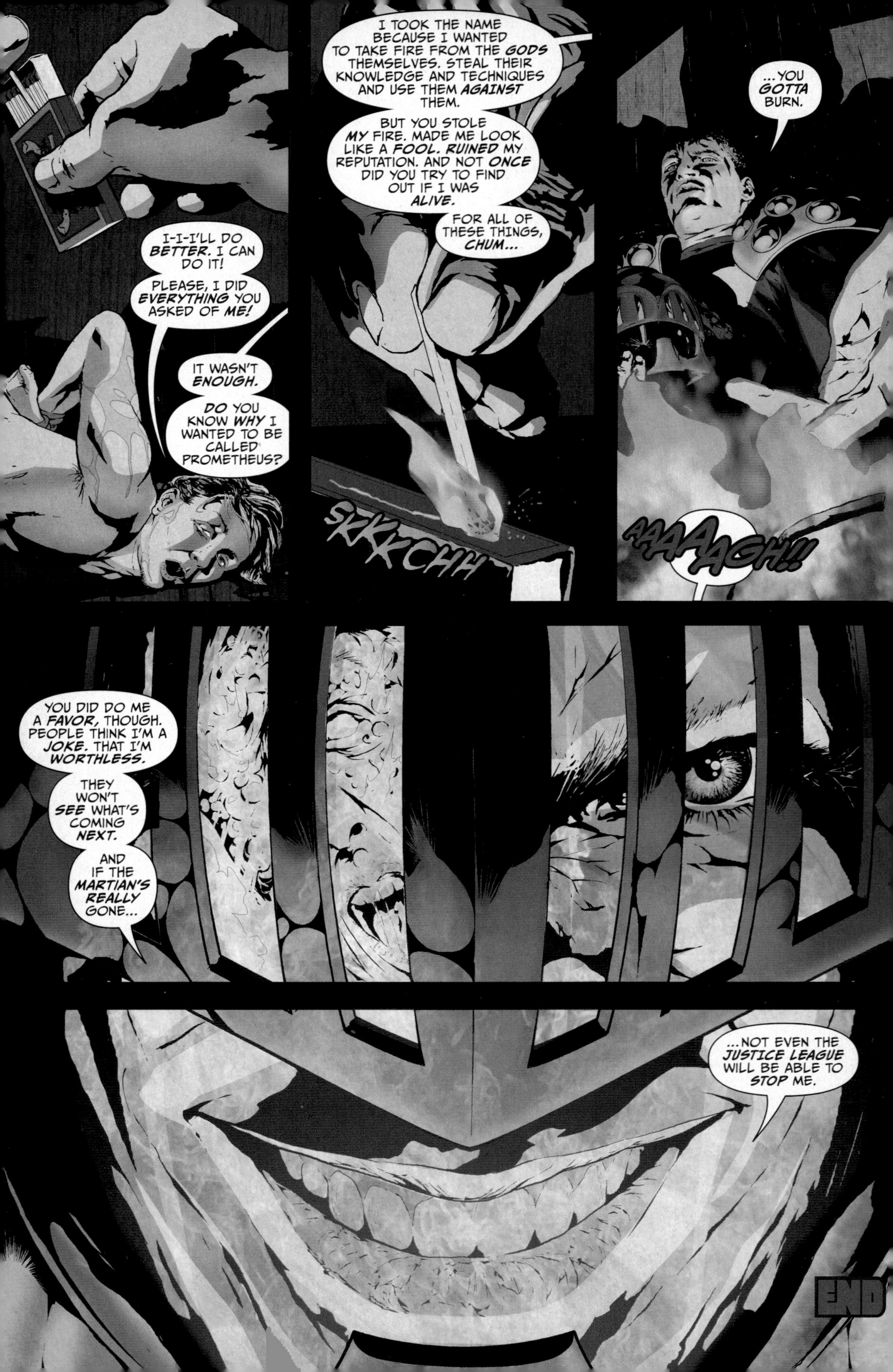
I-I-I'LL DO BETTER. I CAN DO IT!
PLEASE, I DID EVERYTHING YOU ASKED OF ME!
IT WASN'T ENOUGH.
DO YOU KNOW WHY I WANTED TO BE CALLED PROMETHEUS?
I TOOK THE NAME BECAUSE I WANTED TO TAKE FIRE FROM THE GODS THEMSELVES. STEAL THEIR KNOWLEDGE AND TECHNIQUES AND USE THEM AGAINST THEM.
BUT YOU STOLE MY FIRE. MADE ME LOOK LIKE A FOOL. RUINED MY REPUTATION. AND NOT ONCE DID YOU TRY TO FIND OUT IF I WAS ALIVE.
FOR ALL OF THESE THINGS, CHUM...
SKKKCHH
...YOU GOTTA BURN.
AAAAAAGH!!
YOU DID DO ME A FAVOR, THOUGH. PEOPLE THINK I'M A JOKE. THAT I'M WORTHLESS.
THEY WON'T SEE WHAT'S COMING NEXT.
AND IF THE MARTIAN'S REALLY GONE...
...NOT EVEN THE JUSTICE LEAGUE WILL BE ABLE TO STOP ME.
END

JUSTICE LEAGUE ORIGINS

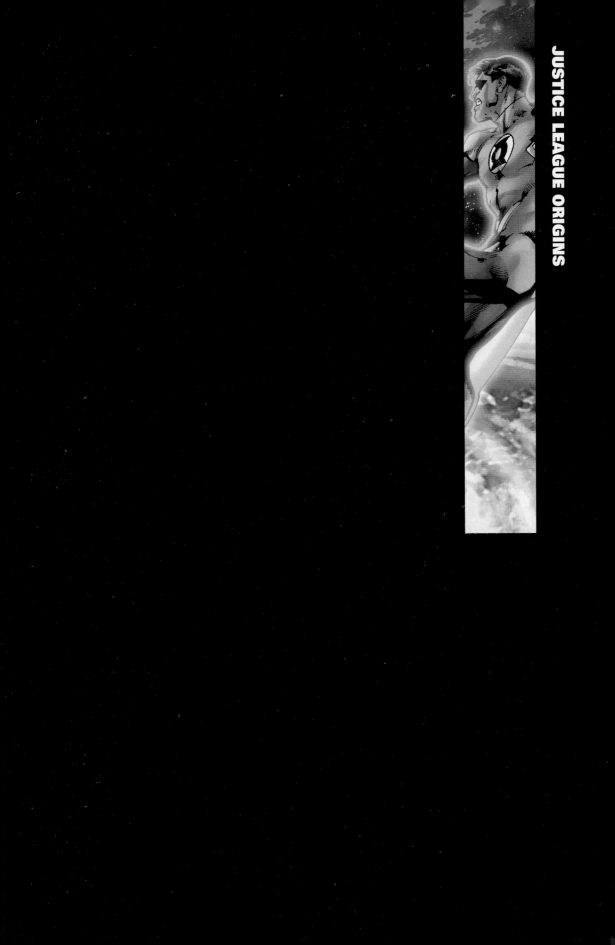

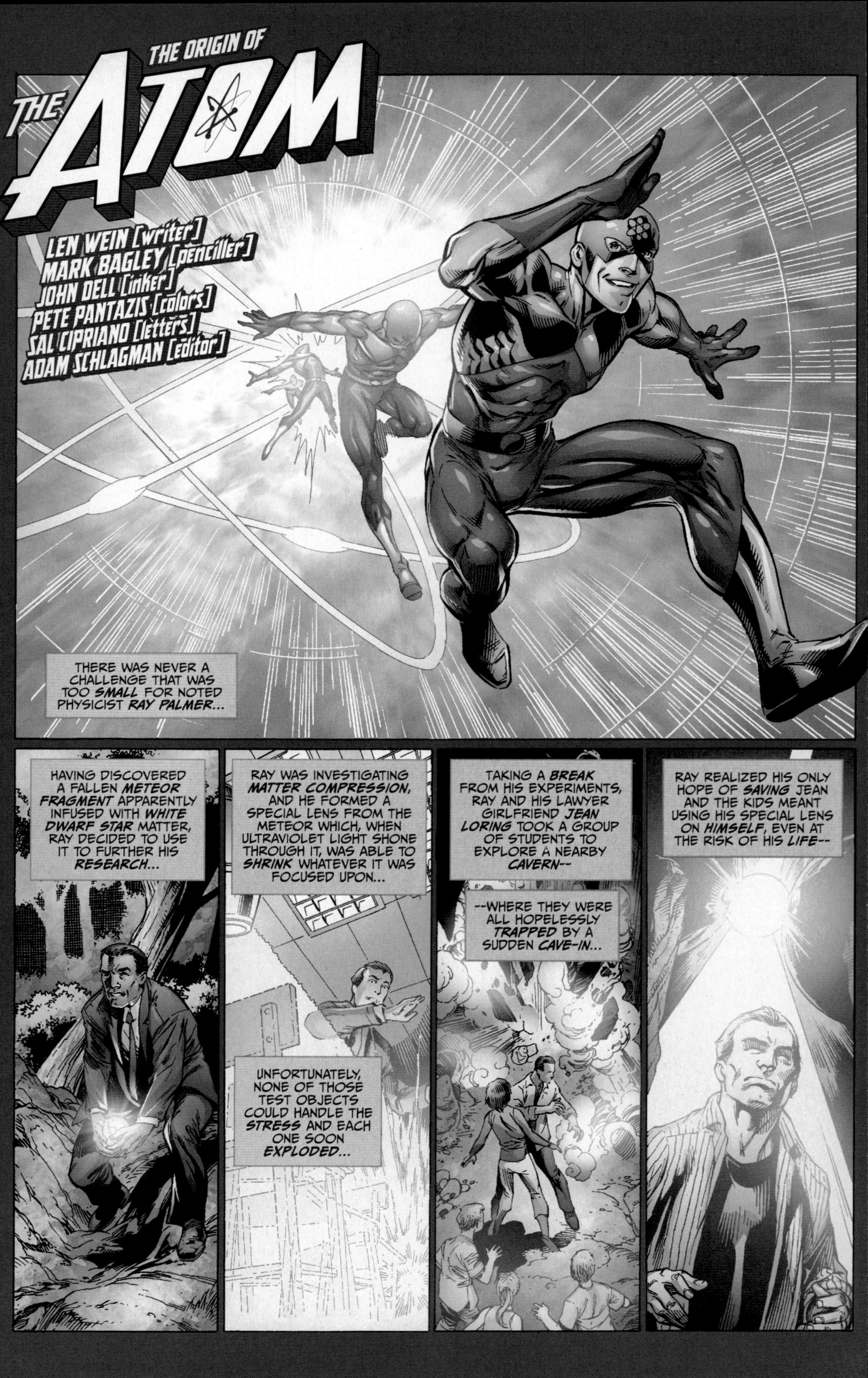
THE ORIGIN OF
THE ATOM
LEN WEIN [writer]
MARK BAGLEY [penciller]
JOHN DELL [inker]
PETE PANTAZIS [colors]
SAL CIPRIANO [letters]
ADAM SCHLAGMAN [editor]
THERE WAS NEVER A CHALLENGE THAT WAS TOO SMALL FOR NOTED PHYSICIST RAY PALMER...
HAVING DISCOVERED A FALLEN METEOR FRAGMENT APPARENTLY INFUSED WITH WHITE DWARF STAR MATTER, RAY DECIDED TO USE IT TO FURTHER HIS RESEARCH...
RAY WAS INVESTIGATING MATTER COMPRESSION, AND HE FORMED A SPECIAL LENS FROM THE METEOR WHICH, WHEN ULTRAVIOLET LIGHT SHONE THROUGH IT, WAS ABLE TO SHRINK WHATEVER IT WAS FOCUSED UPON...
UNFORTUNATELY, NONE OF THOSE TEST OBJECTS COULD HANDLE THE STRESS AND EACH ONE SOON EXPLODED...
TAKING A BREAK FROM HIS EXPERIMENTS, RAY AND HIS LAWYER GIRLFRIEND JEAN LORING TOOK A GROUP OF STUDENTS TO EXPLORE A NEARBY CAVERN--
--WHERE THEY WERE ALL HOPELESSLY TRAPPED BY A SUDDEN CAVE-IN...
RAY REALIZED HIS ONLY HOPE OF SAVING JEAN AND THE KIDS MEANT USING HIS SPECIAL LENS ON HIMSELF, EVEN AT THE RISK OF HIS LIFE--

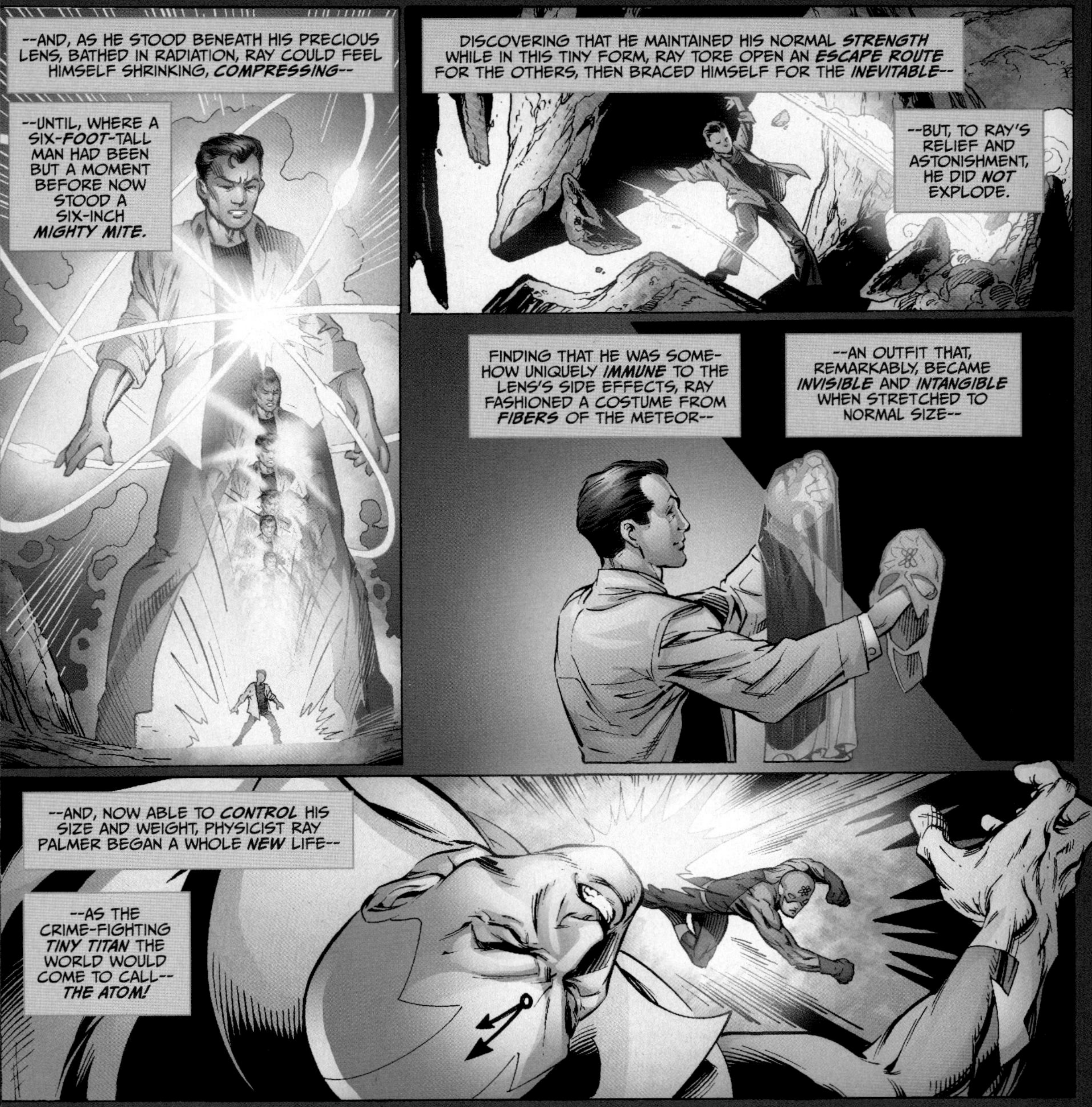
--AND, AS HE STOOD BENEATH HIS PRECIOUS LENS, BATHED IN RADIATION, RAY COULD FEEL HIMSELF SHRINKING, *COMPRESSING*--
--UNTIL, WHERE A SIX-*FOOT*-TALL MAN HAD BEEN BUT A MOMENT BEFORE NOW STOOD A SIX-INCH *MIGHTY MITE.*
DISCOVERING THAT HE MAINTAINED HIS NORMAL *STRENGTH* WHILE IN THIS TINY FORM, RAY TORE OPEN AN *ESCAPE ROUTE* FOR THE OTHERS, THEN BRACED HIMSELF FOR THE *INEVITABLE*--
--BUT, TO RAY'S RELIEF AND ASTONISHMENT, HE DID *NOT* EXPLODE.
FINDING THAT HE WAS SOME-HOW UNIQUELY *IMMUNE* TO THE LENS'S SIDE EFFECTS, RAY FASHIONED A COSTUME FROM *FIBERS* OF THE METEOR--
--AN OUTFIT THAT, REMARKABLY, BECAME *INVISIBLE* AND *INTANGIBLE* WHEN STRETCHED TO NORMAL SIZE--
--AND, NOW ABLE TO *CONTROL* HIS SIZE AND WEIGHT, PHYSICIST RAY PALMER BEGAN A WHOLE *NEW* LIFE--
--AS THE CRIME-FIGHTING *TINY TITAN* THE WORLD WOULD COME TO CALL-- *THE ATOM!*

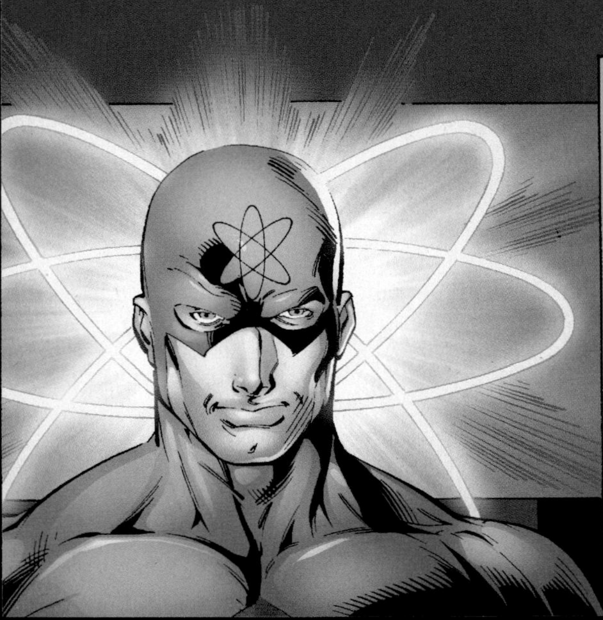

POWERS AND WEAPONS:

BY MANIPULATING HIDDEN CONTROLS IN HIS COSTUME, RAY PALMER CAN ADJUST HIS SIZE AND WEIGHT, ALLOWING HIM TO FLOAT ON AIR CURRENTS OR STRIKE WITH THE FORCE OF A FULL-SIZED MAN, DEPENDING ON HIS NEED. BECAUSE OF AN UNKNOWN FACTOR IN ITS MAKEUP, HIS COSTUME ORIGINALLY REMAINED BOTH INTANGIBLE AND INVISIBLE AT PALMER'S SIX-FOOT SIZE NOW AFTER RAY'S TRAVELS IN THE MULTIVERSE, HIS COSTUME CAN APPEAR WHEN HE GROWS TO NORMAL SIZE.

ALLIANCES:

- JUSTICE LEAGUE OF AMERICA

ESSENTIAL STORYLINES:

- SHOWCASE PRESENTS THE ATOM
- IDENTITY CRISIS
- COUNTDOWN VOLUMES 1-4
- JUSTICE LEAGUE: CRY FOR JUSTICE

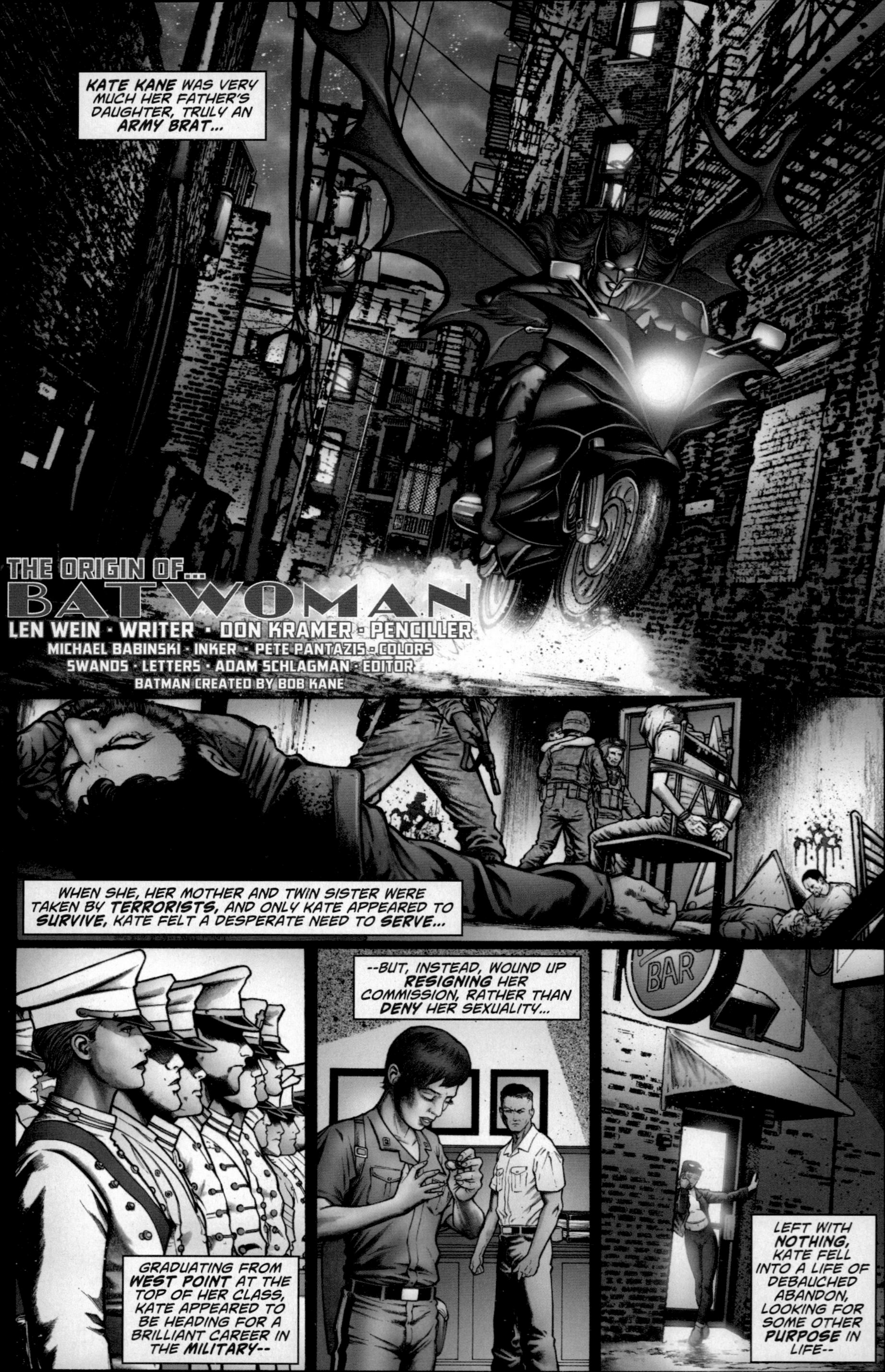
KATE KANE WAS VERY MUCH HER FATHER'S DAUGHTER, TRULY AN ARMY BRAT...
THE ORIGIN OF... BATWOMAN
LEN WEIN · WRITER · DON KRAMER · PENCILLER
MICHAEL BABINSKI · INKER · PETE PANTAZIS · COLORS
SWANDS · LETTERS · ADAM SCHLAGMAN · EDITOR
BATMAN CREATED BY BOB KANE
WHEN SHE, HER MOTHER AND TWIN SISTER WERE TAKEN BY TERRORISTS, AND ONLY KATE APPEARED TO SURVIVE, KATE FELT A DESPERATE NEED TO SERVE...
GRADUATING FROM WEST POINT AT THE TOP OF HER CLASS, KATE APPEARED TO BE HEADING FOR A BRILLIANT CAREER IN THE MILITARY--
--BUT, INSTEAD, WOUND UP RESIGNING HER COMMISSION, RATHER THAN DENY HER SEXUALITY...
BAR
LEFT WITH NOTHING, KATE FELL INTO A LIFE OF DEBAUCHED ABANDON, LOOKING FOR SOME OTHER PURPOSE IN LIFE--

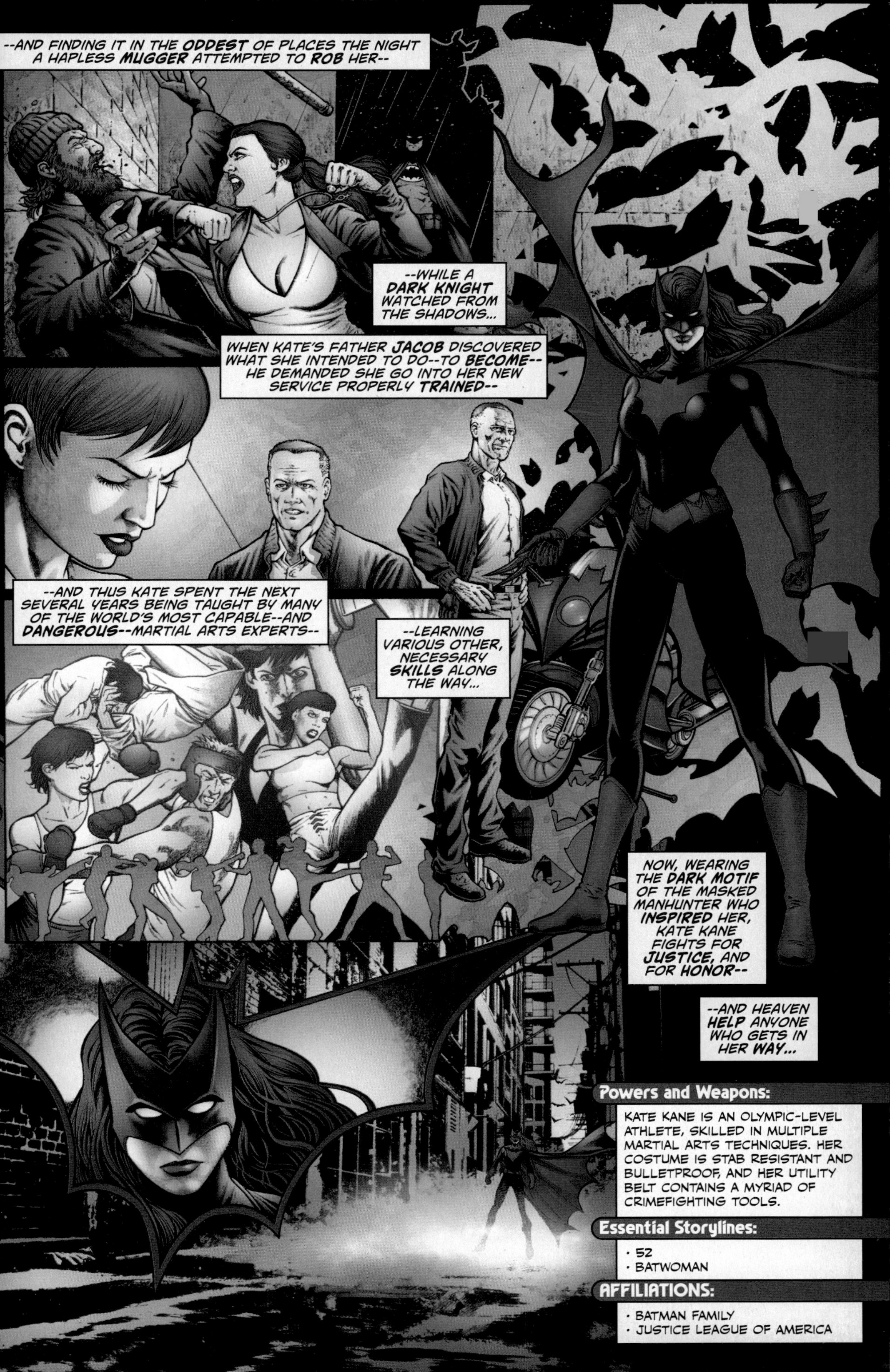
--AND FINDING IT IN THE ODDEST OF PLACES THE NIGHT A HAPLESS MUGGER ATTEMPTED TO ROB HER--
--WHILE A DARK KNIGHT WATCHED FROM THE SHADOWS...
WHEN KATE'S FATHER JACOB DISCOVERED WHAT SHE INTENDED TO DO--TO BECOME--HE DEMANDED SHE GO INTO HER NEW SERVICE PROPERLY TRAINED--
--AND THUS KATE SPENT THE NEXT SEVERAL YEARS BEING TAUGHT BY MANY OF THE WORLD'S MOST CAPABLE--AND DANGEROUS--MARTIAL ARTS EXPERTS--
--LEARNING VARIOUS OTHER, NECESSARY SKILLS ALONG THE WAY...
NOW, WEARING THE DARK MOTIF OF THE MASKED MANHUNTER WHO INSPIRED HER, KATE KANE FIGHTS FOR JUSTICE, AND FOR HONOR--
--AND HEAVEN HELP ANYONE WHO GETS IN HER WAY...

Powers and Weapons:

KATE KANE IS AN OLYMPIC-LEVEL ATHLETE, SKILLED IN MULTIPLE MARTIAL ARTS TECHNIQUES. HER COSTUME IS STAB RESISTANT AND BULLETPROOF, AND HER UTILITY BELT CONTAINS A MYRIAD OF CRIMEFIGHTING TOOLS.

Essential Storylines:

- 52
- BATWOMAN

AFFILIATIONS:

- BATMAN FAMILY
- JUSTICE LEAGUE OF AMERICA

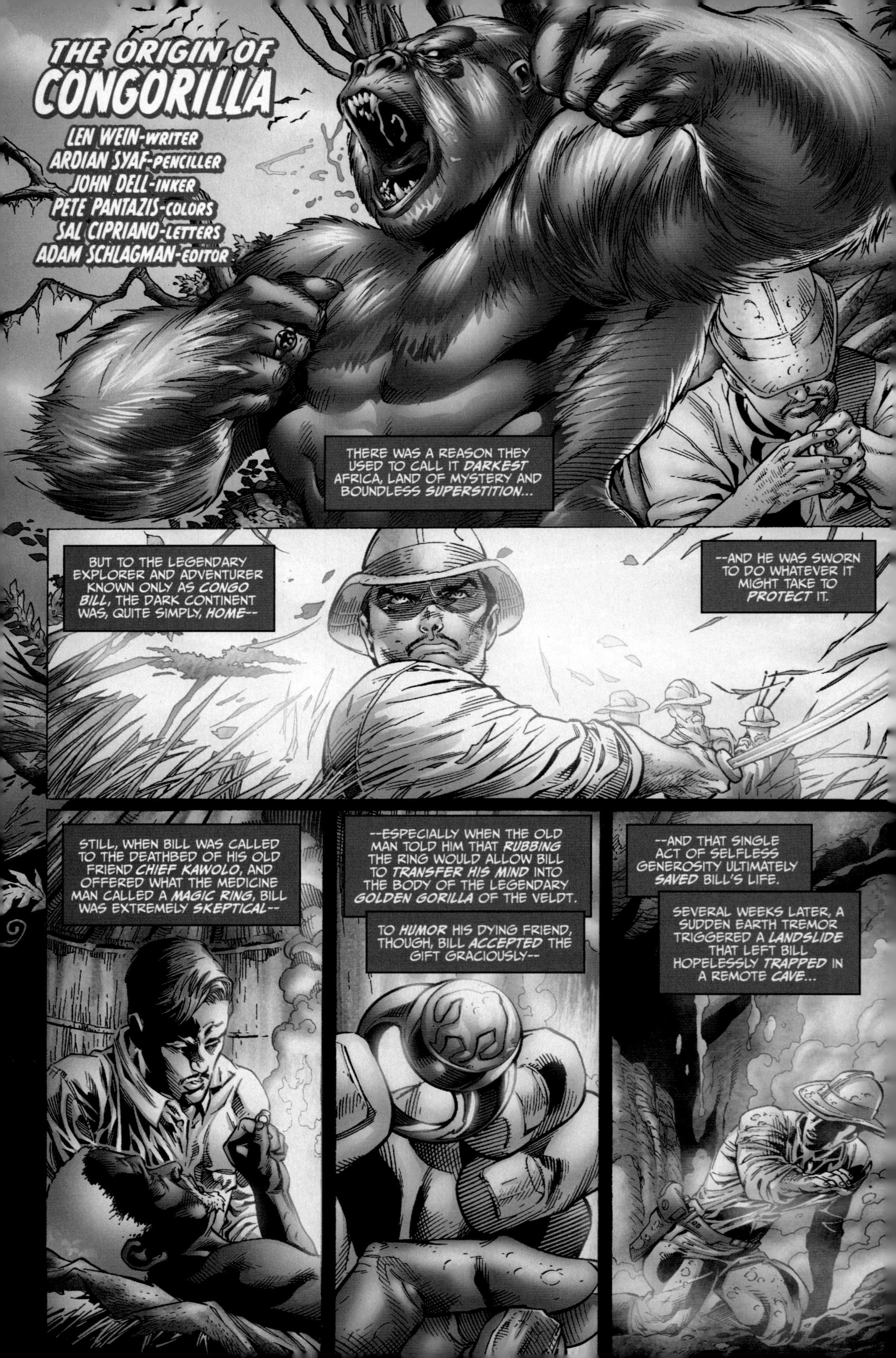

THE ORIGIN OF CONGORILLA
LEN WEIN-WRITER
ARDIAN SYAF-PENCILLER
JOHN DELL-INKER
PETE PANTAZIS-COLORS
SAL CIPRIANO-LETTERS
ADAM SCHLAGMAN-EDITOR
THERE WAS A REASON THEY USED TO CALL IT DARKEST AFRICA, LAND OF MYSTERY AND BOUNDLESS SUPERSTITION...
BUT TO THE LEGENDARY EXPLORER AND ADVENTURER KNOWN ONLY AS CONGO BILL, THE DARK CONTINENT WAS, QUITE SIMPLY, HOME--
--AND HE WAS SWORN TO DO WHATEVER IT MIGHT TAKE TO PROTECT IT.
STILL, WHEN BILL WAS CALLED TO THE DEATHBED OF HIS OLD FRIEND CHIEF KAWOLO, AND OFFERED WHAT THE MEDICINE MAN CALLED A MAGIC RING, BILL WAS EXTREMELY SKEPTICAL--
--ESPECIALLY WHEN THE OLD MAN TOLD HIM THAT RUBBING THE RING WOULD ALLOW BILL TO TRANSFER HIS MIND INTO THE BODY OF THE LEGENDARY GOLDEN GORILLA OF THE VELDT.
TO HUMOR HIS DYING FRIEND, THOUGH, BILL ACCEPTED THE GIFT GRACIOUSLY--
--AND THAT SINGLE ACT OF SELFLESS GENEROSITY ULTIMATELY SAVED BILL'S LIFE.
SEVERAL WEEKS LATER, A SUDDEN EARTH TREMOR TRIGGERED A LANDSLIDE THAT LEFT BILL HOPELESSLY TRAPPED IN A REMOTE CAVE...

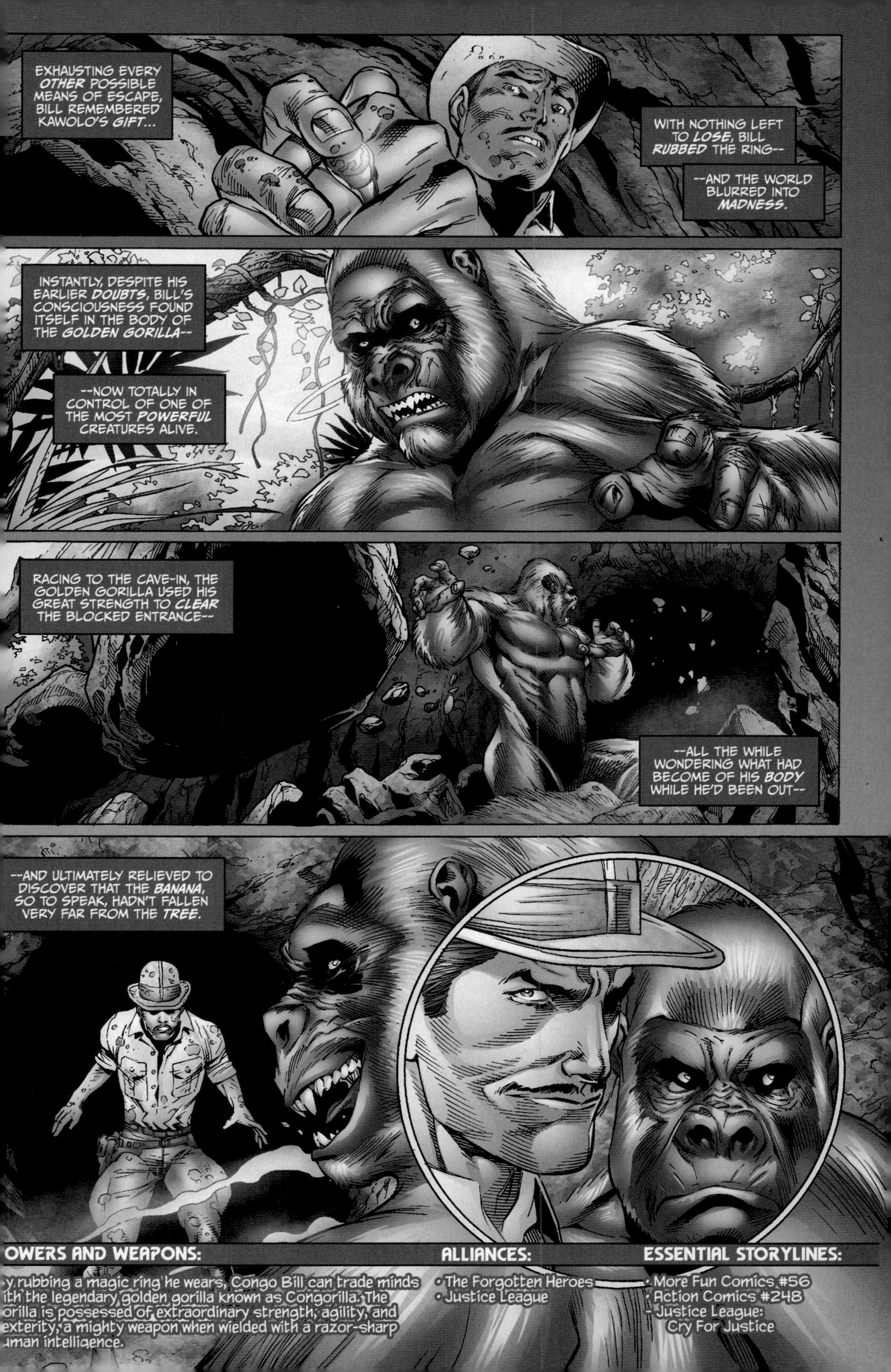
EXHAUSTING EVERY OTHER POSSIBLE MEANS OF ESCAPE, BILL REMEMBERED KAWOLO'S GIFT...
WITH NOTHING LEFT TO LOSE, BILL RUBBED THE RING--
--AND THE WORLD BLURRED INTO MADNESS.
INSTANTLY, DESPITE HIS EARLIER DOUBTS, BILL'S CONSCIOUSNESS FOUND ITSELF IN THE BODY OF THE GOLDEN GORILLA--
--NOW TOTALLY IN CONTROL OF ONE OF THE MOST POWERFUL CREATURES ALIVE.
RACING TO THE CAVE-IN, THE GOLDEN GORILLA USED HIS GREAT STRENGTH TO CLEAR THE BLOCKED ENTRANCE--
--ALL THE WHILE WONDERING WHAT HAD BECOME OF HIS BODY WHILE HE'D BEEN OUT--
--AND ULTIMATELY RELIEVED TO DISCOVER THAT THE BANANA, SO TO SPEAK, HADN'T FALLEN VERY FAR FROM THE TREE.

OWERS AND WEAPONS:

y rubbing a magic ring he wears, Congo Bill can trade minds ith the legendary golden gorilla known as Congorilla. The orilla is possessed of extraordinary strength, agility, and exterity, a mighty weapon when wielded with a razor-sharp uman intelligence.

ALLIANCES:

- The Forgotten Heroes
- Justice League

ESSENTIAL STORYLINES:

- More Fun Comics #56
- Action Comics #248
- Justice League: Cry For Justice

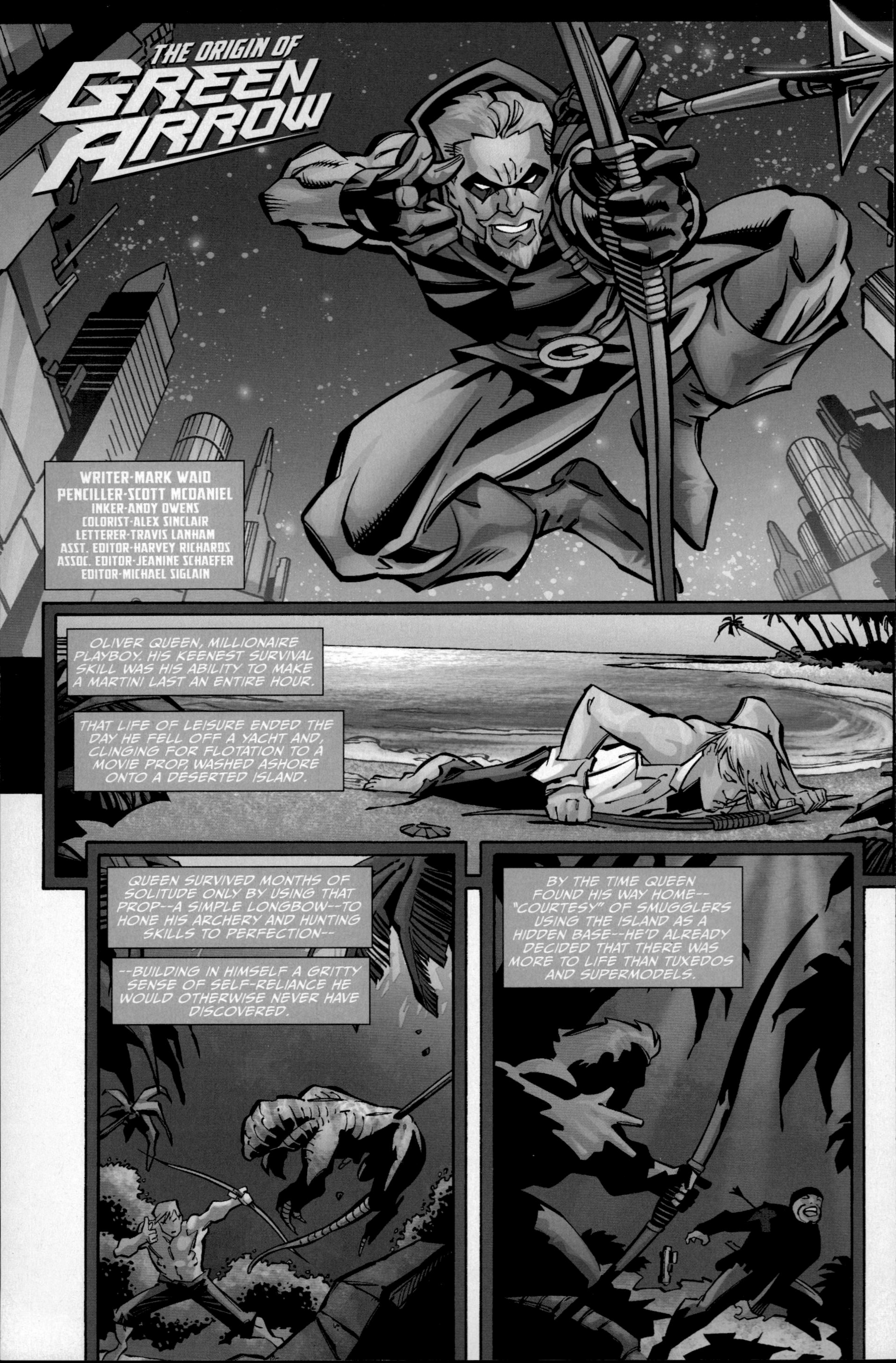
THE ORIGIN OF
GREEN ARROW
WRITER-MARK WAID
PENCILLER-SCOTT McDANIEL
INKER-ANDY OWENS
COLORIST-ALEX SINCLAIR
LETTERER-TRAVIS LANHAM
ASST. EDITOR-HARVEY RICHARDS
ASSOC. EDITOR-JEANINE SCHAEFER
EDITOR-MICHAEL SIGLAIN
OLIVER QUEEN, MILLIONAIRE PLAYBOY. HIS KEENEST SURVIVAL SKILL WAS HIS ABILITY TO MAKE A MARTINI LAST AN ENTIRE HOUR.
THAT LIFE OF LEISURE ENDED THE DAY HE FELL OFF A YACHT AND, CLINGING FOR FLOTATION TO A MOVIE PROP, WASHED ASHORE ONTO A DESERTED ISLAND.
QUEEN SURVIVED MONTHS OF SOLITUDE ONLY BY USING THAT PROP--A SIMPLE LONGBOW--TO HONE HIS ARCHERY AND HUNTING SKILLS TO PERFECTION--
--BUILDING IN HIMSELF A GRITTY SENSE OF SELF-RELIANCE HE WOULD OTHERWISE NEVER HAVE DISCOVERED.
BY THE TIME QUEEN FOUND HIS WAY HOME--"COURTESY" OF SMUGGLERS USING THE ISLAND AS A HIDDEN BASE--HE'D ALREADY DECIDED THAT THERE WAS MORE TO LIFE THAN TUXEDOS AND SUPERMODELS.

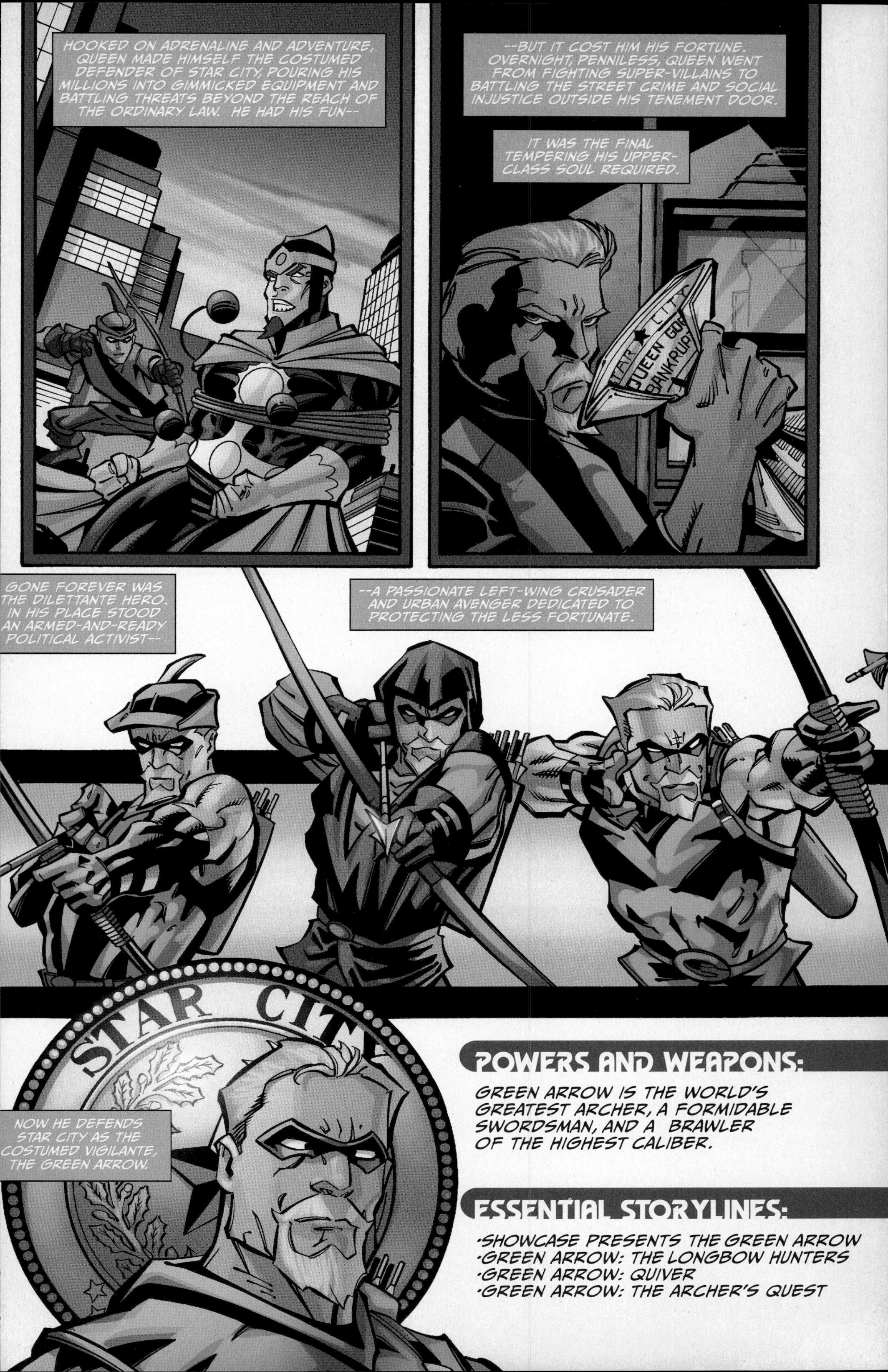
HOOKED ON ADRENALINE AND ADVENTURE, QUEEN MADE HIMSELF THE COSTUMED DEFENDER OF STAR CITY, POURING HIS MILLIONS INTO GIMMICKED EQUIPMENT AND BATTLING THREATS BEYOND THE REACH OF THE ORDINARY LAW. HE HAD HIS FUN--
--BUT IT COST HIM HIS FORTUNE. OVERNIGHT, PENNILESS, QUEEN WENT FROM FIGHTING SUPER-VILLAINS TO BATTLING THE STREET CRIME AND SOCIAL INJUSTICE OUTSIDE HIS TENEMENT DOOR.
IT WAS THE FINAL TEMPERING HIS UPPER-CLASS SOUL REQUIRED.
GONE FOREVER WAS THE DILETTANTE HERO. IN HIS PLACE STOOD AN ARMED-AND-READY POLITICAL ACTIVIST--
--A PASSIONATE LEFT-WING CRUSADER AND URBAN AVENGER DEDICATED TO PROTECTING THE LESS FORTUNATE.
STAR CITY
NOW HE DEFENDS STAR CITY AS THE COSTUMED VIGILANTE, THE GREEN ARROW.

POWERS AND WEAPONS:

GREEN ARROW IS THE WORLD'S GREATEST ARCHER, A FORMIDABLE SWORDSMAN, AND A BRAWLER OF THE HIGHEST CALIBER.

ESSENTIAL STORYLINES:

- SHOWCASE PRESENTS THE GREEN ARROW
- GREEN ARROW: THE LONGBOW HUNTERS
- GREEN ARROW: QUIVER
- GREEN ARROW: THE ARCHER'S QUEST

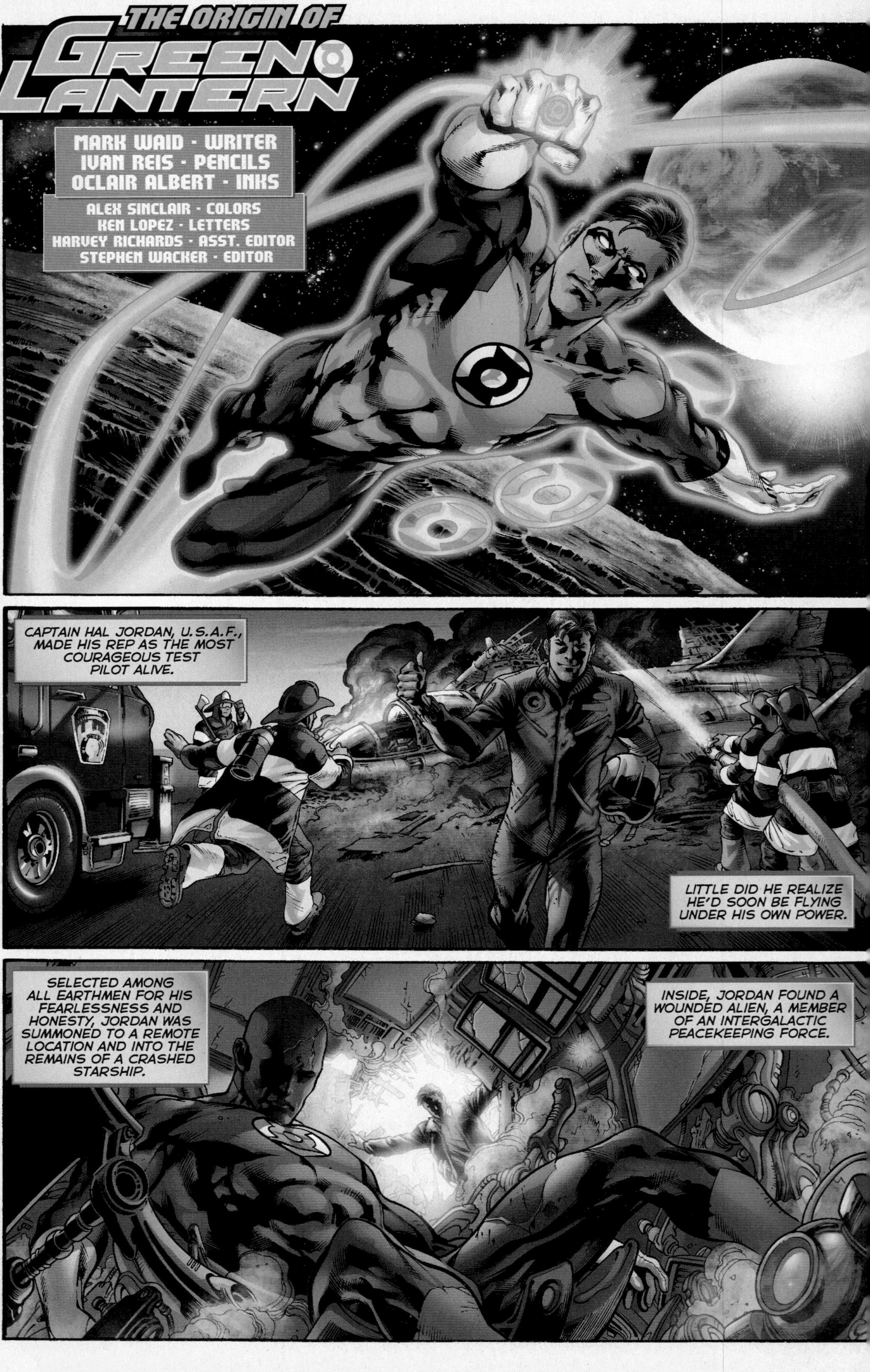
THE ORIGIN OF GREEN LANTERN
MARK WAID · WRITER
IVAN REIS · PENCILS
OCLAIR ALBERT · INKS
ALEX SINCLAIR · COLORS
KEN LOPEZ · LETTERS
HARVEY RICHARDS · ASST. EDITOR
STEPHEN WACKER · EDITOR
CAPTAIN HAL JORDAN, U.S.A.F., MADE HIS REP AS THE MOST COURAGEOUS TEST PILOT ALIVE.
LITTLE DID HE REALIZE HE'D SOON BE FLYING UNDER HIS OWN POWER.
SELECTED AMONG ALL EARTHMEN FOR HIS FEARLESSNESS AND HONESTY, JORDAN WAS SUMMONED TO A REMOTE LOCATION AND INTO THE REMAINS OF A CRASHED STARSHIP.
INSIDE, JORDAN FOUND A WOUNDED ALIEN, A MEMBER OF AN INTERGALACTIC PEACEKEEPING FORCE.

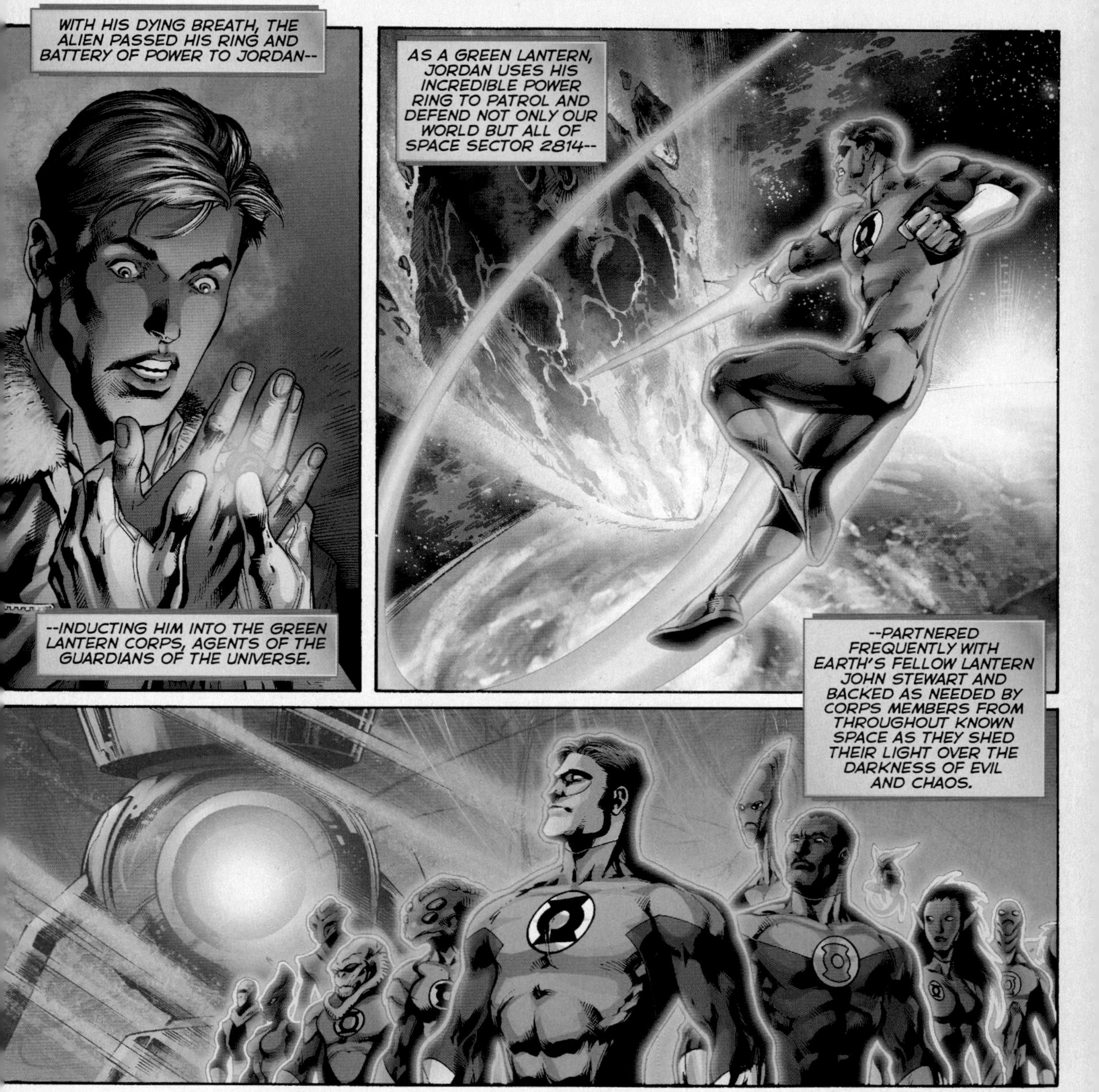
WITH HIS DYING BREATH, THE ALIEN PASSED HIS RING AND BATTERY OF POWER TO JORDAN--
--INDUCTING HIM INTO THE GREEN LANTERN CORPS, AGENTS OF THE GUARDIANS OF THE UNIVERSE.
AS A GREEN LANTERN, JORDAN USES HIS INCREDIBLE POWER RING TO PATROL AND DEFEND NOT ONLY OUR WORLD BUT ALL OF SPACE SECTOR 2814--
--PARTNERED FREQUENTLY WITH EARTH'S FELLOW LANTERN JOHN STEWART AND BACKED AS NEEDED BY CORPS MEMBERS FROM THROUGHOUT KNOWN SPACE AS THEY SHED THEIR LIGHT OVER THE DARKNESS OF EVIL AND CHAOS.

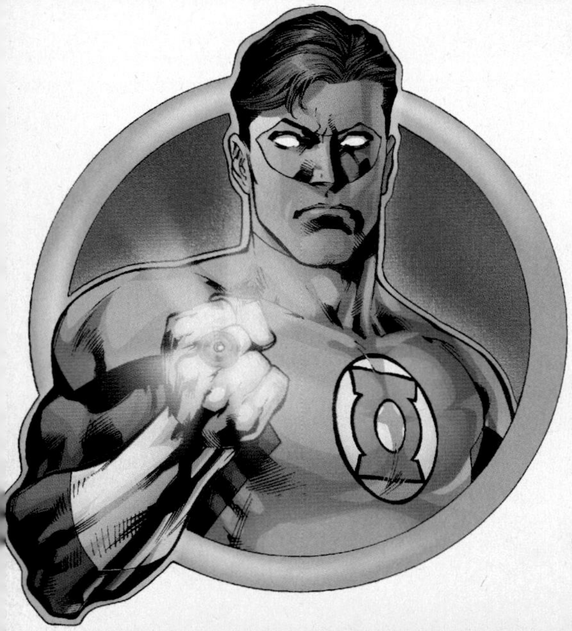

POWERS AND WEAPONS:

Green Lantern is armed with a ring the abilities of which are limited only by his imagination and will power.

Chiefly, the ring is used for antigravity, to unleash torrents of energy, to translate alien dialects and to create hard- light replicas of any shape.

The ring must be periodically charged by contact with a Power Battery which, in turn, draws energy from the Guardians' Central Power Battery on the planet Oa.

ESSENTIAL STORYLINES:

GREEN LANTERN: REBIRTH
GREEN LANTERN: NO FEAR
GREEN LANTERN: THE SINESTRO CORPS WAR
GREEN LANTERN: SECRET ORIGIN

ALLIANCES:

Justice League of America, Green Lantern Corps

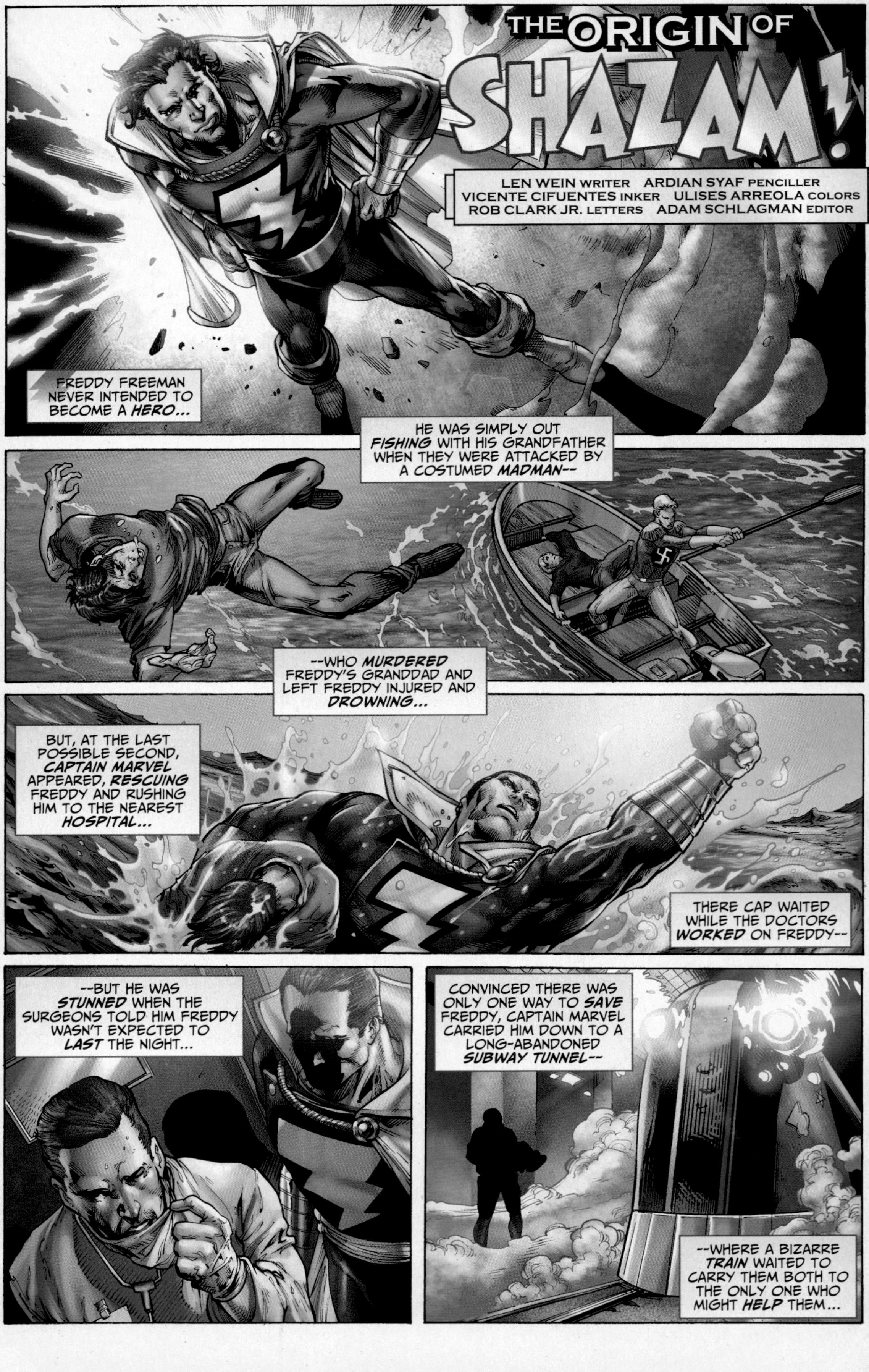
THE ORIGIN OF SHAZAM!
LEN WEIN WRITER ARDIAN SYAF PENCILLER VICENTE CIFUENTES INKER ULISES ARREOLA COLORS ROB CLARK JR. LETTERS ADAM SCHLAGMAN EDITOR
FREDDY FREEMAN NEVER INTENDED TO BECOME A HERO...
HE WAS SIMPLY OUT FISHING WITH HIS GRANDFATHER WHEN THEY WERE ATTACKED BY A COSTUMED MADMAN--
--WHO MURDERED FREDDY'S GRANDDAD AND LEFT FREDDY INJURED AND DROWNING...
BUT, AT THE LAST POSSIBLE SECOND, CAPTAIN MARVEL APPEARED, RESCUING FREDDY AND RUSHING HIM TO THE NEAREST HOSPITAL...
THERE CAP WAITED WHILE THE DOCTORS WORKED ON FREDDY--
--BUT HE WAS STUNNED WHEN THE SURGEONS TOLD HIM FREDDY WASN'T EXPECTED TO LAST THE NIGHT...
CONVINCED THERE WAS ONLY ONE WAY TO SAVE FREDDY, CAPTAIN MARVEL CARRIED HIM DOWN TO A LONG-ABANDONED SUBWAY TUNNEL--
--WHERE A BIZARRE TRAIN WAITED TO CARRY THEM BOTH TO THE ONLY ONE WHO MIGHT HELP THEM...

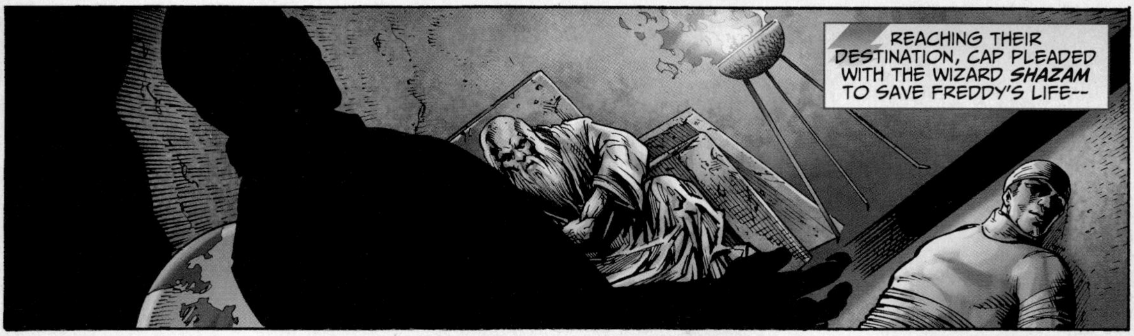
REACHING THEIR DESTINATION, CAP PLEADED WITH THE WIZARD SHAZAM TO SAVE FREDDY'S LIFE--

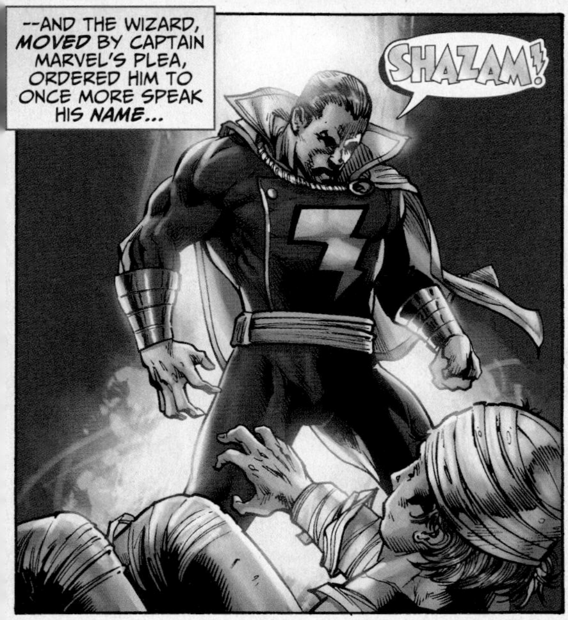
--AND THE WIZARD, MOVED BY CAPTAIN MARVEL'S PLEA, ORDERED HIM TO ONCE MORE SPEAK HIS NAME...
SHAZAM!

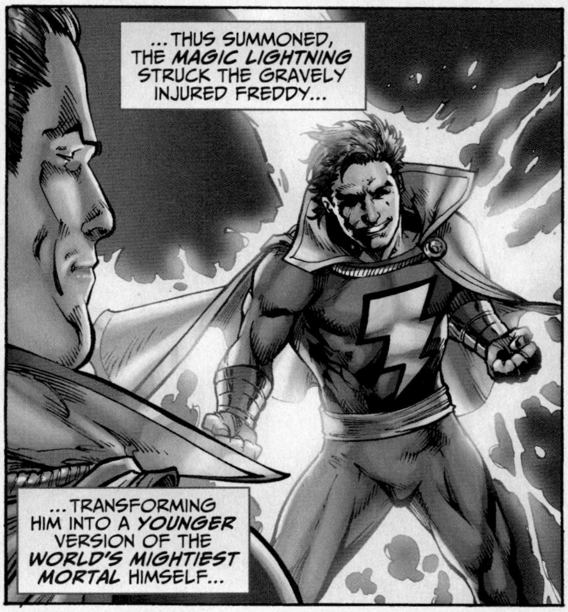
...THUS SUMMONED, THE MAGIC LIGHTNING STRUCK THE GRAVELY INJURED FREDDY...
...TRANSFORMING HIM INTO A YOUNGER VERSION OF THE WORLD'S MIGHTIEST MORTAL HIMSELF...

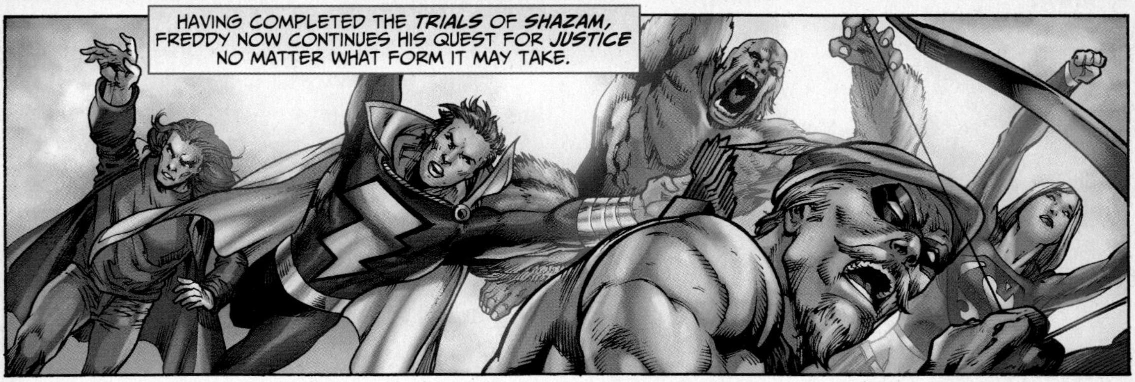
HAVING COMPLETED THE TRIALS OF SHAZAM, FREDDY NOW CONTINUES HIS QUEST FOR JUSTICE NO MATTER WHAT FORM IT MAY TAKE.

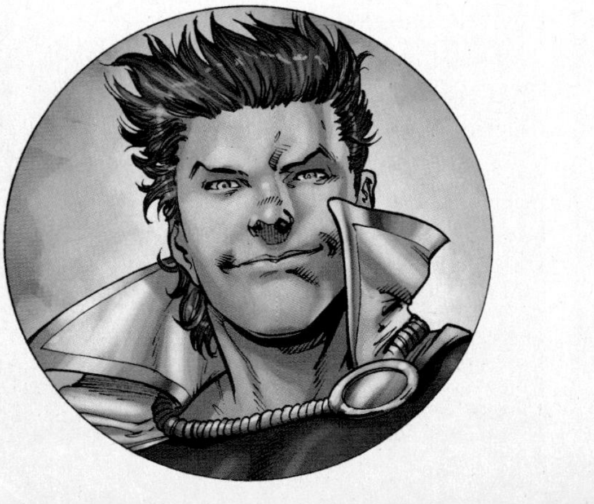

POWERS AND WEAPONS:

GRANTED THE POWERS OF THE ANCIENT GODS, FREDDY FREEMAN POSSESSES THE WISDOM OF SOLOMON, THE STRENGTH OF HERCULES, THE STAMINA OF ATLAS, THE POWER OF ZEUS, THE COURAGE OF ACHILLES, AND THE SPEED OF MERCURY, AS WELL AS INVULNERABILITY AND THE POWER OF FLIGHT.

ESSENTIAL STORYLINES:

- JUSTICE LEAGUE: CRY FOR JUSTICE
- THE TRIALS OF SHAZAM!

AFFILIATIONS:

- JUSTICE LEAGUE OF AMERICA
- THE MARVEL FAMILY
- THE OUTSIDERS
- TEEN TITANS

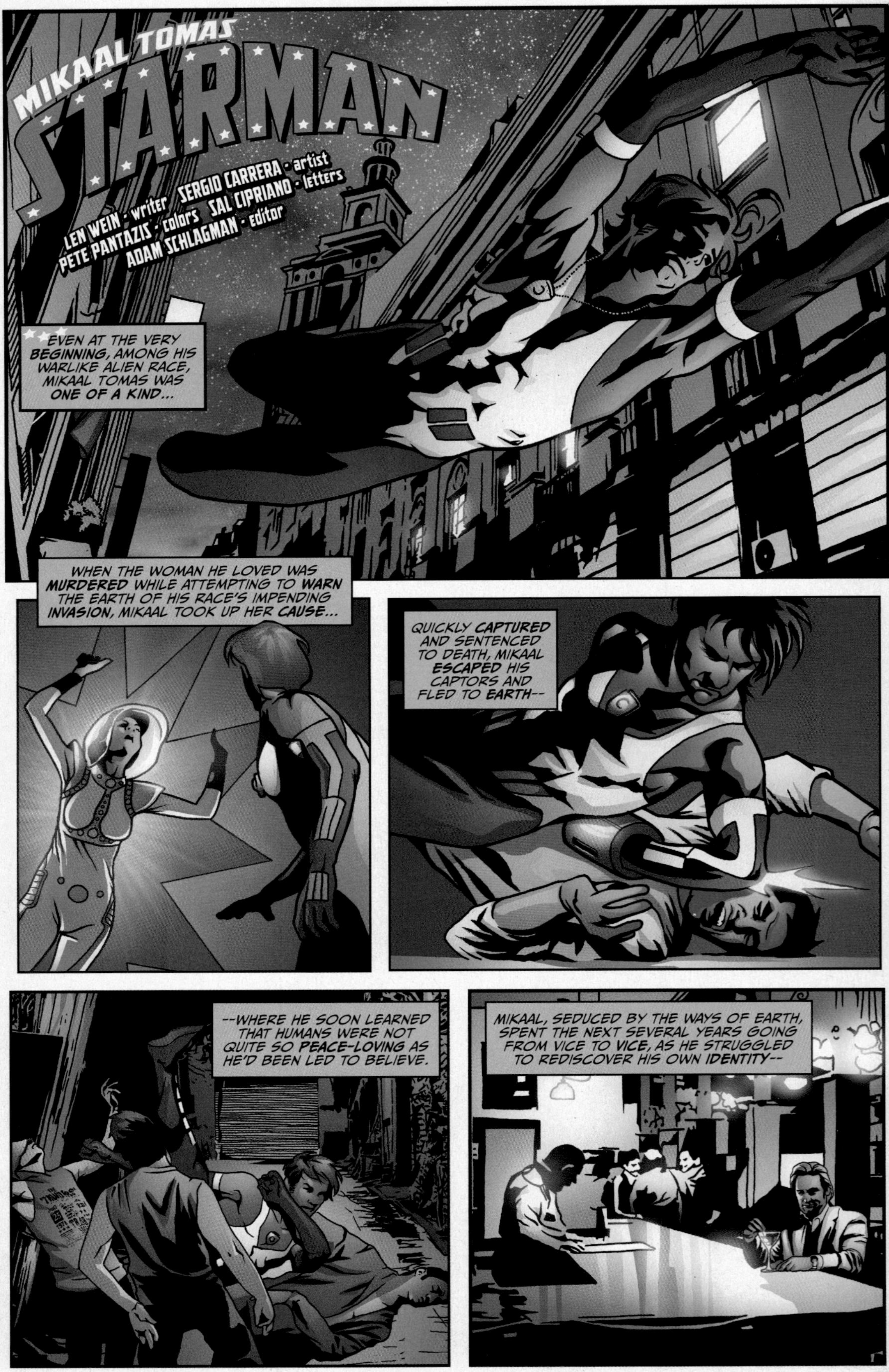
MIKAAL TOMAS
STARMAN
LEN WEIN · writer SERGIO CARRERA · artist
PETE PANTAZIS · colors SAL CIPRIANO · letters
ADAM SCHLAGMAN · editor
EVEN AT THE VERY BEGINNING, AMONG HIS WARLIKE ALIEN RACE, MIKAAL TOMAS WAS ONE OF A KIND...
WHEN THE WOMAN HE LOVED WAS MURDERED WHILE ATTEMPTING TO WARN THE EARTH OF HIS RACE'S IMPENDING INVASION, MIKAAL TOOK UP HER CAUSE...
QUICKLY CAPTURED AND SENTENCED TO DEATH, MIKAAL ESCAPED HIS CAPTORS AND FLED TO EARTH--
--WHERE HE SOON LEARNED THAT HUMANS WERE NOT QUITE SO PEACE-LOVING AS HE'D BEEN LED TO BELIEVE.
MIKAAL, SEDUCED BY THE WAYS OF EARTH, SPENT THE NEXT SEVERAL YEARS GOING FROM VICE TO VICE, AS HE STRUGGLED TO REDISCOVER HIS OWN IDENTITY--

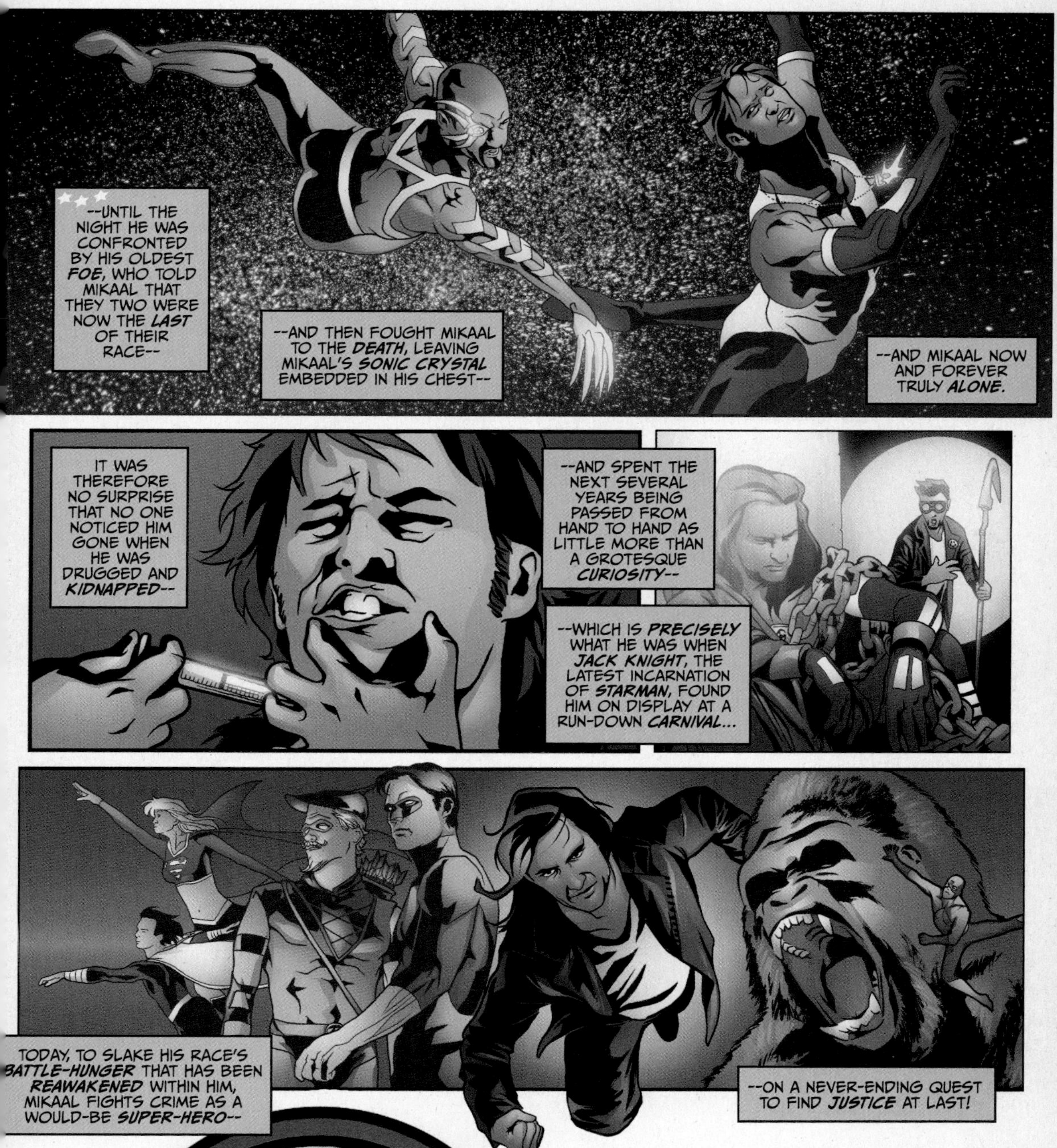
--UNTIL THE NIGHT HE WAS CONFRONTED BY HIS OLDEST FOE, WHO TOLD MIKAAL THAT THEY TWO WERE NOW THE LAST OF THEIR RACE--
--AND THEN FOUGHT MIKAAL TO THE DEATH, LEAVING MIKAAL'S SONIC CRYSTAL EMBEDDED IN HIS CHEST--
--AND MIKAAL NOW AND FOREVER TRULY ALONE.
IT WAS THEREFORE NO SURPRISE THAT NO ONE NOTICED HIM GONE WHEN HE WAS DRUGGED AND KIDNAPPED--
--AND SPENT THE NEXT SEVERAL YEARS BEING PASSED FROM HAND TO HAND AS LITTLE MORE THAN A GROTESQUE CURIOSITY--
--WHICH IS PRECISELY WHAT HE WAS WHEN JACK KNIGHT, THE LATEST INCARNATION OF STARMAN, FOUND HIM ON DISPLAY AT A RUN-DOWN CARNIVAL...
TODAY, TO SLAKE HIS RACE'S BATTLE-HUNGER THAT HAS BEEN REAWAKENED WITHIN HIM, MIKAAL FIGHTS CRIME AS A WOULD-BE SUPER-HERO--
--ON A NEVER-ENDING QUEST TO FIND JUSTICE AT LAST!

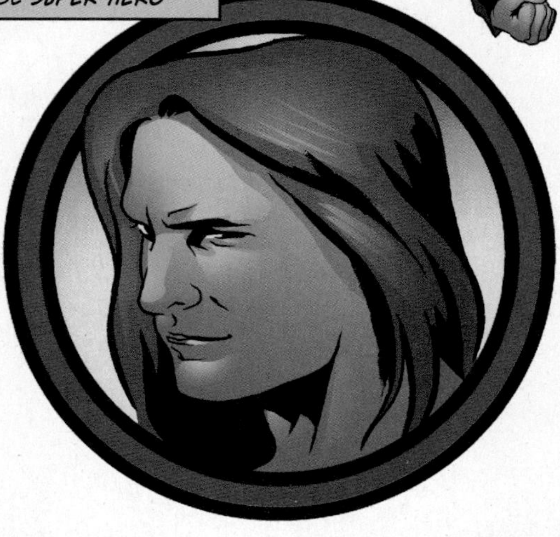

POWERS AND WEAPONS:

THE LAST SURVIVOR OF THE PLANET TALOK III, MIKAAL TOMAS POSSESSES SUPER-HUMAN STRENGTH AND THE POWER OF FLIGHT. MIKAAL ALSO HAS A UNIQUE SONIC CRYSTAL EMBEDDED IN HIS CHEST, WHICH ALLOWS HIM TO FIRE CONCENTRATED BEAMS OF ENERGY.

ALLIANCES:

- JUSTICE LEAGUE OF AMERICA

ESSENTIAL STORYLINES:

- FIRST ISSUE SPECIAL # 12
- JUSTICE LEAGUE: CRY FOR JUSTICE
- STARMAN OMNIBUS VOLUMES 1, 2, 5, 6

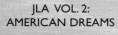